Foundations of Anasazi Culture

Foundations of Anasazi Culture

The Basketmaker–Pueblo Transition

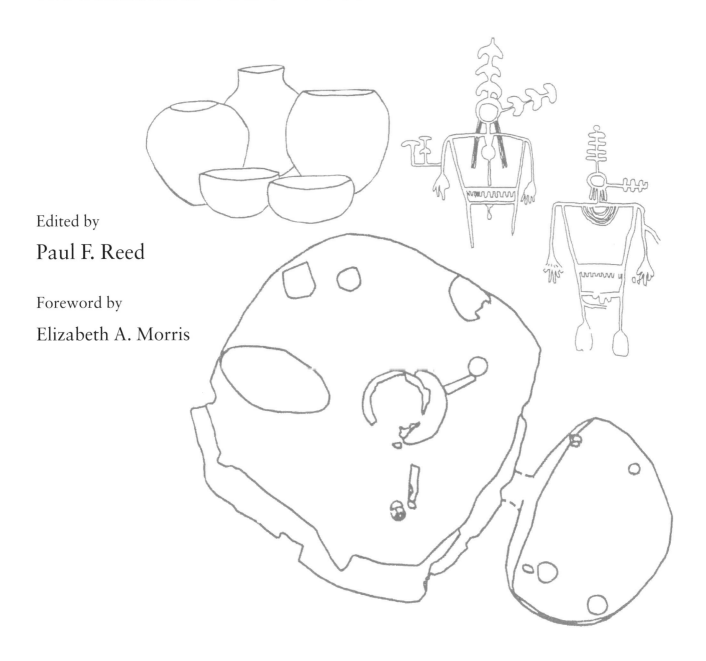

Edited by

Paul F. Reed

Foreword by

Elizabeth A. Morris

THE UNIVERSITY OF UTAH PRESS

Salt Lake City

01 02 03 04 05 06
4 3 2 1

LIBRARY OF CONGRESS CATALOGING-IN-PUBLICATION DATA

Foundations of Anasazi culture : the Basketmaker-Pueblo transition / edited by Paul F.
Reed ; foreword by Elizabeth Morris.
     p. cm.
    Includes bibliographical references and index.
    Contents: Fundamental issues in Basketmaker archaeology / Paul F. Reed — Locational,
architectural, and ceramic trends in the Basketmaker III occupation of the La Plata
Valley, New Mexico / H. Wolcott Toll and C. Dean Wilson — Colonization, warfare, and
regional competition : recent research into the Basketmaker III period in the Mesa Verde
Region / Mark L. Chenault and Thomas N. Motsinger — Distinctive and intensive : the
Basketmaker III to early Pueblo I occupation of Cove-Redrock Valley, Northeastern
Arizona / Paul F. Reed and Scott Wilcox — Socio-economic organization of a late
Basketmaker III community in the Mexican Springs area, Southern Chuska Mountains,
New Mexico / Jonathan E. Damp and Edward M. Kotyk — The early to late Basketmaker
III transition in Tohatchi Flats, New Mexico / Timothy M. Kearns, Janet L. McVickar,
and Lori Stephens Reed — Economics, site structure, and social organization during the
Basketmaker III period : a view from the Lukachukai Valley / Jeffrey H. Atschul and
Edgar K. Huber — Juniper Cove and early Anasazi community structure west of the
Chuska Mountains / Dennis Gilpin and Larry Benallie Jr. — The Basketmaker II–III
transision on the rainbow plateau / Phil R. Geib and Kimberly Spurr — From brown to
gray : the origins of ceramic technology in the Northern Southwest / Lori Stephens Reed,
C. Dean Wilson, and Kelley Hays-Gilpin — Changing lithic technology during the
Basketmaker-Pueblo transition : evidence from the Northern Southwest, Arizona / John
A. Torres — The bird in the basket : gender and social change in Basketmaker III
iconography / Michael R. Robins and Kelly Hays-Gilpin.
   ISBN 0-87480-656-9 (alk. paper)
    1. Basket-Maker Indians. 2 Pueblo Indians—Antiquities. 3. Southwest,
New—Antiquities. I. Reed, Paul F.

E99.B37 F68 2000
978.9'01—dc21

99-050687

Contents

Figures

Tables

Foreword

The old Morris pickup wound its way along a sandy track through sagebrush, juniper, and piñons. Vertical walls of red-orange sandstone closed in on both sides. Somewhere ahead of me was Broken Flute Cave and more than a dozen other rock shelters that had yielded an enormous amount of information about Basketmaker culture. The Ford had been here before but I had not. I had photographs though, taken with Earl Morris's long-enduring 4"× 6" Kodak plate camera. There were notes and floor plans too, to confirm the identity of individual caves when and if I got there. It was 1957. Earl Morris (my father) had passed away the year before after having published on part of his finds made in 1930 for the American Museum of Natural History and in 1931 for the Carnegie Institution in Washington. I inherited the task of writing them up for my dissertation at the University of Arizona, and several publications followed.

Stopping in front of a Navajo hogan, I was hoping for more directions. A grandmotherly soul with a load of firewood came up and I greeted her with "Yah-ta-hey." "Good morning," she said. The turquoise at her throat was the color of the Arizona sky. It turned out that we both knew Mary Bernard at the Bruce Bernard trading post in Shiprock. She told me that the Atahonez that I was seeking was indeed the canyon in front of us but I would not be able to drive much further. There were only sheep trails crossing the deeply cut arroyos. However, I could walk.

Hours later, dusty, hot and footsore, I climbed the steep talus slope at the end of Broken Flute Cave and stepped into the cool level shade. The sight before me made my jaw drop and wiped away the grime and fatigue. Pit house floors were spread out ahead of me for more than a thousand feet! They looked as though they had just been cleaned up for photography! Stone metates, manos, mortars and pestles, part of what I had come to record, were still in place. After 25 years, the shelter was in an excellent state of preservation. I felt awe and exultation as I picked my way between the features.

This was the site that had contained vast quantities of Basketmaker II and III artifacts, including scores of rarely found baskets, textiles, sandals, atlatls, bows and arrows, digging sticks, fur and feather blankets, leather containers, and the flute for which the site was named. The catalog listed thousands of specimens, early pottery was present in abundance.

The excellent state of preservation of roof and wall timbers has provided exquisite chronological detail. In 1936, this same pickup had brought Earl Morris and Emil W. Haury in to collect dendrochronological specimens that clearly reflected building dates for the structures. In the late 1940s, Willard F. Libby used some of this same wood to calibrate the accuracy of the emerging radiocarbon dating method. Then, in the 1980s, Jeffrey L. Eighmy and I returned to take archaeomagnetic samples from the well-dated hearths and burnt floors, thereby extending that chronology back into the A.D. 600s.

Now, at the beginning of the next millennium, researchers doing excavation and interpretative work for the Navajo Nation Archaeological Department and other archaeological institutions are using these same tightly controlled dates, the architectural details, and the rest of the archaeological inventory to reconstruct in previously unattempted detail the evolution of Basketmaker culture from prepottery through later developments forming the foundations of Anasazi culture.

This volume presents a wealth of data and a number of fascinating interpretive hypotheses focused on the Basketmaker period in Anasazi culture. The geographic area included centers on the Four Corners region of the American Southwest. The 21 authors of the 13 contributions represent a considerable number of tribal offices, state agencies, museums, and contracting companies. Research was conducted mostly in the 1990s on the Navajo Indian Reservation. Much information was obtained on the eastern and western sides of the Chuska mountain range, roughly running north-south along the Arizona-New Mexico border. Other information comes from nearby localities, including the La Plata River valley in New Mexico and Colorado, the Mancos Valley near Mesa Verde in Colorado, the Juniper Cove area west of Kayenta, Arizona, and the Rainbow Plateau in Arizona and Utah.

The descriptions and interpretations are relevant to the broader Anasazi area in these four states as well as neighboring areas, including, particularly, the Mogollon culture area to the south. Most of this recent research was done for and by the Navajo Nation Archaeology and Historic Preservation departments.

The Southwest is one of the best-known archaeological areas in the world, in part because of the plethora of sites with excellent conditions of preservation, but also due to the precise chronological controls of dendrochronology, radiocarbon and archaeomagnetic dating, and typological development. So many anthropologists have been working in this optimal context for so long that the Southwest is known for being an important setting for the formulation of sophisticated interpretive hypotheses. This volume is a seminal contribution. Additionally, the text is refreshingly readable in these times of frequently employed technological obscurities.

Several chapters describe recent research published here for the first time. Many include data extracted from contributions to the "gray" literature of contract archaeology. Others cite published sources heavily. These include virtually all of the classical Basketmaker references written during the last 100 years. Some chapters also include less-available information gleaned from the most recent work presented at professional meetings.

Several authors have used precise chronological controls and large numbers of sites to establish temporal subdivisions of the traditional Basketmaker periods based on the presence and absence of attributes. The reconciliation of these newer definitions with more traditional usage is usefully addressed.

Of particular interest are the synthetic discussions and interpretive hypotheses incorporating these new subdivisions. One major topic is settlement patterns, with an emphasis on architectural details, use of internal and external space, community size, composition and location, great kiva communities, stockade occurrences, and burning and abandonment details. The transition between and occasional coincidence of atlatl and bow-and-arrow artifacts are presented with precision. Lithic studies, particularly debitage analysis, have been used to analyze procurement strategies reflecting changing subsistence economies from early to late Basketmaker times. Also discussed are turkey acquisition and domestication, and the association of the introduction of beans and ceramics. Analyses of decorative art—including rock, textile, and ceramic renditions, derived from a huge, well-studied database—are extrapolated into provocative inferences about gender roles and social organization. This reconstruction of nonmaterial attributes from the inevitably incomplete material cultural and contextual remains of the prehistoric record promises to stimulate attention far beyond Basketmaker archaeology in the American Southwest.

The wealth of information available for current research is impressive. In earlier attempts to summarize the Basketmaker III period in the same region, the data were far leaner. For example, when my dissertation (Morris 1959) was published (Morris 1980), only a few additional references could be added. Suggestions about cultural content and dynamics, largely based on ceramic and architectural details, were very cautiously stated and barely departed from factual documentation.

In contrast, the interpretive hypotheses presented here, based on many more carefully produced site reports and more adventurous anthropological theory derived locally and from a broader perspective, suggest previously unheard of cultural dynamics in possible terms. Many of these ideas were impossible to conceive a few decades ago; had they had been launched, they would have been received as impractical flights of fancy. The hypotheses included here do occasionally diverge from each other in major and minor respects, but they do not invalidate each other as products of the foundation premise. Among other contributions they suggest directions for future research.

Although I found it tempting to assume the role of discussant or reviewer of this fascinating textual material, even more tempting is the desire to accumulate the voluminous references cited here, and others that might be useful, and plunge into the myriad pregnant research directions touched upon in this volume. However, rationality indicates that it is better to leave this work to the contributors and others who have professional and mitigational goals and support, as well as more years ahead of them. They will focus pertinent perspectives on subjects of Basketmaker archaeology and cultural dynamics. Research designs will be composed that address the ever-burgeoning questions. Some of these enhanced queries and challenges are included in specific and inspiring detail in this volume.

Elizabeth A. Morris, Ph.D.
Bayfield, Colorado 1999

Preface

Unlike many edited volumes, this book did not spring from a symposium or a conference session. Rather, I conceived the idea in the spring of 1996 as I spoke with colleagues at the annual meeting of the Society for American Archaeology in New Orleans. It was clear to me then that several new and important Basketmaker III studies were being completed. From what I knew of this recent work, the need to publish these innovative findings was immediate and critical. Rather than organize a symposium, I chose to seek a publishing outlet immediately. "Immediately," in this case, took more than three years because of the process of soliciting papers, waiting for drafts, writing, rewriting, and editing. Nevertheless, our perseverance, and that of the University of Utah Press, paid off, and the result is this volume.

As we enter the new millennium, I see Basketmaker archaeology where Chacoan studies were about 20 years ago—on the edge of a new frontier. In the late 1970s, the Chacoan road system was newly discovered and archaeologists were beginning to see that culture's full range of complexity. Today, Basketmaker archaeology is poised on the edge of a similar threshold: new discoveries are being made, and old assumptions are being questioned. I believe the following chapters give us strong hints of where things are headed, but many possibilities remain.

The findings presented herein represent a diversity of approaches to archaeology, but most fall under the rubric of cultural resources management (CRM). As CRM studies have multiplied in the last twenty years, fewer projects can be described as "pure" research. Furthermore, many archaeologists currently practicing in the academic, CRM, and government domains cut their teeth on CRM. It is perhaps fitting, then, that CRM work has produced most of the findings that are driving new research into the Basketmaker realm.

This book does not present a unified or conclusive view of the lengthy Basketmaker interval. Rather, the authors have drawn on a variety of backgrounds, interests, skills, and data to address a wide range of issues related to Basketmaker sites in the Anasazi heartland. I think I can speak for all contributors by saying that what is presented here represents only the beginning of a new era of Basketmaker research. We are building on the foundation laid by the early researchers (see chapter 1) and questioning old (and relatively new) hypotheses about the nature of the Basketmaker adaptation. In no way will this work be the final word on any particular issue. I would hope, however, that this volume has captured the excitement of the new findings and hypotheses concerning Basketmaker archaeology, and that it will help to guide research in the new millennium.

Many people contributed to this undertaking. All of the volume contributors deserve thanks for following my often demanding schedule and producing outstanding work. Lacking the usual and clear motivation of a symposium or conference deadline, the authors instead made due with my arbitrary but necessary deadlines and responded well.

The volume benefited from the comments of several reviewers, including Chip Wills, Richard Wilshusen, and Deborah Nichols. All reviewers offered solid suggestions for improving individual chapters and the entire manuscript. Several colleagues read and commented on various chapters, and I am indebted for their input. Doug Dykeman and Kris Langenfeld offered useful criticism on many of the chapters. Dave Breternitz, Deb Gibson, Kelley Hays-Gilpin, Kathy Hensler, Tony Klesert, and Marilyn Joslin Sklar provided input on the chapters I wrote, and their comments were very helpful. Jeff Grathwohl of the University of Utah Press offered good advice and support throughout the process. Jeff and his staff are to be commended for producing an outstanding book. Alexis Mills technically edited the volume, and her work contributed significantly to the final product. The Navajo Nation Archaeology Department and Animas Ceramic Consulting provided essential support. Last, but certainly not least, I want to thank my wife, Lori Stephens Reed, for helping in a variety of ways. Lori designed the cover, using Basketmaker rock art, pottery forms, and a Basketmaker III pit house. She also compiled references and took on the horrific job of producing a single, cohesive bibliography for the book. Lori also read and commented on most of the chapters, as well as writing and contributing to two of them. I truly could not have produced the book without her. My two young sons, Kevin and Sean, also deserve my thanks for getting by with much less of my attention over the last couple of years, especially the last three months.

Paul F. Reed

Farmington, New Mexico, October 1999

Part I

Introduction

I

Fundamental Issues in Basketmaker Archaeology

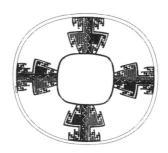

Paul F. Reed

Archaeologists' understanding of the Anasazi Basketmaker period stems from the pioneering work of T. Mitchell Prudden (1897) and Richard Wetherill (see Blackburn and Williamson 1997; McNitt 1966) in the late nineteenth century, and the formalization of the Basketmaker concept by George Pepper (1902). Subsequently, the seminal investigations of Earl Morris (e.g., Morris 1939; Morris and Burgh 1954; E. A. Morris 1980); A.V. Kidder (1924, 1927; Kidder and Guernsey 1919), Samuel Guernsey (1931; Guernsey and Kidder 1921), J. O. Brew (1946), and Frank Roberts (1929), among others, ensued in the early- to mid-twentieth century. Research by this latter group of archaeologists fleshed out the basic concepts put forth around the turn of the century and laid the groundwork for years of Anasazi Basketmaker studies to follow. Continued inquiry into the Basketmaker period from the 1940s to early 1960s (e.g., Amsden 1949; Bullard 1962; Carlson 1963; E. A. Morris 1959) expanded the original concept and increased our knowledge. With the advent of large-scale cultural resource management projects in the 1960s and 1970s (e.g., the Navajo Reservoir Project [Eddy 1966]; the Black Mesa Archaeological Project [Gumerman 1988; Plog and Powell 1984]; and the Dolores Archaeological Program [Breternitz 1986]) previously uninvestigated geographic areas containing substantial Basketmaker remains were studied.

Collectively, these projects and other recent research endeavors, especially during the last 10 years, have revealed the presence of large and varied Basketmaker III populations across the entire northern Southwest (figure 1.1). In particular, large-scale surveys and excavations have revealed Basketmaker remains in settings not previously known to hold such remains, under those of later periods and in "open" settings, as opposed to the classic cave and rock shelter sites upon which the original

Basketmaker concept was built. The outcome of this recent work is an expanded view, both conceptually and geographically, of the Basketmaker III period. The following chapters describe and explore these new findings, elaborating and refining our understanding of this critical period in Anasazi development. All of the chapters contribute to the dominant theme of the book: the foundations of Anasazi society and culture, including an early dependence on maize agriculture; construction and use of substantial pit house structures and storage facilities; production of ceramics; a commitment to a sedentary lifestyle; and an intricate economic, social, and community organization were in place and developed by the Basketmaker III period, if not sooner.

Before discussing the research presented in this volume, a brief summary of the classic view of the Basketmaker III period is warranted. My intent in this chapter is not to provide an exhaustive review of previous Basketmaker III research; this task has been accomplished in several other recent publications (e.g., Blackburn and Williamson 1997; Cordell 1997; Vivian 1990). Rather, I wish to emphasize several issues that emerge from recent studies.

Four recent publications address aspects of the Basketmaker II period: the dedicated *Kiva* issue (volume 60, winter 1994) entitled "Anasazi Origins: Recent Research on the Basketmaker II"; R.G. Matson's (1991) book *The Origins of Southwestern Agriculture*; the Utah Bureau of Land Management (BLM) published volume *Anasazi Basketmaker: Papers from the 1990 Wetherill-Grand Gulch Symposium* (Atkins 1993); and *Cowboys and Cave Dwellers* (Blackburn and Williamson 1997). Although some chapters in the BLM publication touch on the Basketmaker III period, the focus is on the Basketmaker II interval. Similarly, the entire *Kiva* issue is devoted to the Basketmaker II period. Matson's book does

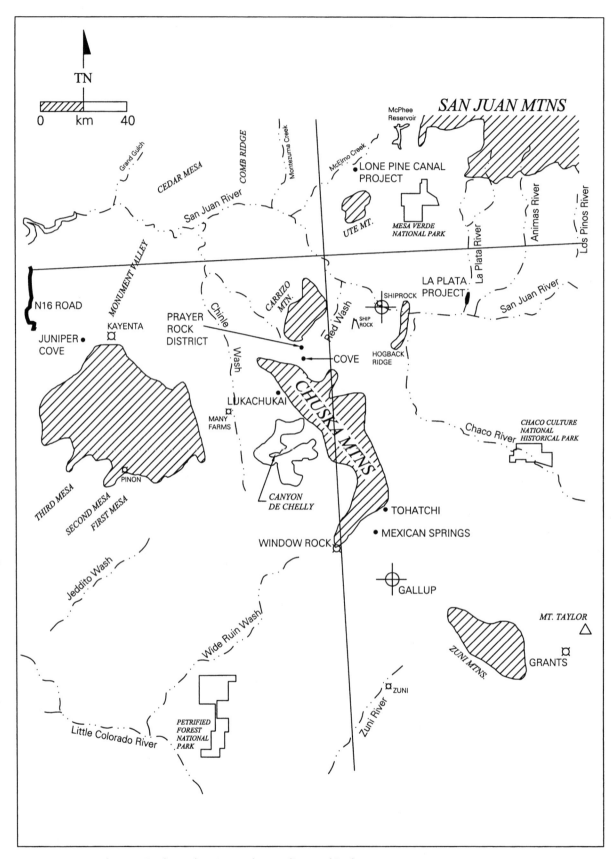

Figure 1.1. Map showing Basketmaker sites and areas discussed in the text.

not address strictly the Basketmaker II period, but he provides an excellent summary work on the period. Lastly, the recent popular book by Blackburn and Williamson (1997) follows up the BLM publication and details Basketmaker archaeology in the Grand Gulch area. The book details the efforts of the Wetherill-Grand Gulch Research Project, a dedicated group of mostly amateur archaeologists who set out to retrace the steps of late-nineteenth-century archaeological expeditions to Grand Gulch. Project participants rediscovered several rock shelters that had not been seen since the original expeditions; rephotographed many of the sites; tracked artifacts and archival notes at the American Museum of Natural History, the Field Museum in Chicago, and several other institutions; and essentially reconstructed the lost and scattered history of Grand Gulch Basketmaker archaeology.

Clearly, the earliest Anasazi period—Basketmaker II—has received considerable recent attention. What is lacking, however, is any attempt to describe, summarize, and provide a perspective on new Basketmaker III material that has come to light. Thus, the need for a synthetic volume, specific to the Basketmaker III period, was clear. Several chapters contained herein discuss the Basketmaker II period, mostly in an evolutionary fashion to illustrate some important aspects of the Basketmaker III period. Nevertheless, all of the chapters focus primarily on the Basketmaker III period.

PECOS CLASSIFICATION AND THE BASKETMAKER PERIODS

As defined by Kidder (1927) in his Pecos Classification (a series of developmental stages for the Anasazi), Basketmaker III was the last pre-Puebloan stage, before the emergence of what Kidder and his contemporaries saw as the "true Anasazi path" during Pueblo I. Kidder's formulation continued a division between Basketmaker and Puebloan peoples that many archaeologists before Kidder had identified: the two groups were viewed as culturally distinct, merely occupying the same basic geographic area. We must remember, of course, that the earliest Basketmaker remains found, predominantly in cave or rock shelter settings and lacking pottery, did stand out significantly from those of the Puebloans (most of what was initially identified dated to Pueblo II and III). Kidder and his contemporaries viewed the groups as largely distinct; some archaeologists of the time, in fact, proposed an invasion of "round-headed" Puebloans who replaced the early, "long-headed" Basketmakers (see Brew 1946). Once sites intermediate between Basketmaker and Pueblo were found (identified initially as modified or post-Basketmaker [Basketmaker III] and pre-Pueblo [now Pueblo I]), the evolutionary nature of the sequence became more clear. The key physical trait separating the

Basketmakers from the Puebloans was supposedly head shape (long and narrow for the Basketmakers compared to short and broad for the Puebloans), which was later determined to be a result of the practice of strapping young infants into differently shaped cradleboards during the Puebloan periods. Brew (1946), drawing on the work of several physical anthropologists studying cranial morphology, demonstrated that the supposedly round-headed Puebloans were statistically indistinguishable from their allegedly long-headed Basketmaker predecessors. Nevertheless, architectural differences, including the apparent lack of aboveground structures among the Basketmakers and the predominance of multiroom, aboveground masonry dwellings in the Puebloan periods, were the other main criteria for differentiating Basketmakers from Puebloans. The architectural differences are still apparent after 70 years of additional study, although both early and late Anasazi groups built and used both subterranean and surface dwellings.

Within the larger Basketmaker interval, the critical trait separating the Basketmaker III period from the earlier Basketmaker II, to Kidder and his contemporaries, and to later generations of archaeologists, was the presence of pottery (Kidder 1927). Recent work shows that pottery does occur in Basketmaker II settings (this volume: Geib and Spurr; Reed et al.). A secondary trait, the construction and use of native-walled or slab-lined pit houses, also was invoked for the later Basketmaker period. At the time, Basketmaker II pit houses were not yet known; all the Basketmaker II caves excavated to that time (late 1920s) lacked habitation structures and contained only cists, other storage features, and burial pits (e.g., Kidder and Guernsey 1919; Guernsey and Kidder 1921). Later work (e.g., Morris and Burgh 1954) identified Basketmaker II sites with pit houses and other habitation structures.

CULTURE HISTORY OF THE EARLY ANASAZI

In this next section, building on the classic view, I provide a brief cultural background on the early Anasazi periods (Basketmaker II through Pueblo I). Although counter-arguments have been made (e.g., Berry and Berry 1986; Matson 1991), many Southwestern archaeologists support the position that the Anasazi developed from late Archaic groups practicing incipient agriculture across the northern Southwest between ca. 1500 and 500 B.C. (see Irwin-Williams 1973; Wills 1985, 1988). Contrary to the in situ development model, Berry (1982) has criticized the use of gradualistic models of Anasazi development, much in the same way that Berry and Berry (1986) did with the Archaic period. Although more dated (and concomitantly less current) than the review undertaken by Berry and Berry, Berry's work nevertheless merits discussion.

Berry (1982) undertook a chronological reassessment of the Anasazi period on the Colorado Plateau and throughout the Southwest. He concluded that the evidence does not support a gradual development of Anasazi culture. Rather, the actual sequence consists of a series of periods punctuated by episodes of abandonment. Berry linked these abandonments to widespread drought conditions that caused large groups of people to migrate to more mesic areas.

Berry's work is not without problems. First, the only sites used in his analysis were those that had been securely dated by either radiocarbon or tree-ring dating. While his intentions were good, Berry undoubtedly excluded from his analysis numerous sites that would impact the patterns he has identified, particularly those sites dated with other reliable methods such as archaeomagnetic dating. Second, Berry's periods are arbitrarily defined, and appear designed to minimize the number of dated sites that occur in transitional periods. Third, in the 18 years since Berry's work was published, numerous additional tree-ring samples have been dated, and other reliable chronological data have been compiled. As a result, many of Berry's gaps have been partially or completely closed (e.g., Berry's early Basketmaker III–Sambrito phase gap in the Navajo Reservoir District [Hammack 1992]; see also Matson 1991; Geib and Spurr, this volume). Nevertheless, Berry's work is important insofar as it encourages archaeologists to consider their chronological data carefully and avoid a priori assumptions concerning the development of cultural sequences.

Basketmaker II

The Basketmaker II period is variously dated between 1000 B.C. and A.D. 500 in different parts of the northern Southwest. Basketmaker II, as currently defined at maximum, is as long as the later Anasazi sequence (Basketmaker III through Pueblo V). Clearly, temporal and spatial differentiation of the period is desirable. Matson (1991) has identified a number of Basketmaker II variants, organized around an east-west spatial division and three temporal stages (table 1.1). Matson's division is well supported geographically but is less certain temporally. He describes the variants (in capital letters with related variants below) as phases but is less certain about their evolutionary relationships (e.g., did the White Dog Cave variant evolve into the Lolomai, which then became the Grand Gulch phase?).

Basketmaker II is a critical stage in Anasazi development because it was during this time that the use of cultigens became a significant part of subsistence. The spread of agriculture, in turn, led to a more sedentary lifestyle (Lipe 1983). General traits of the period include construction and use of small pit houses, large storage cists, shallow grinding slabs, corner- and side-notched dart

TABLE 1.1
Matson's (1991) Basketmaker II Variants

WEST	EAST
GRAND GULCH	LOS PIÑOS
Cedar Mesa	Durango
LOLOMAI	??
Black Mesa	Gallegos Mesa
WHITE DOG CAVE	??
Grand Gulch	
Marsh Pass	
Kanab	

points, the atlatl, one-hand manos, and cradleboard burials (Cordell 1984). The importance of agriculture, along with the initial use of crude ceramics, is what separates the Anasazi during the Basketmaker II period from earlier Archaic populations.

Various models relating to the adoption of agriculture among the Anasazi have been proposed (e.g., Glassow 1980; IrwinWilliams 1973; Matson 1991; Smiley 1994; Wills 1988), many of which have overlapping elements. From an evolutionary point of view, the adoption of agriculture must be seen as providing some selective advantage for the Anasazi that the gathering of wild plant foods did not. Without strong selective pressure, an explanation for why cultigen use became important is difficult. The most important selective advantage of cultigens is their dependability and predictability as contrasted with natural plants (Minnis 1985). Thus, initial use of cultigens probably relates to their seasonal predictability in given areas. It has also been suggested that hunter-gatherers who could most easily fit the demands of cultivation into their seasonal rounds would be most likely to practice agriculture (Wills 1988). There are, of course, other parameters involved in the adoption of agriculture (e.g., environmental limitations, territorial constraints, and social factors), but for the present discussion, understanding that the predictability of cultigens was a key factor is sufficient. In any case, there is good evidence that the Anasazi in certain areas (e.g., Cedar Mesa, Black Mesa) were dependent on maize agriculture by the early Basketmaker II period (Damp and Kendrick 1998; Gumerman and Dean 1989; Matson 1991, 1994; Nelson 1994).

A large Basketmaker II population is inferred for Black Mesa; a dramatic increase from Archaic times is apparent (Smiley and Andrews 1983). Gumerman and Dean (1989) suggest that a firm commitment had been made to agriculture by 600 B.C. on Black Mesa specifically, and more generally, across the Western Anasazi area. Recent dates (2420 ± 100 B.P. and 2320 ± 80 B.P.) from Basketmaker II sites in the Glen Canyon area (Geib 1990; Nickens et al. 1988) support this position. Furthermore, this proposed initiation of Basketmaker II around

600 B.C. is compatible with early dates obtained from northern New Mexico, which suggest a beginning date between 600 and 200 B.C. (Berry and Berry 1986; Irwin-Williams 1973; Vogler et al. 1993). Geib and Spurr (chapter 9, this volume) provide significant new data on the Basketmaker II period on the Rainbow Plateau.

Basketmaker II settlements across the Southwest generally occur on terraces above major drainages and have been documented throughout the San Juan Basin (Judge 1982) and in the Gallegos Mesa area south of the San Juan River (Vogler et al. 1993). In the Redrock Valley area, a possible Basketmaker II occupation underlying the Basketmaker III remains at Broken Flute and Obelisk caves has been tentatively identified (Morris 1980). At least 10 additional Basketmaker II sites have been recorded in Redrock Valley, including camps, pit house habitations, and specialized activity sites (P. Reed and Hensler 1999; P. Reed and Wilcox, chapter 4, this volume).

Basketmaker III

Basketmaker III remains (generally dated from A.D. 400/450 to 700/750) in many areas of the northern Southwest represent in situ continuity from Basketmaker II (see Geib and Spurr, chapter 9, this volume; L. Reed et al., chapter 10, this volume). Important characteristics of this period across the Southwest include use of larger, more elaborate pit houses, upright-slab storage cists and rooms, introduction of the bow and arrow, two-hand manos and trough metates, gray ware and early red and unslipped white ware ceramics, and an increasing dependence on agriculture (Cordell 1984). On Black Mesa, Basketmaker III represents a continuation of Basketmaker II traits, along with the development of pit house villages, use of fired ceramic vessels, and increased trade for shell and lithics (Gumerman and Dean 1989). Sites are relatively common on southern Black Mesa (Linford 1982) and in the Low Mountain area (Anderson 1987), but are apparently absent from northern Black Mesa (Powell 1980). In Glen Canyon, bean agriculture also became important during this period (Lipe 1983). Continuing the pattern established during Basketmaker II, Basketmaker III sites are rare in lower Glen Canyon.

In the San Juan Basin, Basketmaker III sites are relatively common and are scattered throughout the area (Wait 1982). In the Cove-Redrock Valley area, sites dating to this period are quite common, including the Prayer Rock caves (Morris 1980), several sites along the Navajo Route 63 (N63) road (Hildebrant 1989), a number of sites across Buffalo Pass at Lukachukai, Arizona (Altschul et al. 2000), several sites (AZ-I-25-47, AZ-I-26-3, AZ-I-26-5, AZ-I-26-37 and AZ-I-26-41; all Navajo Nation [NN] site numbers) excavated during the Navajo Route 33 (N33) Project (P. Reed and Wilcox, chapter 4, this volume), and elsewhere in the area (cf. Elson 1981;

McEnany 1985; Popelish and Fehr 1983; Warner and Elson 1982).

Pueblo I

The Pueblo I period in the Southwest is generally characterized by the extensive use of surface rooms and pueblos, constructed predominantly of masonry, jacal, or both. Pueblo I is dated between A.D. 750 and 900 in Cove–Redrock Valley and adjacent areas (P. Reed 1999a). "Kivas" of various sizes (presumably the focus of religious ceremonies) became common during this period (Cordell 1984). The widespread production and use of both neckbanded gray ware and early black-on-white painted ceramics are also defining traits of the period. Agricultural production continued to be important for Anasazi subsistence. Areas with significant Pueblo I populations include Mesa Verde (Rohn 1977), the Dolores area (Kane 1986), the upper La Plata River valley (Morris 1939), and parts of Chaco Canyon (Hayes et al. 1981).

In the Western Anasazi area, Gumerman and Dean (1989) see Pueblo I as an elaboration of patterns established during the preceding period. This period apparently represents a time of continued low population density in the Glen Canyon area. Site frequencies are low, similar to areas further to the north and east (see Brew 1946; Lipe and Matson 1971; P. Reed 1990; Winter 1975, 1976). It is possible, of course, that many Pueblo I sites are obscured by the more obtrusive Pueblo II deposits and simply have not been identified. However, certain areas of Glen Canyon do exhibit sizeable Pueblo I occupations; for example, the tributaries of Navajo Canyon (Miller and Breternitz 1958a, 1958b) and the southern end of Paiute Mesa (Stein 1966).

In the San Juan Basin, Pueblo I sites, while not as common as those of earlier or later periods, are present in moderate numbers, and because of this, little population change is inferred for the basin during this period (Cordell 1982). A large Pueblo I occupation does not appear to be present in Cove-Redrock Valley. Most sites dating to the period were either established in Basketmaker III times and extended into Pueblo I or began in late Pueblo I and continued into Pueblo II (Hildebrant 1989; McEnany 1985; Popelish and Fehr 1983; P. Reed et al. 1994; Warner and Elson 1982).

Several chapters in this volume address the evolution of Basketmaker II into Basketmaker III (e.g., Geib and Spurr, chapter 9); others document the transition into Pueblo I in the middle A.D. 700s (e.g., Toll and Wilson, chapter 2). As traditionally applied, the Pecos Sequence, like any trait-based phase sequence, emphasizes the normative character and distinctiveness of both Basketmaker periods, while minimizing variability within each and largely ignoring transitional characteristics. Adherence to such a normative scheme, while having its advantages, has hindered our understanding of the critical changes that define the transition from Basketmaker II to III. Several authors in this volume attempt to redress this shortcoming (e.g., Geib and Spurr, chapter 9; L. Reed, Wilson, and Hays-Gilpin, chapter 10; Robins and Hays-Gilpin, chapter 12) and shed greater light on the nature of the transition. Pivotal issues related to this transition included the initial production and use of pottery, increased reliance on agricultural products, the construction and use of more complex architecture, and the adoption of a more sedentary lifestyle.

Going beyond the Basketmaker II to III transition, the period from A.D. 550 to 750 represents the heart of the Basketmaker III period. During this time, key elements of the Anasazi lifeway were refined and became entrenched: (1) the production and use of gray, red, and white ware ceramics; (2) construction and use of pit structures, large storage cists, and, late in the period, surface rooms; (3) a full commitment to and dependence on the agricultural production of maize, squash, beans, and other crops; and (4) the emergence of varying degrees of economic and sociopolitical differentiation. All of the chapters in this volume contribute new data relating to these basic building blocks, the foundations of Anasazi culture. Below, I briefly highlight several of these issues vis-à-vis previous research and the contributions in this volume.

THE ORIGINS OF CERAMIC PRODUCTION

Discussion of ceramic production in the volume is more limited than many of the other topics of concern here. Nevertheless, one chapter (L. Reed, Wilson, and Hays-Gilpin, chapter 10) is devoted to this subject, and several other authors provide some discussion. In particular, Geib and Spurr (chapter 9) document the earliest known production of ceramics on the Colorado Plateau at Navajo Mountain. Between the second and fourth centuries A.D., a crumbly brown paste pottery was being produced on at least one site on the Rainbow Plateau. The pottery is classified within the Obelisk Utility category, as defined and extended by L. Reed, Wilson, and Hays-Gilpin.

In chapter 11, L. Reed and her coauthors provide evidence of a pan-Colorado Plateau ceramic tradition that began early (A.D. 200 to 400) on the Rainbow Plateau and is dated to the A.D. 500s in most other areas. This tradition used iron-rich, self-tempered alluvial clays to produce an early brown ware, similar to but of much poorer quality than Mogollon Brown Ware made to the south. The authors further document an evolution of this initial technology into the later gray, red, and white wares that typify Basketmaker III assemblages. The strength of the ceramic chapter is its broad, synthetic perspective and the clarity achieved by collapsing numerous local types into larger categories, thus allowing for a

much better understanding of the growth and development of Anasazi ceramic technology.

The production of durable ceramic containers goes hand in hand with reliance on agriculture and increased sedentism (see Crown and Wills 1995). As L. Reed and her colleagues (chapter 10) explain, the earliest brown wares represent the first step in a progression of technological changes that yielded a maintainable, easy-to-make container. The cultivation and consumption of beans, beginning in the early 500s, required a container more durable than the tarred/pitched baskets used to cook previously (Skibo and Blinman 1999). Furthermore, as Gumerman and Gell-Mann (1993:19) pointed out, beans require nearly constant tending to produce a crop and were perhaps the final crop that made sedentism fully necessary. Thus, the development of fired, durable pottery in the northern Southwest went hand in hand with consumption of beans (a dietary complement to maize) and assumption of a fully sedentary lifestyle.

Following Mills (1989) and Hays (1993), L. Reed and her colleagues view ceramic production within the suite of traits that define the early Basketmaker III populations. The initial production and use of ceramic containers, even those as crude as the early brown wares, mesh with the reinterpreted view of Basketmaker III presented here. With an earlier commitment to corn and bean agriculture and sedentary living than previously thought, the earlier production and use of durable ceramic containers are logical accompaniments, one of many technological changes necessary to meet the storage and processing needs of an agricultural, sedentary people.

SUBSISTENCE AND AGRICULTURAL DEPENDENCE

The cornerstone of all Anasazi developments was the initial acceptance and later fluorescence of an agricultural lifeway. As such, the degree to which early Anasazi groups (i.e., during Basketmaker II and III) depended on agriculture is a contentious issue in Southwestern archaeology. Two main positions bracket the issue: (1) Anasazi groups (some if not all) were fully dependent on maize agriculture by at least A.D. 200, during the Basketmaker II period (Matson 1991), and earlier (600 B.C.) in some places (Gumerman and Dean 1989); and (2) the Anasazi were not dependent on agriculture until Pueblo I and perhaps Pueblo II (Plog 1979; Wills 1992). As Matson (1991) notes, these contending views also generally correspond with two primary theories regarding the origin of the Anasazi: in situ development from an Archaic lifeway versus in-migration of a new cultural group. In general, proponents of the in situ model (including Irwin-Williams [1973] and many other Southwestern archaeologists) also support a gradualistic incorporation of maize into the Anasazi diet, with full dependence coming only after A.D. 1000 (Plog 1979). In contrast, those who believe a new cultural group initiated the Anasazi phenomenon (Berry 1982; Berry and Berry 1986) also tend to view the adoption of and dependence on maize as an early occurrence. For my purpose here, the contrast between views of the relative dependence of the Anasazi on maize is the primary concern.

The work of Matson and his colleagues (Chisholm and Matson 1994; Matson 1991; Matson and Chisholm 1991; Matson et al. 1988) on Cedar Mesa makes it clear that the Basketmaker II groups inhabiting the area were fully dependent on maize agriculture by A.D. 200. Matson cites four main lines of evidence: (1) overwhelming abundance of maize remains in analyzed coprolite and pollen samples from Cedar Mesa; (2) isotopic evidence that shows similar levels of maize dependence in the diet of Basketmaker II and Pueblo II populations on Cedar Mesa; (3) similarities in settlement patterns between the Basketmaker II populations and later Anasazi occupations, implying similarities in adaptation (Matson 1991:90); and (4) the lack of late Archaic remains on Cedar Mesa, along with an environment that does not seem to have been favorable for hunting and gathering. Although the same conditions certainly do not apply to all Anasazi groups, it seems clear that assuming a dominant hunting-gathering component for all Basketmaker III groups (as have several authors over the last 15 years; e.g., Gilman 1987; Plog 1997; Reid and Whittlesey 1997; Wills 1992; Wills and Windes 1989) is no longer tenable.

Smiley (1993), discussing work from the Marsh Pass area north of Black Mesa, Arizona, reaches many of the same conclusions as Matson and his colleagues regarding the nature of the Basketmaker II adaptation: "The evidence seems to indicate a rapid transition to agriculture if the radiocarbon data are correct. Further, the indications are unequivocal that relatively intensive agriculture was practiced right from the outset, judging by the large storage facilities associated with all but the smallest sites" (Smiley 1993:253). Smiley's findings, then, do not support a gradual transition to full agricultural dependence, with a peak in later Puebloan times. These Basketmaker II developments, termed the Lolomai phase on Black Mesa, led right into the Basketmaker III occupation of the area, with population aggregation at large sites such as Juniper Cove (Smiley 1993; see also Gilpin and Benallie, chapter 8, this volume).

Gilpin (1994) provides intriguing evidence of an even earlier maize-using Basketmaker II adaptation in the Chinle Valley. Using data from two locales, Gilpin (1994:216) reports direct radiocarbon dates on corn between 1485 and 1109 B.C. at Lukachukai, and 1049 to 1 B.C. (with three dates later than 788 B.C.) at Salinas Springs. Because of the limited work undertaken at these sites, it is unclear to what extent maize dominated the diet. Nevertheless, the presence of numerous maize remains, along with pit house architecture, indicates the

initiation of the Basketmaker II Anasazi lifeway earlier than previously thought.

Recent work on the Zuni Indian Reservation has revealed an early agricultural system, including field systems, associated with pit houses dated to 200 B.C. (Damp and Kendrick 1998). Two Basketmaker II sites (LA 26306 and LA 115330) with pit houses were excavated. The structures contained maize in both micro- and macrobotanical form, and ground stone indicative of maize processing. A nearby site (LA 48695) contained several check dams and was trenched to look for evidence of field systems. Using geomorphological, palynological, and paleoethnobotanical results from this work, Damp and Kendrick (1998:9) interpret LA 48695, and the associated habitation sites, as a household unit "that practiced floodwater irrigation and maintained formal fields."

Jumping ahead in time several hundred years, we find maize-growing, sedentary Anasazi peoples established across the Colorado Plateau: at numerous localities on both sides of the Chuska Mountains, in the La Plata Valley, in the Mesa Verde area, on Cedar Mesa, and on the Rainbow Plateau during the A.D. 600s. Many chapters in this volume provide evidence of reliance on maize agriculture by Basketmaker III peoples. Although none of the studies reported herein have undertaken isotopic work, as did Matson and Chisholm (1991), to confirm the level of maize dependence in the diet, the other evidence presented is compelling and hard to ignore.

I have suggested elsewhere (P. Reed 1999a) that Basketmaker III represented the "golden age" of Anasazi agriculture in the Cove-Redrock Valley and across the Colorado Plateau for several reasons. First, the lands that were extensively exploited beginning in the A.D. 500s had never before been farmed in such a manner. Thus, the problems that vexed later Anasazi populations (e.g., soil salinity, depletion of nitrogen and other nutrients, and the need to bring increasingly marginal lands under production) were not known to the Basketmakers. Second, the overall level of population ca. A.D. 600 was relatively low compared with later periods, and thus good agricultural lands were probably easily obtained. In addition, if problems such as poor or depleted soils arose, migration to other lands was a ready option. Lastly, because of these two reasons, there was little need for sophisticated agricultural technologies (such as planting in a variety of microenvironments [in the modern Hopi fashion], use of labor-intensive mulching methods, or construction of terraces and bordered gardens). We can infer, then, that Basketmaker III agriculture was a relatively simple and straightforward process and that, given the right conditions, was extremely successful with a minimum of labor input.

With this background, do we find evidence for a full commitment to agriculture at Basketmaker III sites? The answer is yes. Several chapters in this volume provide data indicating a clear commitment to agriculture in different areas across the northern Southwest. Altschul and Huber (chapter 7) found evidence of a strong commitment to corn agriculture at a large Basketmaker III village site (AZ E:12:5; Arizona State Museum [ASM] site number) in the Lukachukai Valley. This evidence included all parts of the maize plant (kernels, cobs, stems, and stalks) found in virtually every feature context sampled (pit house floors, hearth features, storage features, milling features, etc.). In addition, large storage features associated with house clusters were identified at AZ E:12:5 (ASM) with maize capacity sufficient to feed the resident households for almost two years. It is unlikely that such large-capacity facilities would be built for every pit house in the absence of the expectation (and the ultimate realization) of filling them with surplus corn.

At Mexican Springs, New Mexico, Damp and Kotyk (chapter 5, this volume) document an extremely diverse assemblage of macrobotanical remains, including large amounts of corn, beans, and squash. These findings indicate that full-scale agriculture occurred at the Basketmaker III sites. Like the Lukachukai sites, macrobotanical remains from cultivated plants were recovered from all feature contexts sampled, again indicating the ubiquity of these resources. Storage features also were abundant at the Mexican Springs Basketmaker III sites, both inside houses (in the form of pits, cists, and bins) and extramural surface storage facilities. In short, the data from the Basketmaker III occupation at Mexican Springs clearly indicate a sedentary population fully dependent on agriculture (while still utilizing abundant wild plant and animal resources).

In chapter 6, Kearns, McVickar, and L. Reed make a convincing case for yet another sedentary Basketmaker III population fully dependent on agriculture. Maize ubiquity of 94 percent for Muddy Wash phase (early Basketmaker III) contexts in the Tohatchi area is a clear indication of its dominance in the subsistence realm. In addition, the large number of internal and extramural storage features at the Tohatchi sites provides additional testimony to the importance of agricultural products in the subsistence economy.

Other volume authors offer data on sedentary, agriculturally dependent Basketmaker III populations. P. Reed and Wilcox (chapter 4) document a sedentary, maize-growing adaptation that began in Basketmaker II in the Cove-Redrock Valley area. Both pollen and macrobotanical data from the N33 project indicate dependence on maize agriculture by the early Basketmaker II period (dated between 350 and 50 B.C.) at two sites, and continuing into the Basketmaker III period. The N33 pollen data show great similarity in Basketmaker and Puebloan structures and storage features regarding economic taxa richness and average maize percentages. Even comparing small Basketmaker II and III sites to the much larger, multicomponent Cove Community site (AZ-I-26-3 [NN]), the "pollen concentrations and economic taxa richness indicate that the subsistence base, or at least what was stored, did not significantly change between Basketmaker and Pueblo times" (Smith 1999:866).

Macrobotanical data from the N33 Project studies also indicate a significant investment in maize agriculture early in the Basketmaker II period (McVickar 1999a; P. Reed and Wilcox, chapter 4, this volume). Maize ubiquity of 81 percent from the structural Basketmaker II site (AZ-I-26-30 [NN]) and nonstructural site (AZ-I-26-24 [NN]) demonstrates a clear commitment early in the Anasazi occupation of Cove-Redrock Valley. As McVickar (1999a:835) notes, "the high value for maize provides convincing evidence for cultivation of maize being fully embraced by the Basketmaker II population." In Basketmaker III, the pattern continues, and dependence on maize is even more pronounced, with ubiquity rising to 90 percent (McVickar 1999a: 835). This percentage almost matches that for Cove Pueblo II period sites (92 percent). Thus, the Basketmaker III inhabitants of Cove-Redrock Valley depended on maize agriculture as much as the later Puebloans.

Geib and Spurr (chapter 9) address the issues of agricultural dependence and permanence of occupation in the Navajo Mountain area. They found evidence of substantial pit houses and large storage features early (around 300 B.C.) during the Basketmaker II period. They also found that the most substantial houses with the largest storage features occurred next to the best agricultural lands, again emphasizing the importance of maize production in the overall subsistence and settlement pattern on the Rainbow Plateau.

In chapter 11, Torres uses data from chipped and ground stone tool assemblages to demonstrate that the Basketmaker III inhabitants of Cove-Redrock Valley were as agriculturally dependent as later Puebloan groups. Torres finds significant correlation between the early and later Anasazi periods regarding raw material usage, utilization of flake and formal tools, and mano and metate configuration. In addition, similar data from Basketmaker II sites in the area indicate that even these earlier populations were practicing an Anasazi adaptation. Data from Cove-Redrock Valley, then, indicate that the transition from a hunter-gatherer to an agriculturalist lifeway was well underway by 200 B.C. This date correlates well with Geib and Spurr's findings on the Rainbow Plateau.

In short, many of the chapters in this volume provide unequivocal support for the hypothesized full-scale agricultural adaptation of Basketmaker III people across the areas under study and, by extrapolation, much of the Colorado Plateau. Other resources were clearly important as well, including a variety of naturally occurring plant foods and animal resources. Nevertheless, the data at hand indicate that Basketmaker III people were as dependent on agriculture as later populations, and probably were just as sedentary, the next issue to be considered.

SEDENTISM, MOBILITY, AND SEASONALITY

A considerable literature on sedentism, mobility, and seasonality exists. Rafferty (1985) and Kelly (1992) have recently summarized this literature, and together their findings provide a good precis. Rafferty (1985) addresses the archaeological record on sedentariness. (Following Cohen [1977] and most archaeologists, I prefer the more parsimonious, if less accurate, term "sedentism.") Rafferty makes several good points. First, the terms "sedentary" and "sedentism" (and synonyms of these words) are frequently used by archaeologists, but are rarely defined explicitly. Thus, adaptations described as sedentary and permanent vary from the city-states of the Near East and Mesoamerica to pit house villages in the American Southwest occupied for only a few years. Rafferty's solution to this problem? She asks archaeologists to define their terminology explicitly. Her own solution is to adopt a definition from Rice (1975:97): "Sedentary settlement systems are those in which at least part of the population remains at the same location throughout the entire year." This definition is very useful, and I borrow it here. Beyond definitions, Rafferty discusses the origins of sedentism and the reasons mobile populations, who have dominated the history of human occupation of the earth, would "settle down." The key to the emergence of sedentary adaptations, in Rafferty's view, is the concentration and availability of resources in a constricted area. Beyond mere abundance, the ability to collect and store resources is critical in the development of sedentary systems. Population pressure, of course, also played a role as hunter-gatherers formerly able to exploit larger areas saw limitations emerge as other groups impinged on their territories. While certainly not causing sedentism, this process dramatically reduced the available territory for hunter-gatherers.

Rafferty discussed different types of sedentary systems, including those that are dispersed. Such systems are likely to develop in areas characterized by high resource diversity but relatively low productivity and reliability (Rafferty 1985:126). The Anasazi of the Southwest met this expectation and were characterized predominantly by dispersed yet sedentary systems until the aggregation that occurred late in the Pueblo III period. Rafferty (1985:144) identified the three most important changes arising from sedentism: population growth, the development of agriculture, and growth in organizational complexity. Regarding agriculture, sedentism "is usually necessary before crop agriculture can develop because to get a yield productive enough to make cultigens the primary food source, people need to be nearby year-round to plant, weed, irrigate, chase away pests, fertilize, harvest, and store...seeds...for planting in the next cycle" (Rafferty 1985:142–143). As I discuss below, the Basketmaker II and III periods provide good test cases for exploring the relationship between sedentism and the development of agriculture.

Kelly (1992) focused on mobility and its varying manifestations to gain insight into sedentism. Following Binford (1980) and others, Kelly identified four types of mobility: residential, logistical, long-term, and migration. As such, mobility is multidimensional and should not be placed at one end of a continuum with sedentism on the other end. No society, even our own, can be considered fully sedentary (Kelly 1992:60). Sedentism can occur in many different forms (e.g., seasonal), and individual members of a society are more or less mobile or sedentary depending on their age, gender, position in the group, and skill level (i.e., highly skilled hunters will hunt more and thus be less sedentary). Based on the work of Powell (1983) and Wills (1988, 1991), among others, Kelly (1992:51) suggests that "seasonal rather than year-round sedentism might account for the archaeological record of the Basketmaker and Puebloan periods." Several chapters in this volume, in contrast, identify early sedentary communities during the Basketmaker III period.

Wills (1985, 1988, 1991, 1995) has written extensively on the transition to food production in the Southwest and on mobility and sedentism. Beyond questioning the level of sedentism of early agriculturalists in the Southwest (see discussion below on Wills and Windes's assessment of Shabik'eshchee Village), Wills's contribution lies in turning the equation around. Rather than asking why hunter-gatherers would take up agriculture and become sedentary, he asked how foragers could incorporate agricultural products into their subsistence pattern. Wills found greater utility in a model that posits foragers using agricultural resources in the same environment and the same season, year after year. Ultimately, Wills hypothesized that competition for resources and land, through increased population density, caused populations to settle down and become sedentary.

Gilman (1983, 1987) influenced the Southwestern archaeological community with her seminal study of architecture. As a result of her work, based on a large cross-cultural ethnographic sample and archaeological data from Black Mesa, Gilman concluded that Southwestern pit houses were most likely winter residences for the Anasazi. Largely because of Gilman's work, and that of others, archaeologists routinely assume that Anasazi pit houses are winter residences, implying, therefore, a biseasonal pattern of residential mobility. Several issues arise from such a blanket assumption, particularly during the Basketmaker III period, by which time many regional Anasazi groups were fully dependent on maize and bean agriculture (as documented by several chapters in the volume).

Given this background, I want to discuss these issues briefly. First is mobility: residential versus logistical, leaving behind Kelly's (1992) other mobility categories for now. Binford (1980) defined the difference between these two modes of mobility based on work with hunter-gatherer groups. His formulation nevertheless can be applied to agricultural groups like the Anasazi. At its simplest, the difference between residential and logistic mobility concerns why people move and how they move. Groups who were residentially mobile, as we assume Archaic populations were, moved their residences several times a year, often within a planned, seasonal round. Logistically mobile people, on the other hand, do not move their primary places of residence very often. Instead, task-specific groups leave home for periods of time, sometimes extended, on various procurement trips: to obtain faunal or vegetal resources, to participate in trade, or to obtain other resources (stone, minerals, etc.) necessary for living. Considering our study of Basketmaker III groups, then, this distinction is critical. Gilman's view of Anasazi pit houses as winter residences in a summer-winter biseasonal pattern assumes residential mobility. Despite her extensive analysis, and that of others (e.g., Wills and Windes 1989), there is no compelling evidence that such a pattern was dominant among the Basketmaker III Anasazi. Specific cases have been made (e.g., the Anasazi of Black Mesa figured prominently in Gilman's study), but most of these involve adaptations to areas marginal for agriculture. The areas under study in this volume cannot be considered marginal. Furthermore, research by Toll and Wilson, Altschul and Huber, Damp and Kotyk, Kearns et al., P. Reed and Wilcox, and Chenault and Motsinger (all in this volume) provide evidence of large and sedentary Basketmaker III populations.

Another issue related to mobility is the seasonality of occupation. Again, if one assumes a biseasonal pattern of residential movement, then the next logical step is to determine the seasonality of use of a given structure. This determination is typically done by examining micro- and macrobotanical remains to see what types of plants are dominant (spring, summer, or autumn), and faunal remains to see, for example, how many young, immature animals might be present, indicating a spring occupation. A major problem with this approach, of course, is the assumption that the remains present in a structure at abandonment (and later excavated by archaeologists) represent both the diversity and the seasonality of subsistence items. The work of Schiffer (1987) and his University of Arizona colleagues and students over many years now clearly illustrates the problems inherent in such a

"Pompeii premise." In short, pit house assemblages can rarely be relied upon to indicate the full range of activities and resources in use. Nevertheless, some archaeologists seem willing to assign a season of use to a structure based entirely upon negative evidence (e.g., "the lack of late spring through early fall plants or animals in the house assemblage indicates a winter occupation"). Many archaeologists, then, are in the habit of making arguments for seasonality because of the attribution of a biseasonal pattern of site occupation, and the resulting need to identify the season of use for every structure. By contrast, I would propose that many Basketmaker III houses were permanent structures occupied year-round by logistically mobile, but residentially sedentary, populations undertaking various resource procurement tasks during seasons of the year.

Support for this hypothesis can be found in several volume papers. Altschul and Huber (chapter 7) document a large, permanent, and year-round occupation at AZ E:12:5 (ASM). Damp and Kotyk (chapter 5) identified several contemporaneous structures, a large communal structure (that could be described as a great kiva), and massive storage features at LA 61955, near Mexican Springs, New Mexico. Based on this evidence, and data from other sites in the area, Damp and Kotyk conclude that the Mexican Springs Basketmaker III occupation was permanent, and not seasonal. Kearns and his colleagues (chapter 6) also document large, permanently occupied Basketmaker III sites in Tohatchi Flats, as do P. Reed and Wilcox (chapter 4) in Cove, Arizona, and Chenault and Motsinger (chapter 3) in the Mesa Verde area.

Were other Basketmaker III populations more mobile than those documented in this volume? Given what we know about the Anasazi of Black Mesa (e.g., Powell 1983), the answer is yes. Upham's (1984) concept of adaptive diversity, with sedentary groups practicing agriculture, while hunter-gatherers lived on the periphery and interacted with these groups, is applicable to the Basketmaker period. Upham postulated that some groups could maintain flexibility in their approach to subsistence and make relatively quick transitions (archaeologically speaking) between adaptations. At this early stage of Anasazi development, then, variability in adaptation was probably the norm. Sites like Shabik'eshchee Village may represent the remains of a more mobile component to the Basketmaker adaptation. Nevertheless, to assume that either Black Mesa or Shabik'eshchee Village is representative of all Basketmaker III groups would be a mistake. The transition to sedentary villages and multihabitation sites with heavy reliance on maize agriculture and the establishment of more-complex economic systems did not occur simultaneously across the Colorado Plateau. For many of the areas studied in this volume, however, which lie predominantly within less than 100 kilometers of the Chuska Mountains, the transition was complete (although not final or necessarily permanent) by the early A.D. 600s.

COMMUNITY ORGANIZATION AND SOCIOPOLITICAL STRUCTURE

Several of the following chapters directly address community organization and social structure. Although no consensus is apparent, what emerges is the sense that Basketmaker III organization was more complicated, if not necessarily more complex, than previously thought. Little has been written on Basketmaker III social organization; most standard texts seem to assume a rudimentary social structure that evolved into the later Puebloan form during Pueblo I, after which time significant changes are inferred (see Cordell 1984). More recent work makes the same assumption: "in general, villages are thought to characterize the Anasazi only after about A.D. 700" (Dohm 1994:257, citing Wills and Windes 1989).

Several case studies presented herein, however, offer good arguments for the existence of Basketmaker III villages (e.g., Altschul and Huber; Damp and Kotyk; Gilpin and Benallie; Kearns et al.; and P. Reed and Wilcox [all this volume]; see also Robins and Hays-Gilpin, this volume, for a different perspective on the evolution of Basketmaker social organization). All of these authors document substantial Basketmaker III villages that consisted of contemporaneously occupied houses, large storage facilities, and great kivas or oversized pit structures. At Kiva Mesa in Cove, Arizona, for example, P. Reed and Wilcox documented a large Basketmaker III village on a low mesa with three great kivas and nine pit houses, several of which are arranged around two plazas. The existence of villages during the mid-to-late Basketmaker III period can no longer be questioned.

Steward (1937, 1955) was perhaps the first archaeologist explicitly to address Basketmaker III social organization. The cultural-ecological framework advanced by Steward, emphasizing environmental and technological parameters, laid the foundation for most later classificatory studies of Southwestern societies (Altschul et al. 2000). Because they practiced agriculture, Steward suggested that the Basketmakers were unlikely to have been organized at the band level of society. He believed that the organizational requirements were simply too great, requiring a higher level of organization: the lineage. While not wishing to propose the lineage as a true stage between band and tribal level societies, Steward nevertheless saw the concept of the lineage as critical to an understanding of early agricultural peoples (like the Anasazi during the Basketmaker III period). Steward (1937) reasoned that the large pit houses and agricultural commitment of the Basketmaker III period indicated a much more sedentary lifestyle than that of the previous Basketmaker II period. Thus, he saw the local lineage as the basic Basketmaker social unit, and envisioned growth occurring through the budding of new lineages. These new lineages then moved to new settlement areas in relative proximity to the parent lineage (Steward 1955:162). In this fashion, Steward could account for large Basketmaker III villages (like Shabik'eshchee Village, Tohatchi Village, or Kiva Mesa) with the lineage model by invoking a large, multifaceted, but single lineage community.

Interestingly, "Steward did not see any organizational differences between these Basketmaker villages and the early Pueblo ones" (Cordell 1984:241). He suggested, instead, that the later, large villages of the Pueblo periods were a result of amalgamation of lineages and other groups, but that the basic structure remained intact. This view suggests that the basic Anasazi social unit at the village level was present and fully developed by at least A.D. 600. Indeed, several chapters herein provide further elaboration on this point. Gilpin and Benallie, P. Reed and Wilcox, and Altschul and Huber all document large, permanently settled Basketmaker III villages.

Birkedal (1976) offered several suggestions about Basketmaker III social structure based on work in the Mesa Verde area. In general, he disagreed with Steward (1937, 1955) that Basketmaker III groups were organized on a lineage model. Instead, Birkedal inferred a band level of organization, invoking lack of organized site layouts and high variation in pit house construction. In this view, the evolution of social structure is predicated on competition for scarce resources and population pressure, two components Birkedal found absent during the Basketmaker III period.

Lightfoot and Feinman (1982) addressed leadership in early Mogollon villages, and their discussion represents the most complete treatment of early social structure in the Southwest. Essentially, they suggested "that social differentiation and specialized decision-making were present in parts of the prehistoric Southwest by at least A.D. 600" (Lightfoot and Feinman 1982:80). Evidence supporting this conclusion comes primarily from differences between large and small pit houses at several Mogollon villages (and at Shabik'eshchee Village). As a rule, the larger houses (inferred to be the residences of local leaders): (1) had substantially more internal area than the other houses (more than twice the floor area), (2) were associated with oversized pit houses or great kivas, (3) had more storage capacity, (4) had greater access to nonlocal trade goods, and (5) contained more evidence of subsistence intensification. Lightfoot and Feinman (1982:81) emphasized the importance of competition between local leaders for (1) attract individuals to their villages through migration, (2) increase regional exchange ties, and (3) encourage the production of [agricultural] surplus. In this view, these leaders played a pivotal role in the sociopolitical changes that occurred during the A.D. 600s (the Basketmaker III period) and that led to all subsequent Mogollon and Anasazi developments.

Looking briefly at Lightfoot and Feinman's "leadership model" vis-à-vis the large Basketmaker III villages discussed in this volume is revealing, but not conclusive. P. Reed and Wilcox (chapter 4) discuss two large Basketmaker III villages in Redrock Valley: Broken Flute Cave and Kiva Mesa. Both sites meet many "leadership model" criteria discussed by Lightfoot and Feinman. Broken Flute Cave is the largest site in the Prayer Rock District, contains a great kiva, has many other pit houses that are larger than average, and has a huge volume of storage capacity. Kiva Mesa, as discussed above, contains three great kivas, many larger than average houses (depressions 10–12 m in diameter), and two plaza areas. The layout of both villages was influenced by topography: the limits of the cave for Broken Flute, and the edge of the mesa for Kiva Mesa. Nevertheless, both sites show evidence of planning in the arrangement of houses with associated storage units and, at Kiva Mesa, in the location of houses relative to plazas and great kivas.

Gilpin and Benallie (chapter 8) and Altschul and Huber (chapter 7) specifically discuss Basketmaker III communities with great kivas or other communal structures (see also Burton 1993). Some Southwestern archaeologists downplay these structures and prefer to avoid the "great kiva" terminology, apparently because of the perceived lack of clear connection between these structures and the later Pueblo I through III great kivas (e.g., Wills and Windes 1989). In contrast, I think these structures logically must be seen as an earlier form of great kiva. This view is not mine originally; earlier archaeologists made the connection between earlier and later great kiva structures. In discussing the four early Anasazi examples (at Broken Flute Cave, Juniper Cove, Blue Mesa, and Shabik'eshchee Village) of great kivas known at the time, Vivian and Reiter (1965) suggested that the origin of these large structures probably predated Basketmaker III.

> There is a span of about 100 years between the village at Broken Flute Cave and Shabik'eshchee. Into this span, based on structural development toward a coalescing great kiva form, we have forced four structures. This is too much, we think, to attribute to a single line of development. It is evident that the great kiva was a not a purely Chaco development. To have great kivas in various stages of growth spread through areas later ascribed to the Chaco, Kayenta, and Mesa Verde branches demonstrates that even at this date the idea of a great kiva—a separate ceremonial structure—was not a newly infiltrating structural form and ritual practice, but that it already possessed time-depth at this point. (Vivian and Reiter 1965:102)

McLellan (1969) undertook a comparative study of Anasazi great kivas from Basketmaker III though Pueblo III. He analyzed 21 characteristics (e.g., size, bench size, presence of sipapu) from a sample of 26 great kivas from across the Southwest. Like Vivian and Reiter, McLellan found evidence for significant continuity through time, concluding that the earlier, Basketmaker III great kivas had evolved into the later, classic great kivas of Pueblo II and III.

Inferring exactly how these large structures may have functioned is difficult, but given their association with large villages, there can be little doubt that they served to integrate Basketmaker III communities along social, political, ritual, and economic axes. Clearly, additional study is necessary to more fully understand Basketmaker III and early Pueblo I great kivas. Nevertheless, Gilpin and Benallie (chapter 8) and Altschul and Huber (chapter 7), among others, offer a substantial beginning.

Wills and Windes (1989) also considered Basketmaker III social structure. They pondered but failed to find support for Lightfoot and Feinman's model. In their view, Shabik'eshchee Village was the locus of temporary gatherings of large numbers of people (to take advantage of piñon nuts), with a small resident population but no aggregated village. Agriculture was not considered by Wills and Windes to have been the dominant means of subsistence for the residents of the village, hence the need for extensive reliance on wild plant foods. Relying largely on a hunter-gatherer model, Wills and Windes did not infer sufficient resources available in the Shabik'eshchee Village area to support a large, permanent settlement or more than temporary leadership. Because of this, they viewed Shabik'eshchee Village as a locale that periodically drew larger numbers of folks (when piñon nuts or other resources were abundant) but which was occupied by only a small resident population.

Other recent publications by Southwestern archaeologists also have described Basketmaker III peoples as mobile and largely dependent on hunting and gathering. Stephen Plog (1997:61), in a recent overview of Southwestern peoples, stated that "sites like Shabik'eshchee were probably established by groups that came together in the fall to collect piñon nuts and perhaps other wild resources." Thus, similar to Wills and Windes, Plog viewed Basketmaker III villages as the result of the temporary aggregation of people still relying primarily on wild plant resources. In other words, Basketmaker III populations are seen essentially as hunter-gatherers who practiced some agriculture. Reid and Whittlesey (1997:167) expressed a similar view of the Basketmakers, indicating that "they were mobile hunters and gatherers who depended heavily on corn agriculture." It is unclear how the Basketmakers could have been both mobile hunter-gatherers and heavily dependent on a sedentary activity like agriculture. Nevertheless, the prevailing Southwestern perspective continues to view Basketmaker III populations as mobile hunter-gatherers who occasionally practiced agriculture. This view is contradicted by several chapters in this volume, which, as noted above, provide interpretations of sites as large, integrated Basketmaker III villages, and present evidence of dependence on maize agriculture.

The view of Basketmaker III social organization offered in this volume has several main components. First, despite the prevailing view to the contrary, the following chapters document several examples of integrated villages during the Basketmaker III period. These villages were occupied permanently, depended predominantly on maize agriculture, and had large numbers of storage facilities upon which the sedentary residents drew. Regarding Birkedal's (1976) band model of organization, these villages were too large and required more-complex mechanisms for conflict resolution than those found in typical band-level groups. Steward's (1937, 1955) lineage model, then, seems more applicable to these Basketmaker III villages, with several lineages probably coming together to comprise the largest villages. Of particular interest is Steward's view that the Basketmaker III groups were not organizationally distinct from later Puebloan populations. Following Steward, we can infer that the larger social unit, the Anasazi village, was present in Basketmaker times, although we cannot yet specify its nature or define all the mechanisms behind it.

Additional research is necessary to clarify these issues. Some late Basketmaker II and early Basketmaker III groups were undoubtedly organized at the "band" level envisioned by Birkedal, while others, particularly those who built large settlements and villages, appear more complex, and perhaps had local leaders similar to those conceptualized by Lightfoot and Feinman. Although these views appear competing and mutually exclusive, it is unlikely that all Basketmaker groups across the northern Southwest experienced the social changes that went along with a more settled life and agricultural dependence at the same time. Thus, flexible organization was probably the rule during this early period in Anasazi development (see Robins and Hays-Gilpin, chapter 12), and we should expect to find different levels of social, political, and ritual organization in different areas.

Before outlining the contributions of specific chapters in this volume, I would like to address the use of the term "Anasazi." In the last few years (but see Brew 1946 for an early objection to use of the Anasazi moniker), many Southwestern archaeologists have abandoned use of this term—the National Park Service has done so programmatically—largely because of the objections of modern-day Puebloan peoples of the Southwest (e.g., the Hopi Tribe). In place of "Anasazi," some archaeologists favor, and many Native Americans support, use of the apparently neutral phrase "Ancestral Puebloans." With all due

respect to the Hopi and other contemporary Native peoples who might object, in this volume we continue to use the word "Anasazi" to describe the prehistoric inhabitants of the Colorado Plateau for the following reasons. First, the prehistoric populations discussed in this book lived and died between 1200 and 1800 years ago. As such, these Basketmaker and early Pueblo I groups have no direct and unequivocal link to any single, modern Native American group. Undoubtedly, many of the Basketmaker populations who produced descendants hundreds of years later are the ancestors of the modern-day people known as the Puebloans. But given the passage of time since these groups inhabited the Southwest, it is also likely that some of the "Basketmakers" evolved through the years into the groups we identify today as non-Puebloan (e.g., the Ute, Paiute, Hualapai, and Mohave). The prehistory and history of the Southwest are complex and document significant population movement, intermarriage between apparently distinct ethnic groups, and fluidity in cultural boundaries. In this light, drawing a direct and exclusive link between the prehistoric Basketmakers and any particular group of present-day Native Southwestern people through use of the phrase "Ancestral Puebloans" seems presumptuous.

Second, although it has come to be imbued with cultural and even ethnic significance, the term "Anasazi" is best viewed as a description of a lifeway. This past lifeway is defined by a number of traits; for example, dependence on primarily maize agriculture for subsistence, construction and use of a variety of permanent dwellings and storage facilities, and a rich ceremonial and ritual life expressed via a number of media, including decorated artifacts, rock art, and kiva murals. In short, far from defining a specific ethnic group, "Anasazi," at one level, is simply a cultural-historical description of the primary adaptation to the northern portion of the American Southwest in prehistoric times. Used as such, "Anasazi" can be a very limiting term, and in some areas (e.g., along the Mogollon Rim in east-central Arizona), in the vicinity of other, similarly defined groups (such as the Mogollon), the distinctiveness of "Anasazi" begins to fade. Nevertheless, the term has historical precedence and serves as a useful shorthand that neither reflects nor implies any specific (and ultimately unprovable) relationship to modern groups. For these reasons, other viewpoints notwithstanding, we use the term "Anasazi" herein.

VOLUME OUTLINE

Following this introduction, the middle section of the book (parts 2, 3, and 4: chapters 2 through 9) presents eight case studies from different geographical areas around the northern Southwest (see figure 1.1). In every case, the chapters present data from a specific area that has seen little prior research. Part 2 documents

Basketmaker landscapes of the northern San Juan region. In chapter 2, Wolky Toll and Dean Wilson use data from sites in the La Plata Valley of New Mexico to suggest refinement of the Basketmaker III concept, conceiving of at least three distinct, temporal configurations. Mark Chenault and Tom Motsinger (chapter 3) discuss the Basketmaker III presence to the north, beyond the limits of Mesa Verde National Park, encompassing a much larger area in southwestern Colorado.

Part 3 of the volume explores Basketmaker archaeology to the south, on the eastern slopes of the Chuska Mountains. In chapter 4, Scott Wilcox and I examine the distinctive Basketmaker III occupation of Cove-Redrock Valley, Arizona, identifying a large community at Cove, within a stone's throw of the Prayer Rock caves excavated by Earl Morris. Jonathan Damp and Ed Kotyk (chapter 5) explore the social and economic differentiation of Basketmaker III populations further south along the eastern Chuska Slope, in the Mexican Springs, New Mexico, locale. Also focusing on the southern Chuska Valley are Tim Kearns, Janet McVickar, and Lori Reed (chapter 6), who document an early, large Basketmaker III population at Tohatchi, tracking its origin, growth, and development through the A.D. 500s and 600s.

Part 4 of the book investigates Basketmaker adaptations west of the Chuska Mountains and beyond. Jeff Altschul and Ed Huber (chapter 7) tackle Basketmaker III social complexity and residential stability, using Lukachukai, Arizona, as their point of focus. Dennis Gilpin and Larry Benallie (chapter 8) document the large site of Juniper Cove, further west in Arizona, and discuss Basketmaker III great kivas and community organization. Finally, Phil Geib and Kimberly Spurr (chapter 9) complete the Western Anasazi case study section by illustrating the transition from Basketmaker II to III on the Rainbow Plateau, emphasizing changes in ceramic and lithic technology, settlement, architecture, and subsistence.

Part 5 of the book consists of three synthetic studies of material culture that crosscut the geographic areas out-lined in part 2. Addressing early ceramic technology, Lori Reed, Dean Wilson, and Kelley Hays-Gilpin (chapter 10) demonstrate that early brown ware ceramics are found in virtually every Basketmaker III locale, reflecting a common origin, perhaps, and indicating that ideas and people moved freely during this period. John Torres (chapter 11) illustrates the importance of Basketmaker III lithic technology in the context of increased resource procurement and processing efficiency, emphasizing Basketmaker III tool use as a stepping stone to later Anasazi developments. Chapter 12, by Mick Robins and Kelley Hays-Gilpin, closes the synthetic section of the book, finding two distinct styles of decorative media, and clear associations with household and community levels of integration.

The final section of the book is a summary paper by Gwinn Vivian (part 6, chapter 13). Vivian ties together many of the threads that run through the volume: dating and chronology, Basketmaker III as a transitional period, settlement structure, evidence of conflict and warfare, the existence of multiethnic communities, and the significance of the cultural boundaries (e.g., Anasazi versus Mogollon) that archaeologists draw.

A complete understanding of the Basketmaker III period is critical for comprehending all subsequent Anasazi and Puebloan developments. The foundations discussed in this book—an early dependence on maize agriculture, construction and use of substantial pit house structures and storage facilities, production of ceramics, a commitment to a sedentary lifestyle, and an intricate economic, social, and community organization—all began in the late Basketmaker II and early Basketmaker III periods (ca. A.D. 200–500) and were well established across the Colorado Plateau by A.D. 600. Thus, the conventional view of the Basketmaker III period as just another step in the process prior to the true emergence of the Anasazi lifeway in Pueblo I seems no longer tenable. Following Earl Morris (1939; quoted at the beginning of chapter 2), I would argue that Basketmaker III is the critical period in Anasazi development.

Part II

Basketmaker Landscapes of the Northern San Juan

2

Locational, Architectural, and Ceramic Trends in the Basketmaker III Occupation of the La Plata Valley, New Mexico

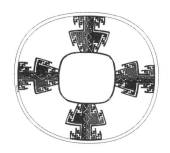

H. Wolcott Toll

C. Dean Wilson

Basketmaker III remains have proved to be extremely plentiful and widely distributed. The period is by far the most important of the entire culture series. So many and such varied events took place before its close that to trace the changes in physical stock and the amplification in material arts in full detail cannot be done at the present time, chiefly because the results of a great amount of fieldwork remain only partially digested and published. (Morris 1939:19)

Much of Morris's assessment remains true, though people who have become fixated on the Chaco phenomenon or who do not like to single out the most important 150 years might cavil with parts of it. Basketmaker is indeed widespread. Partial digestion and publication of work since Morris's time remain a problem, but we are able to add considerable detail to the foundation he laid.

Located in northwestern New Mexico and southwestern Colorado, the La Plata Valley (a part of the La Plata District) was occupied from Archaic through Pueblo III times and remains in use by modern farmers. Present knowledge of sites in the valley suggests that, as at Chaco Canyon and elsewhere, Basketmaker III was the earliest period in which sizable communities were present where several concentrated settlements organized around clusters of public architecture eventually were established (figure 2.1). The area directly south is known as "the Totah." *Totah* is a Navajo word meaning "rivers coming together," here referring to the confluence of the San Juan, Animas, and La Plata Rivers. It is a useful term for the archaeologically important area surrounding modern Farmington, New Mexico (see McKenna and Toll 1992:133). The La Plata Valley is an especially interesting laboratory because of the presence of a permanent stream, a feature that sets it apart from much of the Four Corners region. This chapter examines Basketmaker III settlement patterns using data from the La Plata High-

way Project and other studies. We discuss ceramic changes within the period called Basketmaker III, describe sites and settlement patterns associated with various periods, place aspects of Basketmaker III structures in the context of other recent work done with Basketmaker III and climate, and examine similarities and differences in site locations and social situations with Pueblo II in the valley.

Basketmaker III is defined here temporally, lasting from around A.D. 400 to around 725. This time period was first identified ceramically by the presence of plain ware and Chapin Black-on-white, and the absence of neckbanding and red ware. The A.D. 400 beginning of the period is quite speculative, as dates for Basketmaker III sites are most commonly in the A.D. 600s. Though the timing of architectural variability is a matter of interest and should not be used as a criterion for period definition, the normative Basketmaker III pit structure is a rectangle with rounded corners, an antechamber, a bench, and some sort of floor partition, and is well under 2 m in depth. Usually there are also ground surface storage features.

After the La Plata River emerges from a narrow canyon in the La Plata Mountains in Colorado, it makes its way to the confluence with the San Juan River through a valley that varies considerably in width, dropping in elevation from around 8000 feet to around 5300 feet (2440 to 1615 m). The 6000-foot line (1830 m) seems to form a remarkably good dividing line between portions of the valley occupied at different Anasazi periods. Coincidentally, the river crosses the 6000-foot line very near the New Mexico–Colorado state line. State-based archaeology *should* be assiduously avoided, but there is some chance that this artificial line has had an effect on what we know about the area. The porous and fuzzy 6000-foot "boundary" will be used during

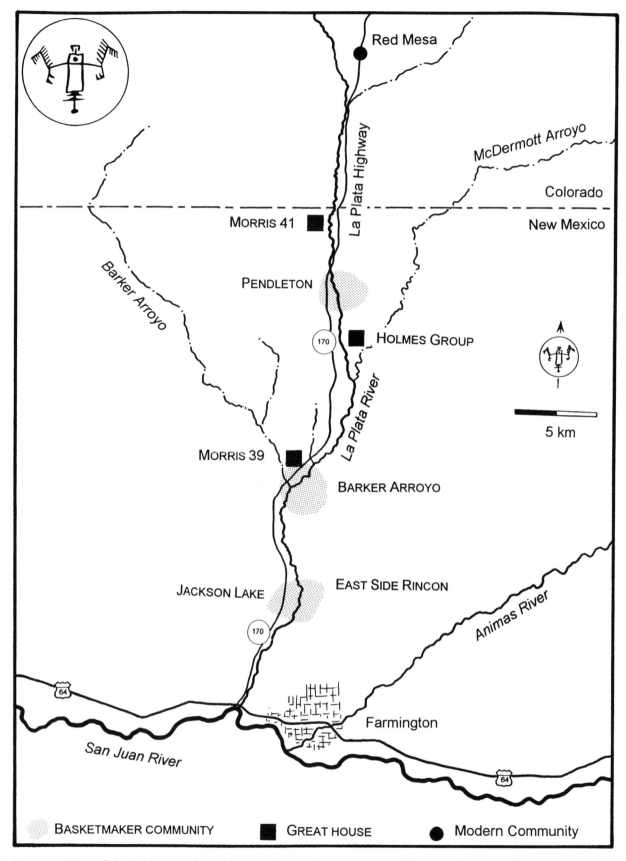

Figure 2.1. Map of the Totah area—the confluence of the La Plata, Animas, and San Juan Rivers—indicating the areas of Basketmaker III settlement in the La Plata Valley, as discussed. La Plata Basketmaker logo is from a Chapin Black-on-white bowl from LA 60751 at Jackson Lake.

discussion here to separate the upper from the lower valley. Hancock et al. (1988) term the portion of the valley just below this boundary "the middle La Plata Valley," which in some contexts is a useful subdivision, but upper and lower suffice here. Based on reconstructions of frost-free periods and precipitation, Schlanger (1986:502, 1988b) has suggested extended periods during which a lower limit for dry farming in the Dolores area is 6000 feet in the early A.D. 700s and the middle 800s, which corresponds to known site distributions in the La Plata. Schlanger's reconstruction also shows a 6000 feet lower limit at A.D. 980–1025 and from ca. 1110 to 1175, neither of which fits as well with known site locations in the La Plata Valley.

Antecedents to Basketmaker III occupation of the lower La Plata Valley are nearly absent from the currently known archaeological record. Given the presence of Archaic and Basketmaker II sites to the south of the San Juan and in the upper reaches of the valley, there can be no doubt that people at least passed through the lower parts of the valley during these periods. Kearns (in Hancock et al. 1988:993–995) suggests that the short-term sites excavated in the La Plata Mine area represent way stations used in transit between summer occupations of the San Juan Basin and wintering sites in the piñon-juniper uplands to the north. The density of later Anasazi and historic use of the river valley itself greatly diminishes the likelihood of survival and recognition of the more ephemeral sites of the Archaic and Basketmaker II, but there does seem to be a pattern of these earlier sites being found in better-forested locations. Data from the region leave no doubt that horticulture and structure building were both practiced before the time of Christ.

DISCOVERING AND DOCUMENTING BASKETMAKER TEMPORAL VARIABILITY

There has long been a tendency to place sites in the La Plata Valley dating as early as A.D. 300 and as late as A.D. 800 into a single Basketmaker III period (Morris 1927, 1939; Shepard 1939). Important clues concerning ceramic change during the early ceramic occupations of the La Plata Valley are presented by Shepard (1939) in her technological study of La Plata Valley pottery. Shepard noted a surprisingly high amount of technological variability in Basketmaker III ceramics from La Plata sites as compared to those from later components. She noted that Basketmaker III assemblages dominated by white wares with iron-based mineral-painted sherds were concentrated in different areas in the La Plata Valley than those dominated by organic- or glaze-painted white wares. These differences were attributed to variation in techniques employed by contemporaneous potters residing in different locations of the La Plata Valley. Shepard felt that this variation reflected the experimental nature

of Basketmaker III, during which a variety of pottery materials were being tested. She proposed that these different spatial distributions could reflect the work of two distinct groups of people with different ceramic traditions (Shepard 1939:284–285). Despite her wide experience with chronological issues, Shepard assumed all assemblages lacking San Juan Red Ware or textured gray ware were roughly contemporaneous, and she assigned them to a single Basketmaker III period, reflecting the broad definition of the Basketmaker III phase during the time of her study (Kidder 1927; Morris 1927, 1939).

More recent investigations verify Shepard's (1939) observation of considerable variability among early ceramic assemblages from La Plata Valley sites. However, this variability probably reflects ceramic change within the long span usually attributed to the Basketmaker III period rather than areal differences in production (Wilson and Blinman 1993). The Navajo Reservoir Project made the first attempts in the region to recognize distinct phases from sites assigned to the Basketmaker III period (Dittert et al. 1963; Eddy 1966). During the project, ceramic distributions were used to place early sites into a series of distinct phases including the Los Piños, Sambrito, and Rosa phases, and were further divided into a series of subphases based on minor differences in ceramic distributions (Dittert et al. 1963; Eddy 1961, 1966).

This scheme appears to be applicable to other areas of the northeastern part of the San Juan Basin, where similar changes occurred, including the La Plata Valley. As is the case for the Navajo Reservoir Project, the earliest ceramic-bearing phases in the La Plata Valley can be distinguished by differences in the frequencies of utility wares (brown ware versus gray ware) as well as the frequencies and associated technologies of decorated white wares. During investigations of the La Plata Highway Project, these differences were utilized to recognize three distinct early ceramic phases that would have earlier been subsumed as simply Basketmaker III. The sequence of ceramic change in the La Plata Valley appears to have been similar to that noted during the Navajo Reservoir Project, although we use terminology not tied to local phases. Sites in the La Plata Valley that would have been previously assigned to the Basketmaker III period were divided into three phases based on associated ceramics: Transitional Basketmaker, Classic Basketmaker III, and Early Pueblo I.

CHRONOLOGY, ARCHITECTURE, AND CERAMICS

While the number of early contexts excavated during the La Plata Highway Project was small, structures associated with all three of these phases were encountered, providing information concerning recognition and dating of early phases in the La Plata Valley (table 2.1). This

Site/ structure	N-S axis/ E-W axis (m)	Bench width (m)/style	Floor partition/ area (m²)	Antechamber/ chamber/	Pits[a] (n)	Sipapu	Date (A.D.) basis
Jackson Lake							
LA 37594/ Pit Structure 5	5.0/ 5.0	no bench	bump	entry?	6[b]	no	539±50 $_{14}$C
LA 60751/ Pit Structure 1	4.5/ 4.25	1.1/ 3/4	wing wall, bin/4.0	ante.	11	no	654–695 dendro.
LA 37595/ Pit Structure 3	4.42/ ?	± .85/ 3/4	wing wall/ 2.1[c]	ante.	10[b]	yes	BM III ceramic archit.
East Side Rincon LA 3131[b]	—	—	—	—	—	—	600s archeomag.
Barker Arroyo							
LA 37605/ Pit Structure 2	5.2[c] 5.4[c]	.75-.90/ 3/4	wing wall/ 7[c]	vent	1[d]	?	Late BM III? ceramic archit.
LA 37605/ Pit Structure 5	5.75[c]/ 6.[c]	.80/ 3/4	wing wall, bin/ 8[c]	ante.	3[b]	no?	Early PI? ceramic archit.
Pendleton							
LA 45687 (DCA-83-211)/ Feature 7	4.08/ 4.40	no bench ?	none	vent	2	no	693 dendro.
LA 45689 (DCA-83-214)/ Feature 1	4.45/ 4.95	no bench	wing wall, bin/ 5	ante.	2	yes	BMIII–PI ceramic 600s $_{14}$C
State Line							
LA 1897 (Morris 39)/ Pit Room J	5.80/	no bench ?	none?	ante.?	?	no?	BM III ceramic
Morris 41/ Pit Room D	2.68/ 2.06	?	bins	?	?	?	BM III–PI position
Morris 19/ Protokiva 3	7.92/ 6.93	.66-.90/ 3/4	wing wall/ 9	ante.	?	no	BM III–PI

[a]"Pits" are defined here as unburned subfloor features; does not include features termed pot rests, ash pits, heating pits, sipapus, or postholes by their excavators. See also Hancock et al. 1988:1020.
[b]Limited data are available from this site.
[c]Estimated.
[d]Partial floor.

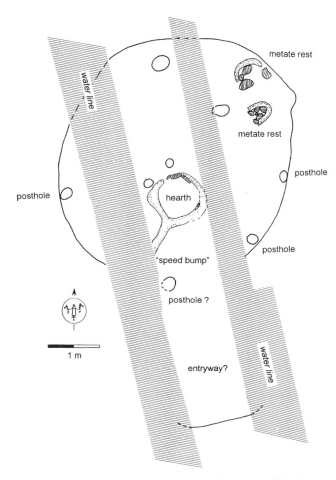

Figure 2.2. Pit Structure 5, LA 37594, a Transitional Basket-maker structure. Floor pits of unidentified function are not labeled.

information may also be used to date collections from other early sites reported for the La Plata Valley and to examine patterns of settlement location and growth.

Transitional Basketmaker: The Earliest Ceramic Occupation

The first temporal group contains a single structure in the La Plata Project sample, LA 37594, Pit Structure 5. This structure is distinctive for several reasons: it is circular with postholes around the periphery, relatively shallow, and has cobble and adobe, horseshoe-shaped metate rests in the main chamber (figure 2.2). It appears to have had an entryway at the south, but the area is sufficiently disturbed by subsequent Pueblo II occupation and then by modern activity to make this unclear. Though the exact roofing pattern is unknown due to modern disturbance, the roof was supported by posts around the edge and perhaps a large central one. The hearth is adobe and cobble lined, with a "speed bump" extended from the adobe lining to the southwest (and probably to the southeast, though this area was cut by a water line). "Speed bumps" are raised, smooth, linear features that partition the floor space (these are the "clay radials" discussed by Kearns et al. and P. Reed and Wilcox, this volume). Their location

seems to anticipate the wing walls found in subsequent structures, although they are also found in later structures. In general plan, diameter (5–6 m), and depth (40–50 cm), this structure is more similar to the aceramic structures located about a kilometer east of the Pendleton Site complex (see below; Foster et al. 1983) than to the Basketmaker III structures of the second temporal group discussed here.

Most of the features and materials at this site come from its Pueblo II occupation. Ceramics in clear association with Pit Structure 5 at LA 37594 were scarce, and the presence of this early component was not recognized until the structure was excavated. All the sherds associated with the early component of LA 37594 exhibit very distinct and limited ranges of characteristics, and are similar to pottery previously classified as Sambrito Brown or Utility Ware (table 2.2; Dittert et al. 1963; Eddy 1961, 1966; Wilson 1989a; Wilson and Blinman 1993). On the surface these sherds are dark gray, brown, to red, and the paste profile is usually dark gray to dark brown. Surfaces are undecorated and polished (in tables 2.2 and 2.3 these sherds are listed as "polished gray"). These sherds appeared to be thick relative to vessel shape. Temper consists of a fine sand or crushed sandstone, in contrast to most of the ceramics from later structures where the vast majority of temper is crushed rock. A subsample of sherds subjected to refiring analysis in a controlled oxidation atmosphere all fired to red colors.

As had the Basketmaker II structures adjacent to the La Plata Valley reported by Foster and his colleagues (1983) and Brown (1991:260), this structure had burned, and both the Tree-ring Lab and the excavators anticipated that it would date well, but the tree-ring specimens could not be temporally placed. We therefore submitted a radiocarbon sample of outer rings from probable structural wood, which dated at 1530 ± 50 BP (Beta-41360), with a two-sigma calibrated range of A.D. 410–630, and a mean of A.D. 544. Although old wood could, of course, be a problem with this sample, and we do not have multiple dates, the ceramics and architecture suggest that this date is reliable. The date and the distinctiveness of the ceramics suggest that this structure represents an occupation that took place early in the use of ceramics in this part of the Southwest. The structure, the ceramic assemblage, and the absolute dates at LA 37594 form a very close fit with a structure excavated by the University of Colorado in Mancos Canyon (Hallisy 1974) and with the majority of the pit structures dating to the Muddy Wash phase in the Chuska Valley (see Kearns et al., this volume). The ceramics in the Mancos structure were all polished brown ware, and the tree-ring dates are in the 470s (Breternitz 1986). The similarities to the example in Mancos Canyon and the considerable settlement in the Chuska Valley are consistent enough that this seems to be more than one or two pioneer families making things up

TABLE 2.2

Overall Ceramic Counts for La Plata Highway Sites with Basketmaker III Components

	LA 1897		LA 37594		LA 37595		LA 37605		LA 60751		Total	
	Count	%	Count	%	Count	%	Count	%	Count	%	Count	%
Plain Rim	6	.1	5	.1	—	—	13	.0	8	1.0	32	.1
Plain Gray	1245	16.4	717	8.4	317	12.1	3718	13.9	237	30.5	6234	13.5
Banded	95	1.2	1	.0	—	—	6	.0	—	—	102	.2
Corrugated Gray	3555	46.9	5222	61.0	1463	55.9	12,434	46.5	225	28.9	22,899	49.5
Polished Gray	—	—	162	1.9	—	—	5	.0	119	15.3	286	.6
BM III B/w	1	.0	—	—	—	—	73	.3	12	1.5	86	.2
P I B/w	1	.0	—	—	—	—	15	.1	1	.1	17	.0
Kana-a Style B/w	—	—	—	—	—	—	1	.0	—	—	1	.0
BM III–P I B/w	1	.0	—	—	—	—	2	.0	1	.1	4	.0
P I–II B/w	2	.0	2	.0	—	—	1	.0	—	—	5	.0
P II B/w	439	5.8	401	4.7	124	4.7	3090	11.6	5	.6	4059	8.8
P II–III B/w	799	10.5	325	3.8	211	8.1	1643	6.1	3	.4	3015	6.5
Misc. White Ware	1409	18.6	1721	20.1	490	18.7	5570	20.8	129	16.6	9319	20.1
Abajo R/o	—	—	—	—	—	—	2	.0	—	—	2	.0
Mesa Verde Red Ware	10	.1	2	.0	6	.2	57	.1	—	—	75	.2
Cibola Red Ware	6	.1	1	.0	1	.0	34	.1	2	.3	44	.1
Kayenta Red Ware	7	.1	8	.1	1	.0	8	.0	1	.1	25	.1
Mogollon Brown	3	.0	—	—	—	—	1	.0	1	.1	5	.0
Mud Ware	1	.0	—	—	2	.1	47	.2	—	—	50	.1
Total	7580	100.0	8567	100.0	2615	100.0	26,720	100	778	100	46,260	100

Note: PS = pit structure; % = percentage of collection.

TABLE 2.3

Ceramic Types in Relatively Unmixed Proveniences in Basketmaker III Pit Structures

	37594 PS 5		37595 PS 3		60751 PS 1		37605 PS 2		37605 PS 5		Total	
	Count	%	Count	%	Count	%	Count	%	Count	%	Count	%
Plain Rim	—	—	—	—	5	3.5	3	.3	—	—	8	.5
Plain Gray	1	.9	—	—	92	63.9	654	60.3	161	48.1	908	54.0
Corrugated Gray	1	.9	—	—	—	—	19	1.8	52	15.5	72	4.3
Mud Ware	—	—	—	—	—	—	29	2.7	18	5.4	47	2.8
Polished Gray	112	95.7	—	—	22	15.3	5	.5	—	—	139	8.3
BM III B/w	—	—	—	—	11	7.6	60	5.5	1	.3	72	4.3
Pueblo I B/w	—	—	—	—	—	—	14	1.3	—	—	14	.8
Pueblo II–III B/w	—	—	—	—	—	—	19	1.6	16	4.8	35	2.1
BM III–P I B/w	—	—	—	—	1	.7	1	.1	—	—	2	.1
Pueblo I–II B/w	—	—	—	—	—	—	1	.1	—	—	1	.1
Painted B/w	—	—	—	—	2	1.4	5	.5	—	—	7	.4
Polished White	2	1.7	1	100.0	10	6.9	269	24.8	87	26.0	369	22.0
Polished B/w	—	—	—	—	1	.7	1	.1	—	—	2	.1
Mesa Verde Red	—	—	—	—	—	—	2	.2	—	—	2	.1
Abajo Red	—	—	—	—	—	—	2	.2	—	—	2	.1
Total	117	100.0	1	100.0	144	100.0	1084	100.0	335	100.0	1681	100.0

Note: PS = pit structure; % = percentage of collection.

as they went along (as per Eddy 1966). As noted by Breternitz (1986), these sites are invisible from the surface, and it is likely that other examples conforming to this pattern exist (see Kearns et al. and Geib and Spurr, this volume).

During investigations of the Navajo Reservoir Project, sites yielding similar ceramics were assigned to the late Los Piños and early Sambrito phase component between A.D. 200 to 550 (Dittert et al. 1963; Eddy 1961, 1966: 352). This period spanned considerable architectural change. Generally, structures dating to before A.D. 550 are characterized by circular forms, depths of less than a meter, and a low frequency of brown ware ceramics, all of which correspond to the structure at LA 37594 (see also Fenenga 1956:205–207).

The dating and relationship of the earliest ceramic occupations to other Anasazi phases are controversial. Based on a perceived absence of sites dating from the fifth to sixth century A.D., Berry (1982) suggests a major occupational gap between the Basketmaker II or Los Piños phase containing early plain brown ware, and the Basketmaker III period consisting of gray and white wares. Our view is that such gaps are the result of archaeological constraints on the identification of such components, and that the earliest ceramic sites span the period between aceramic Basketmaker II to the Classic Basketmaker III periods, dating sometime between A.D. 300 to 550 (Wilson and Blinman 1993). Sites occupied during this period exhibit similar characteristics, including the presence of shallow pit houses and undecorated, polished brown ceramics, and are found throughout the Southwest (Dittert et al. 1963; Eddy 1961; Fowler 1988; Haury and Sayles 1947; Martin and Rinaldo 1947; Morris 1980; Varien 1990; Wendorf 1953; Wheat 1955a; Whittlesey et al. 1994). We feel that the presence of brown ware indicates a transitional phase between Los Piños and Basketmaker III, which we call Transitional Basketmaker (and the Navajo Reservoir Project called the Sambrito phase). The existence of this phase implies a long Basketmaker occupation continuous in time, but not necessarily in space. There is also at least some spatial continuity, since many Transitional Basketmaker structures have been found in the vicinity of Classic Basketmaker sites, as reported for Tohatchi Flats (Kearns et al., this volume).

The early structure at LA 37594 may be placed into an early ceramic phase that postdates many aceramic Basketmaker II occupations but precedes the Basketmaker III period as usually described. LA 37594 and other early ceramic-bearing sites in the northern Anasazi country appear extremely similar to aceramic Basketmaker II sites, except they contain low amounts of plain brown ware ceramics. It is likely they developed directly out of local aceramic Basketmaker II occupations (Matson 1991; Wilson and Blinman 1993). While aceramic

Basketmaker II contexts were not encountered during investigations of the La Plata Highway Project, several aceramic Basketmaker II sites have been excavated in the La Plata Valley (Brown 1991; Foster et al. 1983; Hancock et al. 1988; Reed and Horn 1987) and nearby Animas Valley (Fuller 1988; Morris and Burgh 1954; Winter et al. 1986). Probable Sambrito Brown sherds have been reported in the East Side Rincon across the river from LA 37594 (D. D. Dykeman, personal communication, 1988), indicating the presence of at least a multifamily settlement in the sixth century. Sambrito Brown is also present at a multicomponent site near the confluence of the La Plata with the San Juan, although no features from this time period were identified (Vierra 1993a).

Field and lab recognition of Sambrito Brown is critical to enhancing understanding of settlement during Transitional Basketmaker. Sambrito is one of many variations of early brown wares found in much of the Southwest. Its brown paste, self-temper, and polish make it relatively distinctive (see Wilson 1989a; L. Reed et al., this volume), although it sometimes overlaps with early gray ware types in appearance and probably production technology. Vessels tend to be thick, and vessel forms include seed jars, cooking and storage jars, and bowls. Pastes are soft and silty, and cross-sections tend to be dark. Surface colors include brown, dark gray, and gray-brown.

Classic Basketmaker III

The second temporal group contains two sites for which we have data. These sites are located on either side of LA 37594. Assuming that the structure at LA 37594 dates to the middle A.D. 500s, the features in the second group were in use about a century later, pushing it to the end of the A.D. 600s and, in many schemes, the end of Basketmaker III. The two excavated structures in the vicinity of LA 37594 are rectangular with rounded corners, and have antechambers and benches (LA 37595 Pit Structure 3 and LA 60751 Pit Structure 1, figures 2.3 and 2.4). Pit Structure 1 at LA 60751 has an excellent series of dates showing it was built in A.D. 654 and used until at least 695 (figure 2.5). This structure is the most complete example in the La Plata Highway sample of a Classic Basketmaker structure with an antechamber, four-post roof support (two posts in the wing walls), central hearth, and wide bench. The "La Plata man" figure used on all our maps was from a bowl on the north bench; a grooved maul and a perfect Archaic projectile point (a Jay point) were also found in this structure. Ceramic counts from these two structures are small, particularly at LA 37595, where abandonment and later occupation removed almost all ceramic traces of the Basketmaker occupation (see table 2.2). Although also small, the LA 60751 assemblage is large enough to show some patterns.

This phase is recognized ceramically by the appear-

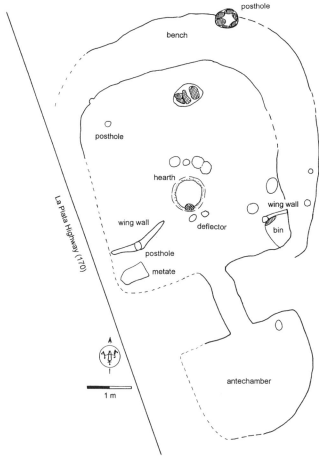

Figure 2.3. Pit Structure 1, LA 60751, a Classic Basketmaker pit house.

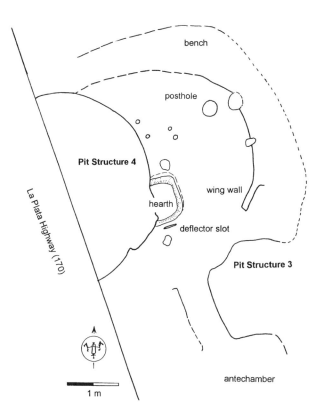

Figure 2.4. Pit Structure 3, LA 37595, a Classic Basketmaker structure. Pit Structure 4, a smaller, deeper Pueblo II "kiva" cuts the middle of Pit Structure 3. The antechamber of this structure was not excavated, but the indications are that it was similar in shape to that at nearby LA 60751, Pit Structure 1 (see figure 2.3).

ance of distinctly Anasazi style pottery at about A.D. 575; it lasts until the beginning of the eighth century. Because this represents the span of time most commonly attributed to the Basketmaker III period of the Anasazi, such occupations are assigned to the Classic Basketmaker phase. Examination of sherds from dated contexts from LA 60751 indicated the presence of a ceramic assemblage characterized by the joint presence of Sambrito Utility with typical Basketmaker III gray ware and white ware types such as Chapin Gray and Chapin Black-on-white. Associations noted between temper and paste colors resulted in the separation of sherds from this site into two distinctive paste groups. Sherds belonging to the high-iron paste group contain sand or sandstone inclusions and may reflect the use of self-tempered clays. These sherds consistently fired to red colors in oxidizing conditions. All sherds belonging to this paste group are unpainted. Many sherds belonging to this group are easily distinguished from gray ware types by a brownish surface color and a polished surface. These ceramics are very similar to sherds from LA 37594 classified as Sambrito Utility and indicate a continuity of technology from the Transitional to Classic Basketmaker III periods. Some of the sherds belonging to this paste group, however, were

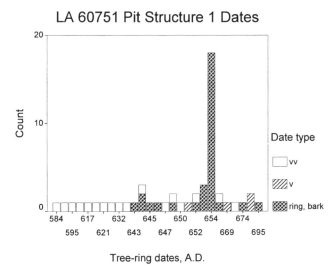

Figure 2.5. Bar chart of LA 60751 Pit Structure 1 tree-ring dates, showing all dates coded by type (vv = very variable, outer rings missing, v = variable, a few outer rings missing, ring, bark = outer ring present). Note that the years are not at equal intervals.

not polished, and exhibited gray pastes. Such sherds were often classified as gray ware during initial analysis where temper was not identified. More detailed examination, however, indicated these sherds contain a combination of sandstone temper and high-iron clays identical to sherds classified as Sambrito Utility. Therefore, such sherds appear to be transitional between sherds normally assigned to Sambrito Utility and Chapin Gray or generic gray body sherds. The presence of these transitional sherds indicates that Chapin Gray gradually developed out of Sambrito Utility, at least in the La Plata Valley. The shift in utility ware types probably reflects gradual changes in resource use and finishing techniques.

A second paste group was represented by most of the sherds assigned to Chapin Gray and Chapin Black-on-white. As is true of the associated brown ware, early gray ware ceramics from the La Plata Valley are utilitarian forms and exhibit no painted or textured decorations. All gray ware sherds from LA 60751 are unpolished. These sherds are consistently tempered with crushed igneous rock probably derived from andesite or diorite cobbles and fire to buff or pink colors when exposed to oxidation conditions. All the painted white ware sherds associated with the early component of this site were classified as Chapin Black-on-white and contained combinations of temper and paste identical to the gray ware from this site. Almost all the white ware from LA 60751 is unpolished and decorated with a dull brown to black mineral pigment. Most of these sherds are decorated with design elements derived from basket-stitching or anthropomorphic designs and are similar to those noted in Basketmaker III sites from other Anasazi areas. Fugitive red is sometimes present on the exterior surface of white ware bowls and on certain gray ware forms such as ollas.

Data from LA 60751 indicate that Classic Basketmaker III ceramic assemblages from the La Plata Valley are easily distinguished from those of immediately earlier and later phases. This is the only phase in the La Plata Valley during which Sambrito Utility occurs along with gray ware and white ware types. Painted ceramics appear during this time and can be distinguished from those associated with later occupations by the general lack of polished surfaces and presence of decorations executed in mineral rather than organic pigment (see Wilson 1996). While trends documented for ceramic pastes and paint use may be useful in differentiating even small assemblages dating to the Classic Basketmaker span in the La Plata Valley and surrounding drainages of the Upper San Juan, such trends may not be applicable in much of the San Juan Basin, particularly in areas to the south and west, where Sambrito Brown was not produced during the Basketmaker III period. Definition of the co-occurrence of early gray and brown wares will be more feasible when archaeological recognition of Sambrito

Brown becomes more consistent (see L. Reed et al., this volume).

EARLY PUEBLO I

The third subdivision of Basketmaker III is represented by two structures at LA 37605 (figures 2.6 and 2.7). These pit structures are also subrectangular with broad benches. The two are very similar in layout and features, and floor elevation. Both have raised partitions on their benches, and both are oriented on the same axis (Akins 1996). We refer to these adobe partitions, which are similar to the separators on a cafeteria plate, as "Bitsue bumps," after Alvin Bitsue, the excavator of several of them. The raised areas run along the edge of the bench, as well as going across the bench, connecting the bench-edge bump with the wall. At the base these bumps are 12–18 cm wide, and they are 3–8 cm high. In Pit Structure 5, where we were able to more fully excavate the bench, a combination of Bitsue bumps and small, upright slabs divided the bench into eight compartments. The similarity of the structures and the unusual features in both make their pairing very likely: they were certainly built in the same tradition, if not by the same people. Pit Structure 2 had a vent rather than an antechamber, while Pit Structure 5 probably had an antechamber (subsequent construction in Pueblo II, and a 1982 water line placed here made this somewhat difficult to ascertain). Both of these structures have archaeomagnetic dates. These plots have nearly identical center points nearest the early A.D. 800s part of the curve (A.D. 760–835 and 770–835; Akins 1996). It seems quite likely that the structure lacking an antechamber (Pit Structure 2, see figure 2.6) was abandoned before the other (Pit Structure 5, see figure 2.7), since it contains a trash deposit immediately above the fill resulting from the dismantling of the roof. It is also quite possible that Pit Structure 5 was built before Pit Structure 2; Pit Structure 5 is larger and has an earlier style. Perhaps Pit Structure 2 represents a "daughter" structure built to accommodate a growing family; a similar pattern is visible at 29SJ629 in Chaco Canyon (Pit Structures 2 and 3; Windes 1993).

In previous studies in the La Plata Valley, schemes allowing for the distinction of components dating to the Classic Basketmaker III from Early Pueblo I assemblages dating after A.D. 725 have been inconsistent to absent. The absence of such differentiations may reflect the rarity of ceramic types such as Moccasin Gray and San Juan Red Ware, often used to identify Early Pueblo I components in areas of the northeastern Anasazi such as the La Plata Valley. Data concerning the recognition of Early Pueblo I contexts were evaluated through the examination of ceramic distributions from the early component at LA 37605. The early component at this site

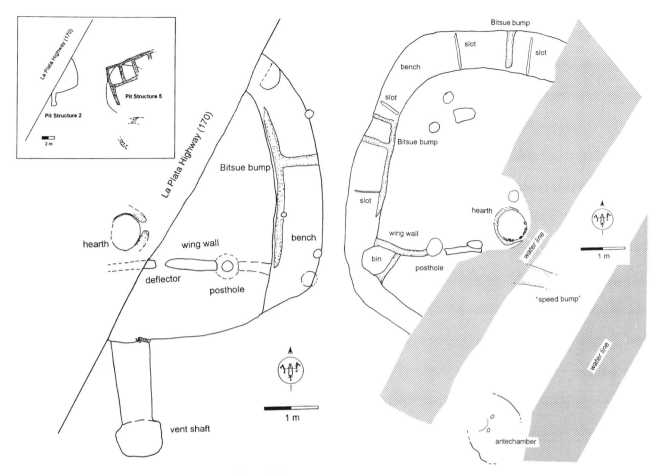

Figure 2.6. LA 37605, Pit Structure 2, an Early Pueblo I structure. Inset shows the general site plan: a Pueblo II room block was superimposed on the main chamber of Pit Structure 5, and a Pueblo II pit structure was superimposed on its antechamber (Pueblo II features shaded).

Figure 2.7. LA 37605, Pit Structure 5, a late Classic Basketmaker to Early Pueblo I structure. The size, architecture, and location of this structure make it look earlier than Pit Structure 2, although it was apparently used later than Pit Structure 2. In addition to Bitsue bumps partitioning the bench surface, there are four slots which could have held slabs or boards.

spans the late Basketmaker III and Early Pueblo I transition, as usually defined. The ceramic assemblages of this component are distinct from those described for LA 60751 and indicate that it is possible to differentiate assemblages associated with Basketmaker III–Pueblo I or Early Pueblo I occupations from those dating to the Classic Basketmaker III period. Ceramic distributions at LA 37605 indicate that three criteria may be particularly helpful in distinguishing Early Pueblo I components from earlier Classic Basketmaker III occupations in the La Plata Valley and surrounding areas. These include the absence of Sambrito Brown, the dominance of organic-painted over mineral-painted white wares, and higher frequencies of white wares at Early Pueblo I components.

White ware types associated with the Early Pueblo I occupation include sherds classified as both Chapin Black-on-white and Piedra Black-on-white. The total frequency of white ware sherds was markedly higher than that noted at LA 60751 (see table 2.3). Characteristics of painted sherds are different at Classic Basketmaker III

and Early Pueblo I assemblages. For example, the great majority of painted sherds from LA 60751 exhibit designs executed in organic or glaze paints as opposed to the iron-based paint dominating assemblages at LA 37605. Thus, white ware pigment type appears to represent a useful attribute for recognizing the very beginning of the Pueblo I period (Wilson 1996). Stylistically, many of the sherds from this site exhibit characteristics intermediate to Chapin Black-on-white and Piedra Black-on-white, as normally defined. Many of these sherds exhibit very slight surface polishing. Basket-stitch elements common in Basketmaker III types tend to be absent. Painted designs more closely resemble designs described for glaze-painted Rosa Black-on-white dominating Early Pueblo I sites in areas just to the east (Wilson and Blinman 1993) and usually differ from this type only by the presence of crushed andesite or diorite temper and the absence of glaze paint (Carlson 1963; Eddy 1966, 1972;

TABLE 2.4
Distribution of Early Pottery-bearing Sites in the La Plata Valley

Area	Transitional Basketmaker		Classic Basketmaker		Early Pueblo I		Total
	Trace	Dominant	Trace	Dominant	Trace	Dominant	
San Juan–La Plata Confluence–5 miles	—	4	5	7	5	2	23
6–10 miles Jackson Lake	—	1	13	20	13	2	49
11–15 miles Barker Arroyo	—	—	17	17	23	7	64
16–20 miles to Colorado state line	—	—	12	16	12	11	51
From Colorado state line–5 miles	—	—	26	21	28	52	127
6–10 miles	—	—	37	16	43	63	159
Total	0	5	110	97	124	137	473

Note: Includes only sites from Nusbaum's survey; probably includes many of the sites discussed from other discovery contexts.

Ellwood 1980; Lucius 1982; Peckham 1963; Wilson 1988; Wilson and Blinman 1993). Neckbanded ceramics and San Juan Red Ware are present in extremely low frequencies.

BASKETMAKER III SETTLEMENT PATTERN

As is true of much of the Totah area, survey data are scant in the La Plata Valley (McKenna and Toll 1992). There are numerous transects of varying width and orientation but little broad areal coverage in the valley itself. Given the lower visibility of Basketmaker III sites, it is especially difficult (perhaps even foolhardy?) to discuss Basketmaker III settlement pattern. The most complete coverage of the La Plata drainage comes from a survey conducted by Deric Nusbaum in 1935. Nusbaum covered a great deal of area in a short time, recording nearly a thousand sites. His maps were inadequate by modern standards, and few of the sites he recorded can be confidently relocated (Dykeman and Langenfeld 1987; Hannaford 1993). A reexamination of the sherd collections by Wilson and Hannaford, however, allows an assessment of temporal settlement trends within the valley (table 2.4; Hannaford 1993). Nusbaum surveyed from the confluence of the La Plata with the San Juan to near the modern settlement of Red Mesa in Colorado (see figure 2.1). Within the constraints of coverage, visibility, and the difficulties of establishing contemporaneity, the data indicate that Basketmaker III occupation occurred in clusters, and thus suggest that some sort of community organization existed.

Four areas in the La Plata Valley contain suggestions of Basketmaker III settlement concentrations: in the vicinity of Jackson Lake, in the vicinity of the entrance of Barker Arroyo, in the vicinity of the old town of Pendle-

ton, and perhaps in the vicinity of the large Pueblo II–III site Morris 41 (see figure 2.1). In both areas where structures have been excavated, they are in the vicinity of other probable Basketmaker features on both sides of the La Plata River. The temporal groups defined here have clear geographical affinities: all known Transitional Basketmaker sites are in the lower valley, Classic Basketmaker III extends from the lower end to perhaps the Colorado–New Mexico line, and Early Pueblo I sites are by far most abundant in the upper end of the valley. Even accounting for the especially low visibility of Transitional Basketmaker sites, there seems to have been a substantial increase in population between Transitional and Classic Basketmaker times.

Jackson Lake/East Side Rincon

Two settlements of both Transitional and Classic Basketmaker age are indicated in this broad stretch of the valley characterized by ample bottom land and a broad lower terrace. The East Side Rincon community is east of the La Plata River. Six Classic Basketmaker pit structures on a sloping terrace have been exposed by a large dissecting arroyo. Chapin Gray and Chapin Black-on-white were noted at these structures (Dykeman and Langenfeld 1987). One of these structures was partially excavated by San Juan College, yielding an archaeomagnetic date in the A.D. 600s (Richard Watson, personal communication, 1991; Daniel Wolfman, personal communication, 1991). Though there is minimal surface indication for the structures exposed by the arroyo cut, Dykeman and Langenfeld suspect that numerous other early structures could be present. A Pueblo II–III site is present in the immediate vicinity, but the degree of reuse is apparently less than across the river. This location is a good candidate for a Basketmaker III community including an integrative structure, but at present we have no way of knowing whether the structures were contemporaneously or sequentially used.

A second group of Basketmaker III structures is within clear view of the East Side Rincon Site on the west side of the river. These include the two rectangular structures described above, at closely spaced "sites" LA 37595 and LA 60751. We can be certain that Basketmaker III structures of which we are unaware exist on both sides of the river.

In addition to being unable to judge contemporaneity of Classic Basketmaker structures, we cannot say whether occupation was continuous from Transitional Basketmaker to Classic Basketmaker in the Jackson Lake area, or whether there was a hiatus. The presence of Sambrito Brown in both types of sites suggests continuity, while changes in pit structure form suggest otherwise. Early Pueblo I sites are apparently absent from Jackson Lake to the La Plata–San Juan confluence.

Barker Arroyo

The confluence of Barker Arroyo with the La Plata River was the focus of intensive settlement during several parts of the Anasazi sequence. The area is best known for Morris 39, located on the promontory overlooking the confluence. Site 39 includes two Pueblo II–III great houses, at least one, and perhaps as many as five great kivas, and a number of associated smaller house mounds (Morris 1939; see also Dykeman and Langenfeld 1987). Knowledge of Basketmaker III sites in this area is quite similar to that at Jackson Lake: three structures have been excavated on the west side of the river, and surface remains suggest that a large settlement may be present immediately across the river to the east. East of the river a site covering 30,000 m² (LA 49603) was recorded during survey by San Juan College; they dated this site to Pueblo I. The survey form lists only one pit house, but in the age of the remains, the location, and the generally smaller amount of surface material from such sites suggest that this could have been a substantial settlement.

West of the river, very little is known about a subrectangular structure excavated in 1916 by Morris at Site 39. Morris (1939:54) was quite certain in retrospect that it was a Basketmaker III house, though it was not excavated fully. Given the scant knowledge of this structure, its main importance now is that it probably indicates settlement of this location in Basketmaker III.

The evidence obtained at Site 39 is incomplete, since only a portion of it was excavated and because field methods have been much improved in the 20 years since the work there was done. Nevertheless the following outline of events is evident enough. During Basket Maker III, probably late in the period, there was a small settlement on the tip of the Mesa. Abandonment followed with reoccupation on the border line between Pueblo I and II. During the latter and early Pueblo III nearly all the structures in evidence at the surface came into being. (Morris 1939:55)

Our analysis of ceramic samples from the edge of the terrace and a site below it, at the edge of Barker Arroyo (LA 37603), supports Morris's assessment. Basketmaker III ceramics from the edge of the terrace form only a trace percentage of the assemblage.

Especially to the north, at sites he excavated in the upper La Plata Valley, some of what Morris called Basketmaker III we would now call Early Pueblo I. The structures we excavated just below Morris 39 fit into that time slot. The La Plata Highway Project excavated two structures located side by side at site LA 37605 (see above), which lies at the foot of the slope from the terrace on which Morris 39 is located. The structures are deep, a few red ware ceramics are present (see table 2.3), as is a small corner-notched projectile point, making Early Pueblo I a better fit than Classic Basketmaker. This appears to be the only area with Early Pueblo I settlement in the lower valley; cumulative surface evidence suggests that occupants of this part of the valley at this period would have had few neighbors (see table 2.4).

Pendleton

The Pendleton area (named for a now dismantled historic settlement) is located where several large arroyos enter the La Plata River, and at the north end of where the valley floor widens and bottom land is currently farmed. The Division of Conservation Archaeology (DCA) excavated two pit structures at Pendleton (LA 45687, LA 45689), and the Basketmaker II structures investigated by Foster and his colleagues (1983) and Brown (1991) are to the east of the valley. Both of the DCA structures lack benches, though that may be due to postoccupational damage. The earlier of the two structures dates clearly to A.D. 693 (LA 45689), and it lacks an antechamber. The second is placed later due to the presence of some Piedra Black-on-white and a single red ware sherd pendant. Neckbanding is absent (though some vessels have a neck fillet left showing, probably representing the "incipient" stages of this manufacturing technique [Hancock et al. 1988:444–446]), indicating the latest possible date is in the late A.D. 700s. The antechamber and the scarcity of Pueblo I in the vicinity could indicate an earlier date (Hancock et al. 1988). A 120 by 220 m portion of a 600 by 450 m site (LA 38541) east of the river proved to consist of a number of corn planting and processing areas. Scheick (1983:90–91) interpreted these remains as a repeatedly used agricultural area that probably served a population with more-permanent residences nearby. Use of the area during Basketmaker III–Pueblo I was sufficiently heavy to form shallow midden deposits. In addition to these confirmed uses during late Basketmaker III, other sites with plain gray pottery on the surface have been located in the area and may represent further Basketmaker III sites. It is also quite possible that Basketmaker III features underlie the extensive Pueblo II–III site LA 37610, about 0.4 km from LA 45689 (Toll 1993). Sites LA 51805 and 58106, just north of and adjacent to LA 37610, contained both Basketmaker III and Pueblo I pit structures (Hancock et al. 1988:755–773). Although there appear to be Classic Basketmaker and perhaps Early Pueblo I occupations in the main river valley, materials from this time span appear to be absent in the woodlands to the east in the areas surveyed and tested for the La Plata Mine, although Archaic, Basketmaker II, Pueblo II–III, and protohistoric occupations are all represented (Brown 1991:74).

LA 45867, a Pendleton area pit structure built in A.D. 693, contains no red ware and no neckbanded vessels (Hancock et al. 1988:345–357); the structure has a vent shaft rather than an antechamber. No brown ware was recorded in the analysis, but about a third of the vessels contain sandstone rather than crushed rock temper, and many of these vessels could be Sambrito Brown. Although no mention is made of polishing, some pastes are described as brown ware. During the analysis of the LA 60751 ceramics, sherds initially called plain gray were reassessed, and it was determined that they were in fact Sambrito Brown. This process of recognition will change the general view of ceramic development and make refined dating possible.

State Line and Beyond: Pre- and Post-Basketmaker III

Survey coverage of the valley is decidedly insufficient, but there is a clear impression that during the A.D. 700s and 800s the Anasazi preferred to live in Colorado, or at least above 6000 feet (see figure 2.1). While Morris suspected that Pueblo I occupations might be present at Morris 39 and 41, clear examples of structures dating to this period are absent at those and other sites he excavated south of Morris 41. Just a few kilometers north of Morris 41, however, Pueblo I sites are suddenly abundant, and this pattern continues up to the Durango area, around Mancos Canyon, and, of course, in the Dolores area (see Fuller 1988; Morris 1939). Absence of Pueblo I in the lower valley is repeated in the La Plata Highway excavations, where reuse of Basketmaker III locations by Pueblo II occupations is common, and these locations frequently extend to Pueblo III in the immediate vicinity, but Pueblo I occupations are absent.

Earl Morris suspected that Basketmaker remains underlay some of the extensive late Pueblo remains at his Site 41, a little south of the Colorado state line, though he excavated no Basketmaker III structures during his extensive work there. He attributed some materials from that period to disturbances beneath the later structures he excavated, and found a few burials (Morris 1939:88, 91, 95–96, 106). Pit Room D was a rough pit lacking wall and floor preparation, with no mention of a hearth. Morris (1939:91) suggests this structure was Basketmaker III or Pueblo I, though the size, the presence of bins and metate fragments, and the lack of a hearth suggest that it could have been a Pueblo II mealing room. Morris thought that Basketmaker structures were most likely to be near the edge of the terrace, as they were at Morris 39. Plain gray pottery has been observed on the surface at various places above the valley floor in this area, but, as noted, sites that date to the A.D. 700s and 800s have not been found. Pueblo I sites are common beginning at this part of the valley, making the settlement implications of these surface sherds ambiguous. Based on elevation, known site distribution, the Pueblo II settlement location "model," and little else, we suspect that Basketmaker III sites are few and temporary north of the state line.

Morris (1939) reports a number of Basketmaker III sites in the La Plata drainage north of the state line, but tree-ring dates and architecture indicate that most of the more fully known of these should be considered Pueblo I under current definitions. Morris's two primary criteria for assignment to Basketmaker III were pottery and lack of cranial deformation. Thus, all the structures at Site 23, called by Morris (1939:57) "a pure Basketmaker III horizon," have vents rather than antechambers, associated blocks of surface rooms (Morris 1939:67–65), and tree-ring dates in the 740s, 760s, and 780s (Robinson and Harrill 1974:34–35). Morris refers to the pit structures at sites as "protokivas," and they range from 1.60 to 2.29 m deep. These sites fit well into the Pueblo I time period of the "Basketmaker III" sites near Durango (Gooding 1980) in that pit structure form and tree-ring dates are very similar (760s–770s), and cranial deformation seems to be absent. The ceramics at the Durango sites include some red ware but do not include neckbanded types, leading to their classification as Basketmaker III. Morris Site 19, near the confluence of Cherry Creek with the La Plata, has a 1.5 m deep pit structure with an antechamber (Morris 1939:63–64) and is the most likely of Morris's sites north of the state line to date to before A.D. 700–750. Therefore, we maintain that the majority of Basketmaker III occupation in the La Plata was south of the state line, below 6000 feet.

Patterns

Transitional Basketmaker III remains are scarce in the valley, and all seem to be toward its southern end. Classic Basketmaker III and Early Pueblo I structures have been investigated in three topographic situations in the La Plata Valley: on top of the high second terrace west of the river (Morris 39, LA 45687, LA 45689), on the fans at the base of the slope to the upper terrace (LA 37594-5, LA 60751, LA 37605) adjacent to extensive arable bottom land, and on the sloping first "terrace" east of the river (East Side Rincon, LA 49603). Each of the three areas in which some excavation has taken place contains structures with little or no surface visibility. East of the river, structures show as relatively confined surface remains; west of the river, surface scatter is much more extensive, although Basketmaker materials are still rare.

The areas designated by archaeologists for the East Side Rincon Site and LA 49603, both on the east side of the river, are large enough to encompass a site the size of Shabik'eshchee Village in Chaco (see Wills and Windes 1989). The differing depositional conditions between mesa-top Shabik'eshchee Village and these terrace sites make it difficult to compare their sizes. It is possible, however, that the La Plata sites are in the Shabik'eshchee Village size range. Because of the number of structures exposed by the arroyo at the East Side Rincon, it seems likely that there, at least, a large settlement was present. Larger than normal Basketmaker community pit structures have not been recorded in the valley, though Dykeman and Langenfeld (1987) suggest that a large Pueblo II structure may have been placed over a Basketmaker III community structure. In view of the relative densities of Basketmaker III and Pueblo II structures in the immediate vicinity, it is more likely that a Basketmaker III community structure would have been present here than a Pueblo II great kiva. If the hypothesis that sizable Basketmaker III communities were present in the La Plata Valley is correct, the La Plata probably contained a larger population during this time than did the Dolores Valley, where the Basketmaker population was quite small (Kane 1986:363).

Wills and Windes (1989) suggest that Shabik'eshchee Village was located to be near piñon-gathering areas. Judging from current vegetation, proximity to piñon might have been a factor for the sites east of the river, or in the Pendleton group, but the sites on the west side of the river in the Jackson and Barker groups seem more likely to have been located for their proximity to good farmland. Were we better able to judge contemporaneity of use, questions we could address would include whether sites on both sides of the river were part of one large settlement. For most of the year, the La Plata River is unlikely to have been a barrier to movement, so that differences in distances to piñon from the settlement clusters defined here seem inconsequential.

Wills and Windes also suggest that antechambers may signal structures that were used by "storagers" (1989: 357) who spent more time at given sites than other members of the group. Excavations in two of the settlement areas revealed pit structures that apparently contravene the accepted architectural trend from antechamber to vent shaft. At LA 37605 and at LA 45687 and 45689,

earlier structures have vents while later ones have antechambers. The structures with antechambers are slightly larger than those without (see table 2.1), in accordance with another pattern identified by Wills and Windes. The structures at LA 37605 are a clear pair, but the two Pendleton sites are around 0.4 km apart. If, as we suspect, the use of the structures at LA 37605 overlapped, it may be significant that the structure with the antechamber (which was presumably the first of the two to be built) continued in use later than the one with the vent. If antechambers were a particular kind of storage unit during Basketmaker III, it may be that the large off-chamber storage facilities briefly described below were analogous means of in-structure storage after antechambers were no longer built. Perhaps with the expansion and contraction of the population at LA 37605, needs for storage declined, or use of the site changed.

PUEBLO II AND BASKETMAKER III: ADAPTIVE TWINS OR COUSINS?

Settlement Location

Basketmaker III structures are found with remarkable consistency to directly underlie Pueblo II structures. The superimposition of Pueblo II habitations on Basketmaker structures is so regular in our sample that there can be little question that it was intentional. Of five Basketmaker–Early Pueblo I pit houses excavated by the La Plata Highway Project, four are directly beneath or within meters of Pueblo II construction. The antechamber of LA 37605 Pit Structure 5 is underneath Pueblo II Pit Structure 1, and the main chamber is under a Pueblo II room block, and the central hearth of LA 37595 Pit Structure 3 is cut in half by Pueblo II Pit Structure 4 (see figures 2.4, 2.6). The Transitional Basketmaker structure at LA 37594 was in the midst of Pueblo II features; the fifth structure, at LA 60751, was surrounded by Pueblo II materials with known structures surrounding the site, although no intact Pueblo II features were located immediately adjacent to the Basketmaker structure, perhaps because of extensive modern disturbance (the structure was partially under the pavement). Further, the probable Basketmaker structure Morris excavated at Morris 39 was located under the corner of Building I, a Pueblo II–III great house.

This pattern is not confined to the La Plata Valley. It recurs in the bean field country of southwestern Colorado to the extent that some early investigators thought that the production of Chapin Black-on-white and Mancos Black-on-white overlapped temporally (Martin 1938). The site of Sikyatuupela on Second Mesa north of the present Hopi villages contains a pit structure labeled Basketmaker III, about a third of which has been removed by a deeper Pueblo II pit structure (Sebastian 1985:50–55). Although the architecture of the earlier structures and their clear construction date of A.D. 805 make a chronological (as opposed to ceramic) designation of Pueblo I seem more appropriate, making the interval between earlier and later occupations probably less, the pattern is similar. There is another example of a Pueblo II pit structure cutting a Basketmaker III structure at the Cerro Colorado Site in the Quemado area (Bullard 1962:26–27).

There is, of course, a strong possibility of a sampling bias here. Pueblo II sites are often easily visible, and thus found and excavated, leading to the excavation of the underlying Basketmaker III site, whereas single-component Basketmaker III sites are far less evident from surface remains and are more likely to get passed over by surveys or excavation plans (see also Bullard 1962:9). These superimpositions have a very important implication for attempts to understand Basketmaker III settlement distribution. Survey and excavation reports consistently remark on the difficulty of projecting Basketmaker III remains from surface materials; survey, testing, and even substantial excavation gave no indication of the presence of Basketmaker III components at any of the four La Plata sites where they were present.

Basketmaker III and Pueblo II similarities aside, there is a major difference in the sheer quantities of ceramics associated with the two periods. Examination of ceramic collections from full excavations (see tables 2.2 and 2.3) shows how Basketmaker III ceramics can be virtually invisible even in tables (see especially site LA 37595), and how few ceramics are actually associated with structures themselves. In areas such as the La Plata Valley where reoccupation by Pueblo II–III pot breakers is the rule, survey sherd counts are guaranteed to greatly underrepresent actual Basketmaker III occupation.

As noted, sites from the A.D. 700s and 800s are uncommon in site inventories in areas below 6000 feet (1825 m). The superimposition of post-A.D. 900 structures on pre-A.D. 700 structures, then, probably represents the recolonization of locations that had been unoccupied for some time. It is quite clear that locations considered optimal by people during Basketmaker III were the same as those so considered in Pueblo II. It appears that archaeological survey was a part of resettlement in Pueblo II, used as a means of selecting building locations. It is likely that this practice had some basis in tradition, and it is even more likely that it had to do with similarities in agriculture and settlement strategies (Schlanger 1988a).

Architecture

The relationship between population, settlement pattern, seasonality of use, storage, and food preparation is clearly complex (Gilman 1987; Wilshusen 1989a). Site locations indicate affinities between Basketmaker III and Pueblo II use of the land, but architecture is different in

the two periods. Pueblo II features provide an abundant sample with which to compare Basketmaker materials. Comparison of surface, as opposed to subterranean, facilities is compromised in our sample. Shallow features such as surface storage facilities or masonry rooms are under-represented in the highway corridor for either period, and Basketmaker surface cists probably were mostly erased during Pueblo reoccupations. Considering only the features that would survive surface disturbance, there are still several classes of features in La Plata Pueblo II sites that are relevant to Basketmaker III and Pueblo II comparison.

Storage location and volume.
In addition to storage in surface rooms, cists up to 2 m deep and nearly 2 m in diameter at the base are present at most of the Pueblo II sites in the La Plata Highway sample. Similar, though probably smaller and less common, features are reported for Basketmaker sites (Bullard 1962:25, 34; Roberts 1929:91–97). We found no Basketmaker examples in our excavations in the La Plata. A feature type that was in use at least by the A.D. 1000s is a high-volume cist or chamber excavated off the main chamber that was entered through a floor-level opening. These features are generally below floor level and are often larger than 1 by 1 m, and around a meter below the level of the structure floor. Structures in both periods possess substantial floor cists as well. Large interior cists are absent in Basketmaker structures, but large storage volumes behind wing walls, especially in wing-wall bins (see figure 2.3; figure 2.7, Pit Structure 5) and in antechambers (Wills and Windes 1989), would have provided at least equivalent volumes. Structures from both periods, then, exhibited substantial in-structure storage volumes; the combination of larger extramural cists and surface rooms would have given Pueblo II larger total volumes, on the whole in less visible locations.

Food processing location.
From the A.D. 500s to the 1300s a regular progression in grinding equipment location is apparent. In the earliest structure in our sample, the pit structure at LA 37594, metate rests are in the main chamber of the room, northeast of the hearth (see figure 2.2). The numerous metates in Area 1 of Talus Village, a Basketmaker II structure north of Durango, are north and northeast of the hearth, with a similar horseshoe-shaped metate rest (Morris and Burgh 1954: figure 5). Kane (1986:404) states that most milling equipment in Dolores Basketmaker III pit structures is found in the northeast portion of the floor as well. Beginning in later Basketmaker pit structures, milling features became established behind (south of) chamber partitions, which are wing walls or ridges (Bullard 1962:154–155; Kane 1986:407), where they remained in Pueblo I. Partly because of the vicissitudes of

later occupations both in Pueblo II and the modern era, our sample of the areas south of wing walls is patchy, and grinding facilities and equipment are notably scarce in our sample from Basketmaker contexts. The prominence of metates in Transitional Basketmaker structures suggests that corn was already a major element of subsistence (as per Gilman 1987). A complete trough metate was found south of the wing wall in the structure at LA 60751 (see figure 2.3), indicating that the shift in grinding location had taken place by the second half of the seventh century.

In Pueblo II, grinding took place in full-sized pit structures, specialized mealing pit structures (Mobley-Tanaka 1993; Schlanger 1995), and eventually mostly in surface rooms. The continued presence of grinding equipment in pit structures suggests continuity in structure use from Basketmaker III and Pueblo I. Increased formalization and separation of grinding activities suggest expanded use of this type of food processing requiring at least more space and perhaps indicating greater cultural and dietary significance.

Structure depth.
As is most graphically illustrated by the structures at LA 37595, there is a clear trend for Pueblo II pit structures to be deeper than their Basketmaker III predecessors in the same locations (see figure 2.4). The floor of the Pueblo II pit structure bisecting the Basketmaker III structure at this site is 0.7 m deeper than that of the Basketmaker III house. Wilshusen (1988a, 1989a) suggests that deeper structures in later periods resulted from greater need for dirt for building larger room blocks. The cobble masonry of the La Plata Valley did in all likelihood require more mud to hold it up than did a structure built of square sandstone blocks. Our imperfect evidence, however, suggests rather minimal surface structures with these deeper pit structures; in combination with still more fill from the large cists discussed above, it seems likely that a superfluity of dirt would have been produced in early Pueblo II. Thus, while Wilshusen's suggestion has much to recommend it, it seems likely to also be true that there is more to the architectural changes that took place than a dirt shortage (see also Gilman 1989). Perhaps a deeper structure required less wood to roof; certainly the Pueblo II population was much more conservative of structural wood than the Basketmaker III population.

Structure occupation span and abandonment.
The length of time pit structures were used is, of course, critical to understanding population size and use patterns (see Cameron 1990a). The two best indices of length of use for these structures are chronometric date brackets and frequency of remodeling. Most of the structures included in table 2.1 had only a single floor, and while modifications were made to features, the overall impression is that these structures were not used for long periods of time. The well-dated structure at LA 45687, with its tight cluster of tree-ring dates at A.D. 691–693, fits the contention of short use (Hancock et al. 1988:346, 390). The pit structure at LA 60751 shows that Basketmaker III structures could, however, experience much longer use. This structure is also well dated, with a clear clustering of dates at A.D. 653–654 marking its initial construction (see figure 2.5). In addition to the cluster, there are five dates ranging from A.D. 666 to 695 that are very likely to represent roof repair. This structure stands apart from the others in having three floors, two of which are separated by a unit that could represent a period of disuse of the structure. Thus, though the use span for the structure indicated by the tree rings is more than 40 years, during part of that span the structure may have been "abandoned." We have few clear absolute dating profiles from Pueblo II or Pueblo III structures. The dates from the single well-dated pit structure (Pit Structure 2 at LA 37600) suggest a first construction event at 1033 followed by a second construction 11 years later, and minor repairs two years after that. Little remodeling is evident in the structure, in spite of the apparent 12-year span of the roof. Other pit structures exhibit a range of remodeling, although remodeling seems more common in Pueblo III than in Pueblo II. Somewhat subjectively, structure-use spans seem likely to have been similar in Basketmaker III and Pueblo II.

A far less precise measure of length of use is midden accumulation. One reason the counts of Basketmaker III sherds in tables 2.2 and 2.3 are so low is that none of the three sites included middens in the areas excavated. LA 45687 in the Pendleton area produced a total of about 350 sherds, a count in the neighborhood of those from the Jackson Lake sites. Both LA 37605 and LA 45689 included midden deposits. The relatively unmixed Basketmaker III–Early Pueblo I deposits in Pit Structure–2 at LA 37605 contained 1084 sherds, though at least 4 percent of these date to the Pueblo II occupation (table 2.3). Pit Structure 2 contains the closest approximation to a Basketmaker III–Early Pueblo I midden in the La Plata Highway sample. More than 2000 sherds were collected from LA 45689, about a fourth of which were from the pit structure and rooms (Hancock et al. 1988:429–448). It is possible that the slightly later dates of these two sites may also contribute to the greater quantities of ceramic trash present.

Whitten estimates that the 332 sherds at LA 45687 represent 70 to 84 vessels (Hancock et al. 1988:356). At the relatively extravagant consumption rate of 10 vessels per year, then, this estimate suggests a use of seven to eight years. While this figure corresponds to the time spans suggested, about the same number of sherds were recovered from LA 60751, which was in use, at least sporadically, for 40 years. The two periods obviously need

TABLE 2.5

Site/ Structure	Abandonment	Filling	Reoccupation
LA 37594/ Pit Structure 5	leisurely abandonment, burned	aeolian/alluvial (shallow)	P II rooms superimposed
LA 37595/ Pit Structure 4	leisurely abandonment, timbers removed	aeolian/alluvial P II material	Cut by P II pit structure
LA 60751/ Pit Structure 1	leisurely abandonment, burned	aeolian/alluvial	BM III remodel? P II vicinity
LA 37605/ Pit Structure 2	leisurely abandonment, timbers removed	BM III/Early P I trash aeolian/alluvial (includes flood gravels)	P II immediate vicinity
LA 37605/ Pit Structure 5	leisurely abandonment, timbers removed	aeolian/alluvial	P II room superimposed
LA 45687 (DCA-83-211) Feature 7	planned abandonment? burned	alluvial on top of burned roofing	None
LA 45689 (DCA-83-214) Feature 1	orderly abandonment, timbers removed	aeolian/alluvial	P I reoccupation?
LA 1897 (Morris 39)/ Pit Room J	orderly abandonment, timbers removed?	aeolian/alluvial followed by trash filling	P II room and pit structure superimposed
Morris 41 Pit Room D	unburned, no roof in evidence	clean fill, some earlier artifacts	P II and P III immediate vicinity

Note: BM = Basketmaker; P = Pueblo.

different standards for comparing trash accumulation: the midden alone at LA 37592 contained 18,000 sherds, and the trashy fill of Pit Structure 1 at LA 37600 nearly 4000 sherds. These differences suggest smaller populations on Basketmaker sites, but also a rather different attitude toward producing, breaking, and throwing away pottery.

Abandonment of Basketmaker III structures within this sample shows a rather different profile from the Pueblo II structures in the same area. Of the nine Basketmaker III structures with sufficient data to make a confident determination, three were burned, whereas only one of 34 Pueblo II–III pit structures excavated by the La Plata Highway Project was burned. The burned Basketmaker structures were all burned shortly after use. Varying quantities of floor artifacts were present in each, but even LA 45687, which had the largest quantity of material on its floor, was thought unlikely to have been catastrophically abandoned (Hancock et al. 1988:358). Virtually all of the Pueblo II–III structures, and all of the unburned Basketmaker III structures, have clear indications that roofing was removed, probably for reuse (table 2.5). Burning a resource that seems to have been scarce even in Basketmaker III might relate to the anticipated permanence of abandonment, or perhaps to extinguishing (through incinerating) a claim of previous inhabitants to a particular area (Schlanger 1988b; Schlanger and Wilshusen 1993). This pattern of burning is similar to

that noted by Chenault and Motsinger, and Reed and Wilcox (this volume), although the frequency of burned structures is greater than that observed here. Our best-dated structure (LA 60751) certainly falls into the terminal A.D. 600s period that Chenault and Motsinger note to have contained numerous burned structures. However, our sample of burned structures also includes the earliest one (LA 37594), and neither of the early A.D. 700s structures at LA 37605 is burned. No stockades were observed at any of our sites, but all of these sites have experienced extensive modern surface alteration. No individuals are present in the burned structures, and, as in the sites mentioned above, abandonments were not deemed catastrophic. A complex set of abandonment behaviors, perhaps including hostilities but other conditions as well, is indicated.

Climate

The similarities discussed between Pueblo II and Basketmaker III raise the question of whether temporally separated populations were responding to similar climatic regimes. The answer to this question is complicated by numerous practical problems, most of which have only partial solutions, summarized in table 2.6.

Using the climatic reconstructions based on tree-ring data for the Dolores area, about 75 km to the northwest, we are able to obtain a good proxy for the climatic history of the La Plata area. The Dolores data are the only

TABLE 2.6

Climatic Data Problems and Means of Redress	
Problem	"Solution"
No La Plata Valley–specific climatic or tree-ring index series has been created.	Sequences for a number of neighboring areas have been worked out (Petersen 1986, 1987). Though the difference in latitude makes it a far-from-perfect proxy, the Dolores sequence is used here both for its appropriate span and its location north of the San Juan River. There are similarities in source and flow between the Dolores and the La Plata, but the Dolores is on the whole at a higher elevation.
Since exact occupation spans are unknown, it is very difficult to know exactly which periods of what length would be meaningful to compare.	Periods such as "Basketmaker III" or "900–1100" are clearly only conveniences, but they do grossly reflect adaptive units. We need to strive to define meaningful spans.
Meaningful comparison is also hampered by the difficulty of translating indices and deviations into humanly important measures.	Table 2.8 isolates good and bad periods and gives mean figures for them.
Does a tree-ring index signify anything in terms of farming conditions?	Blinman (1988:22–26) found that there is a reasonable correlation between tree-ring indices and regional precipitation projections (r^2 = .60).

reconstructions available for before A.D. 900; Blinman (1988:22–26) found that five-year running means for Dolores were closely correlated (r^2 = .60) to those for the Colorado Plateau south of the La Plata between A.D. 900 and 1000. Comparison of the five-year running mean departures for Basketmaker III and Pueblo II allows some characterization and subdivision of the two periods (figure 2.8). Basketmaker III experienced much less variability than did Pueblo II, with relatively more time spent above the overall mean. As is argued by Berry (1982), the break point at A.D. 700 appears to be more than just a convenient number, since the first 25 years of the eighth century are marked by consistently below average moisture and include some markedly bad years. Petersen's 1986:315) reconstructions for the Dolores area show the A.D. 800s as particularly dry, with considerable decline in moisture during the A.D. 700s. Burns's (1983:197, 203, 237, 561, 691) crop and storage simulation, also for southwestern Colorado, show that there were only two years from 705 to 726 when there would not have been shortfalls, even with a three-year storage capacity, making this period one of the worst in the 1317-year span he covered. Our sample from the lower La Plata Valley contains virtually no materials from the early A.D. 700s to 900. Petersen's curves indicate steady increase in moisture through the A.D. 900s; our sample contains only one well-documented provenience from the A.D. 900s, followed by greatly increased occupation in the A.D. 1000s.

Although date ranges for periods used by various researchers are converging, consensus has not been achieved. Wilson (1996:87, 90) published dates for the La Plata material to categorize surface sherd collections. That scheme shows Transitional Basketmaker as A.D. 300–550, Classic Basketmaker at 550–725, and Early Pueblo I at 725–825. Using these brackets, the tree-ring indices are very close to the theoretical average (1.0) for the span from Transitional Basketmaker through Pueblo II. Kearns and McVickar use A.D. 500–600 and 600–725 for two divisions of Basketmaker, and 725–775, 775–850, and 850–920 for subsets of Pueblo I. For table 2.7 here, we have adjusted the dates for several reasons: Wilson's published date span for Transitional Basketmaker begins early to include sites from the Petrified Forest in Arizona and early sites in the Navajo Reservoir. Dates from LA 37594 and from the Chuska Valley (Kearns and McVickar 1996; see also Kearns et al., this volume) suggest a later starting date and somewhat later termination. The splendid series of pit structures reported by Kearns and McVickar (1996: figures 5.23–5.61) suggest that the Classic Basketmaker form of pit house (as at LA 60751) was in use by the early A.D. 600s in the Chuska Valley. Reduction-fired gray wares seem to appear around A.D. 575, and we have used 575 for a starting date for Classic Basketmaker.

The beginning of Early Pueblo I is often placed at 725. Including the first 25 years of the A.D. 700s in calculation of mean tree-ring indices improves the mean index from .967 to 1.023, but the period from A.D. 700 to 725 has by far the lowest mean index for selected groups of years (table 2.8). Chronometric dates from the early A.D. 700s seem to be scarce in the region (see Robinson and Cameron 1991). Lacking dated structures, whether

Mean Departure 525–800

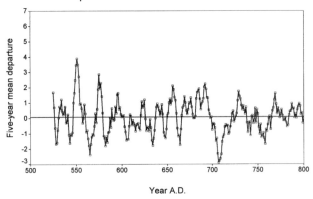

Mean Departure 801–1075

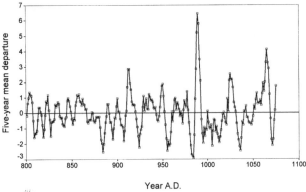

Figure 2.8. Five-year running means for Dolores tree-ring index departures for the periods A.D. 550–800 and 800–1050. Each point is the mean number of standard deviations from the mean (.9911) for the four years preceding and the data point year. The preceding years are used in the mean in order to reflect experienced years, and the process of calculating a running mean smooths the trend (see Blinman 1988 and Petersen 1987 for selection of intervals).

Transitional Basketmaker ends with a bad stretch of years, or Early Pueblo I begins with one, is a philosophical rather than archaeological question. Because of the apparent abandonment of the lower La Plata Valley around A.D. 700, changing phases at A.D. 700 makes sense in this context. Table 2.7 shows two date ranges for Classic Basketmaker and Early Pueblo I: A.D. 576–699 and 700–800, and 576–725 and 726–800, showing the effects of including two and a half dry decades in a time period. However we start and end our time segments, we must suspect that the dry period from A.D. 700 to 725 had an effect on settlement location and other aspects of residents' lives, apparently driving them to higher elevations.

Amounts of variability on the broad scale can be gauged by means and standard deviations for units corresponding to parts of Pecos periods that seem to have some meaning (tables 2.7 and 2.8; figure 2.9). The

Dolores tree-ring data show that Basketmaker III from A.D. 575 to 699 has a high mean tree-ring index and one of the lower standard deviations. In terms of percentages of good and stressful years (see figure 2.9), Basketmaker III has more years above a half a standard deviation over the mean, and fewer below 1.5 standard deviations below the mean than any of the other periods included in the groups. The tree-ring index for early Pueblo II is below average, and the standard deviation is higher than that for Basketmaker III, while later Pueblo II (A.D. 1026–1100) shows as a highly favorable period.

Figure 2.9 contains some surprising and possibly important suggestions. Since we know that settlement shifted to higher elevations in the A.D. 700s and 800s, and we can see from the overall trend line that there were spans of apparently dry years during that time, we might expect that Early Pueblo I and Pueblo I would have large numbers of years in the negative bars on the histogram. This is, however, not the case: these two periods have the highest percentages of years around the mean and, in fact, have low frequencies in the most severe (two standard deviations below the mean) part of the graph. Where these periods are greatly underrepresented is in years receiving well over the mean precipitation; such years were few in Early Pueblo I, and none occurred during Pueblo I as defined for this graph. This suggests two things: mean precipitation is, as is frequently stated in regional literature, marginal for agriculture, especially using dry farming methods. Second, occasional years of well above average moisture were necessary to maintain habitation of the lower elevations; such years would have allowed periodic bumper crops that could have been used to tide the population through years with small crops or no yield at all. Pueblo II and Classic Basketmaker experienced more years well below the mean than Pueblo I, but also considerably more years well above. Transitional Basketmaker, during which we know only of sites in the lower end of the valley, has by far the most even spread of years in each departure group; this regime may have fit well with a subsistence pattern that was less reliant on crops than in later periods, since wild products were probably a larger part of the base and could be more easily emphasized to make up for crop shortfalls. The lower La Plata River is known to go dry in historic times, but the extent to which historic irrigation practice accelerates this is unknown. With smaller upstream demands, the growing Pueblo II population, were it using irrigation, might have been in a better position to weather dry years lower in the valley.

In order to evaluate what a "good" tree-ring index profile is, Toll (1991) attempted to select a few periods in which it might have been a good idea or a bad idea to farm in the Four Corners. Armed with hindsight and charts and tables, spans of 30 years or more that con-

TABLE 2.7

Means for Various Yearly Groupings of Dolores Tree-ring Indices					
Whole Series:	Tree-ring index A.D. 371–1136				
	Mean	Std. Dev.	Minimum	Maximum	*n*
Tree-ring index	.99	.46	.04	2.94	766
5-year mean departure	.00	1.25	−3.1634	6.4559	762
Transitional Basketmaker:	Tree-ring index A.D. 450–575				
	Mean	Std. Dev.	Minimum	Maximum	*n*
Tree-ring index	1.00	.52	.08	2.30	176
5-year mean departure	.02	1.40	−3.1634	3.8946	176
Classic Basketmaker III:	Tree-ring index A.D. 576–699				
	Mean	Std. Dev.	Minimum	Maximum	*n*
Tree-ring index	1.02	.41	.10	2.03	124
5-year mean departure	.20	.99	−1.8057	2.2866	124
	Tree-ring index A.D. 576–725				
	Mean	Std. Dev.	Minimum	Maximum	*n*
Tree-ring index	0.98	.42	.10	2.03	150
5-year mean departure	.26	1.08	−2.8939	2.2866	150
Early Pueblo I:	Tree-ring index A.D. 700–800				
	Mean	Std. Dev.	Minimum	Maximum	*n*
Tree-ring index	.96	.37	.17	1.60	101
5-year mean departure	−.15	.91	−2.8939	1.7570	101
	Tree-ring index A.D. 726–800				
	Mean	Std. Dev.	Minimum	Maximum	*n*
Tree-ring index	1.02	.34	.10	2.03	125
5-year mean departure	.20	.99	−1.8057	2.2866	125
Late Pueblo I:	Tree-ring index A.D. 801–925				
	Mean	Std. Dev.	Minimum	Maximum	*n*
Tree-ring index	.96	.39	.14	2.06	125
5-year mean departure	−.11	.95	−2.5375	2.8451	125
Early Pueblo II:	Tree-ring index A.D. 926–1025				
	Mean	Std. Dev.	Minimum	Maximum	*n*
Tree-ring index	1.00	.55	.08	2.94	100
5-year mean departure	.03	1.61	−2.9226	6.4559	100
Late Pueblo II:	Tree-ring index A.D. 1026–1100				
	Mean	Std. Dev.	Minimum	Maximum	*n*
Tree-ring index	1.04	.54	.13	2.41	75
5-year mean departure	.29	1.64	−2.7975	4.1257	75

tained runs of years above or below the mean were identified. This exercise shows several things (see table 2.8):

1. Mean indices of more than 1.1 characterize good periods, with the maximum being 1.3. Bad periods have means of 0.95 or less. Thus, apparently small changes in tree-ring index means may have climatic significance.
2. The latter parts of both Basketmaker III and Pueblo II contain some of the highest mean indices.
3. The period between A.D. 641 and 695, which

spans most of the firm dates for Basketmaker III in the La Plata Valley, also has a relatively high index.
4. Unlike Basketmaker III, except for the rather variable period from A.D. 1050 to 1080, it is hard to find prolonged "good" stretches in Pueblo II.
5. The best mean index is for the 31-year period A.D. 1050–1080. Since this period immediately predates what seems to be the onset of larger communities and construction of public architecture, its timing is suggestive.
6. A.D. 850–900, a span for which there is very little

Good Basketmaker III

Tree-ring index A.D. 641–695

	Mean	Std. Dev.	Minimum	Maximum	n
Tree-ring index	1.13	.37	.10	1.72	54
5-year mean departure	.64	.96	−1.7383	2.2289	54

Tree-ring index A.D. 665–695

	Mean	Std. Dev.	Minimum	Maximum	n
Tree-ring index	1.22	.28	.52	1.72	31
5-year mean departure	.96	.69	−.7080	2.2289	31

Good Pueblo II

Tree-ring index A.D. 931–975

	Mean	Std. Dev.	Minimum	Maximum	n
Tree-ring index	1.03	.39	.27	1.83	44
5-year mean departure	.08	.99	−2.4508	1.8822	44

Tree-ring index A.D. 1050–1080

	Mean	Std. Dev.	Minimum	Maximum	n
Tree-ring index	1.30	.55	.25	2.41	31
5-year mean departure	1.30	1.70	−2.0946	4.1257	31

Bad Basketmaker III

Tree-ring index A.D. 601–647

	Mean	Std. Dev.	Minimum	Maximum	n
Tree-ring index	.91	.44	.10	2.03	47
5-year mean departure	−.26	.75	−1.7864	1.1985	47

Early A.D. 700s (Classic Basketmaker–Early Pueblo I Transition)

Tree-ring index A.D. 700–725

	Mean	Std. Dev.	Minimum	Maximum	n
Tree-ring index	.78	.39	.17	1.59	26
5-year mean departure	−.99	.94	−2.8939	0.4667	26

Late Pueblo I

Tree-ring index A.D. 850–900

	Mean	Std. Dev.	Minimum	Maximum	n
Tree-ring index	.95	.32	.25	1.70	51
5-year mean departure	−.24	.86	−2.5375	1.2178	51

Bad Pueblo II

Tree-ring index A.D. 975–1036

	Mean	Std. Dev.	Minimum	Maximum	n
Tree-ring index	.93	.63	.08	2.94	62
5-year mean departure	−.13	1.98	−2.9226	6.4559	62

evidence of occupation in the lower La Plata Valley, has a low mean index.

It is of considerable interest that river valleys such as the La Plata and the Dolores seem to be very much affected by variation in precipitation. That is, it seems plausible to suggest that the presence of permanent streams should buffer periods of little rainfall, but that does not seem to be the case. The two firmly dated pit structures in the La Plata Valley (A.D. 654 and 693) were constructed after periods of five out of six, and 11 out of 12 above-average years, suggesting at least that these structures were not built near permanent water as a response to poor conditions elsewhere. Moreover, the lower valley seems to have been little occupied—though not abandoned—for more than 100 years, starting in the A.D. 700s. Given the greater population densities in the valley in late Pueblo II and Pueblo III in the face of continued high climatic variability, it seems reasonable to suggest that some form of irrigation may have developed after early Pueblo II in order to take advantage of the presence of the river (see Schlanger 1988a:789). Because of the location of our sample, the active nature of the river, the presumably small scale of early irrigation fea-

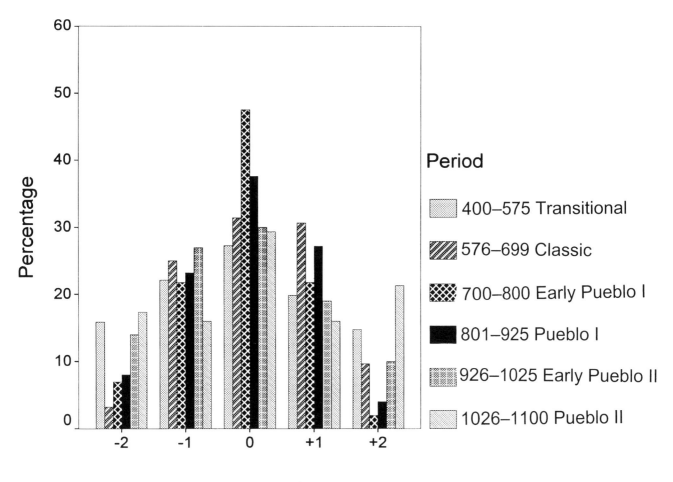

Figure 2.9. Summary of tree-ring index departures by cultural period, displayed as percentage within each group of standard deviations from the mean index. The 0 ranges include departures of .5 standard deviation or less; the ± 1 ranges include from .5 to 1.5; the 2 ranges are values greater than ± 1.5. The lowest value in this series is -3.16 s.d., while the highest is + 6.46 s.d.

Basketmaker III-Pueblo II Comparison

Patterns of Basketmaker III and Pueblo II settlement in the La Plata Valley fit well into the long-term correspondence between settlement location and climate discussed by Schlanger (1986, 1988a). That the Basketmaker III population in the lower La Plata Valley was apparently greater than that in the higher and cooler Dolores Valley also seems to fit with this climatic model.

The similarities in site distribution, and perhaps length of site use, between Basketmaker III and Pueblo II (in the A.D. 1000s) in the La Plata suggest similar conditions and strategies. During each period, sites and entire areas were being reinhabited, including both reoccupation after long periods of little habitation, and, more difficult to discern, reoccupation after shorter "abandonments." If site occupations tended to be relatively brief, relatively mobile subsistence strategies are likely during both periods. The presence of considerable numbers of Basketmaker pit

tures, and the intense historic agricultural use of the valley, we have no physical evidence for this speculation.

structures on the floor of the La Plata Valley adds a dimension to the settlement pattern noted by Chenault and Motsinger (this volume) in the immediately adjacent area. Their survey showed the majority of habitations on mesa-top centers on high ground. The valley-bottom locations of the sites in our sample show use of many niches during Basketmaker III.

Although the precipitation records for the A.D. 600s and 1000s are in some ways similar, there are some important differences as well. Most important among those differences is the fact that there are far more periods of subnormal moisture in the A.D. 1000s (see also Petersen 1986:321). Judging from the frequency of remains, the population during the A.D. 1000s was considerably greater than during the A.D. 600s, though that impression may stem in part from more frequent structural abandonment and reestablishment in the A.D. 1000s. These relocations seem likely to have resulted at least in part from the higher frequency of stress periods, though the presence of a greater population would make the process of relocation more complicated.

Further complicating the picture in the A.D. 1000s is that nearly continuous occupation of the valley extended for more than a century instead of being followed by the two-century hiatus in local occupation that followed the A.D. 600s. Nonetheless, as graphically shown by the superimposition of structures, patterns of settlement location had been established by Basketmaker times and were closely followed for several hundred years. Modifications in architecture—including larger intra- and extramural cists, and larger surface rooms—provided for increased storage in Pueblo II and Pueblo III, which may have made possible the continued occupation using similar location and farming strategies, with the important addition of irrigation in Pueblo II, in spite of an increase in drought periods.

CONCLUSIONS

Ceramic data accumulated during investigations of the La Plata Highway Project provide important clues concerning continuity of occupation and settlement patterns in the La Plata Valley. Ceramic evidence from La Plata Valley sites indicates a long and apparently continuous occupation beginning with the earliest ceramic-bearing phases. Continuity of occupation is indicated by similarities in ceramic distributions between successive phases, showing a gradual sequence of change. For example, Sambrito Utility sherds from the two earliest ceramic components exhibit similar characteristics, indicating continuity between the Transitional Basketmaker and Classic Basketmaker III periods. Similarities in early gray and white ware types indicate continuity between Classic Basketmaker III and Early Pueblo I occupations. These similarities reflect continuity of resource use, manufacturing conventions, and firing technology through time. Within the context of changing climatic conditions, site location choice further shows great time depth. This evidence contrasts greatly with some previous characterizations of a lack of continuity between early ceramic phases (Berry 1982).

The existing sample from the rich archaeological record of the La Plata Valley gives a good idea of the complexity of a period long lumped under the rubric "Basketmaker III." Although only a few early Anasazi sites were excavated during the La Plata Highway Project, ceramic data from three sites provided information allowing for the ceramic differentiation of three distinct early ceramic phases for assemblages that would have been assigned to the Basketmaker III period in previous schemes. In most cases, it should be possible to distinguish assemblages associated with these phases, even with small sample sizes.

Ceramic data also indicate both a gradual increase in population as well as shifts in overall settlement patterns. Ceramic evidence of occupation during the Transitional Basketmaker III period is limited to a very small number of sites along the lower-most part of the La Plata Valley. While the low number of Transitional Basketmaker sites may partially be a reflection of difficulties in identifying such occupations, it is very likely the total population represented during this time is much lower than for other periods. Increases in population resulted in the appearance of a series of small communities spread fairly evenly across the La Plata Valley during Classic Basketmaker times. These communities appear to represent the only Anasazi occupation in which a similar settlement system extended over both the lower and upper La Plata Valley. Climatic reconstruction indicates that this period was the least variable and most favorable during Anasazi occupation of the region. The Early Pueblo I period saw population increase and settlement shift to fairly large communities mostly located in the upper valley north of the New Mexico–Colorado border. These movements are similar to shifts to larger communities in higher elevations noted in other areas of the Anasazi and probably reflect regional responses to drying environments. Settlements continued to be located in the upper La Plata Valley until the early Pueblo II period, during which movement to the lower part of the La Plata Valley began a long period of large-scale occupation. Many of the people reoccupying the lower valley located their structures directly on top of earlier settlements.

The architecture of the period is also complex. During the A.D. 500s, "Transitional Basketmaker" shallow, round pit structures were in use. By the A.D. 600s, deeper rectangular structures with antechambers had come into use, and by the late A.D. 600s to early 700s, structures with both antechambers and vent shafts were being constructed. By Early Pueblo I (which Morris and others still called Basketmaker) still deeper pit structures were being used, and surface architecture was considerably more substantial. Variability in the occurrence of food processing facilities may indicate cyclical reliance on corn rather than the unidirectional increase we often assume, or it may just show that different structures had different functional emphases beginning in Basketmaker times. Increased storage volume in less visible contexts appears to have developed, perhaps in connection with increased reliance on single-harvest staples (as per Gilman 1987).

While the occupation of the valley was never simple, there were clear trends of use of the higher elevations in the 400s and before, and movement lower in the A.D. 500s. During the A.D. 600s population was more widely distributed, appearing at most elevations, while during the A.D. 700s and 800s there was a clear preference for higher-elevation habitations. In both Classic Basketmaker and as substantial occupation of the lower valley was reestablished in the A.D. 1000s, numerous communities were present. Although there are a few suggestions of public architecture, hard evidence is currently slim. These settlements were probably characterized by considerable fluidity of size and occupation. None was probably very large, but their number was substantial, and occupation of the valley as a whole continuous. The Pueblo II trajectory was longer, and led to a larger population, because of regional dynamics and perhaps the critical addition of irrigation. The striking similarities between Classic Basketmaker III and Pueblo II show that by the A.D. 600s, residents of the La Plata Valley had adopted a fully Puebloan lifestyle (as discussed by P. Reed, this volume). Patterns and practices, of course, continued to be elaborated and changed, but the essentials were in place. These similarities also remind us that the lifestyle continued to require a flexible mix of subsistence strategies tailored to short-term conditions long after the Basketmaker period.

Places made significant by use in the past are important in modern Pueblo consciousness and have been for many centuries (Fowler et al. 1987; Lekson 1996). While there are contextual reasons such as access to cropland and avoidance of cold air drainage for reusing site locations, the presence of ancestral occupation probably was a further inducement to occupy certain locations. The La Plata data suggest that this predilection existed in Pueblo II with their reuse of Classic Basketmaker sites, and may be indicated in the reuse of Transitional Basketmaker locations during Classic Basketmaker.

ACKNOWLEDGMENTS

The New Mexico State Highway and Transportation Department has funded the Office of Archaeological Studies' excavation and analysis in the La Plata Valley. Chuck Hannaford provided data from the Nusbaum survey. Eric Blinman provided listings of climatic data and helped with their use and interpretation. Sarah Schlanger was liberal with good ideas about Basketmaker, and Paul Reed provided helpful comments and suggestions. Rob Turner helped with the "La Plata man" figure used on the maps.

3

Colonization, Warfare, and Regional Competition

Recent Research into the

Basketmaker III Period

in the Mesa Verde Region

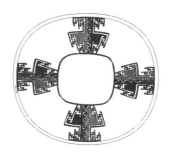

Mark L. Chenault

Thomas N. Motsinger

Although the Mesa Verde region is best known for its extensive Pueblo II and Pueblo III Anasazi ruins, the Basketmaker III period represents the first substantial Anasazi occupation of the area. For this discussion we draw upon the data and conclusions of previous researchers, but most of our information comes from two large survey projects and the excavation of four Basketmaker III sites by archaeologists from SWCA, Inc., Environmental Consultants (figure 3.1). The work was conducted by SWCA under contract with the Bureau of Reclamation.

We begin this chapter with a general discussion of the Basketmaker III period in the Mesa Verde region. Included in the discussion are sections on site structure, the location of use and activity areas in typical Basketmaker hamlets, and Basketmaker III architecture and material culture. We also discuss the evidence for what subsistence resources were used and how they were obtained. In addition, we address the colonization of the region by the Basketmaker III people and the patterns of settlement identified through archaeological survey. The final major topic addressed is regional competition and the onset of warfare. Our excavations revealed that three of the four sites appeared to have been stockaded, and that those three hamlets had been destroyed by fire. Data from this work, along with information from the work of others in the region, lead us to the conclusion that warfare was a part of life during the Basketmaker III period in the Mesa Verde region and that stockades were constructed at many sites as a means of defense. We also conclude that conflict, in spite of the defensive measures, is the most probable explanation for the abandonment and destruction of the sites we studied.

The larger of SWCA's two archaeological surveys was a Class II (sample) survey of approximately 88,000 acres for the proposed Animas-La Plata water project. The

purpose of the survey was to obtain an estimate of the cultural resources within the portion of the proposed water project that is slated for irrigation agriculture. We surveyed approximately 8800 acres (a 10 percent sample) of the project area in 55 systematically selected quarter-section blocks. Of the 372 archaeological sites recorded by our crews, 15 were assigned to the Basketmaker III period (Chenault 1996). The systematic sample afforded a look across both the Mancos River drainage basin and the La Plata River basin.

The second survey, the Huntington Land Evaluation Project, was a Class III (100 percent) inventory of 6020 acres in the upper La Plata River drainage basin in southwestern Colorado. The Bureau of Reclamation is considering purchasing the privately owned land to provide suitable wildlife habitat in compensation for land that might be inundated by the proposed Ridges Basin Reservoir, a component of the Animas-La Plata Project. The survey crews discovered and recorded 10 Basketmaker III sites within the project area (Mabry et al. 1997).

More detailed information for this chapter was obtained from the excavation of the four Basketmaker III habitation sites. The sites—Big Bend (5MT9387), the Rabbit Site (5MT9168), Dead Dog (5MT11,861), and Dancing Man (5MT9343)—were located within the right-of-way of the Lone Pine Canal, a component of the Dolores Project.

SITE STRUCTURE

Basketmaker III site structure in the Mesa Verde region appears to have been fairly standardized. Most Basketmaker III sites in the area were hamlets, as defined by the Dolores Archaeological Program (DAP). According to the DAP systematics, hamlets consisted of one to three dwelling units or household clusters (Kane 1986:355).

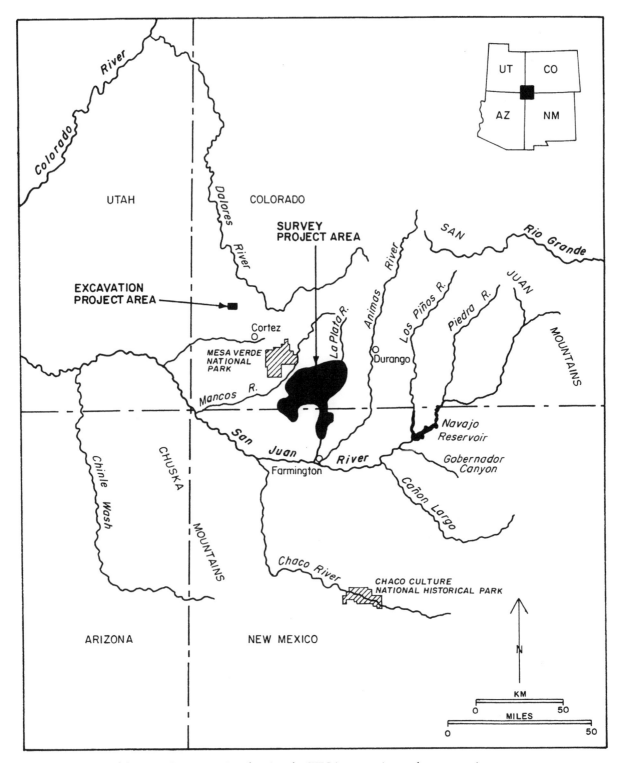

Figure 3.1. Map of the Four Corners region showing the SWCA excavation and survey project areas.

Thus, for our purposes, Basketmaker III hamlets typically consisted of one to three pit structures with an arc of noncontiguous pit rooms located to the north and west of the pit structures (figure 3.2). Trash deposits were found scattered throughout these sites, but in higher concentrations to the south and east of the pit structures. Features such as fire pits and hearths are typically scat-tered throughout the sites. This pattern has been found at Basketmaker III hamlets on Mesa Verde (Hayes and Lancaster 1968; Jennings 1968; Lancaster 1968; Lancaster and Pinkley 1954; Lancaster and Watson 1943, 1954; Nordby and Breternitz 1972; O'Bryan 1950; Smiley 1949), in the Yellow Jacket area (Rohn 1975; Wheat 1955b), and along the Dolores River (Brisbin and Varien

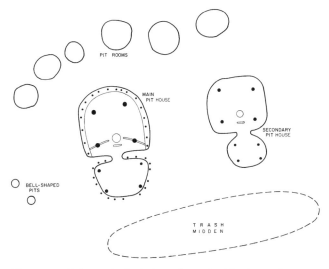

Figure 3.2. Schematic depiction of a typical Basketmaker III hamlet in the Mesa Verde region.

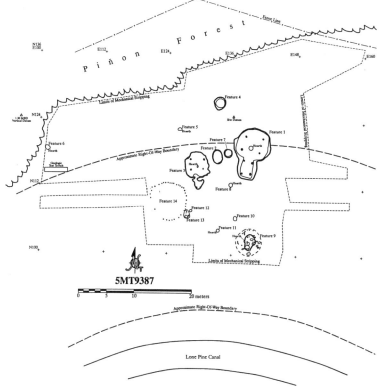

Figure 3.3. Plan map of Big Bend (Site 5MT9387).

1986; Tucker 1983). In addition, there is evidence that some Basketmaker III hamlets were enclosed by stockades (Fuller and Morris 1991; McNamee et al. 1992a, 1992b; Motsinger and Chenault 1995; Rohn 1975). We obtained most of our data for this discussion from the four sites described below. In this chapter we compare the Basketmaker III remains we recovered with those found during other projects, including the many excavations on Mesa Verde and those done by the DAP. Although there are many similarities among our sites and those at Mesa Verde and in the DAP project area, there are some differences, such as the presence of stockades at our sites.

Four Excavated Basketmaker III Sites

Big Bend was a small Basketmaker III habitation site named for the distinctive bend in the nearby Lone Pine Canal. Fourteen features comprised the site (figure 3.3), including two pit houses, three pit rooms, four thermal pits, three pit features, one extramural occupation surface, and one ramada (Motsinger and Chenault 1997). Unlike the three sites described below, Big Bend did not burn; therefore, we did not obtain any tree-ring dates for the occupation of the site. However, ceramics and architecture placed it earlier in the Basketmaker III period than the other three sites, possibly in the sixth century A.D.

The Rabbit Site was a Basketmaker III hamlet consisting of two pit houses, six surface rooms, and several pit features surrounded by a stockade (figure 3.4). The site had been destroyed by an intense fire that consumed the main pit house, several pit rooms, and the stockade (Chenault 1997a). The site's occupants apparently escaped the fire, which burned so hot that some of the adobe used in construction vitrified. As with our other burned sites, we recovered an extensive assemblage of

artifacts from the main pit house. Tree-ring cutting dates place construction of the main pit house at A.D. 632.

The Dead Dog hamlet—named for several dog burials found during excavation (Chenault 1997b)—consisted of three pit houses, a dozen surface rooms, numerous pit features, and many postholes (figure 3.5). The postholes were concentrated along the margins of the site and could have constituted either a full or partial stockade. However, the postholes did not form a clear linear arrangement like those found at other stockaded sites in the region. Dead Dog was also destroyed by fire, which apparently trapped one of the occupants in the main pit house. We found the remains of an adult male on the floor, draped across the hearth in the main chamber. Dendrochronological samples from the main pit house date the occupation of the site from A.D. 640 to 680.

Dancing Man was a Basketmaker III habitation site that derived its name from an anthropomorphic element painted on a sherd recovered during excavation. The site consisted of two pit houses (one with an antechamber and one without), four surface rooms, two inhumations, a ramada, and several pit features (Motsinger 1997).

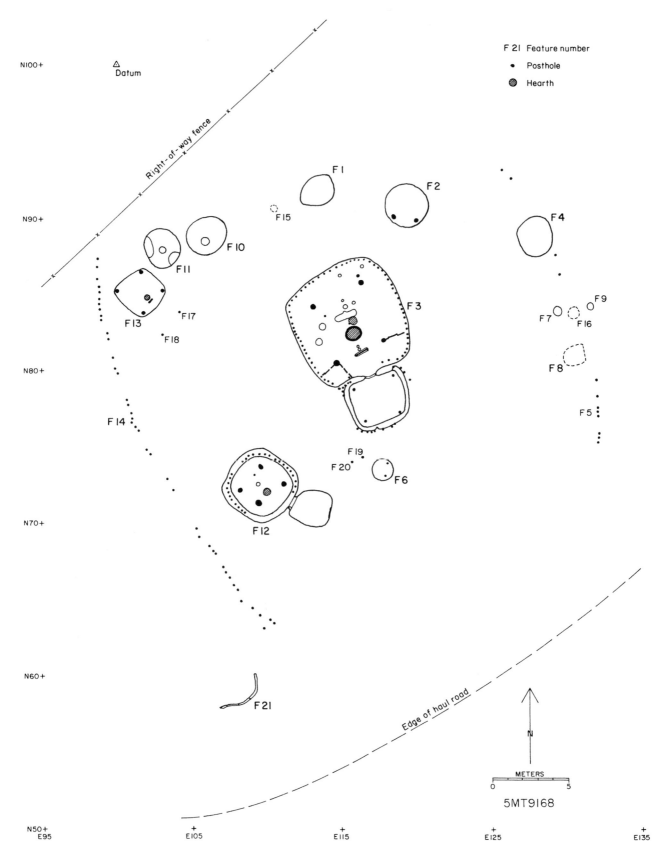

N100+

△
Datum

F 21 Feature number
•   Posthole
▨   Hearth

Right-of-way fence

N90+

F I

F 2

F 4

F 15

F 10

F 11

F 3

F 9

F 7   F 16

F 13

F 17

N80+

F 18

F 8

F 5

F 14

F 19

F 20

F 6

N70+

F 12

N60+

Edge of haul road

N

F 21

METERS
0   5

5MT9168

N50+
E95

+
E105

+
E115

+
E125

+
E135

Figure 3.4. Plan map of the Rabbit Site (5MT9168).

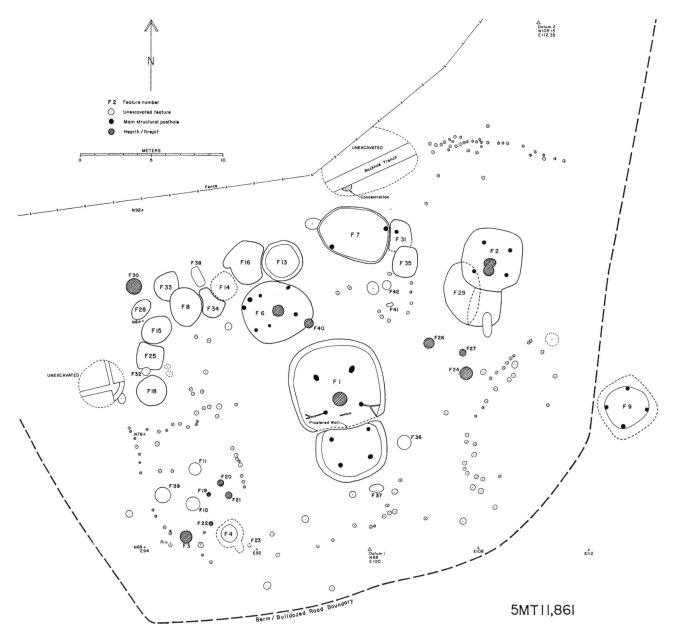

Figure 3.5. Plan map of Dead Dog (5MT11,861).

Many of the features at the site had been surrounded by a stockade (figure 3.6). Most of the site, including the stockade and the main pit house, had been destroyed by fire. Within those burned remains, we discovered a remarkable assemblage of perishable and nonperishable artifacts. Tree-ring dates place the construction of the main pit house at or shortly after A.D. 685. The presence of three intrusive cists in the main pit house and one pit house outside the stockade suggests a later reoccupation.

Use of Indoor Space

Kane (1986:356) presented a model of Basketmaker III use of space and illustrated it with a schematic map of a Basketmaker III household cluster. Based on data from

DAP sites, Kane infers that tool storage occurred in the antechambers of pit houses. He also infers that bins and the areas behind the wing walls were used for storage. According to Kane, the Anasazi slept in the area northwest of the hearth, and the milling of grain was performed north of the southwest wing wall. Other activities included tool manufacture and maintenance, which were performed north of the hearth, and cooking, which occurred around the hearth. Food and water were stored in the eastern portion of the structure, and ritual activities took place around the sipapu (Gilmore and Chenault 1993).

Most archaeological discussions of the use of space in Basketmaker III structures identify the area south of the

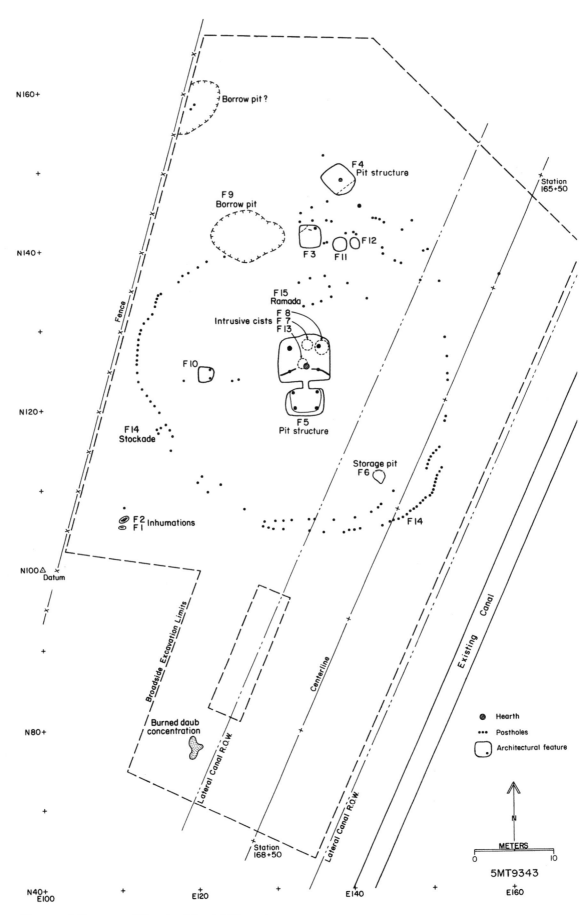

Figure 3.6. Plan map of Dancing Man (5MT9343).

wing walls as the place where the Anasazi used ground stone tools to grind maize and other grains (e.g., Morris 1939). Evidence of milling has often been identified in that portion of pit houses, as stated by Daifuku (1961: 43): "This partition usually separated the southern or eastern portion of the pit house from the rest of the structure. In this section manos and metates have frequently been found, which suggests that the partition may have set off an area devoted to women's work." Bullard (1962:154–155), Morris (1939:25), and Lancaster and Pinkley (1954:50) had similar interpretations. Among the modern Pueblo Indians, women do the corn grinding, and it is likely that they did so prehistorically (Woodbury 1954:61).

Our interpretations of activity and use areas within the pit structures match those depicted by Kane (1986) fairly closely. SWCA excavators found large ceramic vessels that might have been used to store food and water on the east side of the main pit house at Dead Dog. Ceramic vessels were found in the bins formed by the wing walls in several of the main pit houses, supporting the idea that the bins had been used for storage. In addition, we found a dozen complete but unfired ceramic pots in various locations in the main chamber of the primary pit house at Dead Dog. Those items were apparently in the process of manufacture and were being allowed to dry when fire destroyed the structure.

SWCA crews found charred basket fragments on the west side in several of the main chambers of Basketmaker III pit houses. Although we did not find evidence of matting in the northwest quarters of the main chambers, those areas were the most devoid of artifacts and may have been where the inhabitants sat and slept. In the southwest corner of the main pit house at Dancing Man, four awls, two cobble lap stones, and some cordage were found on and around a thick wooden plank, suggesting that weaving or leather working was taking place there just before fire consumed the house.

We found metates standing upright against the southern wall of the main pit houses at the Rabbit Site and at Dead Dog, and metates on rests were located in the southeast bin at Dancing Man and both the southeast and southwest bins at Dead Dog. We recovered numerous manos in the same areas. Two metates—one lying flat and one leaned against a wall—were found in the antechamber at Dancing Man. Those ground stone artifacts provide evidence that the Anasazi milled grains behind the wing walls in Basketmaker III pit houses (Gilmore and Chenault 1993) and possibly in the antechambers.

Extramural Use Areas

The patterns we found at our Basketmaker III sites fit those described above. Site-wide activity was similar to that shown schematically by Kane (1986: figure 5.1), with storage located in rooms north and west of the main pit houses, and trash deposition southeast of the structures. In addition, we found bell-shaped pits in the southwest part of Dead Dog, suggesting that storage also took place in that area of the site. Kane shows outdoor food processing as having taken place north of the primary pit houses; however, our excavations show that the location of food processing may have been more variable. For example, extramural fire pits at Dead Dog were located throughout the site, but were more numerous in the southwest portion (Gilmore and Chenault 1993). At the Rabbit Site, fire pits were located in the southeast part of the site.

To begin to examine the use of extramural space during the Basketmaker III period, a study of the distribution of surface artifacts was carried out at Big Bend. This type of study lends itself well to sites with minimal or moderate natural deposition, and minimal or moderate postoccupational disturbance. It is only at such sites that the distribution of surface artifacts can be presumed to generally reflect their distribution at the time of site abandonment. Although particularly useful for interpreting sites with purely surficial deposits (Phillips 1993; Motsinger and Mitchell 1994), artifact distributions can also provide useful information on how outdoor activities were arranged at pit house and pueblo sites. A similar study was carried out at Tres Bobos Hamlet, a Basketmaker III site in the Dolores Project area (Brisbin and Varien 1986).

Currently, the most useful tool available for visually analyzing the distribution of a large number of artifacts across two- or three-dimensional space is the computer graphics package SURFER, an interactive program that can generate either contour maps or three-dimensional surfaces from any set of X, Y, and Z coordinates. For our purposes, the X and Y coordinates represent the metric northing and easting of the center points of the 112 5-by-5 m sample collection units that were laid across the site in a 7-unit by 16-unit grid. The Z coordinate represents the number of artifacts per 25 m² (the area of each collection unit) across the site's surface. These data were entered into a spreadsheet, then imported into SURFER, which then uses one of several mathematical interpolation methods to create a contour plot. The locations of site features were then digitized and overlaid atop the contour plot.

This exercise yielded some promising results. As figure 3.7 shows, there were several peaks in the distribution of all artifact types across the site. The most dramatic of these was centered atop Feature 13, an amorphous pit, indicating that the pit was last used for depositing trash. Another, more subtle peak on the east side of Feature 5, a roasting pit at the north end of the site, probably represents ceramics that were broken or spalled in the course of using the roasting pit. Trash was also deposited immediately north of Feature 4, a slab-lined pit room, and about 30 m northeast of Feature 1, the main pit house.

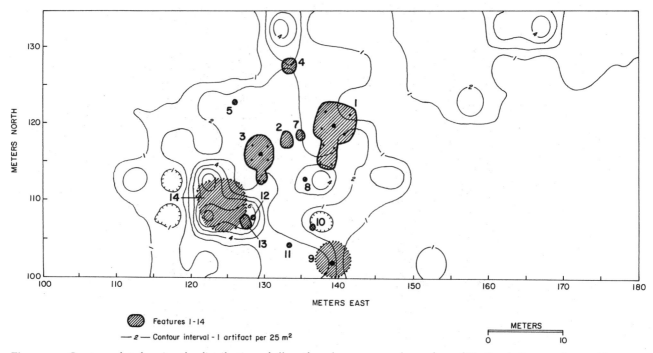

Figure 3.7. Contour plot showing the distribution of all artifact classes across the surface of Big Bend. Contour interval is 7.5 artifacts per 25 m^2.

When we limit our view to only lithic artifacts and debitage (figure 3.8), other subtle patterns emerge. The three collection units atop the ramada (Feature 14) had a dramatically elevated lithic count, indicating that lithic tool manufacture was among the activities carried out inside the ramada. Slight concentrations south of the antechambers of the two pit houses (Features 1 and 3) might be attributed to the sweeping of lithic debris from inside these structures. Interestingly, trash deposition at Big Bend was not concentrated south or southeast of the site as at many other sites, including Tres Bobos (Brisbin and Varien 1986). This suggests that outdoor activities such as trash disposal were less formalized early in the Basket-maker III period.

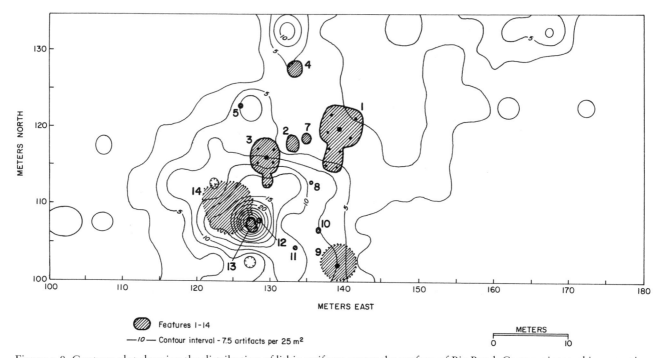

Figure 3.8. Contour plot showing the distribution of lithic artifacts across the surface of Big Bend. Contour interval is one artifact per 25 m^2.

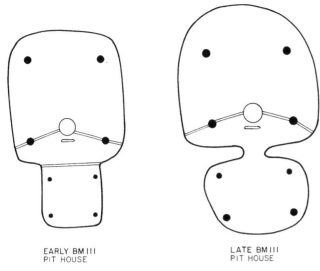

EARLY BM III
PIT HOUSE

LATE BM III
PIT HOUSE

Figure 3.9. Schematic depiction of an early Basketmaker III pit house and a late Basketmaker III pit house (after Cassells 1983:117).

ARCHITECTURE

Basketmaker III architecture consists for the most part of four feature types: pit houses, pit rooms, ramadas, and stockades, each of which is discussed separately below.

Pit Houses

There typically was one primary pit house at Basketmaker III hamlets. Primary pit houses consisted of a large main chamber (usually approximately 6 m in diameter) with a smaller antechamber located to the south or southeast of the main chamber and connected to it by an opening or short passageway. Early in the Basketmaker III period, the two chambers were roughly rectangular in plan, becoming more D-shaped (figure 3.9) later in the period (Cassells 1983:117). Also, in the early Basketmaker III pit houses, the two chambers were often separated by a partition wall rather than being separate structures connected by a short tunnel or opening as in the later Basketmaker III structures. The main pit house at Big Bend (figure 3.10) is an example of an early Basketmaker III structure, and the primary pit house at Dancing Man (figure 3.11) is a late Basketmaker III pit structure.

The floors of the main chambers of the pit houses were fairly shallow, having been built one meter or less below the prehistoric ground surface. The floors were sometimes plastered, but often merely consisted of packed earth. Antechamber floors were similar, although they were sometimes less well prepared than those in the main chambers. Antechambers were often shallower than the main chambers.

Roofs in the pit houses were almost always supported by four main support posts, with the two chambers hav-

ing separate (but connected) superstructures. The Anasazi built the roofs by laying primary beams across the tops of the four main support posts. They then placed secondary beams in a contiguous parallel pattern. In some cases, the builders placed a thick layer of adobe directly over the secondary beams. In other instances, they placed reeds, grass, or maize husks over the beams and then applied the adobe covering (Phillips 1997). Burned adobe chunks in the fill of the pit houses at the three burned sites displayed the impressions of both parallel beams and of the various kinds of closing materials.

The Basketmaker III Anasazi built the walls of their pit house main chambers by leaning a series of upright posts from the floor at the base of the sides of the pit over to the edge of the roof, or they placed the bases of the posts on a bench. In both cases, the posts were set into postholes. Because the upright posts were spaced several centimeters apart, it is inferred that brush would have been woven in between the posts, and the whole thing covered with adobe to form jacal walls. Figure 3.12 is a plan map of the main pit house at the Rabbit Site showing postholes encircling the main chamber at the base of the pit wall.

In some Basketmaker III pit houses, benches were built into the walls on three sides of the chamber; benches are found in both chambers of some structures, but in only one chamber of others. Benches in Basketmaker III structures do not appear to have functioned as platforms for sitting or storage as they appear to have in the kivas of later periods. Instead, when they do occur, benches were used as a shelf into which wall posts were set (figure 3.13). Benches were cut into the native soil and usually were not built from soil or adobe after the structure pit had already been dug. The vertical sides of some benches appear to have been plastered.

The Basketmakers usually constructed two partitions, called wing walls, in the southwest and southeast quarters of the main chambers. These partitions were made of jacal or of upright stone slabs covered with adobe. The two southern roof-support posts usually were incorporated into the wing walls. In some pit houses, the wing walls extended to the main hearth, although the sections from roof-support posts to the hearth were short to allow the inhabitants to step over them. In fact, those sections were sometimes no more than ridges sticking up from the floor, as was the case in the main pit house at Dead Dog (figure 3.14). In other pit houses, additional partitions extended from the roof-support posts to the southern wall of the main chamber, forming bins behind the wing walls, as in the main pit house at the Rabbit Site (see figure 3.12).

Hearths in the primary pit houses were circular, basin-shaped pit features. The hearths in each of our main pit houses were lined with an adobe coping material that

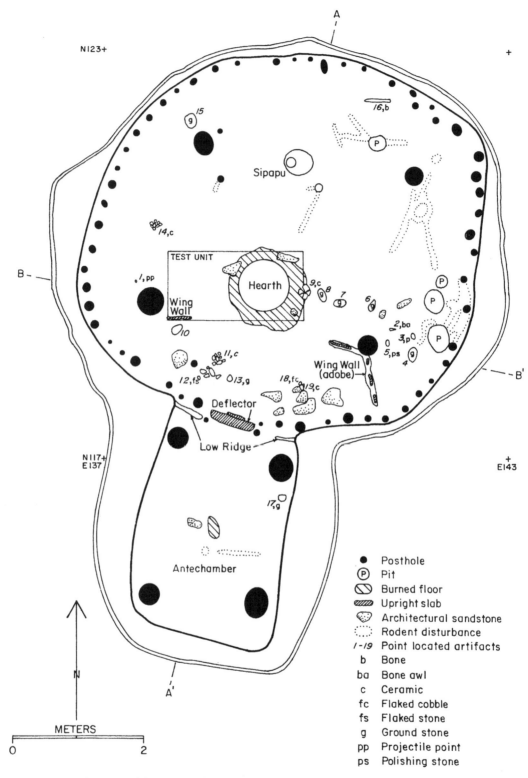

Figure 3.10. Plan map of the main pit house at Big Bend (5MT9387), an early Basketmaker III structure.

had become fire hardened through use. Hearths no doubt provided warmth and light to the inhabitants of the structures, who probably did some food processing and cooking with those features, especially during the colder months of the year. Deflectors, usually consisting of up-

right stone slabs, were located to the south of the hearths. These stones would "deflect" air passing through the antechamber and into the main chamber, and keep it from blowing directly across the hearth. This would have helped to keep smoke from filling the cham-

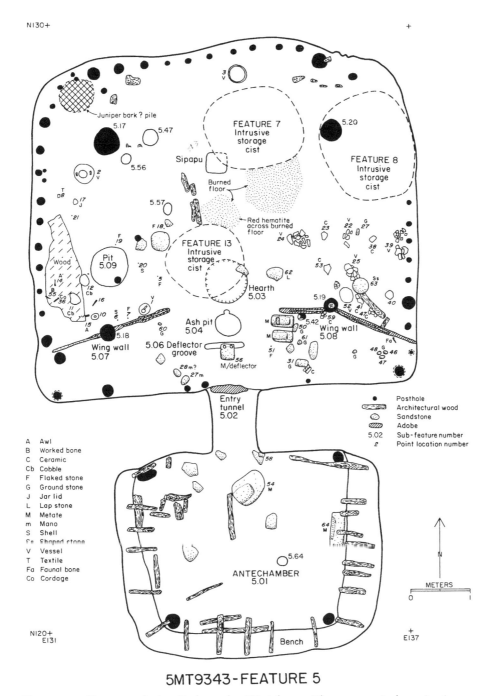

Figure 3.11. Plan map of a late Basketmaker III pit house. The structure is the main pit house at Dancing Man (5MT9343.).

ber. It is hypothesized that there were smoke holes in the roofs of the main chambers, directly above the hearths (e.g., Birkedal 1976).

Sipapus have long been identified as ritual features in Anasazi pit structures (Fewkes 1898; Wilshusen 1988a). The feature type was first identified in ethnographic contexts (Mindeleff 1891; Parsons 1939) and applied through analogy to similar features found in Anasazi structures. *Sipapu* is a Hopi word for the pit shrines found in many Hopi kivas. The sipapu symbolizes the

place of emergence where the original people came up to the surface of the world (Smith 1972:120; Wilshusen 1988a:650). Sipapus in Basketmaker III pit houses, when such features can be identified, are usually of the type Wilshusen refers to as simple sipapus. "Sipapus of this type are recognized as small, cylindrically shaped pits located to the north of the hearth and generally in line with the hearth and ventilator. Some pits are lined with plaster or with the neck of a broken jar, and often the pits are filled with a clean sand" (Wilshusen 1988a:650). This is

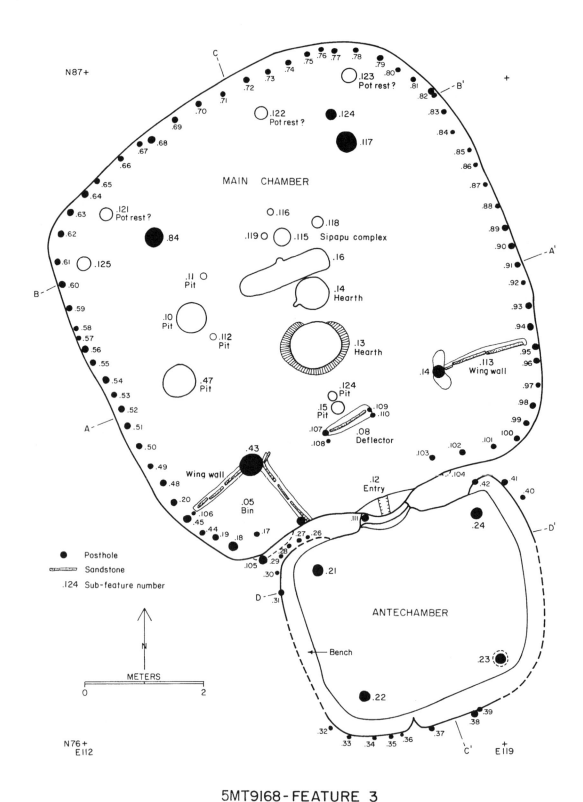

MAIN CHAMBER

.123
Pot rest ?

.124

.117

.122
Pot rest ?

.121
Pot rest ?

.116

.118

.119

.115   Sipapu complex

.84

.125

.16

.11
Pit

.14
Hearth

.10
Pit

.13
Hearth

.112
Pit

.47
Pit

.113
Wing wall

.124
Pit

.15
Pit

.109
.110

.107

.08
Deflector

.108

.43

.12
Entry

Wing wall

.05
Bin

.111

.24

●   Posthole

▭   Sandstone

.124   Sub-feature number

N

METERS

0   2

.21

Bench

.23

ANTECHAMBER

.22

.32

.39

.38

.33   .34   .35   .36   .37

C'   E119

5MT9I68-FEATURE 3

Figure 3.12. Plan map of the main pit house at the Rabbit Site (5MT9168).

not always the case, however. In the main pit house at Dancing Man, we found a square pit feature directly north of the hearth, midway between the hearth and the north wall of the main chamber. We interpret that feature as having been a sipapu, even though it was like some of

the more complex sipapus found in later pit structures (Wilshusen 1988a). In general, Birkedal's (1976:172) statement that "each pit house may also contain a sipapu; but this is not certain," holds true for our structures. In some of our pit houses we found one or more

Figure 3.13. Photograph of the main pit house at Dead Dog (5MT11,861).

pits in the location where one would expect to find a sipapu. But, for example, in the main pit house at the Rabbit Site, it is open to interpretation as to which of the small pits north of the hearth might have been the sipapu, whether all of them together constituted a sipapu complex, or whether none was a sipapu. As Wilshusen (1988a:650–651) said, quoting Smith (1952), some archaeological features are interpreted as sipapus on the weakest of evidence, often simply their position within the pit structure.

In addition to the main pit houses, each of the four sites had at least one secondary pit house (also called Pocket pit houses [Kane 1986; Shelley 1990]). These secondary pit houses ranged from smaller versions of the main pit house, complete with similar internal features, such as Feature 12 at the Rabbit Site, to square pit structures largely devoid of internal features, such as Feature 9 at Dead Dog or Feature 4 at Dancing Man. There is more variation in size and morphology in secondary pit houses than in primary pit houses at Basketmaker III sites. We are not certain of the function of the secondary pit houses, although many of them show evidence of domestic use similar to that which took place in the primary

structures. We discuss the role of secondary pit structures in more detail in the final section of this chapter.

The above description of Basketmaker III pit houses, based largely on data from four sites, in many ways reiterates the description given by Birkedal (1976:166–183) in his dissertation on the Basketmaker III of Mesa Verde. And while we have all been admonished to "escape the confines of normative thought" (Cordell and Plog 1979), comparison of our data with Birkedal's points out the remarkable consistency in Basketmaker III architecture throughout the Mesa Verde region.

Pit Rooms

Surface structures at Basketmaker III habitation sites in the Mesa Verde region can best be described as pit rooms. They were circular to oval in plan view, 3 to 4 m in diameter, and the pits forming the lower part of the structures were shallow, usually 50 cm or less in depth. The limited evidence concerning superstructure for the rooms suggests a variety of construction. Some of the rooms at Dead Dog had numerous unshaped stones in the fill, suggesting that at least the lower portions of the walls outside of the pits were constructed of rough masonry or upright slabs. Other rooms, like those at the Rabbit Site, appear to have had superstructures entirely of jacal, based on the structural remains found in several of the rooms that had burned. Some of the pit rooms, such as the one from Dead Dog shown in figure 3.15, were slab lined both on their floors and the pit walls. Slab-lined pit rooms were common in the Basketmaker III component at Site 5MT3 at Yellow Jacket (Joe Ben Wheat, personal communication, 1983). The superstructures for slab-lined rooms were also apparently made of jacal. The superstructures of those and other pit rooms were probably beehive shaped. Charred maize and other vegetal materials recovered from burned pit rooms at our sites indicate that most of the structures were used as storage areas. An exception to this is Feature 6 at Dead Dog, which was a circular, shallow pit room with a central hearth. The structure was located between the pit rooms and the main pit house. The hearth and use-compacted surface in Feature 6 suggested that domestic activities such as food processing took place there, and that it might have been a habitation structure for at least part of the year, such as during the warm summer months. Feature 6, along with the storage rooms behind it and the pit structure to the south, presages the unit pueblos of Pueblo I and subsequent pueblo periods.

Ramadas

We had evidence of ramadas at both the Rabbit Site and at Big Bend; however, the evidence at our sites and at other Basketmaker III sites in the region appears to be limited largely to alignments of postholes. At Big Bend there was a circular arrangement of postholes, along

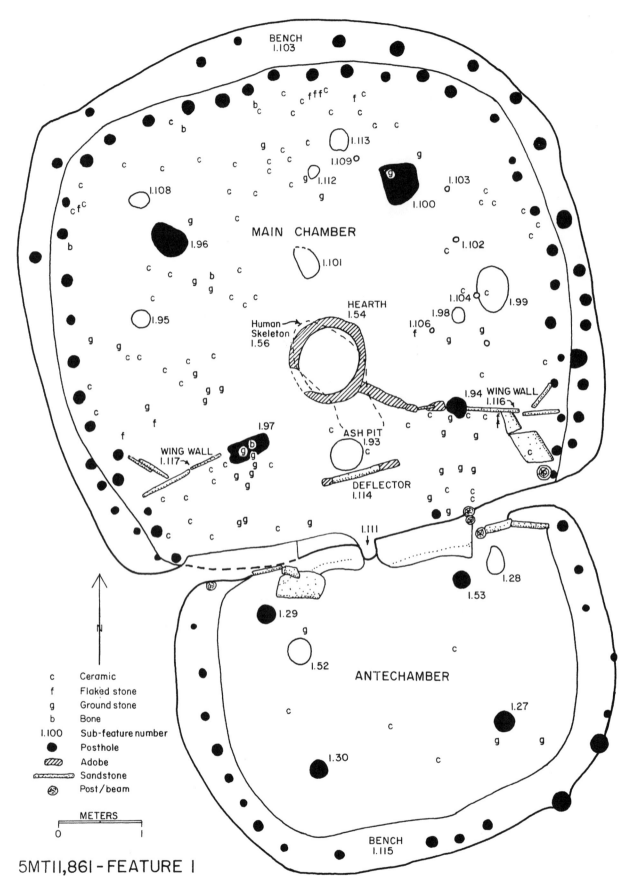

BENCH
1.103

MAIN CHAMBER

1.108

1.113

1.109

1.112

1.100

1.103

1.96

1.102

1.101

1.95

1.104

1.99

HEARTH
1.54

1.98

1.106

Human
Skeleton
1.56

1.94 WING WALL
1.116

1.97

ASH PIT
1.93

WING WALL
1.117

DEFLECTOR
1.114

1.111

1.28

1.53

1.29

1.52

ANTECHAMBER

1.27

1.30

1.115

BENCH

N

c   Ceramic
f   Flaked stone
g   Ground stone
b   Bone
1.100   Sub-feature number
●   Posthole
▨   Adobe
        Sandstone
⊗   Post/beam

METERS
0   1

5MT11,861—FEATURE 1

Figure 3.14. Plan map of the primary pit house at Dead Dog (5MT11,861) showing ridge connecting the southeast wing wall and the hearth.

Figure 3.15. Photograph of slab-lined pit room at Dead Dog (5MT11,861).

with a higher frequency of flaked stone, and at Tres Bobos (Brisbin and Varien 1986), four postholes formed a square in an area southwest of the pit house of Element 2. Ramadas probably provided a shaded work area during the summer months.

Stockades

The lines of postholes we found surrounding many of the features at several Basketmaker III sites suggest that they were protected by stockades; however, we have little information on how Basketmaker III stockades were constructed or what they might have looked like. Rohn (1975:113) reported that the Gilliland Site was "completely encircled by a stockade of vertical poles averaging some 15 cm in diameter and spaced about 20 to 30 cm apart. Presumably the upright poles were interlaced with branches and smaller poles to form a fence, or plastered over with mud to make a wall." Morris (1991:642) agreed with this, stating that "Basketmaker III stockades presumably were lattice works of small poles and brush woven into and supported by closely spaced posts." Hall (1944) described the evidence for this type of construction for a Pueblo I site in the Gobernador District of New Mexico (Morris 1991:642). Hall (1944:28) found a burned stockade at the site and, through careful excavation, identified an area of charcoal fragments spread as far as 5 m on either side of the line of postholes. This strongly suggested that the stockade had been made primarily of wood, or wood and brush, and had stood a meter or two in height. Hall did not report finding large amounts of burned adobe in association with the stockade, leading us to assume that the stockade had not been constructed of jacal.

It has been suggested that most Basketmaker III sites were surrounded by stockades and that excavators have failed to identify them (Rohn 1975). However, as Morris (1991:643) stated, the extensive excavations of the DAP and the MAPCO Project found little evidence of stockades at the Basketmaker III sites investigated. Similarly, many of the Basketmaker III houses reported in this volume had no evidence of stockades.

ECONOMY AND SITE-LEVEL SUBSISTENCE

Material Culture

Because several of the chapters in this volume are concerned with Basketmaker III ceramics (e.g., L. Reed et al., chapter 10), there is no need for us to provide an in-depth discussion of Basketmaker III pottery. Basically, ceramics for the time period in the Mesa Verde region consisted of only two types: Chapin Gray and Chapin Black-on-white (Breternitz et al. 1974; Lucius and Breternitz 1992). Lucius and Breternitz (1992) assigned Chapin Gray to the Lino Gray style. According to Wilson and Blinman (1991:7): "Chapin Gray is analogous to Lino Gray as defined for the Cibola and Kayenta traditions, Rosa Gray for the Upper San Juan tradition, and to Bennett Gray for the Chuska tradition." In the Mesa Verde region, Chapin Gray is found at sites dating between A.D. 575 and 950 (Wilson and Blinman 1991). This ceramic type was made by the concentric coiling method, with all coils obliterated. The Anasazi potter scraped and smoothed the surfaces of the pots, but did not apply any surface decoration, with the exception of occasionally applying a "fugitive red" pigment after the vessel had been fired. Tempering material was most often crushed rock, although crushed sandstone and sand were sometimes used (Breternitz et al. 1974:1).

The decorated ceramic type for the period, Chapin Black-on-white, is assigned to the Lino Black-on-white style (Lucius and Breternitz 1992). Chapin Black-on-white is analogous to Lino Black-on-white for the Kayenta tradition, La Plata Black-on-white for the Cibola tradition, Crozier Black-on-white for the Chuska tradition, and Rosa Black-on-white for the Upper San Juan (Wilson and Blinman 1991). "The great majority of Chapin Black-on-white vessel forms are bowls, with rare examples of seed jars, ollas, and effigies" (Wilson and Blinman 1991:17). Sites with this ceramic type date from A.D. 575 to 800, with a few cases as late as A.D. 900. Chapin Black-on-white vessels were produced with the coil and scrape method, and they have crushed igneous rock temper. Surface color is medium to very light gray, and the surfaces of the vessels are not slipped. Paint used by the prehistoric potters consisted primarily of mineral pigments.

The flaked stone assemblages at our sites included both hard-hammer and soft-hammer percussion. Bifaces and unifaces were simple and reflect low levels of production input, and the majority of tools were used flakes. In general, the inhabitants used an expedient core-reduction technology (Berg and Greenwald 1997a, 1997b; cf. Torres, this volume). The assemblage appears to be comparable to those from other Basketmaker III sites in the region (Birkedal 1976; Kane 1986), although in the Dolores area there was a lower frequency of utilized flakes (Kane 1986).

The primary types of ground stone tools from our sites were manos and trough metates. Other ground stone items included axes, mauls, floor-polishing stones, jar lids, palettes, hand stones, and grinding slabs. In addition, we found a carved-stone figurine in the shape of an animal at Dancing Man. Most of the ground stone artifacts were made of sandstone. The metates were of the "Utah" type, with one end open and a shelf at the closed end. SWCA recovered both one-hand and two-hand manos from the four sites. Ground stone assemblages from the Lone Pine sites are typical for the Basketmaker III period in the Mesa Verde region (Greenwald 1997a, 1997b).

Baskets and textiles were a major component of Basketmaker material culture (hence the name), and we recovered several charred fragments of these materials during our excavations. SWCA crews found two fragments of twined yucca sandals at the Rabbit Site and two from Dead Dog. These items follow the standard pattern for Basketmaker III twined sandals. Most twined sandals have scalloped toes (Webster and Hays-Gilpin 1994), although some are rounded. They have colored geometric designs on the upper side of the midsole, and textured patterns on the underside of the heel. The heels are usually cupped, but are sometimes squared off (Webster 1997a). More detailed discussions of Anasazi and Basketmaker III sandals can be found in Deegan (1993, 1995, 1996), Kent (1983), Webster and Hays-Gilpin (1994), and in some of the older literature (e.g., Morris 1944; Morris and Burgh 1941). We also recovered fragments of coiled baskets. The baskets were of two-rod-and-bundle construction with noninterlocking stitches. This was the most common type of coiled basket among the Basketmaker III Anasazi (Webster 1997a). Yucca fiber cordage was also found at the sites, as was twill plaited matting of yucca fiber (Webster 1997a, 1997b).

Other artifacts found in Basketmaker III contexts at our sites include those made of animal bone. Most bone artifacts were awls, although our crews also found bone beads, and a fragment of what may have been a bone flute was discovered at Big Bend (Stratton 1997a). The awls had been made from large animal bones such as deer tibia.

Subsistence

Not surprisingly, the four Basketmaker III sites excavated along the Lone Pine Canal reflect a mixed strategy of wild plant and animal procurement and domesticate pro-duction. At least as represented by Big Bend, the early part of the Basketmaker III period was marked by the cultivation of squash and maize, along with consumption or other use of prickly pear (which was toasted in one roasting pit), piñon nuts, goosefoot and other Cheno-Ams, purslane, knotweed, ground cherry, globemallow, cattail, and tobacco. Many of these species were found to have been stored in pit rooms. The botanical evidence indicates that summer and fall harvests provided cultigens that could be stored for much of the rest of the year. However, pollen evidence indicates that these stores may have been exhausted at least during the late spring, when diet relied most heavily on wild plants. Dietary protein was provided primarily by medium-sized mammals such as jackrabbits and cottontails, whereas large mammals such as deer were nearly absent from the faunal assemblage at Big Bend. The latter suggests that by the early Basketmaker III period, population increases in some areas were already leading to depletion of some faunal resources.

The preservation of the contents of storage vessels recovered from burned pit houses at the Rabbit Site and Dead Dog provide a remarkable snapshot of the wide array of food resources that were stored. Various vessels on the floor of the main pit house at the Rabbit Site were filled with charred remains or pollen of beans, maize kernels, ground corn meal, ricegrass seeds, purslane, pigweed seeds, Cheno-Ams, tansy-mustard, juniper seeds, pine cones, globemallow, wild onion, beeweed, prickly pear, and wild grape (Cummings and Puseman 1997a). Vessels in the main pit house at Dead Dog stored a large quantity of ground meal made from sunflower and pigweed seeds. Also stored in vessels were manzanita seeds or fruits, beeweed, goosefoot, a member of the sedge family, strawberry cactus seeds or fruits, mint, beans, ground cherry seeds or fruits, ricegrass seeds, purslane, globemallow, cattail, maize, and possibly sagebrush and juniper leaves (Cummings and Puseman 1997b). Dietary protein was provided by medium-sized mammals such as jackrabbits, cottontails, and prairie dogs, although 17 different mammal and avian taxa were represented in the assemblages from the three later sites (Stratton 1997b, 1997c).

COLONIZATION, EXPANSION, AND SETTLEMENT PATTERNING

It is not the topic of this study to examine the origins of the Anasazi or of the earliest Basketmaker people. However, the Basketmaker III period does represent the first real period of colonization of the Mesa Verde region by the people we now call Anasazi. As Kane (1986:361) stated: "The transition from Archaic to Anasazi is thought to have occurred via colonization rather than via direct transition." Where the colonists originated is unclear. There are substantive differences between the Basketmaker III remains in the Mesa Verde region and those, for example, in the Navajo Reservoir area (Eddy 1966). And there are also differences in architecture and material culture between Mesa Verde Basketmaker III and Basketmaker III in northeastern Arizona (e.g., Marek et al. 1993). Basketmaker III remains in Chaco Canyon (Roberts 1929), however, appear to be more like those in the Mesa Verde region, and that may be the direction whence the colonists came.

Our sample survey of the approximately 88,000 acres of the portion of the Animas-La Plata Project slated for irrigation, gave us a glimpse of settlement patterns during the Basketmaker III period in southwestern Colorado. On a large scale, our survey detected differences between the Mancos River drainage in the western portion of the project area and the La Plata River drainage in the eastern part. In general, the Mancos drainage exhibited higher site densities than the La Plata drainage during all prehistoric periods, including the Basketmaker III period (Ahlstrom et al. 1996). The data also suggest that the area between the La Plata River and the heads of the canyons that drain into the Mancos River was sparsely inhabited during the Basketmaker III period. It should be noted, however, that our sample of the region between the rivers was limited, and more extensive coverage might find resources that would partially fill the gap. Nevertheless, the interlying area we surveyed appears to have been unoccupied during the Basketmaker III period.

Our explanation for the difference between the western and eastern portions of the project area is largely based on environmental factors. The La Plata River drainage is an area of low relief. It is dominated by the La Plata River and its floodplain, and by the smaller valleys of tributary streams and the rounded, relatively broad interfluves. The relief in the Mancos River drainage is greater, and the mesas there are separated by steep-walled, deeply incised canyons. Except for the river corridor, the La Plata drainage would have been somewhat drier in prehistory than the Mancos drainage, and its vegetation would have included larger areas of shrubs and smaller areas of woodland than the Mancos drainage (Chenault and Ahlstrom 1996:298). Therefore, with more available moisture and greater access to woodland, the Mancos drainage would have been more attractive for Anasazi habitation.

On a smaller scale, our data indicate a movement of Anasazi habitation sites, through time, from the mesa tops to the canyon rims and then to the canyon heads and the overhangs below the canyon rims. During the Basketmaker III period, the Anasazi located the majority of their habitation sites near the center of mesa tops on ridges of high ground. This would have placed them in the best areas for dry farming, with deep, well-drained soils ideal for the construction of pit houses. The central

portions of the mesa tops were also where the best stands of trees were located. Although these site locations would have put the Basketmaker III Anasazi farther from sources of potable water than if they had located closer to the canyons, they would have been close to other needed resources. The Anasazi continued to locate their sites on mesa tops through the Pueblo I period, but by the Pueblo II period they had moved most of their habitations to the canyon rims or the heads of canyons; in Pueblo III they dropped to below the canyon rims. We are, of course, not the first archaeologists to identify this trend. Rohn (1977:249) found a similar pattern on Chapin Mesa, as did Hayes (1964) on Wetherill Mesa, both within Mesa Verde National Park. The same basic settlement pattern for the Basketmaker III period, followed by the move toward the canyons in later periods, was also described for Mockingbird Mesa in southwestern Colorado (Fetterman and Honeycutt 1987).

The Huntington Land Evaluation Survey (Mabry et al. 1997) filled in a small portion of the area between the two rivers that we had not covered with the above Class II survey. Information gained with the Huntington project did not, however, change our interpretations of the settlement data as described above.

REGIONAL COMPETITION AND THE ONSET OF WARFARE

The mode of abandonment of many Basketmaker III sites in the Mesa Verde region presents us with an enigma. At numerous sites it is clear that most, if not all, architectural features had burned at or around the time of abandonment. This is not the case for Big Bend, which appears to have been abandoned in an orderly, planned fashion, but our other three sites exhibit evidence of intense fires that consumed not only structures but also numerous artifacts within them. In fact, large numbers of cultural items—pottery, baskets, sandals, cordage—were lost in the conflagrations at the Rabbit Site, Dancing Man, and at Dead Dog. For example, at least 30 whole and reconstructible ceramic vessels were left on the floor of the main pit house at the Rabbit Site, eight at Dancing Man, and 73 at Dead Dog.

Working with data from the DAP, Wilshusen (1988b: 680–681) identified 15 types or cases of abandonment of prehistoric Anasazi structures. The 15 cases ranged from catastrophic fire to natural collapse of the structure following planned abandonment, and included ritual burning of structures. The traditional interpretation in Southwestern archaeology of burned structures containing numerous artifacts is that accidental, catastrophic burning occurred (Canby 1982:563; Wilshusen 1986). The nature of the large artifact assemblages in the main structures at Dancing Man, the Rabbit Site, and Dead Dog certainly argue for some type of catastrophic

TABLE 3.1

Site Name	Site Number	Date of Occupation	Stockade	Burned Structures	Burned Stockade	Reference
		Selected Basketmaker III Sites from the Mesa Verde Region				
Big Bend	5MT9387	late A.D. 500s (?)	no	no	N/A	Motsinger and Chenault 1997
Dancing Man	5MT9343	late A.D. 600s	yes	yes	yes	Motsinger 1997
Rabbit Site	5MT9168	early A.D. 600s	yes	yes	yes	Chenault 1997a
Dead Dog	5MT11,861	mid to late A.D. 600s	possible	yes	yes—burned posts	Chenault 1997b
Cloud Blower	5DL121B	late A.D. 600s	yes	yes	yes	McNamee et al. 1992b
Palote Azul	5DL112	late A.D. 600s	yes	yes	yes	McNamee et al. 1992b
Chindi Hamlet	5MT4684	A.D. 600s	no	yes	N/A	Tucker 1983
Tres Bobos	5MT4545	late A.D. 600s	no	yes	N/A	Brisbin and Varien 1986
Gilliland	site number unknown	A.D. 600s	yes	unknown	unknown	Rohn 1975

abandonment. However, Wilshusen's (1986) identification of a significant relationship between burning and certain ritual features (sipapus) in Pueblo I protokivas suggests that ritual burning of structures by the Basketmaker III inhabitants cannot be ruled out.

We suggest three possible explanations for the extensive burning at our sites and at other similarly burned Basketmaker III sites in the region: (1) the sites were purposefully burned at abandonment by the inhabitants, possibly for ritual reasons; (2) the sites were destroyed by accidental fires; or (3) the sites were burned by attackers.

Ritual burning of structures is a possibility; the body of the deceased might have been left within the house and the structure collapsed and burned around it. An analogy with Athapaskans, who sometimes abandoned a structure after its occupant died, has been suggested (Jett and Spencer 1981:28; Wilshusen 1988b:676), but this does not seem applicable to the Anasazi. Even though this practice cannot be traced to the Anasazi, we cannot rule out the possibility that this type of abandonment occurred at our burned sites. It is possible that the death of an individual prompted the intentional burning of the pit houses along with their cultural-material contents.

It is possible, of course, that there was some other ritually driven reason for abandoning structures and setting them afire filled with belongings. At Dolores sites, Wilshusen (1986) found that human burials were not commonly found in burned structures, but instead were often in structures where the roof had been purposely collapsed to cover the burials. As it turned out, those

structures usually contained complex sipapus (basin-shaped sipapu features). Conversely, structures in the Dolores area that had burned were primarily those containing central vault features (complex roofed pits). Thus the intentional burning of structures in the Dolores area was probably related to ritual other than human burial. There may have been some ritual or ceremonial reason for the burning that occurred at our Basketmaker III sites, but we have not been able to identify it and have not found any correlation with a particular ritual-type feature. As we discuss below, however, we do see a relationship between burned Basketmaker III sites and a particular architectural feature: the stockade.

It is also possible that the occupants of the sites intentionally burned their homes for nonritual, nonceremonial reasons. For example, McGuire and Schiffer (1983) suggested that insect infestation was a major cause of abandonment of structures, and burning would certainly cleanse a site of vermin. However, we think it unlikely that the Anasazi would have left so many apparently intact belongings to be destroyed along with their houses.

The second of the explanations listed above is that the sites were destroyed by accidental fires. This seems plausible given that Basketmaker III structures were largely made of wood with a covering of adobe. As already stated, this is the explanation that has been favored by many Southwestern archaeologists. However, experimental burning of a full-scale replica of a pit house by DAP archaeologists suggested that such structures did not burn easily (Wilshusen 1988b:677). Wilshusen (1988b) also pointed to cases where structures had burned, but their hearths were filled with sand or other material, or were empty, and had not been in use at the time of the fire. This was the case with the hearth in the main pit house at the Rabbit Site. The hearth was filled with roof fall, indicating that it had been completely empty when the structure caught fire. This might be construed as evidence for intentional burning of the structure, except that nearly every structure at the site had burned, and the fire could have started anywhere in the hamlet and spread to the main pit house.

Wilshusen (1986) argued that most fires in Anasazi pit structures were not accidental. His linking of structure type and function with abandonment mode revealed a significant pattern in Dolores area pit structures during the Pueblo I period. As mentioned above, we did a similar analysis for Basketmaker III sites. Although the sample size is small, there appears to be a correlation between Basketmaker III sites that burned and the presence of stockade features. Table 3.1 presents a sample of Basketmaker III sites in the region, many of which were stockaded and which had burned prehistorically. The sample is not meant to be comprehensive and is limited to sites where we are fairly certain the excavators searched for evidence of stockades.

If Basketmaker III stockades were primarily defensive features (and this seems to be the general consensus: Motsinger and Chenault 1995; Rohn 1975; Wilcox and Haas 1994), then the last of the above explanations becomes the most likely: the sites were destroyed by attackers. Farmer (1997) has argued for indications of warfare in Basketmaker iconography, and Bullock (1991), Wilcox and Haas (1994), and, most recently, LeBlanc (1999) have argued for the presence of warfare in the prehistoric Southwest. Warfare, in turn, led to the need for defensive features. Rohn (1975) stated that there might especially have been such a need at sites located along the northern periphery of the Anasazi world. The extensive burning and rich artifact assemblages at our sites suggest to us that warfare is the best explanation for their destruction. As Wilcox and Haas (1994:224) stated, "A regional pattern of high percentages of burned settlements, particularly when they also contain good floor assemblages or burned bodies, has been regarded as evidence of warfare."

Although defense was likely not the only function of the stockades (Motsinger and Chenault 1995), it is notable that many of the burned Basketmaker sites were also stockaded. The presence of stockades during the late Basketmaker III period suggests that by this time, defense had become a major concern, and the association of catastrophic burning with stockades suggests that site abandonment and destruction may have been caused by enemy raids. As a caveat, we should note that the mere fact that a site was burned probably makes the stockade

postholes more visible archaeologically. In some soil settings, then, an unburned stockade may not be recognized archaeologically, and the site might therefore be erroneously classified as a nonstockaded site. Also, as the reader may have noted, examination of table 3.1 shows that the strongest correlation is not between evidence of burning and stockaded sites, but between burning and sites that date to the seventh century A.D. In other words, there appears to have been a strong likelihood of destruction by fire for hamlets occupied during that time, whether or not they were stockaded. This would seem to bring us back to the point where we started, still not making a strong case for any of the three explanations listed above. However, we believe that the increased destruction by fire, along with the extensive artifact assemblages and the increased occurrence of stockades in the seventh century A.D., points toward hostilities as the best explanation for the catastrophic abandonments of late Basketmaker III sites in the region (LeBlanc 1999). Such cases of catastrophic burning, along with the occasional remains of victims, are all that might be expected as evidence of warfare. Prehistoric warfare in the Southwest was probably small-scale with no armies or large battles; hit-and-run raiding was probably the norm (Wilcox and Haas 1994:235).

We can only speculate as to the causes for the hostilities during the seventh century A.D. LeBlanc (1999:151) sees early warfare in the Southwest beginning with "typical hunter-gatherer carrying-capacity-constrained warfare." We agree, but also see competition for control of new areas and the resources therein as a factor. As stated earlier, the Basketmaker III period is when much of the Mesa Verde area was colonized by the Anasazi. Conflict over land and resources may have arisen among Basketmaker groups moving into the region prior to reaching the point where population had outgrown the carrying capacity. It is hard to imagine that resources were so scarce or times so hard that economically driven fighting would have erupted among the Anasazi given the relatively low population levels at the time. But it may have been competition over resources in general, rather than over "scarce resources," that caused the conflict. Of course, it is possible that ethnic or ideological friction was at the root of the hostilities—a cause difficult to identify in the archaeological record.

It is also possible that Rohn's (1975) assertion that defensive features were most needed along the northern frontier is the key. Perhaps raids by non-Anasazi groups from the north and west were what the Basketmakers needed protection from. Cassells (1983:146) shows the range of the Fremont extending south and east to near the northern periphery of the Anasazi. However, A. D. Reed (1984) describes the Formative culture of west-central Colorado as being distinct from both the Anasazi and the Fremont. In any case, the Mesa Verde Anasazi may have built their defensive stockades to deter raiding by groups inhabiting the region to the north.

SUMMARY AND CONCLUSIONS

Our intention in this chapter has been to synthesize information gained from recent excavations at four Basketmaker III sites northwest of Mesa Verde and the intensive survey of nearly 15,000 acres southeast of Mesa Verde in order to help address both traditional and current issues in the archaeology of the Basketmaker III period in the region. Of at least equal importance, we have tried to point to areas where new work can most fruitfully be brought to bear on research problems. In our view, some of the most fertile ground for enhancing our understanding of these people lies in reconstructing the history of Basketmaker colonization of, and expansion throughout, various parts of the region. One particularly meaningful aspect to this theme is how the early Anasazi responded socially to increasing sedentism and tighter living arrangements with one another. The erection and evidently violent destruction of defensive structures makes it apparent that in at least some areas, this period was a time of great social stress that could have resulted in (or possibly even resulted from) substantial transformations of ideology and socioeconomy.

Future work should focus on determining the distribution of both stockaded Basketmaker III sites and of burned Basketmaker III sites and features within the Mesa Verde region. Such research might reveal whether stockaded sites were concentrated along the northern boundary, were scattered throughout the region, or were limited to certain locales. And, of course, the question of why seventh-century sites were often burned has by no means been answered. Hypotheses for why pit houses and sometimes entire hamlets were destroyed by fire need to be tested with new data obtained through controlled excavation.

Along these same lines, the function of the stockade features themselves should be examined. Elsewhere (Motsinger and Chenault 1995) we came to the conclusion that the stockades were primarily defensive. We acknowledge, however, that Basketmaker III stockades would not have provided complete protection from an enemy determined to gain access to a hamlet; after all, stockades could be burned. Stockades probably had other functions as well as defensive ones. They would also have provided protection from wild animals and would have helped keep children away from dangers such as poisonous snakes. Stockades might also have provided privacy and enabled the occupants to store food and other items out of view (see Damp and Kotyk, this volume). Stockade walls would also have provided protection from the wind. The need for such protection was made clear to us while we were excavating the Rabbit

Site in June 1993. The wind often blew so intensely that we were forced to shut down the excavations because visibility and breathing conditions became unbearable. Although there would have been more vegetation prehistorically than at present, it would have consisted mainly of sagebrush, which would not have provided much of a break from the wind for sites located on ridge tops (Motsinger and Chenault 1995:7).

Finally, we should also consider the possibility that an important function of Anasazi stockades was to conceptually define the living space. This was suggested by Rohn in his discussion of the Gilliland Site. "Whatever its practical functions may have been, the stockade served to delineate the boundaries of an effective social unit, or community, whose material evidence, or settlement, constitute the Gilliland Site" (Rohn 1975:115). Basketmaker III stockades may have defined the boundaries of the Basketmaker "house" and functioned in a manner similar to the walls of houses in the modern developed world, providing privacy, protection from strangers, and protection from the weather. Such functions have been suggested by others working with Basketmaker remains (Damp and Kotyk, this volume).

Another avenue of research concerns the function of secondary pit houses at Basketmaker III sites. The typical pattern in the Mesa Verde region is for sites to have one primary pit house and one or more smaller, secondary pit houses (see Kearns et al.; Damp and Kotyk, this volume, for similar patterns in the southern Chuska Valley). The function of these secondary structures, or Pocket pit houses, is largely unknown. They sometimes exhibit features similar to those of the main structures and display evidence of domestic activities, but, often as not, they are devoid of interior features or have far fewer than the main houses. Were the secondary pit houses merely smaller versions of the main structures, or did they serve some other purpose? In order to address this question, we need to determine if the secondary structures and main structures were occupied contemporaneously. Unfortunately, we did not obtain tree-ring dates for any secondary structures at our sites. Even when there were indications of burning in those structures, the burning was not intense, and it appears in some cases that the larger timbers may have been removed before the structures were set on fire.

Several lines of evidence suggest that main pit houses and secondary pit houses were not occupied at the same time. At the Rabbit Site, the larger of the secondary pit houses appears to have been built after the stockade and the main pit house had been constructed (Phillips 1997). The other secondary pit house at that site appears to have been made from a remodeled pit room, after that room, and presumably the main structure, had burned. The secondary pit house at Dead Dog was intruded upon by a large pit feature containing burned material. Tree-ring dates from wood samples found in the fill of that pit indicate a date in the middle to late A.D. 500s, although they were vv (noncutting) dates and numerous outer rings could be missing. If those dates are close to the time the wood was cut, then both the pit and the secondary pit house it superimposes predated the construction of the main pit house. The lack of outer rings, though, makes this equivocal.

There are several possible interpretations of the function of the secondary structures, and, of course, the function may have been different at each site. One possibility is that the secondary structures predate the main structures, having been occupied prior to or during the construction of the main houses. A second interpretation is that they were occupied after the main structures were destroyed. And a third scenario is that they were occupied at the same time as the main structures and used for different purposes than the larger houses, or were occupied by different people. For example, they may have been inhabited by the parents or grandparents of the nuclear family occupying the larger structure. Or, conversely, the secondary structures might have been used by newlyweds residing in the same hamlet as the young woman's family, if matrilocal residence can be extended back to the Basketmakers.

Another topic deserving of research is the nature of the early Basketmaker III adaptation. Few early Basketmaker III sites in the Mesa Verde region have been investigated. Investigation of Basketmaker III sites should be built into research designs whenever possible in the hopes of gaining data that will help to characterize the nature of Anasazi culture at that time and, as mentioned above, to gain a better understanding of the colonization of the region.

Basketmaker archaeology is not for the indolent. The nondescript scatters of sherds and flakes that mark the surface of Basketmaker III sites belie the amount of information available to those who make the effort to unearth it. The problem-oriented excavation, recording, and analysis of more of these small sites will be our only means of understanding the late Basketmakers in the Mesa Verde region.

ACKNOWLEDGMENTS

SWCA's Animas-La Plata and Huntington Land Exchange surveys and the Lone Pine Canal excavation project were funded by the Bureau of Reclamation, Durango Projects Office. The projects were administrated by BOR archaeologist Warren Hurley, and we thank him for his help and guidance. We also wish to thank our crews, analysts, and laboratory personnel for their hard work. Maps for this paper were drafted by Charles Sternberg and William Grimm. We thank SWCA, Inc., Environmental Consultants for its support of this study, and the reviewers for their constructive and helpful suggestions. Thanks also to Paul Reed for inviting us to participate in the production of this book.

Part III

Basketmaker Archaeology
on the Eastern Slope
of the Chuska Mountains

4

Distinctive and Intensive

*The Basketmaker III
to Early Pueblo I Occupation
of Cove-Redrock Valley,
Northeastern Arizona*

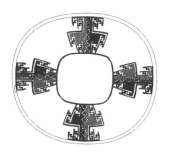

Paul F. Reed
Scott Wilcox

Archaeological research into the Basketmaker III occupation of the northern Southwest has expanded greatly in the last decade (e.g., Altschul 1991; Damp 1999; P. Reed and Hensler 1999; Shelley 1990, 1991; Vivian 1990; Wills and Windes 1989). Researchers have begun addressing questions concerning architecture, site structure, economy, demography, chronology, and community and social organization as never before. In addition, archaeologists recently have identified and excavated Basketmaker III sites in areas not previously investigated or not previously thought to contain significant early Anasazi sites (e.g., Kearns et al., this volume; Damp and Kotyk, this volume). Taken together, this new work indicates that Basketmaker III populations were more widespread and that overall population during the period was higher than previously thought. Recently completed excavations along the N33 road (the Cove-Red Valley Archaeological Project) undertaken by the Navajo Nation Archaeology Department (NNAD) have revealed a large Basketmaker III presence and provided the data to address some of these research concerns (P. Reed and Hensler 1999; figure 4.1).

The N33 Project excavations took place just a stone's throw from the Prayer Rock District, where Earl Morris found a wealth of undisturbed Basketmaker III remains in sites such as Broken Flute Cave, Obelisk Cave, Cave 1, and Cave 2, among others (Morris 1931). These caves largely lacked obtrusive later Puebloan occupations. Thus, the Basketmaker III structures were in good condition, and the deposits were, by and large, not mixed with the refuse of later periods. As such, Morris was able to identify architectural and material culture characteristics of the Basketmaker III interval without significant concern about contamination from later deposits. In addition, most of the caves lacked evidence of prior

Basketmaker II occupation; thus, mixing with earlier materials was not a serious concern. In short, the Prayer Rock caves represented the ideal natural laboratory for Morris to use in defining and differentiating the Basketmaker III period from both earlier and later manifestations. Unfortunately, Morris, a prodigious field-worker, was unable to complete a written report on the Prayer Rock excavations. Nevertheless, his daughter, Elizabeth, compiled the data for her dissertation (Morris 1959, 1980). Earlier, Morris did incorporate findings from the Prayer Rock excavations into his overview of the La Plata Valley Basketmakers (Morris 1939). Because of excellent preservation, numerous ephemeral and fragile textiles, baskets, items of clothing, sandals, and other perishable goods were recovered from the caves, particularly from Broken Flute Cave (see Hays-Gilpin et al. 1998 for a summary of sandals from the area). Earl Morris's excavations revealed a large Basketmaker III community, concentrated in Broken Flute Cave, but also represented by structures in other caves and shelters, and an unfinished great kiva.

In 1987, the Zuni Archaeology Program (ZAP, now known as Zuni Cultural Resource Enterprise) excavated several sites located along the proposed N63 road right-of-way in the Oak Springs area of Redrock Valley, Arizona-New Mexico (Hildebrant 1989). Three of the sites excavated contained Basketmaker III or early Pueblo I structures. These excavations took place 9 km north of AZ-I-25-47, the easternmost Basketmaker III site investigated during the Cove–Red Valley Archaeological Project. Given the distribution of sites along the N33 road and the concentration of sites in the Cove Community, the Oak Springs sites actually lie closer to AZ-I-25-47 than do the other N33 Project Basketmaker III sites (see figure 4.1). AZ-I-25-47, then, provides a very

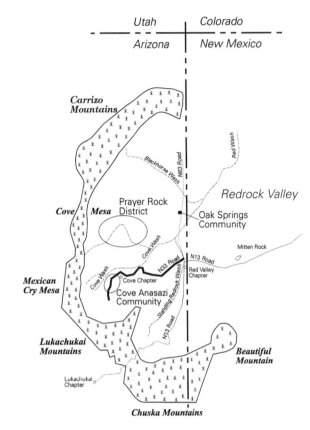

Figure 4.1. Map showing Cove–Redrock Valley area.

ENVIRONMENTAL SETTING

The Cove–Redrock Valley area is located in northeastern Arizona, directly west of the New Mexico-Arizona state line (see figure 4.1). Redrock Valley is a predominantly north-south trending lowland surrounded by the Carrizo Mountains on the northwest, the Lukachukai Mountains on the west and south, and the San Juan Basin on the east. Physiographically, the San Juan Basin is broadly divided into two major zones: the interior lowlands and the encircling uplands. The project area is part of the Four Corners Platform structural subdivision that forms the northwestern rim of the basin (Hunt 1956). The Four Corners Platform is a relatively flat, wide, and low divide between the Chuska Mountains and the San Juan Uplift in Colorado. Vivian (1990) identifies further "subareas" of the San Juan Basin based upon geologic divisions and drainage patterns. The Redrock-Shiprock subarea includes Redrock Valley, which heads between the eastern flanks of the Carrizo and Lukachukai Mountains. Redrock Valley is an irregular lowland formed on red beds of the Upper Triassic Chinle formation and Wingate Sandstone. The Cove–Redrock Valley area is marked by massive, steep-walled canyons with numerous rock shelters. The area is drained by Red Wash to the east, and by Cove Wash and lesser tributaries in the west. Cove Wash itself is tributary to Blackhorse Creek and ultimately to Red Wash, which drains north to the San Juan River. Climate and vegetation regimes within the subarea reflect the more than 700 m of elevational difference between the bordering mountains and the San Juan River.

In geologic terms, Redrock Valley is composed predominantly of Triassic and Jurassic Period formations of sedimentary rock including Chinle, Wingate, Kayenta, Moenave, Navajo, and Summerville formations, as well as associated minor formations. Igneous formations dating to the Tertiary period are present in the Lukachukai and Carrizo Mountains, and as isolated remnants throughout Redrock Valley and the Upper San Juan Basin.

Faunal and floral patterns in the Cove–Redrock Valley area are typical of the Upper Sonoran life zone. Dominant vegetation includes piñon, juniper, and sage on the western end, and snakeweed, rabbitbrush, and a variety of grasses (including Indian ricegrass, muhly, cheatgrass, and grama grass) on the eastern end of the project. Faunal communities are less obvious in the project area due to extensive disturbance by human and domestic animal habitation. Typically present are a variety of mammals including lagomorphs, rodents, deer, and antelope, and numerous species of birds, reptiles, and amphibians.

Sediments in the project area consist largely of deep, well-drained alluvial clay, silt, and sand, particularly on the western end. Aeolian sediments are also represented,

interesting set of comparative data with which to examine the Basketmaker III occupation of the area vis-à-vis the Cove, Oak Springs, and Prayer Rock communities.

During Phase III of the Cove–Red Valley Archaeological Project, 14 archaeological sites ranging in age from Basketmaker II to late Pueblo II–early Pueblo III were excavated (P. Reed and Hensler 1999).[1] Basketmaker III components, including three small pit house villages, two single pit house habitations, and one special-use site, were present at six of these sites. One of the primary foci of this chapter is the three N33 Project habitation sites that contained Basketmaker III and early Pueblo I structural remains. To broaden our perspective and encompass more of the Cove–Redrock Valley area, we also examine data from ZAP's work on the N63 road project (Hildebrant 1989) and Morris's excavations in the Prayer Rock caves (Morris 1980). After providing environmental and cultural background on the N33 sites, we address architecture, ceramic production and use, subsistence, and settlement and community organization, and provide a demographic reconstruction of the early Anasazi occupation of the Cove–Redrock Valley.

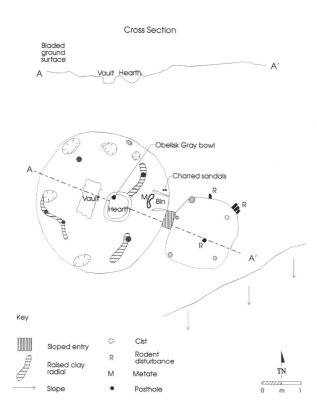

Cross Section

Bladed
ground
surface

A — Vault Hearth — A'

Obelisk Gray bowl

Charred sandals

A —

Vault

Hearth

M Bin

R

R

R

R

A'

Key

	Sloped entry	Cist
	Raised clay radial	R Rodent disturbance
	Slope	M Metate
		Posthole

TN

0   m   1

Figure 4.2. Plan map of Structure 1 at AZ-I-25-47.

especially on the eastern end of the project. In highly
eroded portions of the project area, degraded shale and
clay bedrock are in evidence. Additionally, drainages in
the area frequently contain large sandstone and igneous
boulders that originated in the mountains and testify to
occasional flash flooding and major sediment transport
and deposition.

EXCAVATED COVE–REDROCK VALLEY BASKETMAKER III TO EARLY PUEBLO I COMPONENTS

During Phase III of the Cove–Red Valley Archaeological
Project, Basketmaker III and early Pueblo I pit houses
were excavated at three sites: AZ-I-25-47, AZ-I-26-3,
and AZ-I-26-41 (P. Reed and Hensler 1999). The N33
sites, along with the Basketmaker III to early Pueblo I
sites excavated along the N63 road and by Morris in the
Prayer Rock District, are discussed here.

AZ-I-25-47

AZ-I-25-47 is a Basketmaker III habitation site consisting of at least two pit structures, a midden, and several
extramural features. The site lies on the east bank of Red
Wash, just west of the Arizona-New Mexico state line, at
the point of best topographic access to the Cove portion
of Redrock Valley. Structure 1, a Basketmaker III pit

house, was the primary focus of excavation at the site,
although most of the midden and several extramural
features were also investigated. The house consists of a
circular main structure (4.8 m in diameter) and an antechamber (2.3 m diameter) connected via a narrow (40 cm
by 60 cm) passage (figure 4.2). Although the structure
was originally deeper, the highest remaining wall was
60 cm above the structure floor. The superstructure consisted of a four-post main support system with additional
posts (leaners) leaning inward from outside the structure.
Structural wood elements recovered from within the
structure included *Populus* sp. (38 percent), juniper (27
percent), and piñon (17 percent). Ponderosa pine and
spruce or fir were represented in smaller amounts.

Nine large internal features were identified within the
pit house, including a central hearth, a rectangular floor
vault, a slab-lined bin, a basin-shaped depression, and
five bell-shaped cists (Wilcox 1999). Space within the
main structure was divided by low, mounded partitions.
The area between the hearth and the passage was separated from the rest of the structure by a raised clay radial
extending from the northern edge of the hearth, and a
second radial to the south of the hearth. A main support
posthole was found in each of these partitions. Tree-ring
(noncutting), archaeomagnetic, and radiocarbon dates
place the site within the middle Basketmaker III period,
between A.D. 630 and 675 (Wilcox 1999). The artifact
assemblage and distribution indicate that the structure
suffered a catastrophic fire. Three manos were found in
situ between roof beams, and an incomplete pair of
charred sandals was found on the floor. Several manos
and lithic cores were found on the floor, as well as a
metate and several shaped sandstone cist covers. At least
14 vessels were represented in the ceramic assemblage.
Among the vessels was an Obelisk Utility bowl containing cooked corn that was found in situ in the hearth, indicating that the hearth was in use when the structure
caught fire. Thus, we infer that a catastrophic fire destroyed the structure. There is no indication that the fire
was other than accidental; no indications of conflict or
warfare were identified.

AZ-I-26-3

AZ-I-26-3 is a large, multicomponent Anasazi village
comprising one of the core constituents of the Cove
Community. The site lies due west of Cove Wash and less
than 3 km north of the Lukachukai Mountains. It has
distinct Basketmaker III, Basketmaker III–early Pueblo I,
and Middle and late Pueblo II occupations (P. Reed and
Hensler 1999). The Basketmaker III and Basketmaker
III–early Pueblo I components naturally underlie the later
Pueblo II use of the site and, as a result, have suffered
considerable modification. Present at the site are four
known Basketmaker III or early Pueblo I houses (and

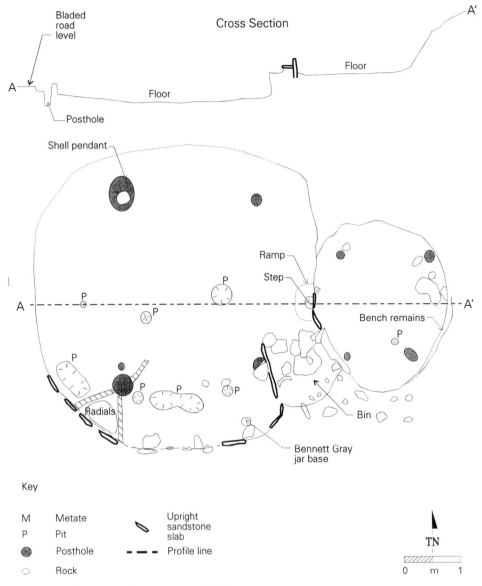

Figure 4.3. Plan map of Structure 7 at AZ-I-26-3.

probably more). NNAD's excavation work focused on the three houses present within the N33 road right-of-way; only the two complete houses are discussed here.

Architecturally, the two excavated houses are different from each other. Structure 7 was a pit house similar to Structure 1 at AZ-I-25-47 with an antechamber that measured 3 by 2.4 m, and a projected main chamber that measured 5 by 4.5 m (figure 4.3). The antechamber floor lay 90 cm below the prehistoric ground surface, but the main chamber was deeper: 1.2 m below the prehistoric ground. The later construction of a Pueblo II period kiva in the same location destroyed most of the main chamber floor. Although much of the main chamber floor and features was destroyed, four central postholes were found, indicating that the roof of the house was supported with a typical Basketmaker III superstructure.

Chronometric dates (including archaeomagnetic, radiocarbon, and ceramic mean dates) indicate that the

structure was constructed and used between A.D. 725 and 800.[2] Internal features within the structure include a wing-wall enclosure, several upright-slab bins, two shallow oval storage pits, a large round pit of unknown function, and numerous postholes. Artifacts present on the floor included an axe and metate in the antechamber, and a shell pendant, a gray ware vessel, a bone awl, and several lithic tools in the main chamber. Because the later, superimposed kiva burned at or around abandonment, determining precisely the abandonment sequence of the house is difficult. Ample evidence of burning was present in both chambers. In addition, the number and diversity of artifacts present in floor context suggest a rapid, unplanned abandonment. If such was the case, then we can perhaps infer that a catastrophic fire similar to that which destroyed Structure 1 at AZ-I-25-47 occurred at Structure 7, ending its use life.

Structure 9 was a subrectangular house, measuring

Cross Section

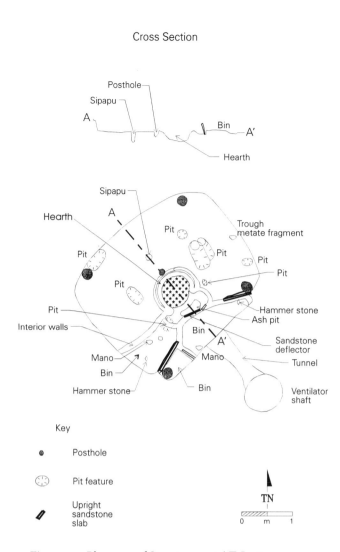

Figure 4.4. Plan map of Structure 9 at AZ-I-26-3.

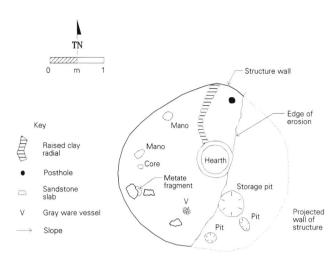

Figure 4.5. Plan map of Structure 1 at AZ-I-26-41.

roughly 3.5 by 2.8 m and oriented northeast-southwest (figure 4.4). The floor of the house was encountered 1.4 m below the present ground surface and about 1 m below the prehistoric surface. The native earth walls of the structure were undoubtedly plastered while in use. The structure lacked an antechamber but had a large ventilator tunnel and shaft on its southeast side. Four main posts set close to the corners of the house comprised the superstructure. A relatively high (ca. 50 cm above the floor) slab and clay radial wing wall separated a small area on the south from the remainder of the house. Drawing on several dating methods (archaeomagnetism, radiocarbon, and ceramic mean dates), we infer that the house was built and used between A.D. 725 and 800 and perhaps was contemporaneous with Structure 7. Internal features, in addition to postholes, include a double-collared hearth, a sipapu, an upright bin, an ash pit, several plastering pits, a metate rest, two vessel rests, and two probable storage pits. Storage inside the house exceeded 0.33 cubic meters. Abandonment of the house appears to have occurred in a relatively slow and planned manner given the limited number of artifacts present in situ on the floor.

AZ-I-26-41

AZ-I-26-41 is a multicomponent Anasazi and Navajo site located about 1 km north of the Lukachukai Mountain front on a fan remnant between two drainages. Two Anasazi components are present at the site: a Pueblo II field house and a Basketmaker III single pit house residence (also interpreted as a field house). Structure 1 was a Basketmaker III pit house situated on a steep hill slope above Cove Wash (figure 4.5). Because of the incline, the southeastern third of the structure was destroyed by natural erosion. The structure was circular, measuring 3 m in diameter, and the highest remaining wall was 41 cm above the structure floor. The superstructure probably consisted of a four-post main support system. Only one posthole was located during excavation. No evidence of burning, intentional or otherwise, was found in Structure 1.

Five internal features were located within the pit house: a hearth, a basin-shaped pit, two circular pits (U-shaped in cross section), and a posthole in the northeast quarter of the structure. The house had little internal storage capacity, less than 0.05 cubic meter. Like Structure 1 at AZ-I-25-47, the space within the pit house was divided by at least one low, raised clay radial partition extending north and east from the collared hearth. The portion of the structure floor to the southeast of the hearth was destroyed by erosion, but it is likely that a second radial partition was present. Unlike the pit house at AZ-I-25-47, however, the main support posts were not incorporated into the partitions.

Chronometric samples recovered from Structure 1 at AZ-I-26-41 included tree-ring, archaeomagnetic, and radiocarbon. Neither the tree-ring nor archaeomagnetic samples produced dates. Based on the radiocarbon date range and ceramic mean dates, we conclude that the house was built and used between A.D. 700 and 775, and may have been contemporaneous with Structures 7 and 9 at AZ-I-26-3. Artifacts recovered from the floor of the

TABLE 4.1

Architectural Attributes of Basketmaker III to Early Pueblo I Structures in Cove–Redrock Valley

Site	Structure No.	Date (A.D.)	Phase	Shape	Length (m)	Width (m)	Burned	Abandonment	Ante-chamber	Bench	Bins	Cists	Storage Capacity (cubic m)
AZ-I-24-7	16	675–750	Broken Flute–View Point	Subrectangular	5.5	5.5	Yes	Planned	No	No	1	1	0.81
AZ-I-24-8	2/25	625–700	Broken Flute	Subrectangular	5	5	Yes	Planned	No	No	4	0	1.02
AZ-I-24-8	4/29	600–675	Broken Flute	D-shaped	6	5.2	Yes	Planned	No	No	4	0	1.18
AZ-I-24-8	7	600–675	Broken Flute	Circular	4.8	4.8	Yes	Planned	No	No	5	1	1.48
AZ-I-24-8	27/35	625–700	Broken Flute	Subrectangular	5.4	5	No	Planned	No	No	5	0	1.87
AZ-I-24-11	20	730–775	View Point	Subrectangular	3.45	3.5	Yes	Catastr.	No	No	0	3	0.47
AZ-I-25-47	1	630–675	Broken Flute	Circular	4.8	4.8	Yes	Catastr.	Yes	No	1	5	0.65
AZ-I-26-3	7	725–800	View Point	Subrectangular	5	4.5	Yes	Catastr.	Yes	??	1	1	0.14
AZ-I-26-3	9	725–800	View Point	Subrectangular	3.5	2.8	No	Planned	No	No	2	0	0.15
AZ-I-26-41	1	700–775	View Point	Circular	3	3	No	Planned	No	??	0	0	0.02
Broken Flute Cave	Great Kiva	623–640	Broken Flute	Circular	14	12	Yes	Unk	No	No	0	0	0
Broken Flute Cave	1	470–520	Obelisk	Subrectangular	4.5	4	Yes	Catastr.	No	No	1	0	0.32
Broken Flute Cave	2	470–520	Obelisk	Circular	2.25	2.25	Yes	Planned	Entry	Yes	0	0	0
Broken Flute Cave	3	470–520	Obelisk	Circular	4.75	4.75	Yes	Planned	No	No	0	0	0
Broken Flute Cave	4	623–640	Broken Flute	Circular	3	2.5	Yes	Catastr.	No	No	0	0	0
Broken Flute Cave	5	623–640	Broken Flute	Circular	5	4	Yes	Planned	No	Yes	0	0	0
Broken Flute Cave	6	623–640	Broken Flute	Subrectangular	7.4	5.5	Yes	Catastr.	No	Yes	0	5	1
Broken Flute Cave	7	623–640	Broken Flute	Subrectangular	8.5	5.25	Yes	Catastr.	No	Yes	4	0	1.07
Broken Flute Cave	8	623–640	Broken Flute	Subrectangular	5.5	5.5	Yes	Catastr.	No	Yes	3	0	0.80
Broken Flute Cave	8A	470–520	Obelisk	Circular	5	5	Yes	Planned	No	No	0	0	0
Broken Flute Cave	9	623–640	Broken Flute	Subrectangular	6.4	6	Yes	Catastr.	No	Yes	1	2	0.45
Broken Flute Cave	10	623–640	Broken Flute	Circular	3.13	3.13	No	Planned	No	No	0	0	0
Broken Flute Cave	11	635–645	Broken Flute	Circular	9	7.5	No	Planned	No	No	1	0	1.50
Broken Flute Cave	12	623–640	Broken Flute	Circular	6.5	6.26	Yes	Planned	No	Yes	4	0	2.42
Broken Flute Cave	13	623–640	Broken Flute	Circular	4.2	2.7	Unk	Unk	No	No	0	0	0
Broken Flute Cave	14	623–640	Broken Flute	D-shaped	3.5	3	Unk	Unk	No	No	2	0	0.10
Broken Flute Cave	15	623–640	Broken Flute	Circular	7.25	7.25	Yes	Planned	No	No	0	0	0

Site	Structure No.	Date (A.D.)	Phase	Shape	Length (m)	Width (m)	Burned	Abandonment	Ante-chamber	Bench	Bins	Cists	Storage Capacity (cubic m)
Broken Flute Cave	16	470–520	Obelisk	Subrectangular	5.5	4.25	Yes	Catastr.	No	No	0	0	0
Cave 1	1	660–700	Broken Flute	Subrectangular	6	3	Yes	Catastr.	No	Yes	0	0	0
Cave 1	2	660–700	Broken Flute	Circular	6.1	6.1	Yes	Unk	No	Yes	0	0	0
Cave 1	3	660–700	Broken Flute	Circular	4	3.5	Yes	Yes	No	No	0	0	0
Cave 2	1	669–700	Broken Flute	Subrectangular	5.65	5.3	Yes	Yes	No	Yes	2	0	0.26
Cave 2	2	669–700	Broken Flute	Circular	6.4	5.8	Yes	Yes	No	No	1	0	0.54
Cave 2	3	650–700	Broken Flute	Circular	3.7	3.7	Yes	Unk	No	Yes	0	0	0
Cave 2	4	650–670	Broken Flute	Subrectangular	5	5	Yes	Planned	No	Yes	1	0	2
Pocket Cave	1	470–520?	Obelisk	Circular	4	4.2	Yes	Catastr.	Entry	Yes	2	0	0.2
Pocket Cave	2	470–520?	Obelisk	Circular	3.79	3.79	Yes	Catastr.	No	No	0	0	0.2
Pocket Cave	3	470–520?	Obelisk	Circular	6	6	Yes	Catastr.	No	No	0	0	0
Pocket Cave	4	470–520?	Obelisk	Circular	7.4	7	No	Catastr.	No	Yes	1	0	0.50

Note: Catastr. = catastrophic burning; Unk = unknown.

structure included a battered cobble, metate fragment, lithic core, and ground stone fragments. The ceramic assemblage consisted of Tallahogan Red, plain gray/brown, and indeterminate Basketmaker III–early Pueblo I black-on-white types. The absence of burning at Structure 1 may indicate that the structure was not intentionally or permanently abandoned. The location of AZ-I-26-41 (overlooking the arable floodplain of Cove Wash), the results of pollen and macrobotanical analyses, and the limited feature and artifact assemblage all suggest that the structure was occupied seasonally and was associated with farming activities.

BASKETMAKER III AND EARLY PUEBLO I SITES ALONG THE N63 ROAD

During excavations along the N63 road between Red Valley and Oak Springs, Arizona, ZAP excavated three sites containing Basketmaker III–early Pueblo I pit structures: AZ-I-24-7, AZ-I-24-8, and AZ-I-24-11 (Hildebrant 1989). AZ-I-24-7 is a Basketmaker III–early Pueblo I habitation site with a single pit house and two associated surface structures. A later Anasazi component was also identified at the site but was not excavated. ZAP's work focused on the pit house and two surface structures. At AZ-I-24-8, another multicomponent village site, four pit houses were excavated. Finally, a single early Pueblo I house (along with associated surface and subsurface rooms) was excavated at AZ-I-24-11.

The variation seen in Basketmaker III and early Pueblo I architecture excavated during the Cove–Red Valley Archaeological Project is apparently common to all of Redrock Valley. Basketmaker III and early Pueblo I pit structures excavated during the N63 road project exhibit similar variability. Six Basketmaker III or early Pueblo I pit structures, each exhibiting a relatively unique suite of attributes, were excavated during the N63 project (table 4.1). The construction of the structures varied from slab-lined to adobe-lined to unlined earthen walls. Antechambers, present on only two of the six structures (Pit Structures 7 and 4/29 at AZ-I-24-8), were attached in a similar fashion to Structure 7 at AZ-I-26-3. The pit house (Structure 20) at AZ-I-24-11 had a vent similar to the one found in Structure 9 at AZ-I-26-3. This similarity seems to reflect temporal factors more than cultural ones, however, as both structures date to the latter half of the eighth century.

PRAYER ROCK DISTRICT BASKETMAKER III SITES

At least 41 pit structures were excavated at eight sites in the Prayer Rock District by Earl Morris in 1930 and 1931 (Morris 1980). Of these, data comparable to the N33 and N63 projects are available from only four sites: Broken Flute Cave, Pocket Cave, and Caves 1 and 2,

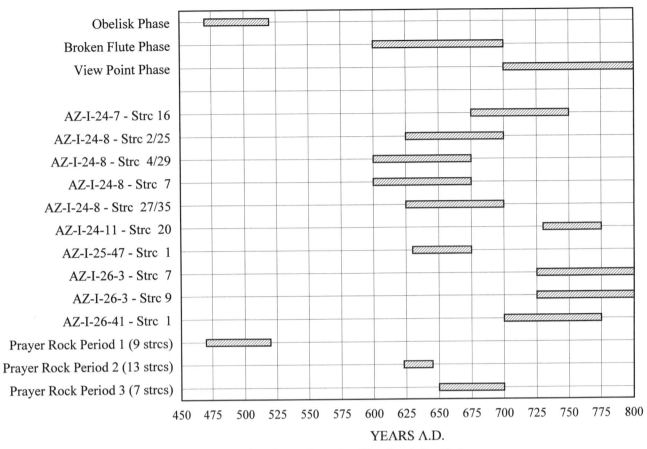

Figure 4.6. Inferred occupations for Cove–Redrock Valley Basketmaker III and early Pueblo I structures.

with a combined total of 29 structures (see table 4.1). Due to excellent preservation, many of the Prayer Rock structures are well dated by dendrochronology. We do not intend to review the chronometric data here (see Ahlstrom 1985; Hays 1992a; Hays-Gilpin et al. 1998; and Morris 1980 for an exhaustive treatment). For our purposes, the Prayer Rock sites can be divided into three periods: Period 1 from A.D. 470 to 520; Period 2 from A.D. 623 to 645; and Period 3 from A.D. 650 to 700. Although individual sites and structures date to different, often shorter intervals, occupation of most of the Prayer Rock sites and structures can be encompassed within these periods.

Like the N63 and N33 sites, the Prayer Rock structures exhibit variability in shape, arrangement of internal features, construction method, and abandonment condition. Some of this variability, of course, was conditioned by building within a confined spaced. Nine of the 18 Broken Flute pit houses burned at abandonment, and at least three of the houses had good evidence of catastrophic abandonments. The shape of the Prayer Rock structures varies from round to subrectangular, and, interestingly, one-third of the structures contain formal benches that were not found at the N63 or N33 sites. Like structures from the other two projects, however, the Prayer Rock structures seem to be evenly divided

between slab-lined, adobe or plaster, and earthen-wall construction. Antechambers were found at only two of the Prayer Rock sites, and these consisted of only a small entry. Above-floor bins seem to have been the preferred method of storage at both the Prayer Rock (due at least in part to the presence of hard cave bedrock) and N63 sites, while subfloor cists were more common at the N33 sites. Interior space at most of the structures discussed was divided using low clay radial floor ridges in varying numbers. In addition, the Prayer Rock sites, particularly Broken Flute Cave, contained significant numbers of both subterranean and aboveground cists in extramural contexts. In fact, Morris identified 65 extramural storage cists in Broken Flute Cave alone (Morris 1980).

Although we have briefly discussed the chronology of the Prayer Rock sites, we need to highlight the sequence used for all of the sites in our study. The phase sequence discussed here was developed during work on the Cove–Red Valley Archaeological Project (P. Reed and Hensler 1999). Dates were compiled from the Prayer Rock sites (Morris 1980), the N63 sites (Cox 1997; Hildebrant 1989), and the N33 sites.[3] Once all of the Basketmaker III and early Pueblo I sites and their inferred periods of occupation are graphed, a basic division into three phases is apparent (figure 4.6). The first two phases encompass the three periods used to summarize the Prayer

Rock sequence; the final phase goes beyond the predominantly Basketmaker III occupation of the caves. The Obelisk phase runs from A.D. 470 to 520; next, a hiatus is postulated for the entire area between A.D. 520 and 600; then, the Broken Flute phase runs from A.D. 600 to 700; and, lastly, the View Point phase is dated from A.D. 700 to 800.

COVE–REDROCK VALLEY ARCHITECTURAL PATTERNS

The N33 structures, those excavated by ZAP along the N63 road, and the intact structures excavated by Morris comprise an excellent sample of 39 structures that we used to study architectural patterns across the region (see table 4.1). A number of pit house traits were examined: shape, size, condition (burned or unburned), abandonment mode (catastrophic, planned, or unknown), presence or absence of antechamber and bench, and the number of internal bins, cists, and clay floor radials. These traits, among others, have been used to classify structures in an attempt to identify regional (normative) architectural patterns (see Shelley 1990 for comparison). Given the close proximity of these structures (the three subareas occur within an overall 15 by 15 km area), we expected to find evidence of a strong normative pattern for architecture. Despite this expectation, and although we controlled for changes through time, we found little evidence upon which to infer a strong normative pattern for the area.

As table 4.1 and the above discussion amply illustrate, no distinct architectural pattern predominated during the Basketmaker III–early Pueblo I occupation of Cove–Redrock Valley. The structures studied show similarity with houses from the Kayenta, Mesa Verde, and Chuska Slope regions. Because Cove–Redrock Valley lies roughly equidistant from these three culture areas, this is not an unexpected pattern.

Looking first at pit house shape, we identified three basic configurations: circular (or oval), D-shaped, and subrectangular (including houses that are essentially square). Although shape is assumed during the Basketmaker III to be circular early and becoming subrectangular and rectangular through time, we found a consistent distribution of circular structures through time: about one-third of the total are dated to the Obelisk phase, 62 percent date to the Broken Flute phase, and 5 percent occurred at post-700 structures. Likewise, subrectangular structures are well distributed across the phases: 13 percent of the total occur in the Obelisk phase, 60 percent of the subrectangular structures date to the Broken Flute phase (with 40 percent dating before A.D. 650), and 27 percent to the View Point phase. Thus, no more than 27 percent of the subrectangular structures occurred at late Basketmaker III or early Pueblo I sites, belying a simple

evolution from circular (early) to subrectangular (late). Only two D-shaped structures were included in the study, and both date to the Broken Flute phase.

Overall house size is another characteristic that we used to evaluate architectural patterns in the area. In general, it has been assumed that houses start small in the early Basketmaker III period and increase over time, peaking in Pueblo I, resulting in huge houses like those excavated by the Dolores Archaeological Program in southwest Colorado (Breternitz et al. 1986) and along the N5010 road (Hensler et al. 1999). Data from Cove–Redrock Valley do not support this postulated evolution. Mean house size during the Obelisk phase is 4.8 by 4.6 m (with a range from 2.3 m to 7.4 m for both length and width). An increase occurs during the following Broken Flute phase, with a mean of 5.5 by 4.8 m (and a range from 2.5 m to 9 m). The View Point phase, however, has the smallest mean size of any interval: 4.1 by 3.9 m (with a range from 2.8 m to 5 m), thus reversing the trend seen in earlier periods. We should point out that the View Point phase sample is small, consisting of only four structures, compared with nine Obelisk phase structures, and 24 that date to the Broken Flute phase. A larger sample size might increase the average size of View Point phase structures. On the other hand, many large houses would be necessary to reverse the pattern identified.

Other pit house traits similarly serve to cast doubt on the attribution of a strong normative pattern for the area. Antechambers are rare throughout the Cove–Redrock Valley area in Basketmaker III (only 18 percent of the structures studied had antechambers). Of seven structures with antechambers, two date to the Obelisk phase, four to the Broken Flute phase, and one is late, dating to the View Point phase. The normative pattern for Basketmaker III is for early structures to have antechambers that are slowly replaced, through time, with ventilator shafts. In contrast, the Cove–Redrock Valley sites show continuation of use of antechambers, albeit in just a few structures, throughout the period and into the early Pueblo I period (latter part of the View Point phase).

Moving the discussion inside Basketmaker III houses, we also find considerable variability in internal features. Roughly 37 percent of all the houses studied had benches, 58 percent lacked benches, and 5 percent (two houses) lacked sufficient data to determine presence or absence of benches. The benches identified occur overwhelmingly in houses dated to the Broken Flute phase (79 percent of the total). Benches were identified in three Obelisk phase houses, but no benches were found in View Point phase structures. Thus, construction and use of benches seem to be largely a middle Basketmaker III (A.D. 600–700) or Broken Flute phase attribute in Cove–Redrock Valley.

Use of internal storage and dividing features also varied considerably among the Basketmaker III houses occupied in Cove–Redrock Valley. The number and size of floor cists varied significantly among structures from all three subareas. Above-floor bins seemed to have been in widespread use during much of the Basketmaker III occupation of Redrock Valley, but this also varied. Structure 1 at AZ-I-25-47 had a single slab-lined bin, while Structure 27/35 at AZ-I-26-8 had five. Although most of the bins were constructed of upright sandstone slabs, wattle-and-daub was used to construct some of these features. A great deal of variability also characterized the placement and arrangement of the bins, which varied from adjoining bins to single bins on opposite sides of a structure.

During the Obelisk phase, few internal storage features were used; an average of 0.4 upright-slab bins per structure was recorded, and no subfloor storage cists were documented at the nine structures in the sample. Similarly, an average of only 0.4 clay radial features (sometimes called "speed bumps") per structure was documented, indicating that division of internal space was not of great importance to the inhabitants. Internal storage capacity—using all cists, bins, and other potential storage features—was relatively low during the Obelisk phase, with an average of 0.14 cubic meters per structure.

During the subsequent Broken Flute phase, however, both bins (mean of 1.6 per structure) and cists (mean of 0.5 per structure) increased in use, as did the construction of clay radial dividers (mean of 1.5 radials per structures). Internal storage capacity also increased substantially during the Broken Flute phase, with an average of 0.72 cubic meters per structure. By the View Point phase, use of bins had apparently decreased (mean of 0.8 per structure), subfloor cists were used more frequently (mean of 1) than in earlier phases, and use of clay radials also increased (mean of 2). Storage in View Point phase structures decreased to an average of 0.32 cubic meters per structure. By this time, use of associated surface structures was the norm for Puebloan settlements, and the decrease in internal pit house storage is not surprising. We did not specifically track construction and use of wing walls, a common dividing feature in late Basketmaker III and early Pueblo I structures. Nevertheless, the increasing use of clay radial dividers through time indicates that differentiation of space (the inferred function of the dividers) became more important toward the end of the period.

The varying use of storage features (aboveground bins or subfloor cists) is problematic and difficult to interpret. Given the presence of 65 storage cists in Broken Flute Cave alone, storage features were an important part of Basketmaker III architecture and were frequently located outside structures. Because of the low overall number of internal storage features in Obelisk phase sites, we might infer that the early Basketmaker III inhabitants of these sites were not as dependent on maize agriculture, thus not requiring as much storage capacity as later groups. On the other hand, we know that all of the Obelisk phase sites had extramural storage features. In any case, we doubt that the storage capacity of the earlier Obelisk phase sites surpassed that of Broken Flute Cave and other contemporary sites. There is little doubt, then, that increased storage capacity was more critical later in the period. The differences in internal versus external storage features may relate more to access and control of stored resources (a social issue) rather than merely the quantity of maize and other food stored (a subsistence issue). All of the Broken Flute phase houses examined during this study had numerous internal storage features with an average capacity of 0.72 cubic meters. By the Broken Flute phase, significant quantities of corn and other plant foods were being produced, well beyond normal, daily need. As a result, a significant investment in storage facilities was required.

The presence of such large storage features inside Broken Flute phase structures contradicts prior interpretations of Basketmaker III storage as primarily a caching strategy (Wills and Windes 1989; Wills et al. 1994). Wills and Windes (1989) came to the conclusion that caching was the primary Basketmaker III storage strategy largely through study of Shabik'eshchee Village in Chaco Canyon (originally studied by Roberts 1929). The site contains at least 68 pit houses, a large structure that Roberts (1929) considered a great kiva, and numerous external storage cists (much like Broken Flute Cave). Examination of the floor plans for the houses reveals a smaller number of internal storage features (bins, cists, pits) than seen in structures from the Cove–Redrock Valley area. Nevertheless, at least half the houses illustrated by Roberts (1929) have some internal storage, either bins, cists, or smaller storage pits. Proportionally, Shabik'eshchee has fewer external storage features than Broken Flute Cave (for Shabik'eshchee a ratio of about one extramural cist or bin to one house is maintained; for Broken Flute, the ratio is 3.6 storage facilities to one house). Clearly, the storage needs of Broken Flute Cave were higher and necessitated a greater area both inside and outside houses.

Other large Basketmaker III–early Pueblo I villages have storage unit/house ratios in-between Shabik'eshchee and Broken Flute Cave. Kiva Mesa, as described below, has a ratio of 2.35:1. Tohatchi Village has a ratio of 1.2:1 (storage rooms/cists to houses). Neither of these large village has been excavated, so internal storage cannot be determined. Nevertheless, the variability that exists suggests that characterizing Basketmaker III storage primarily as a caching strategy is inaccurate. Internal, readily accessible, and large-capacity storage features within houses in Cove–Redrock Valley and other areas suggest significant dependence on the stored products of maize agriculture, as well as natural plant and animal resources. A caching approach to storage is apparent in late Basketmaker II to early Basketmaker III (A.D. 400–525) sites studied in Cove–Redrock Valley (e.g., a large storage cist at AZ-I-26-37 with more than two cubic meters of capacity), but while this type of feature occurs on later Basketmaker III sites, they are most commonly associated with a house or cluster of houses (P. Reed and Hensler 1999).

In addition to storage features inside houses, Broken Flute Cave contains, as noted above, more than 65 external storage cists and bins. These features may have served a caching function, as envisioned by Wills and Windes (1989), but probably also served as overflow storage for individual families. Clearly, the Basketmaker III adaptation represents a flexible approach to settlement and subsistence. Given the high percentage of wild plant foods utilized in Cove–Redrock Valley settlements, "individual groups probably experimented with a number of approaches to food production, involving different mixes of cultivated and natural" (Wills et al. 1994:311). But with the evidence for greater sedentism (with construction of substantial houses), increased internal storage, greater population density, and greater overall dependence on maize and other cultivated products, it is equally clear that Basketmaker III populations, while still using the land extensively, had a much reduced mobility compared to their late Archaic predecessors. Thus, it seems unlikely that "the goals of agricultural production…remained essentially the same as during the late Archaic" (Wills et al. 1994:310). Rather, by A.D. 600, many Basketmaker III populations had committed to a settled, agricultural lifeway. Their agricultural goals centered on the production of a surplus that allowed their sedentary lifestyle to continue and provided the time for the rich ceremonial life that we find evidence of throughout the northern Southwest (e.g., Kidder and Guernsey 1919; Morris 1980).

The last two attributes examined for these houses were condition (burned or unburned) and abandonment mode (catastrophic, planned, etc.). We realize that many different factors can account for the burning of a pit house. Unfortunately, for some of the houses in the study, we lack sufficient data to go beyond the simple burned or unburned assessment to ascertain whether a given structure: (1) was burned accidentally and catastrophically; (2) was fired as part of an abandonment ritual; (3) was burned sometime after abandonment, either by the residents or another party; or (4) was burned intentionally by an outside warring party while in use (see Chenault and Motsinger, this volume; LeBlanc 1999). For most of the houses, though, such data are available. Overall, 79 percent of the structures in the study were burned, 16 percent were not burned, and for 5 percent, we could not determine from the data if the structure had or had not burned. For the Obelisk phase houses, the percentage of

burned structures was 88 percent. In the Broken Flute phase, 85 percent of the houses were burned. Interestingly, only 60 percent (three of five) of the View Point phase houses had evidence of burning.

Taking into account the small number of houses in the View Point sample, the basic pattern that emerges includes a high percentage of burned structures both early (Obelisk) and midway (Broken Flute) through the period. Late in the period, burned houses become less common. If the pattern is accurate and not a reflection of small sample size (especially for the View Point phase), we can offer several explanations for the change. First, if we infer that the burning identified is most often accidental in nature, a reduction in house fires later in the Basketmaker III period may reflect a technological improvement that rendered homes less susceptible to fire. Imagining what this might have been is difficult, especially considering that numerous structures continued to be burned in later Anasazi periods. On the other hand, if the fires were ritual or ceremonial in nature, then perhaps at the end of the A.D. 600s a change in ceremonial or ritual behavior occurred, no longer necessitating burning upon abandonment (see Walker 1998). Nevertheless, ceremonial or ritual burning continued and, in fact, intensified later in the Pueblo I through III periods (Walker 1998; Wilshusen 1989b).

The burned or unburned condition of houses relates directly to the mode of abandonment, the next issue we address. We identified several possible modes of abandonment: planned (with most useable artifacts removed, and floor features filled with sand or otherwise capped), catastrophic (unplanned), and ritual. These categories crosscut those identified above for burning. None of the structures had what we considered evidence of a ritual abandonment (per Wilshusen 1989b). Planned abandonments, whether finished by firing the structure or not, occurred in 42 percent of structures across time. Catastrophic abandonments (with most of the household goods left in place on the house floor) occurred in 45 percent of the structures. Finally, abandonment mode could not be determined for 15 percent of the structures. In the Obelisk phase, 22 percent of the structures were abandoned in a planned fashion, 56 percent were catastrophic with the burning of the structure, 11 percent appeared catastrophic without evidence of burning, and 11 percent of the cases were unclear. For the Broken Flute phase, 46 percent of structures had evidence of planned abandonments, 38 percent appeared catastrophic with burning present, 4 percent were catastrophic without burning, and 13 percent of the structures had no clear evidence of abandonment mode. Lastly, during the View Point phase, 60 percent of the structures were abandoned in a planned fashion, while 40 percent were catastrophic. The numbers are consistent across time, and there is not a significant increase in either planned or catastrophic abandonments from the Obelisk phase through Broken Flute and into the View Point phase.

While catastrophic burning of some structures may be related to warfare or conflict, we found no such evidence in our work on the N33 Project. In contrast, Morris (1980:51) reported a male individual killed by a blow to the head in Broken Flute Cave and suggested that this evidence, along with the high percentage of burned houses in Broken Flute and the other Prayer Rock caves, "may have been the result of a successful raid" (Morris, quoted in LeBlanc 1999:137). LeBlanc (1999) identified a pattern of widespread violence and conflict in the "Early Period," which includes Basketmaker II and III. Warfare and conflict undoubtedly played a role in the lives of Cove–Redrock Valley Basketmakers although it is not clear how much impact this conflict had. Finally, none of the burned structures seem to fit a ritual pattern (as defined by Wilshusen 1989b), although some may have been set afire as part of an abandonment ceremony.

The presence of stockades or fences around Basketmaker III sites is discussed by several other authors in this volume (Chenault and Motsinger; Damp and Kotyk; and Vivian). We did not specifically track the presence of such features at Cove–Redrock Valley sites and structures. Nevertheless, no such structures were described by Morris (1980) for the Prayer Rock sites or at the N63 sites, and we found none around the N33 structures.

Discussion

The most striking differences among the structures, both on the N33 and N63 projects, and in those from the Prayer Rock caves, seem to be the use of space within the structures. There appears to have been no formal protocol regarding the interior division of space. Most of the structures had raised clay radials as the primary means of separating space within the structure, but the number and placement of the radials varied from structure to structure. The architectural differences found in structures from all three areas can be viewed as culturally motivated, but in some cases (e.g., the use of vents versus antechambers) these differences are attributable to temporal differences. On the other hand, the division of interior space may reflect nothing more than personal preference and adaptation to the needs of each individual household.

Shelley (1990, 1991) undertook an analysis of Basketmaker III architecture and identified several styles: Northern, Western, Mixed, Pocket, and Other. Northern-style pit houses have separate antechambers at the same level as main chambers, benches, high wing walls, and rectilinear or D-shaped main chambers. Western-style pit houses are typically rounded with attached antechambers, often elevated above the main chamber floor, and have raised clay radials (anachronistically referred to as "speed bumps" by some archaeologists) separating the

space within the structure. The Mixed style combines traits of both the Northern and Western styles. The last style of concern here is the Pocket style (Kane 1986; incorporated by Shelley into his typology). Pocket pit houses are smaller than typical houses, have fewer floor features, and generally lack formal hearths. These latter structures are assumed to have served specialized functions, were not normally used as primary residences, and are often associated with larger pit houses. The Cove–Redrock Valley structures exhibit traits of Northern, Western, and Pocket styles in various combinations, but no specific pattern is evident. Shelley (1990) noted that the Northern and Western styles are restricted geographically, and that outside of Chaco Canyon, these architectural attributes are seldom combined within the same structure. In the Cove area, though, many of these traits are combined in the same structure. Shelley speculated that the reason for the combination of Northern and Western traits at Chaco was related to the cultural backgrounds of the inhabitants, and that intermarriage between people from different culture areas may be responsible.

Shelley's work is not without problems. His assessment is based on a limited sample of slightly more than 60 excavated structures. At least that many structures are reported for the first time in this volume, and most of the structures do not fall neatly into Shelley's categories (see our discussion below; and Damp and Kotyk; Kearns et al.; and Toll and Wilson, all this volume). The use of a "Mixed" category that encompasses a large percentage of the sample is problematic. Furthermore, some of the differences between the Northern and Western variants seem better explained as a function of change over time, and not as a result of true geographic differentiation. As a preliminary look at Basketmaker III architecture, Shelley's typology is useful, but additional work is necessary to see if his concepts of Western and Northern variants can hold up with a tripling or quadrupling of the sample size.

Nevertheless, we can assess the N33 structures for Northern, Western, Mixed, and Pocket characteristics. All of the complete or nearly complete pit houses excavated during the N33 Project were constructed with a four-post support structure and pole leaners (figure 4.7). Two of the N33 Project structures had antechambers, one in the Western style and one in the Northern style. Structure 1 at AZ-I-25-47 was the earliest of the pit houses excavated during the N33 project, dating between A.D. 630 and 675. Except for the detached antechamber, this structure fits the Western pattern, since it was round in plan view, had space divided by radial floor ridges, and lacked a bench. The antechamber was subrectangular, attached to the main chamber via a short passage.

Structure 7 at AZ-I-26-3 dates from A.D. 725–800 and has yet a different combination of Northern and Western

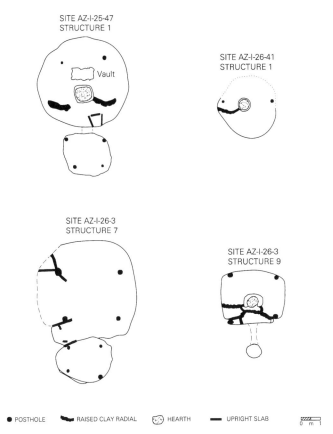

SITE AZ-I-25-47
STRUCTURE 1

Vault

SITE AZ-I-26-41
STRUCTURE 1

SITE AZ-I-26-3
STRUCTURE 7

SITE AZ-I-26-3
STRUCTURE 9

● POSTHOLE   RAISED CLAY RADIAL   HEARTH   — UPRIGHT SLAB   0 m 1

Figure 4.7. N33 Project pit house types by site.

attributes. The house was subrectangular in the Northern style, but had both radial floor ridges and upright-slab wing walls. The antechamber was attached to the main chamber in the Western style, and was partitioned from the main chamber by a wall of upright posts. Architecturally, Structure 9 at AZ-I-26-3 appears to be the latest of the Cove pit houses and dates from A.D. 725 to 800. Like Structure 7, Structure 9 was subrectangular and contained a combination of wing walls and radials. This structure, however, had no antechamber, but instead, a formal ventilator shaft consisting of a large circular vertical shaft connected to the house via a narrow horizontal tunnel. This type of ventilator has been noted by Shelley (1990) and others as associated with the changes in pit structure architecture occurring after A.D. 700. Structure 1 at AZ-I-26-41 dates to the A.D. 700 to 775 interval. The structure was circular and had radial floor ridges extending outward from the hearth. No antechamber or ventilator was present at this structure, nor were any large storage features identified. Although the structure lacked an antechamber and is small, it is the closest of the Cove pit houses to the Western style. A small pit house like this one could be put into the Pocket category, but its formal hearth and the number of floor features present indicate that it probably had more in common functionally with larger pit houses. The inferred field house function of Structure 1 probably explains its small size (built

to accommodate a single individual or two) and the residential features present (sufficient for short-term habitation).

The pit structures excavated during the N33 Project, although a small sample, exhibited a wide variety of architectural styles. This is partially due to temporal changes but, more important, appears to be the result of a blending of culturally determined behaviors. It appears that the construction techniques used by the builders (perhaps the men of the group) were modified to accommodate the needs of other members of the household (the women?) according to the preferred use of space within a given structure.

While we do not intend to individually address the other Cove–Redrock Valley structures used in the study, the discussion above illustrates that the variability seen in the N33 Project structures is present throughout the area. A variety of layouts (circular, subrectangular, and D-shaped) appears, size was quite variable, benches were present in some structures but not in others, and the use of clay radials, bins, and cists was highly variable. In short, our survey of Basketmaker III pit house architecture in Cove–Redrock Valley illustrates the great variability that prevailed and the lack of a strong normative pattern. This blending of traits leads us to conclude that the Basketmaker III inhabitants of the Cove–Redrock Valley area shared cultural affinity with several adjacent Anasazi areas either by marriage, immigration, social ties through trading relationship, or a combination of all of these.

PATTERNS IN CERAMIC PRODUCTION AND USE

To complement our study of Cove–Redrock Valley Basketmaker III architecture as it relates to regional patterns, and to go further in relating the area to adjacent Anasazi traditions, we examine ceramics. The Prayer Rock sites were excluded from this study for several reasons: (1) the ceramic collections are limited and highly variable from structure to structure and site to site; (2) good provenience information is lacking for many of the items collected; and (3) the ceramic analyses completed on the Prayer Rock collections were brief in nature and not comparable to those carried out for the N63 and N33 projects.

Looking at ceramics from the 10 N33 and N63 structures, several patterns are apparent. Table 4.2 shows plain ware ceramics, both gray/brown and brown, by tradition from the 10 structures, arranged in chronological order. Sand-tempered ceramics predominate in the assemblages. Although it is likely that many of these ceramics could be assigned to the Tusayan tradition because of the proximity to the Kayenta area, we prefer to avoid making such an assumption, especially since these sand-tempered ceramics could be of Cibolan origin or might

TABLE 4.2
Ceramics by Tradition for N33 and N63 Structures

Site/Structure	Ceramic Tradition						
	Chuska	Tusayan	Mesa Verde	Cibola	Sand Tempered	Rock Tempered	Indet.
Broken Flute Phase (A.D. 600–700)							
N63 structures							
AZ-I-24-8-4/29	1	0	9	0	90	0	1
AZ-I-24-8-7	0	0	0	0	100	0	0
AZ-I-24-8-2/25	0	0	6	0	93	0	1
AZ-I-24-8-27/35	1	0	1	0	98	0	0
N33 structure							
AZ-I-25-47-1	2	0	0	0	78	19	0
View Point Phase (A.D. 700–800)							
N63 structures							
AZ-I-24-7-16[a]	1	0	7	0	92	0	1
AZ-I-24-11-20	0	0	1	0	99	0	0
N33 structures							
AZ-I-26-41-1	0	0	0	0	96	4	0
AZ-I-26-3-7	10	0	0	0	86	4	0
AZ-I-26-3-9	1	0	0	0	99	0	0

Note: Numbers represent percentages; indet. = indeterminate.
[a]The inferred occupation of this structure began in the late Broken Flute phase, but it falls predominantly within the View Point phase.

have been locally made. Sand-tempered tradition ceramics vary between 78 and 100 percent of the total assemblages for the N33 and N63 structures. Broadly speaking, the N63 sites are more homogenous ceramically than the N33 sites. This is not unexpected, since all three of these sites are located within a one-square-kilometer area. In contrast, 15 kilometers separate sites AZ-I-26-41 and AZ-I-25-47 along the N33 road. All of the N63 structures, even those with View Point phase dates, have about the same percentage of sand-tempered ceramics (low to high 90s). Three of the N63 structures also have relatively high percentages (between 5 and 9 percent) of Mesa Verde ceramics in their assemblages.

The N33 sites, in contrast, show greater variability, due in part to the great spatial and temporal spread of the excavated structures. All of the N33 sites have a high percentage of sand-tempered ceramics, but for Structure 7 at AZ-I-26-3, this percentage was 86 percent. Chuska (10 percent) and rock-tempered sherds (4 percent) round out the assemblage from Structure 7. The structures at sites AZ-I-26-41 (4 percent) and AZ-I-25-47 (19 percent) both have high percentages of rock-tempered ceramics. This latter group of sherds was initially identified as Mesa Verde tradition but was reclassified upon further examination because of the lack of andesite and diorite temper. We interpret this latter group of sherds as locally made, perhaps an attempt to replicate Mesa Verde sherds, but clearly not imported from the Mesa Verde area. A sample of the ceramics identified as Mesa Verde

tradition from the N63 Project was petrographically confirmed to contain andesite and diorite (Wilson 1989b); thus, their designation is not in question (Hensler 1999). This latter group of sherds probably derives from north of the San Juan River, or at least from an area with ready access to andesite and diorite raw materials (perhaps the nearby Carrizo Mountains).

To go beyond the gray ware assemblage, we examined the white ware assemblages from the N33 and N63 projects. Table 4.3 shows the percentage of white ware ceramics by tradition from the sample of 10 structures. Structure 20 at AZ-I-24-11 contained no white ware ceramics. For the other nine structures, considerable variability is present. Some of this variability is due to small sample size. Nevertheless, all structures are discussed to track patterns across the region. Structures 2/25 and 7 at AZ-I-24-8 are completely dominated by sand-tempered, unpainted white ware ceramics, while Structure 1 at AZ-I-25-47 contained only Cibola White Ware, and all of the white ware at Structure 1 at AZ-I-26-41 was rock tempered. Structure 16 at AZ-I-24-7 and Structure 4/29 at AZ-I-24-8 had high percentages (43 and 50 percent, respectively) of Mesa Verde White Ware; Structure 27/35 had a lower percentage (14 percent), but considerably more than some of the other Basketmaker III structures. The latter structure also had a high percentage of Cibola White Ware (57 percent). The two structures from AZ-I-26-3 stand out with high percentages of Tusayan White Ware (83 percent at Structure 7 and 33 percent at

TABLE 4.3
White Ware Ceramics by Tradition for N33 and N63 Structures

Site/Structure	Ceramic Tradition						
	Chuska	Tusayan	Mesa Verde	Cibola	Sand Tempered	Rock Tempered	Indet.
Broken Flute Phase (A.D. 600–700)							
N63 structures							
AZ-I-24-8-4/29	○	○	50	12.5	37.5	○	○
AZ-I-24-8-7	○	○	○	○	100	○	○
AZ-I-24-8-2/25	○	○	○	○	100	○	○
AZ-I-24-8-27/35	○	○	14.3	57	28.7	○	○
N33 structure							
AZ-I-25-47-1	○	○	○	100	○	○	○
View Point Phase (A.D. 700–800)							
N63 structures							
AZ-I-24-7-16[a]	○	○	43	○	28.5	○	28.5
AZ-I-24-11-20	○	○	○	○	○	○	○
N33 structures							
AZ-I-26-41-1	○	○	○	○	○	100	○
AZ-I-26-3-7	3	83	○	14	○	○	○
AZ-I-26-3-9	○	33	○	67	○	○	○

Note: Numbers represent percentages; indet. = indeterminate.

[a]The inferred occupation of this structure began in the late Broken Flute phase, but it falls predominantly within the View Point phase

Structure 9), most of which is Lino Black-on-white (executed in carbon paint) or Kana-a Black-on-white. Structure 9 also had the highest percentage of Cibola White Ware (67 percent) of any of the structures studied.

Beyond demonstrating the great variability in ceramic manufacturing traditions that characterized Basketmaker III sites and houses in the Cove–Redrock Valley area, these data also serve to illustrate the ties that existed between Cove–Redrock Valley and other Anasazi areas. Underlying this discussion of possible ties between the Cove–Redrock Valley sites and other Anasazi areas is the assumption that ceramics described, for example, as Cibola tradition or Tusayan tradition, are truly nonlocal in origin and do not merely represent local adaptations that used the technology of one or another of these traditions.

Petrographic and inductively coupled plasma arc spectrometry (ICP) studies undertaken on the N33 ceramic assemblage provide a partial answer to this issue (Hensler 1999; Hensler and P. Reed 1999). For gray ware from Ceramic Group 1 assemblages (dated between A.D. 500 and 700), a high percentage of the gray/brown sherds studied (79 percent) are local to Cove or derive from somewhere within Redrock Valley. Only one sherd from Mesa Verde was identified, several sherds of Kayenta origin were confirmed, and a small percentage (1.4 percent) came from a source along the south or central slope of the Chuska Mountains. For the following Ceramic Group 2 (A.D. 700–800) assemblage of Bennett

Gray, Lino Gray, and Woodruff Smudged, the identified pattern changed. Seventy-three percent of the Ceramic Group 2 sherds were of local or intraregional origin. The south/central Chuska source produced a small percentage (2.4 percent), similar to Ceramic Group 1. The most dramatic change involved a significant increase in ceramics derived from the Kayenta area (with two distinct sources identified). No gray ware ceramics from a Mesa Verde source were confirmed.

Red ware sherds are so scarce in these assemblages that meaningful discussion in this context is not fruitful. Similarly, so few white ware ceramics were recovered from all 10 N33 and N63 structures (white ware represents less than 2 percent of the entire assemblage from the N63 sites, and less than 4 percent of the N33 assemblage) that the sample size under discussion is very small. Nevertheless, Basketmaker III assemblages across the northern Southwest are dominated by sand-tempered gray ware, and the N33 and N63 structures are not atypical. Thus, the results of white ware sourcing for the N33 sites are presented here. We should also note that the sherds studied were from several sites with Basketmaker III–early Pueblo I occupations, and many are not from the specific structures discussed here. Nonetheless, the patterns identified are representative of the N33 Basketmaker III–early Pueblo I occupation as a whole.

The nature of white ware production and exchange, obtained via petrographic and ICP studies on the N33 Project (Hensler 1999; Hensler and P. Reed 1999), is much more complex than for gray ware. Ceramics from three white ware traditions were studied: Chuska, Cibola, and Tusayan. Mesa Verde White Ware was not present in sufficient quantities on the N33 sites to merit study. Ten distinct sources were found for all periods: four for Chuska White Ware (one local), four for Cibola White Ware, and two for Tusayan White Ware. Two Chuska White Ware types were submitted for ICP analysis: Crozier and Theodore Black-on-white. All sherds analyzed were found to be nonlocal in origin; no sherds from the local source were confirmed. Two of the Crozier sherds were from Structure 7 at AZ-I-26-3. Beyond this, the other three Chuskan sources all contributed ceramics to the N33 sites. For Cibola White Ware, White Mound Black-on-white was studied, and a similar pattern was found. All three identified Cibola sources contributed sherds to the N33 assemblage. Lastly, Lino Black-on-gray, representing Tusayan White Ware, was studied. One of these sherds derived from a Chinle formation clay and is probably local in origin. The remainder are divided between the two Tusayan sources previously discussed. Of these, four sherds were from Structure 7 and one was from Structure 9 at AZ-I-26-3. In sum, most of the early white ware from the N33 sites was derived from nonlocal sources. Later in Pueblo I and II, Cove residents began producing larger quantities of white ware, but this is beyond the scope of this chapter.

Several patterns are apparent in the N33 and N63 ceramic data. Structures 7 and 9 at AZ-I-26-3 show ties to the Tusayan and Cibola areas, given the high percentage of white ware ceramics from these traditions that are present. AZ-I-25-47 also may show ties to the Cibola area, although this inference is based on only one sherd. The only white ware ceramics from AZ-I-26-41 are rock tempered and probably represent locally made items. Of particular note, the N33 sites lack Mesa Verde White Ware, departing significantly from the pattern seen in the N63 assemblage. Judging by the white ware assemblages, then, the N33 sites had ties predominantly with groups to the west and south.

In contrast, the N63 sites have strong evidence of ties to the north. Mesa Verde White Ware is dominant or well represented in the assemblages from three of the structures. Cibola White Ware is present in significant numbers at two of the structures, but no Tusayan White Ware was documented in any of the N63 structures. If we exclude the Cibolan ceramics from the discussion, since both areas possess the latter, and concentrate on the differences, we see a simple relationship: ties for Cove to the west, and ties for Oak Springs to the north. Geographically speaking, these relationships are intuitive. What is most interesting, however, is the nearly complete lack of northern ceramics in the Cove area, and of western ceramics at the Oak Springs sites. This pattern contrasts with that found in architecture, which shows both western and northern influences for Cove, and mostly western influence for the N63 sites.

BASKETMAKER III–EARLY PUEBLO I SUBSISTENCE

Using data derived from the N33 Project, the N63 Project, and the Prayer Rock excavations, subsistence patterns during the Basketmaker III–early Pueblo I occupation of the Cove–Redrock Valley area were examined. Rather than discuss the projects individually, we offer an integrated discussion, since all the sites studied essentially conform to the same basic pattern. In short, all three projects indicate that a full commitment to agriculture was made by A.D. 600, if not earlier. In this case, "a full commitment" means that the inhabitants focused their settlement and subsistence system around the cultivation of maize and other cultigens. Site locations were chosen largely because of the availability of arable land. Further, pit houses and storage facilities were constructed to expedite the processing and storage of large quantities of corn and other crops. Evidence of maize, in the form of both macro- and microfossils from the N33 and N63 projects, and in vast macro quantities from the Prayer Rock caves, is abundant. Beans and squash are less common but have been documented at sites throughout the area and were found in large quantities in the Prayer Rock caves.

Some archaeologists may question the attribution of a full commitment to agriculture in the absence of coprolite studies or isotopic data from human remains in the area. These data are lacking from the Cove–Redrock Valley area and from other areas discussed in this volume. Nevertheless, the work of Matson and his colleagues at Cedar Mesa, Utah (Chisholm and Matson 1994; Matson and Chisholm 1991; see also Stiger 1977), has demonstrated the dependence of Basketmaker II populations on maize at levels comparable to later Pueblo II populations. The supporting data include analysis of plant macrofossils and pollen (we have comparable data from the Cove–Redrock Valley sites), coprolite studies, and study of carbon and nitrogen stable isotopes. Granted, these data come from a single Anasazi area, and isotopic studies from other sites and regions are needed to confirm this pattern. However, additional support for similar levels of dependence on maize agriculture from Basketmaker II and III through Pueblo II come from settlement studies on Cedar Mesa (Matson et al. 1988), in the La Plata Valley (Toll and Wilson, this volume), at Mexican Springs (Damp and Kotyk, this volume), at Tohatchi (Kearns et al., this volume), at Lukachukai (Altschul and Huber, this volume), and in Cove–Redrock Valley. These studies reveal that the same localities were chosen by Basketmaker II and III populations, and by later Pueblo II and III groups that most archaeologists consider maize dependent. Can we explain the selection of the same areas, indeed in certain cases, use of the same structures (e.g., Structure 6/7 at AZ-I-26-3; Hensler and P. Reed 1999) by Basketmaker and Puebloan populations, separated by hundreds of years in time, by other factors? Because of the critical importance of maize agriculture to the later populations, and with access to arable land as the key variable, other explanations seem implausible.

Despite the clear commitment to agriculture, wild plant resources were of critical importance to the Cove–Redrock Valley Basketmakers, as shown by the quantity and diversity of plant resources utilized. These plants included milkweed, bugseed, goosefoot, tansymustard, piñon (nuts), nightshade, dropseed, beeweed, sunflower, Indian ricegrass, purslane, yucca, prickly pear, other cacti, and a host of other, minor plants (McVickar 1999a; Smith 1999). Tobacco also was used, probably ceremonially (Jones 1944; Jones and Morris 1960; McVickar 1999a).

Faunal resources were also pivotal as a source of protein. Large game, such as deer, elk, and antelope, was routinely hunted along with smaller fare such as jackrabbits, cottontail rabbits, gophers, prairie dogs, squirrels, and a variety of rodents (kangaroo rats, white-footed mice, voles, woodrats). Limited evidence of bighorn sheep was recovered, indicating use for subsistence, procurement for horn, or both (Schniebs 1999). Turkeys were certainly consumed, their feathers were used for clothing, and there is good evidence from Pocket Cave that they were kept in pens (Morris 1980). Nevertheless, it is unclear whether or not they were domesticated by the Basketmaker III period (but see Geib and Spurr, this volume). Other faunal remains found relate questionably to subsistence, including a variety of predators such as bobcat, gray fox, badger, and coyote or domestic dog. Dogs were kept for a variety of purposes including, but not limited to, companionship, to provide a source of hair for certain textiles, and as an emergency food source (Morris 1980).

BASKETMAKER III–EARLY PUEBLO I COMMUNITY ORGANIZATION

Although common to many Anasazi research projects, settlement and community organization are only beginning to be explored for Basketmaker sites. In previous studies, researchers have noted the distribution of Basketmaker III sites (e.g., Judge 1982, 1989) and have contemplated the presence of large, great kiva–like pit structures (e.g., Dean and Gumerman 1989), but only limited discussion of settlement or community organization has been offered.

Dohm (1988, 1994) studied Basketmaker II sites on Cedar Mesa to explore the origins of Anasazi village formation. Her review of previous work indicates the possibility of early (Basketmaker II) villages in several areas:

Black Mesa, Talus Village, and Hay Hollow Valley, among others. On Cedar Mesa, Utah, Dohm found evidence for multiple contemporaneous houses with similar layouts of houses, storage units, and trash middens. Dohm (1994:272) described the areas as "neighborhoods" but pointed out that they lack integrative structures such as great kivas or central plazas. Are such sites the first Anasazi villages? Dohm would probably say no to this question, but these Basketmaker II neighborhoods were the precursors to the Basketmaker III villages that arose after A.D. 600.

Archaeologists with the Dolores Archaeological Program (DAP) excavated Basketmaker III and early Pueblo I sites at several locales (Brisbin 1984; Kane 1986; Lipe et al. 1988). In only one area, though, did the remains warrant consideration as a community. At Grass Mesa Village, later the locus of a large Pueblo I village, a Sagehill subphase (A.D. 700–780) community was identified. The site contained 12 pit houses, most of which were believed to be contemporaneous, and a possible integrative structure consisting of an oversized pit house or great kiva (ca. 8 m in diameter). The early Grass Mesa community was organized at the household level, according to the investigators, and had not yet made the jump to the multihousehold organization seen later at the site (Kane 1986). Nevertheless, this village represents the only clustering of residences during this period in the Dolores Valley and was clearly a step in the transition to larger, more complex Anasazi villages.

Building on these studies of early communities, we discuss the Cove Community. Additional study of early communities is provided by Altschul and Huber; Damp and Kotyk, Gilpin and Benallie; Kearns et al.; and Toll and Wilson (all this volume).

Cove Basketmaker III–Early Pueblo I Community

The core of the Cove Community consists of three loci (recorded as sites AZ-I-26-3, -4, and -44) containing 140 structures and features (P. Reed 1999a). Overall, the core of the community measures 750 m north-south by 450 m east-west with a total area of 34 ha. AZ-I-26-47, a large Basketmaker III–early Pueblo I village, lies approximately one kilometer southeast of the community core and occupies an area of about 1 ha on a short mesa called Kiva Mesa. The area of the dispersed community surrounding the core is quite large; an arbitrary 5 km diameter community limit was established to facilitate study. Through archaeological survey related to a variety of projects, including water lines, power lines, home sites, and chapter development projects, a total of 74 Anasazi components have been recorded within the 5 km diameter area. Based upon site density within the community core, block survey of the entire area would probably triple or quadruple the number of identified sites.

The community was established during the Basket-

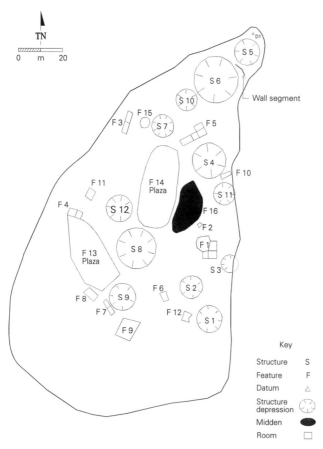

Figure 4.8. Map of central community at Site AZ-I-26-47 on Kiva Mesa.

Key

Structure	S
Feature	F
Datum	△
Structure depression	⊙
Midden	⬤
Room	☐

maker III period, and parts of it were occupied through Pueblo III. Although some use of the community occurred prior to A.D. 600, most of the Basketmaker III features and structures in the community were built and used beginning in the early A.D. 600s. The most intensive Basketmaker III occupation of the community, though, occurred after A.D. 675, especially on Kiva Mesa.

Two forms of public architecture are present in the Basketmaker III community: three great kivas and two plazas, both at the Kiva Mesa community center (figure 4.8). Great kivas are relatively common at large Basketmaker III–early Pueblo I communities in the northern Southwest (i.e., they have been recorded at Shabik'-eshchee Village, 29SJ423 in Chaco Canyon, Bad Dog Ridge, the Ganado Site, Tohatchi Village, Blue Mesa, Juniper Cove, and in Broken Flute Cave, among other sites), but plaza features are almost unknown until the later Puebloan periods.

The Basketmaker III–Pueblo I occupation of the core community probably continued until around A.D. 825 or 850. After 850, occupation and use of the community declined rapidly. Beyond the structures and features that were initially used in late Basketmaker III continuing into Pueblo I, few later Pueblo I features (dating between A.D.

800 and 900) or early Pueblo II features (dating between A.D. 900 and 1000) have been identified. Overall, the Pueblo II period (A.D. 900–1150) represents the peak of occupation at the Cove Community. Since our focus is on the Basketmaker III to early Pueblo I period, the later occupation of the community is not discussed further.

COVE BASKETMAKER III–EARLY PUEBLO I SETTLEMENT

Most of the Basketmaker III to early Pueblo I sites investigated during the Cove–Red Valley Archaeological Project are within the 5 km area defined for the Cove Anasazi Community (P. Reed 1999a; P. Reed and Hensler 1999). AZ-I-25-47, however, is outside the boundary defined for the community, thus providing an interesting comparison. Of a total 77 Anasazi components (including all the Basketmaker III components at AZ-I-26-3 and -4, along with AZ-I-26-47) recorded within the 5 km core of the community, 34 percent (*n* = 26) have Basketmaker III or Basketmaker III–early Pueblo I occupations. Figure 4.9 illustrates the distribution of site types in the core of the community. The central community at Kiva Mesa is the biggest site identified, but four smaller villages have also been identified. In addition, eight single pit house sites and three undifferentiated habitation sites have been documented. The remainder of the community comprises specialized activity sites and camps. Structures and large features identified at habitation sites in the community include 35 pit houses, eight single-room structures, 10 room blocks, 12 middens, three great kivas (all on Kiva Mesa), and two plazas (figure 4.10). A host of smaller features has also been recorded within the community limits including cists, bins, hearths, and miscellaneous burned rock piles.

AZ-I-26-47 located on Kiva Mesa, as discussed above, is the center of the early Cove Community (P. Reed 1999a). This component of the community contains nine pit houses, three pit houses or great kivas with diameters exceeding 15 m, two plaza areas, numerous slab-lined rooms and cists, and various rock alignments, hearths, and other small features (see figure 4.8). In-field ceramic analysis was conducted on a judgmental sample of roughly 60 percent (*n* = 29) of the surface ceramics. Identified types included Lino Gray, La Plata Black-on-white, Bennett Gray, Chapin Black-on-white, and White Mound Black-on-white.

Using a modified version of the mean ceramic date method,[3] a weighted range from A.D. 591–809 was produced (with a mean of A.D. 700) for AZ-I-26-47. Comparing this range with those of the individual types (with the latter means plotted) indicates a period of overlap between A.D. 675 and 800 for the mean dates. Two of the structures at the site (Structures 4 and 10) may date later

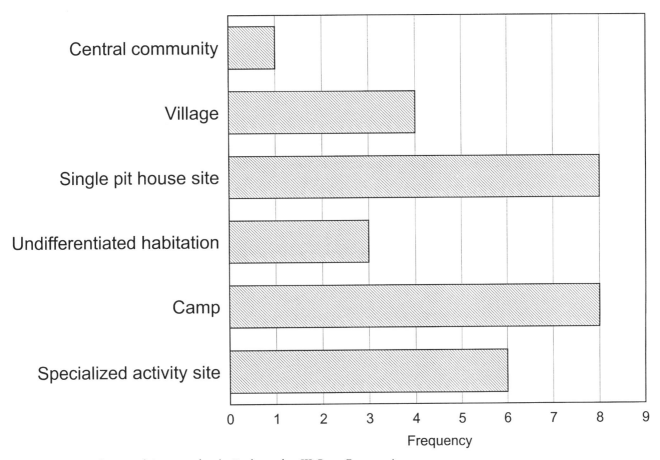

Figure 4.9. Distribution of site types for the Basketmaker III Cove Community.

than this range based on a very small sample of later, predominantly Pueblo I ceramic types. What Kiva Mesa represents, then, is a large Basketmaker III–early Pueblo I community center similar in size and date to Juniper Cove, Tohatchi Village, or Shabik'eshchee Village.

Postulated Oak Springs Community

To date, an Anasazi community has not been defined in the Oak Springs area of Redrock Valley. ZAP's work in the area documented sedentary occupation from Basketmaker III into the late Pueblo II period, but a larger settlement study was not completed, nor was mention made of an Anasazi community in the area. A community, in this case, is defined by the presence of Anasazi public architecture in the form of a great house, great kiva, or both (Pueblo I to Pueblo III periods), a great kiva (Basketmaker III), or by a high density of residential sites. Since no public architecture has yet been found in the Oak Springs area, it is not surprising that no mention has been made of a community. Nevertheless, the density of Basketmaker III–early Pueblo I structures in the vicinity of sites AZ-I-24-7, AZ-I-24-8, and AZ-I-24-11 is high. We estimate that more than 40 structures are present within a 100-acre area at Oak Springs. Even lacking a great kiva, the density of Basketmaker III–early Pueblo I

structures is sufficient in our opinion to infer the existence of a community during this period. This hypothetical Oak Springs Community differs in comparison to the Cove Basketmaker III community since it apparently lacks a discrete center like Kiva Mesa. At this point, there is insufficient data to do more than simply postulate the existence of the early Oak Springs Community.

Broken Flute Cave Community

Although the attribution of a Basketmaker III community may be debatable for the Oak Springs locale, there is no doubt that the structures in Broken Flute Cave, along with those in several other caves, constitute a distinct community. The Prayer Rock Community can be defined by several attributes: (1) a large number of contemporaneous structures in close proximity; (2) the presence of a great kiva; and (3) rock art that is indicative of an integrated settlement (see Robins and Hays-Gilpin, this volume). The designation of the large circular structure in Broken Flute Cave as a great kiva is a point of some contention, mostly because it was apparently never finished or roofed (Morris 1980; see also Dean and Gumerman 1989). Because many pit houses in the cave were burned with numerous items of everyday living in place, it is possible that a catastrophic fire (either accidental or

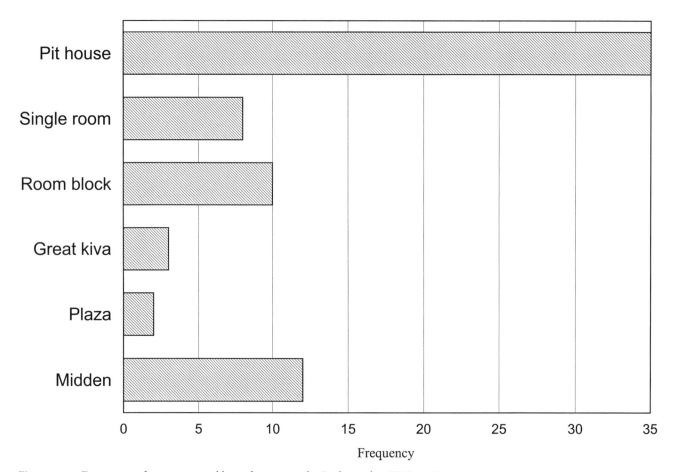

Figure 4.10. Frequency of structures and large features at the Basketmaker III Cove Community.

intentional) rapidly ended the middle A.D. 600s occupation of the cave. If this were the case, then it is reasonable to suggest that the large structure was a great kiva that was being constructed when the catastrophe took place, thus explaining its unfinished state.

Structurally, the Prayer Rock Community was very different from the Cove Community. Whereas Basketmaker III structures at the Cove Community were spread out over a large area, except for the community center on Kiva Mesa, settlement in Broken Flute Cave was dense. A pit house was constructed in nearly every useable portion of the cave. The other Prayer Rock caves are similar in layout, although considerably smaller, packing many Basketmaker III structures into confined areas. It is obvious, of course, that building in caves and shelters requires a different, more conservative use of space. Yet what is more interesting, perhaps, is the underlying reason for choosing such a confined area for habitation. The cave or shelter setting was a draw for the builders of the Prayer Rock Community. Nevertheless, it would be wrong to think that appropriate open settings were unavailable in the area. Flat open land similar in setting to the Cove Community was available no more than 500 m from most of the Prayer Rock habitation sites, so the confined cave settings were clearly preferred.

Reasons for preferring these settings included, no doubt, shelter for protection from the elements, ready access to water (for those caves with springs), and perhaps easier defense of the site.

DEMOGRAPHIC RECONSTRUCTION OF COVE–REDROCK VALLEY

In this section, we offer a demographic reconstruction of the greater Cove–Redrock Valley area during Basketmaker II (to set the stage), and Basketmaker III and early Pueblo I periods (P. Reed 1999b). Because most of the data used in this reconstruction derive from several excavated sites along the N33 road, sampling bias is a concern. In addition, the survey data we compiled do not include a large contiguous block. Thus, the incomplete nature of the data affects our ability to generalize about the greater Cove–Redrock Valley area. Nevertheless, what we provide here is a current summary of archaeological knowledge about the area based on data from several sources: (1) the N33 Project, including excavation data, settlement data from a 5 km diameter area around the Cove Community, and site settlement data from the area covered by the seven USGS 7.5' topographic maps surrounding Cove; (2) the N63 Project; and (3) Morris's

Prayer Rock excavations. Given our incomplete understanding of settlement across the area, the demographic estimates provided represent the minimum number of people and households in residence during any phase. Because our estimates are spread over large periods of time (typically 100 years), the momentary population (e.g., between A.D. 600 and 625) was probably lower than the phase-wide estimates discussed.

Red Valley Phase

The Red Valley phase represents the early portion of the Basketmaker II period, dating between 800 and 390 B.C. in Cove–Redrock Valley. The phase covers a long period of time, mostly because few components are known for the area. Only two components (AZ-I-25-51 and Component 1 at AZ-I-26-34) in the N33 Project area, and in all of Cove–Redrock Valley, are known to date to this interval. Although no maize was recovered in the limited macrobotanical remains from these small sites, the lithic assemblage from Component 1 at AZ-I-26-34 is clearly Anasazi in nature, reflecting cobble core reduction of locally available raw materials (see Torres, this volume). We can conclude, then, that by the time of the Red Valley phase (800–390 B.C.), some inhabitants of the Cove–Redrock Valley area had committed to the "Anasazi path." Given the lack of evidence, we cannot say whether maize or any other cultivated plant was a critical part of subsistence. Additional research should bring more sites from the early Basketmaker II interval to light. Sites dating to this period are, however, very difficult to identify because they lack ceramics and can appear indistinguishable from earlier (or contemporary) Archaic phenomena. Nevertheless, we are encouraged by the results of the lithic analysis, which indicate clear differences between Anasazi and Archaic assemblages (Torres 1999a, this volume). Additional study focusing on these distinctions would no doubt augment the number of early Basketmaker II sites in the database and allow for more inferences about the nature of the Red Valley phase.

With the limited data recovered from Red Valley phase sites, estimating the population during this phase is difficult. At least a few families occupied and used the area. We do not know how many Basketmaker II sites have been recorded in the area. At the survey level, it is nearly impossible to distinguish these sites from those used by groups still practicing an Archaic lifeway, or from lithic sites used by later Anasazi groups. On the basis of limited data, we infer the presence of two to four households or families (between 10 and 20 people) in the greater Cove–Redrock Valley area.

Owl Rock Phase

The Red Valley phase was succeeded by the Owl Rock phase, which lasted from 390 B.C. to A.D. 350 in Cove–Redrock Valley. This phase was characterized by more activity in the area and is represented by a small pit house village with two residential structures, a sweat lodge, and associated extramural processing features; and two associated specialized sites used for floral and faunal processing.

Macro- and microbotanical data indicate substantial reliance on maize during the Owl Rock phase. Maize remains were recovered from 80 percent of the flotation samples and a majority of the pollen samples. Other important plant resources included Cheno-Ams, bugseed, piñon (nuts), and several grasses (e.g., Indian ricegrass). Faunal remains from these sites are limited but indicate use of a variety of animals for subsistence: rabbits, artiodactyls, and smaller mammals. Significantly, the pattern identified is very similar to that seen in the later periods. This evidence, along with the extensive reliance on maize, leaves little doubt that Owl Rock phase remains are Basketmaker II, with the inhabitants on the path to adopting an Anasazi lifeway.

Demographically, we have evidence of an increase in population from the Red Valley phase. The Owl Rock phase site cluster along N33 represents use of the area by at least one household for perhaps a generation or so. Again, we have no reliable data on other late Basketmaker II sites. The initial compilation of data during the N33 settlement study identified about 10 sites recorded as Basketmaker II by the original archaeologists (P. Reed and Torres 1999). Many of these sites probably date to the Owl Rock phase. Caves in the Prayer Rock District have some evidence of Basketmaker II use, involving perhaps a few families. With these limited data, we can perhaps infer a population of multiple households, perhaps seven to 10 (between 35 and 50 people, assuming a household size of five persons), in the greater Cove area. More extensive research into late Basketmaker II sites (through archival and field research) would probably increase this estimate.

Obelisk Phase

The Obelisk phase (A.D. 470–520) initiated the Basketmaker III occupation in Cove–Redrock Valley. The phase is named after Obelisk Cave, which has two probable houses and several storage cists (Morris 1980). Figure 4.11 summarizes demography for the Basketmaker II through early Pueblo I occupation of the area, including the Obelisk phase. The period between A.D. 350 (the end of the Owl Rock phase) and A.D. 470 appears to represent a hiatus; no known sites date to this interval. Additional work, particularly excavation, may fill this gap, but for now it appears real. Two radiocarbon dates from an N33 site (AZ-I-26-37) produced ranges from the middle A.D. 300s to the early 600s. An archaeomagnetic date indicates a largely 600s occupation; thus the early part of the dated range appears too early. The two most likely periods of use, however, fall between the early 400s and

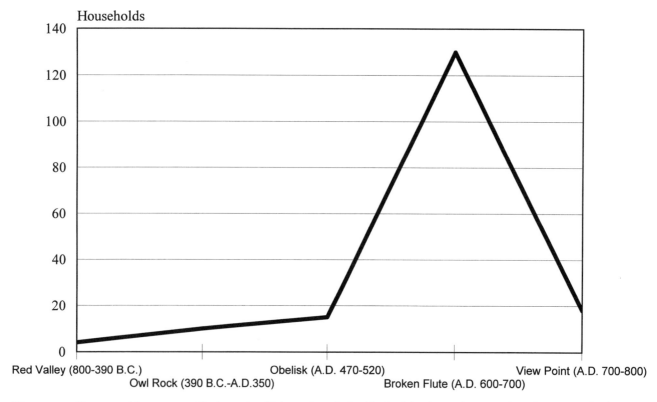

Figure 4.11. Demographic summary (Basketmaker II through early Pueblo I) of the Anasazi occupation of Cove–Redrock Valley.

early 500s, during the Obelisk phase, and between A.D. 600 and 700. The site appears to have an unexcavated pit house outside of the right-of-way, and the excavated portion of the site contains two activity areas with many features.

The remains from Obelisk Cave date between A.D. 470 and 480 (Ahlstrom 1985; Morris 1980). In addition, five houses in Broken Flute Cave and four in Pocket Cave appear to date from the late A.D. 400s to 500 or 520, thus extending the phase boundary to A.D. 520. In the Prayer Rock caves, then, at least 11 pit houses date to the Obelisk phase. No other pit structures dating to this period have been excavated in the area. AZ-I-26-37 is the only N33 site that dates to this phase. In short, almost all the information we have on the phase comes from Earl Morris's work in the Prayer Rock caves almost 70 years ago (see Morris 1980).

Settlement patterns are difficult to discern because the only sites known to date to the Obelisk phase all occur in rock shelters or caves. In addition, the phase encompasses the period of initial ceramic production in the area. Thus it is likely that the inhabitants of some Obelisk phase sites did not use ceramics at all. Identifying Obelisk phase sites at the survey level is as difficult a task as specifying those that date to the Owl Rock phase. Excavation (with absolute or fine-grained relative dating of features and structures) is the only way to isolate additional sites dating to the Obelisk phase.

Using the 11 structures in the three Prayer Rock caves and AZ-I-26-37 to generate a minimum number, we can estimate at least 12 households during the Obelisk phase (assuming one household per structure). Some of the Prayer Rock structures may not be contemporaneous, and all were certainly not occupied for the duration of the phase. Nevertheless, the house counts are a good proxy and lead us to suggest that at least 12 to 15 households, and probably more (with somewhere between 60 and 75 people), were in residence in the Cove–Redrock Valley area during the Obelisk phase.

Broken Flute Phase

Although the Basketmaker III occupation of the Cove Community peaked during the succeeding View Point phase, the Broken Flute phase (A.D. 600–700) represents the peak of Basketmaker III occupation in the remainder of the Cove–Redrock Valley area. As Figure 4.11 amply illustrates, no fewer than 26 excavated and well-dated pit structures were built and used during this phase: 20 in the Prayer Rock District, four in the Oak Springs area, and two along the N33 road (Hildebrant 1989; Morris 1980). An additional 15 houses in the Prayer Rock District probably also date to the latter part of the phase (after A.D. 650). The great kiva in Broken Flute Cave was built during this phase; whether it was ever used is questionable because the floor lacked features, and no evidence of a roof was found by the excavators (Morris

1980). The Prayer Rock phase remains recovered from the Prayer Rock District, the Oak Springs Community, and the N33 sites allow us significant insight into the prevailing lifeway.

Settlement data also can be used to further our understanding of the Broken Flute phase. Although the limitations of the settlement database are clear, it is nonetheless useful. For sites dated strictly to Basketmaker III (A.D. 470–750) we can safely assume that many recorded sites fall within the Broken Flute phase. Looking first at features in the core of the Cove Community, we find 12 that probably date to the phase. The beginning dates for most of these features place them within the Obelisk phase; given the limited early use of the community, they can probably be attributed to the later phase. These features include five middens, four cists, one pit, one hearth, and the Structure 8 pit house at AZ-I-26-3. Most of the features are from the latter site although two are associated with AZ-I-26-4. A much larger group of core community features and structures dates to the Basketmaker III–early Pueblo I interval. The problem, of course, is separating features and structures that are terminal Basketmaker III (Broken Flute phase) from those with occupations that extended into the middle and late 700s. This situation is exacerbated by the paucity of ceramic types in use during Basketmaker III, which renders most ceramic-derived dates imprecise. Using the initiation date (i.e., the earliest part of the chronometric range, whether derived by ceramic mean dating or an absolute dating technique) is perhaps the best way to do this. Thus, using beginning dates before A.D. 650 and excluding all of the features on Kiva Mesa (which, despite the early beginning date for many features, represents a post-A.D. 675 occupation) adds three additional features to the Broken Flute phase occupation of the Cove Community: two middens and an ash stain.

Turning our attention to the 5 km community, 20 sites fall within the Broken Flute phase (using the methodology described above to make phase assignments). Seventy-five percent of these are habitation loci, again reflecting the dominance of habitation sites (compared to specialized activity sites) during this phase. Several specialized activity sites were recorded, along with one camp. Extending the discussion to the surrounding settlement area reveals many Broken Flute phase sites: 65, including 13 camps, 19 habitations (including N33 site AZ-I-25-47), and 33 specialized activity sites. Clearly, settlement across the area during this phase was intensive and diverse.

Demographically, the Broken Flute phase represents the peak of Anasazi settlement across the Cove area. The excavated sample of 41 pit houses (and a great kiva) is augmented by the documentation of an additional 94 structures in the 5 km (*n* = 24) and larger (*n* = 70) settlement areas. Conservatively, these structures suggest a regional population of 100–130 households (500–650

individuals) during this phase. The long span of the phase (100 years) spreads out the inferred population. Nevertheless, a large population was present in the area.

View Point Phase

The View Point phase (A.D. 700–800) represents the peak of occupation at the early Cove Community, although the earlier Broken Flute phase saw the peak of population throughout Cove–Redrock Valley (see figure 4.11). The core of the Cove Community has two excavated View Point phase structures (Structures 7 and 9 at AZ-I-26-3). In addition, ZAP excavated one View Point phase pit house and an associated room block in the Oak Springs area (Hildebrant 1989). No pit houses in the Prayer Rock District are known to date to the View Point phase.

Structures and features (identified at the survey level) in the community core include three great kivas, two plazas, 11 pit houses, several room blocks with more than 30 rooms in use, and several smaller features. As expected, the 5 km and larger settlement areas show relatively light View Point phase settlement (P. Reed and Torres 1999). Only two sites (both single pit house dwellings) dating to the phase are known from the 5 km area, whereas 17 sites (including four habitation sites, 12 specialized activity sites, and one camp) have been recorded in the larger settlement area. Given the patterns identified, perhaps the core community drew settlers away from other areas, thus explaining the growth in the core community and the reduced level of settlement elsewhere in the region.

Population estimates for the View Point phase show a concentration at the Cove Community, specifically on Kiva Mesa. In the hinterlands around the community, only two pit houses from the 5 km area, and four pit structures and 20 rooms from the surrounding settlement area were in use. At the core community, 10 to 12 households are inferred based on the structures occupied. Combining this count with the six households from the surrounding area provides a minimum estimate of 16–18 households (80–90 individuals) in the region during the View Point phase.

CONCLUSIONS

Work on the N33 Project has revealed a large, distinct Basketmaker III and early Pueblo I occupation in the Cove area and has added to our understanding of Basketmaker III to early Pueblo I settlement in the greater Cove–Redrock Valley–Prayer Rock region. When data from the N63 Project and Morris's Prayer Rock excavations are integrated, the picture that emerges is more clear, if still incomplete. Our analyses indicate that with regard to architectural style, the Cove–Redrock Valley inhabitants shared traits with western and northern styles, while conforming exactly to neither. Rather, these structures represent mixtures of both styles, most commonly employing northern structural layouts with western-style internal differentiation. Ceramic data further support the notion of a mixture of cultural elements for the Cove–Redrock Valley Basketmaker III occupation. The N33 Project sites contain predominantly Cibolan and Tusayan White Ware ceramics, while the N63 sites had mostly Mesa Verde White Ware. We infer, on this basis, that the N33 inhabitants had ties mostly to the south and west (through marriage, migration, exchange, or some combination of all) and that N63 groups were linked, via one of these same mechanisms, to the Mesa Verde area to the north. Thus, even within the relatively small space of Cove–Redrock Valley, evidence exists for differential ties to adjacent areas. Further, we would postulate that the variability identified indicates that the area was settled by a mixture of different ethnic groups.

These architectural and ceramic data, along with the presence of the Cove Community center at Kiva Mesa, indicate that the Cove–Redrock Valley area supported a large and diverse Basketmaker III occupation. At least two distinct and very different communities flourished in Cove–Redrock Valley during the Basketmaker III period: an early (ca. A.D. 620–650) community centered in Broken Flute Cave (which includes an unfinished great kiva) as well as other Prayer Rock caves, and a later (mostly post-A.D. 675–775) community in Cove, with Kiva Mesa as its center (which made use of three great kivas). Given the temporal spread, it is possible that the same families or an overlapping group of families built and occupied both communities. The hypothesized Oak Springs Basketmaker III community, dated roughly between A.D. 600 and 675, is more difficult to characterize because of its postulated status. Public architecture has not yet been identified at the community. In terms of density, however, the Oak Springs Community appears similar to the Cove Community, while contrasting with the highly concentrated Prayer Rock Community.

The Basketmaker III and early Pueblo I inhabitants of Cove–Redrock Valley were committed to maize agriculture, although natural plants and faunal resources were important to their subsistence. The construction of large, complex pit houses with significant internal storage indicates a settled lifestyle and the ability to maintain the stored maize and other food products necessary for sedentism. Exchange ties, probably kin-based, were important to the local economy, as seen in the quantities of ceramics, lithic raw materials, shell, and other goods that entered the area (Hensler and P. Reed 1999).

Anasazi settlement of the area began during the Red Valley phase (between 800 B.C. and 390 B.C.; early Basketmaker II) with a few families. Population continued at a low but stable level in the Owl Rock phase, and then expanded during the Obelisk phase. The Broken Flute phase represented the peak of Anasazi occupation

of the greater Cove–Redrock Valley area, with 130 households and 650 individuals in residence sometime during the interval, but a lower momentary population. During the subsequent View Point phase, population leveled off. Later, during Pueblo II, population again increased and led to the peak seen in the Cove and Oak Springs communities during the Cove phase (A.D. 1000 and 1150; P. Reed 1999b).

In summary, Basketmaker III communities in Cove–Redrock Valley, while sharing traits with several adjacent Anasazi traditions (i.e., Mesa Verde, Kayenta, and Chuska), nevertheless represent unique configurations (architecturally, organizationally, and with regard to pottery and other material culture). In Cove–Redrock Valley, the Basketmaker III to early Pueblo I population density was high, certainly comparable to nearby areas along the Chuska Slope, the La Plata Valley, in Chaco Canyon, and elsewhere in the San Juan Basin.

ACKNOWLEDGMENTS

Archaeology for Navajo area roads is funded by the Federal Highway Administration through the Bureau of Indian Affairs-Navajo Region-Branch of Roads and administered by the Roads Planning Program of the Navajo Nation Historic Preservation Department under a P.L. 93-638–Indian Self-Determination and Education Assistance Act (as amended) contract. We acknowledge the support of these agencies and the key personnel therein who have expedited work on the N33 Project. We also wish to thank the Navajo Nation Archaeology Department (NNAD) for providing support and assistance in numerous ways. NNAD employees who aided us in gathering and compiling data include Kathy Hensler, Joell Goff, Patrick Alfred, Vern Hensler, and Alphonzo Benally. Kelley Hays-Gilpin was very helpful with additional, unpublished information about the Prayer Rock caves. Lenora Tsosie CAD-drafted most of the maps used in this paper. Dave Breternitz, Deb Gibson, Kathy Hensler, Deborah Nichols, Lori Reed, and Rich Wilshusen offered useful suggestions. Any errors of omission or content are our responsibility alone.

NOTES

1. The primary source for all of the data presented in the discussion of the N33 Project is P. Reed and Hensler 1999 unless otherwise noted.

2. To provide a chronology for sites not dated by absolute methods, and to supplement dates for all sites, ceramic date ranges were calculated. These dates were generated using a methodology developed by P. Reed (1999a) that represents a modification of the ceramic mean date formula (South 1977). Rather than producing just a mean date, which seemed falsely precise, Reed used Excel 5.0 to generate ceramic ranges for

sites and features. The published date ranges for individual ceramic types and for more generic type and ware categories were put into a spreadsheet that also contained the ware and type frequencies for a given site or provenience. Once type or ware categories with ranges larger than 225 years were eliminated, the remaining type frequencies were weighted by the total number of items per provenience (count frequencies were used for survey data; weight is considered more accurate and was used for excavated proveniences), and a date range based on the weighted scores was produced.

3. Using the original dates and a reassessment of the archaeomagnetic dates by the Archaeomagnetic Dating Laboratory as a starting point, the chronometric data for the N63 sites were reassessed (Cox 1997). As a result of this work, new date ranges were generated for most of the N63 sites. These ranges are different from those originally published by the Zuni Archaeology Program (Hildebrant 1989).

5

Socioeconomic Organization of a Late Basketmaker III Community in the Mexican Springs Area, Southern Chuska Mountains, New Mexico

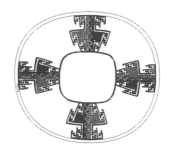

Jonathan E. Damp

Edward M. Kotyk

Status differentiation can be traced to autonomous households (Damp and Kendrick 1998) within the context of a late Basketmaker III community (A.D. 660 to 700) along Mexican Spring Wash in northwestern New Mexico (figure 5.1). Within this late Basketmaker III community, decision making was probably controlled at the household level. The household level is represented archaeologically by pit structures that yielded evidence of year-round settlement, subsistence, vernacular and community architecture, inter- and intrasite variability, and status differentiation. Farming, gathering, and hunting formed the basis of household subsistence strategies within small hamlets, components of an overall community organization. The household economies are measured within the framework of community social dynamics and are shown to exhibit signs of status differentiation associated with the development of settlement aggregates.

The data used in this study were derived from the N30-31 Project, sponsored by the Bureau of Indian Affairs (BIA) and carried out by archaeologists from Zuni Cultural Resource Enterprise between 1989 and 1992 (Damp 1999; Sant 1990, 1999). The project consisted of an archaeological study of the right-of-way for proposed construction on the N30(2) and N31(1) routes across the Chuska Mountains in northwestern New Mexico, between the communities of Navajo and Mexican Springs, New Mexico. The major focus for research questions was the Basketmaker III settlement of the Mexican Springs area, at the base of the Chuska Mountains.

PHYSICAL SETTING

The Chuska Mountains are a gently dipping plateau almost 100 km long and nearly 20 km wide. The mountains rise to over 2700 m above sea level. At the base of

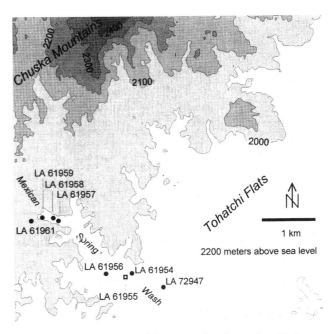

Figure 5.1. Project area and location of Basketmaker III sites along Mexican Spring Wash.

the Chuska Mountains, on the southeast side, lie the open grasslands of the Tohatchi Flats. Between the crest of the mountains and the flatlands is a series of terraces formed out of outwash gravels, sand, and caliche during the early and late Pleistocene. The Quaternary deposits consist of alluvium and aeolian sands. The alluvium is mainly restricted to narrow floodplains, and the aeolian sands are distributed as extensive sheets and coppice dune fields (Huckleberry et al. 1999).

The Upper Nakaibito soil at Mexican Springs is associated with the Anasazi occupation of the area. The soil formed under a cool and semiarid climate. Because of the semiarid nature of the Mexican Springs area, water availability would have been very important during late

Basketmaker times. No perennial streams run in the project area or in the nearby vicinity, but several springs occur in and around the modern-day community of Mexican Springs. Mexican Spring Wash is the major drainage that runs through the area. The wash originates on the east side of Mountain Valley below the crest of the Chuska Mountains. South and slightly east of the community of Mexican Springs, Mexican Spring Wash joins Catron Wash, which becomes Figueredo Wash, flowing east into the flats and the San Juan Basin.

The Mexican Springs area is included in the Great Basin biogeographic province (Brown and Lowe 1980). Two environmental zones are located at lower elevations of Mexican Springs: the Upper Sonoran Zone Great Basin Grassland and Great Basin Woodland vegetation types. The precipitous rise of the Chuska Mountains to the west of Mexican Springs has two additional environmental zones: the Transition Zone Ponderosa Forest and Mixed Conifer Forest vegetation types (Elmore 1976).

N30-31 LATE BASKETMAKER III SITES

The following discussion gives a brief description of the late Basketmaker III components and sites excavated during the course of the project. Only sites with evidence of late Basketmaker III pit structures or features are included, and they are grouped into middle and lower clusters along Mexican Spring Wash. (The Basketmaker III presence in the upper cluster was ephemeral.) Most, if not all, of the sites were occupied at the same time, forming a late Basketmaker III community within the drainage of Mexican Spring Wash. Within this community, differentiation of site structure and material remains is evident in the archaeological record.

Middle Mexican Spring Wash Site Cluster
In the area of this cluster, the Mexican Springs Valley opens up as it comes out of the Chuska Mountains, and the Basketmaker III presence is apparent at four sites containing evidence of late Basketmaker occupation. LA 61958 consists of three pit structures, two Basketmaker III and one other possible Basketmaker III (figure 5.2). Five Basketmaker III pit structures were excavated at LA 61959 (figure 5.3). At LA 61961 a Basketmaker III roasting pit was excavated. Another site with possible Basketmaker III structures is LA 61957. Several areas at this site yielded posthole patterns similar to those at other sites that have been interpreted as fenced areas around domestic quarters; however, no actual pit structure was observed at LA 61957.

Lower Mexican Spring Wash Site Cluster
The largest and most complex sites in the project area are located in the lower cluster near the modern-day community of Mexican Springs. It is here that the late Basket-

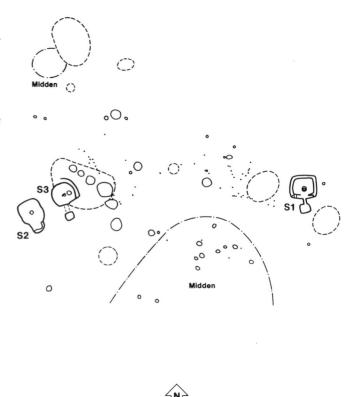

Figure 5.2. Site LA 61958.

maker III settlement of the Mexican Spring Wash area is most pronounced. LA 61954 consists of a limited and small Basketmaker III occupation that includes a pit structure (figure 5.4). The BIA excavated at LA 72947, which is said to have contained up to ten pit structures; it is included here for comparison, but the interpretive data are extremely scarce (Parry 1984). LA 61956 contains five Basketmaker III pit structures, one of which is quite small and may not have been used for residence (figure 5.5). The other four pit structures were residential and were probably occupied year-round; all four were burned. The two largest pit structures were surrounded by a fenced area. A very large Basketmaker III pit structure at LA 61955 (figure 5.6) contained both domestic refuse and ceremonial paraphernalia, and may have served a communal function. It is referred to here as the great pit structure and may have been a protokiva.

LATE BASKETMAKER ARCHITECTURE ALONG MEXICAN SPRING WASH

The following discussion identifies the types of pit structures and other architectural features excavated or

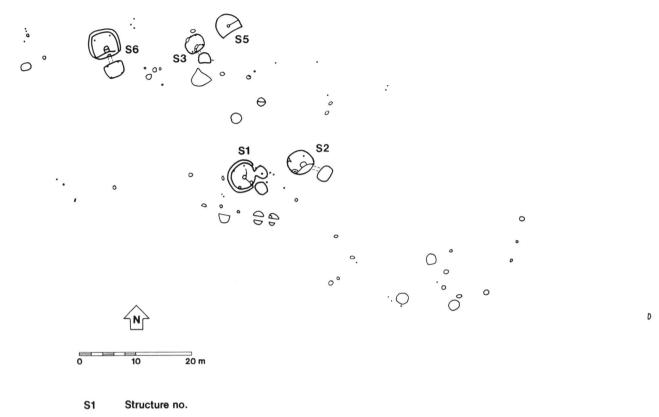

S1   Structure no.

Figure 5.3. Site LA 61959.

mapped for the late Basketmaker III sites within the N30-31 Project area. The discussion documents patterns and variability in architectural form and also provides a comparative basis for viewing the N30-31 architecture within a larger framework of Southwest prehistory.

Pit Structures

Pit structure areas have been categorized as very small, small, medium, large, or very large. Table 5.1 shows the breakdown of Basketmaker III pit structures by size and

Figure 5.4. Site LA 61954.

lists other basic attributes. One pit structure was classified as very small (8.21 m^2), six as small (16.8 to 20.1 m^2), four as medium (26.9 to 34.3 m^2), two as large (40.2 to 44.5 m^2), and one as very large (104.5 m^2). Because dimensions were not available for Structure 7294/-31, it could not be placed into any size category.

The average pit structure size of 30.7 m^2 is skewed by the enormous size of structure 61955-S1. Excluding this structure from the assemblage provides an average of 25 m^2. These categories were calculated by excluding structure 61955-S1 and subdividing the range into four intervals. All of these pit structures are deep, with an average depth of 1.5 m. Structure 61955-S1 is more than twice the size of the next largest pit structure, and more than three times the size of the largest medium-sized pit structure. Its large size and other characteristics indicate that Structure 61955-S1 functioned as a community structure for the local Basketmaker III community along Mexican Spring Wash.

Eleven of the 15 pit structures were burned at abandonment, and an array of features was encountered within this group. Features include hearths, ash pits, wing walls, bins, tunnels, floor vaults, platforms, mealing bins, postholes, and numerous floor pits. Table 5.2 lists the feature types and quantities found within the main chambers of the Basketmaker III pit structures.

Most of the Basketmaker III pit structures are similar in architectural style and appear to represent

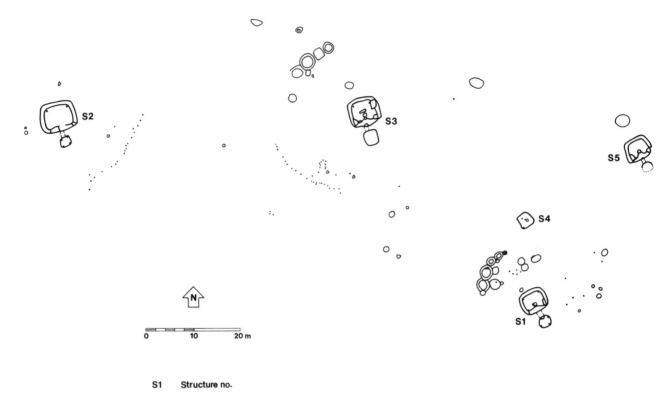

S1   Structure no.

Figure 5.5. Site LA 61956.

single-family occupational units; only two structures deviate from this norm. Structure 61958-S2, which yielded no evidence of a bench or antechamber and lacked significant floor features, appears to have been expediently constructed and used only for a short duration. Structure 61955-S1 also stands out for its uniqueness within the project area. It is larger, has more floor features, and its antechamber is the only one with storage bins. The construction and maintenance (three remodeling episodes) would probably have required a collective effort from more than one family unit. Given these conditions, it appears that Structure 61955-S1 was used by several families or, more likely, was used also as a community structure.

Surface Structures and Extramural Features
Recorded surface structures consist of isolated structures and storage rooms of Basketmaker III origin. Twenty storage rooms, consisting mostly of abutting rooms in the shape of an arc near pit structures, were located at sites LA 61954 (*n* = 3), LA 61956 (*n* = 11), and LA 61958 (*n* = 6). Excavated extramural features associated with the Basketmaker III pit structures included 38 thermal pits, 114 pit features, 187 postholes, and 11 human burials. The size of many of the pit features, such as those forming an arc northwest of Structure 61956-S1 and Structure 61956-S3, is such that sufficient amounts of corn could easily be stored to support the residents for an entire year (see Parsons 1936; Sebastian 1992:100).

The 187 postholes were found as part of the construction of the fences or enclosures surrounding some of the pit structures and associated activity areas. Some researchers have suggested that these enclosures functioned as stockades for defensive purposes. The enclosures observed on the N30-31 Project, however, do not appear to offer any substantial defense based on the sizes of the posts found. It is more likely that these enclosures served a different function, perhaps to keep out wild animals that could threaten food supplies or children. The enclosures may have also served to visually

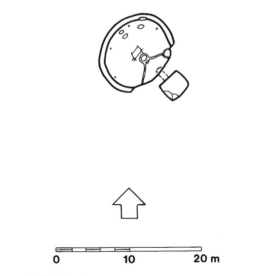

Figure 5.6. Site LA 61955.

TABLE 5.1
Basketmaker III Pit Structures from N30-31

Size Group	Structure	Area (sq. m)	Structure Shape	Antechamber Shape	Post Pattern	Bench Type
Very Small (1)	61959-S3	8.2	Subrectangular	Oval	4	Absent
Small (6)	61958-S1	16.8	Subrectangular	Subrectangular	4	3/4 Contiguous
	61959-S5	17.6	Oval	Unknown	4	Absent
	61959-S2	17.8	D-shaped	Oval	4	Absent
	61959-S1	18.0	D-shaped	Circular	4	3/4 Contiguous
	61959-S6	20.0	Subrectangular	D-shaped	4	3/4 Contiguous
	61954-S4	20.1	Subrectangular	Subrectangular	4	3/4 Contiguous
Medium (4)	61958-S3	26.9	D-shaped	Subrectangular	4	3/4 Contiguous
	61956-S5	29.7	Subrectangular	Subrectangular	4	3/4 Contiguous
	61956-S1	31.3	Subrectangular	Oval	4	3/4 Contiguous
	61958-S2	34.3	Subrectangular	Unknown	4	Absent
Large (2)	61956-S3	40.2	Subrectangular	D-shaped	4	3/4 Contiguous
	61956-S2	44.5	Subrectangular	Subrectangular	4	3/4 Contiguous
Very Large (1)	61955-S1	104.5	Oval	Subrectangular	6	3/4 Contiguous
Unknown (1)	72947-S1	?	Indeterminate	Indeterminate	4	Absent

mark ownership or use areas for a family, much like present-day fences.

SPATIAL ANALYSIS OF LATE BASKETMAKER HOUSEHOLDS

Artifact Distribution

The types and frequency of artifacts within a given pit structure often indicate what activities were carried out there. Artifact frequencies are viewed here in their associ-ation with pit structure floors, and classes include ceramics, flaked stone, ground stone, and faunal remains. Frequency charts demonstrate that certain activities were more prominent in certain pit structures. Possible reasons for differential frequencies are explored later.

Whole Vessels and Pipes.
Examples of vessels with macrobotanical remains included one vessel containing cholla cactus (*Opuntia* sp.) flower buds, and a second vessel containing domesticated

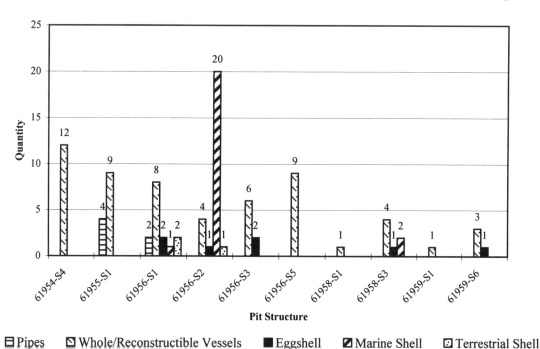

Figure 5.7. Whole vessel, pipe, and egg, marine and terrestrial shell frequencies from pit structure floors.

TABLE 5.2

Feature Types for Main Chambers in Pit Structures

	61954-S4	61955-S1	61956-S1	61956-S2	61956-S3	61956-S5	61958-S1	61958-S2	61958-S3	61959-S1	61959-S2	61959-S3	61959-S5	61959-S6	72947-S1
Hearth	1	1	1	1	1	1	1	1	1	1	1	1	1	1	1
Ash pit	1	1	2	1	1	1	1	—	1	1	—	1	1	1	1
Bin	5	1	4	3	4	2	3	—	2	1	2	—	—	—	—
Floor vault	—	1	1	—	1	—	—	—	—	—	—	—	—	—	—
Mealing bin	—	—	—	—	—	1	—	—	—	1	—	—	—	—	—
Pit	8	140	33	42	32	10	20	6	6	6	17	7	12	7	11
Pit w/in situ vessel	—	—	—	—	—	1	—	—	—	—	—	—	—	—	—
Primary posthole	4	10	4	4	4	4	4	4	4	4	4	4	4	4	2
Bench posthole	33	73	9	44	38	9	51	—	18	26	—	—	—	39	—
Ladder posthole	—	—	2	2	—	—	—	—	—	—	—	—	—	—	—
Posthole	5	10	4	2	3	2	9	45	17	1	—	1	—	6	—
Pot rest w/in situ vessel	—	2	1	—	—	—	—	—	—	—	—	—	—	—	—
Platform	—	—	1	—	1	—	—	—	—	—	—	—	—	1	—
Deflector	—	1	1	1	1	1	1	—	1	1	1	—	—	1	—
Wing wall	1	1	1	1	1	1	1	—	1	1	1	1	1	1	1
Bifurcated tunnel	—	—	—	—	1	1	—	—	—	—	1	—	—	—	—
Tunnel	1	1	1	1	—	—	1	—	1	—	—	1	—	1	—
TOTAL	59	242	65	102	88	34	92	56	52	43	27	16	19	62	16

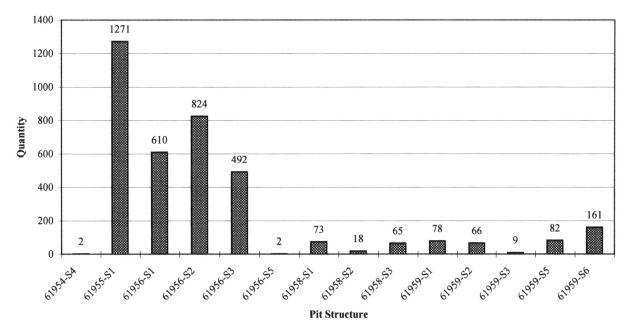

Figure 5.8. Debitage frequencies from pit structure floors.

squash seeds, both from Structure 61954-S4. A vessel from Structure 61955-S1 contained possible tobacco leaves and seeds (*Nicotiana*). A vessel with uncharred squash seeds and fragments of a charred domesticated gourd (*Lagenaria siceraria*) came from Structure 61956-S1.

Another pattern observed was the relative decrease in vessel frequency from one end of the project area to the other (figure 5.7). Those sites closest to the east end of Mexican Spring Wash (LA 61954, LA 61955, and LA 61956) had higher frequencies than those farther west (LA 61958 and LA 61959) and closer to the Chuska

Mountains. Two possible explanations could account for this phenomenon. One is that the frequency of vessels could indicate some form of status or wealth for those residents in the east Mexican Spring Wash area, and that the east was a more favorable location. The second is that certain activities requiring whole vessels (e.g., storage) were centered in the east portion.

Flaked Stone.
For the most part there is a correlation between high frequencies of debitage debris (100+) and high frequencies of cores and hammer stones (15+; figures 5.8 and 5.9).

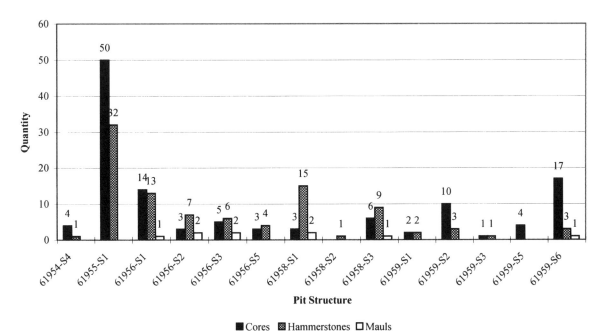

Figure 5.9. Core, hammer stone, and maul frequencies from pit structure floors.

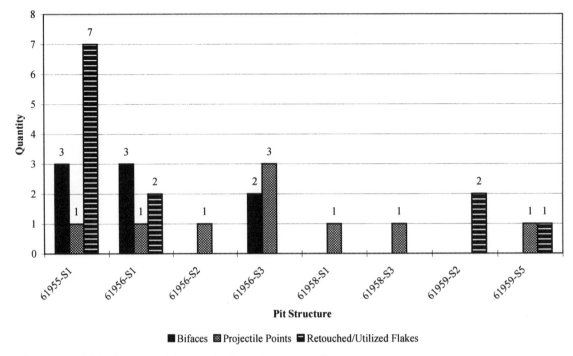

Figure 5.10. Flaked stone tool frequencies from pit structure floors.

However, this association does not correlate with the frequency of formal flaked tools (e.g., bifaces, projectile points; figure 5.10), which, excluding Structure 61955-S1, was extremely low. A similar pattern in frequency is seen for the flaked stone assemblage (debitage and tools) as was seen in the whole vessel assemblage; there tends to be a greater frequency at the east end of Mexican Spring Wash than at the west end.

Ground Stone.
The presence of ground stone has always been associated with food processing and increased sedentism. Considerable amounts of ground stone were recovered from the floor and feature fill of these structures (figure 5.11). However, the frequency of ground stone, specifically metates, is skewed because a number of metates (whole and partial) were found incorporated into the wall construction of storage bins, wing walls, and deflectors.

Faunal Remains.
Two categories were used in separating faunal remains: unmodified and modified bone (figures 5.12 and 5.13). Modified bone includes formal tools such as awls, flakers, or needles, and bones that exhibit shaping through abrasion and polishing. For simplicity, modified bone was categorized as either an awl or modified/worked bone. Worked bone and awls were not commonly recovered from the floor fill of pit structures in this assemblage. However, the frequency is four times higher within the Basketmaker III pit structures (n = 66) than in the later pit structures from the area. The pattern of higher frequency from the east end to the west end is even more

pronounced for the unmodified and modified bone assemblage.

Shell.
This artifact class includes egg shell, marine shell, and terrestrial shell (see figure 5.7). Frequency of shell was extremely low with the exception of one pit structure, 61956-S2, which contained 20 pieces of marine found fairly evenly dispersed across the structure floor. Two explanations are plausible: (1) that some specialized activity (e.g., jewelry production) occurred within this pit structure, or (2) that some ritual/ceremonial abandonment was involved that differed from the abandonment procedures at other pit structures.

Summary of Artifact Distribution
Differences in material frequencies can be accounted for in several ways. Differences in disposal of artifactual materials or in ritual abandonment procedures are likely influencing factors. Another factor that is more theoretical and complicated is status differentiation of resident families within particular houses. Status in this case is defined as "the principles that define worth and more specifically honor, that establish the scales of personal and group value, that relate position or role to privileges and obligations, that allocate respects, and that codify respect behavior" (Goldman 1970:7).

Even given the effect of different methods of disposal or ritual abandonment on the archaeological record, it still appears that some form of status differentiation was present within the Basketmaker III population in the Mexican Spring Wash area. Those structures located in

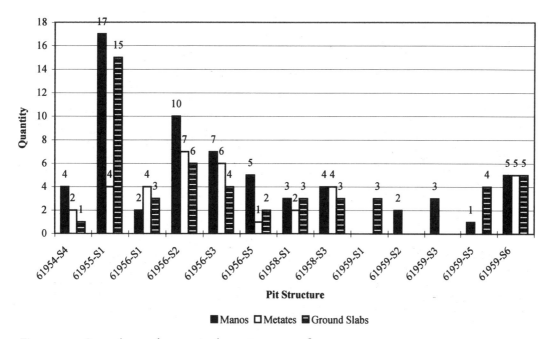

Figure 5.11. Ground stone frequencies from pit structure floors.

the east portion tended to have higher frequencies of artifact materials, and thus status or wealth appears to be associated with this location. This is feasible because the east end of Mexican Spring Wash had control over access between the Chuska Mountains and the Tohatchi Flats. Another possible explanation could be the differentiation of activity from one locale (east end) to another (west end), which might also indicate some form of social or status differentiation.

LATE BASKETMAKER HOUSEHOLD FUNCTION AND ORGANIZATION

A principal question of the N30-31 Project was whether pit structures were occupied seasonally or year-round. Based on the late Basketmaker III pit structure assem-

blage, it is apparent that this population was already sedentary, remaining in one place for an entire year (see Varien 1999:24). But as Varien points out, "threshold definitions do not allow us to distinguish among the relative sedentariness of groups. ...sedentism, unlike mobility, is unidimensional and can be conceptualized as forming a continuum" (Varien 1999:25).

Gilman (1987) argued that Basketmaker III groups, for the most part, occupied areas seasonally, and that the presence of pit structures and storage features are indicative of winter habitation. Rafferty (1985), on the other hand, argued that the degree of labor involved in the construction of pit structures, formalization of storage facilities, and presence of communal structures imply a greater degree of sedentism, possibly year-round. Wills and Windes (1989) suggested that pit structures indicated

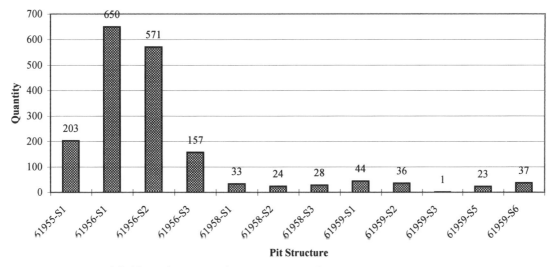

Figure 5.12. Unmodified bone frequencies from pit structure floors.

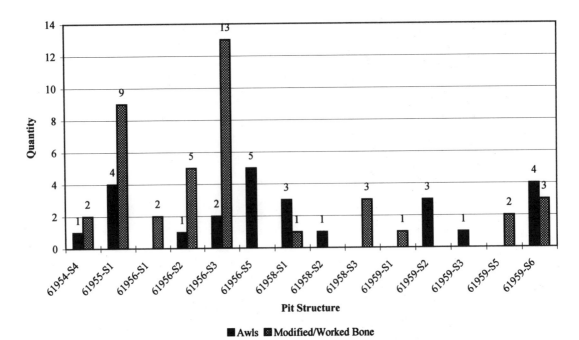

Figure 5.13. Modified bone frequencies from pit structure floors.

long-term use of a localized area but may only have been occupied periodically. In this case, the pit structures may not have been contemporaneous, and apparent villages may have represented small seasonal occupations. Although it is possible that some pit structures were occupied seasonally in areas marginal for horticulture, in more favored areas, such as near springs and other well-watered areas (such as at the base of the Chuska Mountains), it is likely that permanent, year-round Basketmaker III communities existed.

LA 61956 and LA 61958 are the best candidates to address research questions regarding Basketmaker III sedentism for several reasons. First, each site is a single component and not severely impacted by modern activities or later Anasazi occupations. Second, for all practical purposes, LA 61956 could be considered a small hamlet with four pit structures. LA 61958 may also be a small hamlet, but the N30-31 right-of-way limited investigations to only two occupation areas. Third, extensive investigations were conducted in at least one habitation locus at each of the sites, including complete excavation of a pit structure and block excavation in the surrounding extramural activity area and storage facilities.

The pit structures at LA 61956 and LA 61958 were all contemporaneous as evidenced by the chronometric results obtained from the tree-ring samples. All the structures were relatively large, and each had undergone at least two remodeling episodes. Storage facilities were found associated with four of the five pit structures. Two pit structures lacked storage facilities due to (1) previous road construction (61956-S2), which probably removed the storage facilities; and (2) presence of storage facilities outside the area of investigation (61958-S1). The storage

facilities were massive enough to store large quantities of food. In addition, a communal structure (61955-S1) is present in the immediate vicinity. This large structure required extensive labor and materials to construct, suggesting that several sedentary families built and maintained the structure, and that it served a community-wide function for religious, political, or social purposes (see Rafferty 1985). The above evidence indicates that the Basketmaker III occupation within the Mexican Spring Wash was for the most part year-round and not seasonal.

An examination of the extremely diverse macrobotanical data from the Basketmaker III sites indicates that they were occupied most of the year (Brandt 1999). Beans, squash, and particularly maize are ubiquitous, suggesting that enough crops were grown to support the population throughout the year. Although agriculture provided most of the necessary carbohydrates, wild plant collection and processing at different seasons were also important for subsistence. Prickly pear cactus pods were collected during the late spring; goosefoot, pigweed, globemallow, and sunflower seeds between mid and late summer, and piñon nuts from the Chuska slopes during the fall. Pollen found near the hearths of sites LA 61954, LA 61955, and LA 61956 reveal that both storage and processing occurred during the winter months (Dean 1999). Macrobotanical and pollen analyses reveal that maize was the primary domesticated crop, followed by beans, squash, gourd, and possibly domesticated sunflower. Wild plant species included amaranth, beeweed, bugseed, cholla cactus buds, goosefoot, grass, purslane, sunflower, winged pigweed, and yucca.

A mixed subsistence economy is also supported by ground stone types, the diversity of the faunal assemblages, and paleopathology. Although two-hand manos and slab and trough metates (largely used for grinding maize) were predominant during this period, one-hand manos and basin metates (largely used for grinding wild seeds) were also numerous, indicating the continued importance of nondomesticated plant foods. A diversity of animals, including ground squirrel, jackrabbit, and mountain cottontail, were regularly hunted and provided important protein in a diet largely dependent upon maize and other domesticates.

In addition to formalized storage features, the recovery of whole ceramic vessels from sites LA 61954, LA 61955, and LA 61959 also suggest that people were storing or transporting large amounts of subsistence resources. The refuse patterns of lithic debitage may also suggest occupational duration. It has been argued that those sites with formalized middens would show greater occupational intensity than those sites that lack less formalized middens or dispersed sheet trash. The only site that had a formal midden is LA 61954, and as documented above, this Basketmaker III site appears to have been occupied the entire year. High densities of lithic debitage, cores, and hammer stones on house floors may also support residential stability. However, debitage density or diversity may be only indirect evidence of occupational duration (see Jelenik 1976; Lightfoot and Jewett 1984; Schlanger 1988c) because of the different sampling strategies used at several of the pit houses. In addition, much of the debitage was likely due to secondary or refuse (dumping) after house abandonment.

During the late Basketmaker III period, food-processing activity areas were confined largely to pit house floors, as opposed to finished rooms, middens, and extramural activity areas of later occupational periods. Most of the manos and metates were found in these contexts. Likewise, nearly 50 percent of the ornaments are associated with Basketmaker III pit structure floors and extramural activity areas. In addition, 64 percent of the bone awls were found in pit structures, suggesting weaving and hide working, while only a fourth of the assemblage occurs in extramural activity areas, and the rest in antechambers and grid locations. Storage in whole vessels and flake tool reduction and manufacture also occurred primarily on house floors.

Ceramic analysis for the N30-31 Project focused on which decorative, utilitarian, and technological (temper and raw clay data) styles were made locally or were exchanged or introduced into the Chuska region (Waterworth 1999). Cibola White Ware was likely manufactured from local clay sources (although, since the Cibola area is quite large, it may have come from quite a distance), but Kayenta (Tusayan), Chuska, Mesa Verde, and White Mountain Red Ware traditions were definitely nonlocal and traded into the area. In particular, Mesa Verde pottery accounts for nearly 21 percent of the

ceramic assemblages during the late Basketmaker III (and early Pueblo I periods), suggesting trading connections with the north. Brown ware, which suggests trading relationships with the Mogollon or the southern Cibola region, also reaches its highest proportion during the Basketmaker III period.

The presence of exotic and nonlocal turquoise in the Basketmaker III ground stone assemblage suggests that trading may have occurred over a broad region including north-central New Mexico, southern Colorado, and eastern Arizona; nevertheless, the abundance of local raw materials, such as sandstone, suggests that the trading of turquoise (primarily used in the manufacture of jewelry) occurred only rarely.

Other rarely traded items include marine *Olivella* sp. and *Haliotis* sp. shell (also used to make jewelry) from the Gulf of California and the Pacific Coast. Twenty pieces of marine shell were found within pit Structure S2 at LA 61956, but its frequency was extremely low at the rest of the Basketmaker III sites. The presence of these species suggests trading routes from both the south and the west, traversing through California and north of the Hohokam area.

THE LATE BASKETMAKER COMMUNITY

Wills and Leonard (1994:xiii) noted that Southwestern archaeologists use the term "community" to mean "a residential group whose members interact with one another on some regular basis" (e.g., Rohn 1971:40). They further pointed out that two kinds of community analysis are usually embraced by those doing archaeology in the Southwest. The first kind of analysis equates single sites with single corporate units that are residential communities. The other type of community analysis refers to political communities in which individual sites are "linked through intersettlement mechanisms for making social or economic decisions" (Wills and Leonard 1994:xiii).

Archaeologically, political communities are, in essence, clusters of individual archaeological sites. These clusters are assumed to be contemporary in occupation and contain an inherent hierarchy of structure (cf. Breternitz and Doyel 1987:184). In the San Juan Basin the term "community" is generally used in a more specific fashion. Community studies have focused upon outlier complexes containing great houses, great kivas, and surrounding small sites or unit pueblos that are believed to have been participants in the Chaco regional system (Breternitz et al. 1982; Judge 1989; Lekson 1991; Marshall et al. 1979; Powers et al. 1983). Many of the ancestral communities within the San Juan Basin were established as early as Basketmaker III or Pueblo I times, and evidence a long history of development prior to the florescence of the Chaco Canyon area (Vivian 1990).

For our purposes, a concept of community relates

social relationships to the physical factors of location, economy, and material culture. This concept of community puts the focus not on spatial parameters or distance, the site itself, or a grouping of sites, but rather on the common residence group. For the N30-31 Project, the late Basketmaker III community would have included a group of people living and interacting with one another in the same locality or area, such as along Mexican Spring Wash.

Lipe (1994) outlined three kinds of process theory that emphasize different sets of relationships and dynamics in dealing with explanations of change. The first theory "is based on changing relationships between population and resources—as population goes up (or resource supply declines), economic costs and risks rise, the resource economy is intensified, and risk-buffering strategies such as storage and trade become increasingly important" (Lipe 1994:143). The second theory is also density dependent but puts emphasis on the effects of increasing density on interpersonal relations. In this theory, society is required to invest in social control and resolution of conflicts that occur with population growth. The final theory places emphasis on competition: for space, resources, power, and prestige. In this scheme, competition may lead to aggregation, the development of leaders, and other signs of ranking or social stratification. There is also an effect on community organization: settlements may grow or become spatially compact, and lower-ranking individuals or social units may be forced to take up residence in areas determined by the dominant group.

The nature of the late Basketmaker III community as seen in its community composition and dynamic can be explored by revisiting several areas previously discussed: (1) processes of settlement formation; (2) settlement variability; (3) settlement changes; (4) specialization of resource use; and (5) regional interrelationships.

PROCESSES OF SETTLEMENT FORMATION

Site Formation

The settlement of the late Basketmaker III community of Mexican Spring Wash was not preceded by an in situ development in the immediate area. Evidence for an Archaic settlement of the area is extremely limited, and neither the Basketmaker II nor early Basketmaker III period is documented in any way. This lack of evidence for a significant earlier settlement leads to the conclusion that populations moved into the Mexican Springs area around A.D. 650. This hypothesis is strengthened by the identification of a significant earlier Basketmaker III presence just northeast of the project area, on the flats of the San Juan Basin east of Tohatchi during the early A.D. 600s (Kearns et al., this volume). We may interpret this information as indicative that late Basketmaker III move-

ment into the area of Mexican Spring Wash was not a macroregional adjustment (i.e., large-scale migration from a distant source) but, rather, a finer scale adjustment by moving a little higher up into the foothills of the Chuska Mountains. The late Basketmaker III use of the Mexican Springs area ended abruptly around A.D. 700 with burning of most pit structures.

The N30-31 Project provided a wealth of information on pit structure construction, use, and abandonment. As discussed above, the late Basketmaker III pit structure assemblage from the N30-31 Project indicates that this population was already sedentary. This assessment of the archaeological data from the project area is at odds with Gilman's thesis (1987). Gilman argued that Basketmaker III groups were generally seasonal occupants of areas and that the presence of pit structures and storage features are indicative of winter habitation. A different assessment was made by Rafferty (1985), who argued that the degree of labor involved in the construction of pit structures, formalization of storage facilities, and presence of communal structures implies a greater degree of sedentism, possibly year-round. Wills and Windes (1989) suggested that pit structures in the Chaco Canyon area indicated long-term use of a localized area, but that this use may have been periodic, and thus the late Basketmaker pit structures in the Chaco Canyon were not necessarily contemporaneous. They felt that Basketmaker III villages could represent small seasonal occupations by several households over a period of time rather than during the course of an entire year. The evidence from the N30-31 Project provides good information on resolving the issue of length of occupancy for pit structures during this time period.

It is possible that a number of Basketmaker III pit structures were occupied seasonally in areas marginal for horticulture. In more favored areas, such as near springs and other well-watered areas at the base of the Chuska Mountains, permanent, year-round Basketmaker III communities existed. This basically encapsulates the model advanced many years ago by Wendorf (1956:19), who discussed the first appearance of Anasazi traits as representative of "a few fairly large communities located in particularly favorable areas and numerous, widely scattered small villages situated closely adjacent to similarly favorable but small arable plots." Eddy's work (1966) in the Navajo Reservoir area led him to postulate that the smaller sites were part of the overall community during this same time period.

Another aspect of settlement duration and hierarchy that may influence our interpretations is the variation that probably existed within late Basketmaker III communities. For example, if one were to analyze only one or two small pit structures such as those located in the western part of Mexican Spring Wash, it would be feasible to posit a seasonal or limited use of the structures, especially if detailed paleoenvironmental data were lacking. In the case of this project, the data are replete with indications that these pit structures were lived in throughout the year and that the differences in material remains is probably the result of socioeconomic factors rather than seasonal use of the area.

Based on excavations at Shabik'eshchee Village, a Basketmaker III site in Chaco Canyon (Wills and Windes 1989), and at Black Mesa in northeastern Arizona (Gilman 1987) researchers have postulated that pit house architecture and limited storage reflect a biseasonal pattern of site use. Rather than year-round occupation, this pattern is characterized by winter occupation and group mobility during the growing season. Gilman (1987:541–542), using the ethnographic record, argued that pit structures were not used during the summer. Although people depended on stored foods during the winter, they did not depend on storage during the summer because this was the time of year that they foraged for plants and animals and moved to temporary agricultural field houses. Gilman (1987:548) cited evidence from Black Mesa to argue that fully sedentary communities did not commence until Pueblo I, when people switched from pit structures to aboveground pueblos. This switch was the result of population increases, more intensive and consistent farming (with occasional logistic forays for wild plants), and/or use of domestic animals, and more sedentism.

At the N30-31 Project sites, however, the botanical and ground stone data clearly denote dependence upon agriculture at least at the level of subsistence farming, with some logistical forays for wild foods. In fact, many other researchers have argued this for some time now (see Martin and Plog 1973:207), and this view contrasts with Gilman's (1987) argument of intensive agriculture and sedentism not occurring until Pueblo I. Obviously, it is a matter of degree between pit structures and pueblos, as Gilman argues, but there is more variability in the record during the Basketmaker III period than has been argued previously (see P. Reed, this volume).

Furthermore, the high frequency of storage pits and the durability, depth, and quality of pit structure construction at the N30-31 sites strongly suggest permanent villages and substantial populations. Eighteen circular storage rooms with possibly cribbed wooden roofs (i.e., not capped with adobe) at sites LA 61954, LA 61956, and LA 61958, plus 114 earthen, slab, slab and adobe, and slab and earthen pit features provide evidence that storage and food processing were important activities during all seasons. Unlike those at Shabik'eshchee, these storage rooms and pits were found near the houses and not isolated and separate from them. No aboveground storage rooms, which historically kept corn cool and dry,

to be removed almost daily for processing, have been documented at Shabik'eshchee. Shabik'eshchee may have been only seasonally occupied, but this was not true at the N30-31 Project sites.

The pit structures at sites LA 61956 and LA 61958 were all contemporaneous as evidenced by the chronometric results obtained from the tree-ring samples. All the structures were relatively large and each underwent at least two remodeling episodes. Storage facilities were found associated with four of the five pit structures. Road construction probably contributed to the lack of evidence for storage facilities at some pit structures (Structure 61956-S2) and some storage facilities were outside of the area of investigation (Structure 61958-S1). The recorded storage facilities were of sufficient size to permit major food storage. A communal structure (the great pit structure or Structure 61955-S1) required extra labor and materials to construct, suggesting that several sedentary families built and maintained the structure and that it served a community-wide function for religious, political, or a social purposes. The architectural evidence indicates that the late Basketmaker III settlement along Mexican Spring Wash was year-round and not seasonal. This finding contradicts Gilman's (1987) model for pit structure residential patterns in the Southwest and suggests that new models need to be invoked.

The dwellings at sites LA 61956 and LA 61958 yielded well-defined boundaries as seen by the presence of post enclosures (see also Chenault and Motsinger, this volume). Storage facilities were large enough for storing considerable amounts of food for year-round use. In addition, the distribution of associated circular storage rooms in a contiguous arc around the pit structures at LA 61956, and the presence of fenced enclosures around each habitation loci to define use or ownership, also support contemporaneity and year-round occupancy.

Abandonment

Abandonment processes can be complex and are dependent upon the nature of settlement: year-round versus seasonal. Cameron and Tomka (1993) provided an overview of abandonment practices including several cases from the Southwest. The explanation for abandonment of settlements in the Southwest generally centers upon deteriorating climatic conditions although other conditions may have also influenced abandonment, especially during Basketmaker III and Pueblo I times. Morris (1939:41) characterized the end of settlement occupation in the La Plata region by noting that Basketmaker III and Pueblo I sites often showed signs of catastrophic fires that destroyed much of the belongings of the pit structure dwellers. This incidence of burning caused Eddy (1972: 34) to believe that burning or warfare were common reasons for pit structure abandonment (see LeBlanc 1999).

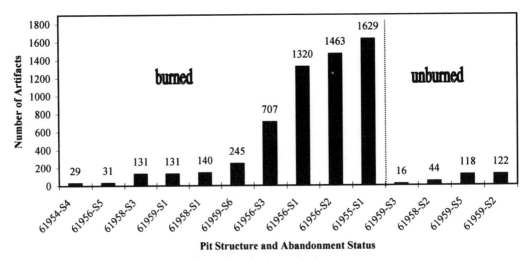

Figure 5.14. Artifact occurrences in burned and unburned pit structures.

In addition to warfare, Cameron (1990b:28) suggests other potential causes for the abandonment of Anasazi sites: (1) problems with obtaining sustenance in the surrounding area; (2) disease or natural catastrophe; or (3) ritual. Wilshusen's (1986) analysis of late Basketmaker and Pueblo I pit structures from the Dolores region showed that pit structures covered with earth are difficult to burn accidentally. He suggested that pit structures showing evidence of burning were abandoned for ritual reasons. Cameron was unable to find unambiguous evidence for abandonment associated with ritual burials within pit structures. Rather, she posited that the deterioration of the structures might be a likely cause for abandonment of unburned structures, and that burned structures may have resulted from either ritual activity associated with the death of the house's owner or a response to insect infestation. Schlanger and Wilshusen (1983:94) looked at Dolores pit structures for correlations between drought conditions and abandonment. They concluded that there were nonpatterned abandonments that may have been "a consequence of the vernacular architecture or of expectations for residential mobility, or of some as yet unrecognized set of circumstances." Abandonment strategy at Dolores was apparently related to intentions of a long-distance move with no anticipation of return.

Another form of ritual abandonment is what Stein and Fowler (1996:116) call "ritual retirement" or the "planned renewal of ritual facilities undertaken on a community and a regional scale" with a shift or relocation of ritual centers at the community or regional level. Stein and Fowler developed this concept to deal with Chacoan systems, but the concept might be equally applicable to earlier phenomena.

Earlier interpretations of Basketmaker III pit structure abandonment considered warfare a viable reason for abandonment. The more recent arguments have sought answers in data derived from examination of site forma-

tion processes. Neither ritual burning nor burning to combat insect infestation appears likely for the pit structure sample because none were associated with interior burials, and the large amount of de facto refuse within some burned pit structures does not appear to be a likely consequence of burning to remove insects. Accidental burning is a possibility, but so is burning due to raiding or warfare. Discrepancies in the amount of de facto refuse may be attributable to socioeconomic differentiation and competition within the Basketmaker II community. The amount of de facto refuse remained the same within pit structures in the upper part of the valley whether or not these structures were burned (figure 5.14). However, the pit structures in the lower Mexican Spring Wash cluster contained large amounts of de facto refuse, and there was also a high incidence of burning. We might suggest, then, that the lower valley pit structures that contained

TABLE 5.3

Pit Structure Size, Burned Status, and Presence or Absence of Fenced Area

Structure	Area (sq. m)	Burned	Fenced Area
61954-S4	20.1	yes	yes
61955-S1	104.5	yes	no
61956-S5	29.7	yes	no
61956-S1	31.3	yes	no
61956-S3	40.2	yes	yes
61956-S2	44.5	yes	yes
61958-S1	16.8	yes	no
61958-S3	26.9	yes	yes
61958-S2	34.3	no	yes
61959-S3	8.2	no	no
61959-S5	17.6	no	no
61959-S2	17.8	no	no
61959-S1	18	yes	no
61959-S6	20	yes	no
72947-S1	?	yes	n/a

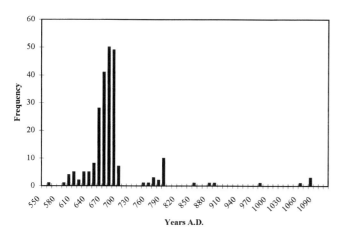

Figure 5.15. N30-31 tree-ring dates (Basketmaker III to Pueblo II).

more material goods were burned through competitive raiding.

Table 5.3 shows the relationship between size and burning of the late Basketmaker III pit structures. All of the pit structures in the lower cluster were burned, whereas only half of those in the middle cluster were. Does the variation in the pattern of burning reflect accident, status differentiation, or unrecognized site formation processes? The N30-31 data would appear to at least open the door again for a bellicose reason for settlement abandonment as noted by others (Chenault and Motsinger, this volume; LeBlanc 1999; Wilcox and Haas 1994). Recent excavations by Zuni Cultural Resource Enterprise in 1999 in the vicinity of Two Grey Hills, roughly 50 km north of Mexican Springs, revealed the presence of a later (late Basketmaker III to early Pueblo I) pit structure that formed part of a hamlet and that was burned. The remains of a family were located in the ventilator shaft. This probably resident family was seemingly massacred or trapped within the pit structure upon burning, suggesting violent abandonment brought about by competing social groups (possibly at the family level).

Perhaps more significant than the nature of settlement abandonment is the timing of this abandonment. Based on the tree-ring data, settlement of Mexican Spring Wash came to an abrupt halt around A.D. 700. On a macro-scale there is a drastic drop in tree-ring dates associated with samples taken from the pit structures (figure 5.15; only Priority 1 and 2 cutting dates as defined by Ruppé 1999 are included in this analysis).

Individual pit structure occupancy can be charted also. Figure 5.16 shows that for nine late Basketmaker III pit structures with tree-ring dates, all but one have final cutting dates around A.D. 690. The exception to this is Structure 61954-S4, which was used earlier. The great pit structure (61955-S1) was apparently used for more than 50 years. Rebuilding of Structure 61955-S1 probably occurred every 10 or 15 years and was apparently associated with the maintenance of this community structure

(Damp 1999). The early dates for Structure 61956-S3 are anomalous and may reflect old wood used in construction. The rest of the pit structures seem to have been used for a 30-year period between A.D. 660 and 690. Sometime around A.D. 690 to 700, all of the pit structures in the project area were rapidly abandoned. Given the differences in content, burned or unburned status, and the rapidity of abandonment, it does not seems likely that ritual burials or insect infestation were factors. Changes in climatic conditions may have affected settlement. However, we would expect that the inhabitants would have taken more of their material goods with them for a long-distance move with no expected return. Long-distance movement in this case probably consisted of relocating to the lower elevations of the Mexican Spring drainage. A rapid move out of the project area is indicated by the condition, content, and chronology of late Basketmaker III pit structures along Mexican Spring Wash.

SETTLEMENT VARIABILITY

The question of settlement variability or community structure within Basketmaker III communities has been approached on a number of occasions. For example, a large number of Basketmaker III sites were recorded in the Chaco Canyon area of the San Juan Basin east of the N30-31 Project area. Two of these sites have great kivas, including Shabik'eshchee Village (Hayes 1981; Roberts 1929; Wills and Windes 1989; Windes 1975). In other areas, such as Redrock Valley, Morris found Basketmaker III sites in a series of rock shelters containing pit houses, cists, and at one site, Broken Flute Cave, a great kiva (Morris 1980). The presence of a great kiva, or in the case of the N30-31 terminology, a great pit structure, implies some sort of communal organization, as do several of the sites discussed in this volume (Altschul and Huber; Gilpin and Benallie; Kearns et al.; P. Reed and Wilcox).

Somewhat different interpretations of settlement organization in the San Juan Basin and its peripheries are available from a number of other sites. Bradley (1994: 385) suggested that early Anasazi settlement in the Standing Rock area of the San Juan Basin was rather dispersed, with most of the late Basketmaker III components lying in the nuclear community, and no evidence of obvious coalition until the Pueblo I period. Nearby, at the late Basketmaker III to early Pueblo I El Llano Community along the lower Indian Creek drainage, there appears to have been a focus of construction at two sites that contained a concentration of domestic space and middens surrounding a probable great kiva. The large house and great kiva represent the earliest known public architecture in the area (Bradley 1994:385).

To the north, in the Dolores region of southwest Colorado, Kane et al. (1986:15) identified the Sagehen phase

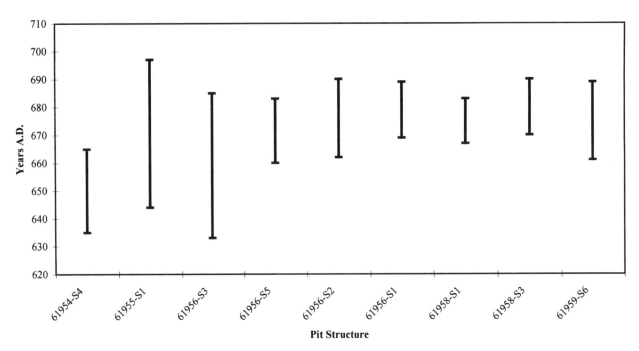

Figure 5.16. Range of Basketmaker III pit structure wood cutting dates.

(A.D. 600–850) as the initial settlement of the project area by Anasazi horticultural groups. Thirty-six Sagehen phase occupations were identified at excavated sites in Sagehen Flats. Sagehen phase habitations were described as small and dispersed, and located on lands with relatively high agricultural potential. The authors considered Sagehen phase communities as groups of contemporaneous small habitations or farming hamlets. Each one of these settlements served as the home base for family groups. Each site may have been occupied for approximately 25 years by mobile family groups. The Sagehen phase hamlet settlements may have been socially connected with other groups at nearby settlements in loosely organized communities or neighborhoods (perhaps five to 10 such units per community). Wilshusen and Ortman (1999) have recently elaborated on the social dynamics of these communities as they relate to aggregation and migration.

Montgomery (1986) provided similar insight on the Basketmaker III to Pueblo I settlement at Apricot Hamlet (Site 5MT2858), also investigated as part of the Dolores Archaeological Project's research in the Sagehen Flats area. Here it is suggested that the inhabitants of Apricot Hamlet were economically self-sufficient and related by kinship ties to other nearby nuclear family households. In addition, political organization may have rested primarily with a "headman"—a leader among equals, and someone who attained more influence than real political authority. According to this scenario, land was held in common as loosely defined "territorial aggregates" (Birkedal 1976:514).

A review of the N30-31 data suggests that there ex-

isted, spread over the landscape, a number of settlements that differed in function, period of use, and social dimension. Some Basketmaker III sites may have only been occupied on a seasonal basis for specific procurement practices. Most of the N30-31 pit structures, however, were occupied for a period that included at least one or two generations. Larger pit structures with fenced enclosures and more material goods were situated around the communal pit structure at LA 61955. This association of artifacts and features suggests status and economic differentiation within late Basketmaker III society.

Differences in pit structure size, nature, and composition indicate that status differentiation may have accounted for settlement hierarchy along Mexican Spring Wash between approximately A.D. 650 and 700. First of all, the largest pit structures were generally located in the lower Mexican Spring Cluster. These pit structures contained the most features, probably because of their size (see tables 5.1 and 5.2). Fenced areas were associated with a number of the late Basketmaker III pit structures (table 5.3; see Chenault and Motsinger, this volume). Within individual sites containing more than one pit structure, the largest pit structures were associated with the remnants of fencing that encircled the domestic area. Within the lower Mexican Spring Wash cluster, the largest pit structures were built with surrounding fences. The great pit structure at LA 61955 (Structure 61955-S1) is an exception, which is not surprising given its probable function as a communal structure. Only the very largest pit structures from the middle Mexican Spring Wash cluster were found to be associated with fenced enclosures. The site with the smallest overall pit structures,

LA 61959, yielded no pit structures with associated fenced areas.

A number of sites have been reported with evidence of fenced areas around Basketmaker III pit structures (Carlson 1963; Chenault and Motsinger, this volume; Rohn 1975), and a number of reasons have been given for their presence. Fenced areas are often referred to as enclosures or palisades, but this implies some sort of defensive function. Wilcox and Haas (1994:218–219) discussed the evidence for fenced areas or palisades and dispensed with the notion that fences were constructed to keep domestic fauna contained. They favor the notion that fences were erected to keep dangerous humans out, thus implying a defensive purpose. The fact that only the largest pit structures at individual sites were associated with fenced areas suggests another alternative. Because the largest pit structures also were found to contain the most material goods and were often associated with large areas for storage, the fences may have been erected as social symbols protecting the occupants' acquired resources from neighbors. Turnbull (1972:115–121) describes the use of fenced compounds around and within a village of the African Ik. In Ik society, fencing and the positioning of gates is used to set each family apart from all others. Basketmaker III social space may not have been as hotly contested as Ik social space, but the possibility exists that fenced areas were expressions of household social space within the late Basketmaker III community. This African analogy may seem inappropriate, but a similar argument has recently been made comparing agricultural strategies from the Wupatki area of northern Arizona to modern-day Tiv villagers of Nigeria (Stone and Downum 1999).

Status differentiation is perhaps attested to by the disparity in pit structure size within the project area, the presence of fenced areas around the larger pit structures at individual sites, the distance of larger pit structures versus smaller pit structures from the probable communal pit structure at LA 61955 (the great pit structure), and the accumulation of more material goods at the larger pit structures.

There is little evidence for the trading, working, or storage of turquoise or other exotic items within households. Some variation in shell distribution is evident between households. The marine *Olivella* sp. and *Haliotis* sp. shells from the Gulf of California and the Pacific Coast were found in high frequencies at Pit Structure S2 at LA 61956, but in quite low frequencies at the other Basketmaker III sites. This evidence may indicate that one household exerted greater control over trade or was better able to hoard exotic resources. Of course, a sampling bias could also account for this variation in shell frequency between households. Regardless, the frequency of material goods was appreciably higher in the downvalley sites clustered around modern-day Mexican

Springs, indicating that preferential access to wealth may have been a factor in community structure and settlement variability.

If individual pit structures or individual sites were interpreted in isolation, it would probably be argued that seasonal resource procurement strategies dictated pit structure construction and design. Pit structures may have been abandoned because of insect infestation, ritual, or environmental deterioration. The evidence from the N30-31 Project, however, suggests that a number of late Basketmaker III pit structures were occupied from approximately A.D. 660 to 700 by several families. Settlement of these sites was year-round and contemporary. Individual pit structures show variability in content and design that is probably attributable to socioeconomic differentiation. The great pit structure at LA 61955 attests to community-oriented functions. Taken as a whole, the late Basketmaker III distribution of households along Mexican Spring Wash illustrates greater settlement variability within a wider community than is typically seen in the study of Basketmaker III sites.

REGIONAL INTERRELATIONS

Establishing boundaries for cultural affiliation has involved studies of the material remains of the Anasazi, including Basketmaker III. Specifically, these studies have focused on the distribution of attributes within ceramics, lithics, and other material goods, as well as architecture. The studies in ceramic assemblages have primarily hinged on determining which styles (decorative and technological) are local manifestations versus introduced or exchanged. Other raw material studies have included identification of lithic sources and how certain lithic materials may have been traded (e.g., obsidian), and tracking the possible trade routes of exotic materials (e.g., marine shell, turquoise, macaw feathers, etc.). Architectural studies have been conducted that try to determine the presence or absence of structural features or styles that are temporal and regional indicators.

Some regional boundaries established in the Southwest are based on trends in architecture styles (Bullard 1962:53). The Basketmaker III structures on the N30-31 Project show variability but are mostly characteristic of the Eastern Anasazi area. Differences are likely due to status differentiation and local family unit expression. The majority of the architectural attributes observed on the N30-31 Project are more similar to the pit structure attributes in the Northern San Juan region, or Vivian's (1990) La Plata subregional variant, than to any other neighboring region. For example, the Basketmaker III pit structures in the N30-31 Project area resemble those found in the Mesa Verde district of the Northern San Juan region more so than those in the neighboring regions of Chaco, Canyon de Chelly, or Cove–Redrock

Valley. Bullard's (1962:179) suggestion that pit structure characteristics may have developed in the north, and were subsequently carried to the south and then east along the slopes of the Chuska Mountains, would explain why pit structure characteristics are more similar to the Northern San Juan region than to the Chaco region.

Ceramic analysis for this project focused on which decorative, utilitarian, and technological (temper and raw clay data) styles were made locally and which were exchanged or introduced into the Chuska region (Waterworth 1999). Cibola White Ware was likely manufactured from local clay sources (although, since the Cibola area is quite large, it may have come from quite a distance), but Kayenta (Tusayan), Chuska, Mesa Verde, and White Mountain Red Ware traditions were definitely nonlocal and traded into the area. In particular, Mesa Verde pottery accounts for nearly 21 percent of the ceramic assemblages during the late Basketmaker III (and early Pueblo I periods) suggesting trading connections with the north. Brown ware, which suggests trading relationships with the Mogollon or the southern Cibola region, also reaches its highest proportion during the Basketmaker III period.

The presence of exotic and nonlocal turquoise in the Basketmaker III ground stone assemblages suggests that trading may have occurred over a broad region including north-central New Mexico, southern Colorado, or throughout east central and southeastern Arizona. However, compared with the abundance of local raw materials, such as sandstone, the trading of turquoise (primarily used in the manufacture of jewelry) occurred only rarely.

The same situation also applies to the presence of marine *Olivella* sp. and *Haliotis* sp. shell from the Gulf of California and the Pacific Coast. Other than most of the material being found within pit structure 61956-S2, the frequency of marine shell (also used to make jewelry) was extremely low at the rest of the Basketmaker III sites. Thus, the presence of these species suggests trading routes from both the south and the west, eventually traversing through California, and ending up north of the Hohokam area.

Finally, connections to the north, especially with the Prayer Rock District/Cove-Red Valley and Canyon de Chelly/Canyon del Muerto, may also be supported by the construction techniques of Basketmaker III coiled basketry assemblages. Although there was no direct trading of basketry techniques or styles between north and south, it is apparent that the Basketmaker III people in the Mexican Spring Wash region shared a widespread pattern of sandal technology with other populations across the Colorado Plateau.

A smaller regional perspective can be invoked to examine the late Basketmaker III settlement of the southern Chuska slope. Few comprehensive surveys have been carried out in the area. Most of the archaeological study de-

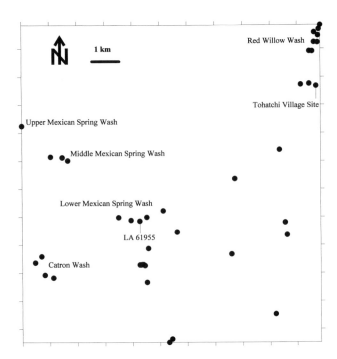

Figure 5.17. Basketmaker sites recorded in the vicinity of Tohatchi and Mexican Springs.

rives from project-specific cultural resource management studies. An examination of the location of known archaeological sites shows distinct clustering in Basketmaker site distribution in the Tohatchi to Mexican Springs area (figure 5.17). Clusters of sites occur in the major drainages and indicate that cohesive community-structured units operated during late Basketmaker III times. The evidence from the N30-31 pit structures suggesting contemporaneity among households indicates that no site existed in isolation, but that each household was part of an overall community pattern that regulated social space, resource procurement, community involvement, and perhaps forms of community leadership.

CONCLUSIONS

The above discussion presents the late Basketmaker III settlement of Mexican Spring Wash as a community that integrated physical space, the environment, the household, groups of households, and ideological concerns of the larger group. Incumbent in this approach is the idea that community analysis focuses on political communities in which individual sites are "linked through inter-settlement mechanisms for making social or economic decisions" (Wills and Leonard 1994:xiii).

Lipe's (1994:143) discussion of three kinds of process theory was also presented above. Lipe emphasizes different sets of relationships and dynamics in dealing with explanations of change. The first theory (based on changing relationships between population and resources) is addressed by the N30-31 data in the evidence for movement into and out of the area, the evidence for storage facilities, and the presence of exotic goods such as shell and obsidian. The second theory, which puts emphasis on the effects of increasing density on interpersonal relations, is manifested in the dispersal of late Basketmaker III households along Mexican Spring Wash and the presence of a community structure at LA 61955. The final theory, placing emphasis on competition for space, resources, power, and prestige, is uniquely addressed by the N30-31 data set. This data set contains signs of competition that led to aggregation and the development of status differentiation and, perhaps, leaders. The distinction between pit structures and sites in the middle and lower clusters of sites along Mexican Spring Cluster suggests that lower-ranking individuals or social units were compelled to take up residence in areas determined by the dominant group near the community structure. The competition theory is also given support by the pit structure and site differentiation, the variation in material goods, the presence of fenced areas around the largest pit structures within individual sites, and the rapid abandonment of the area around A.D. 700.

The advent of agricultural pursuits called for new ways of perceiving the landscape. Although there is considerable evidence for corn cultivation and use of other cultigens in the Archaic and Basketmaker II periods in the San Juan Basin, the evidence for shifting settlement strategies is not as abrupt during these periods. As land became controlled so as to allocate plots for farming, such as during Basketmaker III times, the notion of property may have been introduced. These new relationships between people of the community and between different communities may have led to status differentiation among growing and sedentary populations, as evidenced from the Mexican Springs area.

Lightfoot and Feinman (1982) argued for the appearance of incipient stratification during this time in the Mogollon area. It may be that with a growing population and an increased reliance on agricultural produce, the social relations of production changed, and status differentiation began; or that changes in the social relations of production affected population growth and changes in productive forces such as in agroeconomics. This incipient status differentiation is possibly reflected in pit structure size, content, differentiation, and aggregation in the Mexican Spring Wash late Basketmaker III sites. The observed differences in social distance as measured by pit structure size and physical distance from a communal structure are also indicative of status differentiation, as is the relationship of pit structure size (and richness of artifact content) to the presence of fenced areas around the domestic space. Simply put, the families in the larger houses with more material goods wished to maintain their privacy more than other families of the area. The N30-31 Project data are not precise enough to allow for the identification of individual headmen living in houses associated with exceptional storage capacity (Lightfoot and Feinman 1982:73), but the data suggest that socioeconomic differentiation played a role in settlement logistics and perhaps settlement abandonment between A.D. 660 and 700 along Mexican Spring Wash.

6

The Early to Late Basketmaker III Transition in Tohatchi Flats, New Mexico

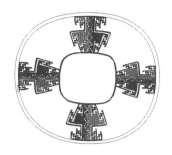

Timothy M. Kearns

Janet L. McVickar

Lori Stephens Reed

Tohatchi Flats, in the southern Chuska Valley of northwest New Mexico, was intensively settled during the Anasazi era. This lowland setting was colonized in the early sixth century A.D. by Basketmaker III agriculturalists following an apparent occupational hiatus during the late Basketmaker II period. Between ca. A.D. 500 and 600, the Ancestral Puebloans established farming settlements in the Tohatchi Flats valley. Although currently speculative, the extant data indicate that during the middle A.D. 600s, the Basketmaker III settlers shifted their residential locations from the valley floor to the valley periphery. Settlement along the valley margin continued, with few exceptions, into the eighth century. The postulated settlement relocation, presumably a response to sociopolitical or environmental perturbations, occurred subsequent to changes in architecture and material culture that differentiate early Basketmaker III from late Basketmaker III. This chapter briefly summarizes the archaeological record of this dynamic period and addresses aspects of change and continuity between the early and late components of the Basketmaker III occupation.

The primary data source for this study is the North System Expansion Project (NSEP), a pipeline development by El Paso Natural Gas Company (Kearns 1995). The NSEP pipeline cut a diagonal swath across the southern Chuska Valley and Tohatchi Flats, prompting excavation of 15 sites with Basketmaker III components (figure 6.1). Additional data pertinent to the Basketmaker III period in the study area are available from pipeline, highway, and other salvage projects conducted in the 1950s, 1960s, and early 1970s (Allen 1972; Benham 1966; Broilo and Allan 1973; Hammack 1964; Johnson 1962a, 1962b, Peekham 1963; Wendorf et al 1956). A significant Basketmaker III occupation has also

been identified in the Mexican Springs area along the western edge of Tohatchi Flats (Damp 1999; Damp and Kotyk, this volume; Sant 1990). Data from the NSEP investigations and other surveys and excavations in Tohatchi Flats are synthesized to examine cultural change during the Basketmaker III period within the context of four research topics: settlement, architecture, subsistence, and exchange.

The extant database represents a fraction of the Basketmaker III archaeological record in Tohatchi Flats, and the current chronological control, while adequate, remains relatively coarse. Also, differences in the integrity and documentation of the earlier data sets necessitated selective use of only the most reliable information. Therefore, this overview is presented as a first approximation. We anticipate that as new data are available, some of the ideas we present will be substantiated and others refuted.

TEMPORAL SETTING

The timing of the Basketmaker III period is traditionally placed between A.D. 500 and 700 but ranges from A.D. 400 to 750 depending on the region and researcher (e.g., Cordell 1984:100–107; McGregor 1965:69; Toll and Wilson, this volume; Reed and Wilcox, this volume; Vivian 1990:3). Unfortunately, poor temporal control, in many cases, has resulted in the masking or oversimplification of events and changes that transpired during the 200 to 350 years assigned to the period. The dating resolution for the Tohatchi Flats data set, albeit far from perfect, is sufficient to differentiate temporal subdivisions and aspects of cultural change within the Basketmaker III period.

The Basketmaker III occupation of Tohatchi Flats is

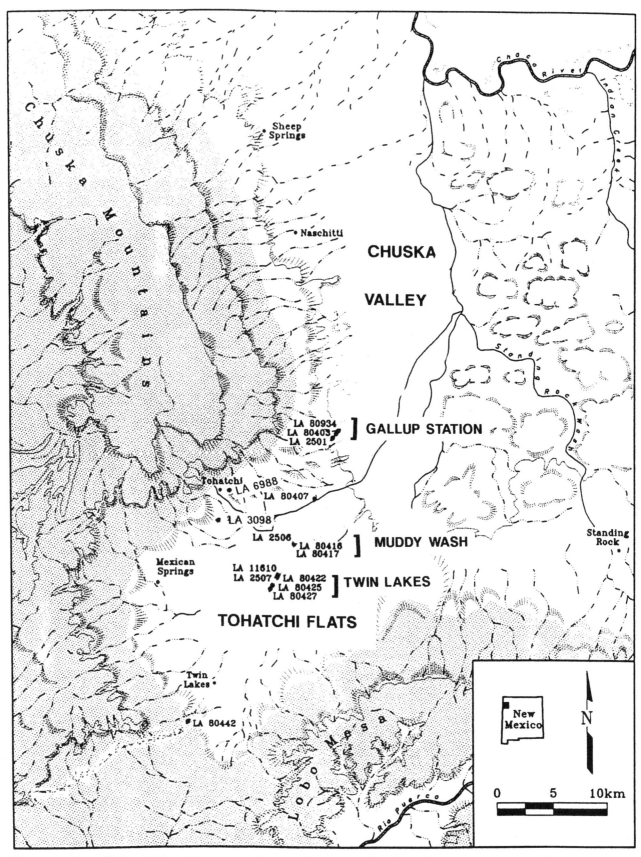

Figure 6.1. Map of Tohatchi Flats, New Mexico, showing the location of Basketmaker III sites and proposed communities

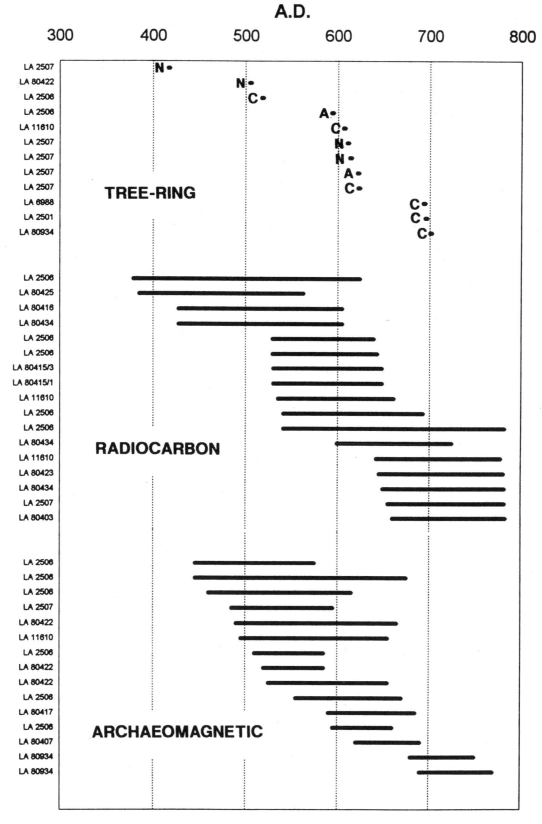

Figure 6.2. Chronometric values for the Basketmaker III occupation of Tohatchi Flats. Letters accompanying tree-ring dates: N for non-cutting, V for near cutting, and C for cutting. The radiocarbon determinations are calibrated, two sigma age ranges.

set between ca. A.D. 500 and 725, based on tree-ring dates from 12 structures, 17 radiocarbon determinations, and 15 archaeomagnetic age ranges (figure 6.2). These chronometric data are complemented by ceramic cross-dating and comparison of architectural styles with dated Basketmaker III sites from other regions. Also, chronometric data from Mexican Springs are directly relevant to the Basketmaker III settlement of Tohatchi Flats (Damp 1999; Damp and Kotyk, this volume).

A cutting date of A.D. 518 is the earliest tree-ring date for the Basketmaker III period in the study area. Although earlier settlement during the fifth century is plausible, discrete evidence has not been recovered. A radiocarbon sample on *Phragmites* sp. that produced a two-sigma age range of A.D. 379–624 was from the pit house that yielded the A.D. 518 cutting date. The possible significance of another potentially early radiocarbon age (from LA 80434) is diminished by a later radiocarbon age from the same feature. Two other seemingly early Basketmaker III radiocarbon determinations, on juniper and juniper and pine, are presumably due to old wood and cross-section effect (Schiffer 1982, 1986, 1987). Unlike the situation on the Rainbow Plateau (Geib and Spurr, this volume), a postulated occupational hiatus between ca. A.D. 150 and 500 (Kearns 1996a, 1996b) would preclude the in situ evolution of the Tohatchi Flats Basketmaker III population from earlier, local Basketmaker II groups. Currently, the Basketmaker III settlement in the early A.D. 500s appears to represent a new period of colonization and the establishment of residential locales in an area that was, at the time, unoccupied.

Two phases, Muddy Wash and Tohatchi, have been proposed for the Basketmaker III period in Tohatchi Flats and the southern Chuska Valley (Kearns 1996a). These designations, based on differences in architecture and other cultural remains, split the Basketmaker III period into pre-A.D. 600 (Muddy Wash) and post-A.D. 600 (Tohatchi) components. For this study, based on the dating and distribution of sites, we have further subdivided the Tohatchi phase into Early Tohatchi (ca. A.D. 600–630/640) and Late Tohatchi (ca. A.D. 630/640–725).

The Muddy Wash phase (ca. A.D. 500–600), or early Basketmaker III, represents the formative period of Basketmaker III development in the study area. Shallow, circular pit houses, a predominance of plain gray-brown and gray ware ceramics, the beginnings of a decorated ceramic tradition (i.e., Tohatchi Red-on-brown; see L. Reed et al., this volume), and small stemmed arrow points are the hallmarks of this phase. Although comparative data are poor, temporal equivalents of the Muddy Wash phase probably include the Lupton phase in the Puerco Valley of east-central Arizona (Wasley 1960), the early ceramic component in the Prayer Rock District of northwest Arizona (Morris 1980), the early Sambrito phase in the Navajo Reservoir District (Eddy 1966), components at

29SJ423 and Shabikk'eshchee Village in Chaco Canyon (McKenna 1986:39–41; Roberts 1929; Truell 1986:218, 235–237; Windes 1975), the early ceramic sites on the Rainbow Plateau (Geib and Spurr, this volume), the transitional Basketmaker phase in the La Plata Valley (Toll and Wilson, this volume), and other early brown ware sites on the Colorado Plateau (Wilson and Blinman 1994).

The Tohatchi phase (A.D. 600–725), which developed directly from the Muddy Wash phase, represents the archetypal manifestation of the Basketmaker III period exemplified elsewhere in the region by the La Plata phase (Gladwin 1945; Gumerman and Olson 1968; Hayes 1964; Hayes and Lancaster 1975; Wasley 1960), Twin Trees phase (Rohn 1977), the Classic Basketmaker III phase (Toll and Wilson, this volume), the Broken Flute phase (P. Reed 1999b; P. Reed and Wilcox, this volume), the Lukachukai phase (Altschul and Huber, this volume), and, perhaps, the Sky Village phase (Irwin-Williams 1973). During this phase, subsquare to D-shaped pit houses with antechambers largely replace the circular forms, plain gray ware ceramics predominate, decorated ceramics (i.e., Lino style black-on-white) become more common, and corner-notched arrow points supersede the stemmed variety. The distribution of dated structures in the study area and the Mexican Springs area (Damp 1999; Damp and Kotyk, this volume; Sant 1990) allows postulation of a division of the Tohatchi phase into Early Tohatchi (ca. A.D. 600–630/640) and Late Tohatchi (ca. A.D. 630/640–725) components. We envision general continuity in material traits and, presumably, resident populations from Early to Late Tohatchi. The distinction between the two components is based on a hypothesized shift in residential location on the valley floor during the Early Tohatchi phase to the valley margin during the Late Tohatchi phase. The interval between A.D. 630/640 and 700 is poorly represented in the current data from the valley floor. The Mexican Springs area and other locales along the valley margin were, however, occupied during this interval (Benham 1966; Cunnar 1996a; Damp 1999; Damp and Kotyk, this volume; Harriman 1996; Jones and Yost 1996; Peckham 1963). A single archaeomagnetic age range of A.D. 620–690 from a hearth in a pit structure at one site (LA 80407) represents the most compelling evidence for occupation of the flats during this period. As noted below, the locational setting of this site represents a distinct departure from other Tohatchi phase site locations.

We have, somewhat subjectively, placed the end date for Basketmaker III in the Tohatchi Flats area at A.D. 725. This is 24 years after the latest cutting date (A.D. 701 from Pit Structure 1, LA 80934) obtained during the NSEP investigations. The transition from Basketmaker III to Pueblo I in the study area appears to be manifested primarily by changes in architecture and settlement but not ceramics. By the late eighth century A.D. the inhabitants of Tohatchi Flats were constructing unit-type pueblos of contiguous living and storage rooms fronted by deep pit structures equipped with ventilator systems, not antechambers (Loebig 1996). The ceramic assemblage is characterized by plain gray ware and unslipped decorated types, however, and the differences between the late eighth century assemblage and the Late Tohatchi phase assemblage are a matter of degree, not kind (L. Reed and Hensler 1998a; also see Toll and Wilson, this volume). Although there are several likely candidates that may mark the Basketmaker III–Pueblo I transition period in Tohatchi Flats (i.e., A.D. 725–775), none of these sites has been securely dated.

PHYSIOGRAPHIC AND PALEOENVIRONMENTAL SETTING

Tohatchi Flats is located at the southern end of the Chuska Valley in northwest New Mexico (see figure 6.1). The Chuska Valley, on the west side of the San Juan Basin, is an elongated, north-trending lowland bordered by the Chuska Mountains on the west, the dissected mesa and bench terrain of the Chaco Slope and Chaco Platform on the east, and Lobo Mesa on the south. Although technically located within the Gallup Sag, Tohatchi Flats, bounded on the northwest by the Chuska Mountains, on the west by the Manuelito Plateau, and on the south by Lobo Mesa, forms a natural southern extension of the Chuska Valley (Kelley and Clinton 1960; Loose 1978). Elevations range from a low of 1800 m (5900 feet), where Tohatchi Flats grades imperceptibly into the Chuska Valley, to ca. 1950 m (6400 feet) around the western and southern periphery. The open valley floor is characterized by deep alluvial and aeolian sediments. Erosional remnants of shale, clay, and sandstone from the Cretaceous Menefee formation punctuate the valley, occurring locally as low mesas, cuestas, ridges, hills, and buttes. These elevated landforms are eroded remnants of the Chuska Mountain pediment and, in the north and west, are capped with outwash gravels.

Although Tohatchi Flats is in the rain shadow of the Manuelito Plateau and Chuska Mountains, ephemeral washes deliver runoff from the uplands to the valley floor, creating an ideal setting for floodwater agriculture. Annual precipitation varies with elevation, and currently ranges from a low of eight inches on the valley floor to 16 to 21 inches in the adjacent uplands. The current growing season averages 157 frost-free days, well within the limits for corn agriculture. Vegetation is currently a mix of sparse grassland and desert scrub. The setting is enhanced by the proximity of piñon-juniper, Ponderosa pine, and spruce-aspen upland environs, and by locally abundant lithic and clay resources.

How different was the environment of Tohatchi Flats during the Basketmaker III occupation? One of our objectives is to identify change in the past environment of the Chuska Valley during the Basketmaker III period and to relate these changes to observed cultural developments. Following McVickar (1996a), we use a variety of studies (Agenbroad et al. 1989; Betancourt and Davis 1984; Betancourt and Van Devender 1981; Betancourt et al. 1983; Dean et al. 1985; Ely et al. 1993; Euler et al. 1979; Grissino-Mayer 1996; Gumerman 1988; Palmer 1965; Petersen 1981, 1988; Petersen and Mehringer 1976) to reconstruct the paleoenvironment of Tohatchi Flats and the southern Chuska Valley during the Basketmaker III period (table 6.1).

Conditions leading into the Basketmaker III period in Tohatchi Flats were less favorable than they are today. Low effective moisture and droughts were prevalent, indicated by a low water table, erosion, and pronounced climatic variability (Dean et al. 1985; Plog et al. 1988; Grissino-Mayer 1996). The lack of dated sites in the study area between ca. A.D. 150 and 500 may reflect these deleterious conditions. The presence of late Basketmaker II and transitional Basketmaker II–III populations at higher elevations (e.g., Durango, Navajo Reservoir District, Cedar Mesa) during this interval complements the absence in Tohatchi Flats. The apparent restriction of the early ceramic period sites to the more elevated southeast portion of the Rainbow Plateau (Geib and Spurr, this volume) may represent an analogous situation.

By the A.D. 500s environmental conditions in Tohatchi Flats were much improved. A rise in the water table, initiated earlier, continued into the sixth century in response to consistent moderate precipitation. Increased alluvial deposition enhanced arable land, and low climatic temporal variability allowed greater predictability for crop production. Basketmaker III populations settled Tohatchi Flats and expanded during this favorable climatic regime.

Tree-ring and regional pollen records indicate a period of high effective moisture for the early A.D. 500s (Dean et al. 1985; Plog et al. 1988; Grissino-Mayer 1996; Grissino-Mayer et al. 1997). An interval of moderate to severe droughts followed in the late A.D. 500s, accompanied by a drop in the water table and evidence of erosion between A.D. 575 and 625 (Dean et al. 1985: figure 1). The Palmer Drought Severity Index (PDSI) for the Chuska Valley shows a period of low effective moisture between ca. A.D. 564 and 570 punctuated by two severe droughts and another brief severe drought at A.D. 590 (figure 6.3). Although these changes presumably affected farming conditions, the dating resolution for Basketmaker III settlement in the A.D. 500s is not sufficiently refined at present to evaluate the impact of these downturns on the local populations.

Archaeological pollen samples from NSEP sites show relative increases in arboreal taxa during the Muddy Wash phase (Holloway 1999), and moisture was

TABLE 6.1

Comparison of Regional Paleoclimatic Reconstructions for the Colorado Plateau

B.P.	A.D.	Betancourt and Van Devender 1981; Betancourt and Davis 1984	Petersen and Mehringer 1976	Petersen 1981, 1988	Ely et al. 1993	Grissino-Mayer 1996	Euler et al. 1979; Dean et al. 1985; Gumerman 1988	Southern Chuska Valley Phase
1700	250					Wet	High effective moisture	
1650	300							Hiatus?
1600	350						Low effective moisture	
1550	400					Severe drought		
1500	450	Warm, dry	Warm, wet	Warm, wet	Dry?			
1450	500							
1400	550						Moderate–high effective moisture	Muddy Wash
1350	600			Cool, dry		Very wet		
1300	650	BMIII						
1250	700							Tohatchi
1200	750					Dry		
1150	800						Low effective moisture	Red Willow

Note: Shading denotes high temporal variability (adapted from Dean et al. 1985: Figure 1).

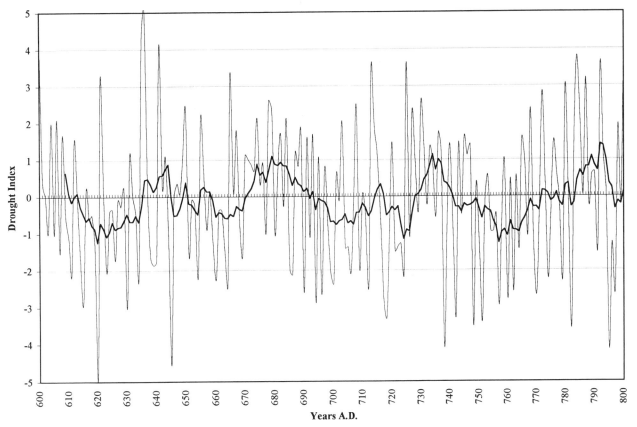

Figure 6.3. Reconstruction of the annual Palmer Drought Severity Index (PDSI) for the Chuska Valley (A.D. 600–800) superimposed by a 10-year running average (dark line).

sufficient to support cottonwood (*Populus* sp.), willow (*Salix* sp.), and reeds (*Phragmites communis*) in well-watered locations (A. C. Reed 1999). Major washes in Tohatchi Flats, now ephemeral, may have flowed year-round. The high water table also contributed to the formation and persistence of standing bodies of water in the valley, and faunal evidence indicates that they were sufficient to support a diversity of waterfowl (McVickar and Wails 1999; Rippel and Walth 1999).

A desert scrub-grassland biotic community was present in Tohatchi Flats during this period, and the NSEP flotation samples indicate that grasses were plentiful (A. C. Reed 1999). Alluvial deposition in the floodplains and the high water table would have provided ideal conditions for agriculture. The NSEP botanical analyses indicate increased crop productivity during this time (Holloway 1999; A. C. Reed 1999). The profusion and diversity of small mammalian remains in Muddy Wash phase NSEP assemblages indicate abundant faunal populations, both in the valley and in the mountains, and favorable environmental conditions and water availability (Murray 1999). Despite occasional short downturns in effective moisture, favorable climatic conditions,

profusion and diversity of flora and fauna, and reliable effective moisture combined to produce an optimal environment during the Muddy Wash occupation that was conducive to population growth.

Data for the A.D. 600s, the Tohatchi phase interval, are varied. PDSI values indicate a period of subnormal moisture in the Chuska Valley between approximately A.D. 612 and 635, and an extreme drought in A.D. 620 (see figure 6.3). Slightly later timing for increased aridity is indicated by the Malpais tree-ring record (Grissino-Mayer 1996; Grissino-Mayer et al. 1997) and other paleo-environmental data from the Colorado Plateau and adjacent mountains (Dean et al. 1985; Euler et al. 1979; Petersen 1987b, 1988; Plog et al. 1988). The drop in effective moisture would have reduced or interrupted recharge of springs, diminished water flow in the washes, and arrested deposition of nutrient-rich sediments necessary for productive agricultural yields. These changes may be reflected in diminished agricultural returns. Flotation samples from NSEP sites show a slight decrease in corn remains from Early Tohatchi phase sites and an increase in grass seeds (A. C. Reed 1999). Dean et al. (1985:543) suggest that the impact of such a downturn would be more severe in more densely occupied areas. Tohatchi Flats appears to have been fairly densely inhabited during this interval. Although problematical, the slightly later timing for the onset of more arid conditions may be more consistent with the archaeological record. It is possible that the deleterious conditions had a sufficiently negative impact on the Tohatchi Flats population to prompt settlement relocation as an adaptive strategy. This may explain the postulated settlement shift from the valley bottom to the valley margin in the middle A.D. 600s (Kearns 1996a, 1996c, 1998; McVickar 1996b). Evidence for a shift to the valley margin is, at present, tenuous, and if the shift occurred, the causal factors, whether sociopolitical or environmental, remain undetermined.

A rise in the water table and return to a depositional environment was initiated by ca. A.D. 640. The El Malpais tree-ring record indicates that the brief moist interval was followed by a prolonged period of below-normal rainfall that lasted from A.D. 661 to 1023 (Grissino-Mayer 1996; Grissino-Mayer et al. 1997). Other records show a notable drop in the water table and low effective moisture until ca. A.D. 670, marking the initiation of a 22-year moist interval (Dean et al. 1985; Euler et al. 1979; Plog et al. 1988). The PDSI for the Chuska Valley generally corroborates these records (see figure 6.3). The presence of LA 80407, a mid A.D. 600s site, on the valley floor (Loebig et al. 1996) may represent an attempt to reestablish settlements in the valley coincident with a rising water table and depositional regime.

Another downturn is indicated in the late seventh century. From about A.D. 690 to nearly 730, available moisture was low until precipitation increased again in the early A.D. 780s (see table 6.1). These conditions may explain the dearth of transitional late Basketmaker III to Pueblo I sites in Tohatchi Flats. After about A.D. 745 a distinct drop in the water table, arroyo downcutting, and a period of pronounced temporal variability (A.D. 750–975) are portrayed in the dendroclimatic and hydrologic records (see table 6.1 and figure 6.3; Dean et al. 1985).

The generally unstable and deleterious climatic regime of the A.D. 600s may have stimulated a general move to the valley margin and possibly additional settlement relocation. This may have culminated in aggregated villages in defensive settings as exemplified by Tohatchi Village, LA 3098 (Gilpin et al. 1996; Marshall et al. 1979; Peckham 1969), a probable transitional late Basketmaker III–Pueblo I site.

SETTLEMENT

Site projections identify Tohatchi Flats as one of the most intensive prehistorically occupied areas of the San Juan Basin (Drager 1983; Drager et al. 1982:235). Survey

records, excavation data, and informal reconnaissance in the region indicate high site densities for the Basketmaker III period. Because of the lack of systematic survey in Tohatchi Flats and the similarity between late Basketmaker III and early Pueblo I ceramics, our assessment of Basketmaker III settlement is based primarily on NSEP data from 10 excavated sites in three spatially segregated communities.[1] Two of the communities are indicative of the Muddy Wash and Early Tohatchi phase settlement in the Tohatchi Flats valley; the third community is representative of the Late Tohatchi phase settlement along the valley margin. The Basketmaker III sites reported in the Mexican Springs area (Damp 1999; Damp and Kotyk, this volume) also represent Late Tohatchi phase settlement of the valley periphery.

The Muddy Wash and Early Tohatchi phase settlements are exemplified by the Muddy Wash and Twin Lakes communities (Kearns 1996a; McVickar 1999b).[2] These settlements are situated on elevated landforms on the valley floor and are roughly 3 km apart (see figure 6.1). The community of Muddy Wash, the largest early Basketmaker III settlement known in the study area, is represented by three excavated sites: LA 2506, LA 80416, and LA 80417 (Latady and McVickar 1999a, 1999b; McVickar 1999b; McVickar and Wails 1999; Olson and Wasley 1956a). The excavated component of the community dates to the A.D. 500s and early 600s and includes 13 pit structures, five surface rooms, three poorly defined structures, nine inhumations, a variety of extramural cists, pits, hearths, roasting pits, postholes, and sheet trash and midden deposits. Pit houses and smaller "Pocket" pit structures are represented. The pit structures are typically shallow, circular, and lack antechambers or ventilators. The two latest pit houses, however, are subsquare, and one has an attached antechamber. The circular to subsquare surface rooms represent a continuum of the pit structure architecture but are generally more shallow and contain fewer features. Two pit structures and one surface structure dating to the Muddy Wash phase and one Early Tohatchi phase pit structure had burned. Also, although the investigations entailed extensive surface stripping, no evidence of stockades or other defensive features was noted. The distribution of structures, the presence of trash-filled and superimposed structures and features, and chronometric data all suggest that the excavated component of the Muddy Wash community represents the growth through time of a small hamlet with contemporaneous occupation by one to several households (McVickar and Wails 1999; L. Reed et al. 1996). The excavated sites are components of a larger cluster of Basketmaker III residential sites that extends 2.5 km along a low, linear cuesta separating two broad floodplains. Although earlier components may be present, the unexcavated sites are tentatively assigned to the Early Tohatchi phase. The number of sites along the ridge suggests the presence of a community of loosely aggregated hamlets.

The community of Twin Lakes is a linear aggregation of at least 10 sites that extends approximately 1.7 km along the eastern edge of a low bench overlooking the Figueredo Wash floodplain (Bullard and Cassidy 1956; Harriman and McVickar 1996; Johnson 1962a, 1962b; Kearns 1996c; Kearns et al. 1991; McVickar 1996b; Olson and Wasley 1956b; Snell and Jones 1996; Snell et al. 1996; Stirniman and McVickar 1996). This community was initially settled in the sixth century and expanded during the early seventh century. The last tree-ring cutting date from the community is A.D. 623 and sometime thereafter (i.e., 5–15 years) the occupation appears to have been temporarily interrupted. This postulated interlude occurred between A.D. 630/640 and the early A.D. 700s. Transitional Basketmaker III–Pueblo I groups established residence in the area sometime after this interval.

The Muddy Wash phase occupation at Twin Lakes is evidenced by one "Pocket" pit structure, one pit house, one probable great pit structure, and a cluster of large, bell-shaped cists. Other excavated cists, pits, surface rooms, and pit structures also may be associated with the early occupation, but the temporal assignments are equivocal. The pit house and the great pit structure both burned. No evidence of a stockade was noted, despite extensive surface stripping. The current data indicate the presence of one or two small hamlets and a possible communal structure that presumably served a larger population. It is likely that additional Muddy Wash phase remains are present and masked by overburden or debris from subsequent occupations.

Fourteen unburned and five burned pit structures are assigned to the Early Tohatchi phase at Twin Lakes; others are undoubtedly present. Other architectural features include noncontiguous storage facilities and pit rooms. Extramural features are common and include large bell-shaped storage cists, a variety of other pits, hearths, and postholes. Sheet trash, trash-filled features, and midden deposits are present. Human burials are interspersed within the residential areas. No evidence of stockades or other defensive features was noted. The density and distribution of structures and features in the Twin Lakes settlement vary significantly. Single pit houses with one to several surface storage facilities and few other features exemplify one end of a continuum (e.g., Snell and Jones 1996; Stirniman and McVickar 1996). These structures and features apparently represent single household residential compounds. Clusters of multiple pit houses, numerous surface storage facilities, and a large number and variety of extramural features represent the opposite end of the continuum (e.g., Harriman and McVickar 1996;

Snell et al. 1996). These locales are the culmination of the accretionary growth, through time, of a small hamlet occupied by one to several households. A large pit house (LA 80422, Pit Structure 1) with numerous exterior storage facilities may be indicative of an influential community member (Lightfoot and Feinman 1982) or simply a large household. The number of pit structures, presence of remodeled and superimposed structures, character and distribution of trash deposits, and the spacing of the residential compounds indicate that the size and composition of the Twin Lakes community fluctuated throughout the Basketmaker III occupation. The maximum size of the community during the Early Tohatchi phase, while larger than the preceding Muddy Wash phase, probably never exceeded 10 contemporaneous households.

Excavations at a third settlement, the Gallup Station community, exemplify the Late Tohatchi phase period in the Tohatchi Flats area. This loosely aggregated settlement near the base of the Chuska Mountains (see figure 6.1) includes four residential sites and an isolated great pit structure situated on low, elevated landforms overlooking the valley floor (Cunnar 1996a; Harriman 1996; Kearns 1996c; Wheeler 1996). An isolated storage locale on a slight rise also may have been part of this Late Tohatchi phase settlement (Cunnar 1996b). The Gallup Station community is one of a series of Late Tohatchi phase residential locales along the western edge of Tohatchi Flats (Benham 1966; Jones and Yost 1996; Peckham 1963). The Mexican Springs community (Damp 1999; Damp and Kotyk, this volume) also exemplifies the Late Tohatchi phase occupation of the valley periphery.

The excavated Basketmaker III component at one of the Gallup Station residential sites (LA 2501) includes a large burned pit house, a smaller Pocket pit structure, an arc of exterior storage facilities, large bell-shaped cists, pits, possibly a roasting facility, multiple inhumations, and sheet trash and midden deposits (Harriman 1996). Tree-ring cutting dates place final construction of the pit house at A.D. 696; the presence of subfloor features indicates an earlier construction episode. The compact arrangement of structures and features within the excavated compound suggests occupation by a single large or influential household. Evidence for rebuilding of the pit house, the array of storage facilities and extramural features, and midden size indicate an extended occupation, but probably no more than 30 years (i.e., ca. A.D. 680–710). Although a sufficient area surrounding the central pit house was stripped, no evidence of an enclosing stockade was noted.

An isolated pit structure (LA 80934) with tree-ring cutting dates of A.D. 701 is roughly 1.25 km northeast of LA 2501 (Cunnar 1996a). The size, construction technique, and constellation of floor features (see architecture section) indicate the structure was a communal or integrative "great" pit structure and not a domicile. This structure also burned.

Generally, the Tohatchi Flats Basketmaker III residential sites are located on elevated landforms adjacent to arable land, although one excavated site is situated directly on the valley floor. The Basketmaker III component at this site (LA 80407) represents a small residential compound with one unburned pit house, two exterior storage facilities, and several extramural features (Loebig et al. 1996). An enclosing stockade was not present. An archaeomagnetic age range from A.D. 620 to 690, obtained from the pit house hearth, places this site in the Late Tohatchi phase (Cox and Blinman 1999). Roughly 0.5 to 0.85 m of alluvial overburden covered this site, and others dating to the same period may be similarly buried on the valley floor.

The interval between ca. A.D. 725 and 775 represents the Basketmaker III to Pueblo I transition in Tohatchi Flats. Although this interval is poorly documented, components at two excavated sites potentially date to this period. At LA 2507 in the Twin Lakes community, a four-room, slab-foundation structure (Bullard and Cassidy 1956) and a nearby pit house with a ventilator (Johnson 1962a, 1962b) indicate a small transitional period hamlet. Several other unexcavated sites in the Twin Lakes community may also contain transitional Basketmaker III–Pueblo I components. Components of this transitional period are also present at the Gallup Station community. The hearth in the deep, ventilator-equipped Pit Structure 3 at LA 2501 (Harriman 1996) produced an archaeomagnetic age range of A.D. 695–755 (Eighmy-Wolfman curve) or A.D. 695–785 (Dubois curve). Also, a slab-lined structure at LA 2501 (Cassidy and Bullard 1956) was destroyed prior to the NSEP investigations.

The unexcavated Tohatchi Village (LA 3098), typically identified as a Basketmaker III site, is an aggregation of approximately 35 pit houses, one great pit structure, and 41 slab- or rock-foundation surface storage units located near the valley margin (Gilpin et al. 1996; Marshall et al. 1979; Peckham 1969; Stuart and Gauthier 1981:90–91). Although rows of slab-lined bins or cists may occur earlier in the Lukachukai Valley (Altschul and Huber, this volume), in Tohatchi Flats contiguous-room, surface storage facilities appear to be a transitional Basketmaker III–Pueblo I development. The location of Tohatchi Village on top of a steep, isolated butte represents a radical departure from the typical Basketmaker III settlement location in Tohatchi Flats. The large number of pit structures at the site may represent the accretionary growth of a small hamlet; however, we think this is unlikely. Alternatively, we suggest that the site represents a large transitional Basketmaker III–Pueblo I village aggregated on top of the butte as a defensive precaution. An unrecorded possible Basket-

maker III–Pueblo I residential site located on a high butte overlooking Figueredo Wash may represent a similar occurrence in Tohatchi Flats. Also, Kiva Mesa, in Redrock Valley (P. Reed and Wilcox, this volume), resembles Tohatchi Village and may be indicative of an analogous response in the northern Chuska Valley area.

The substantial investment in domiciles, the stylistically variable interior and exterior storage facilities, dependence on agriculture, and the location of pit house sites adjacent to prime arable land indicates that the Tohatchi Flats Basketmaker III residential sites were occupied year-round, not seasonally. That is, although some members may have established temporary residence elsewhere, and excepting logistical forays, most of the inhabitants remained at the site throughout the year. Several sites in Tohatchi Flats may represent limited activity or seasonal use locales; however, their functional or temporal designations are equivocal, and their role in Basketmaker III settlement is unclear (Cunnar 1996b; Hammack 1964; Stirniman and Yost 1996).

In summary, Muddy Wash phase settlement in Tohatchi Flats was characterized by small hamlets of one to several households. Great pit structures were present, indicating a level of social integration that transcended the household. Sites were typically situated in the valley on low benches or other elevated landforms that provided well-drained settings with ready access to arable land. Two probable Muddy Wash sites (LA 2547 and an unrecorded site ca. 100 m to the south) located near Coyote Canyon on the southern flank of Tohatchi Flats (Skinner and Gilpin 1997:12; Hammack 1964) may indicate a broader range of settlement locales for this period. Defense does not appear to have been a factor in site location, and there is no evidence of stockades.

Settlement during the Early Tohatchi phase generally followed the earlier pattern. Settlement density increased, however, and small hamlets of one to several pit houses were clustered in large, loosely aggregated villages. The sites were situated in open settings and were not stockaded. Although great pit structures have not yet been identified at Early Tohatchi phase sites, their presence is implied by both earlier and later occurrences.

The general settlement pattern of loosely aggregated hamlets and occasional great pit structures continued through the Late Tohatchi phase. Sometime during the middle A.D. 600s, however, Basketmaker III household locations appear to have shifted closer to the valley margins, although one excavated residential site, dated to the middle A.D. 600s, was situated directly on the valley floor. By the end of the seventh century, and presumably several decades earlier (see Damp and Kotyk, this volume), the open valley setting appears to have been abandoned for locations along the more elevated margins of Tohatchi Flats. Stockades were not discovered during the NSEP excavations; however, their presence at Late

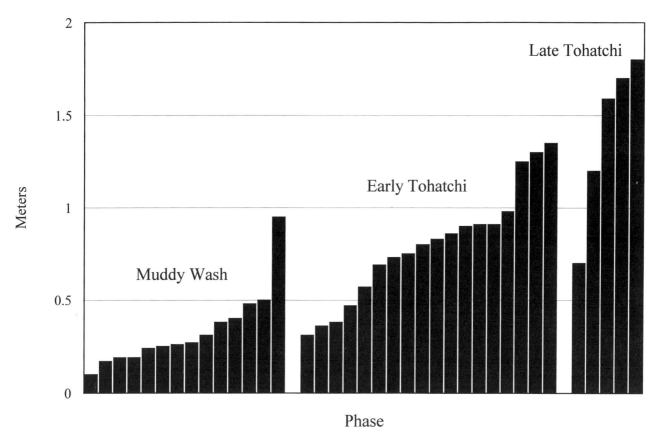

Figure 6.4. Temporal variation in pit structure depth for Basketmaker III sites in Tohatchi Flats.

Tohatchi phase sites in the Mexican Springs area (Damp 1999; Damp and Kotyk, this volume) indicates changes in settlement design and, possibly, social relations. The factors that precipitated the hypothesized mid-to-late-seventh-century settlement relocation also may have prompted a subsequent aggregation of transitional Basketmaker III–Pueblo I households into larger villages in defensive settings during the early to middle eighth century (e.g., Tohatchi Village).

ARCHITECTURE

Basketmaker III architecture in Tohatchi Flats is characterized by pit structures, surface rooms, discontiguous, semisubterranean storage facilities, and extramural features. Architectural styles and construction techniques vary within each temporal division but evidence a general pattern of change through time. Although variability is apparent in the type and density of the surface rooms, storage facilities, and extramural features, the following discussion focuses on the pit structures.

Forty-three Basketmaker III pit structures have been excavated in Tohatchi Flats: 40 along El Paso Natural Gas pipelines and three during other projects (table 6.2). The size of the database and the representation of dated structures from all three Basketmaker III temporal subdivisions allows both a synchronic and a diachronic evaluation of pit structure style and use in Tohatchi Flats. Sample size is a consideration; the temporal periods with the largest sample size, the Muddy Wash and Early Tohatchi phases, also exhibit the greatest variability. Data from Mexican Springs (Kotyk 1999), however, suggest that the Late Tohatchi sample is a generally accurate reflection of pit structure variability during that interval. A general view of pit structure variability is provided by a series of independent attributes. Pit structure depth and floor area vary within and among sites but evidence directional change through time. Structure depth, while variable, generally shifts from shallow to deep through time (figure 6.4). The shallow-to-deep trend is consistent with observations elsewhere on the Colorado Plateau (e.g., Brew 1946:207; Morris 1939:24–25). Although the Tohatchi Flats populations appear to have been sedentary from the onset, increased sedentism through time may be one factor influencing the depth of pit structures. Depth differences within each temporal division are presumably related to ground conditions and structure function.

Pit structure main chamber size also exhibits a considerable range within each temporal period (figure 6.5). The variation in floor space is presumably related to structure function, social unit size and, possibly, status differentiation. The largest structures in the Muddy Wash and Late Tohatchi phase samples are probably

TABLE 6.2

Architectural Attributes of Excavated Basketmaker III Pit Structures in Tohatchi Flats

Site (LA)	Structure	Date (A.D.)	Style	Shape	Depth (m)	Size (sq. m)	Bench	Space Division	Bins	Cists	Ante-chamber	Burned
2501	1	696	Northern	Subrectangular	1.59	39.5	Yes	Upright slab	0	1	Detached	Yes
2501	2	650–700	Pocket	Round	0.7	11.4	No	None	0	0	None	No
2506	1	518	Early Western	Round	0.26	21.2	No	Ridges	3	0	None	Yes
2506	2	500–600	Early Western	Round	0.17	19.6	No	Ridges	5	3	None	No
2606	3	594	Western	Subsquare	0.38	24.7	Yes	Ridges	2	1	Attached	Yes
2506	4	500–600	Early Western	Round	0.48	17.3	No	Ridges	3	4	None	No
2506	5	500–600	Other	Round	0.38	15.4	No	None	1	2	Indet.	Yes
2506	6	500–600	Pocket	Round	0.5	4.9	No	None	0	0	None	No
2506	7	600–610	Early Western	Subsquare	0.86	10.2	Yes	Ridges	2	1	Indet.	No
2506	8	500–600	Other	Oval	0.25	6.0	No	None	0	0	None	No
2506	9	500–600	Other	Round	0.4	8.3	No	None	0	1	None	No
2506	10	500–600	Pocket	Round	0.27	2.2	No	None	0	0	None	No
2506	11	500–600	Early Western	Round	0.31	10.2	Yes	Ridges	0	4	None	No
2506	12	500–600	Early Western	Round	0.24	12.6	No	Ridges	0	0	None	No
2507	50A	610–630	Mixed	Subsquare	0.91	16.9	No	Ridges	1	0	Detached	Yes
2507	53-1	600–700	Other	Subtriangular	0.9	21.4	No	None	0	0	Attached	No
2507	53-2	600–700	Pocket	Oval	NA	20.9	No	None	0	0	None	No
2507	53-3	600–700	Pocket	Oval	NA	9.9	No	None	0	0	None	No
2507	62-5	623	Mixed	D-shaped	0.91	17.6	Yes	Ridges	0	1	Detached	Yes
2507	62-6	550–623	Early Western	Subsquare	NA	14.3	No	Ridges	0	1	None	No
2507	62-7	500–600	Pocket	Round	NA	5.7	No	None	0	0	None	No
2507	92-1	600–700	Mixed	D-shaped?	0.98	10.0	Yes	Ridges	1	0	Detached	No
2507	92-2	622	Mixed	Oval	0.75	8.1	No	Ridges	2	1	Detached	Yes
4473	3	600–700	Other	Oval	0.25	12.2	No	None	0	0	Indet.	Yes
6988	1	694	Northern	Subsquare	1.8	32.8	Yes	Slab/ridges	1	1	Detached	Yes
6989	1	500–600	Mixed	Subsquare	1.6	10.9	No	Ridges	0	1	Detached	No
11610	1	600–650	Mixed	Subsquare	0.57	24.6	No	Ridges	3	1	Detached	Yes
11610	2	607	Mixed	Subsquare	0.47	16.0	Yes	Ridges	4	2	Detached	Yes

TABLE 6.2 continued

Architectural Attributes of Excavated Basketmaker III Pit Structures in Tohatchi Flats

Site (LA)	Structure	Date (A.D.)	Style	Shape	Depth (m)	Size (sq.m)	Bench	Space Division	Bins	Cists	Ante-chamber	Burned
80407	1	620–690	Mixed	D-shaped	1.2	14.3	Yes	Ridges	2	1	Detached	No
80417	1	500–600	Indeterminate	Subsquare	0.1	24.0	No	None	2	0	Indet.	No
80422	1	600–700	Northern	D-shaped	1.35	30.5	Yes	Slab/ridges	6	1	Detached	No
80422	2	500–600	Mixed	Subsquare	0.19	9.6	No	Ridges	0	0	Detached	Yes
80422	3	500–700	Pocket	Oval	0.36	13.2	No	None	0	3	None	No
80422	4	500–600	Great	Round	0.95	45.3	Yes	Indet.	0	?	Detached	Yes
80425	1	500–700	Modified Northern	Subsquare	0.73	17.0	No	None	1	0	Detached	No
80425	4	500–700	Mixed	Round	0.25	9.5	Yes	Ridges	1	2	Detached	No
80425	5	500–700	Mixed	Subsquare	0.83	22.5	Yes	Ridges	2	0	Detached	No
80425	6	500–700	Modified Pocket	Round	0.8	4.4	Yes	None	0	0	Detached	No
80425	7	500–700	Pocket	Oval	0.31	4.2	No	None	0	0	None	No
80425	8	500–700	Pocket	Round	0.69	4.1	No	None	0	0	None	No
80425	9	500–700	Mixed	Round	1.3	14.0	Yes	Ridges	1	0	Detached	No
80442	1	600–700	Modified Northern	Subrectangular	1.25	7.9	Yes	Raised floor	0	0	Detached	No
80934	1	701	Great	Round	1.7	46.6	Yes	None	0	0	Detached	Yes

Note: Pit structure styles include those defined by Shelley (1990); Indet. = indeterminate.

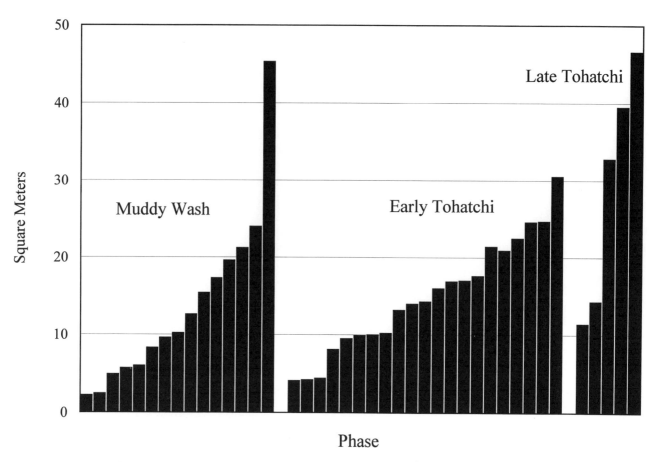

Figure 6.5. Temporal variation in pit structure size for Basketmaker III sites in Tohatchi Flats.

communal facilities (great pit structures or early great kivas) and not domiciles. Similarly, small "Pocket" pit structures (Kane 1986; Shelley 1991) do not appear to have been primary residences. Although the sample is small, Late Tohatchi phase domestic structures are generally larger than the earlier structures. This difference may reflect increases in household size or in the use of interior space.

Three other pit structure attributes—antechambers, floor space division features, and main chamber shape—are significant discriminating variables and are key attributes that differentiate pit structure styles (discussed below). The presence or absence of antechambers may reflect differential storage requirements (Wills and Windes 1989). The Tohatchi Flats sample evidences temporal patterning in antechamber presence and style (figure 6.6), a characteristic that is addressed below.

Upright-slab wing walls and low, rounded clay radials were often used by Basketmaker III households to segregate or define floor space within pit structures. Most pit structures in the Tohatchi Flats sample either lack space division features or are characterized by raised clay radials; only three pit structures have upright-slab wing walls, and two of these exhibit a combination of clay radials and upright slabs (see table 6.2). The use of these features to subdivide the living space is presumably a

functional attribute, but the design of the features is a stylistic variable and is used to discriminate pit structure styles (see below).

The shape of the main chamber is another distinctive stylistic attribute. Four shape groups are recognized in the Tohatchi Flats sample: round or oval, subsquare or subrectangular, D-shaped, and subtriangular (see table 6.2). Evaluation of this attribute relative to pit structure style indicates that shape may be indicative of temporal, cultural, and functional variability (see below).

The construction technique exemplified by the central hearth in the main chamber is a stylistic attribute that is potentially indicative of pit structure variability. Differences in hearth presence and construction technique are apparent in the Tohatchi Flats sample (see table 6.2). No significant changes in construction style through time are evident, however, and increased variability in hearth style co-varies with increased sample size.

To facilitate regional comparisons and evaluate local diversity, the Tohatchi Flats pit structures are compared to four styles proposed by Shelley (1990, 1991). The four stylistic forms—Western, Northern, Pocket, and Mixed—are differentiated by variations in the presence and type of antechamber, floor space division, shape, and other architectural attributes. Shelley (1991) also identifies a category of "Other" pit structures that do not fit

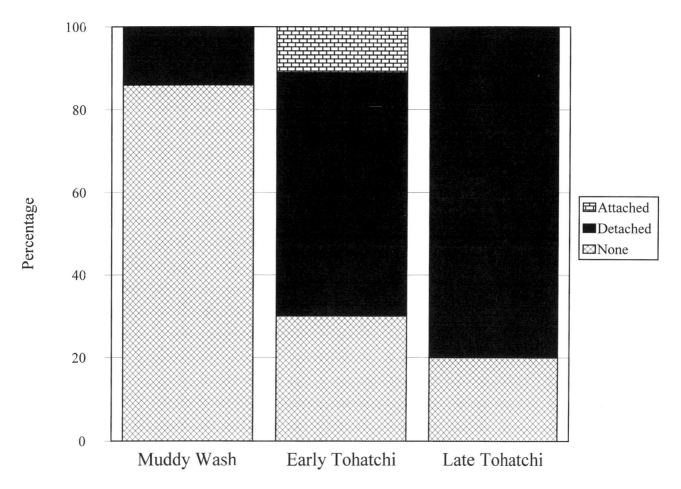

Figure 6.6. Distribution of pit structure antechamber styles through time for Basketmaker III sites in Tohatchi Flats.

the four named styles. Shelley notes that stylistic variation is potentially indicative of regional and temporal patterns in pit house construction. He equates pit house styles with regional variants, associating the Northern style with the La Plata variant, and the Western style with the Lukachukai variant (Shelley 1991). The Mixed style has been identified in Chaco Canyon and several other locales, but its association with a specific regional variant is equivocal (Shelley 1991). Pocket pit structures and great pit structures, a style identified in the Tohatchi Flats sample, are not associated with a specific regional variant.

Shelley's classification provides a useful heuristic tool for examining the Tohatchi Flats pit structures. Twenty-two of the 43 Tohatchi Flats pit structures are classified by the criteria distinguishing the four primary styles; nine others represent stylistic variations of the four types, seven are assigned to the residual Other category, two are identified as "great" style pit structures, and three are too eroded or too problematical to classify (see table 6.2). Attributes used to discriminate stylistic variation in the Tohatchi Flats pit structures include the presence and design of antechambers, the presence and form of floor space division features, hearth style, and main chamber shape and size (figures 6.7 and 6.8; see table 6.2). The follow-

ing section identifies stylistic variability and examines the Tohatchi Flats pit structures relative to three variables: function, chronology, and potential regional affiliation.

Following Shelley (1990, 1991), the typical Western style pit structure is round or subrounded and distinguished by a raised antechamber that is attached directly to the main chamber. A raised clay collar usually surrounds the central hearth, and one or more raised clay radials, not wing walls, extend from the hearth to the structure walls. Only one of the Tohatchi Flats examples is a Western style structure with an attached antechamber (see figure 6.7). Seven examples, termed "Early Western," are similar to Western style pit structures but lack antechambers (see figure 6.7). One indeterminate pit structure is probably an Early Western style structure, but erosion precludes accurate identification. Similarly, two Other pit structures may represent variations on the Early Western theme.

Northern style pit structures are distinguished by the presence of a detached antechamber connected to the main chamber by a short passage; the main chambers are typically D-shaped, subsquare, or subrectangular with a three-quarter or encircling bench; upright-slab or post wing walls physically partition space (Shelley 1990,

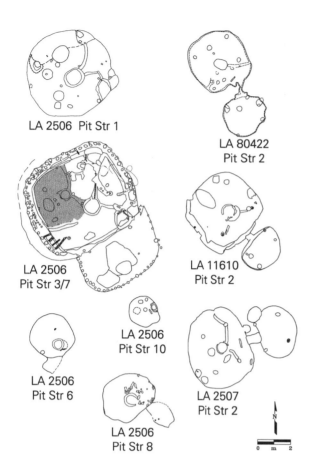

Figure 6.7. Examples of Tohatchi Flats pit structures: Early Western, upper left; Western, center left; Pocket and Other, lower left; Mixed, right.

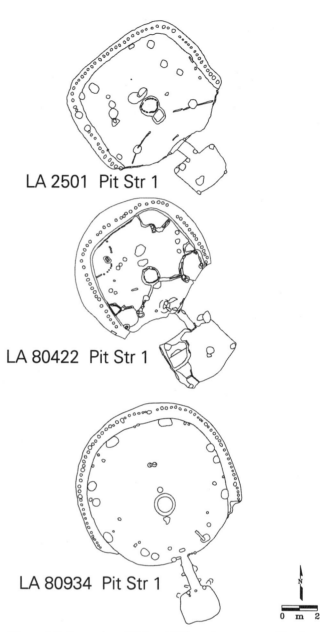

Figure 6.8. Examples of Tohatchi Flats pit structures: Northern, top and center; Great, bottom.

1991). Three of the Tohatchi Flats examples resemble Northern style structures but, contrary to Shelley's (1991:7) definition, have antechambers that are raised above the main chamber floor level and might better fit his Mixed style (see figure 6.8). Two other Tohatchi Flats examples are identified as "Modified Northern" pit structures. These examples approximate Northern style structures; one is subsquare, one is subrectangular, and both possess detached antechambers. Although one example has a raised platform in the southern portion of the main chamber, neither structure has wing walls or raised clay radials, and the antechambers are elevated above the main chamber.

Mixed style pit structures represent a combination of Northern and Western attributes (see figure 6.7). They are characterized by Northern style construction with a detached antechamber level with the main chamber floor, but are distinguished by the presence of Western style raised clay radials, not slab wing walls (Shelley 1990, 1991). Twelve Tohatchi Flats structures (28 percent) are examples of the Mixed style, and depending on the rigor of definition, the three Northern examples and two

Modified Northern examples might also be classified as Mixed style structures.

The Western, Northern, and Mixed style structures and associated variants typify Basketmaker III residential architecture. The size, construction technique, central hearth, and, often, slab-lined bins and other floor features identify these structures as domestic pit houses.

Pocket style pit structures are typically small, often relatively deep, either lack floor features or generally only possess a hearth, and are frequently found in association with larger pit structures (Shelley 1991). Six Pocket style structures are present in the Tohatchi Flats sample. These are typically small (averaging 5.4 m²), and often shallow (averaging 0.5 m deep) circular to oval pit rooms without antechambers or ventilators (see figure 6.7). Floor features, if present, are rare and include hearths or surface burns and various posthole patterns. The small size and presence of interior hearths suggest that some of these structures functioned as supplementary living quarters or sheltered special-use locales (see Altschul and Huber, this volume); others may have served as storage facilities.

Seven Tohatchi Flats structures, classified as Other pit structures, have sufficient differences to preclude assignment to one of the four named styles. For example, one partly slab-lined pit structure (LA 2507: 53-1) is sub-triangular in plan with a large oval entry and only one floor feature, a hearth. The large size (21.4 m^2) of this structure precludes a Pocket style designation. Another example, a small (4.4 m^2) circular pit room lacking floor features (LA 80425:6), resembles the Pocket style but is distinguished by a small raised, detached antechamber. One structure (LA 2506-9) resembled the Early Western style but in place of raised clay radials had two features with raised adobe rims (a bell-shaped cist and a rectangular area) built against the eastern wall. The other examples in this category represent similar atypical expressions of pit structure architecture (see figure 6.7, LA 2506 Pit Structure 8). Six of the seven Other pit structures are from Muddy Wash or Early Tohatchi contexts and may be indicative of a greater range of architectural experimentation during the earlier Basketmaker III period. Five of the Other style structures have hearths. Collectively, these structures appear to include domiciles and special-use shelters.

Two extra large pit structures are present in the Tohatchi Flats sample. These "great" pit structures superficially resemble the Northern style pit structures (see figure 6.8). They are the largest structures in the Tohatchi Flats sample, with main chambers averaging 8.8 m in diameter (46 m^2). Both have relatively deep circular main chambers with three-quarter benches and vertical stringer posts. The large roof-support posts are set against the bench, not centered in the room quadrants. Both possess proportionally small detached antechambers, and both burned. Although two subsequent structures built into the depression of one example obliterated the central floor area (Harriman and McVickar 1996), the preserved attributes are similar to the other intact structure (Cunnar 1996a). The relatively few floor features in the intact example include a circular adobe-coped fire pit, an ash pit, a floor vault, and paired sipapus aligned along the central axis. Wing walls or raised clay radials are absent, but a short wall of post-reinforced adobe turtle-back construction extends 0.77 m off the southeast wall. Other floor features include possible pot rests or small postholes. A cache of Archaic and Basketmaker II projectile points and several stone eccentrics were found on the bench. The relatively large size of the structure, design of the roofing system, number and type

of floor features, and the absence of bins, storage pits, and other hallmarks of Basketmaker III domestic pit houses indicate that this structure was not a domicile.

Both of the great pit structures presumably represent integrative, communal, nonresidential edifices. Comparison of the Tohatchi Flats great pit structures with the few other excavated Basketmaker III–early Pueblo I examples (e.g., Baldwin 1939; Eddy 1966; Gilpin and Benallie, this volume; Lightfoot et al. 1988; Martin and Rinaldo 1939; Morris 1980; Roberts 1929) indicates several shared attributes: large size, circular shape, lack of bins and wing walls or raised clay radials, and limited numbers of floor features. Variability in great pit structure construction techniques are probably more closely related to the individual settings than to stylistic differences. The round shape probably represents a shared symbolic expression. Differences in interior features and floor plans among the excavated great pit structures may be tied to regional style or ritual requirements.

What are the implications of pit structure style for the Tohatchi Flats Basketmakers? At least three functional classes are represented: domestic pit houses, special-use sheltered space (e.g., menstrual huts, bachelor quarters, food-processing rooms, storage rooms), and communal or integrative structures. The variable occurrence of functionally diverse structures presumably reflects differences in the size and composition of the social unit(s) and the placement of settlements in the physical and cultural landscape. Also, it is likely that individual structure use was not static but changed to meet situational needs.

Can stylistic variation in Tohatchi Flats pit structures be used to identify regional affiliation? Shelley (1991) includes the Tohatchi Flats area within his Lukachukai variant. This should be indicated by the common occurrence of Western style pit structures in the study area. The range of styles represented by Tohatchi Flats pit structures is impressive, but no single style dominates the sample (figure 6.9). Pocket pit structures appear to be a pan-Basketmaker III phenomenon (Shelley 1991). Their relatively common occurrence in the Tohatchi Flats sample may be related to use as ancillary domiciles or sheltered space. Similarly, great pit structures (great kivas) are a pan-Basketmaker III architectural style (e.g., Gilpin and Benallie, this volume; Vivian 1990). The relatively infrequent occurrence of great pit structures in Tohatchi Flats presumably reflects communal use. Assuming that the Pocket and great pit structure styles crosscut regional variants, their presence in Tohatchi Flats is not incongruous.

Several explanations may account for the variable occurrence of Western, Northern, Mixed, and Other pit structure styles in Tohatchi Flats: (1) the styles may not be indicative of regional variants but were instead dictated by other ethnic, sociopolitical, or religious association; (2) Tohatchi Flats may have represented a

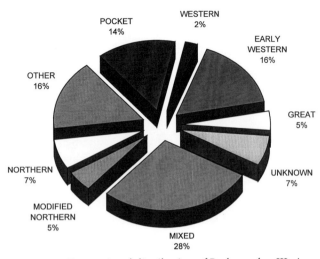

Figure 6.9. Proportional distribution of Basketmaker III pit structure styles in Tohatchi Flats.

"melting pot" of Basketmaker III settlers with diverse origins; or (3) the stylistic differences may be temporal. This latter suggestion, while probably not the sole explanation, does account for much of the stylistic variability in the sample (figure 6.10). Western style structures are an early phenomenon associated with the Muddy Wash

phase and, to a lesser extent, with the Early Tohatchi phase. Mixed style structures appear to be transitional; most are associated with the Early Tohatchi phase, but a small proportion occurs equally in Muddy Wash and Late Tohatchi contexts. Northern style structures are generally late, occurring in equal proportions in Early and Late Tohatchi contexts. Mixed and Northern style pit structures are the predominant styles during the A.D. 600s (Tohatchi phase) in the Mexican Springs area (Kotyk 1999). Although sample size and possibly inaccurate temporal assignments may be skewing the data somewhat, Tohatchi Flats pit structures appear to have generally evolved, through time, from the Western style to the Northern style.

Identifying temporal change does not, however, explain why or how the transformation occurred. Regional interaction may have played a role in the variability evident in the sample. Ceramic and lithic data indicate the Tohatchi Flats populations maintained alliances or exchange relations with groups to the south and north. The influx of ideas or individuals (e.g., through marriage) may have influenced the design template of vernacular architecture. Alternatively, or concurrently, pit structure styles may have changed as a result of population dynam-

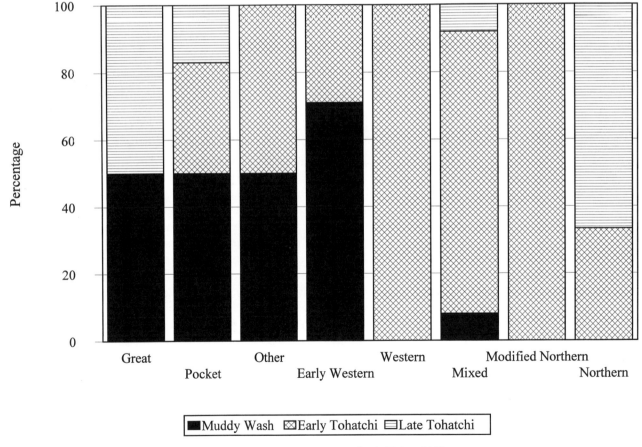

Figure 6.10. Temporal distribution of Basketmaker III pit structure styles in Tohatchi Flats.

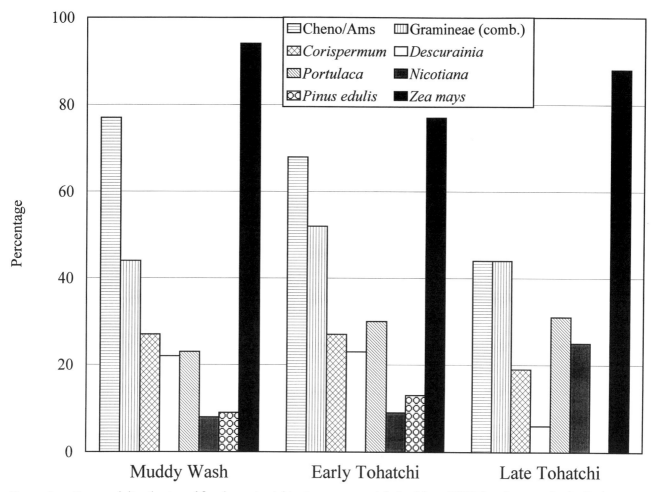

Figure 6.11. Temporal distribution of floral remains (ubiquity percentage) derived from NSEP flotation samples for Basket-maker III sites in Tohatchi Flats.

ics. The temporal control over the length and periodicity of settlement at individual communities, and in Tohatchi Flats in general, is coarse. The tempo or scale of population movement during the Basketmaker III period is unknown. It is conceivable that the movement of households or groups of households in and out of the valley was considerably more fluid than currently envisioned (e.g., Wilshusen and Ortman 1999).

The pit structure sample from Tohatchi Flats most closely resembles the variability in the sample from Chaco Canyon (Truell 1986). Shelley (1991) places Tohatchi Flats within his Lukachukai variant. Vivian (1990:114) includes Chaco Canyon and Tohatchi Flats within the La Plata variant, an areal expression that also includes the Northern San Juan or Mesa Verde region (i.e., Shelley's Northern variant). The similarity between the Chaco Canyon and Tohatchi Flats pit structures and the relatively common occurrence of the Mixed Style in both areas may be indicative of the emergence of a San Juan Basin variant. Chaco Canyon and Tohatchi Flats also share a common ceramic tradition, one that is distinct from the Northern San Juan region.

SUBSISTENCE

Increasing dependence on cultigens is commonly cited as one factor in the origin of the Basketmaker III lifeway, and for the subsequent pit house to pueblo transition (e.g., Cordell 1984:231–233; Gilman 1987; Vivian 1990:111, 132). In this section we examine the role of cultigens and wild resources in the subsistence economy of the Tohatchi Flats Basketmaker III population.

Tohatchi Flats is characterized by ample arable land and is well watered during favorable climatic regimes. Also, access to mountain and lowland biotic communities is relatively easy. Evidence from the NSEP investigations indicates reliance by the Basketmaker III populations on these settings for wild food resources and agricultural produce. Biotic and other remains from NSEP sites in Tohatchi Flats indicate that the resource base remained moderately stable throughout the Basketmaker III period, although, as elsewhere in the region (Bray 1982; A. C. Reed 1999; Ruppé 1989), change in biotic resource use is evident. The composition of botanical and faunal assemblages, measurements of milling equipment, and percentages of projectile points from excavated sites are used to characterize subsistence resource use and change during the Basketmaker III period.

Ubiquity percentages of charred seeds and other potentially edible plant remains recovered from flotation samples were calculated by temporal period to demonstrate change and continuity in the relative importance of these taxa (figure 6.11). Poorly represented taxa were omitted, and some taxa were combined for graphic clarity (e.g., *Chenopodium* and *Amaranthus* are described as Cheno-Ams, and grasses as the combination group Gramineae). Ubiquities and percentages of faunal remains also were calculated, along with counts and percentages of ground stone artifacts and projectile points.

Maize is present in 94 percent of the 107 flotation samples from Muddy Wash phase contexts, providing clear evidence for a commitment to maize agriculture during this period (see figure 6.11). Wild plants also played a significant role in the subsistence of the early residents. *Chenopodium* (goosefoot) seeds are present in 77 percent of the samples, grasses are in 44 percent, and at least four other wild plant resources, while less abundant, were consistently used. The analytical results show a decline in the relative percentage of maize in the 116 Early Tohatchi phase samples. Goosefoot seeds also evidence a moderate decline during this interval, and grass seeds increase. Although the Late Tohatchi phase sample is smaller (*n* = 16), the data indicate the relative occurrence of maize had rebounded almost to Muddy Wash phase levels, goosefoot seed ubiquity evidenced a sharp decrease, and grasses declined slightly. Sample size may be a factor; however, the change in resource ubiquity also may reflect variability in the exploitation of plant food resources. The reliability of the NSEP data is supported by comparable data from 194 flotation samples from Late Tohatchi phase contexts in the Mexican Springs area (Brandt 1999).

Causes for the observed variability in food resource use often are difficult to identify in the archaeological record. Differential preservation and sampling strategy are critical factors, but others include population dynamics, changes in food preparation and consumption behavior, changes in land use or accessibility, and variations in food resource exchange. Climatic change also may have affected subsistence resource use in the study area. The modest decline in maize during the Early Tohatchi phase may be indicative of a climatic downturn between ca. A.D. 610 and 635 (see figure 6.3; Dean et al. 1985; Plog et al. 1988: figure 8.1). Arid conditions and a depressed water table may have resulted in reduced maize yields and required increased reliance on wild food resources. Wild plants tend to be more resistant to high-frequency climatic change.

The increase in maize percentage in Late Tohatchi contexts may coincide with periods of greater effective moisture in the latter A.D. 600s (see figure 6.3) or may be indicative of more favorable growing conditions along the elevated margins of Tohatchi Flats. There is also an increase in tobacco (*Nicotiana* sp.) seed ubiquity after the Early Tohatchi phase. Explanations for this increase are not readily evident, although expanded ritual use of tobacco for rain and crop increase ceremonies is plausible.

Faunal remains are a common constituent in the NSEP assemblages and indicate routine use of animal resources by the Tohatchi Flats Basketmakers (Rippel and Walth 1999). Although small mammals are a consistent component of the Basketmaker III faunal assemblages, reliance upon small mammals is most prevalent during the Early Tohatchi phase. The proportion of jackrabbits is highest in the Early Tohatchi phase interval, as are most of the small mammals, including prairie dogs. Percentages of ubiquity indicate that cottontail rabbit remains occur in roughly the same proportions in Muddy Wash and Early Tohatchi phase assemblages, and they decrease sharply in Late Tohatchi phase assemblages. The increase in most small- and medium-sized mammals during the Early Tohatchi phase may reflect an adaptive response to the decline in botanical resources. Large mammals (e.g., deer and antelope), albeit a small percentage of all the assemblages, were more common in the Muddy Wash and Early Tohatchi phase sites and less common in the Late Tohatchi phase sites. Conversely, large bird remains (including turkeys) are relatively scarce in the early assemblages and are most numerous in Late Tohatchi phase sites. Basketmaker III sites from central Black Mesa (Bray 1982), Redrock Valley (McVicker 1999; Zunie and Hildebrant 1989), Chaco Canyon (Akins 1984), and the southern portion of the San Juan Basin (Brown and Brown 1993) show similar patterns in the relative abundance of small and large mammal remains, although the temporal resolution in these areas is not as refined as in Tohatchi Flats.

The proportion of projectile points in the Basketmaker III flaked stone tool assemblages is used as a proxy measure of the relative importance of hunting in the subsistence economy. The percentages of projectile points from Tohatchi Flats Basketmaker III site assemblages decrease from the early to late components (Kearns 1999a; Kearns and Silcock 1999). Projectile points comprise 13 percent of the Muddy Wash phase flaked tool assemblage, 8 percent of the Early Tohatchi phase assemblage, and only 0.8 percent of the Late Tohatchi phase assemblage. These figures suggest a decline in hunting by Tohatchi Flats Basketmaker III groups through time. The decline in importance of large mammals during the Basketmaker III period parallels the descending numbers of projectile points. Small mammal procurement, significant throughout the period, is more reliant on snares, clubs, and other procurement strategies than on bow and arrow hunting.

The size of milling equipment is another proxy measure of Basketmaker III subsistence practices. Although change in milling equipment size may represent a shift in grinding technology rather than a functional change (Adams 1993), the generally consistent appearance of milling equipment throughout the Basketmaker III period suggests that size differences most likely reflect change in grinding efficiency. Increase in milling equipment size provides greater freedom of movement across the grinding surface and relieves the stress of repetitive grinding movement. Analysis of the NSEP assemblages indicates that the average length of two-hand manos decreased during the Early Tohatchi phase but was identical for the earlier and later assemblages. The average two-hand mano width stayed relatively constant. Both the average length and width of hand stones, or one-hand manos, decreased slightly and consistently through time. Generally, one-hand manos and hand stones are used for grinding small seeds, cracking nuts, and processing other foods (Mauldin 1993). Two-hand manos are typically associated with maize processing.

Average metate width increased somewhat by the Late Tohatchi phase following a slight decrease in metate width and the slight drop in two-hand mano length during the Early Tohatchi phase. Conversely, metate lengths slightly increased between the Muddy Wash and Early Tohatchi phases before sharply increasing in the Late Tohatchi phase. Milling stones or slabs increase notably in length and width from Early to late Basketmaker III, but are the smallest during the Early Tohatchi phase. The general slight decrease in the average size of milling tools during the Early Tohatchi phase coincides with the drop in maize in the flotation samples. The relative consistency in mano size, however, suggests that changes in processing requirements during the Basketmaker III period were minor (Mauldin 1993).

The botanical and faunal remains from the NSEP sites show that the Basketmaker III subsistence strategy was firmly based in maize cultivation and the exploitation of wild plant and animal resources from the valley floor and upland environments, and that this strategy was in place by the Muddy Wash phase (A. C. Reed 1999). The records indicate relatively minor changes during the Basketmaker III period. A small decline in maize in the Early Tohatchi phase is paralleled by a slight increase in the incidence of small mammal remains in the faunal assemblages, suggesting that the procurement of meat became more important in light of the drop of productivity in maize. The reduction of goosefoot seeds in the botanical assemblages throughout the Basketmaker III period suggests either an overall drop in productivity or declining interest in the harvest and consumption of this resource. Grass seed rises in value during the Early Tohatchi phase and stays nearly constant through the remainder of the Basketmaker III occupation. Increased

exploitation of grass seed may have served to offset declines in maize productivity. The pattern evident in the botanical and faunal records, albeit not perfect, may correlate with a period of depressed water tables, drought, and subnormal rainfall during the early A.D. 600s and a subsequent hypothesized shift to the better-watered valley margins.

INTERACTION AND EXCHANGE

The Basketmaker III farmers of Tohatchi Flats were never isolated. Contact, interaction, and exchange with other areas of the Southwest were in place from the onset of settlement in Tohatchi Flats. Imported goods such as ceramic vessels, lithic artifacts, mineral resources, and marine shell are present at Basketmaker III sites in the study area. Evidence of imported ceramic vessels includes sherds and whole vessels from the Northern San Juan (Mesa Verde) region, the northern Mogollon region, and the Kayenta region (L. Reed and Hensler 1998b). Nonlocal lithic tool materials include obsidian, primarily from Grants Ridge near Mount Taylor, Chinle chert (or yellow-brown spotted chert) from the Zuni Mountains, and Narbona Pass chert (formerly Washington Pass chert) from the Chuska Mountains (Kearns 1999b). Imported mineral resources include azurite, malachite, and turquoise, among others (Kearns 1999b). Marine shell, primarily *Olivella* sp. from the Pacific coast or Gulf of California, also was identified in Basketmaker III contexts, particularly in association with burials (Flores and Kearns 1996).

The focus here is on nonlocal ceramic and lithic artifacts and the implications for interaction with other areas. Sourcing mineral resources is problematical, and the likelihood that marine shell items were obtained by down-the-line exchange from multiple sources makes identifying specific routes of exchange for these materials difficult. Sourcing of lithic materials and ceramic vessels is more easily accomplished, and it is assumed that acquisition of these goods occurred through both direct and indirect trade networks with the source areas. Similar to importation of mineral resources and marine shell, however, it is also probable that some of the lithic materials and ceramic vessels were obtained through a series of down-the-line exchanges, and that the established ties associated with these goods are only indirectly related to the source areas.

Although we recognize the complexity of the mechanisms involved in establishing and perpetuating exchange networks (e.g., Blinman and Wilson 1994; Braun and Plog 1982; Lightfoot and Feinman 1982; Plog 1984; Toll 1985; Upham 1982; Wobst 1974) and the importance of placing Basketmaker III exchange in an overall cultural context (e.g., the spatial distribution of nonlocal materials and their association with local culture traits), the

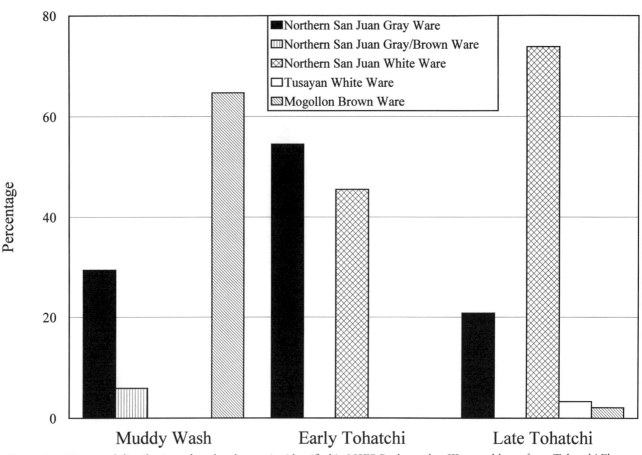

Figure 6.12. Temporal distribution of nonlocal ceramics identified in NSEP Basketmaker III assemblages from Tohatchi Flats.

focus of this discussion is on identifying nonlocal items in Basketmaker III assemblages from Tohatchi Flats, the direction of cultural ties represented by the sources of nonlocal artifacts, and changes in exchange networks from the Early to late Basketmaker III occupation.

Nonlocal Ceramic Vessels

Importation of ceramic vessels from areas outside of Tohatchi Flats began on a small scale early in the Basketmaker III period and increased in intensity throughout the occupation. Clay resources amenable to pottery production occur in the study area as layers in outcrops of the Cretaceous-age Menefee formation or as alluvial deposits derived from those layers. Clays sampled from these layers fire to predominantly yellowish red and red (L. Reed and Hensler 1998b). Locally available temper resources include medium- and coarse-grained sand from washes and sandstone outcrops. Petrographic and inductively coupled plasma arc spectrometry (ICP) analyses indicate that pottery was widely produced at the Basketmaker III sites. These studies demonstrate that most of the locally produced pottery was probably made with yellowish red-firing clays tempered with sand or crushed sandstone.

The NSEP Basketmaker III ceramic assemblage (*n* = 10,992 sherds) is predominantly Cibola series sherds (97 percent); Northern San Juan (Mesa Verde) series sherds

comprise 2 percent, and Mogollon and Tusayan series sherds comprise less than 1 percent each (L. Reed and Hensler 1998b). Although trade ware from Basketmaker III assemblages is represented by relatively few sherds compared to later periods, the presence of sherds from the Northern San Juan, Kayenta, and Mogollon regions suggests that ties with these areas were established early in the Anasazi occupation and that ceramic vessels from these regions were common trade items. There is also evidence to suggest that some of the Cibola series vessels in the assemblage were not locally produced but were imported from other areas of the San Juan Basin or beyond.

Vessels from the Northern San Juan region are present in assemblages from all three Basketmaker III temporal periods (figure 6.12). During the Muddy Wash phase, vessels from both the Northern San Juan and Mogollon regions include gray or brown ware types. Most of the nonlocal ceramics in Muddy Wash phase contexts are from the Mogollon region to the south. The absence of imported white ware vessels is not unexpected considering that during most of this early period the technology for painted vessels was undeveloped (L. Reed et al., this volume). By the Early Tohatchi phase, importation of vessels from the Mogollon region appears to decline accompanied by a significant increase in the importation of Northern San Juan Gray and White Ware vessels.

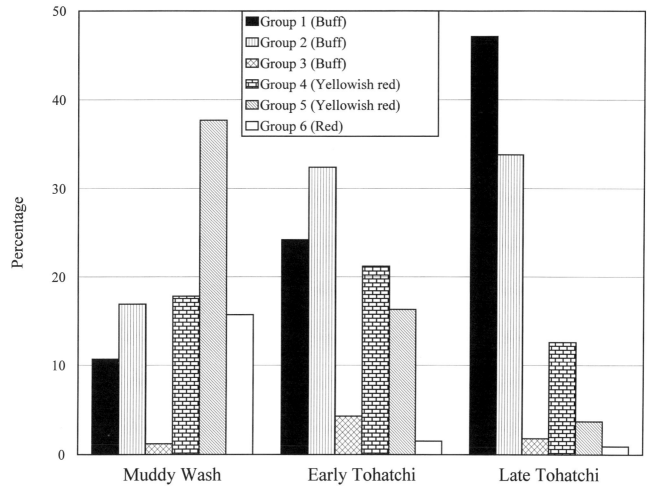

Figure 6.13. Temporal distribution of color groups for refired Cibola series sherds sampled from NSEP Basketmaker III assemblages from Tohatchi Flats. Color groups 1 through 6 correspond to those defined by Windes (1977): Color groups 1, 2, and 3 represent buff-firing clays; color groups 4 and 5 represent yellowish red–firing clays; and color group 6 represents red-firing clays. (Red color group 7 is not represented in the ceramic sample.)

Importation of white ware vessels from the Northern San Juan region increased dramatically during the Late Tohatchi phase. White ware vessels from the Kayenta region (i.e., Tusayan White Ware) were present in the assemblage for the first time, and Mogollon Brown Ware was present in much smaller proportions than in the Muddy Wash phase (see figure 6.12). The increase in imported white ware and a diversity of design styles suggest that nonlocal painted vessels were an important commodity, corresponding with the proliferation of painted design styles across the Colorado Plateau during the Early and Late Tohatchi phases. As suggested by other researchers in the Southwest (Hays 1992a; Hegmon 1995; S. Plog 1980; Robins and Hays-Gilpin, this volume), style (portrayed through painted designs on pottery, rock art, and textiles) may have been important for disseminating culturally meaningful symbols and identifying cultural groups or territories. The emphasis on imported white ware from the Northern San Juan region during the Late Tohatchi phase may have some connec-

tion with exchange of information through pottery designs.

Further evidence for importation of pottery vessels, involvement in exchange networks, and interaction with other Anasazi groups during the Basketmaker III period is found in the oxidation, petrographic, and ICP analyses of Cibola series sherds from NSEP sites. Given the established trade networks for Mogollon, Northern San Juan, and Tusayan ceramic vessels, it is not unexpected that Cibola series vessels were also imported into Tohatchi Flats from other areas. Most of the clay resources from the study area fire yellowish red to red; the few buff-firing clays identified are of poor quality and not amenable to pottery manufacture (L. Reed and Hensler 1998b). Accordingly, roughly 71 percent of the Muddy Wash phase Cibola series sherds refired to yellowish red or red colors (figure 6.13). The remaining sherds refired to buff colors, suggesting that at least some of the vessels were produced outside of Tohatchi Flats. The NSEP petrographic and ICP analyses support the oxidation data from the Muddy Wash phase assemblage and suggest that the ceramic technology for gray/brown and gray ware vessels during this period was experimental (see L. Reed and Hensler 1998b; L. Reed et al., this volume). Potters appear to have been experimenting with local raw materials in an attempt to produce harder, more durable ceramic vessels.

By the Early Tohatchi phase, vessels produced with yellowish red- and red-firing clays decreased, and Cibola series vessels from Tohatchi Flats were more commonly produced with buff-firing clays. Sixty-one percent of the Early Tohatchi phase Cibola series sherds sampled for oxidation analysis refired to buff colors, more than doubling that of the Muddy Wash phase (see figure 6.13). The percentage of red-firing sherds decreases to less than 2 percent by the Early Tohatchi phase. L. Reed and Hensler (1998b) note that the petrographic and ICP data for sites dating to the Early Tohatchi phase support, for the most part, the oxidation data. They suggest that although experimentation with local clay and temper resources continued into the Early Tohatchi phase, in most cases the ICP analysis showed very few matches between local clays and Cibola series sherds.

Increased usage of Cibola series wares of buff-firing clays continued into the Late Tohatchi phase. Eighty-three percent of the Cibola series sherds sampled from Late Tohatchi phase assemblages refired to buff colors (see figure 6.13). Less than 20 percent of the sherds sampled from the study area indicate use of locally available yellowish red- and red-firing clays for pottery production. The refiring data (see figure 6.13), the petrographic data, and the ICP data indicate that, despite experimentation with local resources, the Tohatchi Flats inhabitants were importing significant numbers of Cibola series vessels from other areas in the San Juan Basin or beyond. White, gray, and red ware vessels were produced with buff-firing clays that are scarce in the study area, suggesting that all ware categories were imported into Basketmaker III sites (particularly Early and Late Tohatchi phase sites).

Nonlocal Lithic Raw Materials

Good-quality raw material occurs in outwash deposits along the western periphery of the southern Chuska Valley and on most elevated landforms in Tohatchi Flats (Kearns 1999b). Sandstone, quartzitic sandstone, quartzite, chert, fossiliferous chert, silicified wood, and siltstone are common and represent abundant, easily accessed materials well suited for tool manufacture. Variability in the raw materials used for stone tool manufacture is overshadowed, however, by the overwhelming use of silicified wood for flaked stone tools, and sandstone for ground stone tools, both of which are abundant locally.

Three distinctive nonlocal lithic materials were iden-tified in the Basketmaker III assemblages used for this study: Narbona Pass chert, obsidian, and Chinle chert (Kearns 1999b). Narbona Pass chert (formerly Washington Pass chert) was the closest of the three nonlocal lithic resources to Tohatchi Flats. The typically orangish pink cryptocrystalline material outcrops in the Chuska Mountains in the Narbona Pass vicinity ca. 25 km to the north-northwest and in other localized areas farther north. This distinctive tool stone is commonly identified in Anasazi assemblages from the San Juan Basin (Cameron 1984; Jacobson 1984; Marshall et al. 1979; Powers et al. 1983; Vierra 1993b).

Chinle chert is one of several terms that have been applied to a distinctive yellow-brown or butterscotch chert with black spots that occurs in the Zuni Mountains on the southern periphery of the San Juan Basin (Cameron 1984:141; Green 1985:74; Jacobson 1984:32; Powers et al. 1983:328; Vierra 1993b:163). Chinle chert is also routinely recovered from Anasazi sites in the San Juan Basin (Cameron 1984; Jacobson 1984; Marshall et al. 1979; Powers et al. 1983).

X-ray fluorescence of obsidian (the third nonlocal tool stone) from the Basketmaker III assemblages indicated that the source of most (88 percent) of the obsidian was Grants Ridge near Mount Taylor (Kearns 1999c). Other sources identified in the analysis—including Cerro del Medio, Canovas Canyon, Polvadera Peak, No Agua Peak, and Red Hill—collectively comprise only 12 percent of the Basketmaker III obsidian. Most of the analyzed obsidian from these other sources occurs in Muddy Wash contexts. Obsidian originating from the Grants Ridge source increases in frequency from the early to late Basketmaker III period. The high proportion of Grants Ridge obsidian in Basketmaker III contexts and the occurrence of unmodified Grants Ridge nodules in Basketmaker III sites may be indicative of either exchange or direct procurement.

Despite differences in the number of stone artifacts recovered from Archaic ($n = 4092$), Basketmaker II ($n = 5769$), and Basketmaker III ($n = 40,671$) NSEP contexts, a dramatic proportional increase in the use of all three exotic lithic materials is evident during the Basketmaker III period (Kearns 1999b). The frequency of Narbona Pass chert, Chinle chert, and obsidian in the Basketmaker III flaked stone assemblage indicates that nonlocal materials had assumed a more significant role in the lithic material procurement strategy than in the earlier periods (see Torres, this volume, for a contrasting view). The exotic lithic materials introduced into Tohatchi Flats are not significantly superior, technically, to many of the local lithic resources, and their presence does not appear to have been dictated by the demand for a scarce commodity (e.g., siliceous material with good conchoidal fracture). The routine use of Narbona Pass chert, obsidian, and Chinle chert for mundane utilitarian tasks is exem-

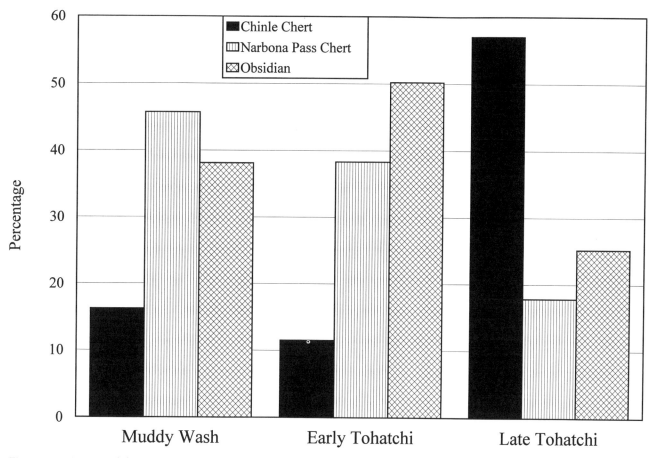

Figure 6.14. Temporal distribution of nonlocal lithic raw materials identified in NSEP Basketmaker III assemblages from Tohatchi Flats.

plified by a high proportion of utilized flakes and other expedient informal tools made from these materials. Also, much of the material was discarded without apparent effort to prolong the use life of the tool or maximize the potential value of the material. These findings suggest that the material itself was not imbued with any exceptional significance. Rather, as demonstrated ethnographically (Paton 1994), the acquisition of exotic materials may have served a symbolic or integrative role rather than being a utilitarian necessity. The casual use and cavalier discard of much of the exotic lithic material may have functioned merely to perpetuate the exchange system and the established social ties.

Temporal change is evident in the distribution of nonlocal lithic materials during the Basketmaker III period (figure 6.14). During the Muddy Wash phase, chert from Narbona Pass and obsidian from Grants Ridge and other sources are the most common nonlocal materials. Chinle chert is present in assemblages from this early period, but comprises less than 20 percent of the nonlocal lithic material. In Early Tohatchi phase sites, the proportional use of Chinle chert and Narbona Pass chert diminishes slightly, and the proportional use of obsidian (primarily Grants Ridge) increases. A dramatic change is evident by the Late Tohatchi phase, when importation and use of

Chinle chert increased by almost 40 percent, making it the most common nonlocal material at Late Tohatchi phase sites. These data show general continuity in the distribution of nonlocal lithic materials between the Muddy Wash and Early Tohatchi phases, and significant differences by the Late Tohatchi phase. The shift in the relative proportions of nonlocal lithic resources in the Late Tohatchi phase indicates, at least superficially, increased interaction with groups to the south, and reduced interaction with groups to the southeast and north.

Shifting Patterns of Exchange

The presence of nonlocal ceramic and lithic artifacts in assemblages from Tohatchi Flats implies active participation by the local Basketmaker III population in widespread exchange networks and, by extension, alliance networks. Although these exchange networks were in place by the Muddy Wash phase, proportional differences through time are evident in the occurrence of nonlocal commodities. During the Muddy Wash phase, the proportions of Grants Ridge obsidian, Chinle chert, and Mogollon ceramics imply ties to the south and southeast. The relative occurrence of Narbona Pass chert also indicates regular interaction with groups to the north along the Chuska Slope. The lower proportions of Northern

San Juan ceramics and Jemez Mountain obsidian indicate that ties further north and east, while evident, were less well developed. Also, the source(s) of the Cibola series vessels imported into Tohatchi Flats during this period remains equivocal.

During the succeeding Early Tohatchi phase, except for a reduction in Jemez Mountain obsidian, there were only slight proportional changes in the importation of nonlocal lithic materials. More conspicuous changes, however, were evident in the ceramic assemblage. Importation of Mogollon Brown Ware appears to have ceased, and exchange for Northern San Juan Gray and White Ware vessels increased dramatically. Also during the Early Tohatchi phase, the occurrence of buff-firing clays increases, suggesting that more Cibola series vessels were imported into the study area.

Another significant shift in exchange patterns appears to have occurred by the Late Tohatchi phase. Chinle chert, imported in proportionally small amounts during the Muddy Wash and Early Tohatchi phases, increases significantly during the Late Tohatchi phase and is accompanied by concomitant decreases in the proportions of obsidian and Narbona Pass chert. White ware and, to a lesser extent, gray ware vessels from the Northern San Juan region comprise the majority of imported ceramic vessels during this interval. Tusayan White Wares, appearing for the first time, and Mogollon Brown Wares are present, albeit in minor proportions. Also during the Late Tohatchi phase, Cibola series vessels produced with buff-firing clays increase dramatically.

The apparent differences in the relative occurrence of exotic ceramic and lithic artifacts from divergent sources indicate that these items circulated via independent networks. The proportional occurrence of nonlocal lithic and ceramic artifacts also implies directional shifts in exchange alliances from the Muddy Wash through Late Tohatchi phases. For example, differences in imported ceramics suggest weakened relationships with southern groups and a strengthening of interaction networks with populations farther north from the Muddy Wash to the Early Tohatchi phase. Conversely, exotic lithic artifacts indicate increasing ties to the south through time. If the paucity of Mogollon ceramics in Tohatchi phase assemblages is taken at face value, then relationships with groups to the south apparently diminished by the Early Tohatchi phase; however, the relatively robust presence of Grants Ridge obsidian during this interval and the subsequent dramatic increase in Chinle chert suggest otherwise. A possible explanation for the seemingly disparate evidence may be the increased technological sophistication of Cibola series ceramic wares by the Early Tohatchi phase. Although archaeological data are scant, the source areas for the southern lithic resources, Mount Taylor and the Zuni Mountains, were presumably within the Anasazi cultural sphere during the Basketmaker III

period (Vivian 1990:129–130). Conceivably, Mogollon ceramics from Muddy Wash phase contexts were obtained via down-the-line exchange along with the lithic materials from Cibola series pottery-producing Anasazi living in the Zuni Mountains and Mount Taylor areas. The Mogollon pottery of this period was technically superior to the early Basketmaker III plain ware and would have been a valued commodity. By the Early Tohatchi phase, however, the Anasazi potters were producing technologically comparable plain and decorated wares. It is possible that nonlocal Cibola series ceramics had replaced the Mogollon wares as exchange commodities and, along with Grants obsidian and Chinle chert, were representative of continuing alliances between Tohatchi Flats and more southern Basketmaker III populations.

In summary, exchange networks were in place during the Muddy Wash phase between Basketmaker III farmers in Tohatchi Flats and contemporaneous populations to the north, south, and possibly, the east. These exchange networks continued throughout the Basketmaker III occupation and were indicative of broader social relationships or alliances. The presence of exotic materials from multiple sources suggests that the extralocal relationships maintained by the Tohatchi Flats Basketmaker III population were not narrowly focused but divergent.

DISCUSSION AND CONCLUSIONS

Tohatchi Flats was settled by early Basketmaker III populations around the beginning of the sixth century A.D. and was one of many early Basketmaker III residential locales on the Colorado Plateau (Wilson and Blinman 1994). Favorable climatic conditions, persisting throughout the first half of the sixth century, may have facilitated the colonization and population growth at Tohatchi Flats. Both stability and change are evident in Basketmaker III culture in the study area between its initiation in the early A.D. 500s and the A.D. 700s. Distinctive transformations in settlement, architecture, ceramic technology, other aspects of material culture, and subsistence occurred from the Muddy Wash to Late Tohatchi phases.

Paleoclimatic and, to a limited degree, floral and faunal data from the NSEP indicate that favorable climatic conditions persisted throughout most of the Muddy Wash phase. From the latter half of the sixth century through the first half of the seventh century, climatic conditions deteriorated and were characterized by a drop in effective moisture and a series of droughts. Erosion was severe, and arable lands may have been scarce. Because Tohatchi Flats appears to have been densely inhabited during this period (the Early Tohatchi phase), the effect of such a downturn should have been keenly felt.

A paucity of residential sites dating between ca. A.D. 630 and 700 in the Tohatchi Flats valley suggests a move sometime in the mid-seventh century to alternate locales.

Albeit tenuous, the apparent settlement decline, coupled with the appearance of populations at this time in the Mexican Springs area (see Damp and Kotyk, this volume), appears to represent the relocation of Basketmaker III households from the valley floor to the valley margins. Although internal community strife (Cameron 1990b:28; Stanislawski 1973) or other sociopolitical circumstances cannot be discounted as causal factors, the postulated relocation was, at least partly, an apparent response to deteriorating climatic conditions. Brief periods of greater effective moisture occurred during the mid and late A.D. 600s and could account for some Late Tohatchi phase settlement on the valley floor. A general deterioration of climatic conditions in the eighth century during the Basketmaker III–Pueblo I transition may have contributed to the development of aggregated villages in defensive locations.

Settlement data from the NSEP suggest that the Muddy Wash phase populations were organized into small hamlets of one to several households distributed across the valley. The settings were not defensive, and no evidence of stockades or other fortifications has been discovered. Although they vary in size, Muddy Wash phase pit structures were generally smaller than those of the succeeding Early and Late Tohatchi phases. A notable exception is an extra large pit structure, analogous to contemporary structures in Chaco Canyon (Roberts 1929; Windes 1975), which is tentatively identified as an early Basketmaker III nonresidential communal structure. The presence of this structure indicates that the organizational level of the Muddy Wash phase populations transcended the individual household.

The settlement system established during the Muddy Wash phase continued through the seventh and into the early eighth century. An increase in the number and size of residential sites in the early A.D. 600s suggests that significant population growth occurred during the Early Tohatchi phase. Although isolated residential sites may have been present at various times, the small hamlets of the Early and Late Tohatchi phases were typically clustered into larger, loosely aggregated communities. The presence of an extralarge Late Tohatchi phase pit house indicates continued integration of households at a community or village level of organization. Domestic pit structures vary in size during the Early and Late Tohatchi phases. Whereas variability in pit structure size may be related to the size of resident social units, differences due to status or rank distinctions cannot be entirely discounted. As in the preceding Muddy Wash phase, however, there is no discrete evidence for hierarchical social differentiation beyond what might be expected by achieved status.

Although the basic settlement system appears to have remained relatively constant throughout the Basketmaker III occupation of Tohatchi Flats, settlement location may have shifted through time. The Muddy Wash and Early Tohatchi phase habitations of the sixth and early seventh centuries were typically situated adjacent to arable land on elevated landforms in the valley. By the Late Tohatchi phase the residential sites appear to have been located along the periphery of Tohatchi Flats. Basketmaker III settlements in the Mexican Springs area, dating from the middle to late A.D. 600s (Damp 1999; Damp and Kotyk, this volume), support this postulated shift to the valley margins. The absence of earlier Basketmaker III residential sites in Mexican Springs and the relatively rapid population growth in that area further support an argument for a shift from the valley floor to the valley margin during the middle to late seventh century. Additionally, all of the other Basketmaker III pit structures along the valley margin that have been dated were constructed in the late seventh and early eighth centuries (Benham 1966; Cunnar 1996a; Harriman 1996). Coincident with the locational shift was the appearance of stockaded or fenced sites (Damp 1999; Damp and Kotyk, this volume). Strategic defensive locations, however, do not characterize the settlement, and a causal relationship of the stockades to strife remains equivocal.

Evidence from the NSEP investigations indicates that commitment to maize agriculture was well established by the Muddy Wash phase, and that reliance upon wild food resources also was common throughout the Basketmaker III period. Maize and wild seeds are abundant at Muddy Wash phase sites and are indicative of reliable arable lands and readily available wild food resources. During the Early Tohatchi phase, a decrease in the percentage of maize in flotation samples and an increase in wild grass seeds and small mammals suggest lower crop yields and an increased reliance upon hunting and gathering of wild resources. This shift in the degree of reliance upon farming, hunting, and gathering strategies appears to correspond to the climatic downturn documented for this period in the Tohatchi Flats region. The increase in Early Tohatchi phase populations early in the A.D. 600s, despite unfavorable conditions, may reflect the use of buffering strategies such as more intensive storage of harvested foods to offset environmental stress. Persistence of deleterious conditions, however, would have eventually reduced stored resources and could have resulted in a variety of cultural responses, including population relocation. Maize remains increased in the Late Tohatchi phase samples although wild resources continued to decline. The increase in maize may reflect better growing conditions along the valley flank or agricultural intensification. The unexpected increase of tobacco seeds in the late Basketmaker III flotation samples may be indicative of ritual behavior, possibly resulting from growing social and political complexity, increased population pressures, or environmental stress.

Architectural data from Tohatchi Flats show a

mixture of styles throughout the Basketmaker III period, but gradual change between the three temporal periods is evident. Comparison of the NSEP architectural data to pit house styles proposed by Shelley (1990, 1991) indicates that Muddy Wash phase pit houses generally correspond to the Western style, Late Tohatchi phase pit houses are similar to the Northern style, and the Early Tohatchi phase pit houses are more varied but have a predominance of the Mixed style. Specific architectural traits—including pit structure size, presence and style of antechambers, and the occurrence of internal and external features—also show considerable variability, although general trends through time are evident. The variability in the Tohatchi Flats sample probably results from a number of sociocultural factors. Stylistic variability, division of space for domestic activities, and the occurrence of certain additional features in contemporaneous pit houses may be attributed to pit house function. It is also likely that some variability was influenced by intermarriage between cultural groups, possibly a contributing factor in alliance formation and establishment, maintenance, and modification of exchange ties (see Hantman 1983; Plog 1983, 1984; Wobst 1974).

Changes in material culture also are evident during the Basketmaker III period. Changes are apparent not only in ceramic technology from the Muddy Wash to Late Tohatchi phases (L. Reed and Hensler 1998b; L. Reed et al., this volume), but also in projectile point style and frequency (Kearns and Silcock 1999), milling equipment size, and the exchange of nonlocal lithic raw materials and ceramic vessels. Examination of nonlocal ceramic vessels and lithic raw materials suggests that economic and social ties were complex and diversified. The evident extralocal interaction may reflect concurrent alliance formations with populations north and south of Tohatchi Flats.

Many variables operated to effect change in Basketmaker III culture in Tohatchi Flats. Environmental stress appears to have been an influencing element at various times, but other factors such as regional interaction, intra- and intercommunity strife, societal norms and tradi-tions, religious beliefs, economic considerations, and political structure undoubtedly precipitated changes during the Basketmaker III occupancy of Tohatchi Flats. Although some changes are evident from the data presented here, there is substantial data suggesting broad cultural continuity from the Muddy Wash through Late Tohatchi phases. This continuity is manifest in the commitment to maize agriculture, the degree of sedentism, the construction and use of great kivas, and the establishment of regional ties. In this chapter we have examined some aspects of the Basketmaker III occupation of Tohatchi Flats. The data for this dynamic cultural period are far from exhausted, and continued investigation in the area will certainly expand and modify the ideas we have presented.

ACKNOWLEDGMENTS

Numerous people along the way have contributed to this paper and to the data presented here. We would like to thank everyone who was involved in the NSEP, and we acknowledge their hard work and dedication. In particular, Western Cultural Resource Management, Inc. (Farmington office), and Animas Ceramic Consulting, Inc., provided technical support for production of the paper. Bob Estes contributed his time and expertise in Autocad to modify the locational map (figure 6.1), and Stephen Yost provided assistance with the NSEP database. Finally, we want to thank Paul Reed for compiling and editing the volume, and for his interest in the NSEP data.

NOTES

1. The term "community" as used in this paper is not synonymous with the definition for Chacoan or outlier communities (e.g., Powers et al. 1983). Rather, it implies a spatially discrete and loosely aggregated constellation of small hamlets.

2. The community of Twin Lakes is not in Twin Lakes, New Mexico, as the name suggests. The name is based on Johnson's (1962a) name for LA 2507. This is an unfortunate historic circumstance.

Part IV

Lukachukai to the Rainbow Plateau:
Basketmaker Archaeology
West of the Chuska Mountains

7

Economics, Site Structure, and Social Organization During the Basketmaker III Period

A View from the Lukachukai Valley

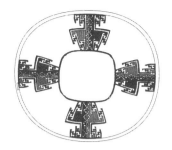

Jeffrey H. Altschul

Edgar K. Huber

Although new information acquired during the past decade has demanded a reexamination of traditional perceptions of Basketmaker III culture, a new theoretical consensus about its organization has been slow to emerge. The forces driving this process of reevaluation have come from two directions. First, new excavations have demonstrated the common occurrence of large Basketmaker III sites. Ten years ago, large Basketmaker III sites such as Shabik'eshchee Village in Chaco Canyon (Roberts 1929) and Juniper Cove near Kayenta, Arizona (Cummings 1953; Gilpin and Benallie, this volume; Haury 1928) were considered to be unusual, if not anomalous. Recent excavations by the Zuni Cultural Resources Enterprise near Mexican Springs on the eastern slope of the Chuska Mountains in New Mexico (Damp and Kotyk, this volume; Damp 1999; Kearns et al., this volume), by Complete Archaeological Service Associates (CASA) in the Dolores region of southwestern Colorado (Morris 1991), and by Statistical Research, Inc. (SRI) in the Lukachukai region of northeastern Arizona (Altschul and Shelley 1995; Altschul et al. 2000) have shown that large, complex Basketmaker III sites are not unusual and, indeed, may be fairly common over much of the Colorado Plateau (table 7.1; figure 7.1).

Second, the wealth of rapidly accumulating Basketmaker III data supports previous theories questioning accepted ideas and offering new notions about the organization of Basketmaker III society. In the mid-1970s, Birkedal (1976) presented a cogent argument using data from Mesa Verde suggesting that Basketmaker III pit structures were occupied by nuclear families and that the localized band probably constituted the maximal level of sociocultural integration. Birkedal's study largely reified and refined the notion of Basketmaker III society as characterized by small-scale, mostly nonaggregated, egalitarian social formations—a view long held by most

Southwestern scholars to be true not only for Basketmaker III on the Colorado Plateau, but in other parts of the Southwest as well. The inference was based on the observation that most Basketmaker III sites were composed of a small number of pit structures and extramural features; only a small social group, which Birkedal associated with families, could be represented. Birkedal acknowledged, however, that some Basketmaker III and early Mogollon sites were relatively large, composed not of three or four pit structures, but many times that number. He argued that such settlements were probably occupied by social formations larger than a primary band or by clusters of primary bands (Birkedal 1976:516).

The egalitarian model of Early Formative cultures in the Southwest was challenged in 1982 by Lightfoot and Feinman (1982). Using data from the Mogollon region at the southern margin of the Colorado Plateau, these authors suggested that the apparent increased size and complexity of early Mogollon pit house villages was largely a response to shifts in the political structure reflecting the development of leaders at a suprahousehold level. Such leadership roles could have developed in some villages because of their proximity to prehistoric trade routes and the need to control increased amounts of interregional trade. Lightfoot and Feinman (1982:78–90) cite Shabik'eshchee Village as evidence that the processes leading to social complexity were not isolated among the Mogollon, but also extended into the Anasazi region.

Based on worldwide ethnographic data, Gilman (1987) argued that pit structures were generally not used on a year-round basis (see also Flannery 1972). Instead, she posits that pit structures tend to be residences occupied in times other than the growing season; they were used primarily by groups not heavily dependent on agriculture and practicing a biseasonal settlement pattern. Gilman (1987:553) offered a settlement model based on

TABLE 7.1
Large Basketmaker III Sites on the Colorado Plateau

Designation	State	Characteristics	Last Tree-ring Date (A.D.)	References
Lukachukai (AZ E:12:5)	AZ	40+ pit structures, surface bins; probable communal structure	691	Altschul & Shelly 1995; Altschul et al. 2000; Robinson & Cameron 1991:4
Prayer Rock District sites (Broken Flute, Obelisk Cave, Red Rock Caves 1–8)	AZ	42+ pit structures in several caves; possible communal structure	676	Morris 1959, 1980; Berry 1982; Ahlstrom 1985; Robinson & Cameron 1991:4
Juniper Cove	AZ	10+ pit structures, surface bins; communal structure	678	Haury 1928; Cummings 1953; Vivian & Reiter 1965; Robinson & Cameron 1991:1
Antelope House	AZ	10+ pit structures, surface bins	776	Robinson & Cameron 1991:4
Klethla Valley (NA8163)	AZ	8 pit structures	555	Ambler & Olson 1977; Berry 1982; Robinson & Cameron 1991:3
Mesa Verde Site 110	CO	10+ pit structures, surface bins	730	Robinson & Cameron 1991:10
Earth Lodge B	CO	8 pit structures, surface bins	595	Rohn 1977:267–269; Robinson & Cameron 1991:10
5MT1	CO	10+ pit structures	676	Robinson & Cameron 1991:12
5MT3	CO	10+ pit structures	638	Robinson & Cameron 1991:12
Gilliland Site	CO	10+ pit structures	709	Robinson & Cameron 1991:12
5MT2525	CO	10+ pit structures, surface bins	644	Robinson & Cameron 1991:14
5MT4545	CO	10+ pit structures	598	Robinson & Cameron 1991:13
5MT8837	CO	10+ pit structures	494	Robinson & Cameron 1991:13
Ignacio Sites (17:10 & 17:12)	CO	10+ pit structures at each site	680	Robinson & Cameron 1991:15
Tohatchi Village	NM	35 pit structures, surface bins; large communal structure	N/A	Roberts 1929; Stuart & Gauthier 1981:90
Shabik'eschee Village	NM	68+ pit structures, surface bins; communal structure	581	Roberts 1929; Stuart & Gauthier 1981
Chaco 29SJ423	NM	7+ pit structures, surface bins; large communal structure	557	Windes 1975; McKenna 1986
Cerro Colorado	NM	25+ pit structures, extramural pits	737	Bullard 1962; Berry 1982; Ahlstrom 1985; Robinson & Cameron 1991:22
LA 16029	NM	10+ pit structures	778	Robinson & Cameron 1991:16
42SA6757	UT	10+ pit structures, surface bins	627	Robinson & Cameron 1991:27
Brew Site 13	UT	9+ pit structures, surface bins; communal structure	778	Brew 1946; Davis 1985:447; Robinson & Cameron 1991:24
42SA8889/8895	UT	10+ pit structures, surface bins; communal structure	684	Davis 1985:445–447; Robinson & Cameron 1991:26

the Western Apache that is applicable to Basketmaker III. She proposed that groups used pit structures primarily as winter residences and practiced residential mobility during the growing season. Gilman (1987:554) further argued that with increasing population and subsistence intensification, winter sedentism by such groups should be characterized by larger, more formal, and more standardized storage facilities.

Gilman's (1987) ideas were applied by Wills and Windes (1989) in a reassessment of the organizational

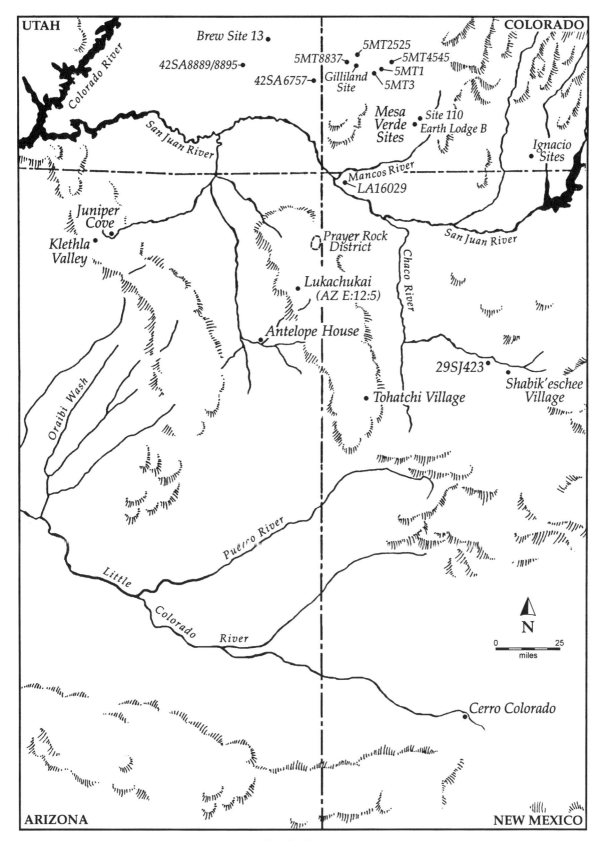

Figure 7.1. Large Basketmaker III sites on the Colorado Plateau.

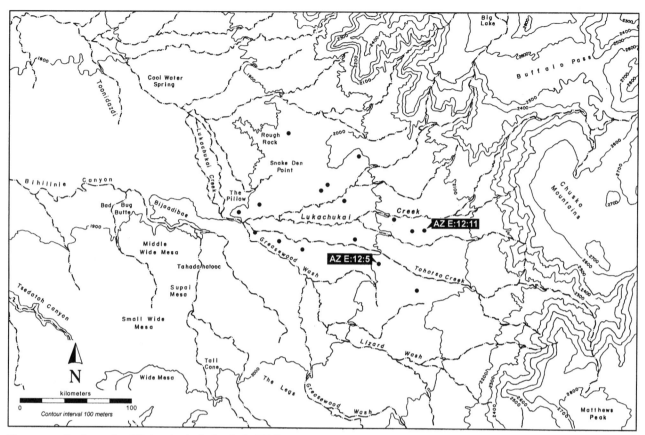

Figure 7.2. Basketmaker III sites in the Lukachukai Valley.

structure of Shabik'eshchee Village. Unlike Lightfoot and Feinman (1982), Wills and Windes (1989) found no evidence at Shabik'eshchee Village to support the development of institutionalized suprahousehold leadership. Rather, they argued that power was contextually based, emerging as the situation dictated. They believed that aggregations such as Shabik'eshchee Village were the exception rather than the rule. In their view, large Basketmaker III sites were not permanent settlements, except for those households in whose home range the aggregated settlements were located. Instead, they contended that the large, architecturally complex sites were seasonal aggregations that occurred only when locally available wild plant resources, especially piñon nuts, were exceptionally abundant.

A decade after Wills and Windes (1989) proposed these ideas, it is now clear that large Basketmaker III aggregations are not exceptional (see table 7.1), and this chapter explores the ways in which traditional notions of Basketmaker society and economy are challenged by the new data. To evaluate previous notions and to offer new ideas concerning village structure, economy, and social organization of Basketmaker III society, we use the results of a large-scale testing and data recovery program carried out by SRI along Navajo Route 13 (N13) near Lukachukai, Arizona (Altschul and Shelley 1988, 1995; Altschul et al. 2000). In particular, we focus on AZ

E:12:5 (ASM) (hereinafter the suffix ASM is dropped), a large, complex Basketmaker III site, bringing in examples from other Basketmaker III sites in the Lukachukai Valley as needed.

THE STRUCTURE OF A LARGE BASKETMAKER III SITE: AZ E:12:5

Site AZ E:12:5 is located on a ridge overlooking the south bank of Tohotso Creek (figure 7.2). The site was originally recorded in the early 1980s by Popelish and Fehr (1983) of the Navajo Nation Archaeology Department in response to proposed road construction along N13. Popelish and Fehr (1983) located eight discrete loci within the proposed right-of-way (ROW) and designated each as a separate site.

In 1986, the Bureau of Indian Affairs contracted with SRI to conduct evaluation and data recovery at 23 sites along the proposed alignment of N13. Upon evaluation, the eight sites on the ridge originally documented by Popelish and Fehr (1983) were combined into a single site labeled AZ E:12:5 that encompassed an area of 300,000 m², covering most of the ridge crest and slope above Tohotso Creek (Altschul and Shelley 1988). The ROW covered about 12,000 m², or 4 percent of the total site area. As part of the project, the entire ROW on top of the ridge was mechanically stripped, thereby exposing

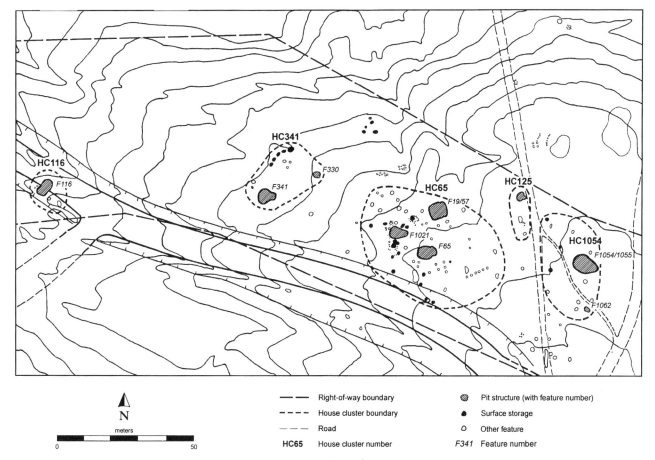

Figure 7.3. House clusters at AZ E:12:5 (ASM). Contour interval is 2 feet.

most, if not all, features in that area. Another 500 m² was visible in an existing northsouth road cut through the southern portion of the site. A variety of obtrusive features, such as room blocks and rock concentrations, were also visible throughout the site area. In all, we estimate that features from about 5 percent of the site were plainly visible on the surface. Excavations were undertaken in and near these features within the proposed ROW.

SRI recorded 390 features at AZ E:12:5 (Altschul et al. 2000). Of these, 40 are historic Navajo dating from the early A.D. 1800s through the mid-1900s, 11 are affiliated with a Pueblo II–III occupation of the Tohotso Creek area, and 333 are known or suspected to date to the Basketmaker III period. Of the features clearly identified as Basketmaker III, nine are pit structures, and one has been interpreted as a very large pit structure, a form of communal structure sometimes referred to as a great kiva. Other Basketmaker features noted at AZ E:12:5 included cists or bins (surface storage structures), hearths, pits of various kinds, post molds, burials, ambiguous rock concentrations, and ash stains. SRI excavated 62 of the Basketmaker III features. All nine pit structures in the ROW, each with a large complement of internal features, were excavated along with a large sample of extramural

features such as surface storage structures, hearths, middens, burials, and pits.

Each pit structure, or series of related pit structures, can be associated with several extramural features based on spatial proximity. We term these groups of related pit structures and extramural features "house clusters." Unlike some other Basketmaker III sites (Shabik'eshchee Village, for example), house clusters at AZ E:12:5 tended to be relatively discrete and were usually separated from similarly defined clusters by areas largely devoid of features (figure 7.3).

In the ROW, five such house clusters have been defined. Figure 7.3 illustrates the house clusters at AZ E:12:5, and table 7.2 lists the tree-ring or ceramic and architectural cross dates for each pit structure. The tree-ring dates comprise a cluster of cutting dates and represent construction date estimates along with possible remodeling or repair events.

AZ E:12:5 was occupied from at least A.D. 600 into the 700s, perhaps as late as A.D. 750. Based on fill sequences in excavated pit structures and changes in pit structure architecture, there might have been an occupational hiatus sometime after A.D. 670 and prior to a reoccupation during the early A.D. 700s. Construction and remodeling or repair events indicate that it was unlikely

TABLE 7.2
Probable Pit Structure Construction and Repair Dates at AZ E:12:5

Household Cluster No.	Pit Structure Feature No.	Probable Date of Construction	Possible Date of Repair	Occupation Span	Repair Occupation Span
65	65	A.D. 602	none indicated	A.D. 602–617	—
	1021	A.D. 624–625	late A.D. 630s	A.D. 624–639	A.D. 640–645
	19/57	A.D. 644–645	early A.D. 660s	A.D. 645–660	A.D. 661–666
1054	1054/1055	A.D. 620s–630s	none indicated	A.D. 630–645+	—
	1062 (Pocket)	A.D. 649	unknown	A.D. 649–664	—
341	341	A.D. 650s	none indicated	A.D. 655–670	—
	330 (Pocket)	pre 750	unknown	unknown	—
125	125	700-750	unknown	unknown	—
116	116	700-750	unknown	unknown	—

Note: Pit structure occupation span is calculated at 15 years (Ahlstrom 1985; Cameron 1990a, 1990b; Schlanger 1985). Repair span is for a moderate repair event resulting in a 5-year extension of structure use-life.

that more than one to three house clusters were ever occupied simultaneously during most of the occupation within the ROW (see table 7.2).

House cluster layout appears to have remained relatively stable throughout most of the occupation. Extramural features—surface structures (large, shallow bins and cists), hearths, and storage pits—were generally located in an arc to the north, west, and south of pit structures, and rarely, if ever, to the east. This pattern appears to be typical of most, if not all, Basketmaker III sites (Kane 1986; Lipe and Breternitz 1980; McKenna 1986; Roberts 1929), and it may first have appeared in late Basketmaker II contexts (Dohm 1994; Matson et al. 1988). This spatial arrangement of pit structures, surface storage facilities, and other extramural features has been related to the positioning of specific household activities (Lipe and Breternitz 1980). At AZ E:12:5, for example, primary storage and outdoor food-preparation activities appear to have taken place along the sides of and behind the houses. Large storage facilities, termed "bins," were placed either as a contiguous row of features or in close proximity to one another to the west or northwest of pit structures. At House Cluster 65, posts were found northwest of the westernmost pit structure. Altschul and Shelley (1995:4–156) suggested that these posts supported a ramada that provided shelter for cooking and food-processing activities carried out nearby in a series of hearths and roasting pits. A similar set of features was found west of the large pit structure in House Cluster 341.

Pit structure entrances at AZ E:12:5 tended to open to the east. The area immediately to the southeast and east of the pit structures was generally clear of features (see figure 7.3), leading us to infer that these areas were preferentially kept clear of extramural features, perhaps because they were used as some type of communal gathering or similar use area. Support for this notion was found at House Cluster 65, where two rows of posts

were found that appear to have enclosed the area east of the pit structures, separating this house cluster from others. Similar stockade or pen-like features have been found at other Basketmaker III sites (see Chenault and Motsinger; Damp and Kotyk; Vivian; all this volume) and have been variously interpreted as defensive stockades, property or residential boundaries, or animal pens. We find little to support the idea that the enclosures at AZ E:12:5 were used for defensive purposes. There is nothing in the material culture or in the mortuary evidence to suggest that warfare or raiding was a primary concern. Moreover, the use of enclosures at one house cluster and not others, some of which are clearly contemporaneous, is inconsistent with a village-wide concern with defense. A cache of turkey bones was found in the pit structure immediately east of the posts. Clearly, inhabitants of this house cluster had access to these animals.

The typical Anasazi refuse-disposal pattern that began in Basketmaker III times, in which middens were placed to the east of structures, is not apparent at AZ E:12:5. Secondary refuse was found primarily as thin sheet deposits that could not readily be associated with a particular house cluster. Refuse was also found in abandoned structures, most of which were burned (Altschul et al. 2000).

All five house clusters contained at least one large pit structure that was 5–6 m in diameter. House Cluster 65 contained multiple large pit structures, and House Clusters 341 and 1054 were composed of a large pit structure and a second, small pit feature. Shelley (1991) termed the small pit features "Pocket pit houses," following terminology used at the Dolores Archaeological Program excavations in southwestern Colorado (Kane 1986). These small structures were 2–3 m in diameter and substantially smaller than the Grass Mesa subphase pit structures for which the term was first coined (Brisbin and Varien 1986; Kane 1986; Kane and Gross 1986). One of the Pocket pit houses at AZ E:12:5 contained a hearth, but the two pit structures were otherwise devoid of internal features.

Shelley (1991) observed that Basketmaker III Pocket pit houses were frequently found in association with larger pit structures. The situation at AZ E:12:5, however, is not clear. Because the small pit structures at House Clusters 341 and 1054 were not well dated, the issue of contemporaneity cannot be resolved (see table 7.2). If the Pocket pit houses were contemporary with the larger pit structures, then it is possible that the smaller features might have been used for specialized functions, such as menstrual huts or bachelor's houses. If the small structures were later than nearby large pit structures, they might represent short-term reoccupations, perhaps to maintain land tenure rights (Adler 1990) or to be used as logistical camps to pursue agricultural or other economic activities.

House Cluster 65 was unique at AZ E:12:5 in containing three large pit structures and no Pocket pit houses. It is possible that a coeval domestic cycle is represented with houses being added as the social unit expanded (Birkedal 1976; Hayes and Lancaster 1975; Kane 1986). A more likely explanation, however, and one that is supported by the tree-ring evidence, is that the structures were used sequentially. As one structure reached the end of its structural use life of approximately 15 years (Ahlstrom 1985; Cameron 1990a, 1990b; Schlanger 1985), another structure was built nearby (see table 7.2).

In sum, the evidence from AZ E:12:5 indicates that the basic architectural unit consisted of a single large pit structure that functioned as a primary habitation, and associated storage, food-preparation, and other activity-related features. Most of the house clusters at AZ E:12:5 (see figure 7.3) appear to represent single occupations, as the entire unit was evidently abandoned along with the main pit structure (House Clusters 116, 125, and 341). House Cluster 65, however, demonstrates that some areas were favored, so that when one large pit structure was abandoned, another was constructed in the same unit. Although most house clusters were probably occupied for no more than 15 to 20 years, others, such as House Cluster 65, might represent more-or-less continuous, seasonal, or permanent occupations for as long as 50 to 60 years. Household residential stability spanning two or more generations is certainly implied.

SEDENTISM AND SETTLEMENT

Did the Basketmaker III residents of AZ E:12:5 occupy the settlement year-round, or did they live there only in the winter of economically favorable years, as argued by Wills and Windes (1989) for Shabik'eshchee Village? Although few plant remains were recovered that bear directly on the issue of seasonality, phytolith, pollen, and macrofossil data from features and pit structures at AZ E:12:5 consistently point to a strong emphasis on maize agriculture accompanied by less-intensive squash cultivation. A variety of wild plant foods complemented the cultivated foods (Bozarth 2000; Johnson and Brooks 2000). Faunal data from sampled contexts at AZ E:12:5 were relatively scant, but on the whole are consistent with a traditional Basketmaker III pattern emphasizing deer and rabbit and moderate use of domesticated turkey (Shelley 2000).

It is not simply the proportion of maize to wild plants at AZ E:12:5 that is striking, but also its ubiquity. Maize, including many parts of the plant—cobs, kernels, stems, and stalks—was recovered throughout the site and from most feature types (Bozarth 2000). Emphasis on maize to this degree traditionally has been associated with the later Pueblo I through Pueblo III periods (Matthews 1986). As many chapters in this volume demonstrate, however, an economic system based on maize agriculture was widespread in Basketmaker III times (see Chenault and Motsinger; Damp and Kotyk; Geib and Spurr; Kearns et al.; P. Reed and Wilcox; Toll and Wilson; all this volume).

At AZ E:12:5, the most compelling evidence for year-round habitation came not from the evidence for a heavy reliance on maize agriculture, nor from the size, diversity, and complexity of the site's features. Instead, it was the emphasis on storage and the storage capacity of each house cluster that led us to the conclusion that AZ E:12:5 should be viewed as a primary village; that is, a habitation composed of multiple domestic groups, some members of which lived there year-round.

Storage features were found within pit structures and in extramural areas around them. The most striking extramural features at House Clusters 65 and 341 were rows of large, slab-lined surface bins (see figure 7.3). These features were so large that some had been interpreted as contiguous room-block segments prior to excavation. We found that each consisted of between two and four shallow, slab-lined structures that were closely spaced or sometimes contiguous. The bins averaged about 3 m^2 in area; based on the amount of associated rubble and comparisons with a Basketmaker III bin found in a nearby rock shelter, each bin was at least 1 m high.

If filled to the top, the gross storage capacity of each bin would have been about 3 m^3. Excavations at other Basketmaker III sites in the region suggest that in many instances these structures may have had conical, wattle-and-daub superstructures (Brisbin and Varien 1986; Damp 1999). It is possible, therefore, that the bins at AZ E:12:5 had an even greater storage capacity than the level filled estimate of 3 m^3.

House Cluster 341, containing two pit structures, had nine surface storage features, and House Cluster 65, containing three pit structures, had 10 surface storage facilities. Other Basketmaker III sites displayed a similar ratio of surface storage structures to pit structures (Damp 1999; Gross 1986:618, 1987). Using the above conservative values, the total storage capacity for House Clusters 65 and 341 in the surface bins alone is estimated at 30 m³ and 27 m³, respectively.

It is likely that pit structures and aboveground storage facilities were built and used contemporaneously. This idea is supported by the overall spatial propinquity of storage structures and pit structures noted in the Basketmaker III archaeological literature. What is unclear, however, is the number of contemporary aboveground storage units that might be associated with each pit structure. At House Cluster 65, for example, although three pit structures and 10 storage structures were present, chronological data (see table 7.2) indicate that only one pit structure was occupied at any single time. Although we suspect that some storage facilities were associated with a nearby pit structure, fine-grained chronological data establishing absolute contemporaneity are lacking. We also assume that the ratio of aboveground storage facilities to pit structures remained relatively constant throughout the Basketmaker III occupation at AZ E: 12:5. The average number of storage structures per pit structure at House Clusters 65 and 341 is 3.3 and 4.5, respectively. Because these were the largest house clusters at AZ E:12:5, it is likely that the ratios overestimate the actual storage capacity at any one time. Therefore, as a conservative estimate, we assume an average of two contemporaneous, aboveground storage structures for each pit structure within a house cluster.

The capacity of each bin is estimated at roughly 84 bushels (3 m³ volume/bin × 28 bushels in one cubic meter = 84 bushels/bin). If we further assume that the bins were used to hold only shelled corn, we can derive an estimate for net caloric storage capacity. According to Lightfoot (1979), there are 88,480 calories per bushel of shelled corn. If filled to the top, each bin could hold approximately 7,732,320 calories of corn. We estimate the average daily individual caloric need for Basketmaker III agriculturalists at 2,400 calories, which is slightly higher than that calculated by Hassan (2,200 calories) for ethnographic hunting-and-gathering populations (Hassan 1981), but similar to estimates used in calculating prehistoric population of Southwest agriculturalists (see Van West 1994; Van West and Altschul 1994, 1997). The daily caloric need for a family of five is approximately 12,000 calories (see below for justification of family size). Thus, if the groups subsisted solely on shelled corn, each bin could supply the needs of the household group for approximately 1.8 years. Following Kohler et al. (1986:528), we assume that a more reasonable estimate of the dietary component represented by corn is around 60 percent. In that case, each bin could hold nearly a

three-year supply. If each contemporaneous household had an average of two extramural storage bins, then enough shelled corn could be stored to last an average of six years.

This exercise begs the question of whether enough corn could have been grown to feed the residents of a house cluster and provide a reasonable surplus. Various researchers have investigated the amount of corn that can be grown on the Colorado Plateau using traditional dry-farming techniques. In perhaps the most exhaustive study, Burns (1983) used historical-period data from five counties in southwestern Colorado. His calculations, which control for technological improvements used during the twentieth century, suggested that 12.77 bushels per acre could be grown in a year of average precipitation and temperature (Burns 1983:179). Using data from two counties in the Dolores River region of Colorado, Petersen (1985:221) calculated the mean production level for the years 1919 and 1960 and arrived at an average yield of 13.98 ± 3.19 bushels of corn per acre.

Estimates based on yields for traditional Hopi farmers tend to be more conservative. Curtis (in Bradfield 1971:39), who worked on First Mesa between 1901 and 1912, put the average yield at 10 bushels per acre. Van West (1994) noted, however, that the turn-of-the-century years 1896–1904 were notably dry, and the period 1905–1920 was particularly wet, especially after 1914. Curtis's estimates, then, were based on the dry years and probably underestimated the long-term mean value. Support for this position derives from Stephen (reported in Bradfield 1971). Stephen, who worked in the 1930s, stated that the average year returned 10–12 bushels per acre, with as many as 15 bushels harvested on the best lands in a good year. Bradfield (1971:39) reported similar figures, with an average yield being 10.7 bushels per acre.

For purposes of this discussion, we assume that about 12 bushels per acre could have been grown in an average year by traditional dry-farming methods in the Lukachukai Valley. If an average family consumed 12,000 calories per day, then in a year this group would need 4,380,000 calories. If 60 percent of this total was supplied by corn, the group would have required 2,628,000 calories from corn, or about 30 bushels (2,628,000 calories divided by 88,480 calories per bushel).

In 1934 and 1935, Hill (1938) found that the average size of a Navajo corn field planted with traditional dry-farming methods in Lukachukai was six acres. If we assume that Basketmaker III fields were approximately the same size, then the average crop yield would have been 72 bushels. If we assume that 10 percent of the harvest was lost to pests and spoilage, and another 5 percent devoted to seed crop, then we are left with about 60 bushels of corn that would have been available for consumption. To store the consumable portion of the average harvest would take up about 70 percent of one bin. Over the course of a year, the family would consume about 30 bushels, leaving approximately 30 bushels in the bin. The next harvest, assuming it was also of average yield, would essentially fill the bin by adding another 60 bushels, at which point a three-year supply of corn would have been available. To fill all six bins at House Cluster 341 would have required 12 years, and it would have taken 10 years to complete this process at House Cluster 65. It is worth noting that to fill a bin in one year would have required planting about nine acres, or an increase in field size of 50 percent.

The above exercise is based on filling the bins to the top with shelled corn. Of course, other storage methods are certainly possible. Indeed, it is likely that a variety of storage methods were used, each associated with a particular stage in the food-processing cycle. The bulk of the corn harvest would initially have been placed in long-term storage. As the Navajo of the Lukachukai Valley did in the early part of the twentieth century, corn for long-term storage was probably stored on the cob (Hill 1938; see also Gross 1987). The most likely place to store such bulk items would have been in the outside bins. Interestingly, corncobs were found in some of the bins. Although data are lacking, it is clear that storing corn on the cob would have reduced the storage capacity of the outside bins considerably. To process the corn, the cobs were probably brought into the structures. Shelled corn may have been stored in the internal bins, as was observed in one such feature. Shelled corn, or in some cases, cornmeal, would probably have been placed in sealed ceramic storage containers—probably gray ware jars—or baskets sealed with a mud coating. The number of vessels or baskets that could have been placed in a bin is unknown, but it is substantially less than the estimates provided above.

Other items besides corn were no doubt stored. Remains of piñon nuts, gourds, cactus pads, and a variety of other items were found at AZ E:12:5. Piñon nuts, in particular, were found in some of the outside bins. The bins, therefore, were probably not all devoted to corn, and this observation should be borne in mind in evaluating the caloric storage capacity of each house cluster.

Regardless of the storage methods that might have been used, the point is that the extramural storage capacity of each house cluster was considerable. The presence of three to four storage bins per pit structure at House Clusters 65 and 341 indicates that some social units might have had the capacity to store sufficient food resources to last their constituent members, and perhaps allied individuals or groups, for several years. If these extramural facilities were used to cache corn—and there is little indication to suggest that corn was not the staple resource at AZ E:12:5 (Altschul et al. 2000; Bozarth 2000; Johnson and Brooks 2000)—such a strategy constitutes a considerable investment, but also a risk, for the household. The surface storage structures were vulnerable to

insect infestation, attack by rodents and large mammals, and human thievery, which would argue strongly against leaving such critical features unprotected for extended periods of time.

Although the considerable investment in stored foods certainly required some form of protection, the degree to which the residents of AZ E:12:5 were sedentary is difficult to determine. The amount of storage is certainly consistent with the notion that the settlement was a winter village housing the entire social group. Moreover, the presence of considerable quantities of stored food surpluses and the presumed importance of these surpluses to the welfare of the social group strongly suggest that some individuals must have stayed at the settlement year-round. How many may have stayed year-round, and where the others may have gone and why, remain unknown.

Another site excavated during the N13 Project, AZ E:12:11 (ASM), may hold answers to some of these questions. The site consisted of a single Basketmaker III pit structure (Feature 74) located on the alluvial fan about 1 km northeast of AZ E:12:5 (see figure 7.2). The pit structure at AZ E:12:11 is tree-ring dated to the A.D. 620s–660s. Although the structure lacked associated extramural surface storage facilities, it was surrounded by rock piles that have been interpreted as agricultural features (Altschul and Shelley 1995; Altschul et al. 2000). The pit structure was relatively large and substantial (figure 7.4). The main chamber measured about 6 m in diameter and more than 1 m in depth. A large antechamber adjoined the main chamber to the east. Although the pit structures at AZ E:12:5 resembled in form and size the structure at AZ E:12:11, they appear to have been much less formal in construction and array of internal features. Two poorly constructed bins defined an entry-way to the main chamber from the antechamber. An irregularly shaped hearth was offset from the entrance and connected to one of the bins. Three-fourths of the floor area was devoid of features. Two metates with manos lying in their troughs were found in or near a human-made depression in the floor along the southern wall. A third trough metate was found leaning against the side of the pit structure a meter away. Altschul and Shelley (1995: 7–30) interpreted the depression as an expedient, informal mealing bin.

The emphasis on grinding in the pit structure and the recovery of a burned corn kernel from one of the extramural features suggest that agriculture was a major, if not the primary, activity conducted by the residents of AZ E:12:11. Agriculture, however, was not the only economic pursuit of the inhabitants of AZ E:12:11; the site yielded a greater ubiquity of native plant seeds than any of the excavated Basketmaker III households at AZ E:12:5. The suite of native plants represented at AZ E:12:11 is strongly suggestive of a summer occupation.

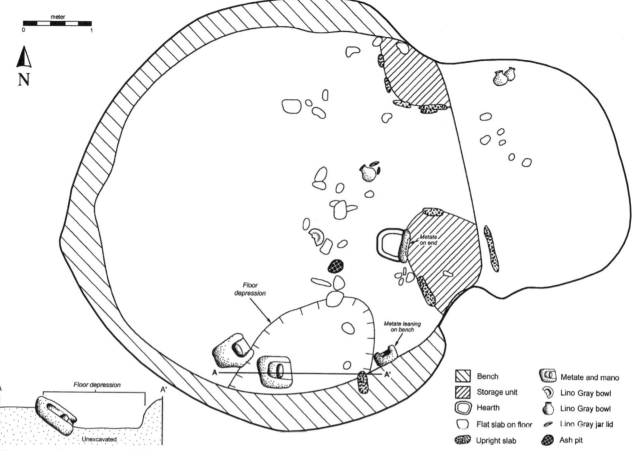

Figure 7.4. Feature 74 at AZ E:12:11 (ASM).

Bench
Storage unit
Hearth
Flat slab on floor
Upright slab
Metate and mano
Lino Gray bowl
Lino Gray bowl
Lino Gray jar lid
Ash pit

Although the site yielded a high relative abundance of medium-sized mammal remains, neither turkey nor rabbit bones were found at AZ E:12:11. The faunal collection is consistent with a logistical strategy placing the site close to procurement zones for wild plant and animal foods (Shelley 2000).

Combining the subsistence results with the architectural data, we interpret AZ E:12:11 as a locale that was used principally during the summer growing season rather than year-round. The site's location in the upper alluvial fan of the Lukachukai Valley placed it in an ideal position for runoff or floodwater agriculture. In his geomorphic reconstruction of the Lukachukai Valley, Johnson (2000) defined cut-and-fill sequences typical for this part of the Colorado Plateau (see Dean 1988). Through a series of radiocarbon dates, Johnson was able to associate the Basketmaker III occupations of the valley with a massive A horizon. He inferred that Tohotso and Lukachukai Creeks were aggrading in the A.D. 600s. Dry and floodwater farming along aggrading streams and washes in the upper part of the Lukachukai Valley would have been relatively easy and productive. AZ E:12:11 was ideally located to take advantage of the geomorphic setting for early agriculture; however, the site, was not likely to have been suitable for long-term winter occupa-

tion. Unlike AZ E:12:5, it was situated in an unprotected part of the valley, vulnerable to the cold winter wind, and away from firewood. The fact that the pit structure at AZ E:12:11 was relatively substantial would seem at odds with this interpretation. It is important to point out, however, that although the shape and layout of the structure were similar to structures at AZ E:12:5, its construction suggests a much smaller investment in time and energy. Its internal features were poorly made, and its floor space unusually devoid of features, suggesting a different range of activities than we think took place in its counterparts at AZ E:12:5 (Altschul et al. 2000). We believe that it was used by a family unit in the course of a growing season, and perhaps served as a situational residence for nonagricultural pursuits in other seasons. It is likely that summer occupants of this structure resided in winter habitations elsewhere. Our guess would be that AZ E:12:5 was such a winter habitation.

In a reconnaissance survey of the Lukachukai Valley conducted in conjunction with the N13 Project, we recorded sites throughout the region (Altschul and Shelley 1995). In addition to the two sites discussed above, another 17 Basketmaker III sites were recorded (see figure 7.2). Most of these were relatively small and were found on the upper alluvial fan of the Lukachukai Creek drainage in geomorphic settings similar to that of AZ E:12:11. We suggest that most of these sites functioned as summer habitations for typically a single nuclear family. It is likely that the pattern of winter residences and summer growing-season loci represents an agricultural risk-minimization strategy similar to that described for later Pueblo period sites in which field locations were diversified in varied locations throughout the upper alluvial fan (Kohler 1992; Ward 1978).

For the Lukachukai Valley, then, we suggest the following settlement model for Basketmaker III period. Dispersed summer habitations were spread along the alluvial fan in areas favorable for agriculture and in proximity to seasonal sources of wild plant and animal foods. Fields were tended on a more or less permanent basis by most, if not all, members of a single social unit, generally a nuclear or extended family. After the harvest, the produce was brought to AZ E:12:5, where it was prepared for long-term caching and then placed in secure outside storage facilities. Individual families living at AZ E:12:5 were likely joined by similarly sized, and probably related, social units. Given the importance of the stored food, it is probable that AZ E:12:5 was inhabited year-round by individual family members who tended nearby fields, or by individuals of special status or rank, such as elders.

POPULATION AND SOCIAL ORGANIZATION

Basketmaker III has long been viewed by anthropologists and archaeologists as a critical transition period in Southwest cultural evolution between the hunters and gatherers of Basketmaker II and the sedentary agriculturalists of the Pueblo periods. Although there is mounting evidence that maize agriculture long preceded Basketmaker III (Matson 1991), the emergence of year-round habitations, such as those represented by AZ E:12:5, is clearly a Basketmaker III phenomenon. As one of the first experiments in communal living on the Colorado Plateau, the type of social organization reflected in these large Basketmaker III villages is of interest. Here we use data from AZ E:12:5 to examine a series of questions:

1. What types of social groups occupied pit structures?
2. How many of these groups lived at the village simultaneously?
3. How were the these groups were integrated into a village-based social organization?

Pit Structures and Village Size

Birkedal (1976, 1982) argued that the nuclear family was the social unit most likely represented by Basketmaker III residential pit structures. His argument is based on several lines of evidence, including internal living space, layout, and associated feature types. The internal organi-

zation of the large pit structures at AZ E:12:5 is consistent with Birkedal's interpretation. Each main chamber had one hearth, which was generally the dominant feature of the chamber. Hearths are often considered to be reliable indicators of nuclear family households. As Birkedal (1976:450) noted, in most nonindustrialized societies each married woman tends one hearth for her family. The average number of metates found in the pit structures and the general pattern of using the main structure as a residence, with storage and ancillary activities taking place in the antechamber, conform to Birkedal's expectations.

Perhaps the most compelling argument supporting the family as the residential unit is the estimated size of the social group occupying a pit structure. Among the wide variety of methods for calculating the resident population of a dwelling (e.g., Clarke 1974; Cook 1972; LeBlanc 1971; Naroll 1962) is Casselberry's (1974) formula. Birkedal found that this method, which is based on a comparative study of eight ethnographic societies with multifamily dwellings, provided the most reasonable estimates for Basketmaker III pit structure population on Mesa Verde. Casselberry (1974) argued that the population of a multifamily dwelling can be estimated at one-sixth of the total floor area measured in square meters.

For pit structures at AZ E:12:5, this method yields an average estimate of 5.85 persons per pit structure, with a range from 3.53 to 11.94. The estimate excludes Pocket pit houses, which are interpreted as special-use features. The average also is skewed by one pit structure, Feature 19 in House Cluster 65, which contained more than twice the floor space compared to the next largest pit structure. The floor of this large square pit structure was littered with rows of post molds. Altschul and Shelley (1995:4–45) argued that these may have been loom holes, and that the pit structure may have been used for textile manufacture as well as other domestic purposes. Eliminating Feature 19, the mean population estimate per pit structure is 4.33, well within the range of a nuclear family.

Corroborating evidence can be drawn from other studies. Based on a comparative analysis of North American tribes, Cook (1972) argued that dwellings of 32.5 m² or less were invariably occupied by nuclear families. Dwellings between 32.5 and 45.5 m² may have been occupied by either a small extended family or a nuclear family with one or more auxiliary members. Houses larger than 45.5 m² were always occupied by extended families. Applying these rules to AZ E:12:5 would suggest that most of the pit structures were occupied by nuclear families, some with auxiliary members.

There is no evidence from AZ E:12:5, then, that would dispute the long-accepted claim that pit structures were used as residences by nuclear families (e.g., Birkedal 1976, 1982; Schiffer 1972; Steward 1937; Wills and

Windes 1989). Judging from the spacing of house clusters in the ROW, the number of depressions elsewhere on the site, and the available land on the ridge top, we estimate that there were between 20 and 25 house clusters at AZ E:12:5. Based on pit structure construction and repair data from the ROW (see table 7.2), we estimate that 40 to 50 percent of the known house clusters were likely to have been occupied contemporaneously; that is, between eight and 12 residential pit structures were occupied at any one time. Rounding the figure of 4.33 people per pit structure calculated above to 5.0 (the number of residents per pit house used by Schiffer [1972] for Shabik'eshchee Village), we arrive at a population estimate of 40 to 60 people for the Basketmaker III occupation at any one time.

Village Organization

Following Birkedal (1976), most archaeologists have argued that Basketmaker III society was relatively simple, organized primarily by family units and, at the most complex level, into lineal, possibly matrilineal, bands. Based solely on the estimated number of inhabitants (40 to 60 individuals) and the number of contemporaneous social units (eight to 12 households), this hypothesis is consistent with the archaeological record at AZ E:12:5. Johnson (1982, 1983) argued that the household or family level of organization with consensual decision making can accommodate camp or village aggregations with populations of six to 14 households, or 30 to 84 individuals. Beyond that size, the number of units with competing needs becomes increasingly difficult to manage with the rudimentary community-wide social institutions that characterize this level of social organization. The inevitable pulls and pushes on the community, termed scalar stress by Johnson (1982, 1983), either lead to a fissioning of the group—with one or more constituent household groups leaving—or a reorganization of the community at a more complex, but not necessarily status differentiated, level of social organization.

There is some evidence that the latter was occurring at AZ E:12:5. First, there is the presence of a great kiva in the southern part of the site. Measuring nearly 12 m in diameter, the great kiva almost assuredly represented a significant amount of communal construction effort. Several of the excavated pit structures to the north were dug deeply (in some cases nearly 50 cm) into the underlying Chinle Sandstone bedrock. Although the great kiva was not excavated, we presume on the basis of its surface size that it could have been as much as 1.5 to 2 m deep, which would place its floor well into the bedrock surface (perhaps a meter or more).

Public architecture of this scale implies that the residents of AZ E:12:5 were committed to the Lukachukai Valley and to their village. The length of continual occupation at AZ E:12:5—at least 75 years—indicates a type of "deep" sedentism that had not characterized previous hunter and gatherers and early agriculturalists. How did a small number of family-based farming groups maintain a community over several generations? We suspect that the great kiva provided one mechanism for resolving community-wide issues such as rights to use certain areas or agricultural fields in the valley; the upkeep and protection of stored produce; allegations of theft, witchcraft, and other misdeeds between households; and finding suitable marriage partners. Within this institution may also have been vested procedures for redistributing food stores between households in time of crisis, as well as for ritual requirements to maintain the community's identity and well-being.

It is not only the presence of a great kiva that argues for a suprafamily level of organization. A second line of evidence was found in the N13 excavations at House Cluster 1054. This cluster consisted of a pit structure (main chamber, Feature 1054; antechamber, Feature 1055), a Pocket pit structure (Feature 1062), three surface storage structures, and eight other extramural features. There is evidence to suggest that Feature 1054/1055 was unique at AZ E:12:5 and was reused as a communal kitchen (Altschul and Shelley 1995; Altschul et al. 2000). At first glance, Feature 1054 appeared similar to many other pit structures at AZ E:12:5 (figure 7.5). It was roughly circular to subrectangular with an antechamber oriented slightly north of east. The similarities, however, end there; its internal structure and assemblage were distinct.

Unlike other pit structures at AZ E:12:5, the main chamber and antechamber at Feature 1054/1055 did not adjoin but were separated by 30 cm. The floor of the antechamber was cluttered with features and artifacts, indicating that the structure was used not for specialized purposes such as storage, but for a myriad of domestic activities. The main chamber was also distinctive. The floor sloped, and there apparently was no attempt to level it. The chamber had four internal bins and two storage units built into the wall. The floor assemblage included a large number of ground stone implements (two metates, eight manos, one mortar, three pestles); numerous shaped, circular discs interpreted as cooking stones; three stacked Lino Gray bowls; and five other reconstructible vessels. Another 18 metates were found in the fill just above and within the roof fall (Altschul and Shelley 1995:4–83).

The hearth also was unusual. It was off centered and lacked the encircling, raised clay ridge and clay radials that are common to the Western style (Shelley 1991) and evident at other pit structures at AZ E:12:5. The walls of the chamber were also blackened. Although it is possible that blackening occurred when the structure burned, it is curious that such characteristics were not noted in the other pit structures on the site, most of which also were

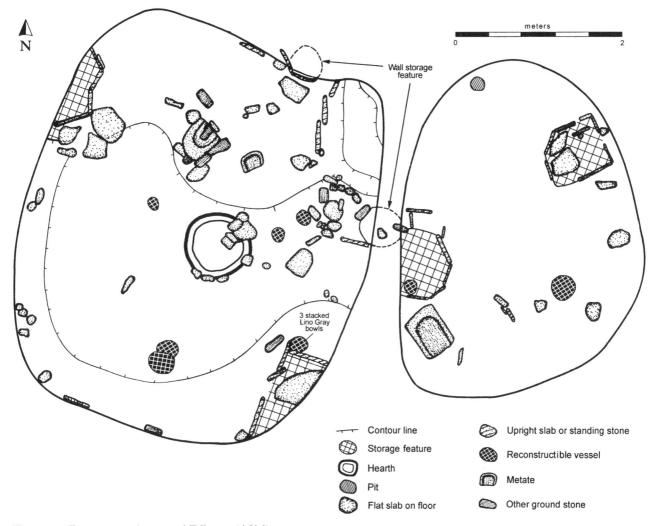

meters
0   2

Wall storage
feature

3 stacked
Lino Gray
bowls

	Contour line		Upright slab or standing stone
	Storage feature		Reconstructible vessel
	Hearth		Metate
	Pit		Other ground stone
	Flat slab on floor		

Figure 7.5. Feature 1054/1055 at AZ E:12:5 (ASM).

burned. The blackening suggests that the chamber was filled with smoke either repeatedly or for one long, sustained period. Although we cannot rule out that the blackening was the result of the conflagration that destroyed the structure, we believe that an equally compelling hypothesis is that it was used as a specialized food-processing and cooking facility. This hypothesis would account for the smoke blackening of the walls, the large amount of ground stone in the main chamber, the lack of a floor assemblage, and the shift of the domestic space from the main chamber to the antechamber.

It is possible, indeed likely, that this specialized function followed the structure's use as a domicile. The layout of the structure, with a central hearth and bins, shares similarities with the other large pit structures at AZ E:12:5. At some point in the history of the feature, domestic activities were moved out into a nearby, but separate, structure. The main chamber was not maintained to the same level as other domestic pit structures, as evidenced by the uneven floors.

It is reasonable to ask what type of social group would

require such a large area for cooking. One hypothesis is that the residents at House Cluster 1054 lived in the slightly smaller antechamber and devoted the entire main chamber to processing and cooking food. It is unlikely that a small unit, such as a family, would need such a large space to prepare and cook meals. A plausible alternative hypothesis is that Feature 1054/1055 was used as a communal kitchen or smoke house. It is further possible that the antechamber may have been part of this communal structure. Although the features in the antechamber were similar in size and characteristics to internal features in the main chambers of other pit structures, their spatial arrangement differed in significant ways. First, storage features were not placed in the corners of the structure but, rather, were scattered over the floor. One bin is freestanding (not attached to any wall). Second, this "jumbled" arrangement precluded any cleared sleeping space in the antechamber. These observations indicate that the antechamber may have served as a communal food-preparation area used prior to cooking the food in the main chamber. The bins in the antechamber may have been owned by different families and used as a type of temporary pantry to store staples or ingredients being used for that day.

We interpret AZ E:12:5 as a village of between eight and 12 economically independent, but socially affiliated, households. What type of social organization best fit this description? A number of investigators have examined this question. Perhaps none have been more influential than Julian Steward's (1937; see also 1955) classic reconstruction of the evolution of the Western Pueblo system of matrilineal clans (see also Eggan 1950).

Steward argued that Basketmaker II society was composed of mobile hunters and gatherers, presumably organized at a band level. The "pit lodge villages" of Basketmaker III are viewed as evidence of increasing reliance on agriculture. With agriculture came heightened concerns over land ownership of small arable fields as opposed to large hunting and gathering tracts. In Steward's model, it would have been possible for Basketmaker III populations to aggregate in fewer and larger villages, but there was no compelling social need to do so. The population, then, was dispersed into small house clusters with "unilateral groups living on or near their farm lands" (Steward 1955:162). When village population increased beyond a certain size, "small lineages budded off, and each set up a new house cluster at no great distance from its neighbors and former kin" (Steward 1955:162).

The increases in population during Pueblo I did not alter the single-lineage social organization. Instead, social units were dispersed across the landscape in small unit-type pueblos in which the lineage composition was formalized in set architectural patterns with five or so rooms associated with a single kiva. Steward views the initial amalgamations of Pueblo II as simply villages composed of distinct lineage-based units. By Pueblo III times, the lineage distinctions in the large villages began to vanish, being replaced by larger social groups whose members assumed a common descent, although they could not demonstrate it. These units, termed "clans," persist today among the Western Pueblo peoples.

Steward's (1937) argument is one of the most elegant of Southwestern archaeology. In the last 60 years it has been refined with new data and interpretations (Chang 1958; Daifuku 1961), but altered little. In one of the rare attacks on Steward's position, Birkedal (1976, 1982) argued that the evidence for Basketmaker III was not consistent with lineage-based organizations. Instead, he maintained that the data overwhelmingly supported the hypothesis that Basketmaker III society was organized in a series of bands. Unlike lineages, which are descent groups in which the actual relationships among members can be demonstrated and not assumed (Fox 1967:49), bands are multifamilial aggregates that are bound together by a loose set of kinship, economic, and ritual re-

lationships (see Fried 1967; Sahlins 1972; Service 1971; Steward 1955). Members of lineages own land in common, share a name, or participate in shared rituals; bands have none of these attributes. The implication for interpreting AZ E:12:5 is that a lineage-based system is more in keeping with a cohesive village, whereas a band organization would be expected if the settlement represented a temporary or seasonal aggregation, such as envisioned by Wills and Windes (1989) for Shabik'eshchee Village.

In his argument, Birkedal (1976, 1982) pointed out that Basketmaker III sites do not follow formal patterns of site layout. In particular, he argued that the formal structure evident at Shabik'eshchee Village (see Chang 1958) was more the result of topography than culture. As long as large Basketmaker sites like Shabik'eshchee Village could be viewed as anomalies, Birkedal's criticism had validity. As AZ E:12:5, Juniper Cove (Gilpin and Benallie, this volume), Kiva Mesa (Reed and Wilcox, this volume), and many other large Basketmaker III sites described in this volume amply demonstrate, however, village sites were not rare; they often contained village-wide features such as great kivas; and they followed similar site layouts (see table 7.1).

Beyond site characteristics, Birkedal's (1976, 1982) argument for bands is based on the notion that competition for scarce resources and population pressure are the two major driving forces behind culture change in the Southwest (see also Harner 1970). The key to evaluating the type of social organization manifested in Basketmaker III society, according to this line of reasoning, is determining whether competition and population pressure accompanied the transition from hunting and gathering to agriculturally based societies. From Birkedal's perspective, the crux of the issue is whether there was competition for agricultural land. He argued that the transition from hunting and gathering to agriculture increased the potential carrying capacity of the land, thereby temporarily decreasing population pressure. A short "free-land" situation, coinciding with the Basketmaker III period, existed as social units shifted economic practices. Thus, whereas the economy was radically transformed during this period, social organization remained stable at the band level.

How much free land was there in the Lukachukai Valley? Our survey of the valley showed that Basketmaker III sites were concentrated in the upper alluvial fan areas. Johnson (2000) argued that these areas would have been favored by agriculturalists for most of the seventh century because water tables were high and streams were aggrading. We have calculated that there are about 350 acres of arable land in the upper fan. If each Basketmaker III family cultivated a field between six and 10 acres in size, and left fallow two additional fields, then each social unit would require about 20 to 30 acres of arable land. The eight to 12 household units at AZ

E:12:5, then, would have needed between 160 and 360 acres to sustain the village. It is possible that other groups could have lived in the valley, particularly if household needs were closer to 20 acres than 30. Alternatively, a critical threshold may have been reached in which the social group based at AZ E:12:5 asserted control over access to all arable land in the Lukachukai Valley. We find the latter hypothesis more in keeping with traditional farming societies. In essence, there was no free land in the valley at the time AZ E:12:5 was occupied.

Our model of AZ E:12:5 is more consistent with a lineage organization than a band. It was necessary for the resident population of the Lukachukai Valley to be sufficiently large to assert and protect land rights to arable land. The need to keep strangers out, however, may have been only slightly more important than the need to define socially acceptable ways of allocating and maintaining land rights within the group. Additionally, labor requirements of agriculture were probably far different from those of hunters and gatherers, possibly requiring communal tasks for clearing, planting, and harvesting.

There undoubtedly was a complex relationship among property rights, land tenure, and communal labor in a larger and more sedentary social group with increased needs for arable land. The lineage system that developed was required to solve problems that simply did not emerge among mobile Basketmaker II bands. The increased number of households needed mechanisms for defining private and public space; these mechanisms were mirrored in needs for balancing the economic self-sufficiency of individual households with social and ritual requirements of maintaining a common identity.

Although a lineage system may represent a major leap in social complexity over the presumed family or band organizations that characterized the Archaic and early Basketmaker II periods, it is questionable whether these units could have been self-sufficient. This issue has economic and social aspects. Self-sufficiency hinges on the productive potential of small valleys, such as the Lukachukai Valley, that were cultivated using relatively simple dry- and floodwater-farming techniques. Johnson's (2000) geomorphic reconstruction of the Lukachukai Valley is consistent with Dean's (1988:156) model, which posits high water tables existing for most of the seventh century for the Colorado Plateau as a whole. High-resolution data are lacking, although Dean and Van West (1999) recently developed a tree-ring-based precipitation reconstruction for the Mesa Verde region that is broadly applicable to the Lukachukai region. These data indicate that precipitation was highly variable in the early A.D. 600s. For the most part, precipitation was above average in the first decade of the A.D. 600s, when AZ E:12:5 was settled; the second decade, by contrast, was consistently dry. The period from about A.D. 620 to A.D. 655, when many of the pit structures were built, was primarily a wet period. Dry conditions prevailed until around A.D. 670, after which precipitation oscillated; rain and snowfall were generally favorable to dry-land and runoff farming until the end of the century. Given high water tables and reasonable precipitation for most of the seventh century, we infer that agricultural productivity was high. For most of the century, then, eight to 12 households at AZ E:12:5 could have produced sufficient food from fields and wild resource procurement to feed their members. In times when one or more households witnessed shortfalls, the remaining domestic groups should have had sufficient stored foods to support not only themselves, but also their neighbors in need. Kohler and Van West (1996) indicated that under such conditions the potential for cooperative food-sharing behaviors should have been relatively high, thereby enabling longer-term aggregations such as that at AZ E:12:5 to come into being.

Even if the lineage could have produced enough food for its members, could a group as small as that inferred for AZ E:12:5 have been socially independent? We think not. Groups of 30 to 50 individuals do not provide sufficient numbers to ensure socially acceptable marriage partners (Wobst 1976). On this basis, then, the population at AZ E:12:5 had to be linked with other habitations to obtain marriage partners. It is possible that this system could have been composed of a relatively large number of small family-based settlements, or one or more similarly larger villages structured along the lines of AZ E:12:5. As this volume makes abundantly clear, Basketmaker III settlement was highly variable, with some valleys organized around large villages, and others around dispersed farmsteads. As these communities were experimenting with economic strategies, we can only assume that they were also struggling to find workable social organizational solutions as well.

CONCLUSION

Traditionally, Basketmaker III is viewed as a transition period between mobile hunters and gatherers and sedentary agriculturalists. Settlements were thought to be small, and society organized at the level of nuclear families or small bands (Birkedal 1976, 1982). People were assumed to be not fully committed to agriculture, with wild resources viewed as an equally important food source (Wills and Windes 1989).

Sites like AZ E:12:5 challenge this conception. AZ E:12:5 was occupied by between eight and 12 households, with at least some of the members living in the village year-round. Particular house clusters may have lasted as long as the village (between 75 and 100 years). Maize agriculture was the dominant economic strategy. Households established fields and field houses in the nearby upper alluvial fans of Lukachukai and Tohotso Creeks.

The evidence does not support recent interpretations of Basketmaker III culture. Episodic abandonment, a central tenant of the argument that Wills and Windes (1989) proposed for Shabik'eshchee Village, is not apparent at AZ E:12:5. There is also little evidence to support Lightfoot and Feinman's (1982) notion that suprahousehold leadership emerged at this time. Each house cluster at AZ E:12:5 appears to have been more or less economically independent; however, Birkedal's (1976, 1982) assertion that these households were also socially independent, or at best loosely tied together, does not follow. The house clusters at AZ E:12:5 shared at least two key aspects of social life: cooking and ritual activities. These two activities may initially appear antithetical, with a common kitchen for food preparation being the epitome of domestic activity, and a great kiva the embodiment of public ritual, but in many societies there is no more common link between related groups than food and ritual. It may be no accident that at AZ E:12:5, a village representing an early Anasazi experiment in communal living, the archaeological record supports a lineage-based system tied by ritual and food preparation. The interweaving of maize and ritual that permeates ethnographic and modern Western Pueblo culture may have very deep roots indeed.

ACKNOWLEDGMENTS

SRI's work along N13 was supported by the Bureau of Indian Affairs (BIA) (contract no. NOO C 1420 X043), with permits and regulatory oversight provided by the Navajo Nation Historic Preservation Department (permit no. C9005). The project lasted from 1986 to 1995 and involved three field seasons (1987, 1988, and 1990). We would like to acknowledge the BIA's contracting officer's technical representatives: Sandra Rayl, Tom Parry, Jim Chase, John Stein, and Donald Sutherland. Also, we want to thank Navajo Nation HPD representatives Mary Bernard Shaw, Chad Smith, and Karen Benally, who commented on various drafts of the technical report. SRI's fieldwork at Lukachukai was directed by Steve Shelley, who also provided comments on this chapter. Others whose comments have improved this chapter include Su Benaron, Carla Van West, and Richard Ciolek-Torrello. Stephanie Whittlesey not only commented on the chapter, she edited it as well. Cindy Elsner drafted the illustrations. We would also like to thank Paul Reed for inviting us to participate in this volume, and for providing valuable advice and comment along the way. Errors are the responsibilities of the authors alone.

8

Juniper Cove and Early Anasazi Community Structure West of the Chuska Mountains

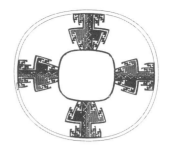

Dennis Gilpin

Larry Benallie Jr.

In 1927, Frank H. H. Roberts Jr. excavated a Basketmaker III great kiva at Shabik'eshchee Village in Chaco Canyon. The following year, Byron Cummings excavated a Basketmaker III great kiva at Juniper Cove (west of Kayenta, Arizona), a site he had been investigating since 1912. In 1931, Earl Morris excavated a Basketmaker III great kiva in Broken Flute Cave, which, although it is in Arizona, is on the east slope of the divide that runs from the Carrizo Mountains south along the crest of the Lukachukai and Chuska Mountains. Thus, in the years from 1927 to 1931, three Basketmaker III great kivas were excavated in the Navajo country, documenting the existence of this type of feature among the architecture of the Basketmaker III period. Roberts quickly published on his excavations (Roberts 1929). Morris's Broken Flute Cave excavations were reported in 1959 as part of his daughter's (Elizabeth Ann Morris) dissertation, which was published in 1980 (Morris 1959, 1980). Cummings's work at Juniper Cove has never been fully reported (but see Baldwin 1939; Bannister, Dean, and Robinson 1968; Cummings 1953; Haury 1928; Vivian and Reiter 1965), and since the time of Cummings's and Morris's work, other examples of Basketmaker III and Basketmaker III–Pueblo I sites with possible great kivas have been identified in northeastern Arizona and northwestern New Mexico. This chapter evaluates the role of the great kiva in the Basketmaker III settlement system of what is now Navajo country by focusing on the area west of the Chuska Mountains (figure 8.1; table 8.1). The key conclusion is that Basketmaker III great kivas were constructed at three known sites in the region, all of which were much larger than the average Basketmaker III farmstead. Sites containing great kivas consisted of 10 to 35 pit houses and 40 to 200 slab-lined storage units. In contrast, numerous farmsteads consisted of one to eight (or more) pit houses and one to 26 storage structures. (And

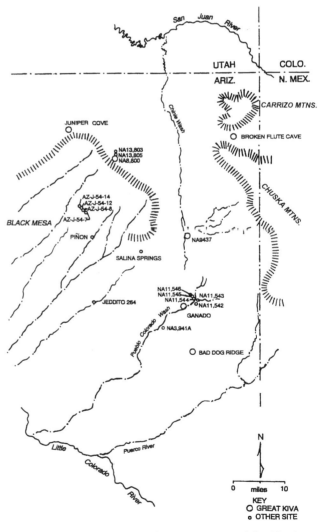

Figure 8.1. Selected Basketmaker III sites west of the Chuska Mountains.

TABLE 8.1
Summary Statistics on Basketmaker III Great Kiva Sites and Other Basketmaker III Sites in Study Area

Site	Date	Size (sq. m)	Great Kivas	Pit Structures	Storage Units
Shabik'eshchee Village	A.D. 537–581	74,800	1	68[a]	45
Broken Flute Cave	A.D. 623–635	3,000	1	17	65
Juniper Cove	A.D. 650–675[b]	60,000	1	6	100
Bad Dog Ridge	BM III[b]	80,000	2	29	40+
Ganado	BM III–PI[b]	490,000	5	17+	539
Kiva Mesa	A.D. 675–775	24,800	3	9	10–15
Tohatchi	BM III	7,500	1	35	41
Mexican Springs	A.D. 640–700	60,000	1 great pit str.	4	79
Twin Lakes	BM III	4,650	1 great pit str.	5	unknown
LA 80422	A.D. 600–725	1,250	1 great pit str.	2	unknown
Electric Raven	A.D. 701	isolated structure	1 great pit str.	0	0
Oak Springs	BM III	unknown	1 great pit str.	4	unknown
Salina Springs	BM III	53,000	0	4	13
Jeddito 264	A.D. 666–736	9,000	0	7	26
AZ-J-54-7 (NN)	BM III	3,600	0	3	16
AZ-J-54-14 (NN)	BM III	2,750	0	6	4
AZ-J-54-8 (NN)	BM III–P I	4,500	0	5	12
AZ-J-54-12 (NN)	BM III–P I	4,320	0	8	1
NA11,780	A.D. 400–600	unknown	0	1	6
NA11,784	BM III–P I	unknown	0	1	0
NA9437	BM III–P I	34,400	1?	5+	12+
NA13,803	BM III–P I	unknown	0	0	0
NA8800	BM III–P I	unknown	1?	8+	0
NA11,545	BM III	400	0	3	3
NA11,542	BM III	1,600	0	1	2+
NA11,543	BM III–P I	1,000	0	2	4
NA11,544	BM III	2,100	0	3	0
NA3941A	A.D. 584–637	unknown	0	1	unknown

Note: NN = Navajo Nation site number; NA = Museum of Northern Arizona site number; BM = Basketmaker; P = Pueblo.
[a]Roberts (1929) excavated 19 pit structures at Shabik'eshchee Village, but Wills and Windes (1989:352) note that the entire site contains 68 pit structures; since Wills and Windes could not identify storage features in the unexcavated portion of the site, the ratio of pit houses to storage features is estimated to be 19 to 45, based on excavations.
[b]Each of these sites has a later component; statistics for only the component listed are presented here.

in Tohatchi Flats and on the southern Defiance Plateau, some hamlets had oversized pit houses.) Finally, a number of seasonal habitations consisting of one or more pit houses with no storage structures were also part of the settlement pattern. Great kiva sites therefore apparently functioned not only as ritual centers but also as storage centers in a process of increasing sedentism and community organization that eventually led to settled village life.

THREE BASKETMAKER III COMMUNITIES IN NORTHEASTERN ARIZONA

Three large Basketmaker III sites with great kivas have been identified in the drainage basins of Chinle and Pueblo Colorado Washes and on the Defiance Plateau. These sites are Juniper Cove, Bad Dog Ridge, and Ganado.

Juniper Cove

Juniper Cove (figure 8.2) consists of a Basketmaker III great kiva, six Basketmaker III pit house depressions, at least 100 Basketmaker III slab-lined features, three Basketmaker III middens, and a Pueblo II room block, pit structure, and midden, all in an area of 14.8 acres (6.0 ha). Tree-ring dates from the site range from A.D. 666 to 678.

History of Research.

Juniper Cove was originally (and most intensively) investigated by Byron Cummings, although the history of Cummings's research at the site is not well understood. Christenson (1987:2.25) says that Cummings made at least five visits to the site. Turner (1962) reports that one visit was in 1912; a diary by Winslow Walker, one of Cummings's students, apparently describes work at the

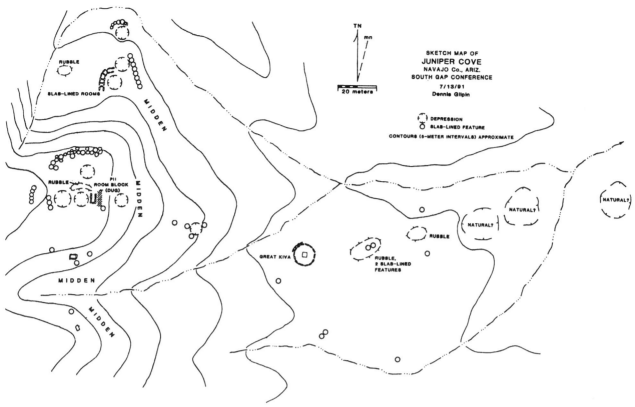

Figure 8.2. Sketch map of Juniper Cove.

site in 1923 (Christenson 1987:2.25); Webster (1991a, 1991b) describes collections from the site made in 1923 and 1926; and, lastly, Cummings himself (1953:68) states that the great kiva was excavated in 1928. (Although Bannister, Dean, and Robinson [1968:21] state that the site was excavated from 1924 to 1926, Cummings was in Mexico in 1924 and 1925.) The Arizona Historical Society in Tucson has a typescript, apparently by Cummings (1926[?]), describing research at Juniper Cove. Someone has penciled "22 or 23" on the typescript, but in 1922 Cummings was at Cuicuilco and did no work in the Southwest. Webster (1991a, 1991b) suggests that the typescript dates to 1923 or 1926 and, based on other sites mentioned and the amount of work that had been completed at Juniper Cove, favors the 1926 date. In addition to the great kiva, Cummings apparently excavated at least four slab-lined circular pit houses at the site (see photographs in Cummings 1953: 18, 23, as well as photographs in the Cummings Photograph Collection [Box 7, File 7; Box 1, File 11; Box 1, File 13] at the Arizona Historical Society in Tucson), one rectangular structure dating to a post-Basketmaker occupation of the site (Cummings 1926[?]; Haury 1928:37 n.7), and presumably other features.

In 1941, Deric Nusbaum of Gila Pueblo collected charcoal for tree-ring dating from the surface of Juniper Cove, which he designated Marsh Pass 7:9. Nusbaum

also filled out a Gila Pueblo site form, including a rough site plan, and made a collection of some 66 sherds; both the site form and the collections are on file at the Arizona State Museum. Nusbaum collected enough charcoal (12 dated pieces) to date the site from A.D. 666 to 678 (Bannister, Dean, and Robinson 1968:21; Robinson and Cameron 1991).

There are no published accounts of fieldwork at Juniper Cove dating after Nusbaum's work, but Alexander J. Lindsay (personal communication, July 13, 1991) states that archaeologists from the Museum of Northern Arizona visited the site, took notes, and made a sketch map. (Bannister, Dean, and Robinson [1968:2] give two site numbers for Juniper Cove: NA3570 and NA7623.) Also, of course, Juniper Cove has been visited regularly by archaeologists, and even if they took no notes, their recollections and impressions of the site may have influenced later, secondary accounts of the site. Nonetheless, all of the descriptions of Juniper Cove published after Cummings's 1953 account appear to be based on Cummings's work at the site, as described by Cummings's book (1953:18, 21, 23, 26–27, 62, 68, 142–143, 144), a Cummings manuscript (Cummings 1926[?]), Haury's 1928 master's thesis, a diary by one of Cummings's students, and an article by Gordon Baldwin on a sandal last from Juniper Cove (Baldwin 1939).

On July 13, 1991, the South Gap Conference (an

Figure 8.3. Cummings's photograph of Juniper Cove great kiva, view to north-northwest. Courtesy of the Arizona Historical Society, Tucson (Accession no. AHS# PC29-F.13a).

informal annual tour of archaeological sites in the Southwest organized by David Breternitz) visited Juniper Cove and other sites in the vicinity. The tour of Juniper Cove provided the opportunity to make a sketch map of the site and record a few notes on it, and also provided the impetus to review the literature on the site (Gilpin 1991).

Location and Environment.
The site of Juniper Cove is located at the base of the southern end of the South Comb, some 14 km southwest of Kayenta, Navajo County, Arizona. It is situated on a ridge top at the heads of several arroyos. The site has approximately 35 m of relief, ranging in elevation from 1840 to 1875 m. Soils are primarily aeolian sands and support a piñon-juniper plant community. Plants observed included piñon, juniper, snakeweed, wolfberry, and prickly pear. Drainage is to the east. The nearest named drainage is Laguna Wash, 1.2 km to the southeast.

Site Description.
Juniper Cove measures approximately 200 m north-south by 300 m east-west. It has three components: (1) a Basketmaker III component consisting of the great kiva, at least six pit house depressions, and at least 100 slab-lined features (mostly circular and often isolated, although four arcs and one straight alignment of slab-lined

features were present), and three middens; (2) a Pueblo II component consisting of an excavated, pot-hunted room block, a possibly associated pit structure, and a midden; and (3) a Pueblo III component consisting of sherds of Tusayan Black-on-red and Tusayan Polychrome, possibly from Happy Valley, a Tsegi phase site on the peak above Juniper Cove.

Cummings (1953:68, 144) classified Juniper Cove as a "circular pit village" of the "circular pit house period" based on the type of dwelling found there. He stated that the site consisted of "112 rooms," including "living rooms, storage chambers and ceremonial and council chambers" (Cummings 1926[?]:2). Haury (1928:27–28) noted that "the main village has 102 rooms, and a smaller one near by has 30 rooms." Baldwin (1939) says that the main village had 105 pit houses and slab-lined features.

The great kiva is located in a flat area between drainages and below the slopes and ridge toes of Comb Ridge (figure 8.3). According to Cummings (1926[?]:2), "The large ceremonial room and council chamber is surrounded by a bauquette [sic] two and one-half feet high. It has a fire-place in the center and a raised oval platform five feet by three feet east of the fireplace. Three large holes in the floor showed where posts had stood to support the roof timbers." According to Cummings (1953: 58), the Juniper Cove great kiva was "36 feet in diameter

Figure 8.4. Cummings's photograph of Winslow Walker at Juniper Cove pit structure, view to west-southwest. Courtesy of the Arizona Historical Society, Tucson (Accession no. AHS# PC29-F.13b.)

and surrounded by a continuous bench." A photograph of the great kiva (Cummings 1953:62) shows the "raised platform, firepit, and prayer stone (deflector)." This photograph, looking roughly north-northwest, shows the shallow, circular, slab-lined feature, with a lower inner ring of upright slabs lining the footings or face of the bench and extending from the floor of the kiva to the front of the bench's earthen seat, while an upper, outer ring of upright slabs lines the wall of the kiva (or the backrest of the bench) and extends from the back of the earthen seat to ground level. Gaps between the irregular tops of the upright slabs were filled with horizontally laid, coursed masonry. The raised platform is a square sandstone pavement one course high. The deflector is an upright slab in the floor to the right of the platform. There are no steps, posts, fire pit, or ventilator visible in the photograph.

On July 13, 1991, the great kiva appeared as a slab-lined depression 11 m in diameter and approximately 50 cm deep with a concentration of sandstone (apparently what is left of the raised platform) in the center. Some gaps between the irregular tops of the upright sandstone slabs were still filled with coursed sandstone, as shown in Cummings's (1953:62) photograph. The ring of upright slabs was probably footings for or the face of the bench. A remnant of the outer wall seemed to be present in the northwest quadrant of the feature, but elsewhere the sandstone slabs of the outer wall appeared to have fallen inward and lay flat just outside of the tops of the upright slabs. No charcoal fragments were present. The great

kiva was fairly small (only 11 m in diameter) and very shallow.

The living rooms were 12 to 20 feet in diameter (Cummings 1926[?]; Haury 1928:28). According to Haury (1928:28), most living rooms were entered "through a door in the side." Two published photographs (Cummings 1953:18, 23) show circular, slab-lined pit houses. One (Cummings 1953:23) is described merely as a "circular, slab-lined pit house, deeply buried," and the photograph shows only a few slabs lining a pit with no floor features or other distinguishing characteristics. Another (figure 8.4, which appears to be the pit house halfway down the ridge, 50 m west-northwest of the great kiva) is described as a "slab-lined circular pit house with storage cists and an alcove" (Cummings 1953:18). Cummings felt that these pit houses had flat roofs supported by four posts. Storage chambers were five to six feet in diameter (Cummings 1926[?]:2). In his book he wrote, "Adjoining this living room, but with a separate entrance, was a storeroom five or six feet in diameter, the floor roughly paved with flat rock. This undoubtedly was the space where their corn and other food products were stored.... The flat roof and separate storage room are characteristic of the circular pit house found at Juniper Cove and in other villages in the vicinity" (Cummings 1953:26–27). This could easily describe the pit house and adjacent slab-lined storage bins just above the great kiva at Juniper Cove. Original photographs of these two "pit rooms" and two additional "pit rooms" are present in the Cummings Photograph Collection (Box 7, File 7;

Box 1, File 11; Box 1, File 13) at the Arizona Historical Society in Tucson.

On July 13, 1991, a few slab-lined features were present south of the great kiva. Some rubble mounds, a few isolated slab-lined features, and three large (ca. 20 m in diameter), possibly natural depressions were east of the great kiva. Some of the rubble mounds contained upright slab-lined features and perhaps represent the remnants of jacal structures with interior slab-lined features.

West of the great kiva, going up the ridge, was a pit house depression and associated slab-lined features. Above this concentration of features was a natural bench that contained an excavated or pot-hunted Pueblo II room block (of two to five rooms) with a pit house or kiva below (east of) it and a midden below (east of) the pit house or kiva depression. This Pueblo II unit could be the one excavated by Cummings. West of the Pueblo II structure were two pit house depressions with an arc of rubble on the north side of them. West of these depressions were three slab-lined features, and west of these slab-lined features, at the western edge of the bench, was a rubble concentration containing several slab-lined features. North of the Pueblo II room block was another pit house depression, and the northern edge of the bench was lined with an arc of perhaps 20 or more slab-lined features ranked two and three deep. At least four slab-lined features were present on the southern edge of the bench, and below (south of) these were dense midden deposits going down into an arroyo. Across the arroyo were additional midden deposits and at least two more slab-lined features.

North of and below the natural bench is a lower bench with three pit house depressions, two arcs and one straight alignment of slab-lined features, and a possible rubble mound. In all, probably a dozen slab-lined features on the site had been dug out.

The Arizona State Museum collections include only 11 items provenienced to Juniper Cove, 10 collected by Cummings, and one donated later. They include four restored ceramic vessels, one ceramic jar effigy neck (donated by a John F. Manley in 1934), a flat piece of fired clay with a sandal impression, a ground selenite animal head (about 2 cm in diameter), a stone bowl, a stone ball, and two bone awls. Pottery includes one Obelisk Gray jar (ASM No. 4573), one Obelisk Gray seed jar (ASM No. 16878), one Lino Black-on-gray bowl (ASM No. 16887), one Lino Gray seed jar (ASM No. 16888), and the Lino Gray bird effigy jar neck (ASM No. 21255). That additional ceramic vessels were collected from the site is evident in photographs and text in Cummings 1953. A photograph (Cummings 1953:144) of five vessels from Juniper Cove includes only one of the vessels currently listed in Arizona State Museum records as coming from Juniper Cove. Therefore, at least four other ves-

sels in Arizona State Museum collections may come from Juniper Cove, including one hemispherical bowl, one seed jar, one recurved rim jar (cf. Morris 1980: figure 26a), and a "feeding cup."

Cummings felt that the plain gray ware pottery found on Juniper Cove was exemplary of the "first fired pottery in the north" (Cummings 1953:144). Cummings (1953: 142–144) identified "the cup, bowl, canteen, olla, ladle, and feeding cup" as characteristic vessel forms. The illustrated "cup" is actually a small jar. The illustrated bowl is a hemispherical bowl, undecorated but similar to the Lino Black-on-gray (and fugitive red) bowl in the Arizona State Museum collections (No. 16887), which is 20 cm in diameter and has a capacity of about 2.1 liters. The illustrated "canteen" is an elongated spherical jar with a small aperture flanked by two vertically pieced lug handles (cf. Morris 1980: figure 29a, b, c). One of the Obelisk Gray jars in the Arizona State Museum collections (ASM No. 4573) is similar to the illustrated example, although it is more spherical. It is 18 cm in diameter and has a capacity of about 3.1 liters. The illustrated "olla" is a spherical vessel with a small aperture and would be called a seed jar today. The illustrated example may be one of the two seed jars (one Obelisk Gray, the other Lino Gray) in the Arizona State Museum collections attributed to Juniper Cove. The Obelisk Gray seed jar (ASM No. 16878) is 23 cm in diameter and has a capacity of about 6.4 liters. The Lino Gray seed jar (ASM No. 16888) is 14 cm in diameter and has a capacity of 1.4 liters. The illustrated ladle or dipper is not represented in the Arizona State Museum collections attributed to Juniper Cove, nor is the "feeding cup." The illustrated ladle appears to have a solid handle. The "feeding cup" is a spherical vessel with a small aperture (essentially a seed jar) with a lateral spout extending from it. Similar examples were recovered from the Prayer Rock District (Morris 1980: figure 28a, c, d, e). One of the most interesting ceramic items that Cummings collected from Juniper Cove was the sandal-impressed slab of fired clay described more fully by Baldwin (1939). The sandal impression preserves a raised design from a sandal sole, like the ones from Basketmaker III sites in the Prayer Rock District described in detail by Hays-Gilpin et al. (1998).

Ceramics collected by Nusbaum for Gila Pueblo and now in the Arizona State Museum were mostly black-on-white and Tsegi Orange ware, representing Pueblo II and III period use of the site. Ceramics observed on July 13, 1991, were overwhelmingly plain gray, and globular vessels were noted. One Lino Black-on-gray sherd and one Kana-a Black-on-white sherd were also seen. Indented corrugated, Black Mesa Black-on-white, and Sosi Black-on-white sherds were observed in association with the Pueblo II room block. Isolated sherds of Tusayan Black-on-red and Tusayan Polychrome were present. Flaked

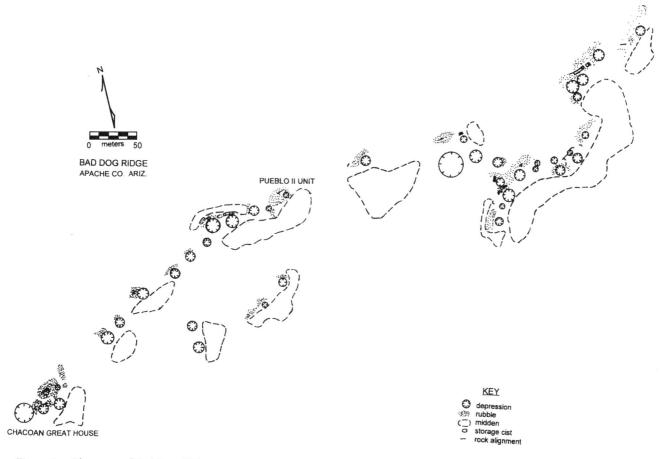

Figure 8.5. Plan map of Bad Dog Ridge.

stone artifacts were relatively rare (and none are present in Arizona State Museum collections attributed to the site). Brushy Basin chert was observed, and one white quartz side-notched point approximately 4 cm long was found. Only a few pieces of ground stone were seen during the 1991 visit. Cummings collected a stone bowl (Arizona State Museum No. 14671), a stone ball (Arizona State Museum No. 14673), and a ground selenite animal head (Arizona State Museum No. 14669) from Juniper Cove.

BAD DOG RIDGE

Bad Dog Ridge (figure 8.5), between Wide Ruins and Klagetoh, contains dwellings ranging in date from Basketmaker III until almost A.D. 1300. The site is unexcavated, but at least 40 pit structures (29 of them Basketmaker III) are present, including a large (24 m diameter, 2 m deep) Basketmaker III great kiva and a possible Basketmaker III–Pueblo I great kiva. Most of these pit structures have associated arcs of rubble and slab-lined storage units; 48 storage bins have been identified. The entire site covers 19.8 acres (8.0 ha) (Benallie 1993).

THE GANADO SITE

The Ganado Site (figure 8.6) covers a 67-acre (27 ha) area measuring 750 m northeast-southwest by 360 m northwest-southeast. The site is located on two mesas and on the northwest bank of the Pueblo Colorado Wash. The Pueblo Colorado Wash flows to the southwest in this area, across a broad sandy bed (300 m wide) that is entrenched as much as 2 m deep. Desert scrub vegetation and grassland dominate the bank of the wash, with isolated juniper and piñon on the mesa tops and slopes.

The Ganado Site is an extremely large habitation complex dating from Basketmaker III through Pueblo II, with isolated yellow ware sherds suggesting some use of the site during the Pueblo IV period. The site is unexcavated; Gilpin recorded it in 1991, and Larry Benallie Jr. mapped and recorded the site in detail in the summer of 1997. The site consists of five Basketmaker III–Pueblo I great kivas, nine pit house depressions, nine arcs of slab-lined storage bins, three trios of storage bins, five paired storage bins, 128 isolated storage bins, 275 upright slabs, 18 rock alignments, 27 rubble areas, 23 middens, 46 ash stains, six thermal features, two Pueblo I room bocks,

N

0 meters 50

THE GANADO SITE
(AZ-P-20-96[NN])
Apache Co., Ariz.

Pueblo Colorado Wash

CHACOAN
GREAT HOUSE

KEY

⊕ depression
▯ enclosed kiva
⟨⟩ rubble
⌐⌐ midden
○ storage cist
╱ upright slab
┬┬┬ stream bank
─∙∙∙─ drainage

CONTOURS (20') BASED ON USGS 7.5' MAP

Figure 8.6. Plan map of the Ganado Site.

five rubble mounds, one room and wall, one Pueblo II Chacoan-style great house, and one Pueblo II walled-in kiva.

Most of the architectural features, including the Pueblo II Chacoan great house, are located along the bank of the Pueblo Colorado Wash. Three great kivas, one arc of rooms, one pit house, 13 isolated slab-lined structures, 31 upright slabs, four rock alignments, eight rubble areas, one hearth, one ash stain, and one walled-in kiva and votive box are located on the mesa to the west of the Chacoan great house. Ceramics and architectural style indicate that all of these features are affiliated with the Basketmaker III–Pueblo I occupation of the site. Based on architectural style, the walled-in great kiva is thought to date to the same period as the Chacoan great

house below. The great kiva adjacent to the walled-in kiva may also date to this period, although it was recorded as a Basketmaker III great kiva.

The top of the mesa on the northwest side of the site contains two room blocks, one room and wall, two Basketmaker III great kivas, six pit houses, three arcs of slab-lined features, one trio of slab-lined features, 12 slab-lined features, 26 upright slabs, five rock alignments, four rubble mounds, four rubble concentrations, one ash stain, and three middens.

Except for Pueblo II ceramics in the vicinity of the Chacoan great house, and a few sherds of Jeddito Corrugated, virtually all of the ceramics on the site are plain gray. In his 1997 recording of the site, Benallie conducted in-field analysis of ceramics in 17 sample units: five in the vicinity of the Chacoan great house, and the other 12 scattered elsewhere across the site. Among the 12 sample units away from the great house, six contained Lino Black-on-gray sherds (from one to 10 sherds), 10 contained White Mound Black-on-white sherds (from one to 11 sherds), 10 contained Kiatuthlanna Black-on-white sherds (from one to 15 sherds), and seven contained neck-banded sherds (from one to five sherds). No unit contained gray ware or Lino Black-on-gray exclusively. Breternitz (1966:102) dates White Mound Black-on-white from A.D. 675 to 900 (although he states that it was most common between about A.D. 750 and 800), Kiatuthlanna Black-on-white to A.D. 850–910 (Breternitz 1966:80), and Kana-a Neckbanded from A.D. 760 to 900 (Breternitz 1966:79). The presence of these types at Ganado suggest that many of the slab-lined structures, pit houses, and early great kivas were in use until A.D. 850 or later.

Eight isolated pit house depressions were identified on the site, and one pit house depression was associated with an arc of storage bins. If even one pit house is associated with each of the other arcs of storage bins, as seems likely, then at least seven additional pit houses are probably present at the site. The arcs of storage bins contain from four to 21 bins each, with an average of 10 bins per arc. In addition, as mentioned above, three trios and five pairs of storage bins were also recorded, as well as 128 isolated storage bins. Finally, if the 275 upright slabs, 18 alignments, and 27 concentrations of rubble also represent storage features, then 539 slab-lined storage bins have been identified at the site. If the average of 10 storage bins per arc equates to the average number of storage bins per pit house, then 54 pit houses might be expected at the site. This would suggest that at least 54 households used the site between approximately A.D. 500 and 850. The duration and contemporaneity of occupation during this period cannot be determined without excavation.

OTHER BASKETMAKER III GREAT KIVAS IN NORTHEASTERN ARIZONA

Possible Basketmaker III great kivas have been noted at two other sites in the Chinle Valley. At Site NA9437—a Basketmaker III–Pueblo I habitation in Beautiful Valley south of Chinle—James (1974) excavated one surface room, one large D-shaped pit house with vestibule, 11 rectangular to square pit structures, two bins, two hearths, and two storage bins in one 15 by 30 m portion of a site that covers 92.4 acres (37.4 ha). To the east of the excavated features, James found a possible great kiva that he was not able to excavate.

At Site NA8800—a Basketmaker III–Pueblo I habitation near Chilchinbito—Gumerman in 1965 excavated two pit houses, one kiva, and 10 surface storage units;

one structure returned a tree-ring date of A.D. 805 (Bond et al. 1977:55–57). In 1977, New Mexico State University (NMSU) excavated three pit houses and found three others; NMSU also reported an arc-shaped alignment of stones that "may represent a large subterranean structure" that can be projected to be about 11 m in diameter (Bond et al. 1977:55–57).

REGIONAL COMPARISONS

Four additional Basketmaker III great kivas have been reported in the Navajo country, all of them in the San Juan Basin. These features occur at Shabik'eshchee Village, Broken Flute Cave, the Tohatchi Basketmaker Village, and Kiva Mesa.

At Shabik'eshchee Village (excavated), in Chaco Canyon, Roberts (1929) excavated 20 pit houses, 48 storage bins, and one great kiva in an area of approximately 2.2 acres (0.9 ha). More recently, Wills and Windes (1989:352, figure 3) have shown that the site covers nearly 18.5 acres (7.5 ha) and contains at least 49 more houses that were not excavated by Roberts. The great kiva, which is 12 m in diameter, is tree-ring dated from A.D. 557 to 581; one of the pit houses dates to A.D. 537.

Broken Flute Cave (excavated), in the Prayer Rock District of northeastern Arizona, contains 17 pit houses, 65 bins, and one great kiva in a cave with a floor area of approximately 3000 m^2 (Morris 1980). The great kiva is 18 m in diameter and lacks floor features (although it has not been fully excavated, only trenched). Four of the pit houses date to the late A.D. 400s; 12 pit houses were tree-ring dated from about A.D. 623 to 635.

The Tohatchi Basketmaker Village (unexcavated), in the Tohatchi Valley of northwestern New Mexico, contains 35 pit houses, 41 slab-lined storage rooms, and one great kiva in an area of 1.9 acres (0.8 ha) (Marshall et al. 1979:285–286; Stuart and Gauthier 1981:90, figure III.15). The great kiva is about 12 m in diameter.

Kiva Mesa (unexcavated), in the Redrock Valley of northwestern New Mexico, contains three great kivas (two are more than 15 m in diameter, one at 22 m in diameter), two plaza areas (one enclosed by a slab boundary), nine pit houses, one large (7 by 8 m) slab-lined room, 21 smaller (2 by 2 m to 5 by 5 m) square rooms, one 5 m diameter bin, and 10 to 15 smaller (1 to 2 m diameter) bins (P. Reed 1999a; P. Reed and Wilcox, this volume). The site covers about 6.2 acres (2.5 ha) on top of a low mesa.

The sites described above with known or suspected great kivas are among the largest recorded Basketmaker III sites in the Navajo country. Because excavations have been conducted at only three of the sites (Shabik'eshchee Village, Broken Flute Cave, and Juniper Cove), comparable statistics on all the sites are not available. Available evidence, however, indicates that sites with great kivas are much larger than the more usual Basketmaker III farmstead (see below). The Basketmaker III sites with great kivas range in size from 0.7 acres (0.3 ha) (at Broken Flute Cave, which is restricted in size because of its setting) to 121.0 acres (49.0 ha) at Ganado. Seven sites for which data are available average 26.1 acres (10.6 ha). The number of identified pit houses at these sites range from six at Juniper Cove to 68 at Shabik'-eshchee Village (although neither of these has been fully excavated). At the seven sites where the number of pit houses is known or estimated, 181 Basketmaker III (or Basketmaker III–Pueblo I) pit houses have been reported, for an average of at least 25.9 pit houses at sites with great kivas. Some 523 storage structures (mostly slab-lined storage bins) have been reported on the seven sites where data are available, for an average of 74.7 storage units per site and 2.9 storage units per pit house. Since excavations have been conducted at only four of the sites, these numbers of pit houses and storage units are considered low estimates. Wills and Windes (1989) did not estimate the number of storage units for the 49 pit houses they added to Shabik'eshchee Village. Roberts (1929) found 45 associated with the pit houses he excavated. Moreover, if upright slabs, rock alignments, and rubble areas are considered evidence of storage features, the Ganado site would have 539 storage features. If the Shabik'eshchee Village excavation data and the projected number of storage features at Ganado are used, the ratio would be 845 storage features per 132 pit houses, or 6.4 storage features per house.

Farmsteads and Seasonal Sites

The Basketmaker III sites with great kivas contrast with other excavated Basketmaker III sites in northeastern Arizona that appear to represent farmsteads and seasonal habitations (Bannister, Hannah, and Robinson 1966; Bond et al. 1977; Daifuku 1961; Fuller and Chang 1978; James 1974; Linford 1982; Trott and Chang 1975a, 1975b). Some 12 excavated Basketmaker III sites in the Chinle and Pueblo Colorado Valleys and on Black Mesa and the southern Defiance Plateau illustrate the variability in Basketmaker III sites west of the Chuska Mountains (see table 8.1).

Nine of these excavated sites consist of from one to eight or more pit houses, and from one to 26 storage units each. On average, each of these sites has four pit houses and 8.4 storage units (or 2.1 storage units per pit house). The largest and best-known of these sites is Jeddito 264 (A.D. 666–736, with 53 dates), which consists of seven pit houses, 16 slab-lined bins, 10 contiguous bins, and one Pueblo II room (Daifuku 1961). Pit houses were all circular with benches, central hearths, and ash pits. Floor ridges, entryways, antechambers, and ventilators were common. Data on site size, available for

eight of these sites, indicate that they are much smaller than sites with great kivas, ranging from 0.1 ha to 0.9 ha and averaging 0.3 ha. Three of these excavated sites consist of from one to three pit houses with no storage facilities. On average, these sites have 1.7 pit houses per site.

COMMUNITIES WITHOUT GREAT KIVAS

A few unexcavated Basketmaker III villages in northeastern Arizona suggest that not all large communities necessarily had great kivas. The Salina Springs Basketmaker Village (AZ-I-64-13 [NN]) on the eastern edge of Black Mesa, southwest of Chinle, contains 13 masonry surface structures, four pit houses, many slab-lined features, and five large and deep middens indicative of long occupation, and covers 5.3 ha, but apparently lacks a great kiva (Gilpin 1989). Nichols and Smiley (1985:62) state that A. V. Kidder reported a Basketmaker III site of more than 100 structures near Cow Springs, and also state that Windham and Dechambre (1978) recorded a Basketmaker III site of more than 30 pit houses at Piñon, on central Black Mesa (Nichols and Smiley 1985:63). Based on the above statistics, the Salina Springs Basketmaker village is within the range of variability of sites lacking great kivas, but the Cow Springs and Piñon sites should have great kivas.

In a number of large, residential Basketmaker III sites in the Navajo country, oversized pit structures or great pit structures have been reported. These structures are typically circular to subrectangular, measuring 6 to 9 m across (compared to great kivas, which range from 12 to 24 m across). They also have wing walls demarcating a chamber between the hearth and the ventilator shaft, and an antechamber connected to the main structure via a narrow tunnel. Examples have been noted at Shabik'-eshchee Village, Mexican Springs, Kiva Mesa, Twin Lakes, Tohatchi, and Oak Springs.

The oversized structure at Shabik'eshchee Village was subrectangular, measuring 6 m across, with a circular alcove connected to the main chamber by a tunnel. The main chamber had four support posts, a central hearth, and wing walls from the hearth to the corners on either side of the tunnel, creating a smaller chamber that contained slab-lined storage bins (Roberts 1929). This structure had been abandoned and filled, and a smaller pit house was later dug into the fill.

In 1990 the Zuni Archaeology Program excavated an oversized pit house at LA 61955 near Mexican Springs, southwest of Tohatchi (Damp and Kotyk, this volume; Damp 1999). The oversized pit house was a large, oval pit structure, 8 m by 11 m, with a central hearth, wing walls demarcating a chamber between the hearth and ventilator shaft, and a rectangular antechamber. The structure had a bench, and the lower bench walls were slab-lined, although the bench was placed where the postholes were, just as at Twin Lakes and Tohatchi. It was associated with a large Basketmaker III community containing multiple pit houses and numerous slab-lined storage units.

The Twin Lakes Site (NM-Q-18-130 [NN], LA 104106) consisted of six pit houses, including one over-sized pit house, and approximately 31 extramural features, including one bell-shaped pit and various pits and fire pits (Lakatos 1998). Structure 2 was a circular pit structure containing several large basin-shaped pits; Structure 3 was a small habitation; Structure 5 was an oval basin, probably a storage pit house; Structure 6 was a small habitation; Structure 7 was a small habitation; Structures 8 and 4 consisted of an oversized pit house (subrectangular and 7 m in diameter) and antechamber; and Feature 1 (5.5 m in diameter) was excavated into Structure 8.

In the Tohatchi area, Basketmaker III sites typically consist of a large pit house surrounded by "Pocket pit houses" (Kearns 1996c; Kearns et al., this volume). Kearns describes two Basketmaker III sites with large pit houses (having antechambers, floor vaults, sipapus, chambers demarcated by low walls, and antechambers) that he thinks may be community-integrative structures. Feature 4 at Site LA 80422 (Muddy Wash phase, A.D. 500–600) was an 8.5 m diameter pit house with an antechamber. Pit Structure 1 at the Electric Raven Site (LA 80934, Tohatchi phase, A.D. 600–725) was a circular 7.7 m diameter pit house with a rectangular antechamber, and was tree-ring dated to A.D. 701.

In the summer of 1999, the Navajo Nation Archaeology Department excavated a Basketmaker III site (AZ-K-12-48 [NN]) north of Oak Springs, Arizona, in the Black Creek Valley. The site consisted of four small pit houses and one large pit house measuring 9 m in diameter (Chuck Amsden, personal communication, 1999).

Although Damp (1999; see also Damp and Kotyk, this volume) and Kearns (1996c; Kearns et al., this volume) suggest that these structures may be community-integrative structures, they appear to have functioned primarily as dwellings, and could be interpreted as representing larger, perhaps extended, families. Moreover, the oversized pit structure at Shabik'eshchee Village had a smaller pit structure constructed in its fill, which supports the likelihood that this was a briefly occupied dwelling rather than a community-integrative structure.

GREAT KIVAS AND COMMUNITY STRUCTURE

As early as about A.D. 550, great kivas were constructed at sites ranging in size from 0.7 to 160.8 acres (0.3 to 49.0 ha) and containing from six to 68 pit houses, and as many as 539 slab-lined storage pits. West of the Chuska Mountains, this pattern is represented at three sites:

Juniper Cove, Bad Dog Ridge, and the Ganado Site. These sites range in size from 19.7 to 160.8 acres (6.0 to 49.0 ha) and contain from six to 29 pit structures and, on average, more than 225 slab-lined storage structures. Other sites west of the Chuska Mountains where possible Basketmaker III great kivas have been reported include Site NA8800, which contains at least eight pit houses, and Site NA9437, which contains at least five pit houses and 12 storage units. Smaller Basketmaker III sites west of the Chuska Mountains, ranging in size from 0.3 to 3.0 acres (0.1 to 0.9 ha) and containing up to eight pit houses, have been excavated, and no great kivas were in association with the sites.

The great kiva sites were thus the largest, most permanent, and most complex sites in a settlement pattern that also included isolated pit houses (single-household farmsteads) and clusters of pit houses (multiple-household hamlets). Assuming a family of four in each pit house and contemporaneity of all the pit houses, populations of these great kiva sites ranged from 24 (at Juniper Cove) to 272 (at Shabik'eshchee Village). Of course, these population estimates are extremely suspect for several reasons, two of which are most important. First, since most of the sites have not been fully excavated (and several have not been excavated at all), the number of pit houses is based mostly on surface manifestations, and pit houses may have been undercounted. Second, contemporaneity of pit houses has not been demonstrated, and if pit houses were occupied sequentially rather than concurrently, then using the number of pit houses on any site as an estimate of momentary population would result in overestimating the population. These two caveats tend to cancel each other, but the real point of the population estimates is to suggest that none of these villages constituted a community. Mahoney (1998) points out that a community needs a population of at least 475 to ensure that each individual can find an unrelated marriage partner of the right age. The population estimates for the great kiva sites suggest that even the largest of these sites housed no more than half of the people constituting a community.

Although the great kiva sites probably housed only a portion of their communities, they may have housed some people year-round and could even have been the location of much of the community's stored resources. Bradfield (1971:8) says that the Hopi required 20 to 24 bushels of maize per person per year. Wills and Windes (1989:357) note that the average storage bin at Shabik'eshchee Village had a volume of 1.6 m³. Since the excavated portion of the site had 2.4 storage bins per house, each house had 3.8 m³ of extramural storage space. Wills and Windes (1989:357) also note that each house had 1.7 m³ of storage facilities inside the house. In total, then, each house had 5.54 m³ of storage, enough to store 177 bushels of maize, or enough for 6.6 people for a year. At Broken Flute Cave, storage bins ranged from 1 to 2.5 m in length and from 0.5 to 1.5 m in width, with depths of as much as 2 m (Morris 1980:41). Using median dimensions of 1.25 by 1.0 by 1.0 m, each storage bin could have held 35.5 bushels. Since there were 3.8 storage bins per house, each house could have stored 134.9 bushels of maize, or enough for 6.6 people for a year. A circular storage unit 1 m in diameter and 1 m in height (or depth) could hold approximately 22 bushels, or enough maize for one person for a year. Cummings (1926[?]:2) says that the storage units at Juniper Cove were from 1.5 to 1.8 m in diameter. Assuming a median diameter of 1.65 m and a depth of 1 m, each storage bin could have held 60.7 bushels. Since there were 16.7 storage bins per house, each house could have stored 1013 bushels of maize, or enough for 42.2 people for a year. Measurements were taken at 27 of 40 storage features (most of which were rectangular) at the Bad Dog Ridge Site, and the average floor area was 5.1 m^2. If each storage unit was only 1 m in height, the average structure would have held 141.9 bushels. There were at least 1.4 storage units per dwelling at Bad Dog Ridge, so each house had enough storage for maize for 8.3 people per year. Some 155 circular storage bins at Ganado were measured and had an average diameter of 1.8 m. If each was 1 m in height, the average circular storage bin could have held 70.9 bushels. Measurements were taken at 37 rectangular structures, each of which had 4.9 m^2 of floor area, at least twice as much as the circular structures. Because of the depositional environment at the Ganado Site, pit houses were generally not visible on the surface, and the amount of storage per structure is difficult to estimate, but with potentially at least 539 storage structures, the Ganado Site clearly had immense amounts of storage capacity. P. Reed and Wilcox (this volume; P. Reed 1999a) indicate that the smaller storage bins at Kiva Mesa are 1 to 2 m in diameter. Assuming a median diameter of 1.5 m and an average depth of 1 m, the average storage bin held 50.1 bushels, and with 1.7 storage bins per house, each house could store 85 bushels, or enough maize for 3.5 persons for a year. The Tohatchi Basketmaker Village is the only great kiva site for which no data are available on dimensions of storage facilities, but with only 1.2 storage bins per house, this site had the lowest storage capacity per house of any of the great kiva sites.

These are admittedly extremely rough estimates, but they suggest that the great kiva sites could have had enough storage capacity to support year-round occupation, and even to store considerable amounts of surplus. Furthermore, the sites with great kivas typically have a much greater ratio of extramural storage bins per house (6.4 bins per house) than sites lacking either great kivas or great pit structures (1.6 bins per house). It thus seems possible that even as early as the Basketmaker III period, sites with ritual architecture may have begun to acquire greater resources than sites lacking ritual architecture.

CONCLUSIONS

In chapter 12 of this volume, Robins and Hays-Gilpin discuss the role of the great kiva in the social and ritual reorganization that characterized the Basketmaker III period. They note that Basketmaker II peoples were relatively mobile, living in small, seasonally occupied settlements. There was little need for rigid sexual division of labor or gender markers. Ritual, particularly as depicted in rock art, focused on shamanic practices. Increasing dependence on agriculture and increasing sedentism in the Basketmaker III period may have led to increased sexual division of labor, matrilineal control of farmland, and matrilocal residence. Individual Basketmaker III settlements would have been exogamous, and communal rituals would have developed to allow the men in those settlements to maintain contacts with consanguineal relatives living in other settlements. Since men would have had the strongest consanguineal relationships with people from other settlements, they would have had the greatest ability and incentive to control communal ritual. Robins and Hays-Gilpin argue that female control of domestic activities and male control of ritual activities constituted an increased differentiation in genders that is manifest in decorative arts. They suggest that decoration of Basketmaker III sandals, textiles, pottery, and baskets, which were probably all made by women and might be considered feminine, contrasts with Basketmaker III rock art, which might therefore be considered masculine. The masculine control of communal great kiva ritual is therefore manifest in the association of a petroglyph showing a procession and located near the great kiva in the "ritual" portion of Broken Flute Cave, some distance away from the domestic portion of the cave (where the dwellings were concentrated).

The size, population, and storage capacity of the Basketmaker III great kiva sites of the Navajo country provide a complementary perspective for understanding the transition to settled village life in the northern Southwest. Specifically, the size, population, and storage capacity of the great kiva sites indicate both the degree of sedentism and the senses in which Basketmaker III populations can be said to have become increasingly sedentary. Estimates of site size and amount of storage taken together suggest that sites with great kivas were only portions of larger communities, but that the great kiva sites could have been occupied year-round and could even have stored community surpluses. In the transition to settled village life, increasing dependence on agriculture led to matrilocality; matrilineal control of farmland; a need for communal ritual to integrate increasingly permanent hamlets and farmsteads that could not persist independently; development of the great kiva, where such rituals could be performed at the largest, most permanent sites; masculine control of the great kiva; and development of site hierarchy, centralization, and unequal concentrations of surplus. The settled village life that characterized Pueblo culture in its various historical and geographic variants was not yet fully developed, but one of the major transformations in its history can be seen in the attributes of Basketmaker III community structure. This study has relied heavily on survey data and excavation data from the early years of Southwestern archaeology, but the picture these data suggest is of significant change in a seminal period of Puebloan history.

ACKNOWLEDGMENTS

The 1991 visit to Juniper Cove was organized by Cory Breternitz and authorized under Navajo Nation Cultural Resources Visitation Permit A9115. John Stein alerted us to the Ganado Site, and Stein and Gilpin first visited it together. Benallie's mapping and recording of the Ganado Site was funded by a grant from the National Park Service. Phil Geib provided a copy of Baldwin's article and some useful corrections to the paper. Laurie Webster provided copies of her notes on Cummings material at the Arizona State Museum and Arizona Historical Society, compiled as part of the Arizona State Museum Cummings Documentation Project. The Arizona Historical Society graciously loaned the photographs (figures 8.3 and 8.4) used in this chapter. Mike Jacobs took Gilpin through the bowels of the Arizona State Museum to see the few artifacts that Cummings collected from Juniper Cove, and suggested other avenues to pursue. Alan Ferg and Beth Grindell directed Gilpin to copies of Nusbaum's site form. Deb Nichols, Chip Wills, and Rich Wilshusen thoughtfully reviewed earlier drafts of this chapter. In addition to organizing this volume and offering many helpful comments on this paper, Paul Reed provided information on Kiva Mesa.

9

The Basketmaker II–III Transition on the Rainbow Plateau

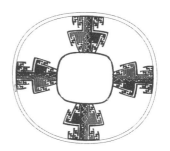

Phil R. Geib

Kimberly Spurr

Subdividing a continuum of cultural development within a region is a common problem for archaeologists. The advent of pottery manufacture traditionally seemed an unambiguous and useful marker for dividing the continuum of Basketmaker cultural development, and was explicitly incorporated into the Pecos Classification for such purpose (Kidder 1927). Most archaeologists working on the Colorado Plateau use ceramics to differentiate between Basketmaker II and III (cf. Berry 1982:88). Pottery occurs on open as well as sheltered sites, making it a more widely documented trait than the many perishable remains (e.g., sandals and feather blankets) that may also serve as markers of this transition. Pottery also seems to have made a rather sudden sweeping appearance across the Four Corners region, so that by A.D. 500 or shortly thereafter it is found nearly everywhere.[1]

But what if you have Basketmaker remains younger than A.D. 500 and no pottery? The impact to archaeological interpretation of just such an occurrence is well illustrated by research on the Rainbow Plateau of northeastern Arizona and southeastern Utah (figure 9.1). The Museum of Northern Arizona's (MNA) excavation of Sand Dune Cave at the foot of Navajo Mountain unearthed Basketmaker materials but no sherds of Lino Gray or Obelisk Gray. Charcoal chunks from a hearth believed to be associated with the Basketmaker remains provided noncutting tree-ring dates up to A.D. 700. On this evidence, Lindsay et al. (1968:364) suggested that "development of the Basketmaker tradition into a later manifestation characterized by ceramics, the bow and arrow, and a different settlement and community patterning is not evidenced on the plateau." To this day there are references to the persistence of a Basketmaker II lifeway beyond A.D. 700 in the Kayenta region (e.g., Dean 1996:29, 32; Gumerman and Dean 1989:111).

In the context of our current understanding of the Basketmaker period, it is reasonable to question what a continuation of Basketmaker II lifeways means. Basketmaker II groups (at least late Basketmaker II) can no longer be considered as modified hunter-gatherers, for evidence indicates that they were nearly as dependent upon maize as were Basketmaker III and later Puebloan populations (Chisholm and Matson 1994; Matson and Chisholm 1991:456; cf. Wills 1992:159). Increased reliance on cultigens, therefore, may not be a distinguishing characteristic of Basketmaker III. Nor is the occurrence of semisedentary habitations, since these have been documented during Basketmaker II on Black Mesa (Smiley 1985), Cedar Mesa (Matson 1991), and the Rainbow Plateau (discussed below). If it is merely the absence of ceramics, beans, and the bow and arrow that indicates a continuation of Basketmaker II lifeways, then no claim for their absence can be made, as this chapter demonstrates. This new evidence highlights the common problem in using stage- or phase-based schemes in our attempt to describe and explain change in cultures. Basketmaker III traits such as pottery, the bow and arrow, beans, and turkey domestication do not appear as a "suite" at a single point in time, nor were these items equally adopted by all contemporaneous households on the Rainbow Plateau.

THE RAINBOW PLATEAU

Environment

The Rainbow Plateau is a broad, generally north-sloping tableland of sandstone and siltstone lying south of the confluence of the Colorado and San Juan Rivers in northeast Arizona and southeast Utah (figures 9.1 and 9.2). A magma intrusion pushed up the ancient sedimentary layers on the northwest edge of the plateau, creating the magnificent dome known as Navajo Mountain. This

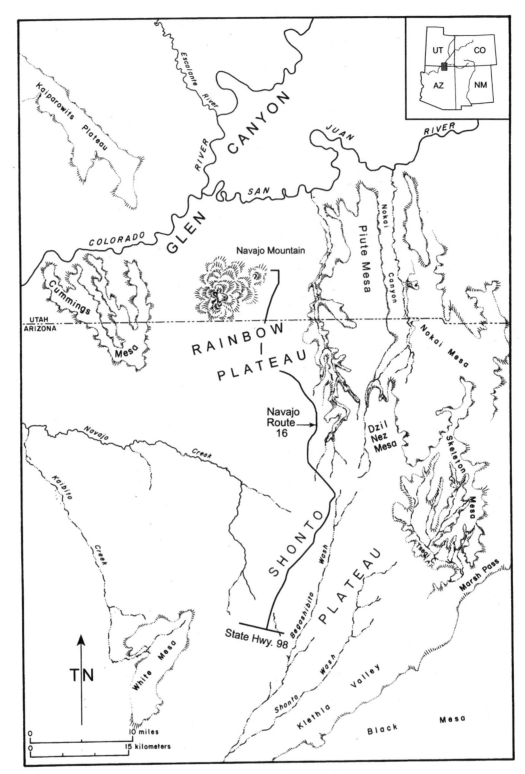

Figure 9.1. General location of Navajo Mountain and the Rainbow Plateau, northeast Arizona and southeast Utah.

singular, dominating topographic feature rises to a height of 3166 m elevation, about 1200 m above the plateau generally and some 2100 m above the Glen Canyon lowlands. These lowlands define the northern limits of the plateau. The south and west sides are defined by a relatively abrupt break known as the Chaiyahi Rim, below which are the labyrinthine canyons that drain into Navajo and Aztec Creeks. The canyon of Aztec Creek, also known as Forbidding Canyon, separates the Rainbow Plateau from the adjacent bedrock platform of Cummings Mesa. The large canyon of Piute Creek defines the eastern edge of the plateau.

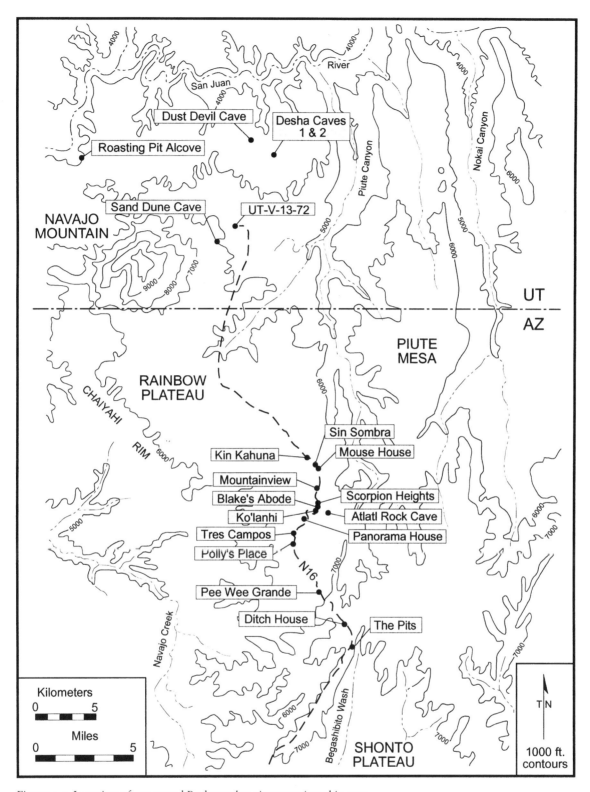

Figure 9.2. Location of excavated Basketmaker sites mentioned in text.

Most of the Rainbow Plateau ranges in elevation from about 1650 m to 2070 m. The highest elevations are along the southeast edge and around the lower flanks of Navajo Mountain. The northern portion of the plateau slopes toward the canyons of the San Juan and Colorado Rivers. Vegetation is mainly characterized by piñon and juniper forest and broad sage flats; a blackbrush community predominates across the northern lower elevation portion of the plateau. Pine, aspen, spruce, and fir cover the mountain.

Opportunities for farmers on the Rainbow Plateau are diverse and include settings suitable for floodwater, dry, and irrigation farming, techniques that local Navajo and Paiute families still use. Runoff from Navajo Mountain and the high divide on the southeast edge of the plateau allow for floodwater farming in the wash bottoms, as do several of the broad washes that cross the plateau. Some of the more productive modern fields are located in such settings. Irrigation and high water table farming is possible in the canyons adjacent to the plateau and draining its northern edge. Prehistoric irrigation features occur at several locations in the area (Lindsay 1961; Lindsay et al. 1968). Extensive dune fields and large falling dunes offer dry-farming opportunities during wetter years.

A massive slickrock divide separating upper Piute Canyon from the western tributaries of Navajo Creek is the one artery of high land connecting the Rainbow Plateau with the Shonto Plateau to the south. Along this route in the 1920s, Hubert Richardson built a road to start a trading business at the foot of Navajo Mountain (Richardson 1986). This historic track doubtless followed a route that natives had used for millennia. Richardson's original road has been improved over the years and is now known as Navajo Route 16 (N16). N16 is currently in the process of further metamorphosis from a graded but rough dirt road to a black asphalt ribbon. It is the excavation of sites threatened by this proposed construction that provides the bulk of new evidence presented here.

Relevant Previous Research

The Rainbow Plateau has been the location of sporadic archaeological research beginning in the early 1900s. The only early activity of particular relevance to our discussion was the excavation of two Basketmaker caves along Desha Creek by the Van Bergen–Los Angeles Museum Expedition. Irwin Hayden's (1930) unpublished manuscript on these two sites, known as Desha Caves 1 and 2, was incorporated into a master's thesis by Allan Schilz (1979). Until now, no chronometric dates were available for these caves; radiocarbon dates presented below demonstrate use of the sites between roughly A.D. 75 and A.D. 630.

During the Glen Canyon Project of the late 1950s and early 1960s, MNA archaeologists assembled the first truly detailed record of the region's prehistoric remains. Part of the project involved survey and excavation on the Rainbow Plateau (Lindsay et al. 1968), including the complete excavation of Sand Dune Cave. Because the findings from this site led to the postulated continuation of Basketmaker II lifeways, it will be further discussed below. Another site excavated by MNA was Roasting Pit Alcove, a site in lower Oak Canyon, at the northern edge of the Rainbow Plateau (Long 1966). Here archaeologists recovered Basketmaker II style sandals and other remains, but no pottery. Charcoal from a large roasting feature yielded a radiocarbon date with a two-sigma cali-

brated range of A.D. 405–670 (1510 ± 80 B.P., Long 1966:60, no laboratory number reported, but assayed by the University of Arizona).

Following the Glen Canyon Project, the next significant work in the area was by Northern Arizona University (NAU) under the direction of J. Richard Ambler. In 1970 he fully excavated Dust Devil Cave (Ambler 1996) and tested several other caves in the area. Recent dating of corn from Dust Devil Cave returned assays within the A.D. 400 to 800 range (Geib 1996a:59–60, table 11). In the 1980s Ambler and students began a multiyear survey of the lush upper Piute Canyon (Fairley 1989), recording several sites with early pottery assigned to the Basketmaker III stage. In 1981, NAU archaeologists excavated eight sites in the construction area for a new Navajo Mountain boarding school, including UT-V-13-72 (NAU), an aceramic site with maize. Wood charcoal from a hearth returned a radiocarbon date with a two-sigma calibrated range of A.D. 265–995 (1400 ± 170 B.P., A-3086, Geib et al. 1985:234), which the authors thought fit the purported lengthened Basketmaker II occupation for the plateau.

The only significant archaeological research on the Rainbow Plateau during the late 1980s and 1990s was the excavation effort for the proposed paving of N16. This project is still in progress, and a final report on the work may not be available until at least 2001. Project findings to date have prompted this revaluation of Basketmaker occupancy on the plateau and provide most of the data for this chapter.

Sand Dune Cave

Excavation of Sand Dune Cave recovered an assemblage of artifacts characteristic of Basketmaker II culture, artifacts resembling those from White Dog Cave and similar sites of the Kayenta region (Lindsay et al. 1968). Significantly, the excavation recovered no early pottery; the earliest types from the cave were late Kana-a Black-on-white (a.k.a. Wepo Black-on-white) and Kana-a Gray (Lindsay et al. 1968:54–55). A twined bag from Cache 1 seemed transitional between Basketmaker II and III: it was "morphologically more similar to Basketmaker III bags than to Basketmaker II ones, although associated with typical Basketmaker II artifacts" (Lindsay et al. 1968:102). Included in the bag were six atlatl dart foreshafts with hafted points and a pouch with 16 dart point preforms. Charcoal from Hearth 9 yielded 28 noncutting (vv) tree-ring dates. The youngest date from this feature was A.D. 701++vv, with the others ranging from 491 to 696 (Harlan and Dean 1968:381). By linking the tree-ring dates with the Basketmaker II remains from the cave, continuation of a Basketmaker II lifeway seemed evident.

There are two problems with this interpretation. First, there is no association between the hearth and the Basketmaker II materials, and second, the dates likely do not accurately represent the true age of the fire. Concerning the first issue, Hearth 9 was situated near the front of the cave where deposits were too shallow to positively correlate the feature with cave strata (Lindsay et al. 1968:41). Lacking secure association with the Basketmaker II remains, the tree-ring dates have no necessary bearing upon the age of these materials. Moreover, even if the hearth could be positively linked to the cave deposits, excavation by arbitrary levels precludes firm association of any remains with the tree-ring dates.

The second question is more critical and was peripherally addressed in the site report with the statement "it is unlikely that 150 or more rings would have been lost from all charcoal specimens" (Lindsay et al. 1968:102). Ring loss is a minor concern compared with the age of the wood before burning. Based on Smiley's (1985) analysis of Basketmaker II dating on northern Black Mesa, we can safely assume that the wood burned in Hearth 9 was at least 200 years dead. This, plus some ring loss, places the true age of the hearth within the time frame represented by the Pueblo I pottery from the cave. It is more tenable that dead wood was burned in Hearth 9 around the tenth century, than to presume that a live tree was cut down and set ablaze shortly after A.D. 700.

There is still the Basketmaker III style twined bag from Cache 1 (see artifact discussion in Lindsay et al. 1968: 89). The problem with this evidence is a virtual lack of chronological control over the materials used for comparison. Recent dating of maize from White Dog Cave and other Marsh Pass sites indicates a considerable time depth for Basketmaker II, back to at least 600 B.C. (Smiley et al. 1986; Smiley 1993). With this stage now spanning more than a millennium, there must be temporal changes in various classes of material culture that have yet to be identified. The Basketmaker II bags described by Guernsey and Kidder (1921:66–74) might all date earlier than the Christian era; thus, the Cache 1 bag from Sand Dune Cave may appear different because it is some 500 years younger, yet still older than A.D. 700 and likely older than A.D. 500. Until we understand how Basketmaker material culture changed through time, something that will doubtless require many direct dates, it is not possible to make a convincing case for the Cache 1 bag being Basketmaker III-like.

CHRONOLOGY

Because chronology is essential to all further discussion, we will treat it first. Prior to 1990, chronological control for Basketmaker occupancy of the Rainbow Plateau was provided by just three radiocarbon dates on wood charcoal from hearths at three sites: a large roasting pit at Roasting Pit Alcove [Long 1966:60]; Hearth 3 at Dust Devil Cave [Lindsay et al. 1968:108]; and Feature 2 at UT-V-13-72 (NAU; Geib et al. 1985:234). During the

past several years the number of Basketmaker radiocarbon dates for the Rainbow Plateau has mushroomed, due mainly to the ongoing N16 excavations. By the end of fieldwork we will have studied portions or all of at least 14 Basketmaker sites; 12 sites have been sampled and radiocarbon dated so far. Although some Basketmaker sites produced tree-ring samples, unfortunately none could be dated. Limited excavation of Atlatl Rock Cave (Geib et al. 1999) and the dating of maize and other remains from previously excavated sites such as Dust Devil Cave (Geib 1996a) and Desha Caves 1 and 2 (Geib 2000) have contributed to a refinement of Basketmaker chronology.

The 68 radiocarbon dates (table 9.1) that currently underlie the Basketmaker chronology for the Rainbow Plateau are largely on maize ($n = 46$, or 68 percent). Most of the other dates are on materials that likewise do not overestimate age and have clear cultural origin. Five are on juniper bark and one on grass used in storage cists, either as fiber temper for mortar of floors and walls ($n = 4$) or as lining for the items being stored ($n = 1$). There are two dates on juniper seeds, one on juniper twigs that represent annual growth, one on a piñon cone scale, one on monocot stems (annual growth), and two on the outer rings of burned posts. Sage used as fuel provides four of the dates, but these assays usually closely accord with maize dates when cross-checks are available. The lowest-quality dates are five on wood charcoal (just 7 percent of the total): three of these are the hearth dates obtained prior to 1990, and two are from recently excavated hearths that contained no carbonized remains other than piñon and juniper charcoal.

One way to examine the date distribution in detail is to plot all dates individually showing both one- and two-sigma calibrated ranges, as done in figure 9.3. All dates were calibrated using the CALIB program, version 3.0.3A (Stuiver and Reimer 1993; 20-year data set, method A). All maize and other nonwood dates, as well as those wood dates obtained by AMS analysis, have been corrected for 13C fractionation based on measured values. Figure 9.3 reveals a nearly continuous series of dates spanning almost 1200 years from roughly 400 B.C. to A.D. 800. Two relatively recent wood charcoal dates, one with a standard deviation of 170 years, account for the portion of the date spread above A.D. 800 and may well correspond to later use intervals than the period of interest here. By eliminating these from consideration, A.D. 800 becomes the terminal end of the date distribution.

Temporal patterning in the remaining 66 radiocarbon dates may be better perceived as graphed in figure 9.4. The interval widths for these histograms are 50 years (Figure 4a) and 100 years (Figure 4b); the former is slightly less than the mean of standard deviations for the sample (62 years), whereas the latter is slightly less than

TABLE 9.1
List of Radiocarbon Dates from Basketmaker Sites of the Rainbow Plateau

Sequence No.	Site	Sample No.	Material	Radiocarbon Age	Calibrated two-sigma range
1	The Pits	B-73979	maize	2230 ± 60	400–110 B.C.
2	Kin Kahuna	B-87904	maize	2210 ± 50	390–110 B.C.
3	Kin Kahuna	B-87905	maize	2210 ± 50	390–110 B.C.
4	Kin Kahuna	B-87903	maize	2190 ± 60	390–50 B.C.
5	The Pits	B-73984	maize	2190 ± 60	390–50 B.C.
6	The Pits	B-73982	maize	2180 ± 60	385–45 B.C.
7	Ditch House	B-102489	sage	2180 ± 40	370–100 B.C.
8	The Pits	B-73983	juniper twigs	2160 ± 60	375–35 B.C.
9	Kin Kahuna	B-87898	maize	2140 ± 50	360–35 B.C.
10	Ko'lanhi	B-94767	juniper seeds	2120 ± 60	360 B.C.–A.D. 15
11	Kin Kahuna	B-94764	maize	2090 ± 80	365 B.C.–A.D. 80
12	Ko'lanhi	B-94768	maize	2080 ± 60	340 B.C.–A.D. 65
13	Kin Kahuna	B-94763	maize	2080 ± 50	195 B.C.–A.D. 55
14	Ditch House	B-94765	maize	2080 ± 40	190 B.C.–A.D. 15
15	The Pits	B-73981	sage	2070 ± 70	350 B.C.–A.D 80
16	The Pits	AA-19519	maize	2035 ± 65	190 B.C.–A.D. 120
17	Ditch House	B-94766	piñon cone scale	2010 ± 60	165 B.C.–A.D. 125
18	The Pits	AA-19522	maize	2005 ± 65	170 B.C.–A.D. 135
19	The Pits	AA-19521	maize	1995 ± 65	160 B.C.–A.D. 140
20	The Pits	B-79145	maize	1990 ± 60	115 B.C.–A.D. 135
21	Kin Kahuna	B-94761	maize	1990 ± 50	90 B.C.–A.D. 125
22	Tres Campos	B-87911	outer rings of post	1980 ± 60	105 B.C.–A.D. 140
23	Kin Kahuna	B-87901	maize	1960 ± 60	60 B.C.–A.D. 215
24	The Pits	AA-19520	maize	1940 ± 65	50 B.C.–A.D. 235
25	The Pits	B-79148	maize	1920 ± 50	5 B.C.–A.D. 230
26	Panorama House	B-101393	outer rings of post	1890 ± 40	A.D. 60–235
27	Desha Cave 2	B-102496	juniper bark	1880 ± 60	A.D. 10–320
28	Sin Sombra	B-94754	maize	1850 ± 60	A.D. 60–335
29	Sin Sombra	B-94755	maize	1840 ± 60	A.D. 65–345
30	Kin Kahuna	B-87902	maize	1840 ± 50	A.D. 75–330
31	Desha Cave 1	B-102492	maize	1840 ± 50	A.D. 75–330
32	Dust Devil Cave	TX-852	wood charcoal	1820 ± 80	A.D. 25–415
33	Sin Sombra	B-94756	maize	1820 ± 60	A.D. 75–385
34	Mouse House	B-94758	twigs	1820 ± 50	A.D. 85–345
35	Panorama House	B-101394	juniper seed	1820 ± 50	A.D. 85–345
36	Atlatl Rock Cave	B-68380	juniper bark	1810 ± 90	A.D. 20–425
37	Atlatl Rock Cave	B-68379	juniper bark	1810 ± 70	A.D. 70–410
38	Mouse House	B-94759	sage	1810 ± 60	A.D. 80–390
39	Mountainview	B-87912	maize	1810 ± 50	A.D. 85–375
40	Scorpion Heights	B-94769	sage	1800 ± 60	A.D. 85–400
41	Kin Kahuna	B-87900	maize	1780 ± 60	A.D. 120–415
42	Mountainview	B-87913	maize	1770 ± 60	A.D. 125–415
43	Panorama House	B-118050	maize	1760 ± 50	A.D. 140–415
44	Mountainview	B-87914	maize	1750 ± 60	A.D. 135–425
45	Sin Sombra	B-94753	maize	1750 ± 60	A.D. 135–425
46	Polly's Place	AA-19524	maize	1750 ± 50	A.D. 145–415
47	Kin Kahuna	B-94762	maize	1740 ± 50	A.D. 150–420
48	Kin Kahuna	B-87899	maize	1730 ± 60	A.D. 145–435
49	Panorama House	B-101396	maize	1730 ± 60	A.D. 145–435
50	Desha Cave 1	B-102493	maize	1730 ± 60	A.D. 145–435
51	Panorama House	B-118051	maize	1720 ± 50	A.D. 225–430

Sequence No.	Site	Sample No.	Material	Radiocarbon Age	Calibrated two-sigma range
52	Atlatl Rock Cave	B-68381	maize	1710 ± 60	A.D. 220–450
53	Panorama House	B-101395	maize	1710 ± 50	A.D. 235–435
54	Desha Cave 1	B-102494	juniper bark	1670 ± 80	A.D. 220–590
55	Pee Wee Grande	B-79153	wood charcoal	1660 ± 50	A.D. 255–540
56	Atlatl Rock Cave	B-68383	grass	1640 ± 70	A.D. 250–595
57	Polly's Place	B-79159	sage	1640 ± 60	A.D. 255–555
58	Polly's Place	B-79160	maize	1610 ± 50	A.D. 345–595
59	Desha Cave 2	B-102495	juniper bark	1590 ± 70	A.D. 265–630
60	Polly's Place	B-79161	maize	1580 ± 50	A.D. 395–605
61	Polly's Place	AA-19523	maize	1550 ± 65	A.D. 395–650
62	Atlatl Rock Cave	AA-19526	maize	1535 ± 65	A.D. 405–655
63	Roasting Pit Alcove	M[a]	wood charcoal	1510 ± 80	A.D. 405–670
64	Atlatl Rock Cave	B-68382	maize	1500 ± 60	A.D. 425–660
65	Dust Devil Cave	B-47893	maize	1480 ± 80	A.D. 420–680
66	UT-V-13-72	A-3086	wood charcoal	1400 ± 170	A.D. 265–995
67	Dust Devil Cave	B-47894	maize	1370 ± 70	A.D. 560–785
68	Pee Wee Grande	B-79154	wood charcoal	1270 ± 70	A.D. 655–970

[a]Assayed by University of Arizona; no sample number reported by Long (1966).

twice this mean. These histograms indicate continuous occupancy of the Rainbow Plateau from almost 400 B.C. up to at least A.D. 700 (the one date in the eighth century is on wood charcoal). There are no clear gaps in the distributions, but there is an obvious increase in dates between about A.D. 200 and 300. This 3rd century spike may relate to a population increase or it may simply be a product of biased sampling. Before graphs such as these will be informative about population trends, we need considerably more dates from a larger sample of sites,

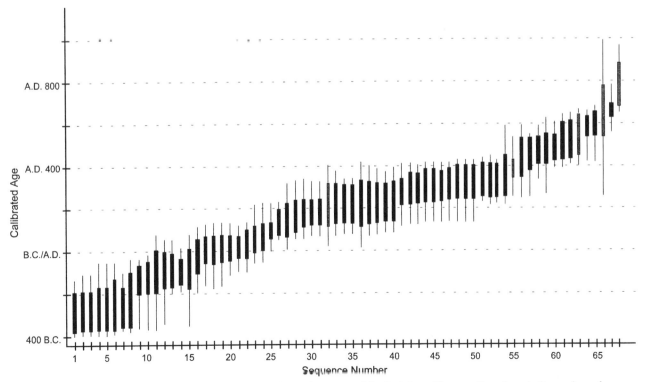

Figure 9.3. Distribution of radiocarbon dates from Basketmaker sites of the Rainbow Plateau. Gray bars indicate dates from wood charcoal; most of the rest are dates on maize or other high-quality materials.

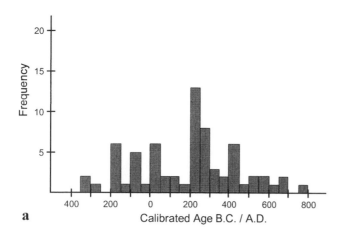

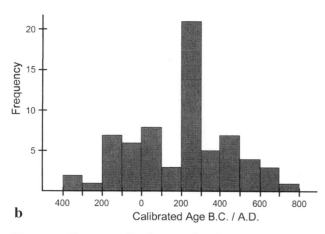

Figure 9.4. Frequency distribution of Basketmaker radiocarbon dates from the Rainbow Plateau: (a) 50-year intervals; (b) 100-year intervals.

from all portions of the plateau. The fall-off in dates after A.D. 700 is an artifact of using 1300 B.P. as the upper limit for inclusion in this analysis, but it may well reflect a real population trend. As yet, few sites are known from the plateau with ceramic assemblages containing Lino Black-on-gray and Kana-a Black-on-white.

The distribution of Basketmaker dates for the Rainbow Plateau stands in marked contrast to Michael Berry's summary of the Basketmaker chronometric data for the Colorado Plateau available in 1980 (see Berry 1982: figure 10). He identified three discrete temporal clusters: Period I, or early Basketmaker II, from about 200 B.C. to the time of Christ; Period II, or late Basketmaker II, from about A.D. 200 to 400; and Period III, or Basketmaker III, from A.D. 500 to 700. Under the working assumption that the patterning disclosed was not sampling error, Berry (1982:87) argued that "occupation occurred in three discrete periods, each separated in time by significant hiatuses." Regarding the topic of our pa-

per, Berry (1982:116–117) stressed that "late Basketmaker II and Basketmaker III cluster tightly into discrete periods; hence it is unnecessary to draw an arbitrary dividing line between these stages.... there are no sites that bridge the greater than two-century gap separating these stages." When we look at the date distribution for the Rainbow Plateau, there are no evident breaks marking a natural line of separation. If one wanted to subdivide this distribution, then an arbitrary line would be called for. Where, though, should such a line be placed? Does the adoption of new material culture items, such as pottery, provide an answer? What about changes in subsistence or settlement? Each of these issues will be examined in turn, starting with settlement, but first, one additional comment is in order.

Although the distribution of Basketmaker dates for the Rainbow Plateau does not support Berry's tripartite temporal scheme, it supports his critique of Glassow's (1972) proposed explanation of the Basketmaker II–III transition as a response to stress resulting from steady population increase. As Berry (1982:89) sees it, Glassow "set for himself the problem of explaining a series of events that probably never happened." With a two-hundred-year gap separating the strong temporal clustering of Basketmaker II sites from Basketmaker III sites, Berry concluded that increasing population density could not be used as an independent variable in an explanatory model. On the Rainbow Plateau, there is no evidence for a two-hundred-year gap in occupancy, but neither is there evidence for steady population increase.

SETTLEMENT

Settlement Types
In a broad summary of Basketmaker II (Lolomai phase) archaeology for northern Black Mesa, Smiley (1985: 261–330; 1993:248–250) identified five general site types based largely on architecture. Generally increasing in size and complexity from small sites with few and simple features to large sites with many and diverse features, these five types are open camps, nonstorage habitations, earthen pit storage habitations, bedrock pit house settlements, and rock shelters. This last category may include sites functionally equivalent to the other types but occurring in naturally sheltered settings. As Smiley (1993:250) suggests, many shelters were probably used for habitation purposes. On the Rainbow Plateau this is true for sites such as Sand Dune and Atlatl Rock Caves, but there are also examples that likely were almost exclusively used for storage, such as the Desha Caves 1 and 2 (Lipe [1970:100–103] discusses similar sites from the Red Rock Plateau).

Based on the N16 excavations, we have identified sites that fit the characteristics for each of the open site types except bedrock pit house settlements, which may not oc-

TABLE 9.2
Basketmaker Sites of the Rainbow Plateau

Site Type	Site Name or Number	Extent of Study	Living Structures[1]	Storage Pits[1]	Storage Cists[1]	Obelisk Utility	Arrow Points	Date Range[2]
Open Habitations with Storage	Kin Kahuna	Excavation	7+	26+			+	390 B.C.–A.D. 435
	The Pits	Excavation	1+	24+	+			400 B.C.–A.D. 230
	Big Bend	Testing	2+	?	1+			unknown
	AZ-J-14-54 (NN)	Survey	5+		+	+	+	unknown
	AZ-D-2-174 (NAU)	Survey	2+		+	+		unknown
	AZ-D-2-200 (NAU)	Survey	1?		+	+		unknown
	AZ-D-2-355 (NAU)	Survey	1		6+	+	+	unknown
Open Habitations without Storage	Blake's Abode	Excavation	1					unknown
	Ditch House	Excavation	2					165 B.C.–A.D. 20
	Mountainview	Excavation	1			+	+	A.D. 145–375
	Panorama House	Excavation	1+					A.D. 240–420
	Polly's Place	Excavation	2			+		A.D. 145–650
	Sin Sombra	Excavation	1					A.D. 130–325
	Tres Campos	Excavation	1					105 B.C.–A.D. 140
Sheltered Habitations with Storage	Sand Dune Cave	Excavation	+[3]		20			unknown
	Atlatl Rock Cave	Testing	2+[4]	1+	21+	+	+	A.D. 20–660
	Ch'íídii Cave	Testing	+[5]		3+			unknown
Sheltered Storage	Desha Cave 1	Excavation			21			A.D. 75–590
	Desha Cave 2	Excavation			12			A.D. 10–630
	Dust Devil Cave	Excavation		+	22		+	A.D. 25–785
	Roasting Pit Alcove[6]	Excavation			2			A.D. 405–670[7]
Open Camps	Ko'lanhi	Excavation						360 B.C.–A.D. 65
	Mouse House	Excavation						A.D. 80–345
	Pee Wee Grande	Excavation						A.D. 255–970
	Scorpion Heights	Excavation						A.D. 90–395
	Windy Mesa	Excavation						unknown

[1] Feature counts are given when known; a count and + sign indicate that additional features are expected but incomplete excavation or no excavation precludes an accurate count; a + sign alone indicates that such features are known but an exact count is not possible.

[2] Date range is based on radiocarbon dates using the calibrated two-sigma range of date averages for short-occupancy sites or the maximum range of oldest and youngest dates for long-occupancy sites.

[3] No structures per se occurred in Sand Dune Cave, but there were sleeping beds, and the nature of Basketmaker cultural deposition in the cave is consistent with a residential role.

[4] One of these structures is located in the open out in front of the cave and is clearly a living structure; the other is located in the cave proper, but whether it was used for living or storage remains unknown because of extensive looter disturbance.

[5] No structures are identified in this cave, but investigation has been limited; the nature of Basketmaker cultural deposition in the cave is consistent with a residential role.

[6] This site is perhaps best characterized as a sheltered camp. It contained more hearths and roasting features than storage cists, and domesticates were almost absent; the site was perhaps principally used by Basketmakers on foraging excursions.

[7] This date range should be considered a bare minimum.

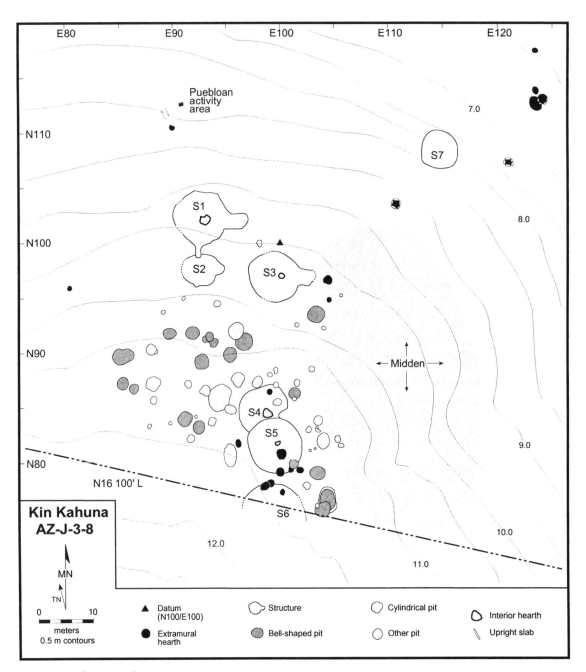

Figure 9.5. Plan map of the northern portion of Kin Kahuna. A large unexcavated portion of the site extends south, outside the N16 right-of-way.

cur in the area. Evidence from surveys and previous excavations rounds out our sample of Basketmaker site variability. With further research, finer or different divisions may allow greater understanding of Basketmaker settlement practices and change therein. At present, however, Smiley's site types seem well suited to the task of summarizing known Basketmaker settlement variability on the Rainbow Plateau, except we prefer to subdivide the rock shelter class into sheltered habitation and sheltered storage. Table 9.2 presents a list of known Basketmaker sites on the Rainbow Plateau; general locations of excavated sites are shown in figure 9.2. This list includes all sites be-

longing to the chronological interval outlined previously and for which we have enough information to make a site type assignment. A brief description of examples from each settlement type provides some essential background information for what follows.

Open Habitations with Storage

The largest and most complex Basketmaker sites on the Rainbow Plateau are residential sites with numerous and large storage features. Two examples have been partially excavated: The Pits and Kin Kahuna. Both are aceramic with initial occupancy during the third or fourth century

B.C. Kin Kahuna continued to be occupied until about A.D. 400, contemporaneous with the first appearance of pottery in the region, whereas The Pits was abandoned by about A.D. 200.

The Pits is situated on a high bedrock ridge (elevation of 2175 m) above two incised drainages. The N16 right-of-way (ROW) crosses the west side of the ridge, bisecting the site. Surface evidence indicates that much of the habitation lies outside the ROW, and excavation confirmed this. Within an area of about 300 m² at the eastern edge of the ROW, we excavated a surface structure almost 5 m in diameter, several hearths, and a cluster of 24 large, bell-shaped storage pits. These pits vary in size from 0.2 to 1.6 m³ (mean of 0.7 m³) and have a combined storage capacity of almost 17 m³.[2] The storage pits are arranged along the crest of a sandy rise that extends outside the ROW, where additional storage pits, most structures, and other features certainly occur. The sandy rise is ideally suited for subterranean storage features: besides being well drained, the deep sand has the property of being easy to dig when damp, but hardening upon drying to form stable walls. The pits appear to have been purposefully laid out in rough north-south and east-west alignments. This may have simplified their relocation once sealed and buried.

We believe that the site minimally served as a winter residence given the abundant storage potential of the pits and the nature of the surface evidence outside the ROW. A midden of abundant burned rock, charcoal-stained soil, and artifacts covers the entire eastern slope of the site, an area 1600 m² in size. Based on this accumulation, we have no doubt that the excavated features represent just the storage component of a major residential site. Unfortunately, excavations could not be pursued outside the ROW; thus, the number and nature of the likely pit houses at this site remain a matter of speculation.

This is fortunately not the case for Kin Kahuna, where excavations revealed seven pit houses, 26 storage pits, 32 other pits, 17 hearths, extensive trash deposits, and human burials (figure 9.5). Because half or more of this site also lies outside the N16 ROW, its true size and complexity remain unknown. Six of the houses were completely excavated, whereas the seventh, which lay mostly outside the ROW, was only sectioned along its northern edge. Surrounding the houses are numerous storage pits of various sizes. Eighteen pits are of the bell-shaped storage variety, like those at The Pits, whereas eight others are shallow with straight sides, but still large. The bell-shaped storage pits range in size from 0.2 to 1.6 m³ (average of 0.6 m³), with a combined storage capacity of 10.4 m³. Estimating storage capacity of the eight other large pits is difficult because they might have had domed superstructures of sticks and mortar as seen in certain sheltered sites (e.g., Guernsey and Kidder 1921: plate 9); such domes would have added considerable volume. Kin

Kahuna has evidence for long-term occupancy based on the superpositioning of structures and other features, and the filling of abandoned structures and storage pits with rich midden accumulation. With maize radiocarbon dates ranging from about 400 B.C. to A.D. 400, it is clear that Basketmaker occupancy of this one location, besides being intensive, was long-term. An obvious reason for long-term occupancy of this location was the prime agricultural land that lay immediately north of the site at the confluence of two small drainages. The importance of maize for the occupants of Kin Kahuna was evident during excavation, because we found corn kernels and cupules (sometimes cobs) in most features, either while digging or in sediment screening (see subsistence discussion below).

Examples of open habitations with storage that also contain early pottery are known from survey evidence, but none have been excavated. They range in size from a single residential structure with associated storage cists, such as site AZ-D-2-355 (NAU) on the west rim of upper Piute Canyon, to sites with multiple residential structures, such as AZ-J-14-54 (NN) located on the southeast edge of the Rainbow Plateau. At this last site there is evidence for at least five structures scattered on level portions of a sandstone ridge. At least one of the houses is entirely lined with upright sandstone slabs. It is impossible to say whether all of the houses were contemporaneous, but the artifact assemblages associated with each are similar and include early brown ware pottery along with arrow and dart points.

Open Habitations without Storage

The list of excavated Basketmaker habitations lacking storage facilities includes Blake's Abode, Ditch House, Mountainview, Panorama House, Polly's Place, Tres Campos, and Sin Sombra.[3] The sites of this class are characterized by a structure or two associated with a small trash midden and extramural hearths; small pits may also be present. The middens are never more than a few paces in front of the houses, immediately east or southeast of the entryways. They are generally artifact poor, characterized mainly by abundant burned rock in a matrix of charcoal-stained and flecked soil. The small size of the middens and comparative scarcity of artifacts seem to indicate temporary habitation, yet the presence of moderately formal structures suggests that the occupants envisioned more than a brief, single use episode. It is possible that this type of site was sequentially occupied over several seasons, or occupied for a month or more during a single season. Lacking storage features, the likely time of site occupancy was summer or fall, when survival would not depend upon stored foods. This type of site evidently served as the domicile of a single residential unit, which, judging from structure size and number, was either a nuclear family or small extended family. The

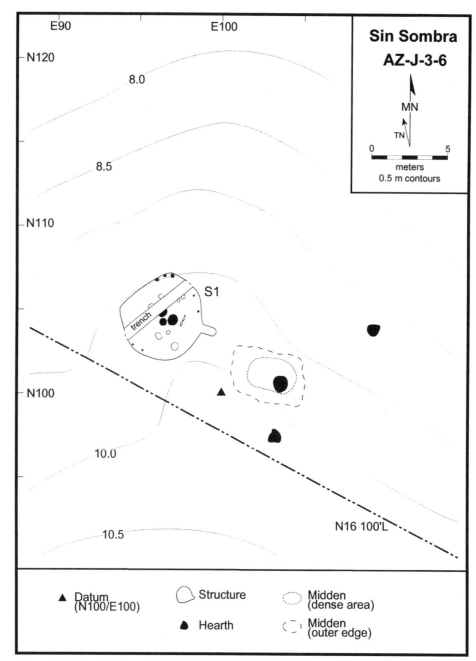

Figure 9.6. Plan map of Sin Sombra.

subsistence-settlement role of these sites remains speculative. Some sites of this class, such as Sin Sombra, are situated close to arable land, allowing for the possibility that
they served as summer field residences. Other examples
of this site class, such as Panorama House, are located on
the dissected high divide between the canyons of Piute
and Navajo Creeks where arable land is in short supply.
Thus, these may have more to do with gathering resources such as piñon nuts.

Sin Sombra provides a good aceramic example of this
sort of site (figure 9.6). The single structure at Sin Sombra was a semicircular pit house, 4.8 by 4.6 m in size and
70 cm deep. It was accessed through its east side by a

narrow, stubby ramp 85 cm long and 45 cm wide. A series of probable shallow postholes along the perimeter
of the structure may mark the position of logs leaned
toward the center to provide a roof similar to that of a
forked-stick hogan. Near the center of the basin-shaped
and slightly irregular floor was a cluster of three partially
overlapping shallow basin hearths. A small deflector constructed of two upright slabs lay between the hearths and
the ramp entry. A few meters southeast of the house was
a small midden up to 20 cm thick, whose main area
measured 3 m in diameter, with a lighter density of material covering an area about 5 m in diameter. The midden
consisted of charcoal-stained sand, charcoal, ash, burned

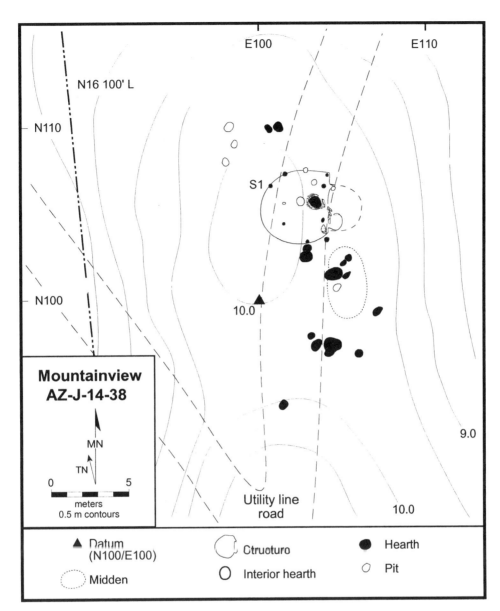

Figure 9.7. Plan map of Mountainview.

rock, flakes, and bone. Three extramural basin hearths lay to the east and southeast of the house.

The best example of a nonstorage habitation with early pottery is Mountainview, one of the most important sites for our topic. Excavation of virtually the entire site revealed a shallow pit structure, a midden, 12 basin hearths, three slab-lined hearths, and four shallow pits (figure 9.7). The single structure occupied a slight level area on the crest of a narrow ridge, with its eastern entryway opening onto a moderately steep slope covered with a thin trash deposit. The structure was a shallow, roughly circular pit house that probably had a superstructure of small logs and brush covered with earth. Interior features of the unprepared sandy floor included a central clay-rimmed hearth, an ash pit, four small pits, and eight postholes. In the southeast corner of the house was a storage area, separated from the main room by a low wall of upright sandstone slabs. A similar storage area was probably present in the northeast corner of the house, but machinery had cut through this portion of the structure during the construction of a nearby power line. The structure's interior measured 3.7 by 4.4 m, providing about 14 m² of floor space. The walled-off storage area(s) added additional use space. The occupants left behind part of their household assemblage upon abandonment. A large metate leaned against the lower wall in the southeast part of the structure, and three manos occurred elsewhere within the floor fill. The southeastern quadrant of the structure floor and floor fill yielded significantly more artifacts than any other area, including several bone artifacts, projectile points, and mineral specimens. Artifacts from the storage area at the southeast edge of the structure included two partially reconstructible Obelisk Utility jars, heavily sooted from use in cooking.

Open Camps

This class of site is peripheral to our topic, thus we will be brief. Based on the few examples of the N16 excavations, there are camps that consist of little more than a hearth or two with next to no artifactual remains, camps with numerous hearths and moderate densities of remains, and camps with hundreds or thousands of flakes and biface production fragments. The latter seem to be the locations of intensive biface reduction and can include dart point bases snapped across the notches. Maize occurs in some hearths at some camps, but is not common. Sites of this kind with early ceramics have yet to be identified, but there are hearths dated by radiocarbon assays to the interval when early pottery was in use.

Sheltered Habitations with Storage

The natural shelter provided by a cave or alcove separates this type of site from those in the open. Both Matson (1991:117) and Smiley (1994:182) argue that shelters were preferred for habitation and storage during the early portion of the Basketmaker stage, with open locations not widely used for residential settlement until around the Christian era. Shelters continued to play an important role during the interval of initial pottery use and throughout Anasazi prehistory.

Sand Dune Cave is the best-known example of a Basketmaker sheltered habitation with storage on the Rainbow Plateau. Here excavations uncovered storage cists, sleeping beds, hearths, and a substantial accumulation of living refuse, leading Lindsay et al. (1968:101) to conclude that the cave "was used largely as a habitation and storage area."

Another site of this class is Atlatl Rock Cave on the southeast edge of the Rainbow Plateau (Geib et al. 1999). The special significance of this cave is that it appears to have been continuously occupied during the transitional interval considered here, and it contains early brown ware pottery. This site is also notable because a slab-lined pit house and other slab-lined features occupy a small flat below the cave. Based on the use of upright slabs to line the entire circumference of the house, we believe that this feature dates to the time that early brown ware was in common use. In the cave proper, Basketmakers constructed numerous storage cists and pits. Radiocarbon dates on maize and construction materials from several of these features indicate rather intensive use of the cave between about A.D. 100 and 600. One of the more interesting finds from the site with regard to our topic came from excavation of a small remnant of a cist formed of slabs plastered over with clay. Resting upon the floor were 10 cm of turkey feces mixed with some feathers, a small amount of sediment, organic remains, and a few artifacts. Organic remains included maize cobs and kernels and a single whole bean. The artifacts included portions of a polished brown ware seed jar and a whole small arrow point of chert.

Sheltered Storage

These are sites that appear to have been principally used for storage, though most also likely served on occasion as temporary resting or camp locations. Importantly, these sites lack substantial living debris. There are at least two dozen examples of Basketmaker storage sites on the Rainbow Plateau, but as yet most are known from survey evidence alone. Two excavated sites of this class include Desha Caves 1 and 2 (Schilz 1979).[4] The Desha Caves are located on the northern portion of the plateau at an elevation of about 1414 m. Irrigated farmland less than 2 km away along Desha Creek (Lindsay et al. 1968: 136–137) is the likely area where Basketmakers raised the produce stored in the caves. Excavation of both caves revealed 33 slab-lined storage cists with a combined storage capacity of about 12 m^3 (this excludes two cists of Cave 1 for which no measurements were provided).[5] The few cists in these caves constructed with fiber-tempered mortar were recently dated by extracting the juniper bark from the clay for radiocarbon analysis (Geib 2000). This, plus the dating of two maize cobs, demonstrates that both caves were used from roughly A.D. 75 to A.D. 630. A distinctive weft-twined sandal with a square bolster-toe and a raised pattern on the sole from one of these caves (Schilz 1979:64–77) may be the sort of sandal style to be expected for a Basketmaker II–III transitional interval (Ann Deegan, personal communication, 1997).

It is worth mentioning that some shelters may appear to fit the sheltered storage class when, in fact, they are part of a habitation that contains structures and trash situated in the open near to the shelter. Atlatl Rock Cave is an example of such a site, and another good example is Hawk's Nest Ruin in Sage Valley on the northern portion of the Shonto Plateau. Several hundred meters can separate shelters from the actual living areas containing structures.

Settlement Distribution

Our understanding of Basketmaker settlement on the Rainbow Plateau is hampered by a lack of intensive regional survey and the problem of positively identifying Basketmaker sites based on surface evidence. We will consider the second problem first, because without positive identification, all else is futile no matter the amount of survey. Most of the sites that we can assign with certainty to the Basketmaker period are those reported above, for which there are radiocarbon dates. Nearly all of these sites were excavated to varying extent, many in the last several years. Minus chronometric dates, the few sites reliably assigned to this interval include several excavated caves that produced typical White Dog Basketmaker perishable remains. The temporal placement of open sites known from surface evidence alone is more problematic.

Aceramic sites with quantities of burned limestone have a good chance of a Basketmaker affiliation, but Archaic foragers or Puebloans on hunting and gathering forays may have created such sites as well. Identification problems extend to Basketmaker sites with early brown ware pottery. These sites not only appear similar to aceramic Basketmaker sites, but also the pottery is often unobtrusive and may occur in such low quantities that it can be overlooked. Earlier surveys also may not have recognized the early pottery for what it is, instead considering it unidentified and undiagnostic.

Survey coverage on the Rainbow Plateau is relatively more thorough north of the Utah state line, but none has been intensive over broad areas. For the Arizona portion of the plateau, survey coverage is limited to small parcels for houses and the like, and linear transects for the N16 road and a power line. Even though MNA and NAU archaeologists have recorded more than 360 sites on the plateau in Utah (Ambler et al. 1985; Lindsay et al. 1968: 16–30), none were positively identified as Basketmaker. A few dozen sites lacking masonry architecture and pottery were considered as probable evidence of Basketmaker II occupation, but a lack of diagnostics precluded positive identification.[6] Many of the probable Basketmaker sites are shelters, some with cists exposed on the surface, but there are also a number of open aceramic sites with burned rock and charcoal-stained soil. The upshot is that we are in a poor position to make any substantive claims about settlement patterning. Current knowledge of Basketmaker settlement remains sketchy and subject to revision once a substantial portion of the plateau has been surveyed and a greater number and diversity of Basketmaker settlement types have been excavated.

With these caveats in mind, it appears that residential sites with storage facilities for overwintering occur in areas of maximum agricultural potential from the earliest part of the Basketmaker period for the Rainbow Plateau. This is best illustrated by Kin Kahuna, which occupies a ridge above the confluence of two drainages that is still farmed. Basketmakers built at least one substantial pit house and several deep storage pits on this ridge sometime around 300 B.C. Other structures and storage pits followed, providing evidence for intensive occupancy of the ridge for some six hundred years. The long-term stability in Basketmaker occupancy of this one location reflects an underlying concern for situating primary residential sites next to prime agricultural land. Not only does this keep transportation costs of produce relatively low (Bradfield 1971), but nearby houses provide a direct marker of land tenure. Matson and Chisholm's (1991: 448) conclusion about Basketmaker II settlement on Cedar Mesa seems most apt to the Rainbow Plateau: "the overall Basketmaker II settlement pattern is consistent with dependence on maize agriculture because it is so similar to later Anasazi settlement patterns."

Known examples of residential storage sites with early brown ware pottery are not located in any more or less productive locations for farming. The largest documented example overlooks the same drainages that flow past Kin Kahuna. Other examples are located in the upper portion of Piute Canyon, where some of the richest farmland in the area is located. Although there are no obvious differences between aceramic and early ceramic Basketmaker residential locations, the latter currently appear to be restricted in distribution to the southeast edge of the Rainbow Plateau and around the head of Piute Canyon. The significance of this pattern is unknown; indeed it may disappear with additional survey.

Although the habitations with storage features seem to be positioned next to prime agricultural land, this is not necessarily the case for those lacking storage features. Many of these are on the high divide between Piute and Navajo Creeks, and these seem better suited to exploit wild resources such as piñon nuts.

ARCHITECTURE

Houses

Pit houses have a long history of use in the Southwest (Wills 1995: table 8.2), and in the mountains of Colorado substantial houses containing subfloor storage pits came into use more than six thousand years ago (Metcalf and Black 1991). Although prefarming hunter-gatherers used pit houses, widespread use of these features on the Colorado Plateau is correlated with the adoption of agriculture. The presence of pit houses with substantial investment in construction has implications for the relative stability and longevity of a residential location, as well as for the resource base and settlement patterns. Gilman's (1987) examination of the conditions surrounding the pit structure to pueblo transition in the prehistoric Southwest focused on subsistence, especially agricultural dependency. It would be equally informative to study changes in the nature and construction of pit houses from Basketmaker II to Basketmaker III to see if patterning relates to changes in agricultural dependency, restrictions in residential mobility, or other factors. A data set on Basketmaker structures of the Rainbow Plateau is beginning to be assembled, but it is still inadequate for broad generalizations. A discussion of excavated Basketmaker houses, however, will help document general trends in house construction on the Rainbow Plateau and enable comparisons with other regions. Temporal changes in construction details and interior features are evident, but how these relate to other

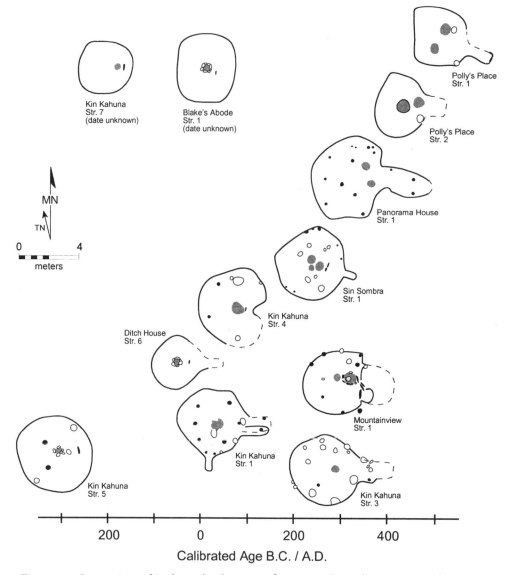

Figure 9.8. Comparison of Basketmaker house configurations through time at sites along N16.

variables is yet unknown. One important consideration is that we lack an equal sample of houses from functionally equivalent sites. Houses dating to the same time might be different because one was built as a long-term winter residence with a planned use-life of a decade or more, whereas another was built as a short-term summer residence with a brief use-life.

Figure 9.8 depicts all completely excavated Basketmaker houses for the Rainbow Plateau ordered by time. Temporal placement for the structures is based on radiocarbon dating of maize or other high-quality remains from hearth and floor contexts. The house at Blake's Abode and Structure 7 at Kin Kahuna are undated because of a lack of high-quality organic remains. All structures are shown at the same scale and orientation. In general the Basketmaker houses are circular, usually about 4 to 5 m in diameter, and from 0.2 to 1 m deep below the prehistoric occupation surface. The oldest house

was also the deepest and had straight walls meeting a level floor with a neat right angle. Most houses, however, had sloping pit walls and saucer-shaped floors. When evident, houses had eastern or southeastern ramp entries. All had at least one centrally located interior hearth. Deflectors occurred between the hearth and the entry for many houses. Most deflectors were expedient, unshaped small slabs, but in the oldest structure, the deflector consisted of a large metate.

Changes in the nature of superstructure construction are difficult to evaluate because the evidence is dependent upon several factors, such as whether a structure burned or was scavenged, whether the substrata helped or hindered preservation of construction details (e.g., clay versus loose sand), and excavator experience. Some houses had no obvious interior postholes; these may have been roofed by leaning-in timbers. Several houses at Kin Kahuna had just two posts that would have supported a single north-south primary beam; this is different from the standard quadrilateral method often discussed for Basketmaker houses.

One of the most obvious temporal trends, although it is not clear in figure 9.8, concerns the use of slabs. In all houses dating before A.D. 200, upright slabs were used only as deflectors. At some point after A.D. 200, slabs started to be incorporated into the construction of entry ramps, such as at Panorama House and Polly's Place. In these examples the entry slabs tend to be quite small, especially compared with those of the Basketmaker houses on Cedar Mesa (Matson 1991: figure 1.3). The structure with the most slabs is Mountainview; this house also appears most similar to Basketmaker houses of the Klethla Valley with tree-ring dates in the A.D. 500s (e.g., Pithouse 1 of NA11,058, Swarthout et al. 1986:426–430). Structures fully outlined by upright slabs occur at the large, early ceramic habitation of AZ-J-14-54 (NN), AZ-D-2-355 (NAU), and Atlatl Rock Cave. These houses are undated, but we anticipate that they date to between A.D. 400 to 600. The increased use of slabs does not necessarily imply greater investment in construction or greater permanency. Indeed, it seems that lining the entire circumference of houses resulted because of relatively shallow depths; the slabs were needed to hold back the loose surface sand. Most of the preceramic Basketmaker houses were excavated into hard, stable sand, reaching depths of up to 1 m.

There is also a clear temporal trend with the central interior hearths of houses. In the early pit houses the hearths consisted of no more than a fire built directly on the floor surface with no prior preparation. In several cases, stones were placed on the floor surface to help contain the accumulating ashes, but these were loose rather than embedded within the floor, and would have allowed for constant rearrangement of the hearth. At the oldest structure at Kin Kahuna, the floor surface under the stones was ash stained, indicating use of the central hearth before placing the stones, or movement of the stones during use. With time, interior hearths became more formalized, consisting of an excavated basin with a clay collar. Hearths of this sort occurred in Structure 2 at Polly's Place and the Mountainview structure. This type of hearth typifies later Basketmaker structures of the Klethla Valley (Ambler and Olson 1977; Swarthout et al. 1986). This change in the nature of interior hearths does connote greater formalization and functional differentiation of interior space—a trend carried forward in later Basketmaker structures with the creation of partitioning walls or ridges and interior bins. The start of this partitioning is seen in the Mountainview structure.

Storage

The introduction of agriculture to the Southwest seems strongly correlated with a vast increase in the number and size of storage features (Wills 1995:231). Therefore, one potentially indirect measure of changing agricultural dependence is storage capacity. To the extent that agricultural dependence increased from Basketmaker II to Basketmaker III, we should expect increasing reliance on storage as part of the Basketmaker II–III transition. Abundant storage, in the form of bell-shaped pits, is an important part of the earliest Basketmaker sites on the Rainbow Plateau. With almost 17 m^3 in 24 large, bell-shaped storage pits, The Pits has more storage pits and the largest storage capacity of any open Basketmaker residential site currently known in the Kayenta Anasazi region.[7] Because of right-of-way limits to excavation, the full size and complexity of this site remain to be determined; with the bulk of the site evidently east of the ROW, true storage capacity must be greater. Contemporaneity among all or most pits is suggested by their systematic layout, as mentioned earlier, and the lack of superposition. They may not have been created all at one time, but it seems likely that most were simultaneously in use. Variable amounts of trash fill and the reuse of some pits for roasting purposes indicate that some of the pits were evidently abandoned earlier than others. An estimate of when these features were used is provided by an unusual maize offering at the bottom of Storage Pit 3.[8] A radiocarbon date on kernels from this offering has a two-sigma calibrated range of 170 B.C. to A.D. 135. Maize from the floor fill of a few other pits produced radiocarbon dates with similar age ranges.

The early abundance of bell-shaped storage pits is also exemplified by Kin Kahuna, where we documented 18 such features with a capacity of just over 10 m^3. Radiocarbon dating of maize from the floor fill of these features indicates that all predate 100 A.D. Another probable storage feature at Kin Kahuna consists of large oval to circular pits with straight sides and flat bottoms; these add an uncalculated amount of additional storage capacity. Given the lengthy Basketmaker occupancy of this one location, the total amount of storage at any one time might have been low. An important unknown is the use-life of storage pits. Were they serviceable for a decade or two, or a year or two? Pit use-life may well be limited compared to cists, but this is a topic needing experimental research.

Slab-lined storage cists become common during the interval in which pottery was adopted, apparently replacing pits. Some unexcavated early ceramic habitations, such as AZ-D-2-355 (NAU), have clustered storage cists. All direct dates on cists constructed with fiber-tempered mortar place construction during the interval of about A.D. 100 to 600. Through time, the form and construction of storage features seem to change, but it remains to be demonstrated whether or not storage volume increased. A lack of excavation of early ceramic Basketmaker habitations with storage features hinders discussion of this topic. There was, however, a clear change from concealed to unconcealed storage, from pits that are easily hidden from view to cists that are not so easily hidden (see discussion in Wills and Windes 1989:357–359). Evidently, there was also a corresponding increase in facility use-life.

MATERIAL CULTURE

Ceramics

The earliest pottery on the Rainbow Plateau is a plain utilitarian ware, usually brownish in color and varyingly burnished. A number of traits distinguish this material from Lino Gray. We classify the early pottery on the Rainbow Plateau as Obelisk Utility (see L. Reed et al., this volume; also Spurr and Hays-Gilpin 1996). It resembles the pottery recovered from Obelisk Cave but differs from much of the pottery previously identified as Obelisk Gray in the Kayenta region—pottery that fits the type description of Lino Gray except for being polished. The primary criterion distinguishing Obelisk Utility from Lino Gray, polished or not, is the use of iron-rich clay containing abundant fine sand and other particles, in addition to poorly sorted quartz and multilithic sand. Lino Gray is made from iron-poor clay, lacks abundant fine sand, and is tempered with well-sorted, usually subrounded quartz sand.

Sites with Early Pottery.

The count of known early pottery sites is currently low, a likely result both of limited survey coverage and identification problems. We have firsthand knowledge of the latter because the site that currently provides the best-dated assemblage of this early pottery, Mountainview, was initially identified as aceramic. It took close inspection of the surface remains during a second visit to notice a few sherds, and excavation to convince us that the pottery was indeed associated with the structure and other features. Except for sparse sherds, the surface appearance of early ceramic habitations may be no different from the surface appearance of aceramic Basketmaker habitations. The most obvious evidence for both is abundant burned rock and darkened soil, along with flaking debris and occasional upright slabs that mark the location of structures, cists, or hearths.

The currently known examples of early pottery sites are clustered at the southeast edge of the Rainbow Plateau and in upper Piute Canyon (see figure 9.2). Several of these are not yet recorded, and for only three is there excavation information: Mountainview, Atlatl Rock Cave, and Polly's Place. Recorded but unexcavated early pottery sites in the area include AZ-J-14-54 (NN), the largest one currently known, and NAU sites AZ-D-2-174, -200, and -355. All of the early pottery

sites thus far documented have evidence for one or more living structures, with upright slabs forming the entryways and at times lining house perimeters. Whether early pottery occurs at nonhabitation sites remains to be seen, but it is absent from Dust Devil Cave and the Desha Caves, sites that likely did not function as habitations.

The best sample of early pottery thus far comes from Mountainview, where excavation of virtually the entire site recovered a small assemblage of Obelisk Utility from a shallow pit structure and associated trash midden. Based on rim sherds, the Mountainview assemblage consists of a minimum of one straight-necked jar and two seed jars from the structure, with at least two more seed jars and two possible bowls or seed jars from the midden. Jar sherds from the structure refit with midden sherds. Several body sherds from the structure do not appear to belong to any of the rims. The vessels from the unburned structure are heavily sooted, indicating use for cooking.

Excavation of a cist remnant filled with turkey feces at Atlatl Rock Cave yielded portions of a polished Obelisk Utility seed jar (Geib et al. 1999). This vessel is quite similar to a polished brown seed jar found by Kidder and Guernsey (1919: plate 59, see figure 35 and page 95 for discussion of recovery location) at Sunflower Cave.[9] There are portions of at least two other Obelisk Utility vessels from the limited testing of Atlatl Rock Cave.

Polly's Place is the third excavated site yielding pottery, but in this case just a single vessel fragment. This is sparse evidence for ceramic use, but the sherd was clearly not intrusive as there was no pottery on the surface of this site or any ceramic sites in the vicinity. The small Obelisk Utility sherd came from a buried occupation surface just outside a structure.

Ceramic Description.

The descriptive characteristics that follow come principally from the Mountainview assemblage because it is the largest sample of brown ware pottery from the Rainbow Plateau and the one for which we have the greatest analytical detail. Examination of sherds from other early ceramic sites of the Rainbow Plateau leads us to conclude that the Mountainview assemblage captures the distinctive essence of this early pottery while at the same time well representing its variability. The observations that follow draw heavily on the findings of Kelley Hays-Gilpin, ceramic analyst for the N16 excavations.

In general, the early pottery on the Rainbow Plateau is a crumbly brown ware with abundant fine sand and surface textures ranging from well polished to rough. Surface color is variable but is most frequently reddish yellow to reddish brown, reflecting a high-iron-content clay.[10] The wide range of color probably results from an uncontrolled firing atmosphere. Splotchy color indicates that vessels were not covered when fired, allowing fuel to touch and reduce some parts of the surfaces, and allowing drafts to oxidize other areas.

Temper consists of very abundant sand that varies from pure, but poorly sorted, quartz, to a mineralogical mixture. Usually there are sparse, moderately large, subrounded quartz grains, with abundant, very fine quartz sand and colored fragments. The fine-grained material is mostly clear and subrounded to nearly spherical. The nature of the clay and the temper indicates that early potters on the Rainbow Plateau used self-tempered alluvial clays. Locally such clay is available in abundance from Piute Canyon, where, after a storm, clay with the perfect moisture content for vessel production can be collected from damp settling basins.

Surface finish varies from a high, shiny polish to smooth and dull with protruding fine temper. Often, surface irregularities are poorly smoothed over. Polishing streaks appear, but not frequently. Surfaces may be bumpy or dimpled, possibly due to forming by pinching. Jar interiors are usually somewhat smoothed, but are often pitted, perhaps from use.

Seed jars seem to be the most common form, but straight-necked jars also occur. Based on sooting and interior surface pitting and spalling, it is evident that all jars were used over fires, probably for boiling food. Simple hemispherical bowls might also be present, but lacking larger vessel portions, possible bowl rim sherds might also be from seed jars. All rims have simple rounded lips that are usually irregular.

Dating.
The age of Obelisk Utility on the Rainbow Plateau is still under study. Current evidence indicates that pottery was in use by A.D. 375 at the latest and perhaps as early as A.D. 145. This date spread comes from the calibrated two-sigma age range for the mean of three statistically equivalent maize AMS dates from Mountainview (see table 9.1). The dated samples consisted of two maize kernels from floor fill of the one structure, and a maize cupule from the midden. Barring systematic laboratory error, there is no reason to believe that the average of these three dates does not accurately reflect the true age of site occupancy. The pottery is certainly associated with the dates because the Obelisk Utility sherds come from the same proveniences that produced the maize samples, and there is no other component at the site from which the pottery or maize could be derived.

Atlatl Rock Cave provides the other good date on Obelisk Utility from the Rainbow Plateau. A maize cob from the floor fill of a cist remnant containing portions of an Obelisk Utility seed jar has a radiocarbon age with a calibrated two-sigma range of A.D. 425 to 660 (Beta-68382, Geib et al. 1999). This date is stratigraphically consistent with two additional assays.[11] The seed jar

from Atlatl Rock Cave may be a few hundred years younger than the Mountainview pottery. In this regard it is notable that the seed jar is better crafted than the vessels at Mountainview, having a harder and more consistent polish, a more even thickness to the vessel walls, and a quite regular rim lip.

The single other piece of temporal information comes from Polly's Place, where one brown ware sherd was found on a buried Basketmaker occupation surface outside of a structure. As previously discussed, there is no evidence that this artifact was intrusive as there was no pottery on the surface of this site, nor are there any ceramic sites in the vicinity. Statistically contemporaneous dates on sage from a hearth within the house (Beta-79159) and maize from a hearth just outside the structure (Beta-79160) have an average calibrated two-sigma range of A.D. 350 to 545 (see table 9.1).

Summary of Ceramic Evidence.
By the fourth century A.D., and perhaps as early as the second century, some Basketmaker occupants of the Rainbow Plateau used pottery. This pottery, designated Obelisk Utility, was produced from an iron-rich, self-tempered clay and fired in a poorly controlled atmosphere, resulting in a brown ware with a crumbly paste. Many sites dating to the first half of the Christian era on the Rainbow Plateau lack pottery, even residential sites. Excavations along the Navajo Mountain road produced no sherds from several structural sites contemporaneous with Mountainview. Panorama House, for example, is quite similar in character to Mountainview, consisting of a single pit structure, a few hearths, a small midden, and no storage facilities. An average of four maize dates for this site place occupancy between A.D. 245 and 405 (calibrated two-sigma range). Kin Kahuna provides an example of a more substantial habitation with abundant trash and storage features that likewise lacks ceramics. There was considerable trash deposition at the site during the interval represented by Mountainview, with one excavated structure (Structure 3) dated by maize at A.D. 145 to 435 (calibrated two-sigma range). Extensive excavation of this site, including the screening of tens of cubic meters of refuse accumulation, recovered not a single sherd of Obelisk Utility. At nonhabitation sites, we expect an even lower probability for pottery to be represented. This seems to be borne out by the findings from Dust Devil Cave and Desha Caves 1 and 2, sites that, as argued earlier, appear to have been used principally for storage. Dating of maize and bark from cist construction reveals that these three sites were occupied during the time that pottery was in use on the Rainbow Plateau, yet no early brown ware pottery was recovered. The maize dates from Dust Devil Cave are late enough (ca. A.D. 400 to 800, Geib 1996a) that pottery was in general

wide use, and Lino Gray was being produced in the Kayenta region.[12]

Bow and Arrow

Traditional culture history holds that the bow was a Basketmaker III addition across the Four Corners region of the Colorado Plateau, being adopted after about A.D. 500 (Cordell 1984:102; McGregor 1965:213; Plog 1979:114). Excavation of Basketmaker II remains from numerous dry caves uncovered abundant and varied evidence of atlatl use (dart points and preforms, dart foreshafts and mainshafts, foreshafts with dart points, atlatls, atlatl weights), but no evidence of bow use (e.g., Guernsey 1931; Guernsey and Kidder 1921; Kidder and Guernsey 1919; Lindsay et al. 1968; Lockett and Hargrave 1953; Schilz 1979). Given the time depth of the Basketmaker II period (e.g., Smiley 1993; Smiley et al. 1986), the lack of evidence for bow use from caves may result because most remains from these sites date from the first millennium B.C. Yet, findings from excavations at late Basketmaker II (ca. A.D. 1 to 400) open sites on Cedar Mesa and Black Mesa follow the traditional framework: plenty of dart points but no arrow points (R. G. Matson, personal communication, 1991; Parry 1987).

Based on Earl Morris's finding of a Basketmaker II burial with an arrow point and foreshaft imbedded between the ribs, Wormington (1961:55) concluded that "although the Basketmakers did not use the bow and arrow, they apparently were in contact with people who did." This was an initial indication that bow technology may have been present in the Four Corners region earlier than generally supposed. Excavation of the Tamarron Site in southwest Colorado led to the first general claim that Basketmaker II populations used the bow (Reed and Kainer 1978). This site remains undated and was assigned to the Basketmaker II period based on architectural similarities between a pit house and tree-ring dated structures of Talus Village and the Falls Creek shelters (Morris and Burgh 1954; Dean 1975). The excavation of 5DL896 provided additional evidence for potential early bow use in southwest Colorado (Reed and McDonald 1988). Here excavations recovered eight arrow points from a stratum radiocarbon dated between A.D. 130 and 430, but the dates are on wood charcoal. Nevertheless, evidence continues to trickle in, especially from northern sites, for the appearance of bow technology during the first several centuries A.D.

On the northern Colorado Plateau it is generally accepted that the bow and arrow began to replace the atlatl and dart by at least A.D. 300 (Holmer 1986:106; Holmer and Weder 1980:60). Closer to the Four Corners region, Geib and Bungart (1989) recovered arrow points from a nonhabitation site in Glen Canyon radiocarbon dated to the first few centuries A.D., and Richens and Talbot

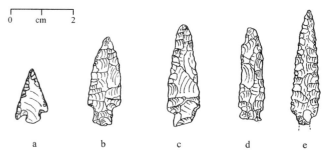

Figure 9.9. Arrow points from Basketmaker sites of the Rainbow Plateau: (a) Atlatl Rock Cave; (b) The Pits; (c—e) Mountainview.

(1989) recovered arrow points from a temporary residential site with a 5 m diameter pit house that was also radiocarbon dated to the first few centuries A.D. The dating for this latter site is quite good because it is based on the average of three statistically contemporaneous assays on burned roof beams.

Sites with Arrow Points and Dating.
On the Rainbow Plateau, Mountainview provides the best evidence for early bow use, but other excavated sites yielding corroborative data include Kin Kahuna and The Pits. The unexcavated large habitation site AZ-J-14-54 (NN) with the same cultural assemblage as Mountainview (Obelisk Utility and arrow points) reveals that Mountainview is not unique, and provides ample opportunity to obtain chronometric dates to check our findings with regard to the age of both arrow points and pottery.

Atlatl Rock Cave yielded a single arrow point (figure 9.9a) in association with Obelisk Utility, but in this case the associated maize has an age in the A.D. 425 to 660 range. Nevertheless, because the cave was occupied during the first several centuries A.D., it may contain perishable components of early bow technology (e.g., nocked ends of arrow points, bow fragments, bow string) that could be directly dated.

The first indication for early bow technology resulting from the N16 excavations came in 1994 from the Basketmaker site known as The Pits. Quite unexpectedly we recovered a whole stemmed arrow-sized projectile point (figure 9.9b) from the floor of a shallow structure. A maize kernel from what was thought to be the principal hearth of this house dated to the first several centuries B.C. Extensive root and rodent disturbance in the area of the point find limited confidence in the actual association between the artifact and the house. Additional dating of maize recovered from the floor surface, and closer to where the point was actually recovered, returned statistically contemporaneous dates, the average of which has a calibrated two-sigma range of 105 B.C. to A.D. 110.

The Mountainview site provides more conclusive evidence for early bow use on the southeast edge of the Rainbow Plateau. From the shallow pit house and associated midden described earlier, we retrieved two whole and one nearly whole arrow-sized points (figure 9.9c–e), a few arrow point fragments, and several small pressure-flaked biface fragments that probably are arrow point preforms broken in production. Recall that the calibrated two-sigma age range for the average of three statistically contemporaneous maize dates is A.D. 145–375. This date range fits quite closely with that for the Sandy Ridge Site (Richens and Talbot 1989). Evidence for continued use of the atlatl by the occupants of Mountainview includes a typical Basketmaker atlatl weight, as well as dart points. Some of the dart points exhibited use-wear traces suggesting tasks other than serving as projectile points, but this is also the case at Basketmaker sites lacking evidence for arrow points.

At Kin Kahuna, the youngest structure is dated by maize at A.D. 145 to 435 (calibrated two-sigma range). No early pottery was recovered in or near this house, or indeed from the site as a whole, but an arrow point came from the floor fill of the structure, and a small pressure-flaked arrow point preform fragment was recovered from the occupation surface just outside the house. The radiocarbon date indicates that this structure was perhaps contemporaneous with Mountainview, and other radiocarbon dates from hearths and trash deposits at Kin Kahuna document substantial use of the site during the first several centuries A.D.

Summary of Bow and Arrow Evidence.
As with Obelisk Utility, arrow-sized points, and bows by implication, were being used by some occupants of the Rainbow Plateau by at least the fourth century A.D. and perhaps as early as the second century. The evidence from The Pits gives cause for speculating that bow technology might have been in limited use even earlier, perhaps around the time of Christ. The early arrow points are for the most part crudely produced, consisting of flakes trimmed to shape with noninvasive, marginal pressure flaking. The same also appears true for the early points from the Sandy Ridge Site (Richens and Talbot 1989: figure 4). A few examples from the Rainbow Plateau, however, are much better made and exhibit overall pressure thinning and shaping.

As with early pottery, not all sites of the early Christian era have evidence for bow technology. Again, the Navajo Mountain road excavations have documented structural sites contemporaneous with Mountainview that did not yield arrow points. The list of excavated structural sites dated to the first several centuries A.D. that lack arrow points includes Blake's Abode, Panorama House, Polly's Place, Sin Sombra, and all but Structure 3 at Kin Kahuna. Most of these sites yielded corner- and side-notched dart points, some being typical examples of White Dog Basketmaker II points (see discussion in Geib 1996b:62–64). Many early Christian era sites lack arrow

points, and those with arrow points might not have pottery, but if early brown ware pottery is present, then arrow points are invariably found. Our tentative interpretation of this pattern is that bows were used in the area before pottery.

SUBSISTENCE

Agricultural Dependence
Increased reliance on domesticates is how many have characterized subsistence change from Basketmaker II to III (Glassow 1972:298; Gumerman and Dean 1989:114; LeBlanc 1982a; Minnis 1989:546). Part and parcel of this view is the notion that new, larger corn varieties were grown, greater efficiency was obtained in corn processing, and storage capacity increased. How archaeologists measure agricultural dependence is a complicated issue, made even more so these days because of the many separate lines of evidence that can be mustered, some of which may give conflicting results. One of the principal measures of agricultural dependence is provided by macrobotanical remains, both from human feces and sediment samples (e.g., Gasser 1982; Minnis 1989; Stiger 1977). Pollen in both fecal and sediment samples can also be related to diet, but interpretation of the findings in terms of agricultural dependence seems even more problematic than for macrobotanical remains. Greater efficiency in maize kernel processing, as evidenced by mano and metate size, is now used as another measure of increased dependency, to the point that it is touted as a more sensitive indicator than bone isotope ratios (Hard et al. 1996).

Our evidence for Basketmaker subsistence on the Rainbow Plateau pertains mainly to preceramic or aceramic sites owing to the small number of excavated early ceramic sites. In particular, although we have data for numerous flotation samples from aceramic habitations with abundant storage, we lack a sample from analogous early ceramic sites. Mountainview, the best example of an early ceramic habitation excavated to date, lacks storage features. Several caves in the area apparently had continuous Basketmaker use during the interval in which pottery first appears, but only Atlatl Rock Cave has been sampled for macrobotanical remains. Unfortunately, the sample size ($n = 3$) for this site is not sufficient to be informative.

The extent to which the presence or absence of storage features at habitations affects the recovery rate of domesticates is well illustrated by N16 excavation results. The two sites yielding the most abundant maize remains are habitations with numerous large storage features: The Pits and Kin Kahuna.

Figure 9.10 presents a plot of *Zea mays* ubiquity values through time for Basketmaker habitations excavated within the N16 ROW; habitations with storage are

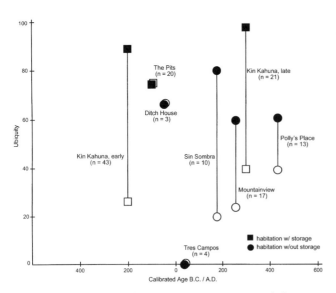

Figure 9.10. Ubiquity of *Zea mays* at sites excavated along N16. Shaded figures represent all *Zea mays* parts; open figures are kernels only.

depicted as squares, nonstorage habitations as circles. Sample size is also shown to provide a perspective on how robust the patterning might be. The blackened squares and circles have ubiquity values calculated using all maize parts (cupules, kernels, glumes, cob portions), whereas the open squares and circles have ubiquity values based only on maize kernels. The presence of kernels alone eliminates the possibility that purposeful burning of maize cobs for fuel, or incidentally by disposal into hearths, might greatly and differentially inflate the incidence of maize. In most cases, representation declines substantially when just kernels are used for calculating ubiquity values. In two instances this did not occur, but one of these (Ditch House) has a minuscule sample size and thus may simply be an aberration. Because it is based on 20 samples, the equal 75 percent ubiquity of kernels and cob portions at The Pits is notable and provides good evidence for the significance of maize during the last few centuries B.C. and the first few centuries A.D.

For this presentation, we separated the lengthy Basketmaker occupancy of Kin Kahuna into two temporal components: early, from about 2200 to 1900 B.P., and late, from about 1900 to 1700 B.P. The late portion is viewed as potentially ceramic, although no pottery was actually recovered from Kin Kahuna. The significance of maize in the diet throughout the occupancy of Kin Kahuna is attested to by finding that 66 out of 72 analyzed flotation samples (92 percent) contained maize (Matthews 1997). Maize kernels occurred in 21 of the 72 samples, or 29 percent. Based on radiocarbon dates and feature attributes, we assigned 43 of the flotation samples to the early component, 21 samples to the later component, and left eight samples unassigned. Some form of

maize was present in 88 percent of the early component samples, and in 95 percent of the later component samples, whereas maize kernels occurred in 26 percent of the early-component samples, and in 38 percent of the later-component samples.

Based on all plant parts, maize ubiquity is high throughout the entire span of Basketmaker occupancy on the Rainbow Plateau represented in our sample. Indeed, maize is the most common food remain other than goosefoot seeds in every flotation sample and at every site. For habitations with storage, maize actually equals or exceeds the percentage presence of goosefoot seeds. Overall, there is not a great difference in ubiquity values between habitations with storage facilities and those without. Nevertheless, this obscures the more basic fact that maize is far more abundant at the former than the latter, something that was unmistakable in the field during excavation. We found maize during excavation of most features at Kin Kahuna and The Pits, whereas maize was rare and often had to be carefully searched for during the excavation of features at nonstorage habitation sites such as Mountainview and Sin Sombra. Quantification of this difference is best provided by Andrea Hunter's (1995) flotation results. In 20 flotation samples (73 liters of sediment) from The Pits (a habitation site with storage), the quantity of maize was 20.8 parts per liter and 1.7 kernels per liter, whereas in 13 samples (47 liters of sediment) from Polly's Place (a nonstorage habitation), the quantity of maize was 2.7 parts per liter and 0.6 kernels per liter. These findings differ somewhat from those reported for northern Black Mesa, where Wills and Huckell (1994:44) report a lack of clear correspondence between site type and maize occurrence.

There is no clear temporal pattern in the ubiquity data supporting an increase in maize use during the Basketmaker chronology for the Rainbow Plateau. Moderately heavy maize dependence appears with the earliest of the open habitations with storage features, sometime around 300 B.C. With maize occurring in 75 to 90 percent of the samples from Kin Kahuna and The Pits, there is little room for an increase in maize representation. Indeed, maize is no more ubiquitous at Pueblo II and III habitations on the Rainbow Plateau, varying between 60 and 90 percent, with a total value of 78 percent for 111 Puebloan samples (Geib and Casto 1985). Other quantification methods, such as ratios, might disclose patterns lost in this analysis, but at present it seems that farming remained consistently important from the start of the Basketmaker period to the end, with no increase in dependency corresponding to the interval during which ceramics were introduced. Moreover, although the incorporation of ceramics seems to have been an individual household decision, maize is no more abundant at early ceramic sites than contemporaneous households

TABLE 9.3

Comparison of Maize Kernel Measurements for Basketmaker II and Basketmaker III Samples, Atlatl Rock Cave

Variables	Basketmaker II, Feature 24 (n=12)				Basketmaker III, Feature 18 (n=26)				T-Test	Prob.
	min.	max.	mean	sta. dev.	min.	max.	mean	sta. dev.		
height	5.33	9.46	6.92	1.01	7.41	11.44	9.97	0.93	8.847	0.000
width	5.18	8.82	6.77	1.08	6.04	10.12	8.36	1.16	4.143	0.000
thickness	4.10	6.22	5.13	0.70	3.28	7.10	4.33	0.92	−2.980	0.006
area (h x w)	33.83	74.17	46.85	10.63	46.09	115.67	83.98	17.14	8.159	0.000
area/thickness	5.94	18.09	9.44	3.23	7.44	31.35	20.21	5.43	7.613	0.000

without ceramics. This is best illustrated by the late component of Kin Kahuna, where maize ubiquity was 95 percent, but no pottery was recovered.

Maize may be equally common to preceramic and ceramic Basketmaker contexts on the Rainbow Plateau, but evidence from Atlatl Rock Cave indicates a significant change in kernel morphology that may have implications for the dietary significance of maize or the processing methods. The sample from this site is small but from well-controlled and -dated proveniences. Table 9.3 presents measurement data on kernels from preceramic and early ceramic contexts. The preceramic Basketmaker kernels tend to be squat and nearly equal in the three dimensions of height, width, and thickness (isodiametric). In contrast, the early ceramic Basketmaker kernels are comparatively thin in relation to their height and width. In addition to the change in kernel morphological, there is a change in kernel color. Most preceramic kernels are reddish, commonly yellowish red (5YR5/6, 5/8) and reddish yellow (7.5YR7/8), with some that are dark red (10R2.5/2, 3/4, 3/6), and a few that are bright red (off the Munsell soil chart). In contrast, most of the early ceramic kernels are yellow (primarily 10YR7/8). The differences in morphology and color also seem to correspond to a shift from a popcorn endosperm (preceramic) to a flour endosperm (early ceramic) (see Benz 1981, and Doebley and Bohrer 1983:32 for endosperm descriptions).

Introduction of Beans

Part of the argument for increased reliance on domesticates during Basketmaker III is the claim that beans were added to the list of cultigens during this stage (Wormington 1961:55). Today we know that beans provided an important source of protein, but prehistoric cognizance of this may have been limited. Simply the satiated feeling one gets with eating beans may have been reason enough for their adoption. Perceived or not, one additional benefit of incorporating beans within subsistence practices may have been their role in maintaining soil fertility by fixing nitrogen. If Wormington's (1961:55) anecdotal account is true, then beans might provide another indirect measure of residential permanence. She relates that "such a crop also indicates a more settled life, for, while corn may be planted and then left for long periods of time, beans require almost constant attention."

The earliest evidence of beans on the Rainbow Plateau comes from Atlatl Rock Cave. A single whole bean was recovered from the previously mentioned cist used to pen turkeys. This item may be classified as Kaplan's (1956) type C11. The radiocarbon date on a corncob in association with the bean suggests an age between A.D. 425 to 660. Cutler (1968:377) reports wads of bean strings containing pod tips and stem ends assigned to the Basketmaker II deposits of both Sand Dune and Dust Devil Caves. The age of these wads must be verified by direct dating.

Some see an obvious functional link between what has seemed to be the contemporaneous introduction of beans and pottery. Linton (1944:377) first expounded upon this, stating that "the relationship of this important protein source [beans] to pottery boiling is of the closest sort." The earliest direct dates on beans from the Southwest deserts (Tagg 1996: table 2; Wills 1995: table 8.1) indicate that this cultigen was in use at or shortly before the adoption of pottery (Deaver and Ciolek-Torrello 1995; and summary in Mabry 1997). The role of beans is little considered in various recent explanations as to why pottery production began in the Southwest (e.g., Crown and Wills 1995; Glassow 1972:297; but see Skibo and Blinman 1999). Arguments for labor efficiency and improved nutrition for women and children are not at odds with a functional relationship between pottery and bean cooking. Beans cooked and mashed into a soupy pulp make an excellent weaning food, something prehistoric women may have found quite useful. Beans clearly fit the expectations of a model outlined by James Brown (1989) for the origins of pottery, wherein one of the motivating factors was the addition of new processing requirements such as long-term boiling.

If there were a functional relationship between pottery and beans, then we would expect beans to first appear on the Rainbow Plateau at the approximate same time as ceramics. So far this is not the case. Flotation samples from excavated early pottery sites have not yielded any bean remains. In particular, the analysis of 19 flotation samples (76 liters) from the Mountainview Site did not reveal any beans (Matthews 1997). These samples came from virtually every feature at the site, including the structure hearth and ash pit, extramural hearths (n = 9), and the midden (n = 6 from different portions of the deposit). Observed floral remains included maize kernels and cupules along with seeds from grasses and several weedy species. Perhaps the lack of beans at Mountainview has to do with its settlement role. Without storage features, this site was probably not occupied in winter, so beans may not have been consumed there. It is worth mentioning that analysis of a considerable number of flotation samples (n = 119) and a large volume of dirt (470 liters) from aceramic Basketmaker habitations has not yielded evidence for beans. Extensive pollen sampling has likewise resulted in negative results from both aceramic and early ceramic sites. We must caution that discovering evidence of beans at open sites is a low probability event. Even at open Puebloan sites, beans are exceedingly rare finds.

Turkey Husbandry

Turkey husbandry is another widely recognized trait of the Basketmaker III period (McGregor 1965:215). Morris (1980:145) recounts how "evidence that turkeys were kept in captivity is first observed in a Basketmaker III context." We include this topic here even though it seems that the motivation behind turkey captivity was for feathers, not food. Feathers were used in the production of feather blankets, which replaced the previously used fur blankets (Guernsey and Kidder 1921:74–75); food use evidently did not occur until roughly the late A.D. 900s (McKusick 1986:151). Evidence for early turkey husbandry on the Rainbow Plateau comes from Atlatl Rock Cave. We previously touched upon the best of this evidence: the cist remnant filled with a 10 cm thick mass of turkey feces mixed with feathers and other organic material, including maize cobs and kernels and a whole common bean. The concentration of feces in this one feature indicates that turkeys were penned in the cave. The A.D. 425 to 660 radiocarbon date (calibrated two-sigma range) on a cob from the fecal mass is consistent with the general view that turkey husbandry began around A.D. 500.

An organic layer (Feature 16) stratigraphically below the cist but horizontally adjacent to it also contained turkey feces and a few feathers, as well as a piece of turkey-feather-wrapped cordage.[13] These remains indicate that turkeys may have been kept within the cave during the time that the organic layer was forming. A radiocarbon date on maize cobs from this layer has a two-sigma calibrated range of A.D. 220 to 445 (Geib et al. 1999). The recovery of scattered turkey feces from deposits immediately underlying the organic layer might support even earlier tending of the birds.

DISCUSSION

The Rainbow Plateau provides evidence that helps bridge the greater than two-century gap between the Basketmaker II and III stages perceived by Berry (1982:117) and other Southwestern archaeologists (e.g., Rohn 1989:154). We doubt that the Rainbow Plateau is exceptional with its record of the Basketmaker II–III transition. Instead, it is likely just one of several localities with sites dating to the transitional interval. Other areas evidently include the Upper San Juan River, from the La Plata Valley (Toll and Wilson, this volume) to the Navajo Reservoir District (Eddy 1966; Wilson and Blinman 1993), and the middle Little Colorado River area around Petrified Forest National Park (Burton 1991; Wendorf 1953). The clearest indication of transitional sites across the Colorado Plateau is the occurrence of brown ware pottery, often in low quantities (see L. Reed et al. this volume; Wilson and Blinman 1993). Most sites with early pottery are in the open; thus details on change in many aspects of material culture and subsistence practices may be poorly represented, if at all. Given a series of fourth-, fifth-, and sixth-century tree-ring dates (Gumerman and Dean 1989:111), Canyon de Chelly should eventually prove important to understanding this transition because of the excellent preservation afforded by its numerous shelters.

Pottery was not widely adopted within a short time frame by all households on the Rainbow Plateau, or elsewhere on the Colorado Plateau, but took several hundred years to become a ubiquitous item of material culture (ca. 200 to 500 A.D.). Consequently, it does not provide a hard and fast marker for distinguishing between Basketmaker II and Basketmaker III. Changing the Basketmaker III criterion from pottery in the generic sense to the advent of gray ware production provides some degree of temporal specificity. With the advent of gray ware, it seems that virtually every household on the Colorado Plateau used pottery, and sherds even occur at seasonal residences and some temporary camps. So, should the Basketmaker III designation be restricted to those sites with gray ware, and should sites with brown ware alone be classified as Basketmaker II or as Basketmaker II–III transitional? For the simple sake of communication, we prefer the latter, but explicit recognition of intermediate stages does not allow greater understanding as to how and why cultures change.

In this chapter, we have attempted to graph and discuss change in Basketmaker culture on the Rainbow Plateau using the culturally independent dimension of time furnished by chronometric dates rather than by phases or stages. In this way it is possible to see that changes from preceramic to ceramic times, or from Basketmaker II to Basketmaker III, took place over the span of several hundred years, or many generations. There was no dramatic or sudden panregional adoption of a new trait complex that ushered in the Basketmaker III stage (contra LeBlanc 1982a). Even within a small area such as the Rainbow Plateau, it is apparent that some households adopted pottery, whereas others did not. On a larger regional scale, it is evident that pottery was more widely accepted earlier in some areas than in other areas. For example, no early pottery is reported from the A.D. 200–400 Grand Gulch phase of Cedar Mesa (Matson 1991; Matson et al. 1988). Whatever selective advantage or benefit of pottery, it was not equally perceived or acted upon in the short run.

Pottery was but one of the technological or biological innovations during the early centuries of the Christian era (ca. A.D. 200–600) that individual households decided whether or not to incorporate into their lives. Some of the new traits may have been directly linked, such as pottery and beans, but apparently not in LeBlanc's (1982a) sense of a trait complex. Innovations were adopted at various times by different households for different reasons, and with different temporal and spatial patterns to acceptance (bow technology also apparently entered the Southwest from the north rather than the south [Blitz 1988]). Attempts to provide a single explanation embracing all or most aspects of change in Basketmaker culture (e.g., Glassow 1972) do not hold up once better temporal control shows that changes in various aspects of culture and adaptation are not necessarily coextensive. Indeed, the notion of temporally coincident changes in several aspects of Basketmaker III culture may be, in large part, an artifact of the stage concept. Intra- and interregional variability in the adoption of new traits likely stems from many different sources, including variations in information flow mediated by kinship or other social forms, proximity to longstanding travel/exchange routes, generational differences in the acceptance of novelties, community/household conservatism, and variable perceptions as to the costs versus benefits of innovation, both from the practicalities of energy expenditure as well as a social concerns. To examine these and more substantive issues, it may help to treat each aspect of culture or each archaeological measure of behavior as a separate variable plotted against the dimensions of time and space.

For examining the Basketmaker II–III transition, we relied upon radiocarbon dating for temporal ordering. We would have preferred the precision of tree-ring dating, but the poor success with this method for the N16 excavations is probably typical for this early time. Reliance on radiocarbon dates is unlikely to change anytime soon, and unfortunately, this technique imposes its own limitations in the form of broad temporal ranges for even the best samples. Because temporal resolution in an ideal case is on the order of about six generations (see Smiley 1985:86–92), we must be circumspect about our ability to describe change, let alone explain it.

Our concept of Basketmaker III seems to be the outcome of the adoption and successful incorporation of technological and biological innovations during the Basketmaker II–III transitional interval. These innovations stimulated subsequent developments, the most important and interesting of which seem to have been social in nature. Rather than population growth being a cause for the adoption of new traits (as per Glassow 1972), the reverse may have happened. Prior adoption of those traits that provide the traditional hallmarks of the Basketmaker III stage may have resulted in population growth during Basketmaker III. This growth would have precipitated experimentation with new social forms evidenced by multifamily settlements and integrative structures (see Altschul and Huber; Gilpin and Benallie, this volume), laying the foundation for future developments.

ACKNOWLEDGMENTS

We would like to acknowledge and thank the Federal Highway Administration, the Bureau of Indian Affairs, and the Navajo Nation Historic Preservation Department for their support of the N16 excavations. Personnel on the project deserving mention include Miranda Warburton (principal investigator), Victoria Clark, Jim Huffman, Lanita Collette, David Ortiz, Ted Neff, and Kerry Thompson. Miranda Warburton and R. G. Matson commented on a draft of this chapter, resulting in several improvements.

NOTES

1. The earliest tree-ring dated pottery is a polished brown ware recovered by Earl Morris from Obelisk Cave in the Prayer Rock District; the available dates indicate that pottery was in use at this site by A.D. 480 (Morris 1980: table 2; Berry 1982:68). This finding is supported by Breternitz's (1986:263) report of brown ware sherds from a pit structure in Mancos Canyon with tree-ring dates in the early A.D. 470s. Specific to the Kayenta region, the earliest tree-ring-dated pottery comes from two sites in the Klethla Valley, NA8163 at A.D. 555 (Ambler and Olson 1977), and NA11,058 in the mid A.D. 530s (Swarthout et al. 1986:426).

2. Storage capacity is calculated using a version of Smiley's (1985:295–297) formula for deriving a conservative estimate for pit volume. Whereas Smiley used an estimate for pit depth in his calculations because of ground surface erosion, we use true pit depths.

3. The lack of storage features at some of these sites, though likely, cannot be considered proven because of ROW limitations to excavation or past disturbances to sites. At Tres

Campos, we excavated the midden and one extramural hearth, but only tested the structure, which largely lay outside the ROW. Nevertheless, the topography at Tres Campos is such that storage pits behind the structure are improbable owing to the shallow depth of soil above bedrock. The current Navajo Mountain road cuts through a portion of Blake's Abode just west of the structure and may have destroyed additional features. ROW restrictions also prevented full exploration of the southern margin of the site area at Sin Sombra, raising the possibility that other features lie outside the ROW. We doubt that storage features exist, but only full exposure along the southern margin of the site can confirm this.

4. Dust Devil Cave also probably functioned principally for storage during Basketmaker times; this site is located in a similar setting as the Desha Caves, but on the opposite side of Desha Creek

5. Schilz (1979) reports 21 cists in Cave 1, and 12 in Cave 2. Eight of these features had no mortar or other caulking between the upright slabs, but the rest had some material sealing the spaces. Juniper bark or other vegetation was packed between slabs for 18 cists; fiber-tempered mortar sealed the spaces for three cists; mortar without fiber was used for another three cists; one had slab fragments as chinking.

6. This is a conservative interpretation of the evidence in several cases, especially based on what we currently know about the surface appearance of Basketmaker sites. The presence of four-warp wickerwork (plain weave) sandals (Lindsay et al. 1968:27) provides fairly conclusive evidence for Basketmaker occupancy of several shelters.

7. By comparison, the Black Mesa Archaeological Project Basketmaker II site with the largest amount of storage in bell-shaped pits is AZ D:11:449 (ASM), where 20 pits provided close to 11 m³ (Smiley 1985). Moreover, this site is an extreme outlier in the sample of BMAP Basketmaker II sites, having several times more storage pits than other sites excavated on the project.

8. In the center of the fire-hardened floor of this pit were three identical siltstone pendants laid out around a small hole (7 cm in diameter and 29 cm deep) that contained three partially carbonized maize ears. Our interpretation of the evidence is that it represents part of a dedication ceremony that involved placing dry corn ears within the hole and arranging pendants around it. This was done prior to fire hardening the pit. The subsequent burning partially carbonized the corn ears.

9. This seed jar is interesting because it provides the first indication of early pottery within the Kayenta region. Kidder and Guernsey (1919:144) state that "the position in which this pot was discovered renders it certain that it is of an earlier period than the main sunflower cliff-house. As Basket Maker remains were noted in the same cave, and as this vessel is unlike any normal Cliff-house product with which we are familiar, it is possible that it may have belonged to that culture."

10. High iron content is verified by refired colors that are all in the yellowish red 5 and red 6 color groups (see Mills et al. 1993:237). Munsell colors of 15 refired nips are 2.5YR5-6/8 and 5YR 7/6-8. The most frequent color ($n = 6$) is 5YR7/6. Munsell color ranges of a sample of 15 sherds from Mountainview before refiring are 2.5YR5/4-6, 5YR2.5-3/1, 6/6, 7.5YR6/2-3, 6/2, 7/3-4, and 10YR7/3, 3/1.

11. These dates are 1710 ± 60 B.P. (Beta-69381) on maize from an organic layer (Feature 16) next to and stratigraphically below the cist, and 1810 ± 70 B.P. (Beta-69379) on juniper bark lining the bottom of a storage pit (Feature 24) that directly underlay the cist (Geib et al. 1999).

12. To be certain that no early pottery occurred in the collections from this site, the authors examined the entire ceramic assemblage but observed no Obelisk Utility or even Lino Gray.

13. This cord was originally made with turkey feathers wrapped with an S-twist around a two-ply Z-twist base cord, but a portion was patched using rabbit fur strips wound over the turkey feathers. Wormington (1961:55) reports that for Basketmaker III, "some blankets were made partially of fur and partially of feather cord."

Part V

Synthetic Studies of
Basketmaker Material Culture

10

From Brown to Gray

*The Origins of Ceramic Technology
in the Northern Southwest*

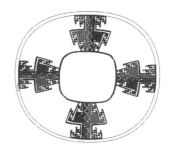

Lori Stephens Reed

C. Dean Wilson

Kelley A. Hays-Gilpin

Across the Anasazi region, accumulating evidence shows that gray, white, and red ware traditions associated with Anasazi ceramic technology evolved from an earlier pan-Southwestern brown ware technology. The growing number of early sites containing brown ware produced with local resources suggests that much of the brown ware identified in late Basketmaker II and early Basketmaker III sites is of local origin. Sites yielding only brown ware date between A.D. 200 and 500. During the A.D. 500s, Anasazi potters in many localities began experimenting with local resources and finishing techniques outside of the brown ware recipe, and began adding temper, slipping surfaces, painting designs, and using different clay resources. The addition of temper and experimentation with geologic clays (as opposed to iron-rich alluvial clays for brown ware) resulted in the transition from brown ware to gray/brown ware and, finally, to the gray ware pottery common in late Basketmaker III (A.D. 600–700) assemblages.

The recognition of a brown to gray ware transition during the larger Basketmaker period has important ramifications concerning the cultural and adaptive transition from Basketmaker II to Basketmaker III. The Basketmaker II period was originally defined as a time of increased reliance on agriculture and use of permanent structures, but was prior to the introduction of ceramics (Kidder 1927). The next defined interval, Basketmaker III, was described as a time of increased dependence on agriculture and population growth and expansion (Rohn 1989). Basketmaker III sites were recognized by the consistent presence of large numbers of distinctive Anasazi gray and white ware pottery. A weakness in the original classification system is that it failed to recognize intermediate developments between the distinct Basketmaker periods, thus masking the sequence of developments. This has contributed to confusion and disagreement regarding

whether the transition between aceramic and ceramic Basketmaker periods resulted in a series of gradual local developments or the sudden replacement of populations (Wilson and Blinman 1994). Proponents of gradual development models have interpreted changes during the Basketmaker periods as reflecting a series of responses to population pressures and deteriorating environmental conditions that followed the introduction of agriculture (Glassow 1972; Irwin-Williams 1973; see also Toll and Wilson, this volume). Others have assumed the absence of a local developmental sequence and have attributed changes associated with the appearance of Basketmaker III groups to sudden regional migrations or expansions from distant regions such as the Mogollon highlands (Berry 1982; LeBlanc 1982b; Lucius 1981). Models of abrupt changes have been inspired by the distinctiveness of sites dating to these two periods, an apparent absence of dates spanning the period between these phases, and the common occurrence of well-developed Anasazi gray and white ware types at Basketmaker III sites.

Data indicating a sequence of gradual change in the Anasazi region were first noted during the Navajo Reservoir Project, which documented a series of ceramic changes during the Basketmaker periods beginning around A.D. 200 (Dittert et al. 1963; Eddy 1961). This view, while initially discounted by many, is rapidly gaining credence as recent projects throughout the Anasazi region have documented similar sequences of ceramic change (Gilpin 1989, 1993; Hammack 1992; Hays 1992b; Hays-Gilpin et al. 1999; Kearns et al., this volume; Morris 1980; P. Reed and Wilcox, this volume; Toll 1991; Toll and Wilson, this volume; Wilson and Blinman 1994). In this chapter we discuss data pertaining to the long sequence of Basketmaker period ceramic developments throughout the northern Southwest. First, Anasazi brown ware is defined and briefly compared with other brown ware technologies (e.g., Mogollon), transitional gray/brown pottery, and gray and white ware. Second, a revised typology is proposed, clarifying the classification of early brown ware and identifying a brown to gray ware transition. Third, data from localities across the Anasazi region are discussed. Finally, the developmental sequence of Anasazi ceramic technology is discussed along with its relationship to models of agricultural dependence, population sedentism, and cultural interaction.

DEFINING BROWN, GRAY/BROWN, AND GRAY WARE TECHNOLOGIES

Classification of early brown ware and transitional gray/brown ware using the existing typological sequence has proven to be very difficult. As research at late Basketmaker II and early Basketmaker III sites increases, the inadequacies of the existing ceramic typology become more obvious. First, regional ceramic traditions defined for gray ware are not suitable for early brown ware ceramic assemblages. Our examination of early brown ware assemblages across the Colorado Plateau suggests that there is little difference between brown and gray/brown ware sherds from late Basketmaker II and early Basketmaker III sites. Recognizable differences are attributed mostly to variable resource availability between localities rather than significant differences in technology or vessel morphology. Thus, the series and type classification (see Colton and Hargrave 1937) developed for later Anasazi periods may not be applicable to brown ware and transitional gray/brown ware assemblages. For the most part, series classification is applicable beginning with late Basketmaker III assemblages, for which regional white ware traditions with specific temper, paint type, and surface treatment technologies develop along with pan-regional design styles. Part of the problem with classifying brown ware within existing ceramic traditions is that gray and white ware series are based on the addition of temper, which, for the most part, is absent from brown ware. We propose a pan-Anasazi brown and gray/brown ware classification that allows for the documentation of changes associated with the evolution of brown to gray ware traditions.

Before outlining a revised typological sequence for early brown ware assemblages, definition of brown, gray/brown, and gray ware ceramics is in order. Anasazi brown and gray/brown ware pottery was produced with clays that tend to have high iron content with dense natural inclusions of sand, silt, or fine volcanic material. Potters frequently, but perhaps not always, selected self-tempered clays, often from alluvial or pedogenic (recently redeposited) contexts. Brown and gray/brown ware vessels were fired in poorly controlled atmospheres; fire clouds and carbon streaks appear frequently. The dominant surface colors include tan, dark brown, red,

Figure 10.1. Paste cross sections of brown ware (top), gray/brown ware (middle), and gray ware (bottom) from the Colorado Plateau (Photographed by Douglas D. Dykeman through a binocular microscope at 20x with fiber optic illumination).

orange, and various shades of gray to black. The characteristic soft, crumbling, porous paste of brown and gray/brown ware vessels was the result of firing conditions that did not promote sintering, along with selection of heavily tempered, high-shrinkage, iron-rich clays. Vessel surfaces are usually polished or smoothed, but can be rough. No specific forming technique is characteristic of early brown ware pottery. Some brown ware pottery was thinned by coil and scrape (e.g., Woodruff Brown, Sambrito Utility, Obelisk Utility), some (probably) by pinching and drawing (i.e., the Hennessey Butte material described below), and some may have been thinned by paddle and anvil (Adamana Brown).

The primary difference between brown and gray/brown ware technology is the intentional addition of temper in gray/brown ware vessels. As shown in figure 10.1 (top), the paste texture of brown ware pottery is homogenous, with naturally occurring silt and fine sand, making the paste appear "dirty." The gray/brown paste in figure 10.1 (center) is similar to a brown ware paste, but with the addition of large temper grains that probably did not occur naturally in the clay. Finally, the gray ware paste shown in figure 10.1 (bottom) appears "cleaner" with no silt or fine sand inclusions, but with intentionally added temper that appears as large grains in the paste. Because paste color is not a reliable criteria for identifying ware categories, the paste cross sections shown in figure 10.1 were photographed in black-and-white to emphasize texture and temper grains without the bias of paste color.

Apparent gray/brown intergrades between specifically brown and gray ware technologies appear in many parts of the Colorado Plateau, especially in areas where low-iron, fine shale clays are rare. In such areas, silty, iron-rich clays were used to produce what is essentially high-iron gray ware that has coarse material (rock, crushed sandstone, sherd, or a combination) added as temper, and that is fired like a gray ware (in a neutral to reducing atmosphere, at a higher temperature, or both) to produce a harder paste than that of brown ware pottery. In such cases, color may remain a warm gray or "gray-brown." Color, then, is unfortunately not a very useful attribute in distinguishing what have become known as brown ware and gray ware pottery. It is important to distinguish these post-A.D. 700 well-fired, iron-rich gray wares from material dating to the 500s that might represent an actual technological transition or period of experimentation. Developing guidelines to make such a distinction will require continued research on sites dating to the A.D. 500s.

In contrast, gray ware pottery was produced with low-iron shale clays with added temper (usually crushed sandstone or other coarse sands, and in some cases, crushed volcanic or metamorphic rock, or crushed sherd). Temper tends to be coarser, better sorted, and less dense than that seen in brown ware pottery. Aplastic inclusions (e.g., silt) in the clay paste are rare. Where low-iron clays were unavailable, two options were available: gray ware was imported (for example, Pueblo II inhabitants of the Navajo Mountain area imported Tusayan Gray Ware from the Black Mesa area), or potters produced gray ware using iron-rich clays but a firing atmosphere that was manipulated to promote sintering. Gray ware vessels were fired in a neutral to reducing atmosphere that allowed sintering at a lower temperature and resulted in gray to black colors. A combination of lower temper density and greater degree of sintering led to hard, shattering fractures. Gray ware pottery in the Anasazi area was usually thinned by coil and scrape and sometimes pinched. For assemblages dating after A.D. 600, the recognition of types belonging to regional traditions, emphasizing paint type for black-on-gray and black-on-white ceramics, is an essential tool for identifying production locales and temporal sequences.

REVISION OF THE CLASSIFICATION SCHEME

The large number of differently defined brown ware types in the Southwest is a reflection of a long, complicated, and confusing history. Colton and Hargrave (1937) name three brown ware types with dates prior to A.D. 800: Woodruff Brown, Adamana Brown, and Rio de

Flag Brown. Most of the material now considered early brown ware was not covered by any of these three types. At that time, anything that looked like polished brown ware on the Colorado Plateau or in the Mogollon highlands was taken to be a product of "ethnically" Mogollon people because polished brown ware appeared in early sites in this area and remained dominant throughout the Mogollon sequence. In addition, most students of Southwestern archaeology are taught that brown ware pottery equals Mogollon peoples, and gray ware pottery equals Anasazi peoples. While brown ware was produced primarily during the earliest part of the Anasazi sequence, in the Mogollon highlands similar brown ware types dominate assemblages throughout the cultural sequence. This technological divergence resulted in the development of plain, polished, neckbanded, and corrugated brown ware in the Mogollon highlands, and plain, neckbanded, and corrugated gray ware in the Anasazi region during the late Basketmaker III through Pueblo III periods.

Emil Haury defined Alma Plain (1936:32–34, 1940: 69–72), a polished, sand-tempered brown ware originating south of the Mogollon Rim, and Martin and Rinaldo (1943) defined Alma Rough (with plain surfaces). Many researchers (e.g., Ferg 1978) have applied "Alma Plain" and "Alma Rough" to quartz sand-tempered, polished, and plain brown wares found in the southern Anasazi area. The term "Alma Plain," as presently used by some researchers working in the Mogollon highlands, refers to brown ware self-tempered with volcanic rock, which is common in Mogollon highland clays (Wilson 1994). The variety system was often used, and continues to be used, to describe local variants, such as a quartz sand tempered Forestdale Variety that is indistinguishable from Woodruff Brown. Colton and Hargrave (1937) noted that the Woodruff series probably represents the northernmost extension of the Alma series of Mogollon Brown Ware. Woodruff Brown and Woodruff Smudged were recognized by the 1961 Third Southwestern Ceramic Seminar: Southwestern Brown Wares as synonymous with Haury's Forestdale Brown, Forestdale Red (highly oxidized but not slipped), and Forestdale Smudged (Dittert 1961; Haury 1940:73–78). The 1995 Chambers-Sanders Trust Lands Ceramic Conference affirmed this decision, but authors of the resulting report (Hays-Gilpin and van Hartesveldt 1998) opted to put Woodruff types in a Puerco Valley Brown Ware tradition to emphasize that production locales for material found in the Puerco Valley are local. Many brown ware sherds in the Museum of Northern Arizona have been labeled Alma, Forestdale, Obelisk, Woodruff, and Lupton by different researchers, but to us they represent areal variants of a coherent brown ware technology in its early stages of development and are often indistinguishable. The materials and techniques used to make polished brown ware pottery were clearly widespread. Therefore, questions about production localities and distribution patterns are very difficult to answer.

Problems with the distinction between brown ware and gray ware is highlighted by Colton's (1955) definition of Obelisk Gray, which he assigned to Tusayan Gray Ware, replacing Lino Polished. In his "remarks" section, Colton (1955: Ware 8A, Type 1) wrote: "Obelisk Gray may belong to Mogollon Brown Ware as some sherds are very suggestive." Colton, however, failed to address which sherds are suggestive of Mogollon Brown Ware, or which attributes he considered indicative of polished Tusayan Gray Ware. Because of his offhand remark about brown ware, subsequent researchers placed soft-paste, polished brown ware sherds from the Lupton to Holbrook area in the Museum of Northern Arizona type collection as specimens of Obelisk Gray. These brown ware sherds are identical to specimens found elsewhere in the repository filed under Lupton Brown (see Wasley 1960) and Alma Plain. In addition, many researchers in the San Juan Basin have used the term Obelisk Gray to classify early brown, gray/brown, and polished gray ware sherds (see Morris 1980; L. Reed et al. 1998; Wilson 1989b). Colton's lack of clarity in defining Obelisk Gray and his comment concerning brown ware has resulted in continued confusion concerning the type and use of the type to classify a variety of brown, gray/brown, and gray ware ceramics.

Originally, Obelisk Gray was named for the polished pottery found in Obelisk Cave, some 6 km north of Cove, Arizona. Because both brown and gray wares were combined by Colton in Obelisk Gray, and because research questions of interest today require their separation, Spurr and Hays-Gilpin (1996) have proposed retiring the term Obelisk Gray. For the N16 Navajo Mountain Road Project, Spurr and Hays-Gilpin (1996) have revived the term "Lino Polished" for polished, sand-tempered gray ware, and have introduced the term "Obelisk Utility" for polished pottery with paste characteristics more commonly noted in brown ware types.

Further east, Dittert and his colleagues defined Sambrito Brown and Los Piños Brown in the Navajo Reservoir area (Dittert et al. 1963). The two types were distinguished by temporally discrete architectural associations and by subtle differences in texture and surface finish. As the result of a 1991 ceramic workshop sponsored by the Bureau of Land Management and the Museum of New Mexico, Wilson and Blinman (1993) collapsed Los Piños Brown and Sambrito Brown into a single category called Sambrito Utility. Twin Trees Gray of the Northern San Juan area (see Abel 1955; Colton 1955; O'Bryan 1950) also is ambiguous, with a similar history and problems like those described for Obelisk Gray. The type is best considered a variant of Obelisk Utility or Sambrito Utility produced in the Mesa Verde region (Wilson and Blinman 1995) with crushed igneous rock temper.

Oral traditions recount that William Wasley named brown ware from the Interstate 40 project in eastern Arizona "Lupton Brown" (A. E. Dittert, personal communication, 1995; see Wasley 1960, wherein the site is described but the pottery remains nameless), but thus far only four type specimens have been located at the Museum of Northern Arizona, and they come from the Holbrook area. Because this material differs from Adamana Brown—the coarser, micaceous material found in and near Petrified Forest—Hays-Gilpin and van Hartesveldt (1998) use the term "Lupton Brown" to describe the earliest sand-tempered brown wares of the Puerco Valley that are distinct from Woodruff Brown. In retrospect, however, this material is barely distinguishable from Obelisk Utility, described above, and the most efficient approach to Western Anasazi brown ware would be to extend the term "Obelisk Utility" to cover sherds identified as Lupton Brown.

As a result, the typological history of smoothed and polished brown ware pottery in both the Mogollon and Anasazi regions is complex and vague. Dittert (Dittert et al. 1963:11; Dittert 1961) proposed that brown wares "underlie the total ceramic development in the Four Corners area," an observation that we believe is confirmed. Whether the widespread brown ware technology is the result of Mogollon migration, diffusion of a Mogollon idea, or part of a larger, pan-Southwestern early brown ware ceramic horizon is a particularly difficult problem to address. The reasons for lack of agreement among researchers are not limited to lack of communication and relative paucity of early brown ware sites. The similarity of brown ware pottery dating ca. A.D. 200 (and possibly earlier) to A.D. 500 across the entire Southwest is due to a shared technology that may have ultimately been derived from northern Mexico (LeBlanc 1982b; Schroeder 1982). Regional differences in early pottery generally reflect variations in geology. Even these geological differences appear to be minor and reflect areal variation in alluvial deposits used during this time.

Recent studies of brown ware sites covering an extensive geographic area indicate that the traditional (regional) type system is not well suited to making fine-grained distinctions of brown ware types. Researchers have tended to force brown ware pottery into the various categories originally defined for what were once a very few sites in widely separate areas. Now, the gaps between brown ware sites are gradually filling as more research is conducted. Typological boundaries, however, are not emerging within the Anasazi brown ware horizon. The regional typologies employed for other ware categories are based on easily observable traits—such as paint formula (e.g., Cibola mineral paints and Tusayan organic paints) and added temper—that emerge in the A.D. 600s.

It could be argued that a single brown ware type with minor, localized varieties is represented.

In an attempt to clarify the typological classification of brown and gray ware ceramics, we propose a revision of the traditional typology, identifying early brown ware and transitional gray/brown ware types. The differences between brown and gray/brown ware sherds are generally difficult to isolate, but the most obvious difference is the intentional addition of temper in gray/brown ware vessels. Nevertheless, identifying what particles were intentionally added and what occurred naturally in the clay source for early brown ware sherds is, to say the least, difficult. We therefore suggest that these two technologically similar wares be subsumed under a single category of Obelisk Utility in the Cibola, Chuska, and Kayenta regions. Because Sambrito Utility is well defined in the literature and has a long typological history, we suggest that the type name be continued in the Northern and Upper San Juan areas.

The differences between brown and gray/brown sherds and typical gray ware are much more distinctive. In assemblages where the differences between brown and gray/brown ware sherds are easily identified, identification of brown paste and gray/brown paste varieties of Obelisk Utility may be used. We also suggest that use of the term "Lupton Brown" be discontinued; it is an ambiguous term that, in many cases, adds to the confusion surrounding typological classification of brown ware. Although this typology combines some types previously considered distinct, the use of numerous brown ware types across the Colorado Plateau merely isolates resource-based traits that are better identified as local varieties of a larger type. The strength of our approach allows for elucidation of broad patterns of early ceramic technology and resource use across the northern Southwest, and is intended to go hand-in-hand with ceramic resource studies.

The temporal sequence for early brown ware begins at approximately A.D. 200 on the Colorado Plateau with sites yielding polished or smoothed brown ware vessels (Geib and Spurr, this volume), and it continues until approximately A.D. 600, when the transition to gray ware vessel production with low-silt- and low-iron-content geologic clays was complete. Between A.D. 200 and 600, variability in resource use and firing atmosphere was great, resulting in the potential for many local varieties of brown ware. During the A.D. 600s, gray ware production increased dramatically, and it became the primary technology for vessel production in the Anasazi region by the end of the Basketmaker III period. The terminal date for Basketmaker III varies between A.D. 700 and A.D. 750, depending on local architectural and ceramic developments. By the end of Basketmaker III in all areas of the Colorado Plateau, the transition to gray ware pottery was complete. Production of brown and gray/brown

ware vessels during the Pueblo I to Pueblo III periods was rare and generally occurred in the form of pinch pots, effigies, miniatures, or pipes (L. Reed et al. 1998). Brown ware vessels from later contexts have been identified as mud ware in many areas; in the Upper San Juan area, for example, these vessels are typed as Rosa Brown (see Eddy 1966; Wilson and Blinman 1993).

Obelisk Utility

For much of the Colorado Plateau, we propose that most early brown ware (including transitional gray/brown pastes) be subsumed under the single category of Obelisk Utility (see Spurr and Hays-Gilpin 1996). This broad type simplifies classification of Anasazi brown ware and eliminates the confusing term "Obelisk Gray." As mentioned above, distinguishing between brown ware pastes with no added temper and gray/brown ware pastes with intentionally added temper (e.g., sand, sandstone, or crushed rock) is generally difficult. In such cases, "Obelisk Utility" as a single typological term is acceptable. When distinctive differences between brown and gray/brown pastes are evident within an assemblage, identification of sherds as Obelisk Utility (brown paste) and Obelisk Utility (gray/brown paste) also is appropriate. The vessels were produced by the coil and scrape method, have an unevenly polished surface that has been described as "bumpy," and have a high silt content and friable paste.

There are some differences between Obelisk Utility and the other brown ware types identified in and near the Mogollon region. In contrast to Obelisk Utility, Adamana Brown of the Petrified Forest and Puerco Valley area was probably produced with the paddle and anvil method and has a distinctively micaceous paste (Mera 1934; Wendorf 1953). Assemblages that include whole Adamana Brown vessels have been described from the Flattop Site (Wendorf 1953) and Sivu'ovi (Burton 1991) in the Petrified Forest National Park. Woodruff Brown (syn. Forestdale Brown) and Woodruff Smudged (syn. Forestdale Smudged) have evenly, highly polished surfaces, medium to coarse sand temper, and fine paste texture (Colton and Hargrave 1937; Wendorf 1953). Woodruff Brown and Woodruff Smudged occur predominantly in bowl forms (figure 10.2), contrasting with the predominantly seed jar form of Obelisk Utility (figures 10.3 and 10.4). Differences in vessel form between Obelisk Utility and Woodruff Brown suggest functional differences between the early brown ware of the northern Mogollon area and Anasazi brown ware. Although seed jars are the most common form for early brown and gray/brown ware, necked jars and bowls also have been documented for Obelisk Utility, Sambrito Utility, Woodruff (Forestdale) Brown, and Adamana Brown (figure 10.5). Alma Plain and Alma Rough of the Mogollon highlands describe a brown ware technology produced with self-tempered

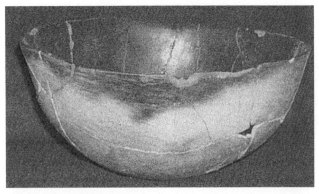

Figure 10.2. Woodruff Smudged bowl (Courtesy of Museum of Northern Arizona Photo Archives, catalog no. NA 5065eb 5-6.1).

(volcanic rock) clays, and having plain or highly polished surfaces. The primary distinction between other brown ware types and Alma Plain and Alma Rough is the occurrence of volcanic temper from the geologic formations of the Mogollon highlands. Thus, we identify Obelisk Utility, Adamana Brown, Woodruff Brown, Woodruff Smudged, Alma Plain, and Alma Rough, along with plain ware from Cienega phase[1] sites in the Tucson Basin (see Heidke 1998; Heidke and Stark 1996), as primarily resource-based variants of an early pan-Southwestern brown ware horizon.

Sambrito Utility

In addition to the type Obelisk Utility, a local variety of Anasazi brown ware from the Upper San Juan area (Navajo Reservoir District) was initially identified by

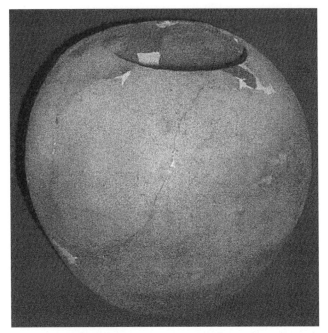

Figure 10.3. Obelisk Utility seed jar (Courtesy of Museum of Northern Arizona Photo Archives, catalog no. NA8671.1).

Figure 10.4. Obelisk Utility seed jar from NM-H-47-102, near Toadlena, New Mexico (Courtesy of NNAD-Farmington Roads Office).

Dittert et al. (1963) and Eddy (1961). Because Sambrito Utility occurs within a distinct geographic area and is generally better polished, the type is considered a useful and recognizable variety of Anasazi brown ware specific to the Upper and Northern San Juan areas. Similar to other brown ware traditions in the Anasazi region, Sambrito Utility appears to be a coherent pottery tradition and does not represent an experimental technology. Thus, production of brown ware pottery in the Upper and Northern San Juan areas was brought in as a preexisting technology rather than being an in situ development. Sambrito Utility was formed by coiling and thinned by scraping. Necked jars are the most frequent vessel form (note that seed jars are most frequent in other areas), but seed jars, bowls, dippers, and pipes also occur. Vessel size is generally small, and walls are thick relative to vessel size.

Vessel surfaces are always smoothed, and at least part of the vessel is polished as well. The paste is soft, with abundant silt and sand that are probably naturally occurring in the raw clay. Petrographic analysis of Sambrito Utility sherds indicates that this material derived from a fine-grained sandstone (Hill 1988). Wilson and Blinman (1993:11) suggest that "most of the sand and rock inclusions occur naturally in the clay sources, and temper was probably not added as a routine step in ceramic manufacture." Sherds tend to break and crumble easily, surfaces often spall, and sherd size is generally small. Paste color ranges from gray to dark gray to brown with occasional dark brown or reddish streaks. Pottery exhibiting similar characteristics described for Sambrito Utility but tempered with crushed andesite from the Northern San Juan area may be classified as Twin Trees Utility.

Lino Polished

In many areas of the Anasazi region, polishing of vessel surfaces continued into late Basketmaker III for gray ware as well as transitional gray/brown ware. Following Spurr and Hays-Gilpin (1996), we suggest reviving the term "Lino Polished" for polished gray ware sherds dating to the late Basketmaker III and Pueblo I periods. Lino

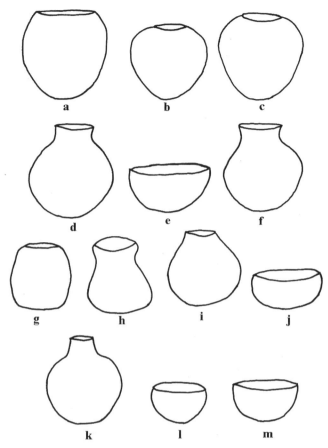

Figure 10.6. Lino Gray seed jar from site LA 2507 in Tohatchi Flats, New Mexico (Courtesy of Western Cultural Resource Management Consultants, Inc.).

Figure 10.5. Examples of early brown and gray/brown ware vessel shapes: (a) Obelisk Utility from Tohatchi Flats (LA 2506; Reed, Goff, and Hensler 1996:G-16); (b–e) Obelisk Utility from the Prayer Rock Caves (Morris 1980:62); (f–h) Sambrito Utility from the Upper San Juan area (Wilson and Blinman 1993:10); (i–k) Adamana Brown from the Petrified Forest (Wendorf 1953:49); (l–m) Forestdale (Woodruff) Smudged from the Petrified Forest (Wendorf 1953:123).

Polished vessels have a distinctive gray ware paste with a hard fracture, temper ranging from medium to coarse sand to crushed sandstone, and an uneven polish similar to Obelisk Utility. This type represents continuation of polishing in utility ware from brown ware to gray ware technologies. In contrast to the plain surfaces of Lino Gray, Lino Polished vessels have distinctive polishing striations that should not be confused with surface "sheen" resulting from some types of use wear. The basic seed jar shape (figure 10.6) remained common for Lino Gray and Lino Polished throughout the Basketmaker III period and into Pueblo I.

Tohatchi Red and Red-on-Brown

Tohatchi Red (L. Reed and Goff 1998) has recently been identified at sites in Tohatchi Flats, northwestern New Mexico (L. Reed and Goff 1998; L. Reed and Hensler 1998b) and in the Cove–Redrock Valley area, northeastern Arizona (Hays-Gilpin et al. 1999). This red ware type is essentially a red-slipped gray/brown ceramic having a

silty brownish paste that is soft and friable, a medium to coarse sand or crushed sandstone temper, and red-slipped surfaces. The red slip is probably a clay and hematite mixture (L. Reed and Goff 1998; L. Reed and Hensler 1998b) that adheres poorly to vessel surfaces and is easily scraped away. In many cases, the fugitive red seen on so called gray/brown and gray ware sherds may be the remains of slips from Tohatchi Red and Tallahogan Red vessels. Tohatchi Red appears in assemblages from Tohatchi Flats as early as A.D. 550 (L. Reed and Hensler 1998b) and in assemblages from the Cove–Redrock Valley area as early as A.D. 575 (Hays-Gilpin et al. 1999).

The primary difference between Tohatchi Red and Tallahogan Red is brown versus gray ware paste. In contrast to Tohatchi Red, Tallahogan Red has a hard gray ware paste with little silt content and a medium to coarse sand temper. At sites in Tohatchi Flats (L. Reed and Hensler 1998b), a local variety of Tallahogan Red has a crushed sandstone temper similar to that of Tohatchi Red; however, Tallahogan Red occurs in assemblages dating to the A.D. 600s and 700s. Production of the red slip on Tohatchi Red vessels improved little in the evolution to Tallahogan Red, on which slips also adhere poorly to vessel surfaces. Essentially, Tohatchi Red is the prototype for Tallahogan Red at sites dating to the middle A.D. 500s in Tohatchi Flats and other areas of the Colorado Plateau. Dolores Red with crushed igneous rock temper is the Northern San Juan equivalent of Tohatchi Red (see Lucius and Wilson 1981).

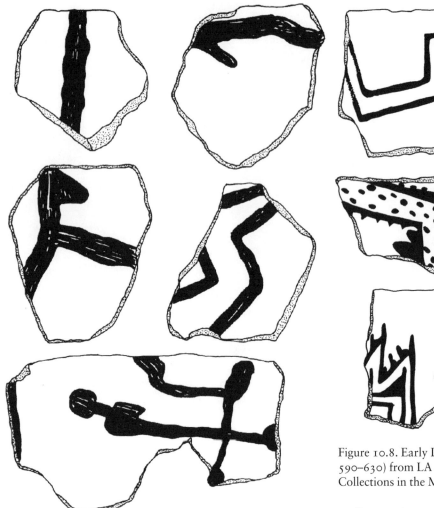

Figure 10.8. Early La Plata Black-on-white designs (A.D. 590–630) from LA 2506 in Tohatchi Flats (Navajo Tribal Collections in the Museum of New Mexico, Santa Fe).

Figure 10.7. Tohatchi Red-on-brown designs (A.D. 550–600) from LA 2506 in Tohatchi Flats (Navajo Tribal Collections in the Museum of New Mexico, Santa Fe).

Shortly after the introduction of red-slipped brown ware at Tohatchi Flats sites (specifically, LA 2506), the red slip mixture (clay and hematite) was used to paint designs on Tohatchi Red-on-brown vessels (Morgenstein 1995; L. Reed and Goff 1998; L. Reed and Hensler 1998b). Similar to Tohatchi Red, Tohatchi Red-on-brown has a silty, brown to gray/brown ware paste that is soft and friable, a medium to coarse sand or crushed sandstone temper, and application of a red pigment that adheres poorly to vessel surfaces. Although chronometric dates from the type site (LA 2506) are not refined enough to confirm use of the clay and hematite mixture as a slip first and then as a paint (McVickar and Wails 1999; L. Reed et al. 1998), it is likely that slipped surfaces occurred first on brown ware, and then shortly after, the slip was used as a paint (see Wilson and Blinman 1994). Painted designs on Tohatchi Red-on-brown sherds (no whole vessels were recovered, but see Morris 1980: figure

30-E, page 65; and Gladwin 1957:42–43) are broad lined and in many cases appear to have been finger painted rather than brush painted. Thick lines and rectilinear lines along with anthropomorphic-looking figures were identified on Tohatchi Red-on-brown sherds (figure 10.7). The majority of Tohatchi Red-on-brown sherds are from bowls, but a few jar sherds also have been identified.

A clear transition in design style, paint type, and clay selection occurred during the occupation of LA 2506. Sherds having gray/brown pastes and red-painted designs that poorly adhere to the surface, but with La Plata style designs, occur as a transitional step toward La Plata Black-on-white, which characterizes later assemblages. These transitional sherds are identified as early La Plata Black-on-white (originally typed as transitional Tohatchi/ La Plata Black-on-white by L. Reed and Goff [1998]) and have design styles that more closely parallel those of later La Plata Black-on-white sherds (figures 10.8 and 10.9).

The change from painted gray/brown ware (e.g., Tohatchi Red-on-brown) to painted gray ware (e.g., La Plata Black-on-white) spans approximately fifty years from A.D. 550 to A.D. 600 (McVickar and Wails 1999).

By A.D. 600, the transition in Tohatchi Flats from painted brown ware (Tohatchi Red-on-brown) to painted gray ware (La Plata Black-on-white) was complete. Tohatchi Red-on-brown is considered the prototype for La Plata Black-on-white at sites in Tohatchi Flats (L. Reed and Hensler 1998b).

Recognition of both Tohatchi Red and Tohatchi Red-on-brown in ceramic assemblages from Tohatchi Flats, Cove-Redrock Valley, and possibly Grand Gulch has important implications for the development of red and white ware technology on the Colorado Plateau. Data from these areas indicate that red and white ware types occurring in late Basketmaker III assemblages (e.g., Tallahogan Red and La Plata Black-on-white) evolved directly from a brown ware technology. Also, the technology of painted brown ware on the Colorado Plateau appears to have occurred earlier than at sites in the Mogollon region. Mogollon Red-on-brown, a red-painted brown ware, dates to A.D. 650–750 (Shafer and Brewington 1995)—at least one hundred years later than the earliest approximate date for Tohatchi Red-on-brown. In contrast to Tohatchi Red-on-brown, Mogollon Red-on-brown has highly polished surfaces, fine-lined designs, and red pigment that adheres well to vessel surfaces.

SPATIAL AND TEMPORAL DISTRIBUTION OF EARLY BROWN, GRAY/BROWN, AND GRAY WARE POTTERY

Production of early brown ware pottery occurs in most major regions of the Southwest between A.D. 200 and 500. Until recently, the appearance of brown ware sherds at Basketmaker II and early Basketmaker III sites on the Colorado Plateau was considered the result of Mogollon migration. More recent research indicates, however, that the appearance of Anasazi brown ware largely represents a local development. The following section provides an overview of Anasazi ceramic developments from early brown ware to gray, white, and red wares at Basketmaker sites. Information regarding this transition is presented for several geographic areas, including the Kayenta, Northern and Upper San Juan, San Juan Basin/Chuska Slope, and Puerco/Little Colorado areas (figure 10.10), but is by no means exhaustive.

Kayenta Anasazi Area

Throughout much of the Basketmaker III through Pueblo III periods, the Kayenta Anasazi area was occupied by smaller, more dispersed populations than the Northern San Juan and San Juan Basin areas. Sparse distribution of Lino Black-on-gray, especially of pots bearing early basketlike designs, suggests that pottery decoration may have begun later in the A.D. 600s, or, perhaps, pottery

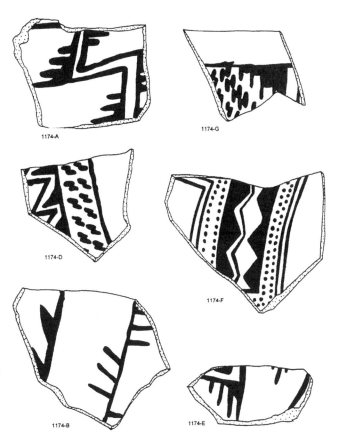

Figure 10.9. La Plata Black-on-white style designs from the Prayer Rock District, Cave 8, A.D. 668 (noncutting date) (adapted from Hays-Gilpin et al. 1999:546; ASM catalog numbers shown).

decoration was simply less frequent at Basketmaker III sites in the Kayenta area. Likewise, the widespread adoption of pottery may have lagged somewhat in this area. Brown ware, however, appears just as early at the Mountainview site near Navajo Mountain (see Geib and Spurr, this volume) as it does in the Upper San Juan area (circa A.D. 200), but at least some of the contemporaneous sites neighboring Mountainview lack pottery. That brown ware finds are rare in the Kayenta area does not appear to be due to gaps in the record for the centuries just prior to the A.D. 600s, but to a lukewarm attitude about pottery; some families made and used pottery, but many apparently did not. Only two brown ware sites in the Kayenta area have produced enough sherds (and no whole vessels) for discussion here. It should be noted, however, that Daifuku (1961:49–50) discusses terminological problems concerning the terms "brown ware" and "red ware" based on his work at Jeddito 264. He describes a slipped red ware with a buff-firing paste which he types as Tallahogan Red, and sherds with an unslipped red-firing paste that he classifies as brown ware. The red and brown ware sherds occur in both early and late Basketmaker III structures at Jeddito 264.

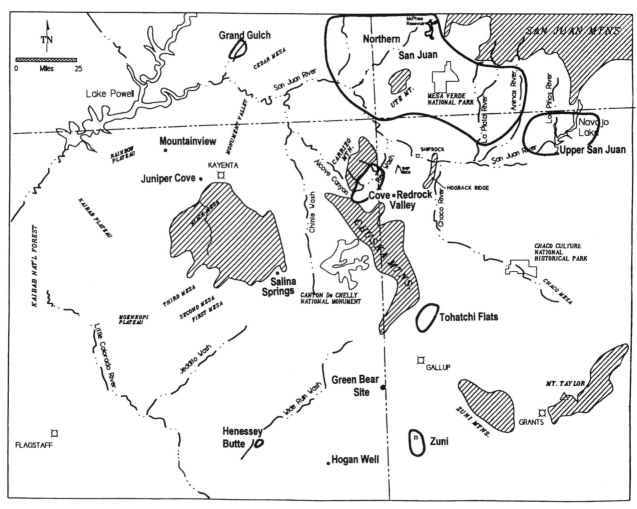

Figure 10.10. Location of early brown ware study areas on the Colorado Plateau.

Unfortunately, the description of these brown ware sherds is brief, and based on petrographic analysis by Anna Shepard, these sherds may be more related to Woodruff Brown than early Anasazi brown ware.

Recent excavation and research at the Mountainview Site (AZ-J-14-38 [NN]), located north of Inscription House and south of Navajo Mountain in Arizona, have identified one of the earliest occurrences of locally produced brown ware pottery in the region. The site consists of a single pit house and midden, dated to sometime between A.D. 145 and 375 (Geib and Spurr, this volume; Spurr and Hays-Gilpin 1996). Testing and data recovery at Mountainview yielded Obelisk Utility, Lino Polished, and tempered mud ware sherds, suggesting a transition from iron-rich, self-tempered alluvial clays to iron-poor geological clays with added temper.

Early brown ware pottery also was recovered at Site AZ-I-63-7 (NN) at Salina Springs, just east of Black Mesa and west of Chinle (Gilpin 1989, 1993). A single radiocarbon date on charcoal from one pit house yielded a date of A.D. 480. Brown ware sherds from the Salina Springs Site have soft and crumbly pastes and primarily fine quartz sand temper. Gilpin (1989, 1993) reports that these sherds variously resemble Obelisk Utility, Alma Plain, and Los Piños Brown.

Northern and Upper San Juan

The sequence of developments in the Basketmaker period in the San Juan region has often been overlooked as the result of a long history of placing sites dating as early as A.D. 300 and as late as A.D. 800 into a single Basketmaker III period (Kidder 1927; Morris 1939; Shepard 1939). In addition, work on Basketmaker II sites in the Durango area by Morris and Burgh (1954) was interpreted as indicating a long aceramic period associated with relatively large pit house villages. Because early ceramic sites in the Mogollon highlands were contemporaneous with Basketmaker II aceramic occupations (Haury and Sayles 1947; Martin and Rinaldo 1947), it was commonly assumed that ceramics were relatively late on the Colorado Plateau, and that the appearance of ceramics at Basketmaker III sites represented an abrupt and sudden development. To the contrary, accumulating evidence from the Navajo Reservoir and Durango areas demonstrates a long developmental sequence of ceramic technology. Recent investigations indicate that sites dominated by Sambrito Utility occur throughout the Upper San Juan as well as in areas of the Northern San Juan region.

During the Navajo Reservoir Project, late Basketmaker II and early Basketmaker III sites were investigated and yielded pottery representing early, locally produced brown ware in the Upper San Juan area (Dittert et al. 1963; Eddy 1966). The revised description of Sambrito Utility presented above is based on examination of the original Navajo Reservoir material together with recent work at the Oven Site (LA 4169; Hammack 1992; Wilson 1989a), along the La Plata Highway (Toll 1991; Toll and Wilson, this volume), and from the Fruitland Coal Gas Excavation Project (Tim Hovezak, personal communication, 1999).

Similar sites occurring in the Durango area date between the first century and late fourth century A.D. (Dean 1975), and formed much of the basis for the recognition of an aceramic Basketmaker II phase in this region. Excavation of a number of sites in this area apparently yielded no ceramics (Fuller 1988; Morris and Burgh 1954), leading to a characterization of Basketmaker II in the Durango area as an aceramic occupation. There is evidence, however, that ceramics were associated with some of the Basketmaker II sites in the Durango area. A small number of sherds probably representing Sambrito Utility were noted on the surfaces of probable Basketmaker II sites in the Ridges Basin and Bodo Canyon area (Fuller 1988). It is also likely that Morris (Morris and Burgh 1954) recovered a small amount of pottery during his excavations of Basketmaker sites in the Durango area that would today be classified as Sambrito Utility. Brown ware sherds were also recovered by Carlson (1963:37) from Basketmaker III sites in the Durango area and described as "similar to Rosa Brown." Given the sporadic association of ceramics and a long temporal span, it is probable that the Los Piños phase as traditionally recognized includes both preceramic and ceramic-bearing subphases.

Excavations conducted along the lower La Plata Valley as part of the La Plata Highway Project resulted in the discovery of a shallow pit house yielding Sambrito Utility as the sole ceramic type (Toll 1991; Toll and Wilson this volume). In addition, recent examination by Dean Wilson of sherds collected during Nusbaum's 1935 survey of the La Plata Valley (Hannaford 1993) indicate the presence of at least four other sites along the lower La Plata Valley dominated by Sambrito Utility.

Other examples of early ceramic occupations are represented by sites in Mancos Canyon south of Mesa Verde National Park. Initial reports described these sites as typical Basketmaker III sites dating sometime between A.D.

600 to 700 (Hallisy 1974). Road construction in Mancos Canyon on the Ute Mountain Reservation of southwestern Colorado in 1973 resulted in excavation of several early Basketmaker III sites (Breternitz 1986). Dendrochronometric samples from these sites indicate that at least one of the sites was occupied in the late A.D. 400s (Breternitz 1986). A second site yielded only plain gray ware sherds, and no cutting dates. One noncutting tree-ring date suggested use of this second site sometime after A.D. 460.

Thus, the examination of data from a number of projects supports existence of an occupational sequence characterized by the presence of distinct brown ware pottery (Sambrito Utility) along the Upper San Juan River and its tributaries, including the Animas, La Plata, and Mancos Rivers. This early pottery has not yet been well documented at sites in the Northern San Juan region west of the Mancos River, which may indicate that ceramic-producing groups moved into these areas slightly later than they did into areas of the San Juan to the east.

An important issue concerns the connection or relationship between Sambrito Utility and Basketmaker III gray and white ware types. A relationship between these types would indicate continuity between the transitional Basketmaker II and Basketmaker III occupations in the Northern and Upper San Juan areas, while the absence of such evidence may indicate a lack of continuity between these occupations (see Berry 1982). A gradualist model of ceramic development is supported by the presence of Sambrito Utility in contexts containing Chapin Gray and Chapin Black-on-white, and by evidence for a transition between brown and gray ware pottery. Sites yielding evidence of the contemporary production of Sambrito Brown and Basketmaker gray and white wares have been documented in the Upper San Juan (Dittert et al. 1963; Eddy 1966; Hammack 1992) and La Plata drainages (Toll 1991; Toll and Wilson, this volume). Evidence also indicates that Sambrito Utility may have been produced at the same sites as Chapin Gray and Chapin Black-on-white, using different locally available resources (Toll and Wilson, this volume; Hill 1988). These sites also contain some pottery exhibiting combinations of pastes and treatments intermediate between Sambrito Utility and Chapin Gray, further substantiating the gradual development of northern and Upper San Juan Gray Ware types out of Sambrito Utility (Toll and Wilson, this volume). Sites exhibiting this combination of Sambrito Utility and Basketmaker III pottery types appear to date from the late sixth to middle seventh century. In addition, the combination of Twin Trees Utility, Chapin Gray, and Chapin Black-on-white documented at sites in Mesa Verde National Park represents a very similar combination of ceramic types (Abel 1955; O'Bryan 1950). These sites exhibit typical Basketmaker

III architecture, and most appear to date to the seventh century.

San Juan Basin/Chuska Slope Area

Most Basketmaker III sites in the San Juan Basin date after A.D. 600. A few sites, however, have early Basketmaker III occupations, specifically Cove-Redrock Valley (Prayer Rock District) on the northwestern periphery of the San Juan Basin and Chuska Mountains (Morris 1980), and in Tohatchi Flats on the southwestern edge of the San Juan Basin (Kearns et al., this volume). Ceramic data from both of these areas are critical in identifying the sequence of ceramic technological development from late Basketmaker II into Basketmaker III throughout the San Juan Basin. Obelisk Utility, under the old type name of Obelisk Gray, has been identified at later Basketmaker III sites in the area; however, many of these sherds are likely examples of Lino Polished. Although few ceramic sites dating to the late Basketmaker II and early Basketmaker III periods have been identified in the San Juan Basin, it is probable that many more of these sites exist but are deeply buried or underlie later Basketmaker III occupations. Early brown ware sites described below include those from the Prayer Rock District and Tohatchi Flats.

The first documented evidence of locally produced brown ware pottery in the San Juan Basin/Chuska Slope area came from Obelisk Cave (the type site for Obelisk Gray, now Obelisk Utility) in the Prayer Rock District. Tree-ring cutting dates from Obelisk Cave indicate a primary occupation between A.D. 470 to 489, with possible earlier use of the cave from the A.D. 430s into the 460s (Ahlstrom 1985; Hays-Gilpin et al. 1999; Morris 1980: 50). Pottery excavated by Earl Morris in 1931 from Obelisk Cave consists almost entirely of polished brown ware seed jars identified as Obelisk Gray (Morris 1980).

Polished gray ware pottery from Broken Flute Cave is relatively frequent, and vessel forms include bowls and seed jars. This material was originally typed as Obelisk Gray, but with the exception of a single brown sherd, it differs from material found in Obelisk Cave, as described above. Based on paste characteristics, Hays-Gilpin et al. (1999) suggest calling this material either polished gray ware as a generic term, or Lino Polished, Cove Variety, where a type name is necessary.

White and red ware pottery from Broken Flute Cave is dominated by deep bowls, having similar pastes to gray ware pottery from the site. Most of the white ware was identified as La Plata Black-on-white, but one shallow bowl has a red slip on its exterior and a simple, tripartite, rotational design on its interior. The dull red design was made by using the same red slip pigment as a paint to cover just part of the interior, leaving "negative" grayish brown triangles of unslipped surface (see Morris 1980: figure 30-E, page 65). Although identified as an untyped

painted brown ware, this vessel essentially fits L. Reed and Goff's (1998) definition of Tohatchi Red-on-brown.

Similar to pottery from Broken Flute Cave, transitional gray/brown ware sherds have been identified at nearby Basketmaker III sites excavated along the N33 road through Cove, Arizona (Hays-Gilpin et al. 1999; P. Reed and Wilcox, this volume). These sites date between A.D. 600 and 700 (P. Reed and Wilcox's Broken Flute phase), representing an occupation later than that identified at Obelisk Cave. Many of the sherds from the N33 Project appear to be transitional between brown and gray ware due to their abundant, poorly sorted temper and occasional high silt content. They may indeed represent a period of experimentation, or they may simply represent the application of gray ware firing technology to "dirtier" materials than those used by potters producing, for example, Tusayan and Northern San Juan Gray Ware at about the same time. Nevertheless, these silty gray/brown ware sherds fit the broad description of Obelisk Utility (gray/brown paste). Sherds that represent the brown ware end of the continuum (soft paste, dense fine temper, tendency to brownish colors) were very rare in the collections from the N33 Project, mostly because no sites dating to the early to middle A.D. 500s were excavated.

The El Paso North System Expansion Project (see Kearns 1995, 1996c; Kearns et al., this volume; McVickar 1999b) yielded a wealth of information on the Basketmaker sequence and the brown to gray ware transition in the western San Juan Basin. More than 100,000 ceramic artifacts from 18 Basketmaker III sites or components were collected and examined (L. Reed and Hensler 1998b). Assemblages dating between A.D. 500 and 600 were dominated by Obelisk Utility (gray/brown paste), Tohatchi Red, Tohatchi Red-on-brown, and plain gray/brown sherds, with smaller amounts of Lino Gray. Late Basketmaker III, Tohatchi phase assemblages (A.D. 600–725) were dominated by Lino Gray, La Plata Black-on-white, Tallahogan Red, and nonlocal types such as Chapin Black-on-white, Lino Black-on-gray, and Chapin Gray.

As described above, data from LA 2506 (Fenenga 1956; McVickar and Wails 1999) indicated that the transition from brown ware to gray ware technology took place during the site's occupation. L. Reed and her colleagues (1996) proposed an occupational sequence for the site that began with construction of a pit house and pocket pit house complex beginning at approximately A.D. 517 (dendrochronologic dates of A.D. 515+v, 517+vv, 518r, and 518v were obtained from structural beams of the pit structure). The sequence of occupation at LA 2506 shows both ceramic and architectural change, beginning with predominantly brown and gray/brown ware sherds associated with the earliest pit structures, continuing into the middle A.D. 500s with a second cluster of pit structures having gray/brown and gray ware sherds, and concluding with a late 500s occupation associated with technological experimentation with early red-slipped and red-painted pottery. The red-slipped and -painted sherds from LA 2506 represent early prototypes (e.g., Tohatchi Red and Tohatchi Red-on-brown) of later red-slipped and painted gray ware vessels. The ceramic assemblage from LA 2506 is distinctive and demonstrates the evolution of classic Basketmaker III gray, white, and red ware from a clearly brown ware technology.

Puerco/Little Colorado Area

Identification of early brown ware in the Puerco/Little Colorado area is frequently more challenging than in areas to the north. The Puerco/Little Colorado area is on the southern periphery of the Anasazi region and is essentially in the transition area between the Anasazi and Mogollon regional traditions. Thus, many sites in this area have architecture and pottery representing an amalgamation of material culture. Differentiating Anasazi and Mogollon occupations, especially sites dating to the late Basketmaker II and early Basketmaker III period, can be difficult and challenging.

Brown ware ceramics were recovered at sites NM:12:K3:201 and NM:12:K3:202 (Zuni site numbers) on the Pia Mesa Road Project on the Zuni Indian Reservation (Varien 1990:88–90). Most sherds were found on the site surface, but at least one sherd appeared in pit structure fill. Tree-ring samples from two of the burned structures produced noncutting dates ranging from the middle A.D. 300s to the early A.D. 400s. Sherds most closely resemble Adamana Brown, Adamana Fugitive Red, and Woodruff Smudged. Varien notes the presence of a floated-surface red sherd that may be analogous to the polished red pottery described by Rinaldo (1943:80–81) as a less well polished variant of San Francisco Red (see also LeBlanc 1982a:110).

The Green Bear Site, AZ K:12:3 (ASM), lies just north of I-40 at Lupton, a few miles west of the Arizona-New Mexico state line. Recorded by Wasley in 1959, it was excavated by Ferg in the 1970s (Ferg 1978). Wasley defined the Lupton phase of Puerco Valley prehistory on the basis of pit houses with early brown ware at nearby AZ K:12:6 (ASM) (Wasley 1960). This phase apparently dates from about A.D. 200 to 500. Wasley initially called the pottery Alma Plain, Forestdale Variety (indicating quartz sand temper), but apparently later named it Lupton Brown, a term that remains obscure and unpublished.

Several sites at Hogan Well, south of Navajo, Arizona, have components with brown ware ceramics dating as early as A.D. 200, and others with classic Basketmaker III gray ware together with brown ware that date at least a few centuries later (Dykeman 1995). Dykeman classifies

the brown ware pottery in the early components as Woodruff Brown and argues that the occupants of the sites were Mogollon. Assemblages from the second time component include Woodruff Smudged bowls as well as Lino Gray jars and Obelisk Gray bowls. Notably, Dykeman (1995:34–53) compared size and density of temper particles in these four types, and his results show this attribute to be useful. Woodruff Smudged has quartz sand temper that is significantly finer and denser than sand in the other types, on the order of 2,429 silt-sized grains per square centimeter. The gray ware types have 78 (Lino Gray) to 87 (Obelisk Gray) coarse grains per square centimeter. The earlier type, Woodruff Brown, has fine to coarse temper. While Woodruff Brown appears to fit the overall description of most early brown wares reviewed here, Woodruff Smudged represents an elaborated brown ware technology for making bowls. Woodruff Smudged evidently appears at about the same time, but as a very different kind of ceramic innovation: the advent of reduction-fired gray wares made with iron-poor shale clays and added coarse quartz temper.

Two sites excavated during the Coronado Railroad Project between Navajo and St. Johns, Arizona, yielded early brown ware assemblages. Two structures at the Cottonwood South Site yielded radiocarbon dates of A.D. 434 to 641 and A.D. 538 to 645 (Marek et al. 1993:179) in association with Lino Gray and sand-tempered brown ware. Beneath these structures were two undated pit houses that yielded only brown ware (Hays 1992b). Some of the brown ware sherds had small amounts of mica visible on their surfaces, and some had large pores (round and linear) visible on both surfaces as well as in their cores, consistent with the use of fiber temper. Sherds closely resemble material called "Lupton Brown" by Wasley and others (i.e., Obelisk Utility), although a few sherds were coarser, had more mica, and could easily be called Adamana Brown. Sherds from upper levels, dating circa A.D. 600, include both rough and polished brown ware that closely resembles the type descriptions for Woodruff Brown and Woodruff Smudged. A few such sherds had red slips and were classified as Woodruff Red. Lino Gray and Lino Fugitive Red had rough, scraped surfaces and hard, light-colored paste. La Plata and White Mound Black-on-white sherds were also present.

Finally, Alan Sullivan described "crude" sand-tempered brown ware pottery recovered at the Hennessey Butte Site (AZ K:13:6 [ASM]) north of Holbrook, Arizona (Hays-Gilpin and Sullivan 1999). Kelley Hays-Gilpin examined the collection of 459 sherds at the Arizona State Museum and later borrowed several sherds and a clay sample for refiring studies. Most of the sherds recovered in and around four small, oval floor surfaces were sand-tempered brown ware. A small number of sherds were red-slipped brown ware and unfired bark-tempered mud ware. The Hennessey Butte brown ware materials most closely resemble pottery from Cottonwood Seep and Cottonwood South. They are considerably more irregular in wall thickness and surface treatment than the Cottonwood materials, however, and include red-slipped pottery, which is absent at the Cottonwood sites.

Of all the Anasazi brown wares, examples from the Puerco-Little Colorado area seem to display the most variability in terms of materials, texture, vessel shape, and forming and finishing techniques. Each variation seems to be localized to a site or group of sites. For example, micaceous paddle-and-anvil-formed Adamana Brown in and around the Petrified Forest contrasts with coil-and-scraped pottery using more sandy, porous materials just to the east of the Petrified Forest, on the west edge of the Chambers-Sanders Trust Lands, while the Hennessey Butte material near Holbrook appears to have been made with similar sandy materials but with different forming, finishing, and firing. Pottery displaying apparent Mogollon technology, such as polishing and smudging, pervades the whole area alongside later Anasazi gray and white ware pottery. Local populations, then, seem to have developed unique variations on a similar brown ware theme. The in situ development of red ware from brown ware, and the longstanding co-occurrence of these wares with white and gray ware that falls solidly into the Anasazi ceramic tradition make questions of Mogollon/Anasazi cultural affiliation and boundaries frustrating and call into question the whole notion of strong association between pottery technology and past "ethnicity."

BASKETMAKER CERAMICS IN AN ANTHROPOLOGICAL CONTEXT

Similar to its origin in other areas of the world, the origin of pottery production in the American Southwest was probably linked to the intensification of agriculture and eventual dependence on domesticated plants such as corn and beans. In western Asia, for example, the beginning of pottery marks the cultural transition between the earlier and later Neolithic (Moore 1995:44–45). Along the Mediterranean, Fertile Crescent, and Anatolian Plateau, earlier Neolithic villages were economically dependent on hunting, gathering, and limited farming. By about 6000 B.C., people in these areas began to abandon hunting and gathering for a full-time farming and herding economy. Although the inhabitants of early villages in the western region of Asia used clay for thousands of years prior to the late Neolithic for making mud bricks (see Kenyon 1981), the use of clay for making vessels did not begin until a full agricultural and herding economy had developed.

It also has been established, however, that the origins of ceramic production and agricultural dependence are not always linked. The earliest ceramic vessels in Japan, Jomon pottery, were produced for cooking and storage by hunting, fishing, and gathering peoples along the coast (Aikens 1995). The adoption of ceramic technology varies between 5000 and 10,000 B.C., depending upon the geographic context of Jomon culture. Jomon pottery was used in the context of storing animal, fish, and wild plant foods until about 2000 B.P., at which time the adoption of wet-rice agriculture changed aspects of local economies and cultures.

The same type of association between pottery production and wild plant foods has been documented in Central America (Cooke and Ranere 1992). Monagrillo ceramics, dated as early as 2800 B.C., are primarily associated with the harvesting of root crops, palms, and other tree crops. Hoopes (1995:189) discusses these data, emphasizing that "Monagrillo pottery has not been found in direct association with maize. Thus, a link between the earliest pottery and the adoption of agriculture has not been identified in the archaeology of Central America." With evidence of feasting and exchange networks among sites, Hoopes and Barnett (1995:4) further point out that "pottery vessels may have enhanced the value of wild food products within the context of social interaction."

The collection of case studies compiled by Barnett and Hoopes (1995) show that, in both the Old and New Worlds, the earliest pottery not only was functional but played an important role in the preparation, serving, and consumption of foods and beverages at social gatherings (e.g., Barnett 1995; Clark and Gosser 1995). Hoopes and Barnett (1995:4) also suggest that the "nutritional advantages of food products made possible by the use of ceramic vessels may well have been secondary to the value of social contexts these foods helped to create."

In the remainder of this section, we place the production of early pottery on the Colorado Plateau within a larger cultural context. At sites across the Southwest, the relationship between agricultural dependence and the need for long-term storage is critical in interpreting the initial production of ceramic vessels. Similar to the early production of pottery in Western Asia (Moore 1995), the inception of ceramic vessel production in the Southwest may have been primarily a functional innovation. On the Colorado Plateau, it appears that the first pottery occurred as a full-blown technology that was slowly adopted by individual households as the need for sturdy storage and cooking pots increased. The spread and adoption of this technology appear to have originated from the south in conjunction with sedentary adaptations associated with dependence on agriculture.

The similarities between the earliest Anasazi pottery and contemporaneous pottery in other areas of the Southwest—particularly the Mogollon highlands, where similar brown ware pottery was manufactured over a longer period—have fueled speculation regarding the origin of pottery-making Anasazi groups and their relationship with other Southwestern cultures. These similarities have been traditionally explained in terms of the spread of people from the Mogollon highlands into the Colorado Plateau, and subsequent differences were attributed to the development of distinct and isolated cultural traditions. Alternative resource- and technology-based models have recently been proposed to explain earlier similarities and later differences for pottery found in different Southwestern regions in terms of the availability and utilization of variable, regional ceramic resources (Wilson et al. 1996).

In the Mogollon area, aspects of the earliest brown ware technology continued in the pottery produced during later periods because they were well suited to local clay resources. The forming, firing, and functional properties of the volcanic-derived, self-tempered alluvial and pedogenic clays occurring throughout the Mogollon highlands were excellent. This resource base contributed to the continuity and conservatism of the ceramic technology practiced in the Mogollon highlands.

Given the poor quality of the alluvial and pedogenic clays found on the Colorado Plateau, Anasazi potters found that they were not as well suited to brown ware technology as resources in other areas of the Southwest. Forming would have been difficult, and the thicker and more uneven vessels would have been weaker and less efficient, as indicated by characteristics noted in Sambrito Utility (Wilson and Blinman 1993). These limitations would have encouraged experimentation with the abundant geologic clay resources on the Colorado Plateau. Between A.D. 500 and 600, this experimentation resulted in a shift in technology to low-iron geologic clays, the addition of temper, and the development of manufacturing conventions more suited for resources available on the Colorado Plateau. Greater control of firing appears to have been achieved shortly after the transition to geologic clays, but there was little change in firing atmosphere.

As a result of geologic variability and the quality of local clay resources, ceramic technology and resource use diverged between the Anasazi and Mogollon regions in the A.D. 500s. While Mogollon potters continued to use the abundant volcanic-derived clays for production of brown ware vessels, Anasazi potters began the transition to gray ware vessels having stronger walls and greater thermal shock resistance.

In most of the areas discussed above, where the transition from Anasazi brown ware to gray ware has been documented, ceramic assemblages dating to the A.D. 200–500 period contain only brown ware sherds with little evidence of added temper. Seed jars appear to be the most common vessel form in assemblages dating to early Basketmaker III. The A.D. 500s in many areas of the Anasazi region was a time of intensive experimentation

with alternative clay and temper resources. At this point, the search for local resources and manufacturing conventions that would produce sturdier vessels was clearly underway. Many of the assemblages dating to the A.D. 500s have sherds that may be described as gray/brown ware, having paste characteristics that fall between true brown and gray ware technologies. By approximately A.D. 600, the transition to a clearly gray ware technology was complete. Gray ware vessels of the late Basketmaker III period have abundant, coarse temper that was intentionally added to low-iron-content clays.

The identification of locally produced brown ware pottery at sites on the Colorado Plateau and the associated technological trajectory characterizing the development of gray ware pastes allows for the examination of various models of Southwestern ceramic technology, reliance on agriculture, and increased population sedentism. Following LeBlanc (1982b) and Wilson and Blinman (1994), we would argue first that polished brown ware in the Anasazi region represents an early pan-Southwestern ceramic tradition using brown-firing, self-tempered alluvial clays. Evidence emerging in the Hohokam area suggests the southern deserts also fit this phenomenon very well (Heidke 1998; Heidke and Stark 1996; Stark 1995). An Early Ceramic Horizon for the U.S. Southwest generally, together with northern Mexico, is discussed by Stark (1994), adding important new data to LeBlanc's earlier formulation. This Early Ceramic Horizon represents adoption of a "mature" ceramic technology, probably introduced from areas to the south, rather than the result of experimentation occurring simultaneously in several areas. Recent work at Early and Late Cienega phase sites from southern Arizona suggests that production of ceramic vessels in the Hohokam region began roughly 1500 years earlier than in the Mogollon and Anasazi regions. Heidke (1998), however, indicates that the earliest vessels were small bowls probably used for rituals, as opposed to domestic cooking and storage vessels. Heidke also suggests that the origins of pottery manufacture in southern Arizona probably diffused from pottery complexes in Mexico dating as early as 1600 B.C. (Clark and Gosser 1995). As discussed below, the origin of pottery as a ritual item rather than a domestic one has been documented in other areas of the world. On the Colorado Plateau, however, the earliest occurrences of ceramic vessels appear in association with cooking and storage of agricultural products.

Brown ware technology, then, apparently developed in northern Mexico and rapidly diffused northward. This diffusion probably occurred through a number of cultural mechanisms—such as interaction between groups, migration, and associated kin ties—and was similar in many ways to the mechanisms associated with the earlier diffusion of corn agriculture. Although migration has been a popular explanation for the spread of cultural traits and ideology, it is probable that migration is only a small part of a larger process in the dissemination of new technologies, material culture, and cultural norms. Along these lines, Skibo and Blinman (1999) suggest that the initial adoption of pottery in the Anasazi region was probably a family-by-family process. Although the evidence for early brown ware is widespread, it nevertheless appears to be scattered. It is likely that during the late Basketmaker II and early Basketmaker III periods, families making and using pottery may have lived next to people who did not adopt pottery technology. Still, the widespread distribution of brown ware pottery technology indicates that by A.D. 200, agricultural developments in most regions of the Southwest had reached a threshold where pottery vessels became important. Local conditions may have contributed to the initial acceptance or rejection of pottery technology. Interestingly, Skibo and Blinman (1999) also suggest that based on the similarity in brown ware technology across the Colorado Plateau (i.e., primarily seed jars with a roughly polished exterior), individual potters may have been copying a standard design using local resources.

Seed jars are the most common form identified in early brown ware assemblages across the Colorado Plateau, continuing in lower frequencies during most of the late Basketmaker III period, after which they became rare. Skibo and Blinman (1999) argue that seed jars are a multipurpose vessel that would perform well in cooking, storage, or food processing. The globular shape and curved surfaces of seed jars result in a strong vessel form that can withstand the strains of thermal shock and physical impact. Brown ware seed jars are in essence, then, an ideal form for a durable and generalized container. Also, the polished exteriors of many brown ware seed jars would have impeded water permeability and prevented leakage (see Schiffer 1988; Skibo 1992). For cooking, however, polished surfaces prevent the escape of steam inside the vessel and can result in spalling of the exterior surface. It is likely that the poorly polished surfaces on Obelisk Utility seed jars, for example, were not the result of poor craftsmanship, but rather served to prolong the use-life of cooking vessels and prevent leakage from storage vessels.

Although the seed jar shape has more strength, the small-diameter opening would restrict access to the contents of a vessel. It is probable that the technological and morphological limitations of brown ware seed jars provided the impetus for the transition to gray and white ware technology in the Anasazi region. In contrast to brown ware, gray/brown and gray ware technology, like that seen in Basketmaker III assemblages from the Cove–Redrock Valley area (P. Reed and Hensler 1999) and Tohatchi Flats (L. Reed and Hensler 1998b), was an in situ development in the Anasazi country, appearing sometime in the A.D. 500s in areas where shale-derived clays were

available. During the A.D. 500s, potters began using coarser temper and experimenting with alternative clay resources and a wider range of vessel forms, possibly in an attempt to produce stronger vessels. By the late A.D. 500s and early A.D. 600s, the transition to geologic clays and coarser temper available on the Colorado Plateau was complete, resulting in vessels that were stronger and better able to withstand thermal shock. In contrast to brown ware, gray ware vessel strength was a product of raw material selection rather than vessel shape. Thus, the all-purpose brown ware seed jar was slowly replaced during the A.D. 600s with other vessel forms having more specific functions (e.g., bowls, ollas, pitchers, wide-mouthed jars). This transition also led to the gradual distinction of specialized forms associated with gray versus white ware vessels.

The adoption of brown ware ceramic technology between A.D. 200 and 500 and the shift to gray ware technology by A.D. 600 in many areas of the Anasazi region were probably responses to changing subsistence patterns and the need for alternative types of storage and cooking tools. Mills (1989) and Hays (1993) have argued that increased sedentism and reliance on agriculture account for a shift from expedient ceramic technology suited to the needs of mobile horticulturalists in the early centuries of the first millennium to more-specialized manufacture of a complex, diverse, and durable ceramic assemblage better suited to the needs of sedentary farmers. Mills argues that Basketmaker III and Pueblo I ceramic assemblages fit a model of "maintainable" technology that includes "ease of manufacture and repair, less temporal lag between manufacture and use, a lack of backup systems, and portability" (Mills 1989:6). We argue that early brown ware technology represents the first step of an even more essentially maintainable technology. Early Anasazi ceramics, especially brown ware, are made of materials that would have been easy to obtain and not very time consuming to prepare; self-tempered clays were commonly used for brown wares. Construction techniques were apparently fairly simple, shapes were simple and restricted to a few vessel forms (primarily seed jars, straight-necked jars, and bowls), decoration was rare, and firing atmosphere seems to have been, for the most part, uncontrolled. Specialist knowledge would not have been necessary to make early containers; with a little knowledge and practice, someone in each household could probably have made ceramic vessels as needed.

In contrast, the introduction of fairly simple gray ware and further changes represented in later Puebloan ceramic assemblages show a gradual shift to an increasingly "reliable" technological system. Ceramics are "sturdier," "over-designed," and have a greater range of shapes and hence a greater range of potential functions. Increasing the size of vessels and the variation of size and shape within assemblages provides a "backup" or "standby" system. Rather than fill a new need with a quickly produced new vessel, one chooses a vessel from a varied stockpile, or obtains one from a specialist potter. "Technological solutions for increasing durability may include the selection of raw materials that promote greater impact, thermal, or abrasion resistance; but also may include the use of higher firing temperatures to produce more indurated pastes" (Mills 1989:7). Indeed, the use of rock temper, corrugated surface texturing, and a better-controlled firing atmosphere seen in later Pueblo period utility vessels resulted in a harder, less porous paste and more resistance to abrasion, thermal shock, and spalling (see Schiffer 1990; Schiffer et al. 1994). Greater time was invested in preparing materials, and in forming, finishing, and decorating vessels, and different wares emerge for different purposes (i.e., white ware and red ware serving vessels). Formal kiln facilities—which allowed for higher temperatures, longer firing duration, and better control of atmosphere and, hence, degree of sintering and color, but requiring greater investment of time, labor, expertise, and possibly special fuels—appear sometime in the late Pueblo II or early Pueblo III period, and increasing craft specialization seems likely in most areas.

Gradual changes associated with this shift include increasing diversity of forms and the development of functionally distinct and specialized ware groups. Mills (1989) argues, then, that changes in ceramic technology in the Anasazi region are part and parcel of changes taking place in the overall adaptive system. Where mobility was once used to even out vagaries in resource distribution, Anasazi people began to replace mobility by investing in "reliable" technology, including agriculture and food-processing systems. With the data presented here, we would suggest that development of a "reliable" ceramic technology on the Colorado Plateau began in the sixth century. Evidence for year-round site occupation and the clear dependence on agriculture by the A.D. 500s and early 600s presented elsewhere in this volume supports a shift to household sedentism through which mobility for resource exploitation would have been achieved by task groups.

Skibo and Blinman (1999) also suggest that cooking of beans, which can often take two to three hours of intense boiling, may have played an important role in the adoption of ceramic technology in the Southwest. Development of gray ware technology, on the other hand, appeared later because it is not as obvious a "recipe" as brown ware. Several generations of potters might have experimented with materials, shaping techniques, and firing processes before the familiar suite of Lino Gray, Lino Black-on-gray, and Tallahogan Red pottery, and its regionally specific counterparts, emerged in the A.D. 600s. In this scenario, changes in pottery resulted from potters seeking greater durability and cooking efficiency

that would have taken place independent of changes in subsistence. Some researchers argue that reliance on agriculture occurred in the A.D. 200s, about the time brown ware pottery emerges on the Colorado Plateau (Matson and Chisolm 1991; see also P. Reed, this volume). Others believe it happened later, in the A.D. 900s (Cordell 1984, 1997; see review in LeBlanc 1982b; Martin and Plog 1973), the period when Mills notes diversification of vessel form and function, refinements of firing technology, and increased labor devoted to ceramic production (for example, preparation of crushed rock or crushed sherd temper). In many chapters in this volume, the authors present data and argue for agricultural dependence by the early A.D. 600s, if not earlier (e.g., Geib and Spurr, this volume).

The adoption of pottery on the Colorado Plateau appears to have been part of a larger suite of cultural changes associated with increased population sedentism, greater reliance on agriculture, and changing roles of individuals. Changes in labor allocation and gender division of labor would have been important in the adoption of pottery technology (Crown and Wills 1995). Crown and Wills examine a number of models relevant to the role of women as potters and subsequent scheduling conflicts (see also Arnold 1985; Brown 1989; Wright 1991). Although Arnold (1985) argues that women are more likely to make pottery because it is compatible with child care responsibilities, is a domestic chore, and is not dangerous, Crown and Wills (1995) present a compelling argument suggesting that the adoption of full pottery production in the American Southwest probably did not occur until a point when the benefits outweighed the scheduling difficulties. In contrast to Arnold (1985) and Brown (1989), they do not believe "that the production and use of the first pottery fit easily into the odd bits of time that prehistoric women had" (Crown and Wills 1995:249). Rather, Crown and Wills outline the many social changes that go along with increased sedentism, dependence on agriculture, and production of ceramic vessels to sustain a single household, concluding that scheduling for all members of a household became more complex. They conclude that the shift to horticulture and eventual agricultural dependence resulted in significant changes in the social roles of household members, including (1) a heavier workload for women; (2) resolution of scheduling conflicts through changes in child care (e.g., early weaning of children); (3) changes in cooking technology and food-preparation time resulting from new varieties of corn and cultivation of beans (beans in particular requiring long periods of boiling, thus the need for ceramic cooking pots); and (4) an improved nutritional quality of foods and greater dietary equality between individuals that may have resulted from cooking with pottery. It is therefore likely that early weaning of children[2] and improved nutrition contributed to population growth, a phenomenon that may have greatly influenced the population increases of the late Basketmaker III period.

CONCLUSION

Based on a growing number of Anasazi sites with early brown ware assemblages, we—along with other researchers in the Southwest (e.g., Dittert et al. 1963; LeBlanc 1982b; Skibo and Blinman 1999; Stark 1994; Wilson and Blinman 1994)—suggest that an Early Ceramic Horizon is represented by brown ware from late Basketmaker II and early Basketmaker III sites from the Anasazi region, early Mogollon sites dating as early as A.D. 200, and Cienega phase sites in the Tucson Basin (Heidke 1998; Heidke and Stark 1996). In the Anasazi region, high-iron clays appear to have been suitable for early brown ware technology and vessel forms, but became an inadequate resource for later vessel requirements. During the A.D. 500s, a gradual transition to gray ware technology occurred at many Basketmaker III sites across the Colorado Plateau. By the beginning of the seventh century, the transition was essentially complete, and production of gray, white, and red ware vessels associated with Anasazi ceramic technology became the norm in most areas of the Colorado Plateau. In other areas of the Southwest, such as the Mogollon and Hohokam regions, clay resources were much more amenable to brown ware technology, and production of brown ware vessels continued.

The classification scheme for Anasazi brown ware has a long and confusing history with the underlying premise that the Anasazi only produced gray ware vessels. With the growing number of early brown ware ceramic assemblages from the Colorado Plateau, the need for a more concise brown ware typology became clear. Because regional Anasazi traditions are based primarily on temper and paint type, classification of Anasazi brown ware necessitates a broader, panregional typological scheme. The modified typology presented above allows for classification of brown and gray/brown ware across the Anasazi region into a small number of types. Isolating early brown ware and transitional polished, slipped, and painted gray/brown ware assemblages is important for understanding the shift in technology that occurred in the Anasazi region, as well as the cultural factors influencing that technological change. These changes were linked to increased agricultural dependence and the development of a more sedentary lifestyle.

ACKNOWLEDGMENTS

During the course of completing recent projects involving Basketmaker III assemblages and undertaking research for this paper, we examined a large number of sherds. We would like to acknowledge the Museum of New Mexico in Santa Fe and the Museum of Northern Arizona in Flagstaff for allowing us to examine and illustrate some of the early brown and gray/brown ware sherds from the Colorado Plateau. Also, Doug Dykeman contributed his time and facilities to photograph the paste cross sections showing the textural differences between brown, gray/brown, and gray ware pastes. A number of individuals—including Chip Wills, Deborah Nichols, Rich Wilshusen, Kris Langenfeld, and Doug Dykeman—reviewed earlier drafts of the chapter and provided helpful suggestions that improved our work. It should also be noted that several other researchers in the Southwest are currently studying early brown ware technology, including James Skibo, Eric Blinman, James Heidke, and Miriam Stark. Many of the ideas in this chapter concerning the gradual transition in ceramic technology and the production of brown ware by early Anasazi groups were initially proposed by Alfred E. Dittert Jr. during the Navajo Reservoir Project. Tim Kearns suggested that material from Grand Gulch, discussed by H. S. Gladwin in 1957, might fit the brown ware profile, and we appreciate his input. Last but not least, we would like to thank Paul Reed for the opportunity to write this chapter, and for his enthusiasm, encouragement, and assistance during the process.

NOTES

1. Heidke (1998) discusses incipient plain ware from the middle and lower Santa Cruz River valley in Arizona. At both Early Cienega phase (800–0400 B.C.) and Late Cienega phase (400 B.C.–A.D. 150) sites, portions of 84 vessels have been recovered. Heidke suggests that this early pottery was used in ritual at least a thousand years before pottery became a functional domestic tool.

2. Early weaning of children generally results in increased fertility in cultures for which other methods of birth control are unavailable. Nursing children for up to three years of age is common in nonindustrial societies and is a natural method of birth control. Prolonged, infrequent breast-feeding with no supplemental feeding suppresses ovulation. Trevathan (1987: 238) notes that the suppression of ovulation is "especially true for women in foraging societies whose nutritional intake is adequate and whose fat reserves are depleted by prolonged lactation. Thus, these women drop below the critical fat level postulated for ovulation (Frisch 1974) and remain anovulatory for the two or three years that an infant is nursed."

11

Changing Lithic Technology During the Basketmaker–Pueblo Transition

Evidence from the Anasazi Heartland

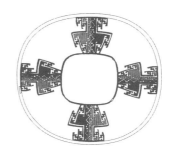

John A. Torres

For archaeologists who have worked in the American Southwest, the term "Anasazi lithic technology" is nearly an oxymoron. It has been called "devolved" and "unremarkable," and with a few notable exceptions has been ignored by most Southwestern archaeologists. In this chapter, I will argue the null hypothesis, if you will, to assert that Anasazi lithic technology was highly evolved and well adapted to meet their specific needs.

The distinctiveness of Anasazi lithic technology can be seen early in their development and is fully recognizable by the Basketmaker–Pueblo transition. The mechanisms that caused changes in lithic technology continued to be refined throughout Anasazi cultural development. Here, I explore these mechanisms and present several hypotheses for the changes in lithic technology during the transition.

The bulk of the data used in this analysis of Anasazi lithic technological change comes from the Cove–Redrock Valley Archaeological Project (CRVAP) (P. Reed and Hensler 1999; Torres 1999a). This project was conducted as part of the N33 road construction for the Navajo communities of Cove and Redrock Valley in northeastern Arizona (figure 11.1), near the Prayer Rock Basketmaker caves explored and excavated by Earl Morris in the 1930s (Morris 1980). The N33 excavations produced a large lithic data set of more than 25,000 items (Torres 1999a). The analysis was conducted using a replicative systems approach (Flenniken 1981) to examine various attributes in order to place tools and debitage within a technological typology. Assuming that material culture is a true reflection of a past lifeway, the lithic technologies employed prehistorically can be interpreted as a signature of that lifeway. These signatures, when interpreted within a cultural ecology paradigm, can be used to address prehistoric culture change. By examining these lithic technological signatures, then, the current synthesis was developed.

BASKETMAKER SITES IN COVE–REDROCK VALLEY

The sites excavated during CRVAP date from late Basketmaker II through early Pueblo III (with most sites dating from Basketmaker III through Pueblo II). Because this span falls short of the time required to examine all of Anasazi development, data from other regions were used to supplement this analysis. Two of the main goals of the N33 lithic analysis (Torres 1999a) were to understand and describe the lithic technological signatures of the Cove–Red Valley Anasazi and to address potential mechanisms for the development of such technologies during the Basketmaker through Pueblo periods. Based on the results of analysis, it was clear that the technological changes that first occurred during the Basketmaker II period set the stage for the adaptations that were fully realized during the Basketmaker III period. During this cultural transition, the Anasazi people went from hunter-gatherers to sedentary horticulturists. The newly sedentary lifeway required a new set of strategies to efficiently utilize their reduced exploitable lithic landscape. As a result, new lithic technologies were developed to better adapt to the new lifeway. It was these early Basketmaker III technological developments that set the stage for development of the distinctive Anasazi lithic technology.

The earliest of the CRVAP sites (AZ-I-26-34 [NN]), dates to 585 B.C. ± 190, a period well after the introduction of corn to the region and presumably after the advent of the cultural adaptations that ultimately led to the Anasazi. However, the introduction of cultigens appears to have had minimal initial impact on the lithic material culture, a pattern observed elsewhere in the Northern San Juan Basin (Simmons 1986; Torres 2000), the Chuska Slope, and the Mesa Verde area (Torres 1999c). Most aspects of the lithic assemblage of AZ-I-26-34 are still very characteristic of a hunting-and-gathering

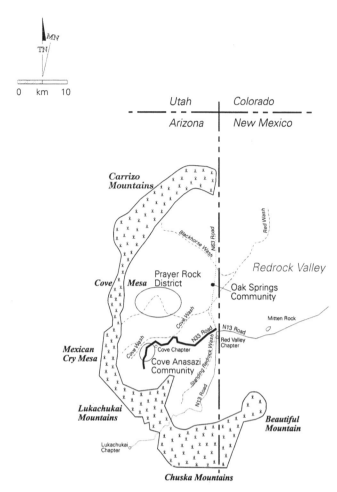

Figure 11.1. Map showing Cove–Red Valley Archaeological Project area in northeastern Arizona.

lifeway. I have argued elsewhere that in the Upper San Juan Basin, the increased use of cultigens by some Archaic groups allowed for the establishment of longer-term residences compared with other groups that were not growing crops (Torres 1999a); however, this pattern has not been documented for other Anasazi areas.

Lithic analysis for AZ-I-26-34 showed that the atlatl and dart combination was still the primary hunting weapon; bifacial cores were still the most common flake production technology; formal, patterned, resharpened, curated lithic tools were still the most common tool type, and exotic lithic raw materials were still commonly used. All of these traits suggest that at least seasonal mobility was still a major part of the settlement system (Kuhn 1994; Lurie 1990). The lack of milling equipment in the assemblage also suggests site specialization. A variety of specialized camps might have served as satellites to a base camp, a settlement pattern characteristic of the Archaic period. In fact, even after nonparametric correlation coefficients were generated, AZ-I-26-34 was consistently the most distant from all other Anasazi sites in the project area (figure 11.2).

The other two Basketmaker II sites excavated as part of the CRVAP (AZ-I-26-24 and AZ-I-26-30 [NN]) date some four hundred years later. Although many aspects of the material culture from these sites are similar to AZ-I-26-34, it is clear that dramatic changes in lithic technology had occurred by this time. The lithic material culture for these two sites is more like the transitional, semisedentary horticulturists predicted by many early investigators (Carlson 1963; Morris 1980). Again, this pattern has been noted throughout the Northern San Juan Basin during the late Basketmaker II period (e.g., Glassow 1972; Simmons 1986). These later Basketmaker II sites were beginning to exhibit a lithic technological signature distinctly Anasazi. By the time large Basketmaker III villages were occupied (e.g., Broken Flute Cave, Juniper Cove, Kiva Mesa, Shabik'eshchee Village), most of the characteristic attributes of Anasazi lithic culture were well established. All three Basketmaker II sites are similar with regard to some tool types (e.g., dart points, flake tools, some bifacial cores), but the technologies employed for tool production follow a significantly different trajectory. The mechanisms that produced the shift in lithic technology and made the later Basketmaker II sites so different from the earlier ones relate to sedentism.

ANASAZI LITHIC TECHNOLOGY

The greatest indicator of mobility in these early Anasazi sites is flake production technology. As demonstrated by Parry and Kelly (1987) for sites on Black Mesa, the lithic technologies of mobile societies are very different from those of settled groups. The change in flake production is the first observable technological shift to occur in these earliest of Anasazi assemblages from the Cove–Redrock Valley area. As during the preceding Archaic period, bifacial cores are the most common flake production technology in early Basketmaker II sites (Phagan 1985; Rozen 1981; Simmons 1982a; Towner 2000). These types of cores are easily portable, and flake production is predictable. Large, thin, expanding flakes can be easily fashioned into dart points or a variety of other tools. Bifacial cores are most advantageous as a flake production technology when people are actively mobile, or at least partially so. Presumably, once food resources became more predictable, mobility decreased, and the need for portable cores also decreased. Bifacial cores, although quite adapted toward a mobile lifeway, are very intensive to configure in terms of labor and raw material (Callahan 1979; Kelly 1988). Therefore, when people begin to settle into permanent habitations, these costs are too great. The result is a shift to a core configuration better adapted to the new flake production needs. Figure 11.3 illustrates this trend through time of reduced usage of bifacial cores at the CRVAP and other sites. The change toward re-

CRVAP Habitation Sites

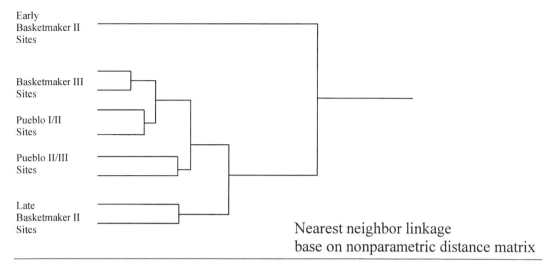

Early
Basketmaker II
Sites

Basketmaker III
Sites

Pueblo I/II
Sites

Pueblo II/III
Sites

Late
Basketmaker II
Sites

Nearest neighbor linkage
base on nonparametric distance matrix

Mesa Verde Area Habitation Sites

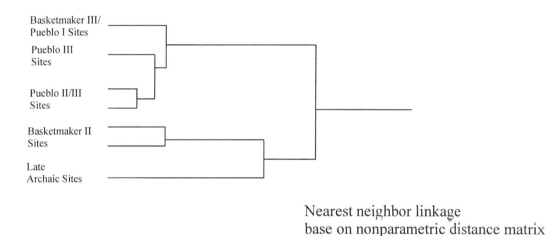

Basketmaker III/
Pueblo I Sites

Pueblo III
Sites

Pueblo II/III
Sites

Basketmaker II
Sites

Late
Archaic Sites

Nearest neighbor linkage
base on nonparametric distance matrix

Upper San Juan Habitation Sites

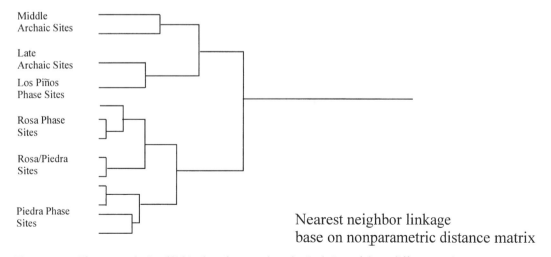

Middle
Archaic Sites

Late
Archaic Sites

Los Piños
Phase Sites

Rosa Phase
Sites

Rosa/Piedra
Sites

Piedra Phase
Sites

Nearest neighbor linkage
base on nonparametric distance matrix

Figure 11.2. Cluster analysis of lithic data from archaeological sites of three different regions.

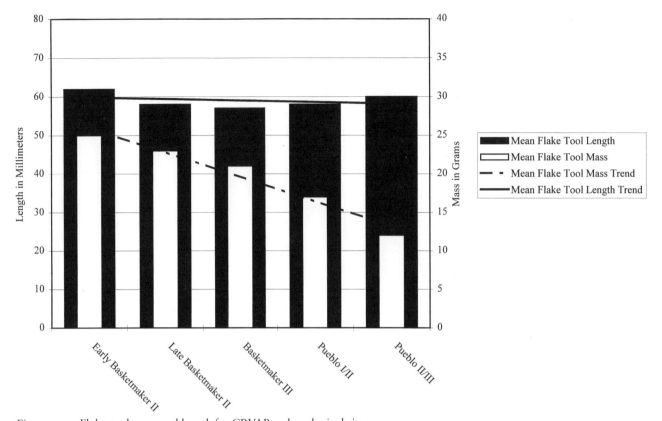

Figure 11.3. Flake tool mass and length for CRVAP archaeological sites.

duced mobility necessitated a new means of lithic raw material procurement. This change in raw material procurement strategy, to better manage a reduced exploitable space, is what initiated an overall trend in various adaptive strategies during the early Basketmaker III period.

Lithic raw material procurement was a major component of settlement and subsistence strategies of prehistoric cultures and varied by differing lithic landscape management strategies. The hunter-gatherer cultures of the Archaic period utilized a wider range of exploitable space, and thus could more easily schedule lithic resource procurement based on other subsistence needs. Known lithic resource procurement areas could be visited indirectly while hunting or gathering, or directly by specifically traveling to known quarries for the sole purpose of extracting raw materials. Lithic resources were also exchanged as part of complex networks. These actively mobile people required portable lithic raw materials often configured into bifacial cores. Excess cortical and waste flakes could be left at quarries, leaving a compact, easily transportable core capable of fulfilling all the lithic requirements until a new procurement area could be reached. Sedentary horticulturalists, however, utilize a reduced exploitable space. This space must be used efficiently to maintain the settlement system over extended periods of time. It is this newly reduced exploitable space that drove the changes in lithic raw material procurement strategies.

While analyzing the lithic resource procurement strategies employed by the CRVAP Anasazi, I explored three different possibilities: nonlocal exchange, direct quarrying, and indirect raw material prospecting. Changes in flake production technologies resulted in observable differences in the early Anasazi lithic material culture. The CRVAP analysis showed that raw material prospecting of the local, patchy lithic landscape in Cove–Redrock Valley was the newly adopted lithic raw material procurement strategy. Raw material prospecting is common in areas of increased sedentism (Parry and Kelly 1987; Torres 1999a) or areas of patchy lithic resources within arid and semiarid environments (Wilke and Schroth 1989).

RAW MATERIAL PROCUREMENT AND CORE EFFICIENCY

Unlike exchange systems and lithic quarrying, raw material prospecting and the mechanisms thereof have only been minimally addressed in the Southwest (Cameron 1987; Simmons 1982a). Raw material prospecting is the process of searching, evaluating, and collecting small packets of tool stone as a means of raw material procurement (Wilke and Schroth 1989). These activities occur as an embedded part of other primary activities in areas with varying lithic material quality, such as the Cove–Redrock Valley area. Once found, these materials

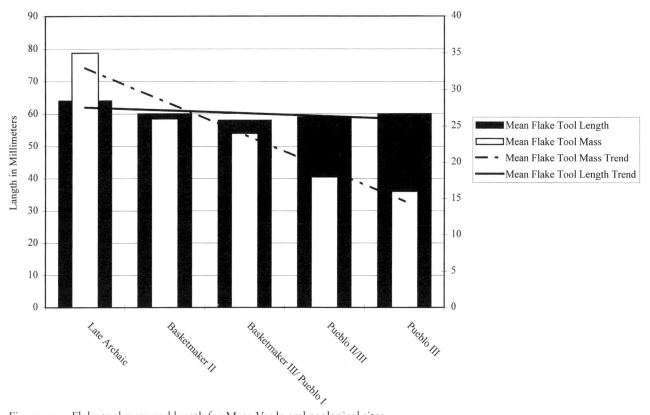

Figure 11.4. Flake tool mass and length for Mesa Verde archaeological sites.

are tested with a few blows, and the result is a tested cobble. The tested cobble is then determined to be of poor quality and discarded, or determined to be of sufficient quality and carried back to the residence for reduction. When these cores are reduced on-site, the appearance is one of opportunistic reduction of cobbles without any formal core production. The resulting implication is that the Anasazi lacked the interest or knowledge to directly extract this resource by other means and were picking up the closest rock and bashing it open. Some have gone so far as to argue that Anasazi lithic technology was "devolved" from their Archaic-period ancestors (Simmons 1982a; Woodbury 1954). Raw material prospecting, however, requires a great deal of knowledge of stone properties and of the local lithic landscape in order to quickly evaluate rock quality and decide which rocks are worth returning to the habitation. Although tested cobbles are found on Anasazi sites, typically they comprise a very small percentage of the assemblage, suggesting that most lithic materials were accurately evaluated while prospecting. This technique would reduce the number of tested cobbles discarded at habitation sites. Although frequently embedded within other behavioral systems (e.g., planting, field maintenance, harvesting), raw material prospecting can be highly productive. Raw material prospecting is not simply rock bashing or a devolved technology; rather it is a complex, efficient, highly

adapted lithic resource procurement strategy designed to meet the needs of a settled community.

The lithic landscape common to most of the Colorado Plateau, consisting of patchy lithic resources, is very conducive to raw material prospecting to most efficiently meet the lithic needs of Anasazi communities. Such a strategy of increased lithic resource procurement efficiency developed during the early Basketmaker III period, when flake production from portable bifacial cores (made mostly of imported raw materials) evolved into use of cobble cores of mostly local raw materials. The maximization of the newly reduced exploitable space as a means of increased efficiency not only shifted the raw material procurement strategy, but also influenced all aspects of stone tool use, including core reduction, flake production, and tool manufacture and use.

On the surface, Anasazi lithic technology appears unremarkable and has been relatively ignored. The complexity of raw material prospecting has only recently been appreciated for its ingenuity, and few studies have examined the evolution of Anasazi lithic technology. One such study explored expedient core technology and correctly argued it to be a by-product of a sedentary lifestyle (Parry and Kelly 1987). The CRVAP lithic analysis showed the same pattern, but also revealed some very significant evolutionary changes in lithic reduction technologies after sedentism was well established. Cobble core reduction remained the flake production strategy,

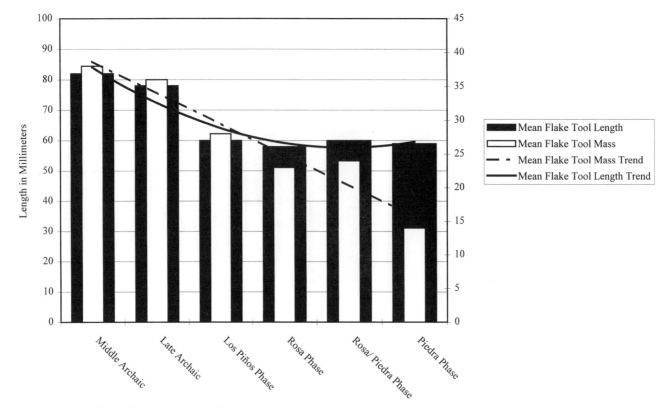

Figure 11.5. Flake tool mass and length for Upper San Juan archaeological sites.

but core configuration continued to change and became more efficient during the Anasazi occupation of the Cove–Redrock Valley area.

Increases in core reduction efficiency resulted from changes in core configuration. These changes were gradual but universal at all N33 sites, regardless of the lithic raw material used. Starting with the earliest Basketmaker III sites, the primary cobble core configuration was unpatterned and multidirectional. Any suitable striking platform was utilized, producing irregular flakes. These cores were produced from the many angular cobbles found in local drainages. By late Basketmaker III, however, core configuration became more patterned and unidirectionally configured. Cobble core reduction efficiency continued to drive lithic technological change among the Cove–Redrock Valley Anasazi. This same trend was taken to an extreme in Mesoamerica, where blade cores (the ultimate unidirectional core) were used to produce very regular, linear flakes.

As use of multidirectional cores decreased through time as a percentage of cores per site, the percentage of unidirectional cores increased (figure 11.4). This trend began during the Basketmaker III period in Cove, and similar trends have been documented during the same period in the neighboring Lukachukai and Red Valley areas, where lithic raw materials were abundant (Foldi 1989; Towner 2000). The same pattern appears in the Mesa Verde region as well (Torres 1999c). Other core types, such as bipolar and bidirectional, were relatively

constant through time. Greater use of unidirectional cores occurred regardless of the raw material preference at these sites, which has been shown to differ geographically (Torres 1999a; Towner 2000). Therefore, the mechanisms driving such a technological change must have been significant.

The mechanisms for such a trend corresponded to increased efficiencies. Unidirectional core reduction is more efficient for the production of regular flakes. Like the development of the predictable bifacial cores for portable efficiencies, use of unidirectional cores develops in areas of increased sedentism. This can be seen among the Mesoamericans (Hester and Shafer 1987), the Hopewellians (Hofman 1987), the Black Mesa Anasazi (Parry and Kelly 1987), and the Mesa Verde Anasazi (Torres 1999c). I have mentioned that the Cove–Redrock Valley area was abundant in patchy lithic resources, albeit of mediocre quality, and that these resources were easily procured and returned to habitation sites for flake production. The angular nature of these materials gave the flintknapper several options for reduction. The multifaceted cobbles would have most easily lent themselves to multidirectional core reduction, as was common during the early transition to cobble core technology. Therefore, the flintknapper would have needed to make the conscious decision to produce unidirectional cores by choosing cobbles with suitable striking platforms. Given that the quantity and quality of the lithic materials did not change through time, there must have been significant motivation to cause such a shift in core configuration. Indeed, one of the major advantages of flake production from unidirectional cores was the consistency in flake size and margin lengths, both of which allowed for easy tool production and use.

FLAKE TOOL USE AND EFFICIENCY

Many Southwestern archaeologists have noted the trend through time for greater use of flake rather than formal tools among the Anasazi. Most of the typical tool types (scrapers, drills, and cutting tools) are present in Anasazi assemblages, but they rarely show evidence of curation or continued use. Use of an expedient flake tool production strategy goes hand-in-hand with the previously discussed patterns of raw material prospecting and cobble core production and reduction. It should be no surprise, then, that there is a direct relationship between the two. How could the increase in use of expedient flake tools have resulted in an increase in use of unidirectional cores, and vice versa? The answer lies again in flake tool production efficiency. Just as unidirectional cores were more efficient in regular flake production, so too were expedient flake tools more efficient because new tools with superior edges could be produced with a single blow.

A decrease in seasonal mobility reduced the need for portable and curatable lithic flake tools. This is equally true for the need to maintain tools, when a new flake tool can be produced with much less effort and with an edge much superior to a retouched one. Flake tools as a percentage of the entire lithic assemblage increase through time in the Cove–Redrock Valley area, but the length of tool edge remains relatively constant. However, when one examines the mean mass of flake tools, it becomes quite apparent that flake production efficiency is the primary objective. Mean mass decreases through time, despite the fact that mean tool length remains constant (figure 11.5). This is a direct result of the increased regularity of the flakes capable of being produced from unidirectional cores. Similarly, these thinner flakes could be used more productively for projectile point and other formal tool manufacture. Greater lithic tool efficiency, in turn, probably contributed to the quick adoption of a new hunting technology during the Basketmaker III period.

Two different hunting systems were employed during the early Anasazi occupation of the Cove–Redrock Valley area: the atlatl and dart, and the bow and arrow. The dart points recovered from the Basketmaker II and early Basketmaker III contexts are essentially unchanged from their Late Archaic period counterparts. They are large, and were hafted to foreshafts with the aid of corner or side notches. Most fall within the Elko series (Holmer 1980; Thomas 1981), Elko Corner-notch/Northern Side-notch (Flenniken and Wilke 1989), San Jose (Irwin-Williams 1973), or Early Ceramic "types" (Parry and Christenson 1987). The only important difference between projectile points of the two periods is that Basketmaker II dart points were made from large biface thinning flakes, whereas the early Basketmaker III dart points were made from cobble core flakes, with some exhibiting a distinctive arris running down the center of the point.

The switch to bow and arrow, at least as demonstrated by these assemblages, was rapid. Sometime between A.D. 500 and 600, the first arrow points appear in Basketmaker III assemblages. The arrow points, like the Basketmaker III dart points, were made on cobble core flakes. These earliest arrow points are small, with stems, straight or concave lateral margins, and corner notches. These forms have been called Rose Spring (Lanning 1963; Yohe 1992), Rosegate (Thomas 1981), or Early Ceramic (Parry and Christenson 1987). These points represent essentially diminutive forms of the earlier dart point forms and quickly gave way to smaller, side-notched and unnotched triangular forms by the early Pueblo I period. It has been shown that smaller points have longer ranges than larger points when used for hunting large game (Christenson 1987). Again, with the quick adoption of a new, more efficient hunting technology, the early Anasazi went further to increase efficiency by making their projectile points smaller and lighter. In the Upper San Juan, a possible Pueblo I hunting camp yielded a collection of arrow points about 1 cm in length (Torres 1999b).

PATTERNS IN CRVAP DEBITAGE

Examination of the CRVAP debitage assemblages revealed that nearly all of the observations noted above regarding Anasazi lithic technology were mirrored in the debitage analysis, and it is here that a technological approach shows its merit. The debitage analysis of the Cove–Redrock Valley sites examined various technological aspects of Anasazi lithic technology through a replicative systems analysis approach (Flenniken 1981). Replicative systems analysis compares archaeologically recovered debitage data to replicated debitage data in order to make inferences about potential lithic technologies. This analysis showed three major trends in the lithic technologies among the Cove–Redrock Valley Anasazi assemblages: (1) changes in raw material frequencies; (2) changes in technology; and (3) changes in debitage percentages. All of these aspects have been addressed above in the tool discussion, but without corroborating debitage data, the argument falls short.

As discussed above, the Basketmaker II–III transition showed a reduced exploitable space and a change in raw material procurement strategies. This reduced exploitable space was also shown by the decrease in raw

Technology	Early BM II	Late BM II	Early BM III	Late BM III	Pueblo I–II	Pueblo II–III
Dart point Production	X	X	X			
Bifacial core Reduction	X	X	X			
Arrow point Production			X	X	X	X
Bipolar Reduction	X	X	X	X	X	X
Cobble core Production/ Reduction		X	X	X	X	X
Unidirectional core Reduction				X	X	X

material variability during this same transition. During the Archaic and Basketmaker II periods, lithic raw materials were procured over a wider landscape, and hence many more exotic lithic material types are present at these sites. By late Basketmaker II and early Basketmaker III, a dramatic increase in locally available lithic material is apparent. In fact, it has been demonstrated during the CRVAP analysis and on other projects that only the most immediately local lithic material was used, even when better-quality materials were less than 1 km away (Torres 1999a). Even during Pueblo IV times at Jemez Pueblo when knappers were just a few kilometers from literally mountains of obsidian, the people used only the most immediately available local lithic materials (Torres 1999d). The same technological trends observed in the recovered core data were demonstrated with the debitage data (table 11.1). Bifacial core reduction debitage is common in early Basketmaker II, but is absent by the late Basketmaker III and Pueblo I periods. Similarly, evidence of dart point production becomes undetectable, and arrow point production becomes dominant during the Basketmaker III period.

Another trend, directly related to core reduction efficiency through time, was observable only by methodologically controlling for excavation screen size. This was a change in debitage frequency through time. Early Basketmaker III sites in the Cove–Redrock Valley area have more waste flakes than do later Pueblo periods, and debitage as a percentage of lithic assemblage decreases. This was a product of the increased efficiency in unidirectional core reduction over multidirectional core reduction. Additionally, this suggests that some core configuration was occurring while prospecting, and that not all stages of core production were conducted at the habitation. Therefore, the debitage data support the patterns seen in the tool data; only through a replicative systems approach could these specific reduction technologies be observed. Core and debitage data have shown that maximizing reduction efficiency was important to the early Anasazi people of the Cove–Red Valley area. This increase in flake production efficiency allowed more of these flakes to be used as newly adapted, expedient flake tools.

ANASAZI MILLING EQUIPMENT TECHNOLOGY

Not only chipped stone data suggest the Basketmaker III Anasazi adopted lithic technologies for efficiency. Many researchers have observed greater efficiency in the Basketmaker III milling implement assemblages (Adams 1993; Kearns et al., this volume). Recent studies of lithic technologies have focused on milling implements, with a particular interest in the Southwest. Although milling gear, in the form of manos and metates, has been used by prehistoric peoples for thousands of years, only within the last two millennia have cultigens had an impact on the role of botanical resources in the diet. In the American Southwest, the rise of agriculture and sedentary lifeways directly influenced milling technology. Just as they made flake production technologies more efficient in response to changing lithic resources, Basketmaker III populations began to make milling equipment more efficient for the processing of the new botanical resources that dominated their economy.

Recent milling implement studies have suggested that apparent changes in milling implement technology were a product of agricultural intensification (Adams 1993; Mauldin 1993). Therefore, not only does the number of milling implements as a proportion of Anasazi lithic assemblages increase through time, but milling tool efficiency increases through time as well (Bartlett 1933). This trend is also apparent at the Cove–Redrock Valley sites and several other sites in the San Juan Basin and Mesa Verde areas.

Milling implements as a percentage of the entire assemblage, including complete tools and discarded fragments, increase through time. This pattern is seen across the Southwest. Milling implement morphology also changes through time, presumably as a result of a conscious attempt to increase efficiency; however, efficiency is more difficult to demonstrate for milling implements than for chipped stone technologies. Two methods have been commonly used: changes in milling technology as a whole (Adams 1993), and changes in surface area of milling implements, particularly of manos (Plog 1974; Hard 1990; Mauldin 1993). Using metate morphology, Adams (1993) demonstrates how milling behavior, as reflected in grinding methods, changes through time. These adaptations result in changing milling technology that starts with basin shapes during the Archaic and Basketmaker II periods, followed by the development of more-efficient trough shapes during the Basketmaker III period. Adams documents how this change in metate morphology is directly related to increased milling efficiency, which is hypothesized to reflect the increased reliance on cultigens and, thus, agricultural intensification. Although the N33 assemblage of metates is small, changes in metate forms through time show a similar pattern. Basin metates as a percentage of milling implements decrease through time, while the percentage of trough and slab metates increases. Similarly, the surface area of manos increases through time. These, again, appear to be innovations developed during the Basketmaker III period.

CONCLUSIONS

So what do these findings indicate in terms of Anasazi cultural development? Clearly, during the late Basketmaker II and early Basketmaker III periods, a new way of life was developing in the Cove–Redrock Valley area. These early Anasazi people began to utilize a reduced exploitable space by choosing a horticultural, sedentary lifeway. Early in the Basketmaker III period, the transition was complete, and the Anasazi adapted several strategies capable of maximizing the efficient use of their reduced exploitable space.

The first of these observable changes was a shift in lithic raw material procurement strategies. Directly quarried and exchanged portable cores were no longer adaptive in the new settlement system. Raw material prospecting and cobble core reduction of immediately local raw materials evolved to more efficiently provide resources in a reduced exploitable space. This pattern has subsequently been observed in other Anasazi areas outside the Cove–Red Valley area. The Anasazi continued to increase efficiency by adopting core configurations that produced more flakes per core and less waste. More of these flakes could then be used as expedient flake tools with superior edges without the need to retouch and manufacture formal tools. Also, more of these thinner flakes could be made into small arrow points as a new and efficient hunting technology was adopted. Crop production also became more efficient and productive, and a set of better-adapted milling tools was developed and manufactured to process more resources, more efficiently.

These early Basketmaker III Anasazi adapted several new strategies to maximize the resource abundance from the landscape immediately surrounding their new habitations. Via their highly adapted and efficient lithic technologies, the Anasazi were capable of redirecting the energy formerly utilized in the management of their lithic landscape into other aspects of their culture. Thus, Anasazi lithic technology was not devolved but actually highly evolved in the biological sense of the word: it was the most adaptive technology for the needs of the culture.

ACKNOWLEDGMENTS

I appreciate the opportunity provided by Paul Reed to contribute to this volume. I would also like to thank the reviewers for their thoughtful and constructive comments. Although many of the ideas expressed in this chapter are built upon many others, any shortcomings are my own.

12

The Bird in the Basket

Gender and Social Change
in Basketmaker Iconography

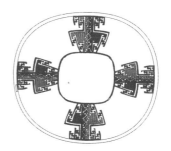

Michael R. Robins
Kelley A. Hays-Gilpin

One of the most important transitions in Southwest prehistory is the development of agricultural intensification leading to sedentary farming villages. In this chapter we explore this transition from the perspective of social change and ritual. Since the late nineteenth century, for example, archaeologists have recognized that kivas in prehistoric ruins were ritual rooms, and that many artifacts had ritual functions, such as the painted and feathered sticks still used today as prayer offerings among the pueblos. The transformation of pit houses into "clan kivas" during the pit house to pueblo transition, and identification of "great kivas" in Basketmaker III sites, suggested to archaeologists that ritual was a key component in the development of sedentary villages. We demonstrate here that analysis of parietal art (i.e., rock art and decorative arts, including baskets, textiles, and pottery) may provide evidence for the kinds of rituals that facilitated the shift from nomadic to sedentary lifeways in the northern Southwest.

Our analysis of rock art and decorative arts suggests that: (1) early Basketmaker II bands had shamanic rituals that emphasized the power and prestige of individuals, primarily men, but iconography did not initially emphasize sex or gender; and (2) the shift to increased sedentism in small, exogamous communities probably resulted in a predominantly matrilocal residence pattern and was facilitated by gender differentiation in the visual arts and rituals. Feminine rituals apparently focused on female puberty, perhaps as early as the A.D. 200s, while masculine rituals after about A.D. 600 emphasized communal processions of men who gathered from different communities. Bird images of this era crosscut masculine and feminine ideational domains, and household or community levels of integration.

METHODS AND ASSUMPTIONS

Shifting land-use patterns and agricultural methods characteristic of the transition from Basketmaker II to Basketmaker III undoubtedly involved reorientation of the ideological and economic domains of men and women, not just as individuals (e.g., spouses), but as dynamic actors who created the culture in which they lived.

The use of such gendered approaches has only recently been explored (e.g., Claassen and Joyce 1997; Conkey 1978, 1991; Wright 1996; and for a Southwestern example, Hays-Gilpin 1996, 2000). These domains are exemplified through the dialectical interplay between parietal and decorative imagery that survives in the archaeological record: rock art and textile/basket design, respectively. We use the words "art," "design," and "decorative" cautiously. Although more convenient and concise than expressions like "visual media that carry symbolic meaning, stylistic information, or both," present-day Euro-American values admittedly taint these terms. "Decoration" may invoke ideas of passivity, especially with regard to women, and "art" may invoke ideas of largely masculine inspiration, creativity, and aesthetic (rather than practical or social) functions, and may be construed as individualistic.

Although we do not advocate loading these terms with any presentist or otherwise biased meanings, contemporary Hopi men identify rock art as a masculine production (anonymous personal communication to K. Hays-Gilpin), and worldwide ethnographic studies suggest that men usually make most rock art (Lewis-Williams 1996; Whitley 1994; but see Bass 1994; Smith 1991; Whitley 1992), and that women usually make most pots and baskets in societies where these media are not produced by full-time craft specialists (Rice 1991; Wright 1991). According to Whitley (1994), in historic Great Basin cultures, men made rock art in part to affirm their status as shamans. Male status was based on access to ritual knowledge and skill. Shamans apparently appealed to women as potential spouses, even though women did not need husbands for subsistence purposes. Gender is, after all, about more than the division of labor. Gender is also about sexuality, reproduction, socialization, and even cosmology.

Gender categories assigned to humans are usually, but not always, based on genital sex, and North American gender categories are unusually flexible (see, for example, Blackwood 1984; Epple 1998; Roscoe 1991; Whitehead 1981). When we refer to "men" and "women" here, we are referring to social and cosmological, not biological, categories, unless otherwise noted (by use of the terms "male" and "female," for example). These categories may have been negotiable, rather than fixed. For example, Epple (1998) argues that Navajo cosmology admits two genders, masculine and feminine. They are not opposed, but integrated, each containing something of the other. Individual Navajos may identify more with one or the other, or may consider themselves in the process of becoming one or the other. The Navajo term *nadleehi* may be used to refer to "cross-dressers," but one translation of the term is "one who is always changing" (Epple 1998). In the absence of such insightful and informative ethnography, we cannot know how individual Basketmaker people classified themselves and other individuals, but we can learn something about the relative importance of gender in remaining evidence for symbolic expression by: (1) identifying depictions of sexed humans; (2) identifying artifacts associated with biological sex, such as menstrual aprons and items with sexed burials; and (3) cautiously applying ethnographic and historical analogies about division of labor, craft production, ritual, and social organization.

BASKETMAKER II AND III CHRONOLOGY AND BACKGROUND

We begin this chapter by examining the chronology of Basketmaker II and III. From this chronology we discuss the kind of farmer/forager economic structure that might have existed in Basketmaker II times. We analyze the rock art of this early period in the context of that economy, which subsequently forms the historical backdrop from which we view the Basketmaker II–III transition.

Our understanding of the time depth of agriculture in the Four Corners region has undergone substantial revision as a result of Smiley's (1985) chronological work at Black Mesa and Marsh Pass. This work established the surprising antiquity of the early Basketmaker II period, or White Dog phase (after Colton 1939; Lipe 1967). The

White Dog phase is characterized by a suite of material items that includes twined bags, atlatls with corner-notched dart tips, rabbit fur blankets, fine basketry, and by the use of dry rock shelters as storage, habitation, and burial locations (Kidder and Guernsey 1919). More recently, Gilpin (1994) and Geib (1996b) have shown that early Basketmaker II habitation and storage were not restricted to dry rock shelters, but can appear in open sites. However, the prevalence of both burials, many of which show complex ritual treatment (see Cole 1993; Kidder and Guernsey 1919; Morris 1934), and distinctive rock art (discussed below) indicates the importance of dry rock shelters as both economic and ceremonial loci. We should note, too, that such rock shelters abound throughout the numerous canyons and drainages of the northern Southwest.

Within Smiley's (1985) new chronological framework, Lipe (1993) identifies two Basketmaker II phases: an early White Dog phase from about 1500 B.C. to A.D. 50, and a later Basketmaker II phase from A.D. 50 to 500. The later interval subsumes the Lolomai and Cedar Mesa phases and is synonymous with the appearance of mesa-top dry farming and clustered pit house habitations (Gumerman and Dean 1989; Lipe and Matson 1971; Matson 1991; Nichols and Smiley 1984).

A definitive difference between the early and later Basketmaker II periods is the former's reliance on a more simple agricultural technique based on the use of aggrading floodplains (Lipe 1967; Gumerman and Dean 1989; Matson 1991; Van West 1994) and subirrigated localities having high water tables (Huckell 1995). In terms of a broad pan-Southwestern chronology, however, Matson (1991) has argued that such simpler technologies were not widely adaptive for the far northern Southwest climate. Thus, Basketmaker people did not establish early agriculture in places like Cedar Mesa until late in the early agricultural period (ca. 80 B.C. Rock shelters north of the San Juan River, however, have long been known to contain the cultural remains associated with the White Dog phase (see Lipe 1967).

Many, if not most, of these rock shelters are badly damaged from intensive looting and prescientific archaeology. For this reason archaeologists have tended to avoid them, thereby skewing the chronometric record. Most recently, Smiley (1997), Smiley and Robins (1997, 1999), and Robins and Smiley (1998) established the presence of the White Dog phase at looted rock shelter sites in the Butler Wash drainage (figure 12.1), where radiocarbon assays have yielded dates as early as 2520 ± 100 BP (Beta-95277) for domestic squash (*Curcubita* sp.) and 3060 ± 90 BP (Beta-115672) for charcoal. While by no means conclusive, the argument that the White Dog phase was well established throughout the northern Southwest is gaining more support. The distribution of the distinctive style of rock art associated with this period

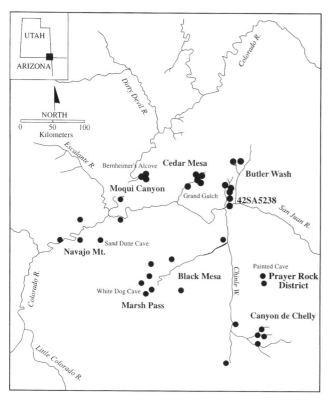

Figure 12.1. Map of the Four Corners region showing many of the Basketmaker rock shelter sites.

also supports this scenario as we will argue here (see also Robins 1997).

Subirrigated Agriculture

Subirrigation resources can be typified as self-sustaining agricultural systems. Runoff regularly adds nutrients that sustain vegetation, which in turn maintains a high and stable water table (Hack 1942). Short side-canyon drainages, which contain many Basketmaker rock shelter sites (Kidder and Guernsey 1919), allow even high-energy runoff to dissipate quickly, creating areas of aggradation typified by abrading streambeds. These areas are highly suited for akchin floodwater farming (Doyle 1993; Hack 1942). Agriculturally, these resources require minimal

maintenance, which alleviates scheduling and logistical conflicts for foraging tasks (see Welch 1991). There is good evidence (Robins and Smiley 1998) that White Dog phase Basketmakers selected storage sites at, or with easy access to, lower elevations (ca. 1450 m), giving them ready access to large cool-season resources such as ricegrass (*Stipa hymenoides*) and tickseed (*Corispermum hyssopifolium*). Large open-air rock art panels—such as Bernheimer's Alcove (42SA736) in Moqui Canyon, the Butler Wash Site (42SA52883), and Castleton's Site No. 30 in Grand Gulch (Castleton 1987)—also occur at low elevations, as do large rock shelter panels such as those at Monument Valley (NA8067) and Morss's Site 1 (Morss 1927) in the middle Chinle near Rock Point, Arizona. Gathering from these rich grassland areas requires only short, intensive trips, thus foraging may have only minimally interfered with crop tending and monitoring.

Although archaeologists have viewed the adoption of maize as a critical step in stabilizing food supplies in marginal regions, the social implications of predictable surplus and its role in hunter-gatherer social life have received less attention. By providing predictable surpluses, highly productive areas such as the Butler Wash Site may have become the focus of large-scale social and ritual activities. Predictable surplus of some kind is necessary to underwrite such activities. Surplus maize crops compete well with other more sparse and stochastic natural resources like piñon nuts.

Predictable Surplus, Territoriality, and the Formation of Social Boundaries

Steward (1938) demonstrated that through their cultivation of wild plants like sunflower and mentzilia, the northern Great Basin Paiute increased predictability and productivity. This change was followed by increased territoriality and aggression between discrete sociopolitical groups. Exclusively male activities, such as community sweat houses, also became more commonplace as males gained political power and prestige. Increasing aggression was offset by the need to crosscut social boundaries, particularly for exogamous band-level communities. For

Figure 12.2. Example of the San Juan Anthropomorphic Style (from Robins 1997).

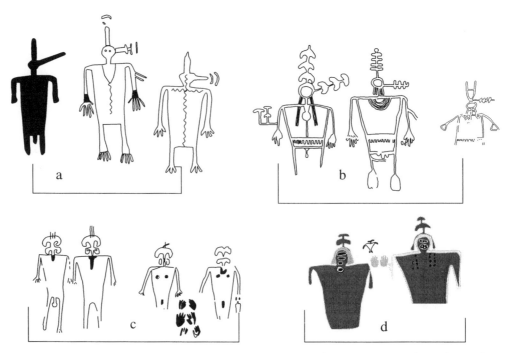

Figure 12.3. Examples of headdresses: (a) Canyon de Chelly (after Grant 1978); (b) Butler Wash; (c) detail from the Green Mask Site, Grand Gulch (after Cole 1993); (d) detail from Bernheimer's Alcove, Moqui Canyon (from Robins 1997). (Figure 12.3c adapted from a drawing by Dennis Hadenfeldt and used with permission of Sally Cole, from Atkins 1993).

the Northern Paiute, crosscutting opportunities took place through mourning ceremonies and fall festivals. Fall festivals have long been noted as a venue for the exchange of marriage partners, trading, gaming (Steward 1938; Thomas 1973), and political maneuvering among shamans (Bender 1985), and form the adaptive basis of macrosocial behavior among hunter-gatherer groups.

Macrosocial venues, or feasts, provide opportunities to reduce tensions that arise through uneven access to predictable surplus foods. There is considerable evidence that open-air Basketmaker II rock art panels were constructed in part around these activities: Basketmaker rock art exhibits spatially idiosyncratic characteristics. These characteristics cross over apparent spatial boundaries that they define. The rock art panels also can be linked to potentially high agricultural productivity (Robins 1997). Macrosocial events may also provide opportunities for trading and pooling seed corn. Though the adaptive properties of this type of trade need further research, some Navajo families hold a taboo on the planting of seed corn from the field in which it was grown. They say seed corn must be traded, or corn plants will grow shorter and shorter (anonymous communication to Michael Robins, 1999).

SAN JUAN BASKETMAKER ROCK ART STYLE

Rock art imagery often portrays the unequivocal material culture of its producers. This, together with the re-

peated association of distinctive rock art styles with single-component archaeological sites, has led to the establishment of a sound stylistic seriation for northern Southwest rock art (Cole 1990, 1993; Grant 1978; Kidder and Guernsey 1919; Robins 1997; Schaafsma 1980; Turner 1963). Referred to by Schaafsma (1980) as "San Juan Anthropomorphic Style," this rock art occurs in nearly all sites linked to the White Dog phase. Though simply referred to by early archaeologists as "square-shouldered anthropomorphs," the style was used to initially identify sites that would yield Basketmaker remains (Kidder and Guernsey 1919; Morss 1927).

The San Juan Anthropomorphic Style is characterized by large, heroically proportioned, often life-sized, static frontal facing anthropomorphs with spadelike, drooping hands and feet (Schaafsma 1980;figure 12.2). Zoomorphic images appear in conjunction with these figures, as do handprints, occasional geometric figures, and masks, yet primary attention is drawn to the body, its clothing, and ornamentation. Ornamentation includes pendants, aprons, medicine bags, hairstyles, and headdresses that in some instances are very elaborate (e.g., figure 12.3).

The spadelike, drooping hands and feet convey a "floating" or "weightless" characteristic that is a cross-cultural feature common to hunter-gatherer rock art throughout western North America (Whitley 1998). This depiction of floating may reflect a trance state symbolizing the shaman's journey to the supernatural for the purposes of healing, rainmaking, or other activities.

Hunter-gatherer references like this, and the representation of hunter-gatherer material culture in the rock art imagery, further bind the San Juan Anthropomorphic Style to the White Dog phase, for which a band-level social organization is inferred (Smiley 1985).

San Juan Rock Art and Band-Level Society

Robins (1997) recently completed preliminary analysis of the spatial and contextual distribution of the San Juan Anthropomorphic Style across the northern Southwest. This analysis concluded that, without exception, the large, life-sized, open-air occurrences of groups of anthropomorphic figures correlate with areas suitable for floodplain, *akchin,* and subirrigated agriculture. Hyder (1997) noted a similar contextual relationship for his study of a single rock art panel in the Grand Gulch drainage. The association of the large San Juan Anthropomorphic panels with the White Dog phase and areas of apparent high agricultural productivity have important implications for social as well as economic uses of maize in emergent agricultural societies. While pursuing these implications, however, we should keep in mind the following points:

1. Agricultural loci of the type mentioned above occur in canyons for which, especially in the Four Corners area, there is no shortage of suitable surfaces for rock art production; thus, these localities create a unique ready-made environment for the coexistence of agriculture and rock art.
2. Basketmaker rock art, and the polysemous nature of rock art in general, marks many things besides agricultural resources (rock art may mark burial places, ancestor spirits, and shamanic visions).
3. It appears that only selected and especially productive subirrigated resources are marked with rock art. This last point suggests a correlation between the scales of maize production and the marking of these sites with elaborate and often complex rock art (see figure 12.2).

Spatial Patterning of the San Juan Rock Art Style

Robins (1997) explored spatial patterning by comparing San Juan Anthropomorphic rock art imagery at several sites across the Four Corners region (see figure 12.1). These sites include Moqui Canyon, Grand Gulch, Canyon de Chelly, the confluence of Butler Wash and the San Juan River, and more recently, Monument Valley, Chinle Wash, and Kin Boko Canyon (Robins 1999). While imagery at these locations shares the characteristics of the overall style horizon described above, certain details remain distinguishable or idiosyncratic. The most explicit example of this can be found in the headdresses worn by the anthropomorphs (see figure 12.3), though overall design elements such as the in-filling of torsos

with zigzag lines and imprinting of torsos with handprints may also be spatially idiosyncratic.

Rock art researchers often comment on these headdresses. Schaafsma (1980), for example, has suggested that they might be emblematic. Grant (1978) has commented on the similarity in headdress features among the rock art at Canyon de Chelly and the rock art panel at the Butler Wash Site, suggesting interaction and a flow of ideas between these two regions (see figure 12.3a and b). In respect to these headdresses, Cole (1990), Schaafsma (1980), Grant (1978), and Hyder (1997) have all used similar terms, such as "tabular," "fountainheads," "earmen," and "crescents."

The distributions of these headdress styles within and among Butler Wash, Grand Gulch, and Canyon de Chelly—in both open-air and rock shelter locations—indicate that distinct headdress styles predominate at specific locations. In Grand Gulch and the nearby Moqui Canyon, the plumed, or crescentic, form is dominant, with at least one occurrence of the tabular form (see Cole 1993: figure 9.10). Kin Boko Canyon, which flows into Marsh Pass, has a characteristic inverted, trapezoidal head figure with zigzag in-filling, and solid white figures similar to those at Monument Valley (Robins 1999). Also at Cave II in Kin Boko Canyon is a large petroglyph, apparently not reported by Kidder and Guernsey in 1919, sharing similar stylistic in-filling and the characteristic linear treatment typical of sites along the San Juan River. A single tabular headdress can be observed among the numerous figures at Monument Valley. Canyon de Chelly anthropomorphs display the bifurcated "earmen" forms, while the Butler Wash Site anthropomorphs, in addition to many tabular forms, display most of the other headdress styles. Such complexity at the Butler Wash Site, while not as apparent elsewhere, may have important social implications. The people for whom the Butler Wash Site was a socially and ritually significant location may have been better "integrated" with people from Grand Gulch and Canyon de Chelly than either the Grand Gulch or Canyon de Chelly groups were with each other.

ROCK ART AND THE BASKETMAKER II SOCIAL LANDSCAPE

Open-air rock art production in the White Dog phase may have been associated with the social dimensions of maize cultivation, particularly in areas of high productivity where surplus production increased and became more predictable. Such areas include the rich, spring-fed alluvial fan at the confluence of Butler Wash and the San Juan River, as well as rich riparian ecozones in Grand Gulch, Kin Boko Canyon, Chinle Wash, and Canyon de Chelly. Territoriality is clearly implied in the distribution of stylistic variability of Basketmaker parietal art, and parallels the expected increase in social tension that comes with agriculture. By itself, social tension is extremely maladaptive, particularly in exogamous band-level social systems, although displayed low-intensity aggression may be common (see Geib 1996a:70 for a valuable discussion on ritual warfare among the Basketmakers). One function of feasting is to mediate these tensions, and the co-occurrence of different emblematic rock art features, particularly at the Butler Wash Site (though common in other areas), suggests that social relations among competing groups were created and reproduced in the rock art panels.

San Juan Basketmaker rock art provides a plausible model of the social landscape during the White Dog phase, and changes in this social landscape—the social relations implied in the spatial distribution of the rock art style—may be reflected in the appearance of new rock art styles, trends, and motifs. In many instances the plethora of narrative, representational, and enigmatic imagery that characterizes much of the late Basketmaker II and early Basketmaker III periods—and, therefore, as we believe, much of the transition from one to the other—are clearly superimposed over the San Juan Basketmaker images. Radiocarbon data from Butler Wash (Smiley 1997; Smiley and Robins 1997) allow for a continuous occupation of the lowland areas of the region where much of this newer rock art (and social change) occurs.

Important at this time of change was the increasing commitment to dry farming. Data from the higher elevation areas of Cedar Mesa show punctuated use beginning around 80 B.C., with a commitment to dry farming appearing around A.D. 200 (Matson et al. 1988). Dry farming no doubt diminished the importance of highly productive subirrigated and *akchin* farming localities. Economic change of this magnitude would have eroded the implicit hegemony underlying San Juan Basketmaker rock art, forcing new solutions to problems of community integration and land tenure. The most notable stylistic anomaly to occur in the rock art in the San Juan River and Grand Gulch region is in the representation of female gender.

Gender in Basketmaker II Rock Art
Most Basketmaker II figures are sex neutral or phallic, while some references to women, breasts, and menstrual aprons do exist in the San Juan Anthropomorphic Style (Cole 1989, 1990). The San Juan Anthropomorphic "tradition" refers to female aspects, but this reference tends to be overshadowed by the "heroic," large, masculinized, trapezoidal figures. In a small geographic region along the San Juan River, and in parts of Grand Gulch, we see a unique "trajectory" in the form of a spatially homogenous class of female images that feature beaded jewelry, sashes, and women's aprons (see Cole 1990, 1993). These images are unique not only in their spatial homogeneity, but in the near absence of the physical body (heads, arms, and legs) and the representation of eyes, some of which appear to be weeping (Cole 1990, 1993). A second class of female-related imagery "behaves" in much the same way: the lobed circle (Hays 1992a; Hurst and Pachak 1989; Manning 1992).

Both the lobed circle and specific stylized images of women may have appeared late in the Basketmaker II period and continued, if differentially, into the Basketmaker III period. As such, they may have important implications in changing ritual, ideology, and community levels of organization. Their homogenous distribution relative to the San Juan Anthropomorphic Style (Robins 1997) and their possible appearance late in the Basketmaker II period suggest that these images and their ritual use are related to changes in residential patterns. We suggest that perhaps with increasing commitment to dry farming during the late Basketmaker II period, men may have had to develop new forms of community ritual for the purpose of meeting new integrative challenges. These challenges may have involved the need to crosscut restricted natal groups that had formed during the early Basketmaker II period—older forms that were no longer suited to the needs of spatially more bounded social groups that formed around the more-intensive agricultural practices of the late Basketmaker II period. In similar ethnographic contexts, men often clear fields, but it is women's labor that increases most dramatically in planting extensive crops (Watson and Kennedy 1991) and processing maize by grinding.

TRANSITIONAL BASKETMAKER II–III ROCK ART

The timing of the transition between Basketmaker II and III (defined in part by the appearance of brown ware ceramics at some sites, followed by widespread appearance of gray ware ceramics; see L. Reed et al., this volume) appears not to have been synchronous throughout the Colorado Plateaus (Matson 1991; see also Geib and Spurr; L. Reed et al., this volume). Table 12.1 summarizes the phase sequence and sequences of change in material culture, settlement patterning, and proposed social organization for the time periods discussed in this paper.

Sometime between about A.D. 1 and 500, Basketmaker people began to make undecorated, polished brown ware pottery (L. Reed et al., this volume) and small fired-clay figurines of women (Hays 1992a; Hays-Gilpin 2000; Morris 1951; Morss 1954). As we have indicated, images of women and other gendered icons such as lobed circles also appear in rock art. Human figures retain many stylistic attributes of the preceding San Juan Anthropomorphic Style, but new themes and emphases emerge in the rock art of some areas. We will consider first the lobed-circle motif and then the images of women.

TABLE 12.1

Proposed Sequence of Material Culture, Environmental, and Social Changes from Basketmaker II to III

	Basketmaker II (2000 B.C.–A.D. 200)	Basketmaker II–III Transition (A.D. 200s–400s)	Basketmaker III (A.D. 500s–600s)
Rock art	Large scale, static, iconic, emphasizes adorned humans.	Most like earlier style, with anomalous female figures in some areas.	High variety, small scale, narrative; birds, animals, humans, ritual items, tools frequently depicted.
Bags	Stripes. Occasional complicated designs in Kayenta area.	Mostly stripes?	Stripes and fringed lines, checkerboards.
Baskets	Most elaborate in Kayenta area, geometric, black designs.	Elaborate black and red counterchanged designs, more similar to later style. Occasional birds?	Elaborate black and red counterchanged designs, occasional birds and animals.
Aprons	Undecorated	Occasionally decorated.	Occasionally decorated.
Tump bands		Some decorated, like later style.	Some decorated, mostly painted.
Pottery	None	Brown ware, undecorated.	Gray ware and early white ware, some painted with designs similar to baskets; few life forms include birds, humans.
Sandals	Rarely decorated, square toes and square heels.	Colored decoration rare, but soles usually have raised pattern; shallow-scalloped toes and square heels.	Often have four-color decorated tops and usually have raised patterned soles; scalloped or round toes and puckered heels.
Architecture	Small scattered pit houses and cists.	Small pit houses and cists.	Large, internally differentiated pit houses with internal storage features; great kivas in some larger communities.
Environmental and demographic conditions	Unspecified	Alluvial downcutting resulting from possible lower effective moisture.[1]	Aggrading conditions and increased precipitation.[1]
Proposed social organization	Patrilocal, and/or ambilocal, bands. Evidence for violence in some areas.	Unstable period of increasing sedentism and probable social pressures.	Increasing sedentism, larger communities, larger households; matrilocal residence becomes dominant or at least frequent? Social pressures continue, and evidence for violence appears in some areas.

[1]From Dean et al. (1985).

Lobed Circles

Manning (1992) interprets the lobed circle as a symbol of fertility and even as a representation of the uterus (figure 12.4). Though he further notes that lobed circles resemble the floor plans of ceremonial kivas, particularly the keyhole-shaped Pueblo III form, the enigmatic shape of the lobed circle more closely resembles the floor plans of early Basketmaker II pit houses and may even have its origin in these "templates." These pit houses have an eastern stepped or ramped entryway (see Geib and Spurr; Kearns et al., this volume, for specific examples) and a central hearth that is mirrored in the lobed-circle shape.

Entering and leaving domestic and communal spaces has long been noted to have been marked with deep ritual meaning (Eliade 1959). As pit house shape and function changed during the Basketmaker III period, it would not be surprising to find expressed symbolic links to the past, and to find these links related to concepts of emergence and symbolic rebirth (Manning 1992; see also Hays-Gilpin 2000). Joe Pachak (personal communication, 1998) has also commented that the lobed circle bears resemblance to the T-shaped doorways common in many Puebloan sites. This again echoes the idea of emergence themes still important in Puebloan ideology today.

a

b

Figure 12.4. Examples of the lobed circle in probable late Basketmaker II contexts: (a) panel located along a cliff overlooking the San Juan River floodplain just east of Bluff, Utah; (b) the Butler Wash Site (image is approximately 1.5 m tall).

Moreover, evidence from Robins's studies of petroglyph superimposition suggests that the lobed-circle image first appears late in the Basketmaker II period. For example, figure 12.4a shows lobed circles superimposed over a San Juan Style anthropomorph with the characteristically plumed headdress. Figure 12.4b shows a lobed circle from the Butler Wash Site placed over a small anthropomorph, which is in turn placed on the abdomen of a San Juan Style anthropomorphic figure. This arrangement suggests that the lobed circle was not originally part of the large San Juan Style anthropomorph, but instead makes some kind of intended historical connection to it. Regardless of its temporal relationship to the San Juan Style anthropomorph, however, placement of the lobed circle is not random. Rather, as Manning (1992) suggests, its placement makes reference to a womb—perhaps, in this context, the womb of an ancestor. Occurrences of this enigmatic symbol vary considerably. Manning (1992) notes that they often occur in pairs, on the heads of anthropomorphs, upon abdomens, and on chests, where they may, in a very abstracted way, symbolize lactating breasts. We return to these images again in the context of Basketmaker III procession panels, in which they figure more prominently.

Images of Women

Cole (1990) and Grant (1978) recognized certain classes of anthropomorphic imagery as representations of women, particularly with reference to menstruation (figure 12.5). These conclusions were drawn from the triangular "aprons" covering the pubic areas of the an-thropomorphs, which almost certainly represent string and bark-fiber garments found in dry site deposits. These garments typically have a waistband supporting a long fringe in front that was drawn between the legs, forming a triangle shape, and tucked into the waistband in back, leaving a tail-like fringe. Menstrual blood often remains in the middle of the fringes. An exception in the way these female images are depicted occurs at a rock shelter in Butler Wash, in which an abraded body is outlined. Directly over the pubic area of this image, also atypical, is a deep vertical "stick groove" indicating a vagina (figure 12.5c). Some images of women at a site in Cottonwood Wash, where these images occur in large numbers, have drilled holes in their navels and are associated with zoomorphic, abstract, and small "generic" anthropomorphic imagery (figure 12.5d and e). Often the figures have eyes, which in at least two instances appear to be weeping (Cole 1990) (see Figure 12.5a). These images also appear along the San Juan River near its confluence with Butler Wash, in the Butler Wash drainage itself (Castleton 1987; Cole 1990), and in large quantities in Grand Gulch (see Castleton 1987 and Cole 1993 for limited examples; much of the Grand Gulch material has yet to be reported). Within our current database, the Cottonwood Wash Site contains, by far, the largest and most numerous of these images in a single location.

Cole (1990) suggests that these images may be subsumed within the San Juan Anthropomorphic Style in that articles of clothing similar to the rock art (i.e., sashes and aprons) were found in Basketmaker II shelters by Guernsey and Kidder (1921), and Basketmaker III

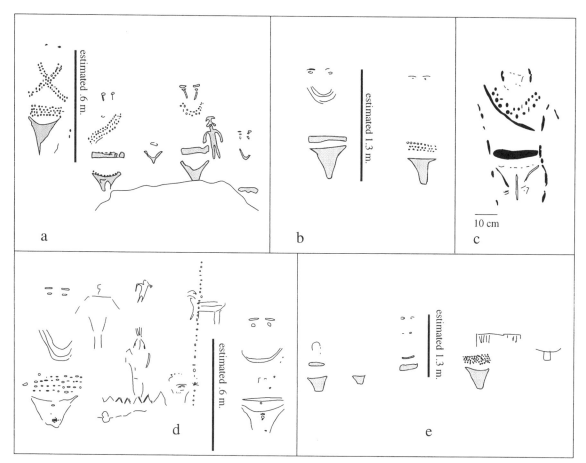

Figure 12.5. Examples of images of women: (a) Butler Wash (see also Cole 1990); (b) Cottonwood Wash; (c) rock shelter in central Butler Wash; (d, e) Cottonwood Wash.

women also wore aprons (Morris 1980). Moreover, these images of women share the San Juan Anthropomorphic Style traits of being depicted in static frontal poses and grouped in rows that in some instances are large and imposing. Unlike the open-air San Juan Anthropomorphic panels previously discussed, however, these images appear to be spatially homogenous within the geographic region in which they occur (Robins 1997).

Importantly, there are several instances where such female images, if somewhat more stylized, appear in conjunction with later Basketmaker II–III images such as the Wolfman Panel (see Cole 1990:116), in which the lobed circle also features prominently. The meanings associated with depictions of women in Basketmaker II imagery therefore continue, if decreasingly, through the Basketmaker III period. However, the lobed circles initially appear in much lower frequencies during the latter part of the Basketmaker II period and become increasingly more prominent in Basketmaker III imagery.

Because these images of women exhibit strong Basketmaker II traits yet appear to overlap in time with the Basketmaker III period, they may represent specific solutions to problems encountered with social and economic change. Such change may have followed the appearance

of dry farming and increasing population densities (see Matson at al. 1988). By A.D. 200 pre-village aggregated groups were established on mesa tops in conjunction with dry farming and possibly with swidden farming techniques in places such as Cedar Mesa (Matson 1991) and Black Mesa (Nichols and Smiley 1984). More recently, an aggregated Basketmaker II site was located near the town of Bluff, Utah, at a much lower elevation (Deborah Westfall, personal communication, 1997). Images of women may have become important at this time and may be related to new forms of community ritual including female puberty rites.

New Ritual Forms and Puberty Rites

Because men moved between residence groups (even as Basketmaker communities moved about the landscape from site to site), one role of men became reproducing the social order on an extra-community scale through rituals (Hays 1992a; Hays-Gilpin 1996). Hays-Gilpin further suggests the possibility that men may have devised communal rituals, some of which are depicted in rock art as "processions" (discussed further below), partly as a means to integrate men from different natal communities into the community of their spouses, and partly to assert their importance against the increasingly formalized economic contributions of women. This is especially apparent in contrast to the structure of early Basketmaker rock art, which we propose reflected restricted intergroup residential mobility for its producers. In asserting their perceived roles as managers of this ritual domain, men may have expropriated symbols of female reproductive powers, including images of puberty rites and the lobed circle.

At the same time, women invested more time and labor in decorating portable artifacts such as containers (especially tray baskets, which may have been used to serve food) and clothing. They also produced another possible marker of female puberty and fertility: the butterfly hairstyle. This symbol also appears in rock art, as discussed in more detail below. Increasing sedentism, larger communities, increasing intercommunity hostilities (evidenced by deliberately burned pit structures and palisades; see Chenault and Motsinger; Damp and Kotyk, this volume), and possible shifts in descent and residence patterns in early Basketmaker III (during the A.D. 400s to 500s) led to social stresses that were, in part, mediated by the development of masculine social groups oriented to the elaboration of ritual as well as defensive or offensive alliances, especially later on during the A.D. 600s.

Cross-cultural studies of female puberty rites have arrived at several different conclusions. Brown (1963) argues that practice of female puberty rites is more frequent than random chance would allow in societies that also practice matrilocal postmarital residence. She reasons that matrilocal societies are more likely to mark a rite of passage to adulthood for young women because they remain in their natal household after reaching adulthood: because no change in residence on marriage marks this transition, the change in social role is marked ritually. Paige and Paige (1981:255) argue that the situation is far more complex, and that all reproductive rituals are "bargaining tactics to resolve critical sociopolitical dilemmas produced by events in the human reproductive cycle." Which kinds of rituals are emphasized depends on stability of subsistence resources, the ability to accumulate surpluses, and the strength of fraternal interest groups. Without access to stable and valuable resources, which was certainly the case for Basketmakers, there is little incentive to protect resources by forming strong fraternal kin groups, and no opportunity to accumulate surpluses. Unpredictable resource bases do, however, encourage formation of a variety of social ties outside the family group.

One means of achieving such ties is sponsoring a public menarcheal ceremony for a daughter. The parents have a chance to display and distribute what wealth they have, to gauge the extent of their support, to garner support by creating indebtedness through gifting, and to find a suitable marriage partner for the daughter just as she

comes into sexual maturity (Paige and Paige 1981:259). Of course, these conditions do not apply only to matrilocal societies, and we would argue on the basis of the chronology of imagery described here that ritual marking of female puberty via aprons and "butterfly" hair whorls appears before any indication of matrilocal residence based on architectural correlates (see table 12.1).[1]

Butterfly Hair Whorls

Butterfly hair whorls may appear earliest in late Basketmaker II rock art in Canyon de Chelly (John Campbell, personal communication, 1997), but examples are more abundant at Basketmaker III sites (see Grant 1978: 178–179 for examples, including some with female genitalia). The figure is well established on Basketmaker III and Pueblo I painted pottery (see below). This hairstyle closely resembles one associated with female puberty in Hopi culture; it is also found in many other historic pueblos. On her first menstruation, a Hopi girl was secluded in her mother's home for four days during which she ground corn. This seclusion is similar to other Hopi initiation rites and mimics the initial rite of passage after birth, when an infant is kept indoors for 20 days before being presented to the Sun and named. Following menarcheal seclusion, the young woman's mother puts up her hair in "butterfly" whorls, which she can wear from this day until her marriage; historically she wore this hairstyle at ritual events if not all the time. No further menstrual taboos or restrictions seem to have been observed.

Butterfly hair whorls appear on a White Mound Black-on-white bowl from a pit house near Houck, Arizona, that also yielded tree-ring samples dating between A.D. 785 and 837 (Hays-Gilpin and van Hartesveldt 1998: figure 5). The hairstyle also appears on other Pueblo I and earlier pottery from the La Plata and Durango Districts (Lister and Lister 1978:11; Morris 1939: plate 224I) and in numerous petroglyphs and pictographs of the Basketmaker III through Pueblo IV styles. Some of these are associated with sites that probably date to the A.D. 600s, such as Morris Cave 4 in the Prayer Rock District (Hays 1992a) and numerous Canyon de Chelly sites (Grant 1978:179). Female puberty and the status it conferred, then, were important enough to have been depicted graphically in several media. We return to the question of puberty rites below, but here suggest the possibility that hair whorls have symbolized female puberty from at least the seventh century to the present. It is also possible that the meaning of the hairstyle originally indicated femaleness generally and only later became restricted to unmarried women, but many hair-whorled figures have aprons or menstrual flow depicted, and female rock art figures also appear without hair whorls, suggesting not all women wore this hairstyle all the time.

Reinterpretation of a Basketmaker III pictograph in Canyon de Chelly suggests association of hair whorls

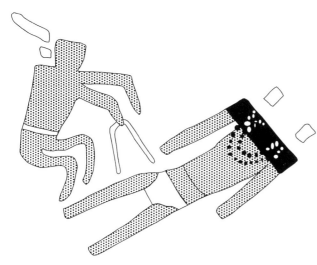

Figure 12.6 Image of "medicine man and woman patient" or female puberty rite, Canyon de Chelly (after Grant 1978, no scale).

with a puberty ceremony (figure 12.6). Originally interpreted by Grant (1978:185) as a shaman exorcising evil spirits from a woman undergoing prolonged or distressed labor, the image shows a figure with a possible hair knot and feather on one side of the head, wearing only a belt, and pointing a U-shaped stick at the pelvic area of a prone figure wearing hair whorls, two bead necklaces, a belt, and an apron. The U-shaped stick looks remarkably like the wooden tool used historically by Hopi mothers to hold the daughter's hair in place while butterfly hair whorls were being tied. There is no indication of the sex of the "shaman," nor of the pregnancy that Grant attributes to the woman figure. Although we can never know what the artist intended here, representation of a puberty event (apron suggesting menstruation, hair whorls, assistant holding stick for putting hair in whorls) seems more plausible than representation of a healing ceremony. In addition, the interpretation of an active and presumed male shaman figure bending over a passive female figure is not based on any further evidence and seems to reflect androcentric Western views of rock art and those who made it.

BASKETMAKER III IMAGERY

Rock art defined here as Basketmaker III dates from the A.D. 500s to 700s, but does not necessarily exclude later Pueblo I material. We rely again on the tree-ring-dated seventh-century occupation of Broken Flute Cave and other Prayer Rock District sites, where domesticated turkey; bow and arrow; large, internally subdivided pit houses; gray ware and black-on-white ceramics; and a great kiva appear together. Basketmaker III rock art here and rock art similar to it elsewhere include numerous depictions of material cultural, including atlatls and spears

(although their use as weapons was probably diminishing due to the probable introduction of the bow and arrow in this era), crook sticks, digging sticks, twined bags, flute players, and representations of agave or yucca plants. Birds and bird-headed anthropomorphs are also thought to date to the Basketmaker III period (Grant 1978:171-174; Schaafsma 1980), although Basketmaker II people also used bird feathers to make feather pahos (prayer offerings), and a ceremonial bird wand appeared in a Marsh Pass area Basketmaker II site (see Cole 1990:125; Guernsey and Kidder 1921). Basketmaker III rock art imagery also emphasizes gender to greater or lesser degrees depending on context. The frequency of butterfly hair whorls is much greater in the 600s than in the earlier transitional period. We also see extensive use of the lobed circle in narrative procession panels, and the appearance of ithyphallic flute players.

The Procession Panels

Lobed circles appear in "procession panels" characteristic of the Basketmaker III Chinle Representational Style (Hays 1992a; Manning 1992; Schaafsma 1980). Schaafsma (1980) noted that many Basketmaker III panels, including the processions, appear narrative in nature. We suggest that this trend reflects the beginnings of a redefined ideology concurrent with changing social and economic patterns. The autocentric and static San Juan anthropomorph is being replaced with more rhetorical discursive constructions: stories, myths, and perhaps reference to cosmic realms. Processions of narrative and discursive anthropomorphic and zoomorphic figures appear over much of the Four Corners region, including Broken Flute Cave (Hays 1992a) and the Butler Wash region (Hurst and Pachak 1989; Manning 1992). Hays-Gilpin (1996) suggests that processions become a popular rock art motif probably sometime in the A.D. 600s, based on examples in Broken Flute Cave where tree-ring dates indicate a primary occupation in the 620s. Often the figures depict group ritual activities undertaken primarily by males (they are often phallic, emphasizing potency).

At least one Butler Wash procession panel (figure 12.7) may have been in use during the seventh century as a focal point for movement and interaction between populations living at Bluff Bench and Cedar Mesa, and possibly on an even larger scale. On the cliff edge beneath the procession panel are toeholds that people used to cross the formidable Comb Ridge at this point. Manning (1992) also notes that this procession panel identifies intercommunity ritual associated with larger circular structures. The four processions in this panel have cardinal direction orientation congruent with the emphasis on four directions (whether cardinal or offset, as at Hopi) found in Puebloan mythologies (Manning 1992).

Another procession panel located at the Butler Wash Site shows the lobed circle as an opening from which a

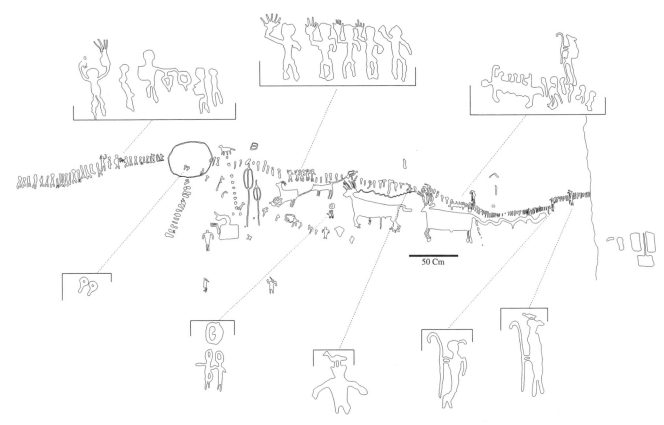

Figure 12.7. Large procession panel located along the Comb Ridge near Butler Wash.

single procession emerges (figure 12.8). This opening has a ladder, noted by Manning (1992) as a reference to a pit house entrance, but it is perhaps at the same time a reference to emergence and the sipapu. Like other procession panels, this one shows humped-back figures holding, or passing, crook sticks. Crook sticks have both utilitarian and ceremonial uses. Crook sticks appear in Hopi culture as a symbol of veneration, and they are often interpreted as canes carried by the elderly. In the more remote past, as seen on Mimbres pottery and actual artifacts found in dry sites like Broken Flute Cave, crook sticks seem to have functioned as general hunting and gathering tools used, for example, to pull small mammals from their burrows or to knock down piñon nuts. They are, then, simultaneously symbols of hunting and gathering activities and of long life. To the right of the kivalike lobed circle (it is conventional for rock art to be viewed as if looking out of the image) we see first a quadruped, possibly a dog or coyote, then humped-backed human figures. These eventually lead to a long procession of stylized anthropomorphs holding hands. These figures stretch for more than a hundred feet across a much earlier panel containing both San Juan Style anthropomorphs and Archaic images. As with the lobed circle on the San Juan Style anthropomorph (see figure 12.4b), this procession also makes a strong connective reference to the past.

Hays (1992a; Hays-Gilpin 1996) noted that the highest density of Basketmaker III (Chinle Representational Style, see Schaafsma 1980) rock art in Broken Flute Cave occurs in the east half of the cave, which holds several fifth-century pit houses, some human burials, and a probable seventh-century ritual structure (a Basketmaker III great kiva). The great kiva, or communal structure, may have been built in this location because of the earlier, perhaps ancestral, structures already there. Some earlier rock art may already have been there as well, or most of the rock art may have been produced during activities that took place in this structure in the seventh century. In any case, most of the rock art appears seventh century in style, and several design elements appear near the great kiva that do not appear in the western half of the site, where the domestic structures are, or in the other inhabited shelters nearby. These images include processions of humans (mostly phallic), possible masks, lobed circles, and a "bird-headed" human.

From site visits to the Butler Wash procession panels, Robins also noted that panels with these icons tend to occur away from any habitation shelters and structures. In a large sandy depression at the base of the large procession panel at Comb Ridge, Robins found camp features and large quantities of lithic reduction debris relative to a few pieces of ground stone. A few hundred meters north of this site another, though much simpler, procession panel was observed, again away from habitation areas

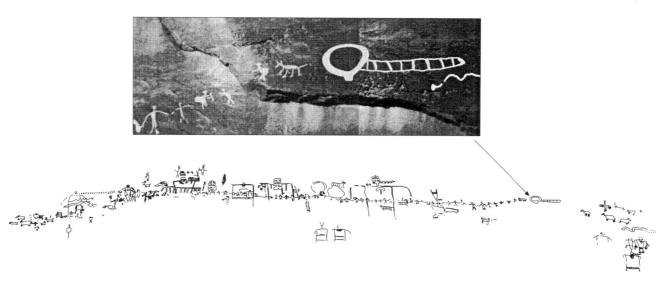

Figure 12.8. Procession panel located at the confluence of Butler Wash and the San Juan River.

(Joseph D. Pachak, personal communication, 1996). Pachak has also mentioned processions of crook sticks in the same area.

Flute Players

Flute players appear in rock art for the first time in the Basketmaker III period (Grant 1978:178), although they become especially numerous and elaborate much later, in Pueblo III and IV times, after about A.D. 1150 (Peter Pilles, personal communication, 1996). Flutes appear to be one of a class of male-gendered "tools" of fertility that also includes staffs, bows, arrows, and at least in Basketmaker II–III times, atlatls (see Loftin 1991:23-28). Flutes appeared in the grave of an adult male in Broken Flute Cave (Morris 1980) and appeared only in male graves at protohistoric Hawikku (Howell 1995). In rock art, flute players are, to our knowledge, never depicted with female genitalia or hair whorls. Many are phallic, and many are ithyphallic.

Hopi has a Flute Clan and flute ceremony, and the flute was the young man's instrument of courtship. Pueblo oral traditions contain many references to flute players (Parsons 1939:41), such as the young male solar deity Paiyatamu at Zuni, who courts young women and lures back the lost Corn Maidens with his flute playing. The Hopi Locust plays his flute to bring warm weather and help crops grow. The handle of a Pueblo II or III period Cibola White Ware effigy pitcher found near Gallup, New Mexico, seems to represent both flute and penis, grasped by a pair of carefully modeled arms and hands (Lister and Lister 1978:47), suggesting that this analogy was not lost on ancient Southwesterners.

WOMEN'S MATERIAL CULTURE

Basketmaker II Textiles and Baskets

Women probably made twined bags, sandals, belts, aprons, other nonloomed textiles, and baskets, based on ethnographic analogs. Tools and raw materials have also been found in sexed burials. We view these objects, like rock art, as part of the Basketmaker environment and as a domain of specialized and meaningful activity. Though poorly provenienced, many baskets and textiles were recovered from Basketmaker shelters in Grand Gulch during the Hyde Exploration Expedition of 1893, and other expeditions of this early period (see Blackburn and Atkins 1993, and Blackburn and Williamson 2000 for excellent summaries). Other collections from Canyon del Muerto (Morris 1934) were also poorly provenienced due to heavy reuse and disturbance.

Webster and Hays-Gilpin (1994) examined these and other materials. They found that basketry and textile design was not consistent throughout the greater Basketmaker II region, yet in the specific culture area defined as the Kayenta-San Juan group (identified temporally as the White Dog phase), baskets and textiles were most highly elaborate and diverse, apparently more so than in any other area. Bag patterns included colored stripes and rows of triangles, while basket designs included zigzags, stepped lines, diamond forms, and circles. Dominant symmetries were finite designs based on rotation, reflection, or both. Investment in decoration of highly visible artifacts such as bags and baskets in the White Dog phase suggests that these items might have been involved in signifying social relationships.

Basketmaker III Textiles, Baskets, and Pottery

Basketmaker III baskets, bags, aprons, and sandals have clear antecedents in Basketmaker II period materials, construction techniques, and decorative conventions, but later items are very often more colorful and have more elaborate designs and, in some cases, constructions. Differentiating Basketmaker II and III artifacts is not always easy, however. Many Basketmaker sites, such as those in

Canyon del Muerto and Grand Gulch, have heavily mixed deposits, so chronological relationships are not clear. Also, many of the collections were made prior to the Pecos Classification of Southwestern prehistory. Consequently, differences between the Basketmaker II period and the early ceramic (brown ware) part of the Basketmaker III period were never considered. We therefore rely heavily on artifacts associated with two tree-ring-dated occupations of Prayer Rock District rock shelters (Hays 1992a; Hays-Gilpin 1996; Morris 1980).

Sandals with shallow-scalloped toes and with square heels appear in Obelisk Cave in the late 400s, together with elaborate colored baskets, decorated aprons, brown ware ceramics, female figurines, and twined bags. Early seventh-century structures in Broken Flute Cave contained similar baskets, textiles, and figurines, together with gray ware and black-on-white ceramics, and deep-scalloped and round-toed sandals with puckered heels (Hays-Gilpin et al. 1998). Baskets described by Pepper from Grand Gulch remain undated, though Pepper (1902:12) comments: "The sandals of the Basket Makers have square toes, apparently without exception." Thus, some of the Grand Gulch baskets date prior to the seventh century and could be contemporaneous with the early Basketmaker III Obelisk Cave baskets, while others could be much older since square-toed, square-heeled sandals were the standard Basketmaker II period footwear. Certainly, further research is needed, including a more careful comparison of the Grand Gulch sandals, especially their heel constructions, with dated specimens and direct AMS dating. With the above cautions in mind, we tentatively explore some relationships between rock art and decoration of baskets and ceramics during the Basketmaker III period.

Basketmaker III textile and basket designs consist almost entirely of small, rectilinear, geometric units such as triangles and stepped triangles (sometimes called keys and terraces) repeated primarily by rotation, but also by reflection, translation, and, only rarely, glide reflection (see Washburn and Crowe 1988 for symmetry terms). Complex red and black color counterchange is a frequent feature of this style. This pattern stands in contrast to Basketmaker II baskets, which tend to have only black decoration, and bags with colored designs are relatively rare. Rectilinearity is in part determined by the gridlike structure imposed by textile and basketry techniques. Nevertheless, many Basketmaker III textiles have painted designs. Curved shapes, including life-forms, would have been easy to paint on the relatively flat surfaces of many twined textiles, but this option was apparently never exercised.

Highly decorated Basketmaker III period artifacts include coiled tray baskets, presumably used for processing and serving food, but also found as burial offerings. Gatherers and farmers carried conical and trapezoidal burden baskets, often decorated, with plain and decorated tump bands. Painted examples sometimes have central stains attesting to sweated brows. Women wore string aprons, but whether all the time or just during their menstrual periods, we do not know. Most aprons bear blood stains, and some contain the bones of miscarried fetuses. After use, aprons were carefully rolled and tucked away in cracks in bedrock or tumbles of boulders, or included in deposits of domestic trash, suggesting little to no concern for menstrual seclusion or "pollution." Of hundreds of aprons recovered in Prayer Rock District rock shelters dating to the A.D. 400s and 600s, only nine are decorated. One is painted, and the rest have four-color counterchanged designs produced by twining dyed yarns. Were decorated aprons worn on special occasions, such as first menstruation, marriage, or return of fertility after childbirth, or were they simply individual expressions of pride in workmanship? We may never know. After the 400s, aprons are rare in rock art, and no depictions show colored designs.

Although Basketmaker people learned to make polished brown ware pottery as early as the A.D. 200s (L. Reed et al., this volume), painted pottery does not appear until the late 500s and early 600s, perhaps even later in some parts of the Western Anasazi area. The earliest pottery designs appear primarily on bowls. They mimic coiled basket decoration, with narrow bands of small, repeated geometric units radiating in a spiraling fashion from the base to the rim. Pottery decoration at this time is a very simplified and poorly visible version of designs seen on baskets and textiles, and so probably had little social importance other than to provide an emphatic link between these media—a link that probably signified women's concerns. The designs that appear most frequently in these portable containers and items of clothing, probably made and used by women, do not appear in Basketmaker III rock art, which if not entirely the domain of men and masculine concerns, was certainly a domain of ritual and suprahousehold organizational scale.

Anomalies in Basketmaker III Material Culture

The exceptions to stylistic partitioning between rock art on the one hand, and textiles, baskets, and painted pots on the other, are almost as patterned, and surely as significant, as the rules they break. Birds are the single most frequent motif to crosscut media. Depictions of birds are frequent in Basketmaker III rock art, at least within the Grand Gulch, Moqui Canyon, Butler Wash, Canyon de Chelly, and Prayer Rock areas, where Grant (1978) and Hays (1992a) have identified turkeys, ducks, and cranes. Human figures with birds on their heads or in place of heads are frequent (Grant 1978:173). Grant notes worldwide occurrences of bird-headed humans in which a bird's head replaces the human head, but in the Basketmaker case, a whole bird sits atop the human body like a headdress. Grant (1978:187-188) argues that this icon represents the shaman's magical soul flight, but also notes the religious importance of birds in Puebloan myth and of feathers in ritual practice. Parsons (1939:186) notes that at Zuni, birds are referred to as "little servants" and as messenger scouts "sent to find lost Corn Maidens or any stray girl." Emergence stories identify a variety of birds sent to look for the sky-opening to the next world, and the turkey is said to have white-flecked tail feathers because the foaming waters of the flooding underworld splashed him as he struggled to escape. Birds often serve as clan symbols in the historic pueblos, and so birdheaded people may have signified the identity of a Basketmaker social group at some scale, if not exactly a clan, or may have signified a social role, such as a ritual specialist of some kind, including but not limited to a shaman with a bird spirit helper.

Birds in rock art most frequently appear singly or in rows, and unaccompanied by humans. Their rare occurrences in other media show them paired or in rows. Wetherill's Grand Gulch collection, from the 1893 Hyde Exploration Expedition, contains a basket from a burial described by Pepper (1902:18): "In this instance the basket covered the head and upper part of the body, the remainder being wrapped in a feather-cloth robe. The figures shown in this basket, forty-four in number, were evidently made to represent ducks or other water-fowl... the figures pointing in one direction are black; those facing [the other] are red, and are raised slightly." The feather-cloth blanket indicates a probable Basketmaker III date since Basketmaker II blankets were made from twined strips of fur.

This description of the basket, including specific complementary coloring and directional placement of elements, connotes a meaningful and prescribed construction. Although tray baskets are usually envisioned piled with food at a meal, baskets and their designs need not be excluded from what are clearly ritual contexts. A design similar to that described by Pepper occurs at Broken Flute Cave, at least 150 kilometers away (figure 12.9a). This basket, which held turkey feathers and was cached in the floor of a seventh-century pit house (Hays 1992a), also has alternating red and black birds. They may represent waterfowl but are most likely turkeys, based on the shape of their protruding chests.

The outlined crosses that alternate with the rows of birds are frequent in rock art and also appear in seventh-century sandals (Hays-Gilpin et al. 1998). The outlined cross at Hopi today is a symbol of the four directions and also of the Sand Clan. It often appears with images of women, including the Mother of Game Animals (McCreery and McCreery 1986; McCreery and Malotki 1994) in Pueblo III–IV period petroglyphs of the Little Colorado River area. In these contexts, it may be associ-

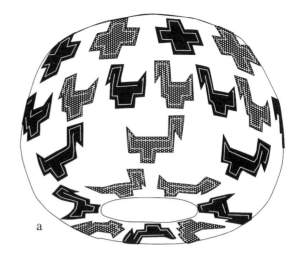

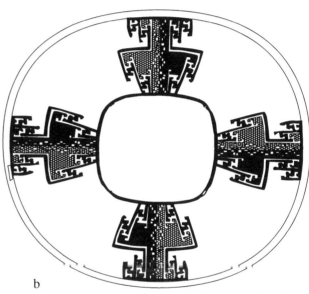

Figure 12.9. Red-and-black baskets (half-tone is red) with bird images from (a) Broken Flute Cave and (b) Canyon del Muerto (after Morris and Burgh 1941

ated with Sand Altar Earth Woman, an earth deity. Perhaps not coincidentally, the turkey is an earth-bound bird, often associated with the earth in Pueblo thought, and opposed to sky- and sun-associated raptors (Tyler 1991).

Ann Axtell Morris (1934) describes a Basketmaker III burial basket from Tseahatso Cave in Canyon del Muerto showing red and black thunderbird-like motifs (figure 12.9b). This same shelter housed the infamous "burial of the hands" in which a pair of adult hands and forearms were "wearing" sandals also patterned in black and red (Morris 1934:204). Twined bags often accompanied burials as wrappings and also are red and black.

Representations of birds and "flight" seem to be a rare yet recurrent theme in basketry design of this period, and like other basket designs, they also appear on pottery bowls. A spread-winged bird appears on a black-on-white bowl from Broken Flute Cave (Arizona State Museum collections; Hays 1992a), on contemporaneous bowls from Chaco Canyon, the La Plata District, and even a site on the Muddy River in southern Nevada. Ducks and birdlike motifs appear in profusion in rock art dating to the Basketmaker III period (Cole 1990; Grant 1978) and also appear in some single-component Basketmaker II rock shelters, such as Bernheimer's Cave 2 in Moqui Canyon (42SA772, some 20 km west of Grand Gulch; Sharrock et al. 1963).

In summary, bird images cross media, and so cross domains of visual expression that were probably gendered (see Braithwaite 1982 for an ethnographic example). Although perhaps most frequent and elaborate in the Canyon de Chelly area, bird images are widespread in rock art, pottery, and possibly basketry (at least, they do occur on Canyon de Chelly, Prayer Rock, and Grand Gulch baskets; perishables from other areas are extremely rare). While some birds had economic uses (turkey feathers for blankets and fletching, ducks and sometimes turkeys as meat), they were clearly valued for ritual uses. These included use of turkey, duck, eagle, and other feathers for prayer sticks and other paraphernalia, and less tangible, "cognitive" uses: birds as metaphors for the changing seasons; as spiritual travelers between sky, earth surface, and underwater worlds; and, at least in historic times, as symbols of social groups such as clans and religious societies. Birds imagery, then, was likely an important ritual and social symbol of concern in many domains of Basketmaker life, including the domains of masculine and feminine gendered activities.

IMPLICATIONS

Conkey (1991:67) has proposed that sexual divisions of labor in situations of social aggregation, where suprahousehold spheres of interaction occur, "carry meanings that structure social action." Division of labor and concepts of gender are usually flexible and in some ways unimportant in small-scale, dispersed settlements. Every individual has the knowledge and ability to carry out any tasks that need to be done and will do so at every opportunity. In contrast, with increasing sedentism and population density, roles usually become less flexible. Although men and women usually have the requisite knowledge to undertake any needed task, opportunities rarely arise, and gender roles tend to be more strictly enforced.

The elaboration of portable artifacts becomes more notable in the late Basketmaker III period (Hays 1992a; Hays-Gilpin 1996). This implicates women in other roles, such as in creating objects used in gift or other forms of exchange. In situations of increasing social interaction, women may produce objects of exchange, objects that carry social meaning, as they were, in Conkey's words (1991:78), "primarily engaged in activities

associated with the use of these products." Webster and Hays-Gilpin (1994:323) note that visual imagery and technologically complicated artifacts such as sandals, baskets, and painted pottery could be manipulated to actively "negotiate the meanings of relationships among individuals, families (kin groups), households (economic groups) and communities (residence groups)."

We should begin to ask whether Basketmaker women were actively mediating social action, in Conkey's terms, through the specialized production and exchange of socially familiar items, or even whether women resisted men's assertion of ritual power, in Hodder's terms (Hodder 1985, 1986:105–116),[2] by elaborating objects they used in social contexts to assert their own interests. Although pottery and baskets have essentially low visibility when compared to rock art, they have higher visibility when traded and exchanged. They are portable, and they may be used in displaying and distributing food in ritual as well as household contexts, especially in the context of intercommunity feasting (see Rice 1999:10–13 for a worldwide review of theories about the role of early pottery in social intensification and competitive feasting). Pottery and basketry may also be displayed in mortuary ritual; loss of an individual in any small community sets in motion a variety of changes in social relationships. These objects, too, may constitute covert discourse in the mediation of social tensions as communities aggregated for ceremonies. The seventh-century great kiva or community structure at Broken Flute Cave, measuring more than 18 meters in diameter, probably served to integrate the inhabitants of Broken Flute Cave and nearby contemporaneous sites. Eating is one the more important activities in highly social settings, including ritual, and decoration of eating utensils used in extrahousehold contexts is frequent in the ethnographic record.

CONCLUSIONS

To summarize, the Basketmaker II period may have been characterized by formalized social and political relationships corresponding to the distribution of different territories. The locations of early open-air rock art panels emphasize the control of maize production, consumption, and distribution in a socioritual context with shamanism and hunter-gatherer lifeways. Within this context, rock art producers may have held positions of power and authority based on the control of subsistence resources and shamanic skill. Because of the strong tendency towards territoriality, movement between different groups may have been restricted, at least for those members who held leadership positions.

As the social and economic system changed during the later part of the Basketmaker II period (between about 200 B.C. and A.D. 200), imagery also changed. While still holding to the San Juan Anthropomorphic Style, differences emerged, such as spatial homogeneity, references to women's puberty, and images representing rebirth and emergence. Much of this imagery appears to make connective references to earlier imagery. This change reflects new forms of ritual that allowed men to create ritual-based crosscutting relationships facilitating mobility between different natal communities and maintaining networks of social ties.

By late Basketmaker III, architecture suggests formalized community integrative rituals, larger household size, and possibly a pattern of predominantly matrilocal residence in at least some areas. Late Basketmaker III images often stress unity and convergence, especially in the form of rows of figures with linked hands and procession panels. These panels depict extrahousehold activities that may be associated with great kivas. In contrast to the inferred highly social context of the San Juan Anthropomorphic Style, where rock art is most prominent in areas of high agricultural production potential, rock art of the Basketmaker III period often occupies more exclusive locations. A ritual community versus household partitioning seems more evident in the Basketmaker III period as people settled into more permanent dwellings.

In contrast to the imagery ascribed to men, or at least to ritual practitioners, whatever their genders, iconography on classes of artifacts considered to be the technological domain of women is probably more consistent through time, at least up until the late Basketmaker III period. Objects made by women may have been used actively in mediating social situations arising from more-formalized aggregations. In situations of aggregation, social life becomes more complex. At such times, styles of both rock art and portable artifacts in the northern Southwest became more diverse and complicated as a result of a combination of factors, including gender and age role differentiation, intracommunity competition for prestige and resource control, intercommunity activities including rituals and feasting, and alliance and conflict.

The substantive contribution of this study is to suggest what kinds of rituals characterized the Basketmaker period, in much the same way that Adams (1991) has shown how the katsina religion pervaded life in Pueblo IV times (ca. A.D. 1300–1540). More broadly, we have demonstrated that analysis of decorative arts and rock art—taken together with more archaeologically familiar approaches to settlement pattern, subsistence practices, and architecture—may provide a way to reconstruct Puebloan ritual history from Basketmaker times to the present.

ACKNOWLEDGMENTS

Illustrations were prepared by Michael Robins from original fieldwork except for figure 12.3c; Sally Cole kindly granted permission to use this image, which was originally adapted from a field sketch by Dennis Hadenfeldt. Robins extends appreciation to the Anthropology Department at Northern Arizona University for support and encouragement during his thesis research, and especially to Kim Smiley, his committee chair, who supported that project throughout its trials and varied forms. Dale Davidson of the BLM also enthusiastically supported that project, and Joe Pachak shared his insights and knowledge of the region. A synthesis of that project is represented here, but should in no way be construed as representative of the views held by those who supported it. Omission or commission is entirely that of the author. Michael Robins also extends a special thanks to Bill Hyder for commenting on a late draft of this chapter.

Kelley Hays-Gilpin's research was supported by the Navajo Nation Archaeology Department—Farmington Roads Office, the Museum of Northern Arizona, and the University of Arizona Graduate College. Thanks are extended to the American Museum of Natural History and Arizona State Museum for access to artifacts, collections, and archives, and to the Navajo Nation, Cove Chapter, for access to sites in the Prayer Rock District. Thanks to Dennis Gilpin, Deborah Nichols, Chip Wills, and Richard Wilshusen for useful comments on the manuscript, and to John Campbell and many other members of the Internet discussion group "rock-art-l" for information about butterfly hair whorls in rock art. The usual disclaimers apply.

NOTES

1. Basketmaker II–III transitional (brown ware horizon, ca. A.D. 200–400) pit houses, like many earlier ones, are small and have fairly simple floor features. Many Basketmaker III pit houses dating to the A.D. 620s in Broken Flute Cave are larger, with floor areas between 33 and 56 m², and interior space divided by low ridges and "wing walls." Ember (1973) (see also Ehrenberg 1989:94–96) proposes crosscultural correlates between floor area of dwellings greater than a cut-off somewhere between 49 and 54 m² and matrilocal residence. Several pit houses in Broken Flute Cave fall into the range for matrilocal residence. Many, however, do not, suggesting a variety of kinds of households resulting from domestic cycle variation (individuals, older couples, etc.) and perhaps flexibility in residence choice.

2. Hodder's ethnographic work among the Ilchamus of Kenya suggested that women began to decorate calabashes at a time in Ilchamus history when their dense, centralized farming villages gave way to dispersed homesteads in which women were able to own resources like cattle for the first time. They silently asserted their growing power and independence, Hodder argues, by decorating calabashes with designs that refer to the powers of sexuality, young warriors, and ritual specialists. Material culture, then, can be manipulated as a form of silent discourse resisting the status quo.

Part VI

Conclusion

13

Basketmaker Archaeology at the Millennium

New Answers to Old Questions

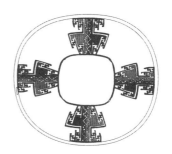

R. Gwinn Vivian

As the Southwestern archaeological database has grown over the past four decades—a process accelerated by contract projects—the assessment or reassessment of chronologically defined periods has become more common (e.g., Adler 1996; Wilcox and Masse 1981). Often there has been a need to establish or to validate the temporal range, spatial scope, defining attributes, and culturally distinguishing processes that marked heretofore relatively unknown segments of time, such as the recent series of analyses (e.g., Matson and Dohm 1994) on the Basketmaker II period. In the case of this volume, we are dealing with a period that has been studied with relative intensity since it was defined in the Pecos Classification (and even earlier; e.g., Pepper 1902), but one now requiring greater scrutiny as its multiple parameters have shifted significantly within the past several decades.

In documenting and evaluating perceived changes, past attention focused on a number of relatively standard issues long associated with the Basketmaker III period. These included, but were not limited to, the early production and use of ceramics, an increasingly complex architecture, a greater reliance on agriculture, and concomitant adjustments to a more sedentary lifestyle. This volume differs in the editor's commitment to include chapters that not only elaborate on these issues but refine our conceptual and geographic understanding of the Basketmaker III period. This is accomplished by presenting new data from areas not previously studied and by moving away from a more traditional normative approach through an emphasis on subregional variability and defining more precisely the implications, relevance, and importance of the transition from Basketmaker II to Basketmaker III. These objectives are achieved in part through synthetic studies of architecture, ceramics, and lithics, and in part by new analyses of Basketmaker community structure and functional organization.

How significant is this new information for the Basketmaker III period and for Anasazi prehistory in general? More specifically, are we any closer to understanding the important processes that were underway during the Basketmaker III period? And, can we determine more precisely the critical changes that characterized the transition from Basketmaker II to Basketmaker III—changes that more firmly positioned the trajectory of Anasazi culture? Rather than attempt to evaluate all of the key elements treated to a greater or lesser degree in individual chapters, I prefer to comment on a few items of general concern as well as a few themes that crosscut a number of the chapters.

GEOGRAPHIC SCOPE

One goal of this book was to expand geographic perceptions of the Basketmaker III period. In one sense, this was accomplished. The zones covered in chapters 2 through 9 do represent, for the most part, areas with limited previous research. In fact, the coverage is in large part limited to a swath of country on either side of the New Mexico-Arizona border stretching from the Four Corners in the north to the Río Puerco of the West in the south, a zone often seen as dividing Western and Eastern Anasazi. The inclusion of the Rainbow Plateau and Juniper Cove in the Kayenta area pays homage to the western zone, but the Eastern Anasazi Basketmaker III is essentially unreported. Thus, geographic coverage is relatively restricted and not representative of all Basketmaker III manifestations in the northern Southwest.

Would greater geographic coverage in this book change the conceptual picture of Basketmaker III that is conveyed largely on the basis of work carried out in the Chuska Valley and the Mesa Verde area? It probably would. For one thing, the relatively stable, year-round occupation of essentially permanent hamlets and villages that has been postulated in many of the chapters may not have characterized all of the northern Southwest. For example, Wills and Windes (1989) have argued that Shabik'eshchee Village, a site comparable in size and complexity to several reported from the Chuska Valley, was not occupied year-round by all residents.

Greater geographic coverage should also inform on the ubiquity of a Basketmaker II–III transition in the Anasazi world. This process has been firmly documented on the Rainbow Plateau by Geib and Spurr, but Chenault and Motsinger report that the Basketmaker III period in the Mesa Verde region represents "the first real period of colonization of the Mesa Verde region by the people we now call Anasazi," implying no direct cultural links to earlier horizons in the area. Similarly, Kearns, McVickar, and L. Reed note an "apparent occupational hiatus" of the Tohatchi Flats during the late Basketmaker II period, followed by a sixth-century colonization of the area by Basketmaker III populations. Though this problem could reflect the lack of site data on earlier periods, the intensity of survey on many of these projects should account for earlier sites. Ultimately, we may discover that very different cultural processes were at work throughout the northern Southwest during the Basketmaker III period as a result of climatic, edaphic, physiographic, and other variables.

DATING

Although the general dating of the Basketmaker III period is not in question, two temporal aspects raised in this volume deserve comment. First, it is apparent that many if not most of the authors are more comfortable lumping some processes over longer spans of time, thereby blurring the older and more conventional divisions between the Pecos Classification time periods. This seems to be particularly true for the transition from Basketmaker III to Pueblo I. At the same time, there is a strong tendency to use shorter, more precisely dated segments for documenting small-scale but critical changes in settlement patterning.

Second, site dating has improved enormously as a result of larger samples for dating (e.g., Damp and Kotyk report 849 dendrochronological samples collected from their work in the Mexican Springs area) and the use of early maize for obtaining radiocarbon dates. One immediate benefit of better dating has been the ability to more securely define the appearance of several hallmarks of the Basketmaker II and III periods. Essentially all authors report heavy dependence on maize at increasingly earlier dates. Geib and Spurr's work on the Rainbow Plateau at a number of well-dated sites has permitted them to hypothesize the replacement of the atlatl by the bow and arrow by at least A.D. 300 and possibly as early as the

second century A.D. Similar early dates have placed the appearance of brown wares on the Colorado Plateau by perhaps A.D. 145.

MATERIAL CULTURE: EMERGING TECHNOLOGIES

Southwestern archaeologists have long acknowledged the importance of new trajectories in Basketmaker III material culture. Two chapters in this volume clarify these processes in two domains and underscore the complex and multiple ramifications of greater sedentism on ceramic and lithic production. First, L. Reed, Wilson, and Hays-Gilpin have produced a most significant contribution to improved understanding of the Basketmaker III period in their confirmation of a brown ware "horizon" among the northern Anasazi and the identification of valid transitional brown/gray wares. Many of the site-based chapters in this volume confirm the presence of brown and brown/gray wares prior to the appearance of long-recognized gray types. The synthesis and evaluation of this information by L. Reed and her colleagues is a gem of succinct thinking and presentation, and they are to be thanked, among other things, for graciously acknowledging Dittert and others' (1963) early recognition that brown wares underlay all ceramic development in the Four Corners area.

This chapter is valuable for several reasons. First, the authors' analysis clarifies the fact that brown ware production was based on a preexisting technology and was not an in situ development. In addition, through tracing the development of the earliest Basketmaker ceramics, the authors make clear for the first time that there was an obvious transition from brown to gray wares. This transition was marked in many areas by a relatively long period of brown/gray ware use, a situation interpreted by the authors as reflecting the problems confronted by Anasazi potters struggling to produce good brown wares when faced with unsuitable clays characteristic of much of the Colorado Plateau. Heretofore, these "mixed" wares had never found a home—"brown" or "gray"; now we know where they belong. We also can thank the authors for "resource-based variants," a most appropriate generic term for these wares.

L. Reed, Wilson, and Hays-Gilpin merit our gratitude as well for creating a coherent albeit simple classificatory system for dealing with brown and brown/gray wares. The system is simple because the authors fortunately lump rather than split wares, and they avoid the color trap by avoiding color. By assigning all brown and brown/gray wares to either Obelisk Utility or Sambrito Utility, the potential for future classificatory problems has been reduced, although future typological boundaries could be drawn on the basis of temper differences in brown/gray wares. Finally, the distinction drawn between "maintainable" and "reliable" technological systems for ceramic production is an especially constructive concept for evaluating the transition from Basketmaker II to Basketmaker III, and beyond to Pueblo I, through ceramics.

Torres investigates this transition in greater depth and argues that it was not so much the introduction of cultigens in Basketmaker II that prompted relatively radical changes in Anasazi lithic technology, but rather the ensuing reduction in mobility and need for portable cores. Greater sedentism and a decrease in exploitable space in Basketmaker III stimulated a pattern of raw material prospecting that, like ceramic technology, was a response to the geologic vagaries of the Colorado Plateau. At the same time, technological efficiency was increased through a shift to unidirectional rather than multidirectional core reduction. Torres says this pattern was "born in" the Cove-Redrock Valley area, although its widespread distribution would point to similar adaptations throughout the Colorado Plateau. If the adoption of a raw materials prospecting strategy, a unidirectional core reduction technique, and an increased use of expedient flake tools can be used as a gauge of the degree of sedentism practiced within a subregion or more circumscribed locales, Torres has provided us with an additional means for determining seasonal or annual use of sites such as Shabik'eshchee Village (see Wills and Windes 1989 and chapters in this volume for differing views).

SETTLEMENT STRUCTURE:
CONFLICT AND RITUAL

A considerable amount of effort was devoted in these chapters to documenting and evaluating Basketmaker architecture, settlement structure, and the local or regional patterning of individual settlements. Two aspects of these investigations—the presence of stockaded hamlets and burned pit structures at some sites, and the identification and distribution of Basketmaker great kivas—are of particular interest.

Several chapters report aspects of Basketmaker III settlement and architecture that suggest a period of conflict that seemingly was short-lived but intense in some areas. The most obvious indications of conflict are living spaces enclosed by fences or post stockades and burned pit structures. At present, stockaded settlements and burned pit houses do not appear to be a Basketmaker III area-wide phenomenon, but as Chenault and Motsinger point out, future work may change this picture. There is, in fact, considerable variation in occurrence throughout the primary regional focus of this book. Chenault and Motsinger cite a high incidence of stockaded villages and burned pit houses (three of four sites discussed) in the Mesa Verde area, whereas Toll and Wilson do not report stockades in the La Plata Valley, and only three of the nine structures they describe were burned "shortly after use."

Even more interesting is the contrast within the Chuska Valley. At the northern end of the valley in the Cove–Redrock area, Reed and Wilcox observe that 89 percent of pit structures in the early Obelisk phase (A.D. 470–520) were burned, a percentage that increased to 95 percent in the subsequent Broken Flute phase (A.D. 600–700). Although the percentage dropped notably (40 percent) in the later View Point phase (A.D. 700–800), the figure is still high when compared to other areas. Stockades are not reported for the Cove–Redrock Basketmaker sites on Kiva Mesa nor for earlier sites, though this is not unexpected given the rock shelter location of many sites known from earlier phases.

The picture is somewhat more confusing in the southern end of the Chuska Valley, where Damp and Kotyk note that 80 percent (12 of 15) of the pit structures in the Mexican Springs area were burned, and many of these were within post enclosures. In the adjoining but lower elevation Tohatchi Flats, Kearns and his colleagues record smaller percentages (28.6 percent) of burned pit houses in the early and middle Basketmaker III periods, but almost 50 percent of the late Basketmaker III houses. Although the sample of late houses (six structures) is too small to warrant much confidence in this apparent trend, it does correlate with the contemporary data from the Mexican Springs area. Kearns et al. also report two burned "great" pit structures in Tohatchi Flats. However, as in the Cove–Redrock Valley area, there was no evidence for stockades at Tohatchi Flats sites, and Kearns and his colleagues (this volume) report that sufficiently large zones around habitation structures were stripped to expose stockade post holes.

If you cross the Chuska Range, however, things change. Altschul and Huber reference neither burned structures nor post enclosures at Lukachukai, a circumstance seemingly paralleled on the somewhat more distant Rainbow Plateau, where Geib and Spurr describe numerous structures. Finally, Gilpin and Benallie do not cite burning or stockades in their larger survey of Basketmaker great kiva literature.

Period of occupation may explain some of the variability. Chenault and Motsinger draw attention to the strong correlation in the Mesa Verde area of burned structures and mid to late seventh-century A.D. dates for these buildings, observing that this correlation is even greater than that between burning and stockaded sites inasmuch as some burned sites were not located within post enclosures. This situation is mirrored in the Cove–Redrock area, where 95 percent of the Broken Flute phase (A.D. 600–700) houses were burned, although an equally high percentage (89 percent) of earlier Obelisk phase (A.D. 470–520) pit structures were destroyed by fire. Less than half of the eighth-century houses were burned. Structure burning in the Mexican Springs area of the lower Chuska Valley occurred primarily "around

A.D. 700," according to Damp and Kotyk. Coincidentally, the percentage of burned structures in the Tohatchi Flats essentially doubles during late Basketmaker III at a time when much of this area was abandoned, and, according to Kearns, McVickar, and L. Reed, local populations relocated to higher elevations on the valley margins—including the Mexican Springs area. Although Altschul and Huber provide no evidence for site loss through burning around Lukachukai, they do report a significant decline in valley habitation sites dating from approximately A.D. 670 into the early 700s. Given the situation in the Chuska Valley, it would be interesting to determine if burned pit structures dating from the late seventh and early eighth centuries were positioned at higher elevations in the Lukachukai area. On the other hand, given the apparent lack of conflict (if conflict can be measured in terms of burned pit structures) on the Rainbow Plateau, confrontation may have been a more "Eastern" than "Western" phenomenon.

Though stockaded hamlets and burned pit structures suggest conflict, only Chenault and Motsinger have no qualms in subscribing to this premise. Their evaluation of three possible reasons for burned pit structures—accidental burning, ritual immolation, and destruction through conflict—convinced them that only the latter explanation could be confirmed by their data. They comment that the total destruction of all architectural features at the Rabbit Site "seems to be purposeful destruction of an entire site with the apparent intention of making the site uninhabitable and destroying all stored resources." P. Reed and Wilcox, in contrast, are hesitant to attribute building destruction to violence. They note that while they do not believe accidental fires account for all burned structures, and evidence for ritual burning is not apparent, only a few structures have good evidence of burning related to conflict. Toll and Wilson likewise observe that all burned structures in the La Plata Valley were destroyed "shortly after use," but they do not believe that the structures had "been catastrophically abandoned," presumably implying that the burning did not represent a hostile act. Although Damp and Kotyk acknowledge the "abrupt" abandonment and burning of most pit structures in the Mexican Springs area, they also are reluctant to relate the cause to conflict, instead identifying the post enclosures around residential areas as "fences" incapable of providing "any substantial defense based on the sizes of the posts found." Kearns (personal communication, 1998) also questions a "direct correlation between burned pit structures and conflict," and observes that "in Tohatchi Flats, at least, there is no other evidence for raiding or hostilities that would support an argument for conflict."

I find it noteworthy that given the evidence, the tack taken by most of this volume's authors with respect to

conflict during Basketmaker III contradicts the recent revival of interest in warfare and intervillage raiding as primary contributors to culture change among the early Anasazi (e.g., Haas and Creamer 1993; LeBlanc 1999; Lekson 1999; Turner and Turner 1999; Wilcox and Haas 1994). Most of these authors, and particularly LeBlanc, see the Basketmaker III period as a time of rather widespread and intense conflict. Lekson (1999) has argued that the traditional "old, idyllic myths" of the ancient Southwest need rewriting so that "its archaeology, at last, can join the real world." The collective perspective conveyed by these chapters appears to me not to be either "old" or "idyllic" but rather reasoned appraisals of empirical data. No one would deny that there is evidence for conflict during Basketmaker III or any period in the prehistoric Southwest, and that conflict was seemingly more intense at certain periods in diverse locales. But we should be cautious about rewriting Southwestern prehistory on the basis of a single, narrowly defined driving force. I do not believe that the multiple interpretations for the archaeological record presented in these chapters reflect a desire to remain comfortably traditional, but rather an obligation to exercise the methodological and theoretical options of our discipline.

It is apparent, for example, that there is an environmental aspect to the temporal occurrence of fenced hamlets and burned pit structures. Climatic data from the Chuska Valley make it clear that the seventh century A.D. was a poor time to be a simple horticulturist in this area. Though moisture levels apparently were not as low in the Mesa Verde region, climatic reconstructions show that relatively normal conditions were punctuated by short intervals of decreased moisture, and there was a relatively severe drought at approximately A.D. 700. Settlement shifts to higher elevations in the La Plata Valley and in the lower Chuska Valley have been interpreted as a response to these conditions. If arable land and other resources were limited at higher elevations, the removal of human competition for those resources may have become a viable survival alternative. The archaeological record may demonstrate the response and the results. Interestingly, the presence of large quantities of portable material culture (e.g., 73 vessels in one pit house at the Dead Dog Site in Mesa Verde) as well as foodstuffs (as reported by Morris [1980] for the Prayer Rock District) in burned houses does not suggest that booty was necessarily the object of house burning, if such burning does represent hostile action taken against residents of these structures.

The limited evidence to date for armed conflict resulting in human death (but see Turner and Turner 1999 for an alternative view) and the destruction of resources, including foodstuffs, tends to reinforce the premise that the intention was to drive off residents, presumably permanently. This is underscored by the fact that all structures at most of the Mesa Verde sites, including the stockades, were burned. If this was happening, the scale of intended "resident removal" is not clear, though the frequency of stockaded settlements during this period suggests that the threat of attack may have been area-wide within certain regions. The very pattern of settlement in many areas—dispersed hamlets—may have invited hostile action if resistance, in terms of numbers of defenders, was minimal. Moreover, site size suggests extended families rather than larger social units capable of mounting a significant defensive force. Most stockaded hamlets in the Mesa Verde area include only one or two pit structures with associated surface and pit storage rooms, ramadas, and refuse zones. Rohn (1975) reported four pit structures from a stockaded Basketmaker site near Yellowjacket in the Mesa Verde region, but it is not clear that they were all contemporaneous. Mapped space enclosed by stockades in the Mesa Verde area was rather consistent at approximately 1500 m².

What has not been determined is whether larger Basketmaker III "villages" such as Shabik'eshchee in Chaco Canyon and the unexcavated Tohatchi Basketmaker Village (LA 3098) in the southern Chuska Valley were also stockaded. Both of these sites were elevated topographically, though Shabik'eshchee was more vulnerable to attack than Tohatchi Village, which was on an isolated and steep-sided butte, creating, according to Kearns and his colleagues, "a defensive precaution." But Kearns does not believe that Tohatchi Village was stockaded. If Morris (1980:148) is correct that the burning of most structures in Broken Flute Cave may have represented a visit "by raiders who captured or drove off the local inhabitants," objectives of attacking parties may have included communities larger than small hamlets. To our knowledge, the Broken Flute Cave community was not fortified other than having a relatively steep access in the front portion of the rock shelter.

Architectural manifestations reflective of a defensive posture may characterize slightly later structures in analogous social and environmental situations. For example, Wilshusen and Ortman (1999) identify an architecturally distinctive mid ninth-century village type in the Dolores River valley that may have been designed to conceal and protect accumulated agricultural surplus. These horseshoe-shaped room blocks were bounded on the southern end by walls "potentially restricting entry into the plaza space" (Wilshusen and Ortman 1999:383). The Dolores plan characterized early Pueblo Bonito and probably other ninth-century Chacoan great houses, although they were built on a more massive and multistory scale. The need to protect resources and human life could have produced both stockaded Basketmaker settlements and Pueblo I enclosed masonry compounds. In essence, room blocks and walls replace stockades, but public space is still defined, and residents and resources are protected. The difference, of course, as far as we know, was the lack of repeated conflict in the Dolores River valley and in Chaco Canyon.

The presence of Basketmaker great kivas in relatively large and complex village settings stands in contrast to the picture of stockaded and often destroyed hamlets. However, the relationship of great kiva presence/absence and periods of possible conflict is not clear. Our ability to support such correlations is hampered by the lack of a more precise taxonomy for large communal buildings dating to the Basketmaker III period. Proceeding from Smith (1952) and Burton (1993), one might ask, "When is a Basketmaker Great Kiva?" Unfortunately, the answer may not be quick in coming. Although Gilpin and Benallie's chapter on great kivas is augmented with additional data on these structures from several of the study areas, 11 of the 15 structures referenced in this book have not been excavated or even tested, making identification on the basis of surface evidence rather problematic.

This situation is well illustrated in the southern Chuska Valley, where three "great pit structures" were excavated. Though Kearns and his colleagues conclude that two "great pit structures" in the Tohatchi Flats community are "analogous to contemporary structures in Chaco Canyon and the Prayer Rock District," they, in fact, are morphologically more like "protokivas" identified in the greater Mesa Verde area (e.g., Site 13 at Alkali Ridge; Brew 1946). Kearns (personal communication, 1998) agrees, but notes a number of structural differences and points out that the Site 13 structures postdate Tohatchi Flats but "may represent a later use of a similar architectural pattern." Damp and Kotyk also note this similarity in their discussion of LA 61955-S1, a "great pit structure" in the Mexican Springs area. The same process of aggregation and use of public architecture late in the Basketmaker sequence (and extending into early Pueblo I) may have been underway in large villages in the northern Chuska Valley. P. Reed and Wilcox identify not only three great kivas but also two plazas as public architecture in the Kiva Mesa community in the Cove–Redrock Valley zone, a site occupied at a time of seemingly decreased conflict. Yet the site lies on an elevated mesa in what can only be described as a defensible location. The picture is less clear for other areas; confirmed Basketmaker great kivas are rare in the La Plata Valley and Mesa Verde region, but large protokivas are known from a number of sites in the northern San Juan Basin.

It is not certain that these structures were in use only during periods of greater stability. For example, the two great pit structures in the Tohatchi Flats community were the only buildings that had burned, whereas the Mexican Springs great pit structure was not burned, had been remodeled at least twice, and was assumed to have been in use for at least 50 years. Kearns and his colleagues (this volume) also believe that Tohatchi Village was intentionally situated in a defensive location, suggesting it was "constructed during a period of stress or conflict." Had the great kiva at Broken Flute Cave in the northern Chuska Valley been in use during the Broken Flute phase, it would have been contemporaneous with living structures, almost 95 percent of which were destroyed by fire; however, this particular great kiva was not burned, possibly reinforcing P. Reed and Wilcox's contention that it was "unfinished." If the intent of burning structures was to permanently drive off local residents, one would assume that communal structures would have been prime targets for destruction.

BASKETMAKER III AS A "TRANSITIONAL" PERIOD

The intentional shift in nomenclature from Basketmaker to Pueblo in the Pecos Classification underscored Kidder's and others' belief that major cultural changes marked this transitional period in Southwestern prehistory. There is some consensus among the authors in this volume that the period was one of change, but the overriding conclusions that can be drawn from these chapters are that the transitional process was initiated earlier in the Basketmaker II period, changes were more gradual, and they extended over a longer period of time. Toll and Wilson, for example, see considerable utility in a long and less strictly divided "Basketmaker" period in the La Plata Valley (see also P. Reed and Wilcox, this volume). In their scheme, the occupational sequence begins in late Basketmaker II (Transitional Basketmaker), extends through the more traditional Basketmaker period (Classic Basketmaker), and concludes in early Pueblo I. Geib and Spurr document an even longer occupation on the Rainbow Plateau, where good chronological controls confirm not only continuous Basketmaker development from approximately 400 B.C. to A.D. 700, but also the presence of Basketmaker II villages with maize agriculture and ceramic production. Based on their review of this development, Geib and Spurr make the cogent argument that "it would probably behoove us to avoid stage-based analyses to the extent possible and try to proceed by treating each aspect of culture initially as a separate variable plotted against the dimensions of time and space."

Although Geib and Spurr state that there is good evidence from several regions for the smooth transition from Basketmaker II to Basketmaker III, the chapters in this volume make it apparent that a pattern of relatively stable, long-term development was not consistent throughout the northern Southwest. The lengthy sequence on the Rainbow Plateau, for example, contrasts markedly with the southern Chuska Valley, where Kearns

and colleagues document an occupational hiatus from A.D. 150 to 500. They believe that the area was colonized by Basketmakers from other areas, a situation similar to that reported by Chenault and Motsinger for portions of the Mesa Verde area. Kearns and his coauthors also note an absence of securely dated transitional Basketmaker III–Pueblo I sites in Tohatchi Flats, but there are sites of this period in the general area. P. Reed and Wilcox, by contrast, see in situ development from the Basketmaker II populations in the area as the prime source of the Basketmaker III "boom" in Cove–Redrock Valley.

REGIONAL VARIABILITY AND MULTIETHNIC COMMUNITIES

Augmenting and clarifying Basketmaker III regional variability was a goal of this book, and several authors dealt specifically with the problem, most often through analysis of pit house architecture. Several referenced an unpublished paper by Steven Shelley (1990) in which he defined several regional pit house styles and then evaluated the potential of using these styles to distinguish between regional or subregional populations. His paper served to test Vivian's (1990) premise of regional variants in the greater Chacoan area. By examining construction styles and variation in interior divisions of pit structures, Shelley concluded that only one of Vivian's four variants, the La Plata, had a significant degree of internal coherence. However, he also defined a new Western variant, the Lukachukai (which was not within Vivian's area of analysis), that conformed to expected patterning. Essentially, Shelley distinguished between an Eastern Mesa Verde style (La Plata) and a Western Kayenta style (Lukachukai).

What made Shelley's analysis intriguing was the association of pit house styles with ethnicity—a premise explored by several of this book's authors. Whereas Chenault and Motsinger noted the remarkable consistency in Basketmaker III architecture throughout the Mesa Verde region, perhaps reflecting a relatively homogenous population, P. Reed and Wilcox found no regional architectural pattern in the Cove–Redrock area and interpreted the presence or blending of two or more pit structure styles as possibly representing multiethnic communities or the results of intermarriage between ethnically distinct groups. A parallel situation occurred in the southern Chuska Valley, where Kearns and his colleagues were unsuccessful in their attempt to use Shelley's pit house styles and proposed that architectural diversity could be related to ethnic, regional, or cultural differences, or to symbolic expression.

Although ceramics are often less persuasive than architectural referents for arguing the case for regional variants, L. Reed, Wilson, and Hays-Gilpin note that pottery becomes an increasingly sound source for distinguishing regional styles through time. They do not go so far, however, as to link defined styles with ethnically defined groups, and they cite the problems caused by the long history of associating brown wares on the Colorado Plateau with "ethnically" Mogollon people—a problem discussed much earlier by Tainter and Gillio (1980). Robins and Hays-Gilpin evaluate yet another potential cause for diversity in material culture in their fascinating analysis of gender-related variability as expressed in rock art, ceramics, and basketry. Most importantly, they demonstrate that styles change as gender roles are altered with increasing sedentism.

It is important to note that Damp and Kotyk, in their perceptive analysis of Basketmaker III settlement patterns, argue that while there was more architectural variability in Basketmaker III than has been proposed in the past, variability in material culture might well represent social inequality based on differential access to resources and other sources of power rather than ethnic expressions of style. These different approaches to interpreting the Basketmaker data are, in a sense, a microcosmic expression of a recent, more seriously considered debate over the merits of citing ranking or stratifying as a cause of perceived variability in certain aspects of the archaeological record, or of seeing this variability as a reflection of ethnic differences. Vivian's (1990) Chacoan hypothesis is considered by some to have pushed the ethnic premise to an extreme, but there is increasing acknowledgment of the potential for closely spaced ethnic groups in the prehistoric Southwest (e.g., Saitta 1997). Wilshusen and Ortman (1999:383), for example, argue that "the ninth century Dolores River Valley was an ethnic landscape populated by communities from at least two distinct cultural backgrounds;" communities that were separated only by the Dolores River. If we are to better understand the dynamics of late Basketmaker III and early Pueblo I, we must acknowledge the presence of ethnically diverse groups and then design mechanisms for identifying those populations and the means they employed for coexisting (e.g., Blanton et al. 1996).

IMPLICATIONS FOR INTERPRETING PUEBLOAN PREHISTORY

Given the new data in these chapters, are we in a better position to measure the magnitude of social processes that were evolving during this period and their relevance for later Puebloan systems? Though the data do confirm, in varying degrees, increased agricultural intensification, larger and more permanently established settlements, and the development of stylistically defined white and gray wares, perhaps what is most significant is the evidence for the accelerated pace of such developments at earlier time periods. Two brief examples serve to illustrate this point.

Relatively recent work by Wills and Windes (1989) and others had questioned the long-held assumption that Basketmaker III settlements had permanent populations. Information from the Rainbow Plateau now makes it clear that the processes leading to greater sedentism were underway in the Basketmaker II period, and data from the Chuska Valley (including botanical remains, large storage facilities, settlement placement near good farming land, and the presence of large communal pit structures) all support, fairly unequivocally, year-round occupation of habitation sites. Long-term use of the Chuska Valley sites does not necessarily obviate arguments for seasonal use of large Basketmaker III sites elsewhere. The potentially greater productivity of the Chuska Valley with a relatively assured water source may have tipped the balance toward ensured sedentism at an earlier time. The archaeological record increasingly manifests a process of variable sedentism during the Basketmaker period that tends to support Stuart and Gauthier's (1981) premise of an early Basketmaker "power drive" and Upham's (1984) concept of adaptive diversity.

Increasing sedentism provides a basis for greater social complexity. The chapter by Damp and Kotyk illustrates the need to acknowledge that variability in Basketmaker material culture may represent aspects of social differentiation. They argue that social inequality evolved early in the Basketmaker III period and is reflected in disparity in pit structure size, the placement of some sites within fenced enclosures, distance to communal pit structures, and the accumulation of large quantities of material goods in larger pit structures. Damp and Kotyk contend that competition for space, resources, power, and prestige led to aggregation; the control of regional ceramic, lithic, and shell exchange; and ultimately the development of ranked or even socially stratified populations. However, others working in the same area and using much the same database (e.g., P. Reed and Wilcox) detect no apparent differences in status or rank among contemporaneous house clusters, while others (Kearns et al.) interpret differences as no more than what would "be expected by age-grading or achieved status."

Finally, the relatively solid evidence for greater regional variability among the Basketmaker III contrasts with the blurring of lines drawn between larger Southwestern "culture areas." The excellent analysis of brown wares reinforces the concept of early Basketmaker participation in pan-Southwestern cultural developmental processes marked by a suite of similar traits. We also may need to change our perception of delayed south to north movement of those traits. The evidence for Basketmaker decorated brown wares predating similar Mogollon wares is a case in point. The broad Basketmaker horizon culminating in Basketmaker III serves as a useful comparative vehicle for charting contemporaneous parallel lines of development in the greater Southwest.

References

Abel, L. J.

1955 *Pottery Types of the Southwest: Wares 5A, 10A, 10B, 12A, San Juan Red Ware, Mesa Verde Gray and White Ware, San Juan White Ware.* Ceramic Series no. 3. Flagstaff: Museum of Northern Arizona.

Adams, E. C.

1991 *The Origin and Development of the Pueblo Katsina Cult.* Tucson: University of Arizona Press.

Adams, J. L.

1993 Technological Development of Manos and Metates on the Hopi Mesas. *Kiva* 58:259–276.

Adler, M. A

1990 Communities of Soil and Stone: An Archaeological Investigation of Population Aggregation among the Mesa Verde Region Anasazi, A.D. 900–1300. Ph.D. diss., Department of Anthropology, University of Michigan, Ann Arbor.

Adler, M. A. (ed.)

1996 *The Prehistoric Pueblo World, A.D. 1150–1350.* Tucson: University of Arizona Press.

Agenbroad, L. D., J. I. Mead, E. D. Mead, and D. Elder

1989 Archaeology, Alluvium, and Cave Stratigraphy: The Record from Bechan Cave, Utah. *Kiva* 54:335–349.

Ahlstrom, R. V. N.

1985 The Interpretation of Archaeological Tree-Ring Dates. Ph.D. diss., Department of Anthropology, University of Arizona, Tucson.

Ahlstrom, R. V. N., M. L. Chenault, and K. P. Gilmore

1996 Settlement and Land-Use Patterns. In *Settlement Patterns in the Mancos and La Plata River Basins: A Class 2 Cultural Resource Survey for the Animas-La Plata Project,* edited by M. L. Chenault, pp. 181–281. Durango, Colo.: SWCA, Inc.

Aikens, C. M.

1995 First in the World: The Jomon Pottery of Early Japan. In *The Emergence of Pottery: Technology and Innovation in Ancient Societies,* edited by W. K. Barnett and J. W. Hoopes, pp. 11–21. Washington, D.C.: Smithsonian Institution Press.

Akins, N. J.

1984 Temporal Variation in Faunal Assemblages from Chaco Canyon. In *Recent Research on Chaco Prehistory,* edited by W. J. Judge and J. D. Schelberg, pp. 225–240. Reports of the Chaco Center no. 8. Albuquerque: Division of Cultural Research, National Park Service.

1996 Excavations at A Room with a Wu, LA 37605. Ms. in preparation. Santa Fe: Office of Archaeological Studies, Museum of New Mexico.

Allen, J. W.

1972 The Mexican Wash Project: Archaeological Excavations along U.S. Highway 666 near Buffalo Springs, New Mexico. Laboratory of Anthropology Note no. 55. Santa Fe: Museum of New Mexico.

Altschul, J. H.

1991 Social Complexity and Residential Stability During the Basketmaker III Period. Paper presented at the 56th annual meeting of the Society for American Archaeology, New Orleans, Louisiana.

Altschul, J. H., and S. D. Shelley

1988 *Research Design: Data Recovery along Route N-13, Navajo Indian Reservation.* Technical Series no. 16, part 1. Tucson: Statistical Research, Inc.

1995 *Data Recovery along N13, Navajo Indian Reservation.* Technical Report no. 95-7. Tucson: Statistical Research, Inc.

Altschul, J. H., S. D. Shelley, and E. K. Huber (eds.)

2000 *Cultural Dynamics in the Lukachukai Valley: The N-13 Project.* Technical Series no. 16, part 2. Tucson: Statistical Research, Inc.

Ambler, J. R.

1996 Dust Devil Cave and Archaic Complexes of the Glen Canyon Area. In *Glen Canyon Revisited,* edited by P. R. Geib, pp. 40–52. Anthropological Papers no. 119. Salt Lake City: University of Utah Press.

Ambler, J. R., H. C. Fairley, M. A. Davenport, and P. R. Geib

1985 Survey. In *Archaeological Investigations near Rainbow City Navajo Mountain, Utah,* edited by P. R. Geib, J. R. Ambler, and M. M. Callahan, pp. 241–258. Archaeological Report no. 576. Flagstaff: Northern Arizona University.

Ambler, J. R., and A. P. Olson

1977 *Salvage Archaeology in the Cow Springs Area.* Technical Series no. 15. Flagstaff: Museum of Northern Arizona.

Amsden, C. A.

1949 *Prehistoric Southwesterners from Basketmaker to Pueblo.* Los Angeles: Southwest Museum.

Anderson, J. K.

1987 *The Archaeological Survey of Several Power Line Systems in the Area of Low Mountain, Arizona (Phases III and IV).* NNCRMP Report 86-287. Window Rock, Ariz.: Navajo Nation Cultural Resource Management Program.

Arnold, D. E.

1985 *Ceramic Theory and Cultural Process.* Cambridge: Cambridge University Press.

Atkins, V. M. (ed.)

1993 *Anasazi Basketmaker: Papers from the 1990 Wetherill-Grand Gulch Symposium.* Cultural Resource Series no. 24. Salt Lake City: Bureau of Land Management.

Baldwin, G. C.

1939 A Basket Maker III Sandal Tablet. *Southwestern Lore* 5:48–52.

Bannister, B., J. S. Dean, and W. J. Robinson

1968 *Tree-Ring Dates from Arizona C-D: Eastern Grand Canyon-Tsegi Canyon-Kayenta Area.* Tucson: Laboratory of Tree-ring Research, University of Arizona.

Bannister, B., J. W. Hannah, and W. J. Robinson
1966   *Tree-Ring Dates from Arizona K, Puerco-Wide Ruin-Ganado Area.* Tucson: Laboratory of Tree-ring Research, University of Arizona.

Barnett, W. K.
1995   Putting the Pot before the Horse: Earliest Ceramics and the Neolithic Transition in the Western Mediterranean. In *The Emergence of Pottery: Technology and Innovation in Ancient Societies,* edited by W. K. Barnett and J. W. Hoopes, pp. 79–88. Washington, D.C.: Smithsonian Institution Press.

Barnett, W. K., and J. W. Hoopes
1995   *The Emergence of Pottery: Technology and Innovation in Ancient Societies.* Washington, D.C.: Smithsonian Institution Press.

Bartlett, K.
1933   *Pueblo Milling Stones of the Flagstaff Region and Their Relation to Others in the Southwest: A Study of Progress Efficiency.* Museum of Northern Arizona Bulletin no. 3. Flagstaff: Museum of Northern Arizona.

Bass, P.
1994   A Gendered Search through Some West Texas Rock Art. In *New Light on Old Art: Recent Advances in Hunter-Gatherer Rock Art Research,* edited by D. S. Whitley and L. L. Loendorf, pp. 67–74. Los Angeles: Institute of Archaeology, University of California.

Benallie, L., Jr.
1993   *An Archaeological Survey of the Klagetoh to Kintiel Water Line System: 91 Scattered Homesites with Septic Tanks and Drainfield Systems (IHS NA-90-630).* NNAD Report no. 89-343. Window Rock, Ariz.: Navajo Nation Archaeology Department.

Bender, B.
1985   Emergent Tribal Formations in the American Midcontinent. *American Antiquity* 50:52–62.

Benham, B. L.
1966   *Excavation of La Plata Phase Pit Houses near Tohatchi, New Mexico.* Laboratory of Anthropology Note no. 38. Santa Fe: Museum of New Mexico.

Benz, B. F.
1981   Five Modern Races of Maize from Northeastern Mexico: Archaeological Implications. Master's thesis, Department of Anthropology, University of Colorado, Boulder.

Berg, C. M., and D. M. Greenwald
1997a   Flaked Stone Analysis. In Excavations at the Rabbit Site (5MT9168), a Basketmaker III Hamlet, edited by M. L. Chenault. In preparation. Durango, Colo.: SWCA, Inc.

1997b   Flaked Stone Analysis. In Excavations at the Late Basketmaker III Hamlet of Dead Dog (5MT11,861), edited by M. L. Chenault. In preparation. Durango, Colo.: SWCA, Inc.

Berry, C. F., and M. S. Berry
1986   Chronological and Conceptual Models of the Southwestern Archaic. In *Anthropology of the Desert West: Essays in Honor of Jesse D. Jennings,* edited by C. J. Condie and D. D. Fowler, pp. 252–327. Anthropological Papers no. 110. Salt Lake City: University of Utah Press.

Berry, M. S.
1982   *Time, Space, and Transition in Anasazi Prehistory.* Salt Lake City: University of Utah Press.

Betancourt, J. L., and O. K. Davis
1984   Packrat Middens from Canyon de Chelly, Northeastern Arizona: Paleoecological and Archaeological Implications. *Quaternary Research* 21:56–64.

Betancourt, J. L., P. S. Martin, and T. R. Van Devender
1983   Fossil Packrat Middens from Chaco Canyon, New Mexico: Cultural and Ecological Significance. In *Chaco Canyon Country, A Field Guide to the Geomorphology, Quaternary Geology, Paleoecology, and Environmental Geology of Northwestern New Mexico,* edited by S. G. Wells, D. W. Love, and T. W. Gardner, pp. 207–217. American Geomorphological Field Group, 1983 Field Trip Guidebook.

Betancourt, J. L., and T. R. Van Devender
1981   Holocene Vegetation in Chaco Canyon, New Mexico. *Science* 214:656–658.

Binford, L. R.
1980   Willow Smoke and Dog Tails: Hunter-Gatherer Settlement Systems and Archaeological Site Formation. *American Antiquity* 45:4–20.

Birkedal, T.
1976   Basketmaker III Residence Units: A Study of Prehistoric Social Organization in the Mesa Verde Archaeological District. Ph.D. diss., Department of Anthropology, University of Colorado. Ann Arbor: University Microfilms.

1982   Basketmaker III Residence Units: A Study of Prehistoric Social Organization in the Northern San Juan Basin. Paper presented at the 47th annual meeting of the Society for American Archaeology, Minneapolis.

Blackburn, F. M., and V. Atkins
1993   Handwriting on the Wall: Applying Inscriptions to Reconstructing Historic Archaeological Expeditions. In *Anasazi Basketmaker: Papers from the 1990 Wetherill-Grand Gulch Symposium,* edited by V. M. Atkins, pp. 41–100. Cultural Resources Series no. 24. Salt Lake City: Bureau of Land Management.

Blackburn, F. M., and R. A. Williamson
1997   *Cowboys and Cave Dwellers: Basketmaker Archaeology in Utah's Grand Gulch.* Santa Fe: School of American Research Press.

Blackwood, E.
1984   Sexuality and Gender in Certain Native American Tribes: The Case of Cross-Gender Females. *The Journal of Women in Culture and Society* 10:27–42.

Blanton, R., G. Feinman, S. Kowalewski, and P. Peregrine
1996   A Dual-processual Theory for the Evolution of Mesoamerican Civilization. *Current Anthropology* 37:1–14.

Blinman, E.
1988   The Interpretation of Ceramic Variability: A Case Study from the Dolores Anasazi. Ph.D. diss., Department of Anthropology, Washington State University, Pullman.

Blinman, E., and C. D. Wilson
1994   Ceramic Perspectives on Northern Anasazi Exchange. In *The American Southwest and Mesoamerica: Systems of Prehistoric Exchange,* edited by J. E. Ericson and T. G. Baugh, pp. 65–94. New York: Plenum Press.

Blitz, J. H.
1988   Adoption of the Bow in Prehistoric North America. *North American Archaeologist* 9:123–145.

Bond, M., T. Sudar-Murphy, and F. P. Frampton
1977   *Highway Salvage Archaeology in the Vicinity of Chilchinbito, Arizona: Excavation and Interpretation of Seven Kayenta Anasazi Sites in Navajo and Apache Counties, Arizona.* Occasional Paper no. 4. Las Cruces: New Mexico State University Museum.

Bozarth, S.
2000   Fossil Pollen Analysis. In *Cultural Dynamics in the*

Lukachukai Valley: The N-13 Project, edited by J. H. Altschul, S. D. Shelley, and E. K. Huber. Technical Series no. 16. Tucson: Statistical Research, Inc.

Bradfield, M.
1971   *The Changing Pattern of Hopi Agriculture.* Occasional Paper no. 30. London: Royal Anthropological Institute.

Bradley, R. J.
1994   Summary and Interpretations. In A Study of Two Anasazi Communities in the San Juan Basin by R. J. Bradley and R. B. Sullivan, pp. 383–408 of *Across the Colorado Plateau: Anthropological Studies along the San Juan Basin and Transwestern Mainline Expansion Pipeline Routes,* vol. IX, J. C. Winter, general editor. Albuquerque: Office of Contract Archeology, University of New Mexico.

Braithwaite, M.
1982   Decoration as Ritual Symbol: A Theoretical Proposal and an Ethnographic Study in Southern Sudan. In *Symbolic and Structural Archaeology,* pp. 80–88, edited by I. Hodder. Cambridge: Cambridge University Press.

Brandt, C. B.
1999   Analysis of Plant Macro-Remains. In *Chuska Chronologies, Houses, and Hogans: Archaeological and Ethnographic Inquiry along N30-N31 Between Mexican Springs and Navajo, McKinley County, New Mexico,* vol. III, part 2, edited by J. E. Damp, pp. 441–492. Research Series no. 10. Zuni Pueblo, N.Mex.: Zuni Cultural Resource Enterprise.

Braun, D., and S. Plog
1982   Evolution of "Tribal" Social Networks: Theory and Prehistoric North American Evidence. *American Antiquity* 47:504–525.

Bray, A.
1982   Faunal Remains. In *Kayenta Anasazi Archaeology on Central Black Mesa, Northeastern Arizona: The Piñon Project,* edited and assembled by L. Linford, pp. 367–385. Navajo Nation Papers in Anthropology no. 10, Window Rock, Ariz.

Breternitz, D. A.
1966   *An Appraisal of Tree-ring Dated Pottery in the Southwest.* Anthropological Papers of the University of Arizona, no. 10. Tucson: University of Arizona Press.
1986   Notes on Early Basketmaker III Sites in Mancos Canyon, Colorado. *Kiva* 51:263–264.

Breternitz, C. D., and D. E. Doyel
1987   Methodological Issues for the Identification of Chacoan Community Structure: Lessons from the Bis sa'ani Community Study. *American Archaeology* 3:183–189.

Breternitz, C. D., D. E. Doyel, and M. P. Marshall (eds.)
1982   *Bis sa'ani: A Late Bonito Phase Community on Escavada Wash, Northwest New Mexico.* Navajo Nation Papers in Anthropology no. 14, Window Rock, Ariz.

Breternitz, D. A., C. K. Robinson, and G. T. Gross
1986   Archaeological Program: Final Synthetic Report. Denver: U.S. Department of the Interior, Bureau of Reclamation, Engineering and Research Center.

Breternitz, D. A., A. H. Rohn, Jr., and E. A. Morris
1974   *Prehistoric Ceramics of the Mesa Verde Region.* Ceramic Series no. 5. Flagstaff: Museum of Northern Arizona.

Brew, J. O.
1946   *Archaeology of Alkali Ridge, Southeastern Utah.* Papers of the Peabody Museum of American Archaeology and Ethnology, vol. XXI. Cambridge: Harvard University.

Brisbin, J. M.
1984   Excavations at Poco Tiempo Hamlet (Site 5MT2378), a Basketmaker III Habitation. *Dolores Archaeological Program Technical Report no. DAP—182.* Denver: U.S. Department of the Interior, Bureau of Reclamation, Engineering and Research Center.

Brisbin, J. M., and M. Varien
1986   Excavations at Tres Bobos Hamlet (Site 5MT4545), a Basketmaker III Habitation. *In Dolores Archaeological Program: Anasazi Communities at Dolores: Early Anasazi Sites in the Sagehen Flats Area,* compiled by A. E. Kane and G. T. Gross, pp. 119–174. Denver: U.S. Department of the Interior, Bureau of Reclamation, Engineering and Research Center.

Broilo, F. J., and W. C. Allan
1973   *An Archaeological Salvage Excavation of a Basket Maker III Site near Naschitti, New Mexico.* Laboratory of Anthropology Note no. 82. Santa Fe: Museum of New Mexico.

Brown, D. E., and C. H. Lowe
1980   Biotic Communities of the Southwest. Map no. GTR-78. Fort Collins, Colo.: Rocky Mountain Forest and Range Experiment Station, U.S. Department of Agriculture Forest Service.

Brown, G. M. (ed.)
1991   *Archaeological Data Recovery at San Juan Coal Company's La Plata Mine, San Juan County, New Mexico.* Technical Report no. 355. Albuquerque: Mariah Associates, Inc.

Brown, J. A.
1989   The Beginnings of Pottery as an Economic Process. In *What's New? A Closer Look at the Process of Innovation,* edited by S. E. van der Leeuw and R. Torrence, pp. 203–224. London: Unwin Hyman.

Brown, J. K.
1963   A Cross-cultural Study of Female Initiation Rites. *American Anthropologist* 65:837–853.

Brown, M. E., and K. L. Brown
1993   Subsistence and Other Cultural Behaviors as Reflected by the Vertebrate Faunal Remains. In *Subsistence and Environment,* by J. W. Gish, J. E. Hammet, M. E. Brown, P. McBride, J. C. Winter, K. L. Brown, J. J. Ponczynski, and J. L. DeLanois, pp. 327–404. Across the Colorado Plateau: Anthropological Studies for the Transwestern Pipeline Expansion Project, vol. XV. UNM Project 185-461B. Albuquerque: Office of Contract Archeology and Maxwell Museum of Anthropology, University of New Mexico.

Bullard, W. R.
1962   The Cerro Colorado Site and Pithouse Architecture in the Southwestern United States Prior to A.D. 900. Papers of the Peabody Museum of Archaeology and Ethnology, vol. 44, no. 2. Cambridge: Harvard University.

Bullard, W. R., and F. E. Cassidy
1956   LA 2507. In *Pipeline Archaeology: Reports of Salvage Operations in the Southwest on the El Paso Natural Gas Company Projects, 1950–1953,* edited by F. Wendorf, N. Fox, and O. L. Lewis, pp. 56–60. Flagstaff: Museum of Northern Arizona.

Bullock, P. Y.
1991   A Reappraisal of Anasazi Cannibalism. *Kiva* 57:5–16.

Burns, B. T.
1983   Simulated Anasazi Storage Behavior Using Crop Yields Reconstructed from Tree Rings A.D. 652–1968. Ph.D.

diss., Department of Anthropology, University of Arizona, Tucson.

Burton, J. F.

1991 *The Archeology of Sivu'ovi: The Archaic to Basketmaker Transition at Petrified Forest National Park.* Publications in Anthropology no. 55. Tucson: Western Archeological Conservation Center, National Park Service.

Burton, J. F.

1993 *When is a Great Kiva? Excavations at McCreery Pueblo, Petrified Forest National Park, Arizona.* Publications in Anthropology no. 63. Tucson: Western Archeological and Conservation Center, National Park Service.

Callahan, E.

1979 The Basics of Biface Knapping in the Eastern Fluted Point Tradition: A Manual for Flintknappers and Lithic Analysts. *Archaeology of Eastern North America* 7:1–180.

Cameron, C. M.

1984 A Regional View of Chipped Stone Raw Material Use in Chaco Canyon. In *Recent Research on Chaco Prehistory,* edited by W. J. Judge and J. D. Schelberg, pp. 137–152. Reports of the Chaco Center no. 8. Albuquerque: Division of Cultural Research, National Park Service.

1987 Chipped Stone Tools and Cores: An Overview of the 1982–1983 Field Seasons. In *Prehistoric Stone Technology on Northern Black Mesa, Arizona,* edited by W. J. Parry and A. L. Christensen, pp. 95–142. Occasional Papers no. 12. Carbondale: Center for Archaeological Investigations, Southern Illinois University.

1990a The Effect of Varying Estimates of Pit Structure Use-Life on Prehistoric Population Estimates in the American Southwest. *Kiva* 55:155–166.

1990b Pit Structure Abandonment in the Four Corners Region of the American Southwest: Late Basketmaker III and Pueblo I Periods. *Journal of Field Archaeology* 12:27–37.

Cameron, C. M., and S. A. Tomka (eds.)

1993 *Abandonment of Settlements and Regions: Ethnoarchaeological and Archaeological Approaches.* Cambridge: Cambridge University Press.

Canby, T. Y.

1982 The Anasazi. *National Geographic* 162:554–592.

Carlson, R. L.

1963 *Basketmaker III Sites Near Durango, Colorado.* University of Colorado Studies, Series in Anthropology no. 8. Boulder: University of Colorado Press.

Casselberry, S. E.

1974 Further Refinement of Formulae for Determining Population from Floor Area. *World Archaeology* 6:117–122.

Cassells, E. S.

1983 *The Archaeology of Colorado.* Boulder, Colo.: Johnson Books.

Cassidy, F. E., and W. R. Bullard

1956 Unexcavated Sites on the New Mexico Survey. In *Pipeline Archaeology: Reports of Salvage Operations in the Southwest on the El Paso Natural Gas Company Projects, 1950–1953,* edited by F. Wendorf, N. Fox, and O. L. Lewis, pp. 6–15. Flagstaff: Museum of Northern Arizona.

Castleton, K. B.

1987 *Petroglyphs and Pictographs of Utah, Volume Two, the South, Central, West and Northwest.* Salt Lake City: Utah Museum of Natural History.

Chang, K. C.

1958 Study of the Neolithic Social Grouping: Examples from the New World. *American Anthropologist* 60:298–334.

Chenault, M. L. (ed.)

1996 *Settlement Patterns in the Mancos and La Plata River Basins: A Class 2 Cultural Resource Survey for the Animas-La Plata Project.* Durango, Colo.: SWCA, Inc.

1997a Excavations at the Rabbit Site (5MT9168), a Basketmaker III Hamlet. In preparation. Durango, Colo.: SWCA, Inc.

1997b Excavations at the Late Basketmaker III Hamlet of Dead Dog (5MT11,861). In preparation. Durango, Colo.: SWCA, Inc.

Chenault, M. L., and R. V. N. Ahlstrom

1996 Conclusions. In *Settlement Patterns in the Mancos and La Plata River Basins: A Class 2 Cultural Resource Survey for the Animas-La Plata Project,* edited by M. L. Chenault, pp. 297–303. Durango, Colo.: SWCA, Inc.

Chisholm, B., and R. G. Matson

1994 Carbon and Nitrogen Isotopic Evidence on Basketmaker II Diet at Cedar Mesa, Utah. *Kiva* 60:239–255.

Christenson, A. L.

1987 Archaeological Exploration and Research in the Kayenta Anasazi Region: A Synoptic History. In *10,000 Years on Black Mesa, Arizona: Prehistoric Culture Change on the Colorado Plateaus,* edited by S. Powell, F. E. Smiley, and G. J. Gumerman, pp. 2.1–2.134. Carbondale: Center for Archaeological Investigations, Southern Illinois University.

Claassen, C., and R. Joyce (eds.)

1997 *Women in Prehistory: North America and Mesoamerica.* Philadelphia: University of Pennsylvania Press.

Clark, J. E., and D. Gosser

1995 Reinventing Mesoamerica's First Pottery. In *The Emergence of Pottery: Technology and Innovation in Ancient Societies,* edited by W. K. Barnett and J. W. Hoopes, pp. 209–221. Washington, D.C.: Smithsonian Institution Press.

Clarke, D. L.

1974 A Method for the Estimation of Prehistoric Pueblo Populations. *The Kiva* 39:233–287.

Cohen, M. N.

1977 *The Food Crisis in Prehistory: Overpopulation and the Origins of Agriculture.* New Haven: Yale University Press.

Cole, S. J.

1989 Iconography and Symbolism in Basketmaker Rock Art. In *Rock Art of the Western Canyons,* edited by J. S. Day, P. D. Friedman, and M. J. Tate, pp. 59–85. Colorado Archaeological Society Memoir no. 3. Denver: Museum of Natural History.

1990 *Legacy on Stone: Rock Art of the Colorado Plateau and Four Corners Region.* Boulder, Colo.: Johnson Books.

1993 Basketmaker Rock Art at the Green Mask Site, Southeastern Utah. In *Anasazi Basketmaker: Papers from the 1990 Wetherill-Grand Gulch Symposium,* edited by V. Atkins, pp. 192–220. Cultural Resources Series no. 24. Salt Lake City: Bureau of Land Management.

Colton, H. S.

1939 *Prehistoric Culture Units and their Relationships in Northern Arizona.* Museum of Northern Arizona Bulletin no. 17. Flagstaff: Northern Arizona Society of Science and Art.

1955 *Pottery Types of the Southwest: Wares 8A, 9A, 9B, Tusayan Gray and White Ware, Little Colorado Gray and White Ware.* Ceramic Series 3A. Flagstaff: Museum of Northern Arizona.

Colton, H. S., and L. L. Hargrave

1937   *Handbook of Northern Arizona Pottery Wares.* Museum of Northern Arizona Bulletin 11. Flagstaff: Northern Arizona Society of Science and Art.

Conkey, M. W.

1978   Style and Information in Cultural Evolution: Toward a Predictive Model for the Paleolithic. In *Social Archaeology,* edited by C. L. Redman and M. J. Berman, pp. 61–85. New York: Academic Press.

1991   Contexts of Action, Contexts for Power: Material Culture and Gender in the Magdalenian. *In Engendering Archaeology: Women and Prehistory,* edited by J. M. Gero and M. W. Conkey, pp. 57–92. Cambridge: Basil and Blackwell.

Cook, S. F.

1972   *Prehistoric Demography.* Addison-Wesley Module in Anthropology 16. Reading: Addison-Wesley Publishing Company.

Cooke, R., and A. J. Ranere

1992   The Origin of Wealth and Hierarchy in the Central Region of Panama (12,000–2,000), with Observations on Its Relevance to the History and Phylogeny of Chibchan-speaking Polities in Panama and Elsewhere. In *Wealth and Hierarchy in the Intermediate Area: A Symposium at Dumbarton Oaks,* October 10–11, 1987, edited by F. W. Lange, pp. 43–84. Washington D.C.: Dumbarton Oaks.

Cordell, L. S.

1982   The Pueblo Period in the San Juan Basin: An Overview and Some Research Problems. In *The San Juan Tomorrow: Planning for the Conservation of Cultural Resources in the San Juan Basin,* edited by F. Plog and W. Wait, pp. 59–83. Santa Fe: National Park Service, Southwest Region and School of American Research Press.

1984   *Prehistory of the Southwest.* New York: Academic Press.

1997   *Archaeology of the Southwest.* San Diego: Academic Press.

Cordell, L. S., and F. Plog

1979   Escaping the Confines of Normative Thought: A Reevaluation of Puebloan Prehistory. *American Antiquity* 44:405–429.

Cox, J. R.

1997   Letter Report Concerning Reassessment of N63 Archaeomagnetic Dates. Archaeomagnetic Dating Laboratory, Museum of New Mexico, Santa Fe. Ms. on file, Navajo Nation Archaeology Department, Farmington Roads Office, New Mexico.

Cox, J. R., and E. Blinman

1999   Results of Archaeomagnetic Sample Analysis. In *Supporting Studies: Nonceramic Artifacts, Subsistence and Environmental Studies, and Chronometric Studies,* compiled by T. M. Kearns and J. L. McVickar, pp. 19-1 to 19-28. Pipeline Archaeology 1990–1993: The El Paso Natural Gas North System Expansion Project, New Mexico and Arizona, vol. XII, T. M. Kearns, general editor. Report no. WCRM(F)074. Farmington, N.Mex.: Western Cultural Resource Management, Inc.

Crown, P., and W. H. Wills

1995   Economic Intensification and the Origins of Ceramic Containers in the Southwest. In *The Emergence of Pottery: Technology and Innovations in Ancient Societies,* edited by W. K. Barnett and J. W. Hoopes, pp. 241–256. Washington, D.C.: Smithsonian Institution Press.

Cummings, B.

1926[?]   Report: Summer Expeditions into the San Juan Valley, in Northern Arizona, by the Arizona State Museum. Ms. on file (MS 200, Box 3, Folder 39), Arizona Historical Society, Tucson. The date for this manuscript is uncertain. A date of 1923 is written across the top of the first page, but this date is too early—Cummings did not work at Juniper Cove in 1923. Gilpin (this volume) and Webster (1991a, 1991b) believe that 1926 is the likely date.

1953   *First Inhabitants of Arizona and the Southwest.* Tucson: Cummings Publication Council.

Cummings, L. S., and K. Puseman

1997a   Pollen Analysis. In Excavations at the Rabbit Site (5MT9168), a Basketmaker III Hamlet, edited by M. L. Chenault. In preparation. Durango, Colo.: SWCA, Inc.

1997b   Pollen Analysis. In Excavations at the Late Basketmaker III Hamlet of Dead Dog (5MT11,861), edited by M. L. Chenault. In preparation. Durango, Colo.: SWCA, Inc.

Cunnar, G.

1996a   LA 80934: Excavations at the Electric Raven Site. In *Excavation of the Gallup Station,* edited by C. W. Wheeler, pp. 4-1 to 4-148. Pipeline Archaeology 1990–1993: The El Paso Natural Gas North System Expansion Project, New Mexico and Arizona, vol. IV, draft report, T. M. Kearns, general editor. Report no. WCRM(F)074. Farmington, N.Mex.: Western Cultural Resource Management, Inc.

1996b   LA 80403: A Basketmaker III and Pueblo II Limited Activity Site. In *Excavation of the Gallup Station,* edited by C. W. Wheeler, pp. 3-1 to 3-31. Pipeline Archaeology 1990–1993: The El Paso Natural Gas North System Expansion Project, New Mexico and Arizona, vol. IV, draft report, T. M. Kearns, general editor. Report no. WCRM(F)074. Farmington, N.Mex.: Western Cultural Resource Management, Inc.

Cutler, H. C.

1968   Appendix 1: Plant Remains from Sites near Navajo Mountain. *In Survey and Excavation North and East of Navajo Mountain, Utah 1959–1962,* by A. J. Lindsay, Jr., J. R. Ambler, M. A. Stein, and P. M. Hobler, pp. 371–378. Museum of Northern Arizona Bulletin no. 45. Flagstaff: Northern Arizona Society of Science and Art.

Daifuku, H.

1961   *Jeddito 264: A Report on the Excavation of a Basketmaker III–Pueblo I Site in Northwestern Arizona with a Review of Some Current Theories in Southwestern Archaeology.* Reports of the Awatovi Expedition no. 7. Cambridge, Mass.: Peabody Museum.

Damp, J. E.

1999   *Chuska Chronologies, Houses, and Hogans: Archaeological and Ethnographic Inquiry along N30-N31 between Mexican Springs and Navajo, McKinley County, New Mexico.* Research Series no. 10. Zuni Pueblo, N.Mex.: Zuni Cultural Resource Enterprise.

Damp, J. E., and J. W. Kendrick

1998   Agricultural Production and Economically Autonomous Households on the Zuni Landscape. Paper presented at the 97th annual meeting of the American Anthropological Association, Philadelphia.

Davis, W. E.

1985   *Anasazi Subsistence and Settlement on White Mesa, San Juan County, Utah.* Lanham, Md.: University of Americas Press.

Dean, G.

1999   Pollen Evidence of Human Activities in the Southern Chuska Mountains from Basketmaker III through Historic Navajo: The N30-N31 Project, McKinley County, New Mexico. In *Chuska Chronologies, Houses, and Hogans: Archaeological and Ethnographic Inquiry along N30-N31 between Mexican Springs and Navajo, McKinley County, New Mexico*, vol. III, part 2, edited by J. E. Damp, pp. 493–601. Research Series no. 10. Zuni Pueblo, N.Mex.: Zuni Cultural Resource Enterprise.

Dean, J. S.

1975   *Tree-Ring Dates from Colorado West, Durango Area.* Laboratory of Tree-ring Research Series. Tucson: University of Arizona.

1988   Dendrochronology and Paleoenvironmental Reconstruction on the Colorado Plateaus. In *The Anasazi in a Changing Environment*, edited by G. J. Gumerman, pp. 119–167. Cambridge: Cambridge University Press.

1996   Anasazi Settlement Transformations in Northeastern Arizona, A.D. 1150–1350. In *The Prehistoric Pueblo World, A.D. 1150–1350*, edited by M. A. Alder, pp. 29–47. Tucson: University of Arizona Press.

Dean, J. S., and G. J. Gumerman

1989   Prehistoric Cooperation and Competition in the Western Anasazi Area. In *Dynamics of Southwest Prehistory*, edited by L. S. Cordell and G. J. Gumerman, 99–148. Washington, D.C.: Smithsonian Institution Press.

Dean, J. S., R. C. Euler, G. J. Gumerman, F. Plog, R. H. Hevly, and T. N. V. Karlstrom

1985   Human Behavior, Demography, and Paleoenvironment on the Colorado Plateau. *American Antiquity* 50:537–554.

Dean, J. S., and C. R. Van West

1999   Environment-Behavior Relationships in Southeastern Colorado. Ms. on file, Crow Canyon Archaeological Center, Cortez, Colo.

Deaver, W. L., and R. Ciolek-Torrello

1995   Early Formative Period Chronology for the Tucson Basin. *Kiva* 60:481–529.

Deegan, A. C.

1993   Anasazi Fibrous Sandal Terminology. *Kiva* 59:49–64.

1995   Anasazi Sandal Features: Their Research Value and Identification. *Kiva* 61:57–69.

1996   Anasazi Square Toe—Square Heel Twined Sandals: Construction and Cultural Attributes. *Kiva* 62:27–44.

Dittert, A. E., Jr.

1961   Third Southwestern Ceramic Seminar: Southwestern Brownwares. Notes on file, Museum of Northern Arizona.

Dittert, A. E., Jr., F. W. Eddy, and B. L. Dickey

1963   Evidence of Early Ceramic Phases in the Navajo Reservoir District. *El Palacio* 70:5–12.

Doebley, J., and V. Bohrer

1983   Maize Variability and Cultural Selection at Salmon Ruin, New Mexico. *The Kiva* 49:19–37.

Dohm, K. M.

1988   The Household in Transition: Spatial Organization of Early Anasazi Residential Units, Southeastern Utah. Ph.D. diss., Department of Anthropology, Washington State University, Pullman.

1994   The Search for Anasazi Village Origins: Basketmaker II Dwelling Aggregation on Cedar Mesa. *Kiva* 60:257–276.

Doyle, D. E.

1993   *Prehistoric Non-irrigated Agriculture in Arizona: A His-*

toric Context for Planning. Prepared for Arizona State Historic Preservation Office. Phoenix: Estrella Cultural Research Paper no. 3.

Drager, D. L.

1983   Projecting Archaeological Site Occurrences in the San Juan Basin, New Mexico. In *Remote Sensing in Cultural Resource Management: The San Juan Basin Project*, edited by D. L. Drager and T. R. Lyons, pp. 123–127. Albuquerque: Remote Sensing Division, National Park Service.

Drager, D. L., J. I. Ebert, and T. R. Lyons

1982   Remote Sensing and Nondestructive Archeology: Approaches to Cultural Resources Management. In *The San Juan Tomorrow: Planning for the Conservation of Cultural Resources in the San Juan Basin*, edited by F. Plog and W. Wait, pp. 219–244. National Park Service, Southwest Region and the School of American Research, Santa Fe.

Dykeman, D. D.

1995   *The Hogan Well Project: Archaeological Excavations at Early Mogollon and Late Anasazi Sites in the Puerco River Valley, Arizona.* Navajo Nation Papers in Anthropology no. 31. Window Rock, Ariz.: Navajo Nation Archaeology Department.

Dykeman, D. D., and K. Langenfeld

1987   *Prehistory and History of the La Plata Valley, New Mexico: An Overview.* Contributions to Anthropology Series no. 891. Farmington, N.Mex.: San Juan County Archaeological Research Center and Library, Salmon Ruins.

Eddy, F. W.

1961   *Excavation at Los Piños Phase Sites in the Navajo Reservoir District.* Museum of New Mexico Papers in Anthropology no. 4. Santa Fe: Museum of New Mexico Press.

1966   *Prehistory in the Navajo Reservoir District.* Museum of New Mexico Papers in Anthropology no. 15. Santa Fe: Museum of New Mexico Press.

1972   Culture Ecology and the Prehistory of the Navajo Reservoir District. *Southwestern Lore* 38:1–75.

Eggan, F.

1950   *Social Organization of the Western Pueblos.* Chicago: University of Chicago Press.

Ehrenberg, M.

1989   *Women in Prehistory.* Norman: University of Oklahoma Press.

Eliade, M.

1959   *The Sacred and the Profane.* New York: Harcourt Brace Jovanovich, Inc.

Ellwood, P. B.

1980   Ceramics of Durango South. In *The Durango South Project: Archaeological Salvage of Two Late Basketmaker III Sites in the Durango District*, edited by J. D. Gooding, pp. 78–102. Anthropology Papers no. 34. Tucson: University of Arizona.

Elmore, F. H.

1976   *Shrubs and Trees of the Southwest Uplands.* Tucson: Southwest Parks and Monuments Association.

Elson, Mark D.

1981   *The Prehistoric and Historic Occupation of the Red Rock Valley, Northeastern Arizona: The Carrizo Flats Survey.* NNCRMP Report 82-181. Window Rock, Ariz.: Navajo Nation Cultural Resource Management Program.

Ely, L. L., Y. Enzel, V. R. Baker, and D. R. Cayan

1993   A 5000 Year Record of Extreme Floods and Climate

Change in the Southwestern United States. *Science* 262:410–412.

Ember, M.

1973   An Archaeological Indicator of Matrilocal Versus Patrilocal Residence. *American Antiquity* 38:177–182.

Epple, C.

1998   Coming to Terms with Navajo Nadleehi: A Critique of "Berdache," "Alternate Gender," and "Two-Spirit." *American Ethnologist* 25(2):267–290.

Euler, R. C., G. J. Gumerman, T. N. V. Karlstrom, J. S. Dean, and R. H. Hevly

1979   The Colorado Plateaus: Cultural Dynamics and Paleoenvironment. *Science* 205:1089–1101.

Fairley, H. C.

1989   Anasazi Settlement Dynamics in Upper Paiute Canyon, Northeastern Arizona. Master's thesis, Department of Anthropology, Northern Arizona University, Flagstaff.

Farmer, J. D.

1997   Iconographic Evidence of Basketmaker Warfare and Human Sacrifice: A Contextual Approach to Early Anasazi Art. *Kiva* 62:391–420.

Fenenga, F.

1956   Excavations on Trunk O. In *Pipeline Archaeology: Reports of Salvage Operations in the Southwest on El Paso Natural Gas Company Projects, 1950–1953*, edited by F. Wendorf, N. Fox, and O. L. Lewis, pp. 204–207. Santa Fe: Laboratory of Anthropology, Museum of New Mexico.

Ferg, A.

1978   *The Painted Cliffs Rest Area: Excavations along the Rio Puerco, Northeastern Arizona.* Contributions to Highway Salvage in Arizona no. 50. Tucson: Arizona State Museum, University of Arizona.

Fetterman, J. E., and L. Honeycutt

1987   *The Mockingbird Mesa Survey.* Cultural Resource Series no. 22. Denver: Bureau of Land Management.

Fewkes, J. W.

1898   Archaeological Expedition into Arizona in 1895. In 17th *Annual Report of the Bureau of American Ethnology* for the years 1895–1896, part 2, pp. 519–742. Washington, D.C.

Flannery, K. V.

1972   The Origin of the Village as a Settlement Type in Mesoamerica and the Near East: A Comparative Study. In *Man, Settlement, and Urbanism*, edited by P. Ucko, R. Tringham, and G. W. Dimbleby, pp. 23–53. London: Gerald Duckworth.

Flenniken, J. J.

1981   *Replicative Systems Analysis: A Model Applied to the Vein Quartz Artifacts from the Hoko River Site.* Reports of Investigations no. 59. Pullman: Washington State University, Laboratory of Anthropology.

Flenniken, J. J., and P. J. Wilke

1989   Typology, Technology, and Chronology of Great Basin Dart Points. *American Anthropologist* 91:149–158.

Flores, P., and T. M. Kearns

1996   *Human Remains, Mortuary Practices, and Burial Goods.* Pipeline Archaeology 1990–1993: The El Paso Natural Gas North System Expansion Project, New Mexico and Arizona, vol. X, general editor T. M. Kearns. Report no. WCRM(F)074. Farmington, N.Mex.: Western Cultural Resource Management, Inc.

Foldi, D.

1989   Flaked Stone Artifacts. In *Archaeology and Ethnohistory of Redrock Valley: A Study of Prehistoric and Historic Land Use in Northeast Arizona*, prepared by B. S. Hildebrant, pp. 333–417. Research Series no. 3, report no. 262. Zuni Pueblo, N.Mex.: Zuni Archaeology Program.

Foster, M. S., R. Knudson, and G. C. Tucker

1983   *Archaeological Investigation of Five Sites within the Cortez CO2 Project Corridor near La Plata, New Mexico.* Montrose, Colo.: Nickens and Associates, no. CR-26.

Fowler, A. P.

1988   *Archaeological Testing of Site NM:12:K3:263 at Blackrock, Zuni Indian Reservation, McKinley County, New Mexico.* Report no. 250. Zuni Pueblo, N.Mex.: Zuni Archaeology Program.

Fowler, A. P., J. R. Stein, and R. Anyon

1987   An Archaeological Reconnaissance of West-central New Mexico: The Anasazi Monuments Project. Submitted to the State of New Mexico Office of Cultural Affairs Historic Preservation Division, Santa Fe.

Fox, R.

1967   *Kinship and Marriage: An Anthropological Perspective.* Baltimore: Penguin Books.

Fried, M. H.

1967   *The Evolution of Political Societies: An Essay in Political Anthropology.* New York: Random House.

Frisch, R.

1974   *Demographic Implications of the Biological Determinants of Female Fecundity.* Research Paper no. 6. Cambridge: Harvard University, Center for Population Studies.

Fuller, S. L.

1988   *Archaeological Investigations in the Bodo Canyon Area, La Plata County, Colorado.* U.S. Department of Energy Uranium Mill Tailings Remedial Action Project. Archaeological Report no. 25. Cortez, Colo.: Complete Archaeological Service Associates.

Fuller, S. L., and C. Chang

1978   Archaeological Excavations at Eleven Prehistoric Sites within the Ganado Sewer Lagoon and along the Right-of-Way of Route N27(1). Flagstaff: Department of Anthropology, Museum of Northern Arizona.

Fuller, S. L., and J. N. Morris

1991   Excavations at Knobby Knee Stockade (Site 5MT2525), a Basketmaker III–Pueblo III Habitation. In Four Corners Archaeological Project, Report no. 16, Archaeological Excavations on the Hovenweep Laterals, by J. N. Morris, pp. 59–325. Cortez, Colo.: Complete Archaeological Service Associates.

Gasser, R. E.

1982   *The Coronado Project Archaeological Investigations: The Specialists Volume.* Research Paper no. 23. Flagstaff: Museum of Northern Arizona.

Geib, P. R.

1990   A Basketmaker II Wooden Tool Cache from Lower Glen Canyon. *Kiva* 55:265–277.

1996a   Glen Canyon Revisited. Anthropological Papers no. 119. Salt Lake City: University of Utah Press.

2000   Radiocarbon Dating of Desha Caves 1 and 2. Ms. on file, Navajo Nation Archaeology Department, Northern Arizona University branch office, Flagstaff.

Geib, P. R. (ed.)

1996b   *Excavations at Nine Sites along Segment 4 of N16: An Interim Report of Data Recovery Findings.* NNAD

Report 95-131. Window Rock, Ariz.: Navajo Nation Archaeology Department.

Geib, P. R., and P. W. Bungart
1989   Implications of Early Bow Use in Glen Canyon. *Utah Archaeology* 2:32–47.

Geib, P. R., and B. Casto
1985   Macrobotanical Remains from Seven Archaeological Sites near Navajo Mountain, Utah. In *Archaeological Investigations near Rainbow City Navajo Mountain, Utah,* edited by P. R. Geib, J. R. Ambler, and M. M. Callahan, pp. 450–469. Archaeological Report no. 576. Flagstaff: Archaeology Laboratory, Northern Arizona University.

Geib, P. R., J. R. Ambler, and M. M. Callahan (eds.)
1985   *Archaeological Investigations near Rainbow City, Navajo Mountain, Utah.* Archaeological Report no. 576. Flagstaff: Archaeology Laboratory, Northern Arizona University.

Geib, P. R., N. J. Coulam, V. H. Clark, K. A. Hays-Gilpin, and J. D. Goodman II
1999   *Atlatl Rock Cave: Findings from the Investigation and Remediation of Looter Damage.* NNAD Report no. 93-121. Window Rock, Ariz.: Navajo Nation Archaeology Department.

Gilman, P. A.
1983   Changing Architectural Forms in the Prehistoric Southwest. Ph.D. diss., Department of Anthropology, University of New Mexico, Albuquerque.

1987   Architecture as Artifact: Pit Structures and Pueblos in the American Southwest. *American Antiquity* 52:538–564.

1989   A Response to Wilshusen. *American Antiquity* 54:834–836.

Gilmore, K. P., and M. L. Chenault
1993   Basketmaker III Use of Space. Paper presented at the 5th Occasional Anasazi Symposium, Farmington, N.Mex.

Gilpin, D.
1989   *The Salina Springs Discoveries: Archaeological Investigations at the Western Edge of the Chinle Valley, Apache County, Arizona.* NNAD Report no. 85-469/86-027, addendum. Window Rock, Ariz.: Navajo Nation Archaeology Department.

1991   *The 1991 South Gap Conference Expedition to Juniper Cove, Navajo County, Arizona.* NNAD Report no. 91-262. Window Rock, Ariz.: Navajo Nation Archaeology Department.

1993   A Brownware Pottery Assemblage from Basketmaker Sites at Salina Springs, Apache County, Arizona. Paper presented at the spring 1993 meeting of the Arizona Archaeological Council, Flagstaff.

1994   Lukachukai and Salina Springs: Late Archaic/Early Basketmaker Habitation Sites in the Chinle Valley, Northeastern Arizona. *Kiva* 60:203–218.

Gilpin, D., D. D. Dykeman, and P. F. Reed
1996   *Anasazi Community Architecture in the Chuska Valley.* Albuquerque: New Mexico Archaeological Council.

Gladwin, H. S.
1945   *The Chaco Branch: Excavations at White Mound and in the Red Mesa Valley.* Medallion Papers no. XXXIII. Globe, Ariz.: Gila Pueblo.

1957   *A History of the Ancient Southwest.* Portland, Maine: The Bond Wheelright Company.

Glassow, M. A.
1972   Changes in the Adaptations of Southwestern Basketmakers: A System Perspective. In *Contemporary Archaeology: A Guide to Theory and Contributions,* edited by

Mark P. Leone, pp. 289–302. Carbondale: Southern Illinois University Press.

1980   *Prehistoric Agricultural Development in the Northern Southwest: A Study in Changing Patterns of Land Use.* Anthropological Papers no. 16. Socorro, N.Mex.: Ballena Press.

Goldman, I.
1970   *Ancient Polynesian Society.* Chicago: University of Chicago Press.

Gooding, J. D. (ed.)
1980   *The Durango South Project: Archaeological Salvage of Two Late Basketmaker III Sites in the Durango District.* Anthropological Papers of the University of Arizona no. 34. Tucson: University of Arizona Press.

Grant, C.
1978   *Canyon de Chelly: The People and the Rock Art.* Tucson: University of Arizona Press.

Green, M.
1985   *Chipped Stone Raw Materials and the Study of Interaction on Black Mesa, Arizona.* Occasional Paper no. 11. Carbondale: Center for Archaeological Investigations, Southern Illinois University.

Greenwald, D. M.
1997a   Ground Stone Assemblage. In Excavations at the Rabbit Site (5MT9168), a Basketmaker III Hamlet, edited by M. L. Chenault. In preparation. Durango, Colo.: SWCA, Inc.

1997b   Ground Stone Analysis. In Excavations at the Late Basketmaker III Hamlet of Dead Dog (5MT11,861), edited by M. L. Chenault. In preparation. Durango, Colo.: SWCA, Inc.

Grissino-Mayer, H. D.
1996   A 2,129-year Reconstruction of Precipitation for Northwestern New Mexico, USA. In Tree Rings, Environment, and Humanity, edited by J. S. Dean, D. M. Meko, and T. W. Swetnam. *Radiocarbon* 38:191–204.

Grissino-Mayer, H. D., T. W. Swetnam, and R. K. Adams
1997   The Rare Old-aged Conifers of the Malpais—-Their Role in Understanding Climatic Change in the American Southwest. In *Natural History of El Malpais National Monument,* compiled by K. Mabery. *New Mexico Bureau of Mines and Mineral Resources Bulletin* 156:155–162.

Gross, G. T.
1986   Technology: Facilities. In *Dolores Archaeological Program: Final Synthetic Report,* compiled by D. A. Breternitz, C. K. Robinson, and G. T. Gross, pp. 611–632. Denver: U.S. Department of the Interior, Bureau of Reclamation, Engineering and Research Center.

1987   Anasazi Storage Facilities in the Dolores Region: A.D. 600–920. Ph.D. diss., Department of Anthropology, Washington State University, Pullman.

Guernsey, S. L.
1931   *Explorations in Northeastern Arizona.* Papers of the Peabody Museum of American Archaeology and Ethnology, vol. 12, no. 1. Cambridge: Harvard University.

Guernsey, S. L., and A. V. Kidder
1921   *Basket Maker Caves of Northeastern Arizona.* Papers of the Peabody Museum of American Archaeology and Ethnology, vol. 8, no. 2. Cambridge: Harvard University.

Gumerman, G. J.
1984   *A View from Black Mesa.* Tucson: University of Arizona Press.

Gumerman, G. J. (ed.)
1988   *The Anasazi in a Changing Environment.* School of American Research Advanced Seminar Series. Cambridge: Cambridge University Press.

Gumerman, G. J., and J. S. Dean
1989   Prehistoric Cooperation and Competition in the Western Anasazi Area. In *Dynamics of Southwest Prehistory,* edited by L. S. Cordell and G. J. Gumerman, pp. 99–148. Washington, D.C.: Smithsonian Institution Press.

Gumerman, G. J., and M. Gell-Mann
1993   Cultural Evolution in the Prehistoric Southwest. In *Themes in Southwestern Prehistory,* edited by G. J. Gumerman, pp. 1–21. Santa Fe: School of American Research Press.

Gumerman, G. J., and A. P. Olson
1968   Prehistory in the Puerco Valley, Eastern Arizona. *Plateau* 40:113–127.

Haas, J., and W. Creamer
1993   *Stress and Warfare among the Kayenta of the Thirteenth Century A.D.* Fieldiana: Anthropology, no. 21. Chicago: Field Museum of Natural History.

Hack, J. T.
1942   *The Changing Physical Environment of the Hopi Indians of Arizona.* Peabody Museum of American Archaeology and Ethnology Papers, vol. 35, no. 1. Cambridge: Harvard University.

Hall, E. T., Jr.
1944   *Early Stockaded Settlements in the Gobernador District, New Mexico.* Columbia Studies in Archaeology and Ethnology, vol. 2, no. 1. New York: Columbia University Press.

Hallisy, S. J.
1974   Salvage Excavations at Sites 5MTUMR2344 and 5MTUMR2347 in Mancos Canyon, Southwest Colorado. Report submitted to Bureau of Indian Affairs, Albuquerque Area Office.

Hammack, L. C.
1964   *The Tohatchi Road Salvage Project; 1963–64.* Laboratory of Anthropology Notes no. 28. Santa Fe: Museum of New Mexico.

Hammack, N. S.
1992   The Oven Site, LA 4169: A Reevaluation Based on Recent Excavations. In *Cultural Diversity and Adaptation: Archaic, Anasazi, and Navajo Occupation of the Upper San Juan Basin,* edited by L. S. Reed and P. F. Reed, pp. 37–53. Cultural Resources Series no. 9. Santa Fe: Bureau of Land Management, New Mexico State Office.

Hancock, P. M., T. M. Kearns, R. A. Moore, M. A. Powers, A. C. Reed, L. Wheelbarger, and P. A. Whitten
1988   *Excavation in the Middle La Plata Valley for San Juan Coal Company.* Studies in Archaeology no. 6. Farmington, N.Mex.: Division of Conservation Archaeology, San Juan County Museum Association.

Hannaford, C. A.
1993   The Long-lived Communities. Paper presented at the Fifth Occasional Anasazi Symposium, Farmington, N.Mex.

Hantman, J. L.
1983   Social Networks and Stylistic Distributions in the Prehistoric Plateau Southwest. Ph.D. diss., Department of Anthropology, Arizona State University, Tempe.

Hard, R. J.
1990   Agricultural Dependence in the Mountain Mogollon. In *Perspectives on Southwestern Prehistory,* edited by P. E. Minnis and C. L. Redman, pp. 135–149. Boulder, Colo.: Westview Press.

Hard, R. J., R. P. Mauldin, and G. R. Raymond
1996   Mano Size, Stable Carbon Isotope Rations, and Macrobotanical Remains as Multiple Lines of Evidence of Maize Dependence in the American Southwest. *Journal of Archaeological Method and Theory* 3:253–318.

Harlan, T. P., and J. S. Dean
1968   Tree-Ring Data for Several Navajo Mountain Region Sites. In *Survey and Excavation North and East of Navajo Mountain, Utah 1959–1962.* Museum of Northern Arizona Bulletin no. 45. Flagstaff: Northern Arizona Society of Science and Art.

Harner, M. J.
1970   Population Pressure and the Social Evolution of Agriculturalists. *Southwestern Journal of Anthropology* 26:67–86.

Harriman, R. G.
1996   LA 2501: Casa de Viento Hamlet. In *Excavation of the Gallup Station,* edited by C. W. Wheeler, pp. 2-1 to 2-111. Pipeline Archaeology 1990–1993: The El Paso Natural Gas North System Expansion Project, New Mexico and Arizona, vol. 4, draft report, T. M. Kearns, general editor. Report no. WCRM(F)074. Farmington, N.Mex.: Western Cultural Resource Management, Inc.

Harriman, R. G., and J. L. McVickar
1996   LA 80422: Aquila Caserio. In *Investigations at an Early Anasazi Community in the Tohatchi Flats,* edited by J. L. McVickar, pp. 3-1 to 3-221. Pipeline Archaeology 1990–1993: The El Paso Natural Gas North System Expansion Project, New Mexico and Arizona, vol. 7 draft report, T. M. Kearns, general editor. Report no. WCRM(F)074. Farmington, New Mexico: Western Cultural Resource Management, Inc.

Hassan, F.
1981   *Demographic Archaeology.* New York: Academic Press.

Haury, E. W.
1928   The Succession of House Types in the Pueblo Area. Master's thesis, Department of Anthropology, University of Arizona, Tucson.
1936   *Some Southwestern Pottery Types, Series IV.* Medallion Papers no. 19. Globe, Ariz.: Gila Pueblo.
1940   *Excavations in the Forestdale Valley, East-central Arizona.* University of Arizona Bulletin 11, no. 4, Social Science Bulletin no. 12. Tucson: University of Arizona.

Haury, E. W., and E. B. Sayles
1947   An Early Pit House of the Mogollon Culture. University of Arizona Bulletin 18, no. 4, Social Science Bulletin no. 16. Tucson: University of Arizona.

Hayden, I.
1930   Preliminary Report on Two Caves in Southeastern Utah, explored in July and August 1930, by the Van Bergen-Los Angeles County Museum Party. Ms. on file, Los Angeles County Museum of Natural History.

Hayes, A. C.
1964   The Archeological Survey of Wetherill Mesa, Mesa Verde National Park, Colorado. Archeological Research Series no. 7A. Washington, D.C.: National Park Service.
1981   A Survey of Chaco Canyon Archeology. In *Archeological Surveys of Chaco Canyon, New Mexico,* by A. C. Hayes, D. M. Brugge, and W. J. Judge, pp. 1–68. Publications in Archeology 17A. Washington, D.C.: National Park Service.

Hayes, A. C., and J. A. Lancaster
1968   Site 1060, a Basketmaker III Pit House on Chapin Mesa. In *Emergency Archaeology in Mesa Verde National Park, Colorado, 1948–1966,* edited by R. H. Lister, pp. 65–68. University of Colorado Studies, Series in Anthropology no. 15. Boulder: University of Colorado Press.
1975   *Badger House Community, Mesa Verde National Park.* Archeological Research Series no. 7E. Washington, D.C.: National Park Service.

Hayes, A. C., D. M. Brugge, and W. J. Judge (eds.)
1981   Archeological Surveys of Chaco Canyon, New Mexico. Publications in Archeology 18A. Albuquerque: National Park Service.

Hays, K. A.
1992a   Anasazi Ceramics as Text and Tool: Toward a Theory of Ceramic Design "Messaging." Ph.D. diss., Department of Anthropology, University of Arizona, Tucson.
1992b   Ceramics from the Coronado Project. In *The Coronado Project: Anasazi Settlements Overlooking the Puerco Valley, Arizona,* vol. 2, edited by R. V. N. Ahlstrom, M. Marek, and D. H. Greenwald, pp. 11–64. Anthropological Research Paper no. 3. Flagstaff: SWCA, Inc.

Hays-Gilpin, K. A.
1993   Pottery Technology and Cultural Affiliation of the Puerco Valley Basketmakers. Paper presented at the 1993 spring meeting of the Arizona Archaeology Council, Flagstaff.
1996   Anasazi Iconography: Medium and Motif. In *Interpreting Southwestern Diversity: Underlying Principles and Overarching Patterns,* edited by P. R. Fish and J. J. Reid, pp. 55–67. Anthropological Research Papers no. 48. Tempe: Arizona State University.
1999   Gender Constructs in the Material Culture of Seventh Century Anasazi Farmers in Northeastern Arizona. In *Gender and Material Culture: Representations of Gender from Prehistory to the Present,* edited by M. Donald and L. M. Hurcombe, pp. 31–44, Hampshire, UK: Macmillan.

Hays-Gilpin, K., and A. Sullivan
1999   The Hennessey Butte Site and Early Ceramics in the American Southwest. Paper presented at the 64th annual meeting of the Society for American Archaeology, Chicago.

Hays-Gilpin, K. A., A. C. Deegan, and E. A. Morris
1998   *Prehistoric Sandals from Northeastern Arizona: The Earl H. Morris and Ann Axtell Morris Research.* Anthropological Papers of the University of Arizona no. 62. Tucson: University of Arizona Press.

Hays-Gilpin, K. A., J. Goff, and K. N. Hensler
1999   Ceramic Analysis from the Cove-Red Valley Archaeological Project. In *Anasazi Community Development in Redrock Valley: Archaeological Excavations along the N33 Road in Apache County, Arizona,* edited by P. F. Reed and K. N. Hensler, pp. 445–550. Navajo Nation Papers in Anthropology no. 33. Window Rock, Ariz.: Navajo Nation Archaeology Department.

Hays-Gilpin, K. A., and E. van Hartesveldt (eds.)
1998   *Prehistoric Ceramics of the Puerco Valley, Arizona: The 1995 Chambers-Sanders Trust Lands Ceramic Conference.* Ceramic Series no. 7. Flagstaff: Museum of Northern Arizona.

Hegmon, M.
1995   *The Social Dynamics of Pottery Style in the Early Puebloan Southwest.* Occasional Paper no. 5. Cortez, Colo.: Crow Canyon Archaeological Center.

Heidke, J. M.
1998   Cienega Phase Incipient Plain Ware from Southeastern Arizona. *Kiva* 64:311–338.

Heidke, J. M., and M. T. Stark
1996   Early Ceramics in Southeastern Arizona: Technology, Iconography, and Function. Paper presented at the 29th annual Chacmool Conference, Calgary, Canada.

Hensler, K. N.
1999   Anasazi Ceramic Traditions: The View from the Cove. In *Anasazi Community Development in Redrock Valley: Archaeological Excavations along the N33 Road in Apache County, Arizona,* edited by P. F. Reed and K. N. Hensler, pp. 551–686. Navajo Nation Papers in Anthropology no. 33, Window Rock, Ariz.

Hensler, K. N., and P. F. Reed
1999   Anasazi Economy and Social Organization in Cove–Redrock Valley: Interaction, Exchange, Specialization, and Subsistence. In *Anasazi Community Development in Redrock Valley: Archaeological Excavations along the N33 Road in Apache County, Arizona,* edited by P. F. Reed and K. N. Hensler, pp. 953–993. Navajo Nation Papers in Anthropology no. 33, Window Rock, Ariz.

Hensler, K. N., P. F. Reed, S. Wilcox, J. Goff, and J. A. Torres
1999   *A Pueblo I Household on the Chuska Slope: Data Recovery at NM-H-47-102, along Navajo Route 5010(1) near Toadlena, New Mexico.* Navajo Nation Papers in Anthropology no. 35, Window Rock, Ariz.

Hester, T. R., and H. J. Shafer
1987   Observations on Ancient Maya Core Technology at Colha, Belize. In *The Organization of Core Technology,* edited by J. K. Johnson and C. A. Morrow, pp. 239–258. Boulder, Colo.: Westview Press.

Hildebrant, B. S.
1989   *The Archaeology and Ethnohistory of Redrock Valley: A Study of Prehistoric and Historic Land Use in Northeastern Arizona.* Research Series no. 3. Zuni Pueblo, N.Mex.: Zuni Archaeology Program.

Hill, D. V.
1988   Being Brown: Technological Analysis of Ceramic Material from the Oven Site (LA 4169). Ms. on file, Complete Archaeological Service Associates, Cortez, Colo.

Hill, W. W.
1938   *The Agricultural and Hunting Methods of the Navaho Indians.* Publication in Anthropology no. 18. New Haven: Yale University Press.

Hodder, I.
1985   Boundaries as Social Strategies: An Ethnoarchaeological Study. In *The Archaeology of Frontiers and Borders,* edited by S. W. Green and S. M. Perlman, pp. 141–159. New York: Academic Press.
1986   *Reading the Past: Current Approaches to Interpretation in Archeology.* Cambridge: Cambridge University Press.

Hofman, J. L.
1987   Hopewell Blades from Twenhafel: Distinguishing Local and Foreign Core Technology. In *The Organization of Core Technology,* edited by J. K. Johnson and C. A. Morrow, pp. 87–118. Boulder, Colo.: Westview Press.

Holloway, R. G.
1999   Synthetic Overview of Palynological Data from the El Paso Natural Gas Project, McKinley and San Juan Counties, New Mexico. In *Supporting Studies: Nonceramic Artifacts, Subsistence and Environmental Studies, and Chronometric Studies,* edited by T. M. Kearns and J. L. McVickar, pp. 13-1 to 13-119. Pipeline Archaeology

1990–1993: The El Paso Natural Gas North System Expansion Project, New Mexico and Arizona, vol. XII, general editor T. M. Kearns. Report no. WCRM(F)074. Farmington, N.Mex.: Western Cultural Resource Management, Inc.

Holmer, R. N.
1980   Chipped Stone Projectile Points. In *Cowboy Cave*, edited by J. D. Jennings, pp. 31–38, Anthropological Papers no. 104. Salt Lake City: University of Utah Press.
1986   Common Projectile Points of the Intermountain West. In *Anthropology of the Desert West: Essays in Honor of Jesse D. Jennings*, edited by C. J. Condie and D. D. Fowler, pp. 90–115. Anthropological Papers no. 110. Salt Lake City: University of Utah Press.

Holmer, R. N., and D. G. Weder
1980   Common Post-Archaic Projectile Points of the Fremont Area. In *Fremont Perspectives*, edited by D. B. Madsen, pp. 55–68. Antiquities Section Selected Papers vol. 3, no. 16. Salt Lake City: Utah State Historical Society.

Hoopes, J. W.
1995   Interaction in Hunting and Gathering Societies as a Context for the Emergence of Pottery in the Central American Isthmus. In *The Emergence of Pottery: Technology and Innovation in Ancient Societies*, edited by W. K. Barnett and J. W. Hoopes, pp. 185–198. Washington, D.C.: Smithsonian Institution Press.

Hoopes, J. W., and W. K. Barnett
1995   The Shape of Early Pottery Studies. In *The Emergence of Pottery: Technology and Innovation in Ancient Societies*, edited by W. K. Barnett and J. W. Hoopes, pp. 1–7. Washington, D.C.: Smithsonian Institution Press.

Howell, T. L.
1995   Tracking Zuni Gender and Leadership Roles across the Contact Period. *Journal of Anthropological Research* 51(2):125–147.

Huckell, B. B.
1995   *Of Marshes and Maize: Preceramic Agricultural Settlements in the Cienega Valley, Southeastern Arizona*. Anthropological Papers of the University of Arizona no. 59. Tucson: University of Arizona Press.

Huckleberry, G., M. McFaul, K. Traugh, and G. Smith
1999   Site-Specific Geomorphology. In *Chuska Chronologies, Houses, and Hogans: Archaeological and Ethnographic Inquiry along N30-N31 between Mexican Springs and Navajo, McKinley County, New Mexico*, vol. III, part 1, edited by J. E. Damp, pp. 347–376. Research Series no. 10. Zuni, N.Mex.: Zuni Cultural Resource Enterprise.

Hunt, C. B.
1956   *Cenozoic Geology of the Colorado Plateau*. U.S. Geological Survey Professional Paper no. 279. Washington, D.C.: U.S. Government Printing Office.

Hunter, A. A.
1995   Appendix B: Flotation Data Tables. In *Excavations at Nine Sites along Segment 3 of N16: An Interim Report of Data Recovery Findings*, by P. R. Geib, V. H. Clark, J. Huffman, K. Spurr, M. Warburton, and K. A. Hays-Gilpin. NNAD Report no. 95-130, Window Rock, Ariz.: Navajo Nation Archaeology Department.

Hurst, W., and J. D. Pachak
1989   *Spirit Windows: Native American Rock Art of Southeastern Utah*. Spirit Windows Project. Blanding, Utah: State of Utah Natural Resources, Division of Parks and Recreation, Edge of the Cedars State Park.

Hyder, W. D.
1997   Basketmaker Social Identity: Rock Art as Culture and Praxis. In *Rock Art as Visual Ecology*, edited by P. Faulstich, pp. 31–42. International Rock Art Conference Proceedings, vol. 1. Tucson: American Rock Art Research Association.

Irwin-Williams, C.
1973   *The Oshara Tradition: Origins of Anasazi Culture*. Eastern New Mexico University Contributions in Anthropology, vol. 5, no. 1. Portales: Eastern New Mexico University.

Jacobson, L.
1984   Chipped Stone in the San Juan Basin: A Distributional Analysis. Master's thesis, Department of Anthropology, University of New Mexico, Albuquerque.

James, C. D., III
1974   Preliminary Report for Archaeological Excavations, NA9437–Ariz. E:14:3(MNA) Route N27. Ms. on file, Department of Anthropology, Museum of Northern Arizona, Flagstaff.

Jelenik, A. J.
1976   Form, Function, and Style in Lithic Analysis. In *Cultural Change and Continuity: Essays in Honor of James Bennett Griffin*, edited by C. E. Cleland, pp. 19–76. New York: Academic Press.

Jennings, J. D.
1968   *Prehistory of North America*. New York: McGraw-Hill.

Jett, S. C., and V. E. Spencer
1981   *Navajo Architecture: Forms, History, Distributions*. Tucson: University of Arizona Press.

Johnson, A. W., and T. Earle
1987   *The Evolution of Human Societies: From Foraging Group to Agrarian State*. Stanford: Stanford University Press.

Johnson, C.
1962a   The Twin Lakes Site, LA 2507. *El Palacio* 69(3):158–173.
1962b   LA 2507: Unpublished Field Notes. On file, Laboratory of Anthropology, Museum of New Mexico, Santa Fe.

Johnson, G.
1982   Organization Structure and Scalar Stress. In *Theory and Explanation in Archaeology: The Southhampton Conference*, edited by C. Renfrew, M. Rowlands, and B. A. Segraves, pp. 389–421. London: Academic Press.
1983   Decision-Making Organization and Pastoral Nomad Camp Size. *Human Ecology* 11:175–199.

Johnson, W. C.
2000   Lukachukai Alluvial Geomorphology. In *Cultural Dynamics in the Lukachukai Valley: The N-13 Project*, edited by J. H. Altschul, S. D. Shelley, and E. K. Huber. Technical Series no. 16, part 2. Tucson: Statistical Research, Inc.

Johnson, W. C., and R. E. Brooks
2000   Macrobotanical Analyses. In *Cultural Dynamics in the Lukachukai Valley: The N-13 Project*, edited by J. H. Altschul, S. D. Shelley, and E. K. Huber. Technical Series no. 16, part 2. Tucson: Statistical Research, Inc.

Jones, J. G., and S. W. Yost
1996   Cold Wind Site: LA 80442. In *Investigations at Nine Sites in the Southern Tohatchi Flats and Adjacent Uplands*, edited by S. W. Yost, pp. 12-1 to 12-14. Pipeline Archaeology 1990 1993: The El Paso Natural Gas North System Expansion Project, New Mexico and Arizona, vol. VIII, general editor T. M. Kearns. Report no.

WCRM(F)074. Farmington, N.Mex.: Western Cultural Resource Management, Inc.

Jones, V. H.

1944 Was Tobacco Smoked in the Pueblo Region in Pre-Spanish Times? *American Antiquity* 9: 451–456.

Jones, V. H., and E. A. Morris

1960 A Seventh-century Record of Tobacco Utilization in Arizona. *El Palacio* 67: 115–117.

Judge, W. J.

1982 The Paleo-Indian and Basketmaker Periods: An Overview and Some Research Problems. In *The San Juan Tomorrow: Planning for the Conservation of Cultural Resources in the San Juan Basin,* edited by F. Plog and W. Wait, pp. 5–57. Santa Fe: National Park Service, Southwest Region.

1989 Chaco Canyon–San Juan Basin. In *Dynamics of Southwestern Prehistory,* edited by L. Cordell and G. J. Gumerman, pp. 209–262. Washington, D.C.: Smithsonian Institution Press.

Kane, A. E.

1986 Prehistory of the Dolores River Valley. In *Dolores Archaeological Program: Final Synthetic Report,* compiled by D. A. Breternitz, C. K. Robinson, and G. T. Gross, pp. 353–435. Denver: U.S. Department of the Interior, Bureau of Reclamation, Engineering and Research Center.

Kane, A. E., and G. T. Gross (compilers)

1986 *Dolores Archaeological Program: Anasazi Communities at Dolores: Early Anasazi Sites in the Sagehen Flats Area.* Denver: U.S. Department of the Interior, Bureau of Reclamation, Engineering and Research Center.

Kane, A. E., G. T. Gross, and N. J. Hewitt

1986 Dolores Archaeological Program Investigations at Early Anasazi Sites in the Sagehen Flats Area: An Introduction. In *Dolores Archaeological Program: Anasazi Communities at Dolores: Early Anasazi Sites in the Sagehen Flats Area,* compiled by A. E. Kane and G. T. Gross, prepared under the supervision of David A. Breternitz, pp. 3–26. Denver: Denver: U.S. Department of the Interior, Bureau of Reclamation, Engineering and Research Center.

Kaplan, L.

1956 The Cultivated Beans of the Prehistoric Southwest. *Annals of the Missouri Botanical Gardens* 43:189–249.

Kearns, T. M.

1996a A Proposed Phase Sequence for Tohatchi Flats and the Southern Chuska Valley, Northwest New Mexico. In *Time, Place, and Society: Project Synthesis,* by T. M. Kearns and J. L. McVickar, pp. 3-1 to 3-27. Pipeline Archaeology 1990–1993: The El Paso Natural Gas North System Expansion Project, New Mexico and Arizona, vol. XIII, draft report, T. M. Kearns, general editor. Report no. WCRM(F)074. Farmington, N.Mex.: Western Cultural Resource Management, Inc.

1996b Hunter-Gatherers and Early Agriculturalists: Paleoindian, Archaic, and Basketmaker II Occupation of the Southern Chuska Valley. In *Time, Place, and Society: Project Synthesis,* by T. M. Kearns and J. L. McVickar, pp. 4-1 to 4-19. Pipeline Archaeology 1990–1993: The El Paso Natural Gas North System Expansion Project, New Mexico and Arizona, vol. XIII, draft report, T. M. Kearns, general editor. Report no. WCRM(F)074. Farmington, N.Mex.: Western Cultural Resource Management, Inc.

1996c Early Villages in the Southern Chuska Valley: Basketmaker III and Pueblo I Periods. In *Time, Place, and Society: Project Synthesis,* by T. M. Kearns and J. L. McVickar, pp. 5-1 to 5-17. Pipeline Archaeology 1990–1993: The El Paso Natural Gas North System Expansion Project, New Mexico and Arizona, vol. XIII, draft report, T. M. Kearns, general editor. Report no. WCRM(F)074. Farmington, N.Mex.: Western Cultural Resource Management, Inc.

1998 In and Out, Up and Down: Basketmaker and Early Pueblo Settlement in Tohatchi Flats, New Mexico. Paper presented at the 63rd annual meeting of the Society for American Archaeology, Seattle.

1999a A Summary of Stone Tool Use Through Time at NSEP Sites. In *Supporting Studies: Nonceramic Artifacts, Subsistence and Environmental Studies, and Chronometric Studies,* compiled by T. M. Kearns and J. L. McVickar, pp. 4-1 to 4-24. Pipeline Archaeology 1990–1993: The El Paso Natural Gas North System Expansion Project, New Mexico and Arizona, vol. XII, T. M. Kearns, general editor. Report no. WCRM(F)074. Farmington, N.Mex.: Western Cultural Resource Management, Inc.

1999b Lithic Resource Procurement: Sources and Selection. In *Supporting Studies: Nonceramic Artifacts, Subsistence and Environmental Studies, and Chronometric Studies,* compiled by T. M. Kearns and J. L. McVickar, pp. 3-1 to 3-37. Pipeline Archaeology 1990–1993: The El Paso Natural Gas North System Expansion Project, New Mexico and Arizona, vol. XII, T. M. Kearns, general editor. Report no. WCRM(F)074. Farmington, N.Mex.: Western Cultural Resource Management, Inc.

1999c NSEP Obsidian Sourcing Study. In *Supporting Studies: Nonceramic Artifacts, Subsistence and Environmental Studies, and Chronometric Studies,* compiled by T. M. Kearns and J. L. McVickar, pp. 8-1 to 8-9. Pipeline Archaeology 1990–1993: The El Paso Natural Gas North System Expansion Project, New Mexico and Arizona, vol. XII, T. M. Kearns, general editor. Report no. WCRM(F)074. Farmington, N.Mex.: Western Cultural Resource Management, Inc.

Kearns, T. M. (ed.)

1995 *Project Overview, Background, and Implementation.* Pipeline Archaeology 1990–1993: The El Paso Natural Gas North System Expansion Project, New Mexico and Arizona, vol. I, T. M. Kearns, general editor. Report no. WCRM(F)074. Farmington, N.Mex.: Western Cultural Resource Management, Inc.

Kearns, T. M., B. E. King, C. A. Kugler, W. R. Latady, Jr., G. C. Nelson, R. M. Van Dyke, and J. J. Wollin

1991 *Evaluation Studies, New Mexico Portion.* Pipeline Archaeology Revisited: Anthropological Investigations Along The El Paso Natural Gas San Juan Expansion Project, New Mexico and Arizona, vol. 2. Technical Report no. 2504. Farmington, N.Mex.: Division of Conservation Archaeology, San Juan County Museum Association.

Kearns, T. M., and J. L. McVickar

1996 *Time, Place, and Society: Project Synthesis.* Pipeline Archaeology 1990–1993: The El Paso Natural Gas North System Expansion Project, New Mexico and Arizona, vol. XIII, draft report, T. M. Kearns, general editor. Report no. WCRM(F)074. Farmington, N.Mex.: Western Cultural Resource Management, Inc.

Kearns, T. M., and D. Silcock

1999 Projectile Points from the North System Expansion Project. In *Supporting Studies: Nonceramic Artifacts, Subsistence and Environmental Studies, and Chronometric*

Studies, compiled by T. M. Kearns and J. L. McVickar, pp. 6-1 to 6-15. Pipeline Archaeology 1990–1993: The El Paso Natural Gas North System Expansion Project, New Mexico and Arizona, vol. XII, T. M. Kearns, general editor. Report no. WCRM(F)074. Farmington, N.Mex.: Western Cultural Resource Management, Inc.

Kelley, V. C., and N. J. Clinton

1960   *Fracture Systems and Tectonic Elements of the Colorado Plateau.* University of New Mexico Publications in Geology no. 6. Albuquerque: University of New Mexico Press.

Kelly, R. L.

1988   The Three Sides of a Biface. *American Antiquity* 53:717–734.

1992   Mobility/Sedentism: Concepts, Archaeological Measures, and Effects. *Annual Review of Anthropology* 21:43–66.

Kent, K. P.

1983   *Prehistoric Textiles of the Southwest.* Santa Fe: School of American Research Press.

Kenyon, K. M.

1981   Excavations at Jericho. Vol. 3. London: British School of Archaeology in Jerusalem.

Kidder, A. V.

1924   *An Introduction to the Study of Southwestern Archaeology, with a Preliminary Account of the Excavation at Pecos.* Andover, Mass.: Yale University Press.

1927   Southwestern Archaeological Conference. *Science* 66:489–491.

Kidder, A. V., and S. J. Guernsey

1919   *Archaeological Explorations in Northeastern Arizona.* Bureau of American Ethnology Bulletin no. 65, Washington, D.C.: U.S. Government Printing Office.

Kohler, T. A.

1992   Field Houses, Villages, and the Tragedy of the Commons in the Early Northern Anasazi Southwest. *American Antiquity* 57:617–635.

Kohler, T. A., and C. R. Van West

1996   The Calculus of Self-interest in the Development of Cooperation: Sociopolitical Development and Risk among the Northern Anasazi. In *Evolving Complexity and Environmental Risk in the Prehistoric Southwest,* edited by J. Tainter and B. Tainter, pp. 169–196. Santa Fe Institute Studies in the Sciences of Complexity, vol. XXIV. Reading: Addison-Wesley Co.

Kohler, T. A., J. D. Orcutt, E. Blinman, and K. L. Petersen

1986   Anasazi Spreadsheets: The Cost of Doing Agricultural Business in Prehistoric Dolores. In *Dolores Archaeological Program: Final Synthetic Report,* edited by D. A. Breternitz, C. R. Robinson, and G. T. Gross, pp. 525–538. Denver: U.S. Department of the Interior, Bureau of Reclamation, Engineering and Research Center.

Kotyk, E. M.

1999   A Study in Anasazi Architecture and Extramural Features along the Chuska Slopes. In *Chuska Chronologies, Houses, and Hogans: Archaeological and Ethnographic Inquiry along N30-N31 between Mexican Springs and Navajo, McKinley County,* vol. 3, part 1, by J. E. Damp, pp. 263–310. Research Series no. 10. Zuni, N.Mex.: Zuni Cultural Resource Enterprise.

Kuhn, S. L.

1994   A Formal Approach to the Design and Assembly of Mobile Toolkits. *American Antiquity* 59:426–442.

Lakatos, S. A.

1998   Preliminary Data Recovery Results for Five Archaeological Resources along U.S. 666, near Twin Lakes, McKinley County, New Mexico. Ms. on file, Office of Archaeological Studies, Museum of New Mexico, Santa Fe.

Lancaster, J. A.

1968   The Salvage Excavations of Sites 353 and 354, Chapin Mesa. In *Emergency Archaeology in Mesa Verde National Park, Colorado, 1948–1966,* edited by R. H. Lister, pp. 57–59. University of Colorado Studies, Series in Anthropology no. 15. Boulder: University of Colorado Press.

Lancaster, J. A., and J. M. Pinkley

1954   Excavation at Site 16 of Three Pueblo II Mesa-top Ruins. In *Archeological Excavations in Mesa Verde National Park, Colorado, 1950,* by J. A. Lancaster, J. M. Pinkley, P. F. Van Cleave, and D. Watson, pp. 23–86. Archeological Research Series no. 2. Washington, D.C.: National Park Service.

Lancaster, J. A., and D. Watson

1943   Excavation of Mesa Verde Pit Houses. *American Antiquity* 9:190–198.

1954   Excavation of Two Late Basketmaker III Pit Houses. In *Archeological Excavations in Mesa Verde National Park, Colorado, 1950,* by J. A. Lancaster, J. M. Pinkley, P. F. Van Cleave, and D. Watson, pp. 7–22. Archeological Research Series no. 2. Washington, D.C.: National Park Service.

Lanning, E. P.

1963   *Archaeology of the Rose Spring Site, Iny-372.* Publications in American Archaeology and Ethnology, vol. 49, no. 3. Berkeley: University of California.

Latady, W. R., and J. L. McVickar

1999a   LA 80416: The Big Bird Site. In *Investigations at Four Sites in the Tohatchi Flats, New Mexico,* edited by J. L. McVickar, pp. 3-1 to 3-25. Pipeline Archaeology 1990–1993: The El Paso Natural Gas North System Expansion Project, New Mexico and Arizona, vol. VI, T. M. Kearns, general editor. Report no. WCRM(F)074. Farmington, N.Mex.: Western Cultural Resource Management, Inc.

1999b   LA 80417: Eastview House. In *Investigations at Four Sites in the Tohatchi Flats, New Mexico,* edited by J. L. McVickar, pp. 4-1 to 4-70. Pipeline Archaeology 1990–1993: The El Paso Natural Gas North System Expansion Project, New Mexico and Arizona, vol. VI, T. M. Kearns, general editor. Report no. WCRM(F)074. Farmington, N.Mex.: Western Cultural Resource Management, Inc.

LeBlanc, S. A.

1971   An Addition to Naroll's Suggested Floor Area and Settlement Population. *American Antiquity* 36:210–211.

1982a   Temporal Change in Mogollon Ceramics. In *Southwestern Ceramics: A Comparative Review,* edited by A. H. Schroeder, pp. 107–128. The Arizona Archaeologist no. 15. Phoenix: Arizona Archaeological Society.

1982b   The Advent of Pottery in the Southwest. In *Southwestern Ceramics: A Comparative Review,* edited by A. H. Schroeder, pp. 27–52. The Arizona Archaeologist no. 15. Phoenix: Arizona Archaeological Society.

1999   *Prehistoric Warfare in the American Southwest.* Salt Lake City: University of Utah Press.

Lekson, S. H.

1991   Settlement Patterns and the Chaco Region. In *Chaco and Hohokam: Prehistoric Regional Systems in the American Southwest,* edited by P. L. Crown and W. J. Judge, pp. 31–56. Santa Fe: School of American Research Press.

1996   Rewriting Southwestern Prehistory. *Archaeology* 50(1):52–55.

1999   War and Peace in the Southwest. *Discovering Archaeology* 1(3):38–40.

Lewis-Williams, J. D.

1996   Modeling the Production and Consumption of Rock Art. Paper presented at the 61st annual meeting of the Society for American Archaeology, New Orleans.

Lightfoot, K. G.

1979   Food Redistribution among Prehistoric Pueblo Groups. *The Kiva* 44:319–340.

Lightfoot, K. G., and G. M. Feinman

1982   Social Differentiation and Leadership Development in Early Pithouse Villages in the Mogollon Region of the American Southwest. *American Antiquity* 47:64–86.

Lightfoot, K. G., and R. A. Jewett

1984   The Occupation Duration of Duncan. In *The Duncan Project: A Study of the Occupation Duration and Settlement Pattern of an Early Mogollon Pithouse Village,* by K. G. Lightfoot, pp. 47–82. Anthropological Field Studies no. 6. Tempe: Arizona State University.

Lightfoot, R. R., A. M. Emerson, and E. Blinman

1988   Excavations in Area 5, Grass Mesa Village (Site 5MT23). In *Dolores Archaeological Program: Anasazi Communities at Dolores: Grass Mesa Village,* compiled by W. D. Lipe, J. N. Morris, and T. A. Kohler, pp. 561–766. Denver: U.S. Department of the Interior, Bureau of Reclamation, Engineering and Research Center.

Lindsay, A. J.

1961   The Beaver Creek Agricultural Community on the San Juan River, Utah. *American Antiquity* 27:174–187.

Lindsay, A. J., Jr., J. R. Ambler, M. A. Stein, and P. M. Hobler

1968   *Survey and Excavation North and East of Navajo Mountain, Utah 1959–1962.* Museum of Northern Arizona Bulletin no. 45. Flagstaff: Northern Arizona Society of Science and Art.

Linford, L.

1982   *Kayenta Anasazi Archaeology on Central Black Mesa, Northeastern Arizona: The Piñon Project.* Navajo Nation Papers in Anthropology no. 10, Window Rock, Ariz.

Linton, R.

1944   North American Cooking Pots. *American Antiquity* 9:369–380.

Lipe, W. D.

1967   Anasazi Culture and Its Relationship to the Environment in the Red Rock Plateau Region, Southeastern Utah. Ph.D. diss., Department of Anthropology, Yale University, New Haven.

1970   Anasazi Communities in the Red Rock Plateau, Southeastern Utah. In *Reconstructing Prehistoric Pueblo Societies,* edited by W. A. Longacre, pp. 84–139. Albuquerque: University of New Mexico Press.

1983   The Southwest. In *Ancient North America,* edited by J. D. Jennings, pp. 421–493. San Francisco: W. H. Freeman and Co.

1993   The Basketmaker II Period in the Four Corners Area. In *Anasazi Basketmaker: Papers from the 1990 Wetherill-Grand Gulch Symposium,* edited by V. M. Atkins, pp. 1–10. Cultural Resources Series no. 24. Salt Lake City: Bureau of Land Management.

1994   Comments on Population Aggregation and Community Organization. In *The Ancient Southwestern Community: Models and Methods for the Study of Prehistoric Social Organization,* edited by W. H. Wills and R. D. Leonard,

pp. 141–143. Albuquerque: University of New Mexico Press.

Lipe, W. D., and C. D. Breternitz

1980   Approaches to Analyzing Variability among Dolores Area Structures, A.D. 600–950. *Contract Abstracts and CRM Archaeology* 1:21–28.

Lipe, W. D., and R. G. Matson

1971   Human Settlement and Resources in the Cedar Mesa Area, southeastern Utah. In *The Distribution of Prehistoric Aggregates,* edited by G. Gumerman, pp. 126–151. Prescott College Anthropological Reports no. 1, Prescott, Ariz.

Lipe, W. D., J. N. Morris, and T. A. Kohler

1988   *Dolores Archaeological Program: Anasazi Communities at Dolores: Grass Mesa Village.* Denver: U.S. Department of the Interior, Bureau of Reclamation, Engineering and Research Center.

Lister, R. H., and F. C. Lister

1978   *Anasazi Pottery.* Albuquerque: Maxwell Museum.

Lockett, H. C., and L. L. Hargrave

1953   *Woodchuck Cave: A Basketmaker II Site in Tsegi Canyon, Arizona.* Museum of Northern Arizona Bulletin no. 26. Flagstaff: Northern Arizona Society of Science and Art.

Loebig, D. E.

1996   LA 80410: A Multicomponent Basketmaker III/Pueblo I Habitation. In *Excavations in the Northern Tohatchi Flats,* edited by S. W. Yost, pp. 5-1 to 5-438. Pipeline Archaeology 1990–1993: The El Paso Natural Gas North System Expansion Project, New Mexico and Arizona, vol. V, draft report, T. M. Kearns, general editor. Report no. WCRM(F)074. Farmington, N.Mex.: Western Cultural Resource Management, Inc.

Loebig, D. E., S. W. Yost, and R. Van Dyke

1996   Flowing Well Hamlet (LA 80407): A Multicomponent Basketmaker III–Pueblo I Habitation Site. In *Excavations in the Northern Tohatchi Flats,* edited by S. W. Yost, pp. 4-1 to 4-173. Pipeline Archaeology 1990–1993: The El Paso Natural Gas North System Expansion Project, New Mexico and Arizona, vol. V, draft report, T. M. Kearns, general editor. Report no. WCRM(F)074. Farmington, N.Mex.: Western Cultural Resource Management, Inc.

Loftin, J.

1991   *Religion and Hopi Life in the Twentieth Century.* Bloomington: Indiana University Press.

Long, P. V., Jr.

1966   *Archaeological Excavations in Lower Glen Canyon, Utah-Arizona 1959–1960.* Museum of Northern Arizona Bulletin no. 42. Flagstaff: Northern Arizona Society of Science and Art.

Loose, R. W.

1978   Physiography/Geology. In *Western Area Survey,* edited by M. A. Tart, pp. 17–54. Albuquerque: Public Service Company of New Mexico.

Lucius, W. A.

1981   Modeling Anasazi Origins: The Frontier Approach. In *Proceedings of the Anasazi Symposium 1981,* edited by J. E. Smith, pp. 51–68. Mesa Verde National Park, Colo.: Mesa Verde Museum Association.

1982   Ceramic Analysis. In *Testing and Excavation Reports: MAPCO's Rocky Mountain Liquid Hydrocarbons Pipeline, Southwestern Colorado,* vol. 2, edited by J. E. Fetterman and L. Honeycutt, pp. 7.1–7.2. San Francisco: Woodward-Clyde Consultants.

Lucius, W. A., and D. A. Breternitz

1992　*Northern Anasazi Ceramic Styles: A Field Guide for Identification.* Publications in Anthropology no. 1. Phoenix: Center for Indigenous Studies in the Americas.

Lucius, W. A., and C. D. Wilson

1981　Formal Descriptions of Mesa Verde Region Ceramic Types: Three New, One Old. *Pottery Southwest* 8(3):4–7.

Lurie, R.

1990　Lithic Technology and Mobility Strategies: The Koster Site Middle Archaic. In *Time, Energy, and Stone Tools,* edited by R. Torrence, pp. 46–56. Cambridge: Cambridge University Press.

Mabry, J. B.

1997　Conclusions. In *Archaeological Investigations of Early Village Sites in the Middle Santa Cruz Valley, Analysis and Synthesis,* edited by J. B. Mabry. In press. Anthropological Paper no. 19. Tucson: Center for Desert Archaeology.

Mabry, J., B. Clark, and M. Lowe

1997　Archaeological Survey for the Huntington Land Exchange. In preparation. Durango, Colo.: SWCA, Inc.

Mahoney, N.

1998　Beyond Bis Sa'ani: Rethinking the Scale and Organization of Great House Communities. Paper presented at the 63rd annual meeting of the Society for American Archaeology, Seattle.

Manning, S. J.

1992　The Lobed-circle Image in the Basketmaker Petroglyphs of Southwestern Utah. *Utah Archaeology* 1992:1–7.

Marek, M., D. H. Greenwald, and R. V. N. Ahlstrom (eds.)

1993　*The Coronado Project: Anasazi Settlements Overlooking the Puerco Valley, Arizona.* Vol. 1. Anthropological Research Paper no. 3. Flagstaff: SWCA, Inc.

Marshall, M. P., J. R. Stein, R. W. Loose, and J. E. Novotny

1979　*Anasazi Communities of the San Juan Basin.* Albuquerque: Public Service Company of New Mexico.

Martin, P. S.

1938　*Archaeological Work in the Ackmen-Lowry, Southwestern Colorado, 1937.* Anthropological Series, vol. 23, no. 1. Chicago: Field Museum of Natural History.

1939　*Modified Basketmaker sites in the Ackmen-Lowry Area, Southwestern Colorado, 1938.* Anthropological Series, vol. 23, no. 3. Chicago: Field Museum of Natural History.

Martin, P. S., and F. Plog

1973　*The Archaeology of Arizona.* Garden City, N.J.: Doubleday/Natural History Press.

Martin, P. S., and J. B. Rinaldo

1939　*Modified Basket Maker Sites: Ackmen-Lowry Area, Southwestern Colorado, 1938.* Anthropological Series, vol. 23, no. 3. Chicago: Field Museum of Natural History.

1943　*The S.U. Site: Excavations at a Mogollon Village, Western New Mexico, Second Session, 1941.* Anthropology Series 32(2). Chicago: Field Museum of Natural History.

1947　*The S.U. Site: Excavations at a Mogollon Village, Western New Mexico, Second Session, 1941.* Anthropology Series, vol. 51, no. 1. Chicago: Field Museum of Natural History.

Matson, R .G.

1991　*The Origins of Southwestern Agriculture.* Tucson: University of Arizona Press.

1994　Anomalous Basketmaker II Sites on Cedar Mesa: Not So Anomalous After All. *Kiva* 60:219–237.

Matson, R. G., and B. Chisholm

1991　Basketmaker II Subsistence: Carbon Isotopes and Other Dietary Indicators from Cedar Mesa, Utah. *American Antiquity* 56:444–459.

Matson, R. G., and K. M. Dohm

1994　Introduction. In Anasazi Origins: Recent Research on the Basketmaker II. *Kiva* 60:159–163.

Matson, R. G., W. D. Lipe, and W. R. Haase IV

1988　Adaptational Continuities and Occupational Discontinuities: The Cedar Mesa Anasazi. *Journal of Field Archaeology* 15:245–264.

Matthews, M.

1986　The Dolores Archaeological Program Macrobotanical Resource Data Base: Resource Availability and Mix. In *Dolores Archaeological Program: Final Synthetic Report,* compiled by D. A. Breternitz, C. K. Robinson, and G. T. Gross, pp. 151–183. Denver: U.S. Department of the Interior, Bureau of Reclamation, Engineering and Research Center.

1997　Appendix A: Flotation Data Tables from Segment 4 of N16. Ms. on file, Navajo Nation Archaeology Department, Northern Arizona University Branch Office, Flagstaff.

Mauldin, R.

1993　The Relationship between Ground Stone and Agricultural Intensification in Western New Mexico. *Kiva* 58:317–330.

McCreery, P., and J. McCreery

1986　A Petroglyph Site with Possible Hopi Ceremonial Association. In *American Indian Rock Art II,* edited by E. Snyder, pp. 1–7. El Toro, Calif.: American Rock Art Research Association.

McCreery, P., and E. Malotki

1994　*Tapamveni: The Rock Art Galleries of Petrified Forest and Beyond.* Petrified Forest, Ariz.: Petrified Forest Museum Association.

McEnany, T.

1985　*An Archaeological Survey of the Northern Portion of the Red Rock Valley, Apache County, Arizona: The Navajo Route N-63 Project.* NNCRMP Report 84-460. Window Rock, Ariz.: Navajo Nation Cultural Resource Management Program.

McGregor, J. C.

1965　*Southwestern Archaeology.* Urbana: University of Illinois Press.

McGuire, R. H., and M. B. Schiffer

1983　A Theory of Architectural Design. *Journal of Anthropological Archaeology* 3:277–303.

McKenna, P. J.

1986　A Summary of the Chaco Center's Small Site Excavations: 1973–1978. In *Small Site Architecture of Chaco Canyon,* edited by P. J. McKenna and M. L. Truell, pp. 5–114. Chaco Canyon Studies, Publications in Archeology 18D. Santa Fe: National Park Service.

McKenna, P. J., and H. W. Toll

1992　Regional Patterns of Great House Development among the Totah Anasazi, New Mexico. In *Anasazi Regional Organization and the Chaco System,* edited by D. E. Doyel, pp. 133–143. Anthropological Papers no. 5. Albuquerque: Maxwell Museum of Anthropology.

McKusick, C.

1986　The Avian Remains. In *Antelope House,* by D. Morris, pp. 142–158. Washington D.C.: Department of the Interior, National Park Service.

McLellan, G. E.

1969 The Origin, Development, and Typology of Anasazi Kivas and Great Kivas. Ph.D. diss. Department of Anthropology, University of Colorado, Boulder. Ann Arbor: University Microfilms.

McNamee, W. D., R. G. Harriman, and R. W. Yarnell

1992a Excavations at Palote Azul Stockade (5DL112), a Late Basketmaker III Habitation. In Four Corners Archaeological Project, Report no. 18, *Archaeological Excavations on Reach III of the Dove Creek Canal,* compiled by W. D. McNamee and N. S. Hammack, pp. 2.1–2.48. Cortez, Colo.: Complete Archaeological Service Associates.

1992b Excavations at Cloud Blower Stockade (5DL121b), a Late Basketmaker III Habitation. In Four Corners Archaeological Project, Report no. 18, *Archaeological Excavations on Reach III of the Dove Creek Canal,* compiled by W. D. McNamee and N. S. Hammack, pp. 3.1–3.33. Cortez, Colo.: Complete Archaeological Service Associates.

McNitt, F.

1966 *Richard Wetherill Anasazi.* Albuquerque: University of New Mexico Press.

McVickar, J. L.

1996a The Changing Environment of the Southern Chuska Valley, Northwestern New Mexico. In *Time, Place, and Society: Project Synthesis,* by T. M. Kearns and J. L. McVickar. Pipeline Archaeology 1990–1993: The El Paso Natural Gas North System Expansion Project, New Mexico and Arizona, vol. XIII, draft report, T. M. Kearns, general editor. Report no. WCRM(F)074. Farmington, N.Mex.: Western Cultural Resource Management, Inc.

1999a Analysis of Plant Macrofossils. In *Anasazi Community Development in Redrock Valley: Archaeological Excavations along the N33 Road in Apache County, Arizona,* edited by P. F. Reed and K. N. Hensler, pp. 809–850. Navajo Nation Papers in Anthropology no. 33, Window Rock, Ariz.

McVickar, J. L. (ed.)

1996b *Investigations at an Early Anasazi Community in Tohatchi Flats.* Pipeline Archaeology 1990–1993: The El Paso Natural Gas North System Expansion Project, New Mexico and Arizona, vol. VII, draft report, T. M. Kearns, general editor. Report no. WCRM(F)074. Farmington, N.Mex.: Western Cultural Resource Management, Inc.

1999b *Excavations at Four Sites in Tohatchi Flats.* Pipeline Archaeology 1990–1993: The El Paso Natural Gas North System Expansion Project, New Mexico and Arizona, vol. VI, T. M. Kearns, general editor. Report no. WCRM(F)074. Farmington, N.Mex.: Western Cultural Resource Management, Inc.

McVickar, J. L., and S. A. Wails

1999 LA 2506: The Muddy Wash Site. In *Excavations at Three Sites in Tohatchi Flats,* edited by J. L. McVickar, pp. 2-1 to 2-410. Pipeline Archaeology 1990–1993: The El Paso Natural Gas North System Expansion Project, New Mexico and Arizona, vol. VI, T. M. Kearns, general editor. Report no. WCRM(F)074. Farmington, N.Mex.: Western Cultural Resource Management, Inc.

Mera, H. P.

1934 *Observations on the Archaeology of the Petrified Forest National Monument.* Technical Series Bulletin no. 7. Santa Fe: Laboratory of Anthropology, Museum of New Mexico.

Metcalf, M. D., and K. D. Black

1991 *Archaeological Excavations at the Yarmony Pit House Site, Eagle County, Colorado.* Cultural Resource Series no. 31. Denver: Bureau of Land Management.

Miller, W. C., and D. A. Breternitz

1958a 1957 Navajo Canyon Survey: Preliminary Report. *Plateau* 30:72–74.

1958b 1958 Navajo Canyon Survey: Preliminary Report. *Plateau* 31:3–7.

Mills, B. J.

1989 The Organization of Ceramic Production in Household Economies. Paper presented at a Symposium in Honor of Lewis R. Binford, Albuquerque, New Mexico.

Mills, B. J., C. E. Goetze, and M. N. Zedeno

1993 *Interpretation of Ceramic Artifacts.* Across the Colorado Plateau: Anthropological Studies for the Transwestern Pipeline Expansion Project, vol. XVI. Albuquerque: Office of Contract Archaeology and Maxwell Museum of Anthropology.

Mindeleff, V.

1891 A Study of Pueblo Architecture: Tusayan and Cibola. In *Eighth Annual Report of the Bureau of American Ethnology* for the years 1886–1887, pp. 3–228. Washington, D.C.: U.S. Government Printing Office.

Minnis, P. E.

1985 Domesticating People and Plants in the Greater Southwest. In *Prehistoric Food Production in North America,* edited by R. I. Ford, pp. 309–339. Anthropological Papers No. 75. Ann Arbor: Museum of Anthropology, University of Michigan.

1989 Prehistoric Diet in the Northern Southwest: Macroplant Remains from Four Corners Feces. *American Antiquity* 54:543–563.

Mobley-Tanaka, J.

1993 Subterranean Mealing Rooms in the Montezuma Valley: Site Patterns and Social Functions. Paper presented at the Fifth Occasional Anasazi Symposium, Farmington, N.Mex.

Montgomery, J. L.

1986 Excavations at Apricot Hamlet (Site 5MT2858): A Basketmaker III/Pueblo I Habitation Site. In *Dolores Archaeological Program: Anasazi Communities at Dolores: Early Anasazi Sites in the Sagehen Flats Area,* compiled by A. E. Kane and G. T. Gross, prepared under the supervision of D. A. Breternitz, pp. 213–256. Denver: U.S. Department of the Interior, Bureau of Reclamation, Engineering and Research Center.

Moore, A. M. T.

1995 The Inception of Potting in Western Asia and Its Impact on Economy and Society. In *The Emergence of Pottery: Technology and Innovation in Ancient Societies,* edited by W. K. Barnett and J. W. Hoopes, pp. 39–53. Washington, D.C.: Smithsonian Institution Press.

Morgenstein, M.

1995 Analysis of Tohatchi Red-on-brown Pigment: LA 2506-4928-0-32-1. Report prepared by Geosciences Management Institute, Inc., Boulder City, Nevada. Ms. on file at Western Cultural Resource Management, Inc., Farmington, N.Mex.

Morris, A. A.

1934 *Digging in the Southwest.* New York: The Junior Literary Guild and Doubleday, Doran, and Co. Inc.

Morris, E. A.

1959 Basketmaker Caves in the Prayer Rock District, Northeastern Arizona. Ph.D. diss., Department of Anthropology, University of Arizona, Tucson.

1980 *Basketmaker Caves in the Prayer Rock District, Northeastern Arizona.* Anthropological Papers of the University of Arizona no. 35. Tucson: University of Arizona Press.

Morris, E. H.

1919 *Preliminary Account of the Antiquities of the Region between the Mancos and La Plata Rivers in Southwestern Colorado.* Bureau of American Ethnology Annual Report no. 53, pp. 155–206, Washington, D.C.

1927 *The Beginnings of Pottery Making in the San Juan Area: Unfired Prototypes and the Wares of the Earliest Ceramic Periods.* American Museum of Natural History Anthropology Papers, vol. 28, part II, New York.

1931 Report on Archaeological Reconnaissance in the Carriso-Lukachukai District of Northeastern Arizona and Northwestern New Mexico. Eighth Bernheimer Expedition of the American Museum of Natural History in 1930 under permit from the Department of the Interior issued to the American Museum of Natural History May 5, 1930. Ms. on file, American Museum of Natural History, New York.

1939 *Archaeological Studies in the La Plata District, Southwestern Colorado and Northwestern New Mexico.* Carnegie Institute Publication no. 519, Washington, D.C.

1944 Anasazi Sandals. *Clearing House for Southwestern Museums News-Letters* 68–69:239–241.

1951 Basketmaker III Human Figurines from Northeastern Arizona. *American Antiquity* 7:33–40.

Morris, E. H., and R. F. Burgh

1941 *Anasazi Basketry, Basket Maker II through Pueblo III: A Study Based on Specimens from the San Juan River Country.* Carnegie Institute Publication no. 553, Washington, D.C.

1954 *Basket Maker II Sites near Durango, Colorado.* Carnegie Institute Publication no. 604, Washington D.C.

Morris, J. N.

1991 *Archaeological Excavations on the Hovenweep Laterals.* CASA Report no. 90-16. Cortez, Colo.: Complete Archaeological Service Associates.

Morss, N.

1927 *Archaeological Explorations on the Middle Chinlee, 1925.* Memoirs of the American Anthropological Association no. 34, Menasha, Wisconsin.

1954 *Clay Figurines of the American Southwest.* Papers of the Peabody Museum of American Archaeology and Ethnology no. 44. Cambridge: Harvard University.

Motsinger, T. N. (ed.)

1997 Excavations at Dancing Man Hamlet (5MT9343). In preparation. Durango, Colo.: SWCA, Inc.

Motsinger, T. N., and M. L. Chenault

1995 Stockaded Basketmaker Sites in the Mesa Verde Region. Paper presented at the 60th annual meeting of the Society for American Archaeology, Minneapolis.

Motsinger, T. N., and M. L. Chenault (eds.)

1997 Excavations at Big Bend Hamlet (5MT9387): A Basketmaker III Site on Reach 1 of the Lone Pine Laterals, Montezuma County, Colorado. In preparation. Durango, Colo.: SWCA, Inc.

Motsinger, T. N., and D. R. Mitchell

1994 *The Clarkdale Pipeline Archaeological Project: Data Recovery at Ten Sites in the Northern Black Hills, Yavapai County, Arizona.* Archaeological Report no. 94-101. Tucson: SWCA, Inc.

Murray, L. K.

1999 Paleoenvironmental Implications of the Faunal Remains: El Paso Natural Gas North System Expansion Project. In *Supporting Studies: Nonceramic Artifacts, Subsistence and Environmental Studies, and Chronometric Studies,* compiled by T. M. Kearns and J. L. McVickar, pp. 15-1 to 15-35. Pipeline Archaeology 1990–1993: The El Paso Natural Gas North System Expansion Project, New Mexico and Arizona, vol. XII, T. M. Kearns, general editor. Report no. WCRM(F)074. Farmington, N.Mex.: Western Cultural Resource Management, Inc.

Naroll, P.

1962 Floor Area and Settlement Population. *American Antiquity* 27:587–588.

Nelson, Reid J.

1994 Basketmaker II Lithic Technology and Mobility Patterns on Cedar Mesa, Southeast Utah. *Kiva* 60:277–288.

Nichols, D. L., and F. E. Smiley

1984 *Excavations on Black Mesa, 1982: A Descriptive Report.* Center for Archaeological Investigations Research Paper no. 39. Carbondale: Southern Illinois University.

1985 An Overview of Northern Black Mesa Archaeology. In *Excavations on Black Mesa, 1983: A Descriptive Report,* edited by A. L. Christenson and W. J. Parry, pp. 49–81. Center for Archaeological Investigations Research Paper no. 46. Carbondale: Southern Illinois University.

Nickens, Paul R., Alan D. Reed, and Todd R. Metzger

1988 Investigations at Rock Creek Alcove: An Early Basketmaker II Burial Site in Glen Canyon National Recreation Area, Utah. *Kiva* 53:235–252.

Nordby, L. V., and D. A. Breternitz

1972 Site MV 1824-71: A Basketmaker III Pit House and Cist on Wetherill Mesa. Report submitted to the Midwest Archeological Center, National Park Service, Lincoln, Neb.

O'Bryan, D.

1950 *Excavations in Mesa Verde National Park, 1947–1948.* Medallion Papers no. 39. Globe, Ariz.: Gila Pueblo.

Olson, A. P., and W. W. Wasley

1956a LA 2506. *In Pipeline Archaeology: Reports of Salvage Operations in the Southwest on the El Paso Natural Gas Company Projects, 1950–1953,* edited by F. Wendorf, N. Fox, and O. L. Lewis, pp. 51–56. Flagstaff: Museum of Northern Arizona.

1956b Further Excavations at Site LA 2507. In *Pipeline Archaeology: Reports of Salvage Operations in the Southwest on the El Paso Natural Gas Company Projects, 1950–1953,* edited by F. Wendorf, N. Fox, and O. L. Lewis, pp. 61–65. Flagstaff: Museum of Northern Arizona.

Paige, K. E., and J. M. Paige

1981 *The Politics of Reproductive Ritual.* Berkeley: University of California Press.

Palmer, W. C.

1965 *Meteorological Drought.* Research Paper no. 45. U.S. Weather Bureau 58. Washington, D.C.: NOAA Library and Information Services Division.

Parry, T.

1984 Site NA10764 (LA 72947) Fieldnotes. Notes on file, Zuni Archaeology Program, Zuni Pueblo, N.Mex.

Parry, W. J.

1987 Technological Change: Temporal and Functional Variability in Chipped Stone Debitage. In *Prehistoric Stone Technology on Northern Black Mesa, Arizona,* by W. J.

Parry and A. L. Christenson, pp. 199–256. Center for Archaeological Investigations Occasional Paper no. 12. Carbondale: Southern Illinois University.

Parry, W. J., and A. L. Christenson

1987 *Prehistoric Stone Technology on Northern Black Mesa, Arizona.* Center for Archaeological Investigations Occasional Paper no. 12. Carbondale: Southern Illinois University.

Parry, W. J., and R. L. Kelly

1987 Expedient Core Technology and Sedentism. In *The Organization of Core Technology,* edited by J. K. Johnson and C. A. Morrow, pp. 285–304. Boulder, Colo.: Westview Press.

Parsons, E. C.

1939 *Pueblo Indian Religion.* Chicago: University of Chicago Press.

Parsons, E. C. (ed.)

1936 *Hopi Journal of Alexander Stephen.* New York: Columbia University Press.

Paton, R.

1994 Speaking through Stones: A Study from Northern Australia. *World Archaeology* 26:172–184.

Peckham, S.

1963 Two Rosa Phase Sites near Dulce, New Mexico. In *Highway Salvage Archaeology* 21, assembled by S. Peckham, pp. 92–122. Santa Fe: Museum of New Mexico.

1969 An Archaeological Site Inventory of New Mexico, part 1. Ms. on file, Laboratory of Anthropology, Museum of New Mexico, Santa Fe.

Pepper, G. H.

1902 The Ancient Basket Makers of Southeastern Utah. *American Museum Journal,* vol. II, no. 4 (supplement), New York.

Petersen, K. L.

1981 10,000 Years of Climatic Change Reconstructed from Fossil Pollen, La Plata Mountains, Southwestern Colorado. Ph.D. diss., Department of Anthropology, Washington State University. Ann Arbor: University Microfilms.

1985 *Agricultural Potential Classification in the Dolores Archaeological Project Area, Southwestern Colorado.* Dolores Archaeological Program Technical Report DA-223. Submitted to the Bureau of Reclamation, Upper Colorado Region, Salt Lake City.

1986 Climatic Reconstruction for the Dolores Project Area. In *Dolores Archaeological Program: Final Synthetic Report,* compiled by D. A. Breternitz, C. K. Robinson, G. T. Gross, pp. 311–325. Denver: U.S. Department of the Interior, Bureau of Reclamation, Engineering and Research Center.

1987a Reconstruction of Droughts for the Dolores Project Area Using Tree-ring Studies. In *Dolores Archaeological Program: Supporting Studies: Settlement and Environment,* compiled by K. L. Petersen and J. D. Orcutt, pp. 89–102. Denver: U.S. Department of the Interior, Bureau of Reclamation, Engineering and Research Center.

1987b Summer Precipitation: An Important Factor in the Dolores Project Area. In *Dolores Archaeological Program: Supporting Studies: Settlement and Environment,* edited by K. L. Petersen and J. D. Orcutt, pp. 73–88. Denver: U.S. Department of the Interior, Bureau of Reclamation, Engineering and Research Center.

1988 *Climate and the Dolores River Anasazi.* Anthropological Papers no. 113. Salt Lake City: University of Utah.

Petersen, K. L., and P. J. Mehringer

1976 Postglacial Timberline Fluctuations, La Plata Mountains, Southwestern Colorado. *Arctic and Alpine Research* 8:275–288.

Phagan, C. J.

1985 Reductive Technology. In *Prehistory and Cultural Dynamics in the Dolores Area: The Dolores Archaeological Program Final Report,* edited by D. A. Breternitz, C. K. Robinson, and G. T. Gross. Ms. on file at U.S. Department of the Interior, Bureau of Reclamation, Upper Colorado Region, Salt Lake City.

Phillips, D. A., Jr.

1993 Interpretation of Surface Artifact Scatters: An Example from Southeast Arizona. Paper presented at the 58th annual meeting of the Society for American Archaeology, St. Louis.

1997 Architecture and Feature Descriptions for Site 5MT9168. In Excavation of the Rabbit Site (5MT9168), edited by M. L. Chenault. In preparation. Durango, Colo.: SWCA, Inc.

Plog, F.

1974 *The Study of Prehistoric Change.* New York: Academic Press.

1979 Prehistory: Western Anasazi. In Southwest, edited by A. Ortiz, pp. 131–151. *Handbook of the North American Indians,* vol. 9, W. C. Sturtevant, general editor. Washington, D.C.: Smithsonian Institution.

1983 Political and Economic Alliances on the Colorado Plateaus, A.D. 400–1450. In *Advances in World Archaeology,* vol. 2, edited by F. Wendorf and A. E. Close, pp. 289–330. New York: Academic Press.

1984 Exchange, Tribes, and Alliances: The Northern Southwest. *American Archeology* 4:217–223.

Plog, F., G. J. Gumerman, R. C. Euler, J. S. Dean, R. H. Hevly, and T. N. V. Karlstrom

1988 Anasazi Adaptive Strategies: The Model, Predictions, and Results. In *The Anasazi in a Changing Environment,* edited by G. J. Gumerman, pp. 230–276. Cambridge: Cambridge University Press.

Plog, S.

1980 *Stylistic Variation in Prehistoric Ceramics.* Cambridge: Cambridge University Press.

1997 *Ancient Peoples of the American Southwest.* London: Thames and Hudson.

Plog, S., and S. Powell

1984 Patterns of Culture Change: Alternative Interpretations. In *Papers on the Archaeology of Black Mesa, Arizona,* vol. II, edited by S. Plog and S. Powell, pp. 209–216. Carbondale: Southern Illinois University Press.

Popelish, L., and R. T. Fehr

1983 *Archaeological Investigations in the Northern Chuska Mountains: The N-13 Road Survey at Red Rock to Lukachukai, Navajo Nation (CRMP-83-039).* Navajo Nation Papers in Anthropology no. 18, Window Rock, Ariz.

Powell, Shirley L.

1980 Material Culture and Behavior: A Prehistoric Example from the American Southwest. Ph.D. diss., Department of Anthropology, Arizona State University, Tempe.

1983 *Mobility and Adaptation: The Anasazi of Black Mesa, Arizona.* Carbondale: Southern Illinois University Press.

Powers, R. P., W. B. Gillespie, and S. H. Lekson

1983 *The Outlier Survey: A Regional View of Settlement in the San Juan Basin.* Reports of the Chaco Center no. 3. Albuquerque: Division of Cultural Research, National Park Service.

Prudden, T. M

1897   An Elder Brother to the Cliff-Dweller. *Harper's Monthly* (June 1897):56–63.

Rafferty, J. E.

1985   The Archaeological Record on Sedentariness: Recognition, Development, and Implications. In *Advances in Archaeological Method and Theory,* edited by M. B. Schiffer, pp. 113–156. New York: Academic Press.

Reed, A. C.

1999   Archaeobotanical Analysis. In *Supporting Studies: Nonceramic Artifacts, Subsistence and Environmental Studies, and Chronometric Studies,* compiled by T. M. Kearns and J. L. McVickar, pp. 12-1 to 12-62. Pipeline Archaeology 1990–1993: The El Paso Natural Gas North System Expansion Project, New Mexico and Arizona, vol. XII, T. M. Kearns general editor. Report no. WCRM(F)074. Farmington, N.Mex.: Western Cultural Resource Management, Inc.

Reed, A. D.

1984   *West Central Colorado Prehistoric Context.* Denver: State Historical Society of Colorado.

Reed, A. D., and J. C. Horn

1987   *A Supplemental Cultural Resource Inventory of the La Plata Mine, San Juan County, New Mexico.* Montrose, Colo.: Nickens and Associates.

Reed, A. D., and R. E. Kainer

1978   The Tamarron Site, 5LP326. *Southwestern Lore* 44:1–47.

Reed, A. D., and S. A. McDonald

1988   Archeological Investigations at Three Lithic Scatters and Eight Culturally Peeled Trees along the West Dolores Road, Montezuma and Dolores Counties, Colorado. Report on file, National Park Service, Interagency Archeological Service, Denver.

Reed, L. S., and J. Goff

1998   Formal Type Descriptions of Tohatchi Red and Tohatchi Red-on-Brown. In *Exploring Ceramic Production, Distribution, and Exchange in the Southern Chuska Valley: Analytical Results from the El Paso Natural Gas North Expansion Project,* by L. S. Reed, J. Goff, and K. N. Hensler, appendix C. Pipeline Archaeology 1990–1993: The El Paso Natural Gas North System Expansion Project, New Mexico and Arizona, vol. XI, T. M. Kearns, general editor. Report no. WCRM(F)074. Farmington, N.Mex.: Western Cultural Resource Management, Inc.

Reed, L. S., J. Goff, and K. N. Hensler

1998   *Exploring Ceramic Production, Distribution, and Exchange in the Southern Chuska Valley: Analytical Results from the El Paso Natural Gas North Expansion Project.* Pipeline Archaeology 1990–1993: The El Paso Natural Gas North System Expansion Project, New Mexico and Arizona, vol. XI, T. M. Kearns, general editor. Report no. WCRM(F)074. Farmington, N.Mex.: Western Cultural Resource Management, Inc.

Reed, L. S., and K. N. Hensler

1998a Pueblo I Ceramic Assemblages. In *Exploring Ceramic Production, Distribution, and Exchange in the Southern Chuska Valley: Analytical Results from the El Paso Natural Gas North System Expansion Project,* by L. S. Reed, J. Goff, and K. N. Hensler, pp. 4-1 to 4-90. Pipeline Archaeology 1990–1993: The El Paso Natural Gas North

System Expansion Project, New Mexico and Arizona, vol. XI, T. M. Kearns, general editor. Report no. WCRM(F)074. Farmington, N.Mex.: Western Cultural Resource Management, Inc.

1998b Basketmaker III Ceramic Assemblages. In *Exploring Ceramic Production, Distribution, and Exchange in the Southern Chuska Valley: Analytical Results from the El Paso Natural Gas North Expansion Project,* by L. S. Reed, J. Goff, and K. N. Hensler, pp. 3-1 to 3-130. Pipeline Archaeology 1990–1993: The El Paso Natural Gas North System Expansion Project, New Mexico and Arizona, vol. XI, T. M. Kearns, general editor. Report no. WCRM(F)074. Farmington, N.Mex.: Western Cultural Resource Management, Inc.

Reed, L. S., J. L. McVickar, and S. A. Wails

1996   Modeling the Basketmaker Transition in the Southern San Juan Basin, New Mexico. Paper presented at the 61st annual meeting of the Society for American Archaeology, New Orleans.

Reed, P. F.

1990   Changing Patterns of Anasazi Settlement in the Middle San Juan from Basketmaker III to Pueblo III. Paper presented at the 55th annual meeting of the Society for American Archaeology, Las Vegas, Nevada.

1999a The Cove Anasazi Community: A Basketmaker III–Pueblo III Period Settlement in Redrock Valley, Northeastern Arizona. In preparation. On file, Navajo Nation Archaeology Department, Farmington, N.Mex.

1999b A Demographic Reconstruction of the Anasazi Occupation of Cove–Redrock Valley. In *Anasazi Community Development in Redrock Valley: Archaeological Excavations along the N33 Road in Apache County, Arizona,* edited by P. F. Reed and K. N. Hensler, pp. 1023–1034. Navajo Nation Papers in Anthropology no. 33, Window Rock, Ariz.

Reed, P. F., A. Anderson, V. Yazzie, K. Langenfeld, and J. J. Ponczynski

1991   *An Archaeological Reassessment of the Cove to Red Valley Road (Navajo Route 33) for Bureau of Indian Affairs, Branch of Roads in Apache County, Arizona.* NNAD Report 93-004. Window Rock, Ariz: Navajo Nation Archaeology Department.

Reed, P. F., and K. N. Hensler (eds.)

1999   *Anasazi Community Development in Redrock Valley: Archaeological Excavations along the N33 Road in Apache County, Arizona.* Navajo Nation Papers in Anthropology no. 33, Window Rock, Ariz.

Reed, P. F., and J. T. Torres

1999   Settlement Patterns in the Greater Cove–Redrock Valley Area. In *Anasazi Community Development in Redrock Valley: Archaeological Excavations along the N33 Road in Apache County, Arizona,* edited by P. F. Reed and K. N. Hensler, pp. 945–952. Navajo Nation Papers in Anthropology no. 33, Window Rock, Ariz.

Reid, J., and S. Whittlesey

1997   *The Archaeology of Ancient Arizona.* Tucson: University of Arizona Press.

Rice, G.

1975   A Systematic Explanation of a Change in Mogollon Settlement Patterns. Ph.D. diss., University of Washington, Seattle. Ann Arbor: University Microfilms.

Rice, P. M.

1991   Women and Prehistoric Pottery Production. In *Gender and Archaeology: Proceedings of the 22nd Chacmool*

Conference, edited by D. Walde and N. Willows, pp. 446–463 Calgary, Canada: University of Calgary.

1999 On the Origins of Pottery. *Journal of Archaeological Method and Theory* 6:1–54.

Richardson, G.

1987 *Navajo Trader.* Tucson: University of Arizona Press.

Richens, L. D., and R. K. Talbot

1989 Sandy Ridge: An Aceramic Habitation Site in Southeastern Utah. *Utah Archaeology* 2(1):77–88.

Rinaldo, J.

1943 Pottery. In *The S.U. Site: Excavations at a Mogollon Village, Western New Mexico,* by P. S. Martin and J. Rinaldo, pp. 78–84. Anthropological Series of the Field Museum of Natural History, vol. 32, no. 1, Chicago.

Rippel, S. P., and C. K. Walth

1999 Analysis of Faunal Remains from Archaic to Modern Times in Northwest New Mexico. In *Supporting Studies: Nonceramic Artifacts, Subsistence and Environmental Studies, and Chronometric Studies,* edited by T. M. Kearns and J. L. McVickar, pp. 14-1 to 14-54. Pipeline Archaeology 1990–1993: The El Paso Natural Gas North System Expansion Project, New Mexico and Arizona, vol. XII, T. M. Kearns, general editor. Report no. WCRM(F)074. Farmington, N.Mex.: Western Cultural Resource Management, Inc.

Roberts, F. H. H., Jr.

1929 *Shabik'eshchee Village: A Late Basketmaker Site in the Chaco Canyon, New Mexico.* Bureau of American Ethnology Bulletin no. 92, Washington, D.C.

Robins, M. R.

1997 Modeling Socio-economic Organization of the San Juan Basketmakers: A Preliminary Study in Rock Art and Social Dynamics. In *Early Farmers of the Northern Southwest: Papers on Chronometry, Social Dynamics, and Ecology,* edited by F. E. Smiley and M. R. Robins, pp. 73–120. Animas-La Plata Archaeological Project Research Paper no. 7. Flagstaff: Northern Arizona University.

1999 San Juan Basketmakers: Rock Art, Food Production, and Social Relations in a Mixed Farming and Foraging Economy. Paper presented at the 1999 International Rock Art Congress, Ripon, Wisc.

Robins, M. R., and F. E. Smiley

1998 The Butler Wash Rockshelters Project: Preliminary Data Recovery from Extensively Looted Contexts. Paper presented at the 63rd annual meeting of the Society for American Archaeology, Seattle.

Robinson, W. J., and C. M. Cameron

1991 *A Directory of Tree-ring Dated Prehistoric Sites in the American Southwest.* Tucson: Laboratory of Tree-ring Research, University of Arizona.

Robinson, W. J., and B. G. Harrill

1974 *Tree-Ring Dates from Colorado V, Mesa Verde Area.* Tucson: Laboratory of Tree-ring Research, University of Arizona.

Rohn, A. H.

1971 *Mug House, Mesa Verde National Park, Colorado.* Archeological Research Series no. 7D. Washington, D.C.: National Park Service.

1975 A Stockaded Basketmaker III Village at Yellow Jacket, Colorado. *The Kiva* 40:113–119.

1977 *Cultural Change and Continuity on Chapin Mesa.* Lawrence, Kan.: Regents Press.

1989 Northern San Juan Prehistory. In *Dynamics of Southwest*

Prehistory, edited by L. S. Cordell and G. Gumerman, pp. 149–178. Washington, D.C.: Smithsonian Institution Press.

Roscoe, W.

1991 *The Zuni Man-Woman.* Albuquerque: University of New Mexico Press.

Rose, M. R., W. J. Robinson, and J. S. Dean

1982 Dendroclimatic Reconstruction for the Southeastern Colorado Plateau. Final report to the Division of Chaco Research, National Park Service.

Rozen, K. C.

1981 Patterned Association among Lithic Technology, Site Content, and Time: Results of the TEP St. Johns Project Lithic Analysis. In *Prehistory of the St. Johns Area, East-central Arizona: The TEP St. Johns Project,* edited by D. A. Westfall, pp. 157–232. Archaeological Series no. 153. Tucson: Cultural Resource Management Division, Arizona State Museum, University of Arizona.

Ruppé, P. A.

1989 Analysis of Archaeobotanical Remains from Redrock Valley, Northeastern Arizona. In *The Archaeology and Ethnohistory of Redrock Valley: A study of Prehistoric and Historic Land Use in Northeastern Arizona,* vol. 1, edited by B. S. Hildebrant, pp. 438–475. Research Series no. 3. Zuni Pueblo, N.Mex.: Zuni Archaeology Program.

1999 N30-N31 Project Chronology. In *Chuska Chronologies, Houses, and Hogans: Archaeological and Ethnographic Inquiry along N30-N31 Between Mexican Springs and Navajo, McKinley County, New Mexico,* vol. III, part 1, edited by J. E. Damp, pp. 311–325. Research Series no. 10. Zuni Pueblo, N.Mex.: Zuni Cultural Resource Enterprise.

Sahlins, M.

1972 *Stone Age Economics.* Chicago: Aldine-Atherton, Inc.

Saitta, D. J.

1997 Power, Labor, and the Dynamics of Change in Chacoan Political Economy. *American Antiquity* 62:7–26.

Sant, M. B.

1990 N30/N31 Project Plan for Recovery of Data at Prehistoric Sites and Prehistoric Components at Multicomponent Sites and Preliminary Results from Previous Testing and Reassessment Phases of the N30/N31 Roadway Project. Ms. on file, Zuni Archaeology Program, Zuni Pueblo, N.Mex.

1999 Research Orientation. In *Chuska Chronologies, Houses, and Hogans: Archaeological and Ethnographic Inquiry along N30-N31 between Mexican Springs and Navajo, McKinley County, New Mexico,* vol. I, edited by J. E. Damp, pp. 67–84. Zuni Cultural Resource Enterprise Research Series no. 10, Zuni Pueblo, N.Mex.

Schaafsma, P.

1980 *Indian Rock Art of the Southwest.* Albuquerque: University of New Mexico Press.

Scheick, C. L. (compiler)

1983 *HR 100: Excavations in the Dead Zone.* School of American Research Report no. 102, Santa Fe.

Schiffer, M. B.

1972 Cultural Laws and the Reconstruction of Past Lifeways. *The Kiva* 37:148–157.

1982 Hohokam Chronology: An Essay on History and Method. In *Hohokam and Patayan: Prehistory of Southwestern Arizona,* edited by R. H. McGuire and M. B. Schiffer, pp. 299–344. New York: Academic Press.

1986 Radiocarbon Dates and the "Old Wood" Problem: The

Case of the Hohokam Chronology. *Journal of Archaeological Science* 13:13–30.

1987 *Formation Processes of the Archaeological Record.* New York: Academic Press.

1988 The Effects of Surface Treatment on Permeability and Evaporative Cooling Effectiveness of Pottery. In *Proceedings of the 26th International Archaeometry Symposium,* edited by R. M. Farquhar, R. G. V. Hancock, and L. A. Pavlish, pp. 23–29. Toronto: Archaeometry Laboratory, Department of Physics, University of Toronto.

1990 The Influence of Surface Treatment on Heating Effectiveness of Ceramic Vessels. *Journal of Archaeological Science* 17:373–381.

Schiffer, M. B., J. M. Skibo, T. C. Boelke, M. A. Neupert, and M. Aronson

1994 New Perspectives on Experimental Archaeology: Surface Treatments and Thermal Response of the Clay Cooking Pot. *American Antiquity* 59:197–217.

Schilz, A. J.

1979 The Desha Caves: Two Basketmaker Sites in Southeast Utah. Master's thesis, Department of Anthropology, California State University. Ann Arbor: University Microfilms.

Schlanger, S. H.

1985 Prehistoric Population Dynamics in the Dolores Area, Southwestern Colorado. Ph.D. diss., Department of Anthropology, Washington State University, Pullman.

1986 Population Studies. In *Dolores Archaeological Program: Final Synthetic Report,* compiled by D. A. Breternitz, C. K. Robinson, G. T. Gross, pp. 493–524. Denver: U.S. Department of the Interior, Bureau of Reclamation, Engineering and Research Center.

1988a Patterns of Population Movement and Long-term Population Growth in Southwestern Colorado. *American Antiquity* 53:773–793.

1988b Recognizing Persistent Places in Anasazi Settlement Systems. Paper presented at the 53rd annual meeting of the Society for American Archaeology, Phoenix.

1988c Site Occupation Duration and Patterns of Sedentism among the Eastern Anasazi. Paper presented at the Southwest Symposium, Arizona State University, Tempe.

1995 Corn Grinding, Mealing Rooms, and Prehistoric Society in the American Southwest. Ms. in possession of author.

Schlanger, S. H., and R. H. Wilshusen

1993 Local Abandonments and Regional Conditions in the North American Southwest. In *Abandonment of Settlements and Regions: Ethnoarchaeological and Archaeological Approaches,* edited by C. M. Cameron and S. A. Tomka, pp. 85–98. Cambridge: Cambridge University Press.

Schniebs, L.

1999 Faunal Analysis for the Cove–Red Valley Archaeological Project. In *Anasazi Community Development in Redrock Valley: Archaeological Excavations along the N33 Road in Apache County, Arizona,* edited by P. F. Reed and K. N. Hensler, pp. 765–808. Navajo Nation Papers in Anthropology no. 33, Window Rock, Ariz.

Schroeder, A. H.

1982 Historical Overview of Southwestern Ceramics. In *Southwestern Ceramics: A Comparative Review,* edited by A. H. Schroeder, pp. 1–26. The Arizona Archaeologist no. 15. Phoenix: Arizona Archaeological Society.

Sebastian, L.

1985 *Archeological Excavation along the Turquoise Trail: The Mitigation Program.* Albuquerque: Office of Contract Archeology, University of New Mexico.

1992 *The Chaco Anasazi: Sociopolitical Evolution in the Prehistoric Southwest.* New York: Cambridge University Press.

Service, E. R.

1971 *Primitive Social Organization: An Evolutionary Perspective.* 2nd ed. New York: Random House.

Shafer, H. J., and R. L. Brewington

1995 Microstylistic Changes in Mimbres Black-on-white Pottery: Examples from the Nan Ruin, Grant County, New Mexico. *Kiva* 61:5–29.

Sharrock, F. W., K. Day, and D. S. Dibble

1963 *1961 Excavations, Glen Canyon Area.* Anthropological Papers no. 63. Salt Lake City: University of Utah Press.

Shelley, S. D.

1990 Basketmaker III Social Organization: An Evaluation of Population, Aggregation, and Site Structure. Paper presented at the 55th annual meeting of the Society for American Archaeology, Las Vegas, Nev.

1991 The Potential for Distinct Populations during Basketmaker III on the Colorado Plateau. Paper presented at the 56th annual meeting of the Society for American Archaeology, New Orleans.

2000 Faunal Analysis. In *Cultural Dynamics in the Lukachukai Valley: The N-13 Project,* edited by J. H. Altschul, S. D. Shelley, and E. K. Huber. Technical Series no. 16. Tucson: Statistical Research, Inc.

Shepard, A. O.

1939 Technology of La Plata Pottery, Appendix A. In *Archaeological Studies in the La Plata District in Southwestern Colorado and Northwestern New Mexico,* by E. H. Morris. Publication no. 519. Washington, D.C.: Carnegie Institute.

1953 Notes on Color and Paste Composition. In *Archaeological Studies in the Petrified Forest National Monument,* by F. Wendorf, pp. 177–193. Museum of Northern Arizona Bulletin no. 27, Flagstaff.

Simmons, A.

1982a Technological and Typological Variability of Lithic Assemblages in the Bis sa'ani Community. In *Bis sa'ani: A Late Bonito Phase Community on Escalante Wash, Northwestern New Mexico,* edited by C. D. Breternitz, D. E. Doyel, and M. P. Marshall, pp. 955–1013. Navajo Nation Papers in Anthropology no. 14, Window Rock, Ariz.

1982b Technological and Typological Variability in the ADAPT I Lithic Assemblages. In *Prehistoric Adaptive Strategies in the Chaco Canyon Region, Northwestern New Mexico,* edited by A. H. Simmons, pp. 731–779. Navajo Nation Papers in Anthropology no. 9, Window Rock, Ariz.

1986 New Evidence for the Early Use of Cultigens in the American Southwest. *American Antiquity* 51:73–89.

Skibo, J. M.

1992 *Pottery Function: A Use-Alteration Perspective.* New York: Plenum Publishing.

Skibo, J. M., and E. Blinman

1999 Exploring the Origins of Pottery on the Colorado Plateau. In *Pottery and People: A Dynamic Interaction,* edited by J. M. Skibo and G. M. Feinman, pp. 171–183. Salt Lake City: University of Utah Press.

Skinner, E., and D. Gilpin

1997 *Cultural Resources Investigations along Navajo Route 9 (N9), U.S. Highway 666 to Standing Rock, McKinley*

County, New Mexico. Report no. 96-144. Flagstaff, Ariz.: SWCA, Inc.

Smiley, F. E.

1985   The Chronometrics of Early Agricultural Sites in Northeastern Arizona: Approaches to the Interpretation of Radiocarbon Dates. Ph.D. diss., Department of Anthropology, University of Michigan. Ann Arbor: University Microfilms.

1993   Early Farmers in the Northern Southwest: A View from Marsh Pass. In *Anasazi Basketmaker: Papers from the 1990 Wetherill-Grand Gulch Symposium,* edited by V. M. Atkins, pp. 243–254. Cultural Resource Series no. 24. Salt Lake City: Bureau of Land Management.

1994   The Agricultural Transition in the Northern Southwest: Patterns in the Current Chronometric Data. *Kiva* 60:165–189.

1997   Toward Chronometric Resolution for Early Agriculture in the Northern Southwest. In *Early Farmers of the Northern Southwest: Papers on Chronometry, Social Dynamics, and Ecology,* edited by F. E. Smiley and M. R. Robins, pp. 13–41. Animas-La Plata Archaeological Project Research Paper no. 7. Flagstaff: Northern Arizona University.

Smiley, F. E., and P. P. Andrews

1983   An Overview of Black Mesa Archaeological Research. In *Excavations on Black Mesa, 1981: A Descriptive Report,* edited by F. E. Smiley, D. L. Nichols, and P. P. Andrews, pp. 45–60. Research Paper no. 36. Carbondale: Center for Archaeological Investigations, Southern Illinois University.

Smiley, F. E., W. J. Parry, and G. J. Gumerman

1988   Early Agriculture in the Black Mesa/Marsh Pass Region of Arizona: New Chronometric Data and Recent Excavations at Three Fir Shelter. Paper presented at the 51st annual meeting of the Society for American Archaeology, New Orleans.

Smiley, F. E., and M. R. Robins

1997   Chronometric Sampling in Disturbed Contexts. Paper presented at the 62nd annual meeting of the Society for American Archaeology, Nashville, Tenn.

1999   Early Agriculture and Intersite Variation: The Basketmaker II People of Southeastern Utah. Paper presented at the 64th annual meeting of the Society for American Archaeology, Chicago.

Smiley, T. L.

1949   Pithouse Number 1, Mesa Verde National Park. *American Antiquity* 14:30–32.

Smith, C.

1991   Female Artists: The Unrecognized Factor in Sacred Rock Art Production. In *Rock Art and Prehistory,* edited by P. Bahn and A. Rosenfeld, pp. 45–57. Oxbow Monograph no. 10. Oxford: Oxbow Press.

Smith, S. J.

1999   Pollen Analysis. In *Anasazi Community Development in Redrock Valley: Archaeological Excavations along the N33 Road in Apache County, Arizona,* edited by P. F. Reed and K. N. Hensler, pp. 850–870. Navajo Nation Papers in Anthropology no. 33, Window Rock, Ariz.

Smith, W.

1952   *Excavations in Big Hawk Valley, Wupatki National Monument, Arizona.* Museum of Northern Arizona Bulletin no. 24, Flagstaff.

1972   *Prehistoric Kivas of Antelope Mesa, Northeastern Arizona.* Papers of the Peabody Museum of Archaeology and Ethnology, vol. 39, no. 1. Cambridge: Harvard University.

Snell, D., and J. Jones

1996   LA 2507: Twin Lakes Site. In *Investigations at an Early Anasazi Community in the Tohatchi Flats,* edited by J. L. McVickar, pp. 4-1 to 4-154. Pipeline Archaeology 1990–1993: The El Paso Natural Gas North System Expansion Project, New Mexico and Arizona, vol. IV, draft report, T. M. Kearns, general editor. Report no. WCRM(F)074. Farmington, N.Mex.: Western Cultural Resource Management, Inc.

Snell, D., B. G. Randolf, and R. Korgel

1996   LA 80425. In *Investigations at an Early Anasazi Community in the Tohatchi Flats,* edited by J. L. McVickar, pp. 6-1 to 6-300. Pipeline Archaeology 1990–1993: The El Paso Natural Gas North System Expansion Project, New Mexico and Arizona, vol. IV draft report, T. M. Kearns, general editor. Report no. WCRM(F)074. Farmington, N.Mex.: Western Cultural Resource Management, Inc.

South, S.

1977   *Method and Theory in Historical Archaeology.* New York: Academic Press.

Spurr, K., and K. A. Hays-Gilpin

1996   New Evidence for Early Basketmaker III Ceramics from the Kayenta Area. Paper presented at the 1996 Pecos Conference, Flagstaff.

Stanislawski, M. B.

1973   Ethnoarchaeology and Settlement Archaeology. *Ethnohistory* 20:375–392.

Stark, M. T.

1995   The Early Ceramic Horizon and Tonto Basin Prehistory. In *The Roosevelt Community Development Study.* Vol. 2, *Ceramic Chronology, Technology, and Economics,* edited by J. M. Heidke and M. T. Stark, pp. 249–272. Anthropological Papers no. 14. Tucson: Center for Desert Archaeology.

Stein, J. R., and A. P. Fowler

1996   Looking beyond Chaco in the San Juan Basin and Its Peripheries. In *The Prehistoric Pueblo World, A.D. 1150–1350,* edited by M. A. Adler, pp. 114–130. Tucson: University of Arizona Press.

Stein, M. A.

1966   An Archaeological Survey of Paiute Mesa, Arizona. Master's thesis, Department of Anthropology, University of Oklahoma, Norman.

Steward, J. H.

1937   Ecological Aspects of Southwestern Society. *Anthropos* 32:87–104.

1938   *Basin-Plateau Aboriginal Sociopolitical Groups.* Bureau of American Ethnology Bulletin no. 120. Washington, D.C.: Smithsonian Institution.

1955   *Theory of Culture Change: The Methodology of Multilinear Evolution.* Urbana: University of Illinois Press.

Stiger, M. A.

1977   Anasazi Diet: The Coprolite Evidence. Master's thesis, Department of Anthropology, University of Colorado, Boulder.

Stirniman, P., and J. L. McVickar

1996   LA 11610: The In-between Site. In *Investigations at an Early Anasazi Community in the Tohatchi Flats,* edited by J. L. McVickar, pp. 1–130. Pipeline Archaeology 1990–1993: The El Paso Natural Gas North System Expansion Project, New Mexico and Arizona, vol. IV, draft report, T. M. Kearns, general editor. Report no. WCRM(F)074. Farmington, N.Mex.: Western Cultural Resource Management, Inc.c.

Stirniman, P., and S. W. Yost

1996 LA 9967: A Pueblo II Food Processing Locale and Basketmaker III Midden in the Tohatchi Flats. In *Excavations in the Northern Tohatchi Flats*, edited by S. W. Yost, pp. 6-1 to 6-109. Pipeline Archaeology 1990–1993: The El Paso Natural Gas North System Expansion Project, New Mexico and Arizona, vol. V, draft report, T. M. Kearns, general editor. Report no. WCRM(F)074. Farmington, N.Mex.: Western Cultural Resource Management, Inc.

Stone, G. S., and C. E. Downum

1999 Non-Boserupian Ecology and Agricultural Risk: Ethnic Politics and Land Control in the Arid Southwest. *American Anthropologist* 101:113–128.

Stratton, S. K.

1997a Faunal Remains. In Excavations at Big Bend Hamlet (5MT9387): A Basketmaker III Site on Reach 1 of the Lone Pine Laterals, Montezuma County, Colorado, edited by T. N. Motsinger and M. L. Chenault. In preparation. Durango, Colo.: SWCA, Inc.

1997b Faunal Remains Analysis. In Excavations at the Rabbit Site (5MT9168), a Basketmaker III Hamlet, edited by M. L. Chenault. In preparation. Durango, Colo.: SWCA, Inc.

1997c Faunal Remains. In Excavations at the Late Basketmaker III Hamlet of Dead Dog (5MT11,861), edited by M. L. Chenault. In preparation. Durango, Colo.: SWCA, Inc.

Stuart, D. E., and R. P. Gauthier

1981 *Prehistoric New Mexico: Background for Survey.* Santa Fe: New Mexico Historic Preservation Bureau.

Stuiver, M., and P. J. Reimer

1993 Extended 14C Data Base and Revised CALIB 3.0 14C Age Calibration Program. *Radiocarbon* 35:215–230.

Swarthout, J., S. Stebbins, P. Stein, B. Harrill, and P. J. Pilles, Jr.

1986 *The Kayenta Anasazi: Archaeological Investigations along the Black Mesa Railroad Corridor.* Vol. 2. Research Paper no. 30. Flagstaff: Museum of Northern Arizona.

Tagg, M. D.

1996 Early Cultigens from Fresnal Shelter, Southeastern New Mexico. *American Antiquity* 61:311–324.

Tainter, J. A., and D. Gillio

1980 Cultural Resources Overview: Mt. Taylor Area, New Mexico. Washington, D.C.: U.S. Government Printing Office.

Thomas, D. H.

1973 An Empirical Test for Steward's Model of Great Basin Settlement Patterns. *American Antiquity* 38:155–176.

1981 How to Classify the Projectile Points from Monitor Valley, Nevada. *Journal of California and Great Basin Anthropology* 3:21–43.

Toll, H. W., III

1985 Pottery, Production, Public Architecture, and the Chaco Anasazi System. Ph.D. diss., Department of Anthropology, University of Colorado, Boulder. Ann Arbor: University Microfilms.

1991 Patterns of Basketmaker III Occupation in the La Plata Valley, New Mexico. Paper presented at the 56th annual meeting of the Society for American Archaeology, New Orleans.

1993 *Results of Resurvey and Evaluation of Archaeological Sites in the Dawson Arroyo Segment of the La Plata Highway Project.* Archaeology Notes no. 67. Santa Fe: Office of Archaeological Studies, Museum of New Mexico.

Torres, J. A.

1999a Lithic Analysis. In *Anasazi Community Development in Redrock Valley: Archaeological Excavations along the N33 Road in Apache County, Arizona,* edited by P. F. Reed and K. N. Hensler, pp. 687–764. Navajo Nation Papers in Anthropology no. 33, Window Rock, Ariz.

1999b Lithic Analysis of LA 81694. In *Cultural Adaptations to Upland Environments in the Upper San Juan Basin: Archaeological Investigations at LA 81694 in Northwestern New Mexico,* edited by D. D. Dykeman and J. T. Wharton, pp. 105–127. Navajo Nation Papers in Anthropology no. 34, Window Rock, Ariz.

1999c Lithic Analysis of the MAPCO Pipeline Archaeological Project. LRI-Report no. 99-11. Farmington, N.Mex.: Lithic Research, Inc.

1999d Lithic Analysis of Horseshoe Springs Archaeological Project. LRI-Report no. 99-8b. Farmington, N.Mex.: Lithic Research, Inc.

2000 Lithic Analysis of LA 71781. In LA 71781 Final Report. In preparation. Navajo Nation Archaeology Department, Window Rock, Ariz.

Towner, R.

2000 Lithic Artifacts. In *Cultural Dynamics in the Lukachukai Valley: The N-13 Project,* edited by J. H. Altschul, S. D. Shelley, and E. K. Huber, pp. 14-1 to 14-55. Technical Series no. 16. Tucson: Statistical Research, Inc.

Trevathan, W. R.

1987 *Human Birth: An Evolutionary Perspective.* New York: Aldine de Gruyter.

Trott, J. J., and C. Chang

1975a Environmental Report for Archaeological Excavations, Prehistoric Site NA11,780, Arizona E:9:5 (MNA) N59-18. Unpublished typescript on file, Museum of Northern Arizona, Flagstaff.

1975b Environmental Report for Archaeological Excavations, Prehistoric Site NA11,784, Arizona E:10:11 (MNA) N59-22. Unpublished typescript on file, Museum of Northern Arizona, Flagstaff.

Truell, M. L.

1986 A Summary of Small Site Architecture in Chaco Canyon, New Mexico. In *Small Site Architecture of Chaco Canyon, New Mexico,* by P. J. McKenna and M. L. Truell, pp. 115–502. Publications in Archeology 18D. Santa Fe: Branch of Cultural Research, National Park Service.

Tucker, A. J.

1983 *Excavations at Chindi Hamlet (Site 5MT4684), a Basketmaker III Habitation Site.* Dolores Archaeological Program Technical Reports DAP-106. Denver: U.S. Department of the Interior, Bureau of Reclamation, Engineering and Research Center.

Turnbull, C. M.

1972 *The Mountain People.* New York: Simon and Schuster.

Turner, C. G., II

1962 *A Summary of the Archaeological Explorations of Dr. Byron Cummings in the Anasazi Culture Area.* Technical Series no. 5. Flagstaff: Museum of Northern Arizona.

1963 *Petroglyphs of the Glen Canyon Region.* Museum of Northern Arizona Bulletin no. 38, Flagstaff.

Turner, C. G., and J. A. Turner

1999 *Man Corn.* Salt Lake City: University of Utah Press.

Tyler, H.

1991 *Pueblo Birds and Myths.* Flagstaff: Northland Publishing.

Upham, S.

1982   *Polities and Power: An Economic and Political History of the Western Pueblo.* New York: Academic Press.

1984   Adaptive Diversity and Southwestern Abandonment. *Journal of Anthropological Research* 40:235–256.

Van West, C. R.

1994   *Modeling Prehistoric Agricultural Productivity in Southwestern Colorado: A GIS Approach.* Reports of Investigations 67. Pullman: Department of Anthropology, Washington State University.

Van West, C. R., and J. H. Altschul

1994   Agricultural Productivity and Carrying Capacity in the Tonto Basin. In *Roosevelt Rural Sites Study: Changing Land Use Patterns in the Tonto Basin,* edited by R.S. Ciolek-Torrello and J. R. Welch, pp. 361–435, vol. 3. Technical Series no. 28. Tucson: Statistical Research, Inc.

1997   Environmental Variability and Agricultural Economics along the Lower Verde River, A.D. 750–1450. In *Vanishing River: Landscapes and Lives of the Lower Verde Valley: The Lower Verde Archaeological Project: Overview, Synthesis, and Conclusions,* edited by S. M. Whittlesey, R. Ciolek-Torrello, and J. H. Altschul, pp. 337–392. Tucson: Statistical Research, Inc.

Varien, M. D.

1990   Ceramics. In *Excavations at Three Prehistoric Sites along Pia Mesa Road,* edited by M. D. Varien, pp. 88–106. Research Series no. 4. Zuni Pueblo, N.Mex.: Zuni Archaeology Program.

1999   *Sedentism and Mobility in a Social Landscape: Mesa Verde and Beyond.* Tucson: University of Arizona Press.

Vierra, B. J.

1993a   *The Excavation of a Multicomponent Anasazi Site (LA 50337) in the La Plata River Valley, Northwestern New Mexico.* Archaeology Notes no. 49. Santa Fe: Office of Archaeological Studies, Museum of New Mexico.

1993b   Lithic Resource Variation across the Colorado Plateau. In *Architectural Studies, Lithic Analyses, and Ancillary Studies,* by B. J. Vierra, T. W. Burchett, K. L. Brown, M. E. Brown, P. T. Kay, and C. J. Phagan, pp. 157–167. Across the Colorado Plateau: Anthropological Studies for the Transwestern Pipeline Expansion Project, vol. XVII, J. C. Winter, principal investigator. Albuquerque: Office of Contract Archeology and Maxwell Museum of Anthropology, University of New Mexico.

Vivian, G., and P. Reiter

1965   *The Great Kivas of Chaco Canyon and Their Relationships.* School of American Research Monograph no. 22. Albuquerque: University of New Mexico Press.

Vivian, R. G.

1990   *The Chacoan Prehistory of the San Juan Basin.* San Diego: Academic Press.

Vogler, L. E., K. Langenfeld, and D. Gilpin

1993   *DA'A' A'K 'EH NITSAA: An Overview of the Cultural Resources of the Navajo Indian Irrigation Project, Northwestern New Mexico.* Navajo Nation Papers in Anthropology no. 29, Window Rock, Ariz.

Wait, W.

1982   The Development and Application of a Computerized Data Base for the San Juan Basin, New Mexico. In *The San Juan Tomorrow: Planning for the Conservation of Cultural Resources in the San Juan Basin,* edited by F. Plog and W. Wait, pp. 171–217. Santa Fe: National Park Service, Southwest Region.

Walker, W. H.

1998   Where Are the Witches of Prehistory? *Journal of Archaeological Method and Theory* 5:245–308.

Ward, A. E. (ed.)

1978   *Limited Activity and Occupation Sites.* Contributions to Anthropology no. 1. Albuquerque: Center for Anthropology Studies.

Warner, L. E., and M. Elson

1982   *The Carrizo Flats Survey: Anasazi and Navajo Occupation of the Red Rock Valley Area of Arizona.* Navajo Nation Papers in Anthropology no. 17. Window Rock, Ariz.

Warren, A. H.

1993   The Pottery of LA 50337. In *The Excavation of a Multicomponent Anasazi Site (LA 50337) in the La Plata River Valley, Northwestern New Mexico,* by B. J. Vierra, pp. 143–184. Archaeology Notes no. 49. Santa Fe: Office of Archaeological Studies, Museum of New Mexico.

Washburn, D. K., and D. W. Crowe

1988   *Symmetries of Culture: Theory and Practice of Plane Patterns.* Seattle: University of Washington Press.

Wasley, W. W.

1960   Salvage Archaeology on Highway 66 in Eastern Arizona. *American Antiquity* 26:30–42.

Waterworth, R.

1999   Ceramic Artifact Materials, Time, and Space Studies. In *Chuska Chronologies, Houses, and Hogans: Archaeological and Ethnographic Inquiry along N30-N31 Between Mexican Springs and Navajo, McKinley County, New Mexico,* vol. III, part 1, edited by J. E. Damp, pp. 1–46. Research Series no. 10. Zuni Pueblo, N.Mex.: Zuni Cultural Resource Enterprise.

Watson, P. J., and M. C. Kennedy

1991   The Development of Horticulture in the Eastern Woodlands of North America: Women's Role. In *Engendering Archaeology: Women and Prehistory,* edited by J. Gero and M. W. Conkey, pp. 255–275. Oxford: Basil Blackwell.

Webster, L. D.

1991a   Accession Notes, Cummings Field Season 1923. Ms. on file, Arizona State Museum, Tucson.

1991b   Accession Notes, Cummings Field Season 1926. Ms. on file, Arizona State Museum, Tucson.

1997a   Textiles and Basketry. In Excavations at the Rabbit Site (5MT9168), a Basketmaker III Hamlet, edited by M. L. Chenault. In preparation. Durango, Colo.: SWCA, Inc.

1997b   Textiles and Basketry. In Excavations at the Late Basketmaker III Hamlet of Dead Dog (5MT11,861), edited by M. L. Chenault. In preparation. Durango, Colo.: SWCA, Inc.

Webster, L. D., and K. A. Hays-Gilpin

1994   New Trails for Old Shoes: Sandals, Textiles, and Baskets in the Basketmaker Culture. *Kiva* 60:313–328.

Welch, J. R.

1991   From Horticulture to Agriculture in the Late Prehistory of the Grasshopper Region, Arizona. In *Mogollon V,* edited by P. Beckett, pp. 75–91. Las Cruces, N.Mex.: Coas Books.

Wendorf, F.

1953   *Archaeological Studies in the Petrified Forest National Monument.* Museum of Northern Arizona Bulletin no. 27. Flagstaff: Northern Arizona Society of Science and Art.

1956   Some Distributions of Settlement Patterns in the Pueblo Southwest. In *Prehistoric Settlement Patterns in the New*

World, edited by G. Willey, pp. 18–25. Viking Fund Publications in Anthropology 23.

Wendorf, F., N. Fox, and O. L. Lewis (eds.)

1956 *Pipeline Archaeology: Reports of Salvage Operations in the Southwest on El Paso Natural Gas Company Projects, 1950–1953.* Flagstaff: Museum of Northern Arizona.

Wheat, J. B.

1955a Mogollon Culture Prior to A.D. 1000. *American Anthropologist* 57(2): part 3, memoir 82.

1955b MT-1: A Basketmaker III Site near Yellow Jacket, Colorado. *Southwestern Lore* 21:18–26.

Wheeler, C. W. (ed.)

1996 *Excavations North of the Gallup Station.* Pipeline Archaeology 1990–1993: The El Paso Natural Gas North System Expansion Project, New Mexico and Arizona, vol. IV draft report, T. M. Kearns, general editor. Report no. WCRM(F)074. Farmington, N.Mex.: Western Cultural Resource Management, Inc.

Whitehead, H.

1981 The Bow and the Burden Strap: A New Look at Institutionalized Homosexuality in Native North America. In *Sexual Meanings: The Cultural Construction of Gender and Sexuality,* edited by S. B. Ortner and H. Whitehead, pp. 80–115. Cambridge: Cambridge University Press.

Whitley, D. S.

1992 Shamanism and Rock Art in Far Western North America. *Cambridge Archaeological Journal* 11:291–329.

1994 By the Hunter, for the Gatherer: Art, Social Relations, and Subsistence change in the Prehistoric Great Basin. *World Archaeology* 25:357–373.

1998 Finding Rain in the Desert. In *The Archaeology of Rock Art,* edited by C. Chippendale and P. S. C. Tacon, pp. 11–29. Cambridge: Cambridge University Press.

Whittlesey, S. M., R. Ciolek-Torello, and W. L. Deaver

1994 Resurrecting the Ootam: The Early Formative Period in Arizona. In *Mogollon VII: The Collected Papers of the 1992 Mogollon Conference Held in Las Cruces, New Mexico,* pp. 31–42. Las Cruces, N.Mex.: COAS Publishing and Research.

Wilcox, D. R., and J. Haas

1994 The Scream of the Butterfly: Competition and Conflict in the Prehistoric Southwest. In *Themes in Southwest Prehistory,* edited by G. J. Gumerman, pp. 211–238. Santa Fe: School of American Research Press.

Wilcox, D. R., and R. B. Masse (ed.)

1981 *The Protohistoric Period in the North American Southwest, A.D. 1450–1700.* Anthropological Research Paper no. 24. Tempe: Arizona State University.

Wilcox, S.

1999 Data Recovery at AZ-I-25-47. In *Anasazi Community Development in Redrock Valley: Archaeological Excavations along the N33 Road in Apache County, Arizona,* edited by P. F. Reed and K. N. Hensler, pp. 83–108. Navajo Nation Papers in Anthropology no. 33, Window Rock, Ariz.

Wilke, P. J., and A. Schroth

1989 Lithic Raw Material Prospects in the Mojave Desert, California. *Journal of California and Great Basin Anthropology* 11(2):146–174.

Wills, W. H.

1985 Early Agriculture in the Mogollon Highlands of New Mexico. Ph.D. diss., University of Michigan, Ann Arbor.

1988 *Early Prehistoric Agriculture in the American Southwest.* Santa Fe: School of American Research Press.

1991 Organizational Strategies and the Emergence of Prehistoric Villages in the American Southwest. In *Between Bands and States,* edited by S. A. Gregg, pp. 161–180. Occasional Paper no. 9. Carbondale: Center for Archaeological Investigations, Southern Illinois University.

1992 Plant Cultivation and the Evolution of Risk-prone Economies in the Prehistoric American Southwest. In *Transitions to Agriculture in Prehistory,* edited by A. B. Gebauer and T. D. Price, pp. 153–176. Monographs in World Archaeology no. 4. Madison, Wisc.: Prehistory Press.

1995 Archaic Foraging and the Beginning of Food Production in the American Southwest. In *Last Hunters, First Farmers: New Perspectives on the Prehistoric Transition to Agriculture,* edited by T. D. Price and A. B. Gebauer, pp. 215–242. Santa Fe: School of American Research Press.

Wills, W. H., P. L. Crown, J. S. Dean, and C. G. Langton

1994 Complex Adaptive Systems and Southwestern Prehistory. In *Understanding Complexity in the Prehistoric Southwest,* edited by G. J. Gumerman and M. Gell-Mann, pp. 297–340. Reading, Mass.: Addison-Wesley Publishing Co.

Wills, W. H., and B. Huckell

1994 Economic Implications of Changing Land-Use Patterns in the Late Archaic. In *Themes in Southwest Prehistory,* edited by G. J. Gumerman, pp. 33–52. Santa Fe: School of American Research Advanced Seminar Series.

Wills, W. H., and R. D. Leonard

1994 Preface. In *The Ancient Southwestern Community: Models and Methods for the Study of Prehistoric Social Organization,* edited by W. H. Wills and R. D. Leonard, pp. xiii–xvi. Albuquerque: University of New Mexico Press.

Wills, W. H., and T. C. Windes

1989 Evidence for Population Aggregation and Dispersal during the Basketmaker III Period in Chaco Canyon, New Mexico. *American Antiquity* 54:347–369.

Wilshusen, R. H.

1986 The Relationship Between Abandonment Mode and Ritual Use in Pueblo I Anasazi Protokivas. *Journal of Field Archaeology* 13:245–254.

1988a Sipapus, Ceremonial Vaults, and Foot Drums (or a Resounding Argument for Protokivas). In *Dolores Archaeological Program: Supporting Studies: Additive and Reductive Technologies,* compiled by E. Blinman, C. J. Phagan, and R. H. Wilshusen, pp. 649–671. Denver: U.S. Department of the Interior, Bureau of Reclamation, Engineering and Research Center.

1988b Abandonment of Structures. In *Dolores Archaeological Program: Supporting Studies: Additive and Reductive Technologies,* compiled by E. Blinman, C. J. Phagan, and R. H. Wilshusen, pp. 673–702. Denver: U.S. Department of the Interior, Bureau of Reclamation, Engineering and Research Center.

1988c Architectural Trends in Prehistoric Anasazi Sites During A.D. 600 to 1200. In *Dolores Archaeological Program: Supporting Studies: Additive and Reductive Technologies,* compiled by E. Blinman, C. J. Phagan, and R. H. Wilshusen, pp. 599–633. Denver: U.S. Department of the Interior, Bureau of Reclamation, Engineering and Research Center.

1989a Architecture as Artifact—Part II: A Comment on Gilman. *American Antiquity* 54:826–833.

1989b Unstuffing the Estufa: Ritual Floor Features in Anasazi Pit Structures and Pueblo Kivas. In *The Architecture of Social Integration in Prehistoric Pueblos,* edited by W. D. Lipe and M. Hegmon, pp. 89–111. Crow Canyon Archaeological Center Occasional Paper no. 1, Cortez, Colo.

Wilshusen, R. H., and S. G. Ortman
1999 Rethinking the Pueblo I Period in the San Juan Drainage: Aggregation, Migration, and Cultural Diversity. *Kiva* 64:369–399.

Wilson, C. D.
1988 Ceramics. In Archaeological Investigations in the Bodo Canyon Area, La Plata County, by S. L. Fuller, pp. 317–333. U.S. Department of Energy Uranium Mill Tailings Remedial Action Project Archaeological Report 25. Cortez, Colo.: Complete Archaeological Service Associates.
1989a "Sambrito Brown" from Site LA 4169: A Description and Evaluation. *Pottery Southwest* 16:4–7.
1989b Ceramics. In *The Archaeology and Ethnohistory of Redrock Valley: A Study of Prehistoric and Historic Land Use in Northeastern Arizona,* by B. S. Hildebrant, pp. 272–317. Research Series no. 3, Zuni Pueblo, N.Mex.: Zuni Archaeology Program.
1994 Implications of a Ceramic Resource Survey in the Northern Mogollon Country. In *Mogollon VII: The Collected Papers of the 1992 Mogollon Conference Held in Las Cruces, New Mexico,* compiled by P. H. Beckett, pp. 73–80. Las Cruces: COAS Publishing and Research.
1996 Ceramic Pigment Distributions and Regional Interaction: A Re-examination of Interpretations in Shepard's "Technology of La Plata Pottery." *Kiva* 62:83–102.

Wilson, C. D., and E. Blinman
1991 Ceramic Types of the Mesa Verde Region. Handout prepared for the Colorado Council of Professional Archaeologists Ceramic Workshop, Boulder, Colo.
1993 *Upper San Juan Ceramic Typology.* Archaeology Notes 80. Santa Fe: Office of Archaeological Studies, Museum of New Mexico.
1994 Early Anasazi Ceramics and the Basketmaker Transition. In *Anasazi Symposium 1991,* compiled by A. Hutchinson and J. E. Smith, pp. 199–214. Published by the Mesa Verde Museum Association.
1995 Changing Specialization of White Ware Manufacture in the Northern San Juan Region. In *The Organization of Ceramic Production in the American Southwest,* edited by B. J. Mills and P. L. Crown, pp. 63–87. Tucson: University of Arizona Press.

Wilson, C. D., E. Blinman, J. M. Skibo, and M. B. Schiffer
1996 Designing Southwestern Pottery: A Technological and Experimental Approach. In *Interpreting Southwestern Diversity: Underlying Principles and Overarching Patterns,* edited by P. R. Fish and J. R. Reid, pp. 249–256. Arizona State University Anthropological Research Papers no. 28, Tempe.

Windes, T. C.
1975 Excavation of 29SJ423, an Early Basketmaker III Site in Chaco Canyon: Preliminary Report of the Architecture and Stratigraphy. Unpublished manuscript on file, Division of Cultural Research, National Park Service, Albuquerque.

1993 *The Spadefoot Toad Site: Investigations at 29SJ629, Chaco Canyon, New Mexico.* Reports of the Chaco Center no. 12. Santa Fe: National Park Service Branch of Cultural Research.

Windham, M., and D. Dechambre
1978 Report on the Cultural Resources in the Former Joint Use Area. Ms. on file, Department of Anthropology, Northern Arizona University, Flagstaff.

Winter, J. C.
1975 *Hovenweep 1974.* Archaeological Report 1. San Jose, Calif.: Department of Anthropology, San Jose State University.
1976 *Hovenweep 1975.* Archaeological Report 2. San Jose, Calif.: Department of Anthropology, San Jose State University.
1994 *Synthesis and Conclusions: Communities, Boundaries, and Cultural Variation.* Across the Colorado Plateau: Anthropological Studies for the Transwestern Pipeline Expansion Project, vol. XX. UNM Project 185-461B. Albuquerque: Office of Contract Archeology and Maxwell Museum of Anthropology, University of New Mexico.

Winter, J. C., J. A. Ware, and P. J. Arnold III
1986 *The Cultural Resources of Ridges Basin and Upper Wildcat Canyon.* Albuquerque: Office of Contract Archaeology, University of New Mexico.

Wobst, M.
1974 Boundary Conditions for Paleolithic Social Systems: A Simulation Approach. *American Antiquity* 39:147–178.
1976 Locational Relationships in Paleolithic Society. *Journal of Human Evolution* 5:49–58.

Woodbury, R. B.
1954 *Prehistoric Stone Implements of Northeastern Arizona.* Papers of the Peabody Museum of American Archaeology and Ethnology, Reports of the Awatovi Expedition, vol. XXXIV, no. 6. Cambridge: Harvard University.

Wormington, H. M.
1961 *Prehistoric Indians of the Southwest.* Popular Series no. 7 (5th printing). Denver: Denver Museum of Natural History.

Wright, R. P.
1991 Women's Labor and Pottery Production in Prehistory. In *Engendering Archaeology: Women and Prehistory,* edited by J. M. Gero and M. W. Conkey, pp. 194–223. London: Basil Blackwell.

Wright, R. P. (ed.)
1996 *Gender and Archaeology.* Philadelphia: University of Pennsylvania Press.

Yohe, R. M., II
1992 A Reevaluation of Western Great Basin Cultural Chronology and Evidence for the Timing of the Introduction of the Bow and Arrow to Eastern California Based on New Excavations at the Rose Spring Site (CA-Iny-372). Ph.D. diss., Department of Anthropology, University of California, Riverside.

Zunie, J., and B. S. Hildebrant
1989 Faunal Remains from Redrock Valley. In *The Archaeology and Ethnohistory of Redrock Valley: A Study of Prehistoric and Historic Land Use in Northeastern Arizona,* by B. S. Hildebrant, pp. 418–437. Research Series no. 3. Zuni Pueblo, N.Mex.: Zuni Archaeology Program.

Contributors

Jeffrey H. Altschul, Statistical Research, Inc., 6099 E. Speedway Blvd., Tucson, AZ 85751

Larry Benallie Jr., Navajo Nation Archaeology Department, P.O. Box 689, Window Rock, AZ 86515

Mark L. Chenault, SWCA, Inc., Environmental Consultants, 8461 Turnpike Rd., Suite 100, Westminster, CO 80030

Jonathan E. Damp, Zuni Cultural Resource Enterprise, P.O. Box 1149, Zuni, NM 87327

Phil R. Geib, Navajo Nation Archaeology Department, Northern Arizona University Branch, P.O. Box 6103, Flagstaff, AZ 86011

Dennis Gilpin, SWCA, Inc., Environmental Consultants, 114 N. San Francisco St., Suite 100, Flagstaff, AZ 86001

Kelley A. Hays-Gilpin, Department of Anthropology, Northern Arizona University, Flagstaff, AZ 86011

Edgar K. Huber, Statistical Research, Inc., 6099 E. Speedway Blvd., Tucson, AZ 85751

Timothy M. Kearns, Western Cultural Resource Management, Inc., 550 Dekalb, Suite A, Farmington, NM 87401

Edward M. Kotyk, Zuni Cultural Resource Enterprise, P.O. Box 1149, Zuni, NM 87327

Janet L. McVickar, National Park Service, P.O. Box 728, Santa Fe, NM 87504

Elizabeth A. Morris, 48 Pine Place, Country Rd. 504, Bayfield, CO 81122

Thomas N. Motsinger, SWCA, Inc., Environmental Consultants, 343 S. Scott Ave., Tucson, AZ 85701

Lori Stephens Reed, Animas Ceramic Consulting, P.O. Box 5893, Farmington, NM 87499

Paul F. Reed, Navajo Nation Archaeology Department, 717 W. Animas St., Farmington, NM 87401

Michael R. Robins, Navajo Nation Archaeology Department, Northern Arizona University Branch, P.O. Box 6103, Flagstaff, AZ 86011

Kimberly Spurr, Navajo Nation Archaeology Department, Northern Arizona University Branch, P.O. Box 6103, Flagstaff, AZ 86011

H. Wolcott Toll, Office of Archaeological Studies, Museum of New Mexico, P.O. Box 2087, Santa Fe, NM 87504-2087

John A. Torres, Navajo Nation Archaeology Department, 717 W. Animas St., Farmington, NM 87401

R. Gwinn Vivian, Arizona State Museum, University of Arizona, Tucson, AZ 85721

Scott Wilcox, Navajo Nation Archaeology Department, 717 W. Animas St., Farmington, NM 87401

C. Dean Wilson, Office of Archaeological Studies, Museum of New Mexico, P.O. Box 2087, Santa Fe, NM 87504-2087

Index

abandonment, of sites: and Basketmaker III sites in Cove-Redrock Valley, 79–80; and Basketmaker III sites with great kivas, 170; and Basketmaker III sites in La Plata Valley, 35–36; and Basketmaker III sites in Mexican Springs area, 107–109; and burning of structures at Basketmaker II sites in Mesa Verde region, 62

Adamana Brown (ceramics), 207, 209

Adams, E. C., 247

Adams, J. L., 229

adaptive diversity, 12. *See also* seasonality

agriculture: and Basketmaker II period, 6, 191–92, 195–98; Basketmaker III and early Pueblo I sites in Cove-Redrock Valley, 84–85; and Basketmaker III sites in Lukachukai Valley, 151, 152–53, 158–59; and Basketmaker III sites in Mexican Springs area, 104, 107, 113; and ceramic production, 8, 216, 217–19; and climate in La Plata Valley, 38; and foundations of Anasazi culture, 8–11; lithic technology and milling equipment, 228; and sedentism, 11; subirrigated forms of, 233; surplus, territoriality, and social boundaries, 233–34. *See also* beans; diet; irrigation; maize; storage; subsistence

Alma Plain and Alma Rough (brown ware), 205, 207–208

Altschul, J. H., 10, 12, 13, 14, 16, 155, 253, 254

Ambler, J. R., 178

Anasazi: and ceramic production, 8, 203, 220; community organization and sociopolitical structure, 13–15; culture history of early, 5–8; and lithic technology, 221, 222, 224; sedentism, mobility, and seasonality, 11–13; subsistence and agriculture, 8–11; and understanding of Basketmaker II period, 16; use of term, 15

Ancestral Puebloans, 15

Animas-La Plata water project, 45

antechambers, and pit houses, 33, 77, 126–27, 128, 129, 130, 156, 157–58

Antelope House, 146

Apricot Hamlet, 110

aprons, and rock art, 237, 238, 239, 244. *See also* textiles

Archaeomagnetic Dating Laboratory, 93n3

Archaic period, and milling equipment, 229

architecture: and Basketmaker II-III transition, 237; and Basketmaker II sites on Rainbow Plateau, 189–92; Basketmaker III and early Pueblo I sites in Cove-Redrock Valley, 74–75, 77–81, 91–92; and Basketmaker III sites in La Plata Valley, 21–28, 33, 42; and Basketmaker III sites in Mesa Verde region, 53–59; and Basketmaker III sites in Mexican Springs area, 96–99; and Basketmaker III sites in Tohatchi Flats, 125–33, 141–42; differentiation of Basketmaker from Pueblo culture, 5; and relationship between Basketmaker III and Pueblo II, 34–36; and residential mobility, 11–12. *See also* great kivas; pit houses; public architecture

Arizona Historical Society, 163

Arizona State Museum, 166, 215

Arnold, D. E., 219

Athapaskans, 62

Atlatl Rock Cave, *180, 181, 183, 188, 191, 192, 193, 194, 195, 197, 198*

AZ-D-2-174, *183*

AZ-D-2-200, *183*

AZ-D-2-355, *183, 191*

AZ E:12:5, 148–60

AZ E:12:11, 153–54

AZ-I-24-7, 74, 75, 87

AZ I 24 8, 74, 75, 82, 87

AZ-I-24-11, 74, 75, 87

AZ-I-25-47, 69–70, 71, 74, 78, 82, 84

AZ-I-26-3, 71–73, 74, 81, 82–83, 84, 86, 91

AZ-I-26-4, 86, 91

AZ-I-26-8, 78

AZ-I-26-24, 10

AZ-I-26-34, 89, 222

AZ-I-26-37, 90

AZ-I-26-41, 71, 73, 75, 81, 82, 84, 86–87

AZ-I-26-47, 86

AZ-I-63-7, 212

AZ-J-14-54, *183, 191, 194*

AZ-J-54-7, AZ-J-54-8, AZ-J-54-12, and AZ-J-54-14, 162

Bad Dog Ridge, 162, 167, 171, 172

bags and bag patterns, 237, 243, 245. *See also* textiles

Baldwin, G., 163, 166

band level, of sociopolitical organization, 15, 158, 159, 235

Barker Arroyo sites, 22, 31

Barnett, W. K., 216

basin metates, 229

Basketmaker II: and agriculture, 9; and architecture on Rainbow Plateau, 189–92;

Basketmaker III and continuation of lifeways, 175; and caching for storage, 79; ceramics and transition to Basketmaker III, 26, 203; chronology of, 179–82, 198–99, 232–34; culture history of, 6–7; gender and material culture, 243–46; lithic technology and milling equipment, 229; and material culture on Rainbow Plateau, 192–95; recent publications on, 3, 5; and Red Valley phase, 89; and Sand Dune Cave site, 178–79; and rock art, 234, 235–36; separation of Basketmaker III period from, 5; and settlement patterns on Rainbow Plateau, 182–89; and subsistence on Rainbow Plateau, 195–98; and temporal distribution of ceramic types, 211–16

Basketmaker III: and Basketmaker II transition, 26, 198–99, 203, 256; chronology of, 179–82, 232–34, 252; culture history of, 7; and demographics in Cove-Redrock Valley, 88–91; and description of sites in Mexican Springs area, 96; and exchange in Tohatchi Flats, 135–40; gender and material culture of, 243–47; and geographic scope of research, 251–52; and great kivas in Chuska Mountains, 161–73; location of sites on Rainbow Plateau, *177*; map of sites and areas discussed in text, 4; need for synthetic volume on, 5; new research on, 69, 145–48; and Pecos classification, 5, 7–8, 252, 256; and Prayer Rock District sites, 75–77; and population in Lukachukai Valley, 155–60; and Puebloan prehistory, 16, 257; and Pueblo II sites in La Plata Valley, 33–42; and regional interrelations, 111–12; regional variability and multiethnic communities, 256–57; and rock art, 234–35, 241–43; 111; settlement structure and ritual, 253–56; and site structure in Mesa Verde region, 45–52, 64; and site structure in Lukachukai Valley, 148–51; temporal definition of, 19; and temporal setting in Tohatchi Flats, 115–19; and temporal variability in La Plata Valley, 21. *See also* architecture; community; ceramics; lithic assemblages; settlement patterns; sociopolitical organization; subsistence

baskets and basketry, 60, 237, 243–44, 245–46

beans, 8, 197–98

bell-shaped storage pits, 191

Benallie, L., Jr., 13, 14, 16, 167, 253, 255

287

III phase, 28; and painted ceramics from Pueblo I sites, 29

deflectors, in pit houses, 54–55, 190

demographics: and adoption of pottery, 220; Basketmaker III and early Pueblo I sites in Cove-Redrock Valley, 88–91; and Basketmaker III sites with great kivas, 171; and Basketmaker III sites in Lukachukai Valley, 155–60

Desha Caves 1 and 2, 180, 181, 183, 188, 192, 193

Desha Creek, 178

diet: and Basketmaker III sites in Mesa Verde region, 60; and capacity of storage bins, 152. See also agriculture; faunal resources; plant resources; storage

Ditch House, 180, 183

Dittert, A. E., Jr., 206, 208, 252

Division of Conservation Archaeology (DCA), 31

dogs, 85

Dohm, K. M., 13, 85

Dolores area, and Basketmaker III sites, 108, 109–10

Dolores Archaeological Program (DAP), 77, 85

Dolores Red ceramics, 209

Durango sites (Colorado), 32

Dust Devil Cave, 178, 180, 181, 192, 193–94, 197, 200n4

Dykeman, D. D., 30, 33, 215

Early Formative cultures, 145

Earth Lodge B, 146

East Side Rincon site, 30–31, 33

economy. See subsistence

Eddy, F. W., 106, 208

egalitarian model, of Early Formative cultures, 145

Electric Raven site, 162, 171

El Paso Natural Gas Company, 115, 214

Ely, L. L., 120

Ember, M., 247n1

entrances, of pit houses, 150

environment: and Basketmaker II–III transition, 237; of Cove-Redrock Valley area, 70–71; and Juniper Cove, 164; of Mexican Springs area, 95–96; of Rainbow Plateau, 175–78; and temporal occurrence of stockades and burned structures, 254; of Tohatchi Flats, 119–22. See also climate; faunal resources; plant resources

Epple, C., 232

ethnicity, Basketmaker III sites and multiethnic communities, 256–57

Euler, R. C., 120

exchange: Basketmaker III and early Pueblo I sites in Cove-Redrock Valley, 92; and Basketmaker III sites in Tohatchi Flats, 135–40, 142. See also trade

Farmer, J. D., 63

faunal resources: and Basketmaker III sites in Lukachukai Valley, 151, 154; and

Basketmaker III sites in Mexican Springs area, 102, 103, 105; of Cove-Redrock Valley, 70, 85; of Tohatchi Flats, 121, 134, 135, 141. See also dogs; turkeys

Fehr, R. T., 148

Feinman, G. M., 13–14, 15, 113, 145, 160

Ferg, A., 215

flute players, and rock art, 243

food processing: and Basketmaker III and Pueblo II sites in La Plata Valley, 34–35, 42; and Basketmaker III sites in Lukachukai Valley, 157; and Basketmaker III sites in Mexican Springs area, 105; and Basketmaker III sites in Tohatchi Flats, 135. See also agriculture; metates; storage

Four Corners region: and Basketmaker rock shelter sites, 233; geography of, 70; and map of Mesa Verde survey areas, 46

Fowler, A. P., 108

Fremont cultures, 63

Gallup Station site, 123, 124

Ganado site, 162, 167–69, 170, 171, 172

Gauthier, R. P., 257

Geib, P. R., 8, 10, 16, 194, 232, 252, 253, 256

gender: and adoption of pottery, 219; flexibility of categories of, 232; and material culture, 243–47; and rituals, 231; and rock art, 231–32, 236–41

geology, of Cove-Redrock Valley, 70–71. See also environment; lithic assemblages

Gilliland Site, 59, 62, 64, 146

Gillio, D., 257

Gilman, P. A., 11–12, 103, 106, 107, 145–46, 189

Gilpin, D., 9, 13, 14, 16, 167, 212, 232, 253, 255

Glasscow, M. A., 182

Glen Canyon, 7, 178, 194

Goff, J., 214

Grand Gulch site, 235, 238, 244

Grand Gulch variant, of Basketmaker II, 5, 6

Grant, C., 235, 238, 241, 244–45

Grass Mesa Village, 85

grass seed, as food resource, 135, 141

gray/brown ware: and Basketmaker III ceramics from Tohatchi Flats, 138; and Basketmaker III material culture, 252–53; definition of as ceramic technology, 204–11; temporal distribution of, 211–16. See also ceramics

gray ware: and Basketmaker III ceramics from Cove-Redrock Valley, 82–83; and Basketmaker III ceramics from Juniper Cove, 166; and Basketmaker III ceramics from La Plata Valley, 24–25, 27, 28; and Basketmaker III ceramics from Tohatchi Flats, 118, 138; definition of as ceramic technology, 204–11; temporal distribution of, 211–16; and transition from brown ware, 203. See also ceramics

great kivas: and Basketmaker III sites in Chuska Mountains, 161–73; and Basketmaker III villages in Cove-Redrock Valley, 86, 87–88, 90; and Basketmaker III villages in Lukachukai Valley, 156; interpretation of at Basketmaker III sites, 255; and settlement variability, 109; and sociopolitical structure, 14. See also public architecture

great pit structures, 131

Green Bear Site, 215

Green Mask site, 234

Grissino-Mayer, H. D., 120

Guernsey, Samuel, 3, 179, 192, 200n9, 235, 238

Gumerman, G. J., 7, 120, 169

Haas, J., 63

hairstyles, 240–41

Hall, E. T., Jr., 59

Hancock, P. M., 21

Hannaford, C. A., 30

Hargrave, L. L., 205

Hassan, F., 152

Haury, E. W., 163, 165, 205

Hawk's Nest Ruin, 188

Hayden, I., 178

Hayes, A. C., 61

Hays-Gilpin, K. A., 8, 166, 172, 192, 206, 208, 214, 215, 218, 239–40, 241, 242, 243, 244, 246, 252–53, 256–57

headdresses, 234, 235

hearths, in Basketmaker pit houses, 53–55, 128, 129, 131, 156, 190, 191

Heidke, J. M., 217, 220n1

Hodder, I., 246, 247n2

Hogan Well site, 215

Hoopes, J. W., 216

Hopi: and agricultural yields, 152; rock art and gender, 231–32; and themes of rock art, 240, 242, 243

house clusters, at Basketmaker III sites, 149–51

Huber, E., 10, 12, 13, 14, 16, 253, 254

Huckell, B. B., 196

Hunter, A., 196

Huntington Land Evaluation Project, 45, 61

Hyder, W. D., 235

Ignacio sites, 146

inductively coupled plasma arc spectrometry (ICP) studies, 83–84, 136, 138

irrigation: and Pueblo II sites in La Plata Valley, 38, 40–41; and Rainbow Plateau, 178. See also agriculture

Jackson Lake sites, 22, 30–31

James, C. D., III, 169

Japan, and Jomon pottery, 216

Jeddito, 264, 162

Jemez Pueblo, 228

Johnson, W. C., 142n2, 154, 156, 158, 159

Jomon pottery (Japan), 216

Juniper Cove, 146, 162–67, 170, 171, 172

Pueblo I sites in La Plata Valley, 29; and transition from brown ware, 203. *See also* ceramics